Software Engineering

Software Engineering

Principles and Practice

THIRD EDITION

Hans van Vliet

John Wiley & Sons, Ltd

Other Wiley Editorial Offices

John Wiley & Sons Inc., 111 River Street, Hoboken, NJ 07030, USA

Jossey-Bass, 989 Market Street, San Francisco, CA 94103-1741, USA

Wiley-VCH Verlag GmbH, Boschstr. 12, D-69469 Weinheim, Germany

John Wiley & Sons Australia Ltd, 42 McDougall Street, Milton, Queensland 4064, Australia

John Wiley & Sons (Asia) Pte Ltd, 2 Clementi Loop #02-01, Jin Xing Distripark, Singapore 129809

John Wiley & Sons Canada Ltd, 6045 Freemont Blvd, Mississauga, Ontario, L5R 4J3, Canada

Library of Congress Cataloging-in-Publication Data

Vliet, Hans van.
   Software engineering : principles and practice / Hans van Vliet. – 3rd
ed.
      p. cm
   Includes bibliographical references and index.
   ISBN 978-0-470-03146-9
   1. Software engineering. I. Title.
   QA76.758.V54 2008
   005.1 – dc22

                                          2008004317

British Library Cataloguing in Publication Data

A catalogue record for this book is available from the British Library

ISBN 978-0-470-03146-9 (pbk)

Typeset in 10/12pt Weiss by Laserwords Private Limited, Chennai, India
Printed and bound in Great Britain by Bell & Bain, Ltd, Glasgow
This book is printed on acid-free paper responsibly manufactured from sustainable forestry
in which at least two trees are planted for each one used for paper production.

To Marjan, Jasper, and Marieke

Contents

Foreword

"Software engineering – what an oxymoron!" and "Let's bury the term software engineering!" are rants that I recently found on blogs. Even today, many people consider that developing software-intensive systems must be more a creative activity – akin to an art or a craft – than an engineering activity in the traditional sense of applying science and discipline for developing useful products or creating value. They argue that putting the "engineering" into software engineering would kill the creative, fluid, dynamic nature of software development, stifle it, sink it under bureaucracy and restraints.

I disagree. Software engineering suffers from several misconceptions. First, it is often confused with programming, or code development – probably due to abuse of the term and job title "software engineer." Well, while programming and all things close to the program do play a part in software engineering, we could almost argue that software engineering encompasses *everything but* programming. You're a programmer, a software developer, good! Now you can start learning software engineering and all the concepts, skills, and techniques that are necessary to make great software products, not just nice piles of code, including the techniques and tools to *avoid* developing code. Second, software engineering suffers from the constant use of analogies to and attempts to pigeonhole it into civil or mechanical engineering. No, it does not require using processes, lifecycles, tools and techniques similar to other engineering disciplines. Over the last 40 years, we have developed approaches to software engineering that acknowledge its specific nature and even take advantage of its "soft" nature. Building software is *not* like building a bridge, because we cannot evolve and modify a bridge the way we do with software. And we have demonstrated that we can bring rigour and discipline to software engineering without having to resort to approaches derived from other engineering disciplines, which have to live within their own constraints, often imposed by the physics involved.

Hans' book on software engineering brings to both the student and the practitioner alike precisely this: a wealth of knowledge on how to *engineer* software – which he has accumulated, refined and decanted over the years – a palette of all the arrows outside of the strict realm of programming that a well-rounded software engineer should have in her quiver.

We are not speaking about a natural science here, where we can slowly get closer and closer to some ultimate truth. Almost everything remains a matter of opinion and is highly dependent on context. Hans and I each have our unique experience of software engineering, so naturally we disagree on some points. Life would be dull and no progress would be made if we were all patting each other on the back and not exercising our critical skills. But I can accept *most* of what he writes, and this is a big book, so that's still a lot.

We all know that this is not the be-all and end-all of software engineering, that our understanding of software development evolves constantly, but this book constitutes a pretty darn good baseline of proven approaches. Far too often I have seen software developers, analysts, and software managers reinventing the wheel or falling in love with a new technique or tool or some other fad. As an alternative, Hans has given a good starting point to learn about what works, and to understand where it comes from.

Yes, software can be engineered, and not quite like bridges and motors. It can be engineered with the approaches, techniques and tools that are specific to the nature of software.

Happy reading!

Philippe Kruchten
Vancouver, Canada

Preface

Around 1990, my wife and I discussed whether or not we should move. We were getting restless after having lived in the same house for a long time. For lack of space, my study had been changed into a child's bedroom. I definitely needed a room of my own in order to finish the first edition of this book. My wife thought her kitchen too small.

The opportunity to buy a building lot in a new development plan arose. We gathered information, looked for an architect, subscribed to the plan. Still, we were not sure whether we really wanted to leave our house. It was situated very nicely in a dead-end street, with a garden facing south and a playground in front. When asked, our children told us they did not want to move to a new neighborhood.

So, we asked an architect about the possibility of rebuilding our house. He produced a blueprint in which the altered house had a larger kitchen and four extra rooms. We were sold on the idea immediately. We told ourselves that this rebuilding would also be cheaper, although the architect could not yet give us a reliable cost estimate.

After giving the rebuilding plan some more thought, we decided this was the way to go. My brother, who is employed in the building industry, warned us of the mess it would create. We thought we could handle it. We started the procedure to get permission, which takes at least half a year in The Netherlands – and costs money (this was not accounted for).

In August, a year later, we were finally ready to start. The rebuilding was estimated to take 60 working days at most. Unfortunately, the contract did not mention any fine should this period be exceeded. We agreed on a fixed price. Certain things, such as the new electrical wiring, a new central-heating unit, and the cost of plumbing were not included. We hardly knew what those 'extras' would cost in the end. We did estimate them on the back of an envelope, and felt confident.

On 15 September, the first pile was driven. Counting on good weather throughout the fall, this should have meant that all would be finished by Christmas. The building contractor, however, had other urgent obligations, and progress was rather slow at the beginning. About one week's work was done during the first month.

In October, part of the roof had to be removed. We could interrupt work until the following spring (the safe option) or continue – rather tricky in a country as wet as ours. We prayed for some dry weeks and decided to go on. The contractor started to demolish part of our house. While doing so, some surprises showed up and an even larger part of the house had to be demolished. We were really lucky – it only rained for two days while our roof was open. Our bedrooms became rather wet and the kitchen was flooded. Some time in November, the new roof was on and we could sleep quietly again.

By the end of November, we were getting nervous. There was still a lot of work to be done but several times the workmen did not show up. In the meantime, we had made arrangements for our new kitchen to be installed the week before Christmas. Before this, a door had to be cut in an existing brick wall. The old central-heating unit was placed right behind that wall and had to be removed first. The new central-heating unit, unfortunately, was not available yet (fall is the peak season for central-heating units).

Work continued as far as possible. A new wall was erected, after which we could enter our (old) kitchen only from the outside. For a while, we even lived with no kitchen at all. To cut a long story short, the contractor made it, but only barely. The new kitchen was installed. Upstairs, however, much work remained. The project was finally finished by the end of January, only six weeks late.

During the rebuilding, life had been rather provisional. My computer was stored away in the attic. The children had virtually no space to play indoors. Dust was everywhere. These circumstances can be tolerated for a while, but we became frantic towards the end. Though the work seemed to be finished by the end of January, a lot still remained to be done: rooms had to be painted and decorated, and all that had been packed needed to be unpacked again. It was several more months before life took its normal course again.

Several months later, some of the new wooden planks on the back façade started to crack. They had expanded during the summer heat; either the tongue was too wide or the groove too narrow. This, and various other minor problems were, eventually, rectified.

On the financial side: various tiny expenses not accounted for added up to a pretty sum. I am still not sure whether we chose the cheapest option, but I am absolutely sure that knocking down a house and rebuilding it while you are still trying to live in it is a nightmare. In that sense, my brother was more than right.

After the house-rebuilding project and work on the first edition of this book was finished, I turned my attention to tidying up our garden. I designed a garden with various borders, terraces, a summer house and a pond. And I carried out all the work. I made one big mistake on this second project, which only manifested itself a couple of years later when I wanted to repaint the back façade. In order to do so, I had to put the legs of the ladder in the pond. So I did some rework and moved the pond.

This story is fairly typical of a software development project. Software too is often delivered late, does not meet its specifications and is, moreover, faulty. Software projects also tend to underestimate the impact of non-technical factors. The growing awareness of this in the late 1960s gave rise to the expression 'the software crisis'.

Fortunately, we have made quite some progress since the term 'software engineering' was first coined back in 1968.

SOFTWARE ENGINEERING

The field of software engineering aims to find answers to the many problems that software development projects are likely to meet when constructing large software systems. Such systems are complex because of their sheer size, because they are developed by a team involving people from different disciplines, and because they will be modified regularly to meet changing requirements, both during development and after installation.

Software engineering is still a young field compared to other engineering disciplines. All disciplines have their problems, particularly when projects reach beyond the engineers' expertise. It seems as if software development projects stretch their engineers' expertise all of the time.

The subject is rapidly moving and there are more questions than answers. Yet, a number of principles and practices have evolved in the 40 years the field has existed. To foster and maintain software engineering as a professional discipline, the IEEE Computer Society and ACM carried out a joint project – SWEBOK – to identify and validate the body of software engineering knowledge. This project ran from 1998 to 2001.

This book addresses all of the knowledge areas identified in the SWEBOK project.[1] Of course, the relative attention paid to individual topics and the way these topics are treated reflects my own view of the field. This view can be summarized as follows:

- What is theory today may become practice tomorrow. For that reason, I have not limited myself to a discussion of well-established practices. Rather, I also pay attention to promising methods and techniques which have not yet outgrown the research environment or have hardly done so: quantitative assessment of software quality, component-based software engineering, and service-oriented software engineering, to name but a few.

- We may learn a lot from our own history. I do not only discuss techniques that have proven their worth and are in wide use today. I also discuss developments that are by now considered dead-ends. Knowing *why* a certain technique is no longer used is often valuable. My discussion of cost estimation models in Chapter 7 is a case in point.

---

[1] The 2004 version of the SWEBOK Guide lists the following knowledge areas: software requirements, software design, software construction, software testing, software maintenance, software configuration management, software engineering management, software engineering process, software engineering tools and methods, and software quality. The software construction area covers both coding and unit and integration testing; of these, only unit and integration testing are covered in this book.
For more information on the SWEBOK project, see www.sWebok.org.

- Everything changes. Requirements change while development is still under way. People enter and leave the project team. The functionality of a toolset changes before the systems developed with it are replaced. And so on. Change is a recurring theme in this book.

- Human and social aspects are central. Most chapters of this book carry titles that sound fairly technical. Within these same chapters, though, I regularly touch upon human and social aspects of the trade. For example, requirements elicitation is by no means a purely technical issue, and the design of a system is heavily influenced by the prior experiences, both positive and negative, of the designer.

- Software engineering is becoming increasingly heterogeneous, as recent developments show (Vliet, 2006):

  - Distributed software development, involving teams from different cultures and scattered around the globe.
  - The combination of software developed in-house with COTS, open source, and other externally acquired software.
  - The combination of traditional, document-driven development approaches with more recent, people-driven agile development approaches.

  As a consequence of this shift, control of software development has become much more difficult.

People actively involved in software development and maintenance – programmers, analysts, project managers – and students of computer science and software engineering alike must be aware of the problems incurred by large-scale software development, and the solutions proposed.

I firmly believe that none of the solutions proposed is a silver bullet: CASE, object-oriented software development, software reuse, architectural design, formal specifications, process models, component-based software engineering, service-oriented software engineering; they each contribute their mite. The fundamental problems will, however, remain. Software systems are extremely complex artifacts. Their successful realization requires experience and talent from their designers. If applied in a thoughtful, conscientious manner, the methods and techniques discussed in this book may help you to become a professional software engineer.

LEARNING ABOUT SOFTWARE ENGINEERING

Most chapters of this book can be read and studied independently. In a classroom setting, the instructor has a large degree of freedom in choosing topics from this book, and the order in which to treat them. It is recommended that a first course in software engineering at least deals with the topics discussed in Chapters 1–3 and 9–14 (in this order). Additional material can be chosen at will from the other chapters or be used as material for a secondary course. Two obvious clusters of material for a secondary course are Chapters 4–8 and 16–20 (see Figure 1).

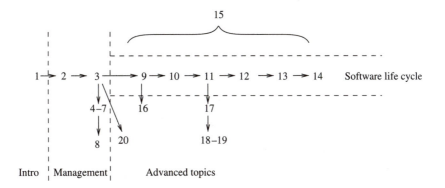

Figure 1 How the book is organized

A recurring problem in teaching software engineering is when and how to address project management issues. Computer science students often have difficulty in appreciating the importance of issues such as team organization and cost estimation. Software professionals know from the trenches that these non-technical issues are at least as important as the technical ones. Students of computer science or software engineering are more likely to understand the importance of management issues near the end of the course, possibly after they have been involved in some sort of practical work. However, a short treatment of the issues raised in Chapters 2 and 3 should be given near the beginning of the course.

Much of what is said in this book sounds obvious. In fact, it is. As one speaker at a software engineering education conference said: 'You cannot teach it, you can only preach it.' So this book is one long sermon on how to practice software development. Just as you cannot become a good hand at carpentry from reading a textbook on the subject, you cannot become a serious software engineer merely by reading and absorbing the material contained in this book. You need to practice it as well.

Doing practical work in a university setting is not easy. The many risks that real-life software development projects run cannot be realistically mimicked in a term project. Yet certain recurring problems in software development can be dealt with successfully. For example, small student teams may be asked to design, implement and test a nontrivial system, which another team is asked to maintain.

Figure 2 depicts how schoolchildren in Amsterdam learned to swim around 1900. My father grew up in the countryside and learned the hard way. His father simply tied a rope around his middle, threw him into the river that ran in front of the house, and shouted, 'Swim.' Nowadays, Dutch schoolchildren, by and large, get their first swimming certificate before entering school. Their swimming lessons start off in

Figure 2 The swimming equivalent of a correspondence course in software engineering ©
The Municipal Archives of Amsterdam. Reproduced with permission

a very gentle way, in a toddler pool, next to mamma and with lots of material to keep
them afloat. Gradually, the amount of floating material is reduced and the pool gets
deeper. They do not get scared and usually enjoy the swimming lesson.

A similar range of possibilities is possible in a software engineering course. The
dry-land swimming equivalent is not to be recommended. Doing it the hard way
by involving the student in a real project has its problems too. The student may,
figuratively speaking, drown in the day-to-day practical intricacies of the project.
Some sort of intermediate scheme involving 'real-life' aspects in a protected setting,
or a sequence of educational experiences with an increasing amount of realism, seems
most appropriate. Issues of software engineering education are addressed in the yearly
Conference on Software Engineering Education. See also (Inverardi and Jazayeri, 2006) for a
state-of-the-art overview.

In addition to this practical work, the exercises at the end of each chapter
provide further learning material. Exercises that are simply numbered ask relatively
simple questions about the chapter just read. Exercises marked with a ♡ or ♠ require
the reader to reflect seriously on major issues or study additional sources to deepen
his or her understanding.[2] Exercises marked with a ♡ may require one hour to answer.
Exercises marked ♠ may require more than a day. The simple exercises give but
a superficial knowledge of the field. Deep knowledge of software engineering will

---

[2]Rather than writing 'his or her' all the time, I will use male pronouns throughout this text for brevity.

only be developed if you cut your teeth on a number of the marked exercises. These exercises force you to think about and reflect on the material discussed. The reflection part is as important as the mere answer. Answers to these exercises and further teaching material may be obtained from `www.cs.vu.nl/~hans/SEbook.html`.

WHAT'S CHANGED?

Software engineering is a rapidly evolving field. Preparing this third edition therefore necessitated changes in every chapter. But some chapters changed more than others. The major changes are as follows:

- I have added material on agile development methods, most notably in Chapters 1–8.

- I have added three completely new chapters, on component-based software engineering, service orientation, and global software development.

- I have considerably updated the chapters on requirements engineering (9) and software architecture (11).

- I have collected the material on notational issues into one chapter (10).

- I have integrated the remaining material on object-oriented analysis and design in the chapter on software design (12).

- I have integrated the material on software reliability in the chapter on software testing (13).

- I have dropped the chapter on formal specification.

ACKNOWLEDGEMENTS

The present text is really a fifth edition. The first two editions appeared in Dutch only. I have used this material many times in courses, both for university students and software professionals. These people have, either consciously or unconsciously, helped to shape the text as it stands. I have received many useful suggestions from Remco de Boer, Rik Farenhorst, Steven Klusener, Philippe Kruchten (University of British Columbia), Patricia Lago, Judith Stafford (Tufts University) and Witold Suryn (University of Quebec). Special thanks go to Gerrit van der Veer, who co-authored Chapter 16, and Michel Chaudron and Ivica Crnkovic, who co-authored Chapter 18.

Shena Deuchars of Mitcham Editorial Services did a great job as copy-editor. Many people from John Wiley & Sons have contributed to this book. Emma Cooper handled all the production work. Claire Jardine dealt with a host of chores. Thanks also go to Commissioning Editor, Jonathan Shipley.

The litho on the front cover is called 'Waterfall' (M.C. Escher, 1961). It is appropriate in name and message alike.

Finally, I thank Marjan, Jasper and Marieke for their patience and support. The schedule overrun of this project has been worse than that of many a software development project.

Hans van Vliet
Amsterdam, October 2007

1

Introduction

LEARNING OBJECTIVES

- To understand the notion of software engineering and why it is important

- To appreciate the technical (engineering), managerial, and psychological aspects of software engineering

- To understand the similarities and differences between software engineering and other engineering disciplines

- To know the major phases in a software development project

- To appreciate ethical dimensions in software engineering

- To be aware of the time frame and extent to which new developments impact software engineering practice

> Software engineering concerns methods and techniques to develop large
> software systems. The engineering metaphor is used to emphasize a system-
> atic approach to developing systems that satisfy organizational requirements
> and constraints. This chapter gives a brief overview of the field and points
> at emerging trends that influence the way software is developed.

Computer science is still a young field. The first computers were built in the mid
1940s, since when the field has developed tremendously.

Applications from the early years of computerization can be characterized as
follows: the programs were quite small, certainly when compared to those that are
currently being constructed; they were written by one person; they were written and
used by experts in the application area concerned. The problems to be solved were
mostly of a technical nature, and the emphasis was on expressing known algorithms
efficiently in some programming language. Input typically consisted of numerical data,
read from such media as punched tape or punched cards. The output, also numeric,
was printed on paper. Programs were run offline. If the program contained errors,
the programmer studied an octal or hexadecimal dump of memory. Sometimes, the
execution of the program would be followed by binary reading of machine registers
at the console.

Independent software development companies hardly existed in those days.
Software was mostly developed by hardware vendors and given away for free.
These vendors sometimes set up user groups to discuss requirements, which they
incorporated into their software. This software development support was seen as a
service to their customers.

Present-day applications are rather different in many respects. Present-day
programs are often very large and are developed by teams that collaborate over
periods spanning several years. These teams may be scattered across the globe. The
programmers are not the future users of the system they develop and they have no
expert knowledge of the application area in question. The problems that are being
tackled increasingly concern everyday life: automatic bank tellers, airline reservation,
salary administration, electronic commerce, automotive systems, etc. Putting a man
on the moon was not conceivable without computers.

In the 1960s, people started to realize that programming techniques had lagged
behind the developments in software both in size and complexity. To many people,
programming was still an *art* and had never become a *craft*. An additional problem
was that many programmers had not been formally educated in the field. They had
learned by doing. On the organizational side, solutions to problems often involved
adding more and more programmers to the project, the so-called 'million-monkey'
approach.

As a result, software was often delivered too late, programs did not behave as the
user expected, programs were rarely adaptable to changed circumstances, and many

errors were detected only after the software had been delivered to the customer. This became known as the 'software crisis'.

This type of problem really became manifest in the 1960s. Under the auspices of NATO, two conferences were devoted to the topic in 1968 and 1969 (Naur and Randell, 1968; Buxton and Randell, 1969). Here, the term 'software engineering' was coined in a somewhat provocative sense. Shouldn't it be possible to build software in the way one builds bridges and houses, starting from a theoretical basis and using sound and proven design and construction techniques, as in other engineering fields?

Software serves some organizational purpose. The reasons for embarking on a software development project vary. Sometimes, a solution to a problem is not feasible without the aid of computers, such as weather forecasting or automated bank telling. Sometimes, software can be used as a vehicle for new technologies, such as typesetting, the production of chips, or manned space trips. In yet other cases, software may increase user service (library automation, e-commerce) or save money (automated stock control).

In many cases, the expected economic gain will be a major driving force for automation. It may not, however, always be easy to prove that automation saves money (just think of office automation) because, apart from direct cost savings, the economic gain may also manifest itself in such things as more flexible production or a faster or better user service. In either case, software development is a value-creating activity.

Boehm (1981) estimated the total expenditure on software in the US to be $40 billion in 1980. This was approximately 2% of the GNP. In 1985, the total expenditure had risen to $70 billion in the US and $140 billion worldwide. Boehm and Sullivan (1999) estimated the annual expenditure on software development in 1998 to be $300–400 billion in the US and twice that amount worldwide.

So the *cost* of software is of crucial importance. This concerns not only the cost of developing the software, but also the cost of keeping the software operational once it has been delivered to the customer. In the course of time, hardware costs have decreased dramatically. Hardware costs now typically comprise less than 20% of total expenditure (see Figure 1.1). The remaining 80% are comprised of all non-hardware costs: the cost of programmers, analysts, management, user training, secretarial help, etc.

An aspect closely linked with cost is *productivity*. In the 1980s, the quest for data-processing personnel increased by 12% per year, while the population of people working in data processing and the productivity of those people each grew by approximately 4% per year (Boehm, 1987a). This situation has not fundamentally changed (Jones, 1999). The net effect is a growing gap between demand and supply. The result is both a backlog with respect to the maintenance of existing software and a slowing down in the development of new applications. The combined effect may have repercussions on the competitive edge of an organization, especially when there are severe time-to-market constraints. These developments have led to a shift from *producing* software to *using* software. We'll come back to this topic in Section 1.6 and Chapters 17–19.

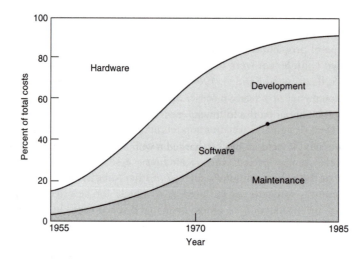

Figure 1.1 Relative distribution of hardware and software costs (*Source*: B.W. Boehm, Software Engineering, *IEEE Transactions on Computers*, © 1976 IEEE. Reproduced with permission.)

The issues of cost and productivity of software development deserve our serious attention. However, this is not the complete story. Society is increasingly dependent on software. The quality of the systems we develop increasingly determines the quality of our existence. Consider as an example the following message from a Dutch newspaper on 6 June 1980, under the heading 'Americans saw the Russians coming':

> For a short period last Tuesday, the United States brought their atomic
> bombers and nuclear missiles to an increased state of alarm when, because
> of a computer error, a false alarm indicated that the Soviet Union had
> started a missile attack.

Efforts to repair the error were apparently in vain, for on 9 June 1980, the same newspaper reported:

> For the second time within a few days, a deranged computer reported
> that the Soviet Union had started a nuclear attack against the United
> States. Last Saturday, the DoD affirmed the false message, which resulted
> in the engines of the planes of the strategic air force being started.

It is not always the world that is in danger. On a smaller scale, errors in software may have very unfortunate consequences, such as transaction errors in bank traffic; reminders to pay a bill of $0.00; a stock control system that issues orders too late and thus lays off complete divisions of a factory.

The latter example indicates that errors in a software system may have serious financial consequences for the organization using it. One example of such a financial loss is the large US airline company that lost $50 million because of an error in their seat reservation system. The system erroneously reported that cheap seats were sold out while, in fact, there were plenty available. The problem was detected only after quarterly results lagged considerably behind those of both their own previous periods and those of their competitors.

Errors in automated systems may even have fatal effects. One computer science weekly magazine contained the following message in April 1983:

> The court in Düsseldorf has discharged a woman (54), who was on trial for murdering her daughter. An erroneous message from a computerized system made the insurance company inform her that she was seriously ill. She was said to suffer from an incurable form of syphilis. Moreover, she was said to have infected both her children. In panic, she strangled her 15-year-old daughter and tried to kill her 13-year-old son and herself. The boy escaped and, with some help he enlisted, prevented the woman from dying of an overdose. The judge blamed the computer error and considered the woman not responsible for her actions.

This all marks the enormous importance of the field of software engineering. Better methods and techniques for software development may result in large financial savings, in more effective methods of software development, in systems that better fit user needs, in more reliable software systems, and thus in a more reliable environment in which those systems function. Quality and productivity are two central themes in the field of software engineering.

On the positive side, it is imperative to point to the enormous progress that has been made since the 1960s. Software is ubiquitous and scores of trustworthy systems have been built. These range from small spreadsheet applications to typesetting systems, banking systems, Web browsers and the Space Shuttle software. The techniques and methods discussed in this book have contributed their mite to the success of these and many other software development projects.

1.1 WHAT IS SOFTWARE ENGINEERING?

In various texts on this topic, one encounters a definition of the term software engineering. An early definition was given at the first NATO conference (Naur and Randell, 1968):

> Software engineering is the establishment and use of sound engineering principles in order to obtain economically software that is reliable and works efficiently on real machines.

The definition given in the *IEEE Standard Glossary of Software Engineering Terminology* (IEEE610, 1990) is as follows:

> Software engineering is the application of a systematic, disciplined, quantifiable approach to the development, operation, and maintenance of software; that is, the application of engineering to software.

These and other definitions of the term 'software engineering' use rather different words. However, the essential characteristics of the field are always, explicitly or implicitly, present:

- *Software engineering concerns the development of large programs.*
  (DeRemer and Kron, 1976) makes a distinction between **programming-in-the-large** and **programming-in-the-small**. The borderline between large and small obviously is not sharp: a program of 100 lines is small, a program of 50 000 lines of code certainly is not. Programming-in-the-small generally refers to programs written by one person in a relatively short period of time. Programming-in-the-large, then, refers to multi-person jobs that span, say, more than half a year. For example:

  - The NASA Space Shuttle software contains 40 million lines of object code (this is 30 times as much as the software for the Saturn V project from the 1960s) (Boehm, 1981);

  - The IBM OS360 operating system took 5000 man years of development effort (Brooks, 1995).

  Traditional programming techniques and tools are primarily aimed at supporting programming-in-the-small. This not only holds for programming languages, but also for the tools (such as flowcharts) and methods (such as structured programming). These cannot be directly transferred to the development of large programs.

  In fact, the term program – in the sense of a self-contained piece of software that can be invoked by a user or some other system component – is not adequate here. Present-day software development projects result in systems containing a large number of (interrelated) programs – or components.

- *The central theme is mastering complexity.*
  In general, the problems are such that they cannot be surveyed in their entirety. One is forced to split the problem into parts such that each individual part can be grasped, while the communication between the parts remains simple. The total complexity does not decrease in this way, but it does become manageable. In a stereo system there are components such as an amplifier, a receiver, and a tuner, and communication via a thin wire. In software, we strive for a similar separation of concerns. In a program for library automation, components such as user interaction, search processes and data storage could, for instance, be distinguished, with clearly given facilities for data exchange between those components. Note that the complexity of many a piece of software is not so much caused by the intrinsic complexity of the problem (as in the case of compiler optimization algorithms or

numerical algorithms to solve partial differential equations), but rather by the vast number of details that must be dealt with.

- *Software evolves.*
  Most software models a part of reality, such as processing requests in a library or tracking money transfers in a bank. This reality evolves. If software is not to become obsolete fairly quickly, it has to evolve with the reality that is being modeled. This means that costs are incurred after delivery of the software system and that we have to bear this evolution in mind during development.

- *The efficiency with which software is developed is of crucial importance.*
  The total cost and development time of software projects is high. This also holds for the maintenance of software. The quest for new applications surpasses the workforce resource. The gap between supply and demand is growing. Time-to-market demands ask for quick delivery. Important themes within the field of software engineering concern better and more efficient methods and tools for the development and maintenance of software, especially methods and tools enabling the use and reuse of components.

- *Regular cooperation between people is an integral part of programming-in-the-large.*
  Since the problems are large, many people have to work concurrently at solving those problems. Increasingly often, teams at different geographic locations work together in software development. There must be clear arrangements for the distribution of work, methods of communication, responsibilities, and so on. Arrangements alone are not sufficient, though; one also has to stick to those arrangements. In order to enforce them, standards or procedures may be employed. Those procedures and standards can often be supported by tools. Discipline is one of the keys to the successful completion of a software development project.

- *The software has to support its users effectively.*
  Software is developed in order to support users at work. The functionality offered should fit users' tasks. Users who are not satisfied with the system will try to circumvent it or, at best, voice new requirements immediately. It is not sufficient to build the system in the right way; we also have to build the right system. Effective user support means that we must carefully study users at work, in order to determine the proper functional requirements, and we must address usability and other quality aspects as well, such as reliability, responsiveness, and user-friendliness. It also means that software development entails more than delivering software. User manuals and training material may have to be written, and attention must be given to developing the environment in which the new system is going to be installed. For example, a new automated library system will affect working procedures within the library.

- *Software engineering is a field in which members of one culture create artifacts on behalf of members of another culture.*

This aspect is closely linked to the previous two items. Software engineers are expert in one or more areas such as programming in Java, software architecture, testing, or the Unified Modeling Language. They are generally not experts in library management, avionics, or banking. Yet they have to develop systems for such domains. The thin spread of application domain knowledge is a common source of problems in software development projects.

Not only do software engineers often lack factual knowledge of the domain for which they develop software, they lack knowledge of its culture as well. For example, a software developer may discover the 'official' set of work practices of a certain user community from interviews, written policies, and so on; these work practices are then built into the software. A crucial question with respect to system acceptance and success, however, is whether that community actually follows those work practices. For an outside observer, this question is much more difficult to answer.

- *Software engineering is a balancing act.*
  In most cases, it is illusory to assume that the collection of requirements voiced at the start of the project is the only factor that counts. In fact, the term 'requirement' is a misnomer. It suggests something immutable, while in fact most requirements are negotiable. There are numerous business, technical and political constraints that may influence a software development project. For example, one may decide to use database technology X rather than Y, simply because of available expertise with that technology. In extreme cases, the characteristics of available components may determine the functionality offered, rather than the other way around.

The above list shows that software engineering has many facets. Software engineering certainly is *not* the same as programming, although programming is an important ingredient of software engineering. Mathematical aspects play a role since we are concerned with the correctness of software. Sound engineering practices are needed to produce useful products. Psychological and sociological aspects play a role in the communication between human and machine, organization and machine, and between humans. Finally, the development process needs to be controlled, which is a management issue.

The term 'software engineering' hints at possible resemblances between the construction of programs and the construction of houses or bridges. These kinds of resemblances do exist. In both cases, we work from a set of desired functions, using scientific and engineering techniques in a creative way. Techniques that have been applied successfully in the construction of physical artifacts are also helpful when applied to the construction of software systems: development of the product in a number of phases, a careful planning of these phases, continuous audit of the whole process, construction from a clear and complete design, etc.

Even in a mature engineering discipline, say bridge design, accidents do happen. Bridges collapse once in a while. Most problems in bridge design occur when designers extrapolate beyond their models and expertise. A famous example is the

Tacoma Narrows Bridge failure in 1940. The designers of that bridge extrapolated beyond their experience to create more flexible stiffening girders for a suspension bridge. They did not think about aerodynamics and the response of the bridge to wind. As a result, that bridge collapsed shortly after it was finished. This type of extrapolation seems to be the rule rather than the exception in software development. We regularly embark on software development projects that go far beyond our expertise.

There are also good reasons for considering the construction of software as something quite different from the construction of physical products. The cost of constructing software is incurred during development and not during production. Copying software is almost free. Software is logical in nature rather than physical. Physical products wear out in time and therefore have to be maintained. Software does not wear out. The need to maintain software is caused by errors detected late or by changing requirements of the user. Software reliability is determined by the manifestation of errors already present, not by physical factors such as wear and tear. We may even argue that software wears out *because* it is being maintained.

Viewing software engineering as a branch of engineering is problematic for another reason as well. The engineering metaphor hints at disciplined work, proper planning, good management, and so on. It suggests we deal with clearly defined needs, that can be fulfilled if we follow all the right steps. Many software development projects, though, involve the translation of some real-world phenomenon into digital form. The knowledge embedded in this real-life phenomenon is tacit, undefined, uncodified, and may have developed over a long period of time. The assumption that we are dealing with a well-defined problem simply does not hold. Rather, the design process is open ended and the solution emerges as we go along. This dichotomy is reflected in the way the view of software engineering has changed over time (Eischen, 2002). In the early days, the field was seen as a craft. In a countermove, the term 'software engineering' was coined, and many factory concepts were introduced. In the late 1990s, the pendulum swung back again and the craft aspect was emphasized anew, in the agile movement (see Chapter 3). Both engineering-like and craft-like aspects have their place, and we will give a balanced treatment of both.

Two characteristics that make software development projects extra difficult to manage are visibility and continuity. It is much more difficult to see progress in software construction than it is to see progress in building a bridge. One often hears the phrase that a program 'is almost finished'. One equally often underestimates the time needed to finish up the last bits and pieces.

This '90% complete' syndrome is very pervasive in software development. Not knowing how to measure real progress, we often use a surrogate measure, the rate of expenditure of resources. For example, a project that has a budget of 100 person-days is perceived as being 50% complete after 50 person-days are expended. Strictly speaking, we confuse speed with progress. Because of the imprecise measurement of progress and the customary underestimation of total effort, problems accumulate as time elapses.

Physical systems are often continuous in the sense that small changes in the specification lead to small changes in the product. This is not true with software. Small changes in the specification of software may lead to considerable changes in the software itself. In a similar way, small errors in software may have considerable effects. The Mariner space rocket to Venus for example got lost because of a typing error in a FORTRAN program. In 1998, the Mars Climate Orbiter got lost because one development team used English units, such as inches and feet, while another team used metric units.

We may also draw a comparison between software engineering and computer science. Computer science emerged as a separate discipline in the 1960s. It split from mathematics and has been heavily influenced by mathematics. Topics studied in computer science, such as algorithm complexity, formal languages, and the semantics of programming languages, have a strong mathematical flavor. PhD theses in computer science invariably contain theorems with accompanying proofs.

As the field of software engineering emerged from computer science, it had a similar inclination to focus on clean aspects of software development that can be formalized, in both teaching and research. We used to assume that requirements can be fully stated before the project started, concentrated on systems built from scratch, and ignored the reality of trading off quality aspects against the available budget, not to mention the trenches of software maintenance.

Software engineering and computer science do have a considerable overlap. The practice of software engineering however also has to deal with such matters as the management of huge development projects, human factors (regarding both the development team and the prospective users of the system) and cost estimation and control. Software engineers must *engineer* software.

Software engineering has many things in common with other fields of engineering and with computer science. It also has many unique facets.

1.2 PHASES IN THE DEVELOPMENT OF SOFTWARE

When building a house, the builder does not start by piling up bricks. Rather, the requirements and possibilities of the client are analyzed first, taking into account such factors as family structure, hobbies, finances and so on. The architect takes these factors into consideration when designing a house. Only after the design has been agreed upon is the actual construction started.

It is expedient to act in the same way when constructing software. First, the problem to be solved is analyzed and the requirements are described in a very precise way. Then a design is made based on these requirements. Finally, the construction process, i.e. the actual programming of the solution, is started. There are a distinguishable number of phases in the development of software. The phases, as discussed in this book, are depicted in Figure 1.2.

The **process model** depicted in Figure 1.2 is rather simple. In reality, things will usually be more complex. For instance, the design phase is often split into a global,

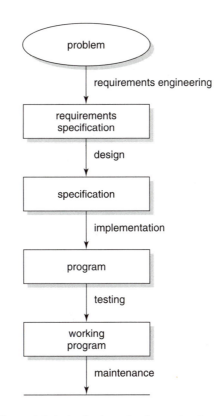

Figure 1.2 A simple view of software development

architectural design phase and a detailed design phase, and often various test phases
are distinguished. The basic elements, however, remain as given in Figure 1.2. These
phases have to be passed through in each project. Depending on the kind of project
and the working environment, a more detailed scheme may be needed.

In Figure 1.2, the phases have been depicted sequentially. For a given project,
these activities are not necessarily separated as strictly as indicated here. They may,
and usually do, overlap. It is, for instance, quite possible to start implementation of
one part of the system while some of the other parts have not been fully designed yet.
As we will see in Section 1.3, there is no strict linear progression from requirements
engineering to design, from design to implementation, etc. Backtracking to earlier
phases occurs because of errors discovered or changing requirements. It is better to
think of these phases as a series of workflows. Early on, most resources are spent on
the requirements engineering workflow. Later on, effort moves to the implementation
and testing workflows.

Below, a short description is given of each of the basic elements from Figure 1.2.
Various alternative process models are discussed in Chapter 3. These alternative

models result from justifiable criticism of the simple-minded model depicted in Figure 1.2. The sole aim of our simple model is to provide an adequate structuring of topics to be addressed. The maintenance phase is further discussed in Section 1.3. All elements of our process model are treated much more elaborately in later chapters.

Requirements engineering: The goal of the requirements engineering phase is to get a complete description of the problem to be solved and the requirements posed by and on the environment in which the system is going to function. Requirements posed by the environment may include hardware and supporting software or the number of prospective users of the system to be developed. Alternatively, analysis of the requirements may lead to certain constraints imposed on hardware yet to be acquired or the organization in which the system is to function. A description of the problem to be solved includes such things as:

- the functions of the software to be developed;

- possible future extensions to the system;

- the amount, and kind, of documentation required;

- the response time and other performance requirements of the system.

Part of requirements engineering is a **feasibility study**. The purpose of the feasibility study is to assess whether there is a solution to the problem which is both economically and technically feasible.

The more careful we are during the requirements engineering phase, the greater is the chance that the ultimate system will meet expectations. To this end, the various people involved (among others, the customer, the prospective users, the designers, and the programmers) have to collaborate intensively. These people often have widely different backgrounds, which does not ease communication.

The document in which the result of this activity is laid down is called the **requirements specification**.

Design: During the design phase, a model of the whole system is developed which, when encoded in some programming language, solves the problem for the user. To this end, the problem is decomposed into manageable pieces called **components**; the functions of these components and the **interfaces** between them are specified in a very precise way. The design phase is crucial. Requirements engineering and design are sometimes seen as an annoying introduction to programming, which is often seen as the real work. This attitude has a very negative influence on the quality of the resulting software.

Early design decisions have a major impact on the quality of the final system. These early design decisions may be captured in a global description of the system, i.e. its **architecture**. The architecture may next be evaluated, serve as a template for the development of a family of similar systems, or be used as a skeleton for the development of reusable components. As such, the architectural description of a system is an important milestone document in present-day software development projects.

During the design phase, we try to separate the *what* from the *how*. We concentrate on the problem and should not let ourselves be distracted by implementation concerns.

The result of the design phase, the (**technical**) **specification**, serves as a starting point for the implementation phase. If the specification is formal in nature, it can also be used to derive correctness proofs.

Implementation: During the implementation phase, we concentrate on the individual components. Our starting point is the component's specification. It is often necessary to introduce an extra 'design' phase, the step from component specification to executable code often being too large. In such cases, we may take advantage of some high-level, programming-language-like notation, such as a **pseudocode**. (A pseudocode is a kind of programming language. Its syntax and semantics are in general less strict, so that algorithms can be formulated at a higher, more abstract, level.)

It is important to note that the first goal of a programmer should be the development of a well-documented, reliable, easy-to-read, flexible, correct program. The goal should *not* be to produce a very efficient program full of tricks. We come back to the many dimensions of software quality in Chapter 6.

During the design phase, a global structure is imposed through the introduction of components and their interfaces. In the more classic programming languages, much of this structure tends to get lost in the transition from design to code. More recent programming languages offer possibilities for retaining this structure in the final code through the concept of modules or classes.

The result of the implementation phase is an executable program.

Testing: Actually, it is wrong to say that testing is a phase following implementation. This suggests that you need not bother about testing until implementation is finished. This is not true. It is even fair to say that this is one of the biggest mistakes you can make.

Attention has to be paid to testing even during the requirements engineering phase. During the subsequent phases, testing is continued and refined. The earlier that errors are detected, the cheaper it is to correct them.

Testing at phase boundaries comes in two flavors. We have to test that the transition between subsequent phases is correct (this is known as **verification**). We also have to check that we are still on the right track as regards fulfilling user requirements (**validation**). The result of adding verification and validation activities to the linear model of Figure 1.2 yields the so-called **waterfall model** of software development (see also Chapter 3).

Maintenance: After delivery of the software, there are often errors that have still gone undetected. Obviously, these errors must be repaired. In addition, the actual use of the system can lead to requests for changes and enhancements. All these types of change are denoted by the rather unfortunate term maintenance. Maintenance thus concerns all activities needed to keep the system operational after it has been delivered to the user.

Project management is an activity that spans all phases. As with other projects, software development projects must be managed properly in order to ensure that the product is delivered on time and within budget. The visibility and continuity characteristics of software development, as well as the fact that many software development projects are undertaken with insufficient prior experience, seriously impede project control. The many examples of software development projects that fail to meet their schedule provide ample evidence of the fact that we have by no means satisfactorily dealt with this issue yet. Chapters 2–8 deal with major aspects of software project management, such as project planning, team organization, quality issues, cost and schedule estimation.

An important activity not identified separately is **documentation**. A number of key ingredients of the documentation of a software project are elaborated upon in the chapters to follow. Key components of system documentation include the project plan, quality plan, requirements specification, architecture description, design documentation and test plan. For larger projects, a considerable amount of effort will have to be spent on properly documenting the project. The documentation effort must start early on in the project. In practice, documentation is often seen as a balancing item. Since many projects are pressed for time, the documentation tends to get the worst of it. Software maintainers and developers know this, and adapt their way of working accordingly. As a rule of thumb, (Lethbridge *et al.*, 2003) state that, the closer one gets to the code, the more accurate the documentation must be for software engineers to use it. Outdated requirements documents and other high-level documentation may still give valuable clues. They are useful to people who have to learn about a new system or have to develop test cases, for instance. Outdated low-level documentation is worthless and programmers consult the code rather than its documentation. Since the system will undergo changes after delivery, because of errors that went undetected or changing user requirements, proper and up-to-date documentation is of crucial importance during maintenance.

A particularly noteworthy element of documentation is user documentation. Software development should be task-oriented, in the sense that the software to be delivered should support users in their task environment. Likewise, the user documentation should be task-oriented. User manuals should not just describe the features of a system, they should help people to do things (Rettig, 1991). We cannot simply rely on the structure of the interface to organize the user documentation (just as a programming language reference manual is not an appropriate source for learning how to program).

Figure 1.3 gives a rough indication of the relative effort usually spent on the various activities up to delivery of the system. From this data, a very clear

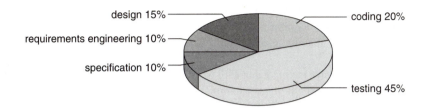

Figure 1.3 Relative effort for the various activities

trend emerges, the so-called 40–20–40 rule: only 20% of the effort is spent on actually programming (coding) the system, while the preceding phases (requirements engineering and design) and testing each consume about 40% of the total effort.

Depending on specific boundary conditions, properties of the system to be constructed, and so on, variations to this rule can be found. For iterative development projects, the distinction between requirements engineering, design, implementation, and (unit) testing gets blurred, for instance. For the majority of projects, however, this rule of thumb is quite workable.

This does not imply that the 40–20–40 rule is the one to be strived for. Errors made during requirements engineering are the ones that are most costly to repair (see also Chapter 13). It is far better to put more energy into the requirements engineering phase than to try to remove errors during the time-consuming testing phase or, worse still, during maintenance. According to (Boehm, 1987b), successful projects follow a 60–15–25 pattern: 60% requirements engineering and design, 15% implementation, and 25% testing. The message is clear: the longer you postpone coding, the earlier you are finished.

Figure 1.3 does not show the extent of the maintenance effort. When we consider the total cost of a software system over its lifetime, it turns out that, on average, maintenance alone consumes 50–75% of these costs; see also Figure 1.1. Thus, maintenance alone consumes more than the various development phases taken together.

1.3 MAINTENANCE OR EVOLUTION

> The only thing we maintain is user satisfaction.
> Lehman (1980)

Once software has been delivered, it usually still contains errors which, upon discovery, must be repaired. Note that this type of maintenance is not caused by wearing. Rather, it concerns repair of hidden defects. This type of repair is comparable to that encountered after a newly built house is first occupied.

The story becomes quite different if we start talking about changes or enhancements to the system. Repainting our office or repairing a leak in the roof of our house is called maintenance. Adding a wing to our office is seldom called maintenance.

This is more than a trifling game with words. Over the total lifetime of a software system, more money is spent on maintaining that system than on initial development. If all these expenses merely concerned the repair of errors made during one of the development phases, our business would be doing very badly indeed. Fortunately, this is not the case.

We distinguish four kinds of maintenance activity:

- **corrective** maintenance – the repair of errors;

- **adaptive** maintenance – adapting the software to changes in the environment, such as new hardware or the next release of an operating or database system;

- **perfective** maintenance – adapting the software to new or changed user requirements, such as extra functions to be provided by the system, increasing the system's performance, or enhancing its user interface;

- **preventive** maintenance – increasing the system's future maintainability, for example by updating documentation, adding comments, or improving the modular structure of a system.

Only the first category may rightfully be termed maintenance. This category, however, accounts only for about a quarter of the total maintenance effort. Approximately another quarter of the maintenance effort concerns adapting software to environmental changes, while half of the maintenance cost is spent on changes to accommodate changing user requirements, i.e. enhancements to the system (see Figure 1.4).

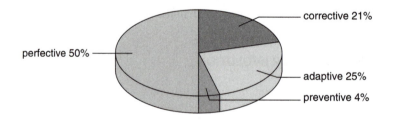

Figure 1.4 Distribution of maintenance activities

Changes in both the system's environment and user requirements are inevitable. Software models part of reality and reality changes, whether we like it or not. So the software has to change too. It *has* to evolve. A large percentage of what we are used to calling maintenance is actually evolution. Maintenance because of new user requirements occurs in both high- and low-quality systems. A successful system calls for new, unforeseen functionality, because of its use by many satisfied users. A less successful system has to be adapted in order to satisfy its customers.

The result is that the software development process becomes cyclic, hence the phrase '**software life cycle**'. Backtracking to previous phases, alluded to above, does not only occur during maintenance. During other phases, also, we will from time to time iterate earlier phases. During design, it may be discovered that the requirements specification is not complete or contains conflicting requirements. During testing, errors introduced in the implementation or design phase may crop up. In these, and similar, cases an iteration of earlier phases is needed. We will come back to this cyclic nature of the software development process in Chapter 3, when we discuss alternative models of the software development process.

1.4 FROM THE TRENCHES

> And such is the way of all superstition, whether in astrology, dreams, omens, divine judgments or the like; wherein men, having a delight in such vanities, mark the events when they are fulfilled, but when they fail, though this happens much oftener, neglect and pass them by. But with far more subtlety does this mischief insinuate itself into philosophy and the sciences; in which the first conclusion colours and brings into conformity with itself all that come after, though far sounder and better. Besides, independently of that delight and vanity which I have described, it is the peculiar and perpetual error of the human intellect to be more moved and excited by affirmatives than by negatives; whereas it ought properly to hold itself indifferently disposed towards both alike. Indeed in the establishment of any true axiom, the negative instance is the more forcible of the two.
> Sir Francis Bacon, The New Organon, *Aphorisms XLVI* (1611)

> Historical case studies contain a wealth of wisdom about the nature of design and the engineering method.
> Petroski (1994)

> Engineers must never assume that their products will achieve perfection.
> Colwell (2002)

In his wonderful book, Henri Petroski tells us about some of the greatest engineering successes and, especially, failures of all time. Some such failure stories about our profession have appeared as well. Four of them are discussed in this section.

These stories are interesting because they teach us that software engineering has many facets. Failures in software development projects often are not one-dimensional.

They are not *only* caused by a technical slip in some routine. They are not *only* caused by bad management. They are not *only* the result of human communication problems. It is often a combination of many smaller slips, which accumulate over time, and eventually result in a major failure. To paraphrase a famous saying of Fred Brooks about projects getting late:

> How does a project really get into trouble?
> One slip at a time.

Each of the stories discussed below shows such a cumulative effect. Successes in software development will not come about if we just employ the brightest programmers. Or apply the newest design philosophy. Or have the most extensive user consultation. Or even hire the best manager. You have to do all of that. And even more.

1.4.1 Ariane 5, Flight 501

The maiden flight of the Ariane 5 launcher took place on 4 June 1996. After about 40 seconds, at an altitude of less than 4 kilometers, the launcher broke up and exploded. This $500 million loss was ultimately caused by an overflow in the conversion from a 64-bit floating-point number to a 16-bit signed integer. From a software engineering point of view, the Ariane 5 story is interesting because the failure can be attributed to different causes, at different levels of understanding: inadequate testing, wrong type of reuse, or a wrong design philosophy.

The altitude of the launcher and its movements in space are measured by an inertial reference system (Système de Référence Inertielle, SRI). There are two SRIs operating in parallel. Their hardware and software is identical. Most of the hardware and software for the SRI was retained from the Ariane 4. The fatal conversion took place in a piece of software in the SRI which is only meaningful before lift-off. Though this part of the software serves no purpose after the rocket has been launched, it keeps running for an additional number of seconds. This requirement was stated more than ten years earlier for a somewhat peculiar reason. It allows for a quick restart of the countdown, if it is interrupted close to lift-off. This requirement does not apply to the Ariane 5, but the software was left unchanged – after all, it worked. Since the Ariane 5 is much faster than the Ariane 4, the rocket reaches a much higher horizontal velocity within this short period after lift-off, resulting in the above-mentioned overflow. Because of this overflow, the first SRI ceased to function. The second SRI was then activated, but since the hardware and software of both SRIs are identical, the second SRI failed as well. As a consequence, wrong data was transmitted from the SRI to the on-board computer. On the basis of this wrong data, full nozzle deflections were commanded. These caused a very high aerodynamic load, which led to the separation of the boosters from the main rocket; this, in turn, triggered the self-destruction of the launcher.

There are several levels at which the Ariane 5 failure can be understood and explained:

- It was a software failure, which could have been revealed with more extensive testing. This is true: the committee investigating the event managed to expose the failure using extensive simulations.

- The failure was caused by reusing a flawed component. This is true as well but, because of physical characteristics of the Ariane 4, this flaw had never become apparent. There had been many successful Ariane 4 flights, using essentially the same SRI subsystem. Apparently, reuse is not compositional: the successful use of a component in one environment is no guarantee for successful reuse of that component in another environment.

- The failure was caused by a flaw in the design. The Ariane software followed a typical hardware design philosophy: if a component breaks down, the cause is assumed to be random and it is handled by shutting down that part and invoking a backup component. In the case of a software failure, which is not random, an identical backup is of little use. For the software part, a different line might have been followed. For instance, the component could have been asked to give its best estimate of the required information.

1.4.2 Therac-25

The Therac-25 is a computer-controlled radiation machine. It has three modes:

- Field-light mode. This position merely facilitates the correct positioning of the patient.

- Electron mode. In electron therapy, the computer controls the (variable) beam energy and current, and magnets spread the beam to a safe concentration.

- Photon (X-ray) mode. In photon mode, the beam energy is fixed. A 'beam flattener' is put between the accelerator and the patient to produce a uniform treatment field. A very high current (some 100 times higher than in electron mode) is required on one side of the beam flattener to produce a reasonable treatment dose at the other side.

The machine has a turntable which rotates the necessary equipment into position. The basic hazardous situation is obvious from the above: a photon beam is issued by the accelerator while the beam flattener is not in position. The patient is then treated with a dose which is far too high. This happened several times. As a consequence, several patients have died and others have been seriously injured.

One of the malfunctions of the Therac-25 has become known as 'Malfunction 54'. A patient was set up for treatment. The operator keyed in the necessary data on the console in an adjacent room. While doing so, he made a mistake: he typed 'x' (for X-ray mode) instead of 'e' (for electron mode). He corrected his mistake by moving the cursor up to the appropriate field, typing in the correct code and pressing the return key a number of times until the cursor was on the command line again. He then pressed 'B' (beam on). The machine stopped and issued the message 'Malfunction 54'. This particular error message indicates a wrong dose, either too high or too low. The console indicated a substantial underdose. The operator knew that the machine often had quirks, and that these could usually be solved by simply pressing 'P' (proceed). So he did. The same error message appeared again. Normally, the operator would have audio and video contact with the patient in the treatment room. Not this time, though: the audio was broken and the video had been turned off. It was later estimated that the patient had received 16 000–25 000 rad on a very small surface, instead of the intended dose of 180 rad. The patient became seriously ill and died five months later.

The cause of this hazardous event was traced back to the software operating the radiation machine. After the operator has finished data entry, the physical set up of the machine may begin. The bending of the magnets takes about eight seconds. After the magnets are put into position, it again checks if anything has changed. If the operator manages to make changes **and** return the cursor to the command-line position within the eight seconds it takes to set the magnets, there will be changes in internal system parameters but the system will nevertheless 'think' that nothing has happened and simply continue, with consequences as described above.

Accidents like this are reported to the Federal Drugs Administration (FDA). The FDA requested the manufacturer to take appropriate measures. The 'fix' suggested was as follows:

> Effective immediately, and until further notice, the key used for moving the cursor back through the prescription sequence (i.e. cursor 'UP' inscribed with an upward pointing arrow) must not be used for editing or any other purpose.

> To avoid accidental use of this key, the key cap must be removed and the switch contacts fixed in the open position with electrical tape or other insulating material. . . .

> Disabling this key means that if any prescription data entered is incorrect then an 'R' reset command must be used and the whole prescription reentered.

The FDA did not accept this remedy. In particular, they judged the tone of the notification not commensurate with the urgency for doing so. The discussion between the FDA and the manufacturer continued for quite some time before an adequate response was given to this and other failures of the Therac-25.

The Therac-25 machine and its software evolved from earlier models that were less sophisticated. In earlier versions of the software, for example, it was not possible to move up and down the screen to change individual fields. Operators noticed that different treatments often required almost the same data, which had to be keyed in all over again. To enhance usability, the feature to move the cursor around and change individual fields was added. Thus, it is apparent, user friendliness may conflict with safety.

In earlier models also, the correct position of the turntable and other equipment was ensured by simple electromechanical interlocks. These interlocks are a common mechanism to ensure safety. For instance, they are used in lifts to make sure that the doors cannot be opened if the lift is between floors. In the Therac-25, these mechanical safety devices were replaced by software. The software thus became a single point of failure. This overconfidence in software contributed to the Therac-25 accidents, together with inadequate software engineering practices and an inadequate reaction of management to incidents.

1.4.3 The London Ambulance Service

The London Ambulance Service (LAS) handles the ambulance traffic in Greater London. It covers an area of over 600 square miles and carries over 5 000 patients per day in 750 vehicles. The LAS receives over 2 000 phone calls per day, including more than 1 300 emergency calls. The system we discuss here is a computer-aided dispatch (CAD) system. Such a CAD system has the following functionality:

- It takes calls, accepting and verifying incident details including the location of the incident.

- It determines which ambulance to send.

- It mobilizes the ambulance and communicates the details of the incident to the ambulance.

- It takes care of ambulance resource management, in particular the positioning of vehicles to minimize response times.

A fully-fledged CAD system is quite complex. In panic, someone might call and say that an accident has happened in front of Foyle's, assuming that everyone knows where this bookshop is located. An extensive gazetteer component, including public-telephone identification, helps in solving this type of problem. The CAD system also contains a radio system, mobile terminals in the ambulances, and an automatic vehicle-location system.

The CAD project of the London Ambulance Service was started in the fall of 1990. Delivery was scheduled for January 1992. At that time, however, the software was still far from complete. Over the first nine months of 1992, the system was installed piecemeal across a number of different LAS divisions, but it was never stable. On 26 and 27 October 1992, there were serious problems with the system and it was decided to revert to a partially manual mode of operation. On 4 November 1992, the system crashed. The Regional Health Authority established an inquiry team to investigate the failures and the history that led to them. They came up with an 80-page report, which reads like a suspense novel. Below, we highlight some of the issues raised in this report.

The envisaged CAD system would be a major undertaking. No other emergency service had attempted to go as far. The plan was to move from a wholly manual process – in which forms were filled in and transported from one employee to the next via a conveyor belt – to complete automation, in one shot. The scheme was very ambitious. The participants seem not to have fully realized the risks they were taking.

Way before the project actually started, a management consultancy was asked for advice. They suggested that a packaged solution would cost $1.5 million and take 19 months. Their report also stated that if a packaged solution could not be found, the estimates should be significantly increased. Eventually, a non-packaged solution was chosen, but only the numbers from this report were remembered, or so it seems.

The advertisement resulted in replies from 35 companies. The specification and timetable were discussed with these companies. The proposed timetable was 11 months (this is not a typo). Though many suppliers raised concerns about the timetable, they were told that it was non-negotiable. Eventually, 17 suppliers provided full proposals. The lowest tender, at approximately $1 million, was selected. This tender was about $700 000 cheaper than the next lowest bid. No one seems to have questioned this huge difference. The proposal selected superficially suggested that the company had experience in designing systems for emergency services. This was not a lie: they had developed administrative systems for such services. The LAS system was also far larger than anything they had previously handled.

The proposed system would impact quite significantly on the way ambulance crews carried out their jobs. It would therefore be paramount to have their full cooperation. If the crews did not press the right buttons at the right time and in the right order, chaos could result. Yet, there was very little user involvement during the requirements engineering process.

The intended CAD system would operate in an absolutely objective and impartial way and would always mobilize the optimum resource to any incident. This would overcome many of the then present working practices which management considered outmoded and not in the interest of LAS. For instance, the new system would allocate the nearest available resource regardless of the originating station. The following scenario may result:

- John's crew has to go to an accident a few miles east of their home base.

- Once there, they are directed to a hospital a few miles further east to deliver the patient.

- Another call comes in and John happens to be nearest. He is ordered to travel yet a few miles further east.

In this way, crews may have to operate further and further away from their home base and in unfamiliar territory. They lose time, because they take wrong turns, or may even have to stop to ask for directions. They also have further to travel to reach their home station at the end of a shift. Crews didn't like this aspect of the new system.

The new system also took away the flexibility of local emergency stations in deciding which resource to allocate. In the new scheme, resource management was fully centralized and handled by the system. So, suppose John runs down to where the ambulances are parked and the computer has ordered him to take car number 5. John is in a hurry and maybe he cannot quickly spot car number 5, or maybe it is parked behind some other cars. John is thinking about the patient waiting for him and decides to take car number 4 instead. This means trouble.

The people responsible for the requirements were misguided, or naive, in believing that computer systems in themselves can bring about changes in human practices. Computers are there to help people do their job, not vice versa. Operational straitjackets are doomed to fail.

The eventual crash on 4 November 1992 was caused by a minor programming error. Some three weeks earlier, a programmer had been working on part of the system and forgot to remove a small piece of program text. The code in itself did no harm. However, it did allocate a small amount of memory every time a vehicle mobilization was generated by the system. This memory was not deallocated. After three weeks, all memory was used up and the system crashed.

The LAS project as a whole did not fail because of this programmer mistake. That was just the last straw. The project schedule was far too tight. The management of both the London Ambulance Service and the contractor had little or no experience with software development projects of this size and complexity. They were far too optimistic in their assessment of risks. They assumed that all the people who would interact with the system would do so in exactly the right way, all of the time. They assumed the hardware parts of the system would work exactly as specified. Management decided on the functionality of the system, with hardly any consultation with the people that would be its primary users. Any project with such characteristics is doomed to fail. From the very first day.

1.4.4 Who Counts the Votes?

> It's not who votes that counts, it's who counts the votes.
> Josef Stalin

Traditional, non-automated election systems leave a paper trail that can be used for auditing purposes: have all votes been counted? have they been counted correctly? Such an audit is done by an independent party. These safeguards serve to build trust in the outcome.

But what if the elections are supported by computers? As a voter, you simply press a button. But what next? The recording and counting is hidden. How do you know your vote is not tinkered with? How can fraud be avoided? For the individual, one needs a voter ballot, a piece of paper similar to an ATM receipt, that serves to verify the voter's choice. The ballots of all voters may be used in an independent audit of the election outcome. Most automated election systems today do not provide these safeguards.

What if we go one step further and provide our voters with a Web application to place their votes? Below is a story about a real system of this kind. The application was developed in Java. Due to governmental regulations, the voting model implemented mimicked the traditional one. The application maintains a voting register, containing the identification of all voters, and a ballot box in which the votes are stored. One of the regulations that the system had to comply with is anonymity: a vote in the ballot box should not be traceable to a name in the voting register. Another regulation concerns security: both registers have to be stored separately.

The technical design envisaged two separate databases, one for the voters and one for the ballots. Placing a vote and marking a voter as 'has voted' should be performed in a single transaction: either both actions are done or neither of them. This design would cater for the correctness requirement: the number of votes in the ballot box equals the number of voters being marked 'has voted'.

At least, this is what we hoped for. Tests of the system, though, showed that, seemingly at random moments in time, there were more votes in the ballot box than there were voters marked as 'has voted'. So the system allowed voters more than one vote.

Taking a look under the hood, a coding error was revealed in the voting process. Part of the algorithm ran as follows:

1. Identify the voter.

2. Match the voter with an entry in the register.

3. If a match is found, check that the voter has not voted yet.

The test in the latter step had the form

```
voter.getIdentification()==identification()
```

instead of

```
equals(voter.getIdentification()==identification())
```

In other words, references were compared, rather than actual values. This is one way to win an election.

1.5 SOFTWARE ENGINEERING ETHICS

Suppose you are testing part of a big software system. You find quite a few errors and you're certainly not ready to deliver. However, your manager is pressing you. The schedule has already slipped by quite a few weeks. Your manager in turn is pressed by his boss. The customer is eagerly awaiting delivery of the system. Your manager suggests that you should deliver the system as is, continue testing, and replace the system by a better version within the next month. How would you react to this scheme? Would you simply give in? Argue with your manager? Go to his boss? Go to the customer?

The development of complex software systems involves many people: software developers, testers, technical managers, general managers, customers, etc. Within this temporary organization, the relationship between individuals is often asymmetrical: one person participating in the relationship has more knowledge about something than the other. For example, a software developer has more knowledge about the system under construction than his manager. Such an asymmetric relationship asks for trust: if the developer says that development of some component is on schedule, his manager cannot but believe this message. At least for a while. Such reliance provides opportunities for unethical behavior, such as embezzlement, even more so if there also is a power relationship between the individuals.

It is not surprising then that people within the software engineering community have been discussing a software engineering code of ethics. Two large organizations of professionals in the field, the IEEE Computer Society and ACM, have jointly developed such a code. The short version of this code is given in Figure 1.5.

In the long version of the code, each of the principles is further refined into a set of clauses. Some of these clauses are statements of aspiration: for example, a software engineer should strive to fully understand the specifications of the software on which he works. Aspirations direct professional behavior. They require significant ethical judgment. Other clauses express obligations of professionals in general: for example, a software engineer should, like any other professional, provide service only in areas of his competence. A third type of clause is directed at specific professional behavior within software engineering: for example, a software engineer should ensure realistic estimates of the cost and schedule of any project on which he works.

There are a number of clauses in this code which bear upon the situation of the tester mentioned above:

- Approve software only if you have a well-founded belief that it is safe, meets specifications, passes appropriate tests, and does not diminish quality of life or privacy or harm the environment (clause 1.03[1]).

- Ensure adequate testing, debugging, and review of software and related documents on which you work (clause 3.10).

- As a manager, do not ask a software engineer to do anything inconsistent with this code of ethics (clause 5.11).

- Be accurate in stating the characteristics of software on which you work, avoiding not only false claims but also claims that might be supposed to be speculative, vacuous, deceptive, misleading, or doubtful (clause 6.07).

---

[1]Clause 1.03 denotes clause 3 of principle 1 (Public).

Preamble

The short version of the code summarizes aspirations at a high level of abstraction. The clauses that are included in the full version give examples and details of how these aspirations change the way we act as software engineering professionals. Without the aspirations, the details can become legalistic and tedious; without the details, the aspirations can become high-sounding but empty; together, the aspirations and the details form a cohesive code.

Software engineers shall commit themselves to making the analysis, specification, design, development, testing, and maintenance of software a beneficial and respected profession. In accordance with their commitment to the health, safety and welfare of the public, software engineers shall adhere to the following eight Principles:

1. **Public.** Software engineers shall act consistently with the public interest.

2. **Client and employer.** Software engineers shall act in a manner that is in the best interests of their client and employer, consistent with the public interest.

3. **Product.** Software engineers shall ensure that their products and related modifications meet the highest professional standards possible.

4. **Judgment.** Software engineers shall maintain integrity and independence in their professional judgment.

5. **Management.** Software engineering managers and leaders shall subscribe to and promote an ethical approach to the management of software development and maintenance.

6. **Profession.** Software engineers shall advance the integrity and reputation of the profession consistent with the public interest.

7. **Colleagues.** Software engineers shall be fair to and supportive of their colleagues.

8. **Self.** Software engineers shall participate in lifelong learning regarding the practice of their profession and shall promote an ethical approach to the practice of the profession.

Figure 1.5 Software engineering code of ethics

The code is not a simple algorithm to discriminate between acceptable and unacceptable behavior. Rather, the principles stated should influence you, as a software engineer, to consider who is affected by your work. The software you develop affects the public. The health, safety and welfare of the public is the primary concern of this code of ethics. Adhering to this, or a similar, code of ethics is not merely something to consider on a Friday afternoon. It should become a way of life.

The code not only addresses software engineers. It also addresses managers, in that the code indicates what might reasonably be expected from professional software engineers.

1.6 QUO VADIS?

A lot of progress has been made over the past 30 years. For each of the major phases, numerous techniques and tools have been developed. A number of these have found widespread use. In their assessment of design and coding practices, for example, DeMarco and Lister found that a number of widely acclaimed techniques (such as the use of small units, strong component binding and structured programming) are applied in practice and also pay off (DeMarco and Lister, 1989). However, the short sketches in Section 1.4 (and the more elaborate discussion in the following chapters) show that a lot of research is still needed to make software engineering into a truly mature engineering discipline.

It takes some time before technology developed in research laboratories is applied in a routine way. This holds for physical products, such as the transistor, but also for methods, techniques, and tools in the area of software technology. The first version of the UNIX operating system goes back to 1971; only since the late 1980s, has interest in UNIX spread widely. Studies of the cost of software were first made in the early 1960s; in the 1980s, there was a growing interest in quantitative models for estimating software costs (see also Chapter 7). Dijkstra's article on programming as a human activity appeared in 1965. In the late 1970s, the first introductory textbooks on structured programming were published. The term 'software engineering' was introduced in 1968. In the 1980s, large national and international programs were initiated to foster the transition of this new technology. The above list can be extended with many other examples (Redwine and Riddle, 1985). This maturation process generally takes at least 10 to 15 years.

In a seminal article, Brooks (1987) discusses a number of potentially fruitful approaches to dramatically increase software productivity. His main conclusion is that there is no silver bullet. But we need not be afraid of the werewolf either. By a careful study of the many innovations and an investigation of their true merits, a lot of improvements in both quality and productivity can be achieved. The remainder of this text is devoted to a critical assessment of these technological and non-technological developments.

Several relatively recent developments have had a dramatic impact on the field:

- The rise of agile methods. As noted before in this chapter, the term 'software engineering' implies an orderly, factory-like approach to software development. This ignores the fact that, for many a project, it is impossible to state the requirements up front. They emerge as we go along. Armour (2001) compares traditional software development with shooting down a Zeppelin and agile approaches with shooting down a supersonic plane. To shoot down a Zeppelin, we collect information on altitude, distance, velocity and so on, relay this information to the gun, aim, and shoot. This approach does not work for supersonic planes. We do not know where the intercept will be, and the missile will have to change direction while in the air. It is a challenge to try to successfully combine engineering and craft-like approaches to software development.

- The shift from *producing* software to *using* software. Time-to-market, cost, and sheer complexity encourage organizations to assemble systems from existing components, rather than developing those components from scratch. Builders build (pieces of) software and integrators integrate those pieces into end-user applications. As one consequence, consumers of software often do not talk to developers any more. Requirements come from a variety of other sources, such as helpdesk call-log analysis or market research (Sawyer, 2001). To the consumer, the software development process is not interesting any more, only the resulting product counts. This shift has given rise to new topics within software engineering, such as component-based software development (CBSD), commercial off-the-shelf (COTS) components, software product lines, and services.

- The success of open source software. Open source software is software whose source code is freely available. Most software developed is closed source software, developed for the purpose of selling it to a client. It is not in the interest of the developing organization or the client to make the software available to others for perusal and change. With open source software, the source code *is* available.

  Individual software developers usually get involved in open source development for personal reasons: hobbyism, higher esteem from colleagues, opportunity to work on challenging tasks, involvement in projects with a high visibility, or better career opportunities. But that is not enough to explain the success of open source projects.

  The success of open source products such as Linux, Apache and Mozilla is partly caused by network effects. These products involve huge numbers of developers that exchange ideas and propose new features. Successful proposals seep through the layers of the open source development organization (see Section 5.2.6) and ultimately become accepted by the core development team. So, rather than having an expensive requirements engineering process with a risky outcome, the requirements *emerge* as a byproduct of the development process. This is also known as *crowdsourcing*: the 'crowd' is the source of the requirements. The crowd of people involved filters the requirements and only those that are widely accepted get through. The end result is a product whose features are valued by a large user community. Many organizations, for instance those in the telecommunications world, have recognized the opportunities of this development model and carefully watch developments in the open source communities in which they are interested. They make strategic deals with communities they deem interesting. In the long run, this value-building aspect of open source software development is likely to be more important for its success than the volunteer aspect.

- The more heterogeneous nature of software development. In the old days, a software development organization had everything under control. Or so it thought. Nowadays, software is developed by teams scattered across the globe. Part of the development may be outsourced to a different organization. Software incorporates components acquired from other suppliers, open source products, or services found on the Web. As a consequence, one organization is not in control any more.

To close this chapter is a list of important periodicals that contain material which is relevant to the field of software engineering:

- *Transactions on Software Engineering* (IEEE) is a monthly periodical in which research results are reported.

- *Software* (IEEE) is a bimonthly journal which is somewhat more general in scope.

- *Software Engineering Notes* (ACM) is a bimonthly newsletter from the ACM Special Interest Group on Software Engineering.

- *Transactions on Software Engineering and Methodology* (ACM) is a quarterly journal which reports research results.

- *The Journal of Systems and Software* (Elsevier) is a monthly journal covering both research papers and reports of practical experiences.

- *Proceedings of the International Conference on Software Engineering* (ACM/IEEE) gives the proceedings of the most important international conference in the field, organized every year.

- *Proceedings of the International Conference on Software Maintenance* (IEEE) gives the proceedings of an annual conference.

- *Software Maintenance and Evolution: Research and Practice* (Wiley) is a bimonthly journal devoted to topics in software maintenance and evolution.

1.7 SUMMARY

Software engineering is concerned with the problems that have to do with the construction of *large* programs. When developing such programs, a phased approach is followed. First, the problem is analyzed, and then the system is designed, implemented and tested. This practice has a lot in common with the engineering of physical products; hence the term 'software engineering'. Software engineering, however, also differs from the engineering of physical products in some essential ways.

Software models part of the real world surrounding us, such as banking or the reservation of airline seats. The world around us changes over time, so the corresponding software has to change too. It has to evolve with the changing reality. Much of what we call software maintenance is actually concerned with ensuring that the software keeps pace with the real world being modeled.

We thus get a process model in which we iterate earlier phases from time to time. We speak about the software life cycle.

Agile methods, reuse of components, open source software, and globalization are some of the relatively recent trends that have a huge impact on the way we view the field. There is a shift from producing software to using software, a major consequence of which is that a development organization loses control over what it delivers.

1.8 FURTHER READING

Johnson (1998) describes the early history of the software industry. Campbell-Kelly (2003) describes the history of the industry until approximately 2000. The more recent state of the practice is described in (Software, 2003). Finkelstein (2000) describes the state of the art as of 2000. Glass (2003) is a very readable overview of the field of software engineering, phrased as a collection of facts and fallacies.

For a more elaborate discussion of the differences and similarities between software engineering and a mature engineering discipline, e.g. bridge design, see (Spector and Gifford, 1986). Leveson (1992) compares software engineering with the development of high-pressure steam engines.

The four kinds of maintenance activity stem from (Lientz and Swanson, 1980).

The Ariane failure is described in (Jézéquel and Meyer, 1997). I found the report of the inquiry team at www.cs.vu.nl/~hans/ariane5report.html. An elaborate discussion of the Therac-25 accidents can be found in (Leveson and Turner, 1993). The inquiry into the London Ambulance Service is described in (Page *et al.*, 1993). Neumann (1995) is a book wholly devoted to computer-related risks. The bimonthly *ACM Software Engineering Notes* contains a column 'Risks to the public in computer systems', edited by Peter Neumann, which reports on large and small catastrophes caused by automation. Flowers (1996) is a collection of stories about information systems that failed, including the LAS system. (Kohno *et al.*, 2004) and Raba (2004) discuss problems with one specific electronic voting system. Further problems of voting systems are discussed in a special issue of the *Communications of the ACM* (Neumann, 2004). Petroski (1994) is a wonderful book on failures in engineering. (Avison *et al.*, 2006) discuss several projects that were catastrophic, or near catastrophic, due to management complacency. Fairley and Wilshire (2003) relate the famous story of the Vasa, a ship that sank right after its launching, to software project failures. (Software, 1999) is a special issue with stories about successful IT projects.

The ACM/IEEE software engineering code of ethics is discussed in (Gotterbarn, 1999). The text of the code can also be found in (Gotterbarn *et al.*, 1999). Epstein (1997) is a collection of (fictional) stories addressing the interaction between ethics and software engineering. Oz (1994) discusses ethical questions of a real-life project.

Exercises

1. Define the term 'software engineering'.

2. What are the essential characteristics of software engineering?

3. What are the major phases in a software development project?

4. What is the difference between verification and validation?

5. Define the four kinds of maintenance activity.

6. Why is the documentation of a software project important?

7. Explain the 40–20–40 rule of thumb in software engineering.

8. What is the difference between software development and software maintenance?

9. ♡ Do you think the linear model of software development is appropriate? In which cases do you think an agile approach is more appropriate? You may wish to reconsider this issue after having read the remainder of this book.

10. ♡ Discuss the major differences between software engineering and some other engineering discipline, such as bridge design or house building. Would you consider state-of-the-art software engineering as a true engineering discipline?

11. ♠ Quality and productivity are major issues in software engineering. It is often advocated that automated tools (CASE tools) will dramatically improve both quality and productivity. Study a commercial CASE tool and assess the extent to which it improves the software development process and its outcome.

12. ♡ Medical doctors have a Hippocratic oath. Could a similar ethical commitment by software engineers be instrumental in increasing the quality of software systems?

13. ♠ Suppose you are involved in an office automation project in the printing industry. The system to be developed is meant to support the work of

journal editors. The management objective for this project is to save labor costs; the editors' objective is to improve the quality of their work. Discuss possible ramifications of these opposing objectives on the project. You may come back to this question after having read Chapter 9 or (Hirschheim and Klein, 1989).

14. ♡ Discuss the difference between requirements-based software development and market-driven software development (Sawyer, 2001).

15. ♡ Discuss the impact of globalization on software development (see also Chapter 20).

16. ♡ Discuss how open source software has changed the software development landscape (e.g., see (Riehle, 2007)).

17. ♠ Study both the technical and user documentation of a system at your disposal. Are you satisfied with them? Discuss their possible shortcomings and give remedies to improve their quality.

18. ♠ Take a piece of software you wrote more than a year ago. Is it documented adequately? Does it have a user manual? Is the design rationale reflected in the technical documentation? Can you build an understanding of the system from its documentation that is sufficient for making nontrivial changes to it? Repeat these questions for a system written by one of your colleagues.

19. ♠ Try to gather quantitative data from your organization that reveals how much effort is spent on various kinds of maintenance activity. Is this data available at all? If so, is the pattern like that sketched in Section 1.3? If not, can you explain the differences?

20. ♠ A 1999 Computer Society survey lists the following candidate fundamental principles of software engineering:

    a. Apply and use quantitative measurements in decision-making.

    b. Build with and for reuse.

    c. Control complexity with multiple perspectives and multiple levels of abstraction.

    d. Define software artifacts rigorously.

e. Establish a software process that provides flexibility.

f. Implement a disciplined approach and improve it continuously.

g. Invest in the understanding of the problem.

h. Manage quality throughout the life cycle as formally as possible.

i. Minimize software component interaction.

j. Produce software in a stepwise fashion.

k. Set quality objectives for each deliverable product.

l. Since change is inherent to software, plan for it and manage it.

m. Since tradeoffs are inherent to software engineering, make them explicit and document them.

n. To improve design, study previous solutions to similar problems.

o. Uncertainty is unavoidable in software engineering. Identify and manage it.

For each of these principles, indicate whether you (strongly) agree or (strongly) disagree, and why. You may wish to re-appraise these principles after having studied the rest of this book.

Part I
Software Management

CONTENTS

Software development projects often involve several people for a prolonged period of time. Large projects may even range over several years and involve hundreds of people. Such projects must be carefully planned and controlled. The main aspects that deserve the continuous attention of project managers are introduced in Chapter 2 and further dealt with in Chapters 3–7: progress, information, people, quality, cost and schedule. The management part ends with Chapter 8, in which the various approaches sketched in Chapters 3–7 are reconciled.

Introduction to Software Engineering Management

LEARNING OBJECTIVES

- To be aware of the contents of a project plan

- To understand the major dimensions along which a software development project is controlled

> Software development projects often involve several people for a prolonged period of time. Large projects may even range over several years and involve hundreds of people. Such projects must be carefully planned and controlled. The main aspects that deserve the continuous attention of project managers are introduced in this chapter.

It is not easy to successfully complete a software development project. This book mainly deals with technical aspects of software development: design, specification, implementation and testing of software systems. As we learn to control these aspects better, we will also learn to satisfy our customers' demands better. The organizational and managerial aspects of software development projects are at least as important as the technical aspects, though.

Before we embark on a discussion of these organizational and managerial aspects, let us first pay some attention to the boundaries of a software development project as they are drawn in this book.

A software development project is usually not started in complete isolation. There are other projects within the organization that this particular project needs to be tuned to, priorities between projects have to be decided upon, etc. The term **'information planning'** is often used to refer to this meta-project planning process.

Also in a more technical sense, projects are not started in isolation. To increase interoperability between systems, overall guidelines regarding the use of certain standards, data interchange formats, security policies, Web page layout, and so on are laid down for the whole organization and imposed on every project. In product-line development, the architecture of the product line guides the development of individual products.

These project-exceeding rules result in a set of boundary conditions for each project, much like the zoning regulations set the conditions for a building project. Establishing these company-wide rules is a problem on its own, and will not be addressed here. (We will, however, pay ample attention to some issues which generally surpass the boundaries of individual software development projects, such as configuration control, quality assurance and product-line development.)

In a more technical sense, software is also not generally developed in isolation. In most cases, software is not written from scratch. It must interface with existing software, extend existing software, use existing subroutine libraries, build upon an existing framework, and so on.

In some sense, the notion of a 'software development project' is a misnomer. We do not just develop software, we develop systems. Broadly speaking, a system transforms inputs into outputs. Software is an important ingredient of the systems we develop, but it is by no means the only ingredient. The technical and user documentation, the hardware, the procedures that govern the use of the system, and even the people using the software, may be considered as part of that same system.

Consider, for example, a system for library automation. The system will contain various software components, such as a database component to store information on books and customers and an interaction component to process user requests. As well as the development of these components, attention should be paid to matters such as:

- techniques to identify books electronically, such as a bar-code scheme;

- the selection and acquisition of special hardware both to produce an identification code for new books and to scan the identification code;

- setting up a scheme to provide all books with an identification code;

- instruction of library employees to handle the new types of equipment (training material and courses, operating procedures, and so on);

- production of user-friendly documentation for the library customers;

- Web-accessibility issues, such as whether the catalog can be browsed, or books can be reserved online.

Whenever the notion 'software development project' is used in the following text, it should be understood in this wider sense. This is graphically illustrated in Figure 2.1.

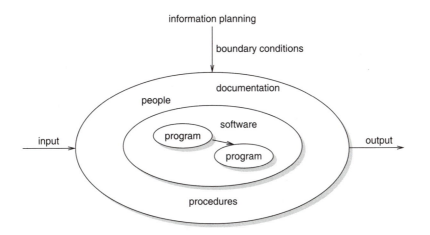

Figure 2.1 The systems view of a software development project

Thus, our systems encompass a number of components. In a narrow sense, the software component itself may also consist of a number of interacting components. These latter components correspond to programs as we know them from introductory computer science textbooks. In general, a software development project results in a set of components which collectively provide us with the desired functionality.

Given a project's boundary conditions, a software development project may get started. Planning the project is the very first step to be undertaken. Part of this planning process is to identify the project characteristics and their impact on the development process. The result of the planning phase is laid down in a document, the **project plan**, which aims to provide a clear picture of the project to both the customers and the development team. The contents of the project plan are discussed in Section 2.1.

During the execution of the project, a number of elements have to be managed: time, information, organization, quality, and money (see Section 2.2). Each of these elements is further elaborated upon in a separate chapter.

2.1 PLANNING A SOFTWARE DEVELOPMENT PROJECT

Before we embark on a software development project, it has to be carefully planned. Planning entails, amongst other things, an assessment of project properties that may affect the development process. A number of properties, however, will not be sufficiently well understood until the requirements engineering phase has ended. As with many other aspects of a software development project, planning is not a one-shot activity. Rather, it is highly dynamic in nature. The project plan can serve as a guide during the project.

The amount of upfront planning depends on characteristics of the problem at hand. In highly explorative projects, where requirements are largely unknown at the start, a too rigorous early planning can be stifling and may increase the probability of major failures. A strict 'plan the work and work the plan' attitude does not work in these circumstances. Rather, such projects call for nominal early planning and a management style that encourages responding to change. This is reflected in the content and size of the project plan. Chapters 3 and 8 further discuss differences between the so-called agile and planning-driven approaches to software development.

The major constituents of a project plan are:

1. **Introduction** In the introduction to the project plan, the background and history of the project are given, together with its aims, the project deliverables, the names of the persons responsible, and a summary of the project.

2. **Process model** In Chapter 1, we introduced a simple life cycle model in order to discuss the various activities to be dealt with in a software development project. There exist many variations of this process model, some of which are discussed in Chapter 3. For each project, one has to decide upon the exact process model to be followed: which activities are to be undertaken, which milestones can be identified, how we ascertain whether those milestones are reached, and which are the critical paths.

Different types of projects have different characteristics and so call for different process models.

3. **Organization of the project** The relationship of the project to other entities and the organization of the project itself are dealt with under this heading. The project will have a relationship with the user organization, the parent organization, and possibly with other organizations.

   The prospective users will, from time to time, be involved in the project. The project plan has to state which information, services, resources and facilities are to be provided by the users and when these are to be provided.

   Within the project team, various roles can be identified: project manager, tester, programmer, analyst, etc. One has to clearly delineate these roles and identify the responsibilities of each of them. If there are gaps in the knowledge required to fulfill any of these roles, the training and education needed to fill these gaps have to be identified. Different forms of team organization are discussed in Chapter 5.

4. **Standards, guidelines, procedures** Software projects are big projects. Usually, a lot of people are involved. A strong working discipline is therefore needed, in which each person involved follows the standards, guidelines and procedures agreed upon. Besides being stated on paper, many of these can be supported or enforced by tools. Of extreme importance are clear agreements about documentation: when is documentation to be delivered, how is the quality of the documentation to be assessed, how does one ensure that the documentation is kept up to date?

   To a large extent, these standards and procedures will be described in separate documents, such as the Configuration Control Plan or the Quality Assurance Plan.

5. **Management activities** Management activities are guided by goals and priorities set for the project. For example, management will have to submit regular reports on the status and progress of the project. It will also have to follow certain priorities in balancing requirements, schedule and cost.

6. **Risks** Potential risks have to be identified as early as possible. There will always be risks: hardware may not be delivered on time, qualified personnel may not be available when required, critical information may be lacking when it is needed, and so on. It is rather naive to suppose that a software development project always runs smoothly. Even in well-established fields, such as construction, there is always something that goes wrong. One should diagnose the risks of a software project early on, and provide measures to deal with them; see also Chapter 8.

   The more uncertain various aspects of the project are, the larger the risks.

7. **Staffing** At different points in time, the project will require different amounts of personnel, with different skills. The start, duration, amount and expertise of personnel categories are listed under this heading.

8. **Methods and techniques** Under this heading, the methods and techniques to be used during requirements engineering, design, implementation and testing are given. Typically, the way version and configuration control for software components is dealt with is described here too. A large proportion of the technical documentation will be produced during these phases. One thus has to state how this documentation will be taken care of.

   The necessary test environment and test equipment is described. During testing, considerable pressure will normally be put on the test equipment. Therefore, this activity has to be planned carefully. The order in which components are integrated and tested has to be stated explicitly. Also, the procedures to be followed during acceptance testing, i.e. the testing under user supervision, have to be given. Testing is discussed in Chapter 13.

9. **Quality assurance** Which organization and procedures will be used to assure that the software being developed meets the quality requirements stated? The many aspects of a Quality Assurance Plan may also be dealt with in a separate document. The topic of quality assurance is discussed in Chapter 6.

10. **Work packages** Larger projects must be broken down into activities, manageable pieces that can be allocated to individual team members. Each of these activities has to be identified in the project plan. The hierarchical decomposition of the project is depicted in a work breakdown structure (see also Section 8.4).

11. **Resources** During the project, many resources are needed. The hardware, CPU-cycles and tools needed to support the project are listed under this entry. One should also indicate the personnel needed for the various process phases.

12. **Budget and schedule** The total budget for the project has to be allocated to the various activities as indicated in the work breakdown structure. The activities also have to be scheduled in time, e.g. using a PERT chart (see Section 8.4). The way in which resources and other expenditures are tracked is also indicated under this heading. The topic of cost and time estimation are dealt with extensively in Chapter 7.

13. **Changes** It has been stated before that changes are inevitable. One has to ensure that these changes are dealt with in an orderly way. One thus needs clear procedures on how proposed changes will be handled. If the process is agile, every iteration involves changes, and these are dealt with in a lightweight manner. In fact, they are not seen as changes. In more heavyweight processes, each proposed change must be registered and reviewed. When a change request has been approved, its impact (cost) has to be estimated. Finally, the change

has to be incorporated into the project. Changes that are entered via the back door lead to badly structured code, inadequate documentation, and cost and time overruns. Since changes lead to different versions of both documentation and code, the procedures to be followed in dealing with such changes are often handled in the context of a Configuration Control Plan.

14. **Delivery** The procedures to be followed in handing over the system to the customer must be stated.

The project plan aims to provide a clear picture of the project to both the customer and the project team. If the objectives are not clear, they will not be achieved.

Despite careful planning, surprises will still crop up during the project. However, careful planning early on leads to fewer surprises and makes the project less vulnerable to these surprises. The project plan addresses a number of questions that anticipate possible future events. It gives orderly procedures for dealing with those events, so that justifiable decisions can be reached.

2.2 CONTROLLING A SOFTWARE DEVELOPMENT PROJECT

After a project plan has been drawn up and approved, the execution of the project may start. During the project, control has to be exerted along the following dimensions:

- time,

- information,

- organization,

- quality,

- money.

The progress of a software development project (the **time** aspect) is hard to measure. Before the proposed system has been finished, there is only a (large) pile of paper. Utterances such as '90% of the code has been written' should be taken with a pinch of salt. A much too rosy picture of the actual state of affairs is usually given. The phased approach introduced in Chapter 1, and its variants, aim at providing the manager with an instrument to measure and control progress. The time needed to build a system is obviously related to the size of the system, and thus to the total manpower required. Larger systems require more time to develop, although we may try to shorten development time by allocating more personnel. Part of the control problem for software development projects is to trade off time against people. Adding more people to shorten development time does not come for free. The more people that are involved, the more time will be needed for coordination and communication. After a certain point, adding more people actually lengthens the development time. Part of the time-control problem is phrased in Brooks' Law: 'Adding people to a late project only makes it later'. We will come back to this issue in Chapter 7.

The **information** that has to be managed, above all, is the documentation. Besides technical and user documentation, this also entails documentation on the project itself. Documentation concerning the project includes such things as: the current state of affairs, changes that have been agreed upon, and decisions that have been made. This type of documentation can best be handled in the context of configuration management. In agile projects, less attention is given to documentation during development. Necessary knowledge is tacit; it resides in the heads of the people involved. But here too, once the system is ready and handed over to its customers, documentation has to be provided.

All members of the development team must understand their role in the team and what is expected of them. It is very important that these expectations are clear to all the people involved. Unspoken and unclear expectations lead to situations in which individual team members set their own goals, either consciously or unconsciously. These **organizational** aspects deserve the continuous attention of the project manager. The organization of a team and the coordination of the people involved will, at least partly, depend upon characteristics of the project and its environment. This dependence has to be recognized and taken into account when setting up a project team.

The **quality** aspect is of paramount importance. Customers are not satisfied with purely technical solutions offered by computer specialists. They want systems that fit their real needs. The quality requirements for software and for its development process often conflict with one another. At architecture time, quality requirements are balanced in a dialog with all stakeholders involved. During a project, we have to assess whether or not the quality requirements are being met. This quality assessment has to occur on a regular basis, so that timely actions can be undertaken. Quality is not an add-on feature, it has to be built in.

Controlling expenses (the **money** aspect) largely means controlling labor costs. Though the cost of hardware and tools cannot be ignored, these can usually be estimated fairly precisely early in the project. Moreover, these are usually much less of an issue than personnel costs.

Estimating the cost of software means that we must estimate the manpower required to build the software. The manpower needed is very much dependent on the size of the software, for instance measured as the amount of code to be delivered. Many other factors, though, influence this cost or, alternatively, the productivity with which the software can be produced. A well-balanced team with experienced people will be much more productive than a newly formed team with inexperienced people. Extremely strict quality constraints, such as very high reliability or a very fast response time, may also severely reduce productivity.

A number of models have been proposed that try to quantify the effect of those different cost drivers on the manpower required (see Chapter 7). Rather than estimating the size first, and then its cost, one may also set a cost threshold first, and work incrementally, first on the most pressing user requirements and, if time allows, on less pressing ones. Or one may agree on a first threshold, and decide whether more money will be spent when this threshold is reached. These incremental approaches to cost estimation fit in well with agile project development.

Software development is a very labor-intensive process. One of our hopes is that better tools and the increased use of those tools will lead to a significant increase in productivity and, consequently, a significant decrease in the cost involved in developing software. A second way to increase productivity dramatically is to use software rather than build it yourself. Both these topics are discussed in later chapters. As these trends continue, software development starts to become a capital-intensive activity, rather than a labor-intensive one (Wegner, 1984).

Continuous assessment of the project with respect to these control aspects is of the utmost importance and will, from time to time, lead to adjustments in time, cost, organization, information, or quality, or some combination thereof. Project management is a very dynamic activity.

In order to be able to adequately control a project, we need quantitative data, which is collected while the project is being executed. For instance, data about errors discovered during unit testing may help us in estimating further test effort needed. Data about the time and effort spent up to a specific point will guide us in re-estimating the schedule and cost. To measure is to know.

This data is also valuable in a postmortem evaluation of the project. In a postmortem evaluation, we assess the present project in order to improve our performance on projects yet to come: what did we do wrong, what have we learned, what needs to be done differently on the next project?

Unfortunately, in practice very little hard data is ever gathered, let alone retained for later use. Most software development organizations have little insight into what they are doing. They tend to operate in a somewhat chaotic way, especially when facing a crisis. By identifying key factors that affect the controllability of the software development process, we may find ways to improve on it. This topic is further treated in Section 6.6, where we discuss the Capability Maturity Model.

2.3 SUMMARY

This chapter provides an introduction to the management of software engineering projects.

Before we embark on a software development project, it has to be carefully planned. This planning process results in a document, the project plan, which provides a clear picture of the project to both the customers and the project team.

Once the project plan has been drawn up and the project has started, its execution must be controlled. We identified five entities that require our continuous attention for project control:

- Time: How do we assess progress towards the project's goals? Usually, some phased approach is followed which aims to provide management with a way of measuring and controlling progress.

- Information: How do we handle the documents that are produced in the course of a project? In planning-based development, maintaining the integrity of the set of documents and handling all change requests require careful procedures.

- Organization: How do we organize the project team and coordinate the activities of team members?

- Quality: How do we define and assess quality requirements for both the development process and the resulting product?

- Money: How do we estimate the cost of a project? These costs are to a large extent determined by the size of the software.

Each of these controlling aspects is further elaborated upon in a separate chapter (Chapters 3–7). The various dimensions of project control are then reconciled in Chapter 8.

Exercises

1. In what sense is the phrase 'software development project' a misnomer?

2. What are the major constituents of a project plan?

3. List five dimensions along which a software development project has to be controlled.

4. How may software development become a capital-intensive activity, rather than a labor-intensive one?

5. ♠ Consider a software development project you have been involved in. Did the project have a project plan? Did the project plan address the issues listed in Section 2.1? If some of these issues were not addressed, do you think it would have helped the project if they had been?

6. ♡ Do you think quantitative project data is important? In what way can it contribute to project planning?

7. ♡ How would a project plan for an agile project differ from that for a planning-driven project?

8. ♠ Consider once again a software development project you have been involved in. To what extent were any environmental issues, such as user training and working procedures, adequately dealt with in the project?

9. ♡ A program written for personal use imposes rather less stringent requirements than a product that is also to be used by other people. According to (Brooks, 1995), the latter may require three times as much effort. Discuss possible reasons for this considerable increase in cost.

3

The Software Life Cycle Revisited

LEARNING OBJECTIVES

- To be aware of a number of generic models for structuring the software development process

- To appreciate the pros and cons of these models, in particular those of the planning-driven and agile methods

- To understand the similarities between software maintenance and software evolution

- To recognize that it is profitable to apply software product-line engineering when developing a series of similar systems

- To be aware of process modeling as a way to describe software development processes explicitly

To be able to assess progress during software development, one opts for a phased approach with a number of well-defined milestone events. The linear ordering of activities which underlies the traditional software development model, the waterfall model, renders it an impossible idealization of reality. It assumes software development proceeds in an orderly, sequential manner. Real projects proceed in far less rational ways. The waterfall model of software development is not feasible, much as Escher's Waterfall, on the front cover, is infeasible. This chapter discusses various alternative models of the development process.

In Chapter 1, we introduced a simple model of the software life cycle. We distinguished several consecutive phases: requirements engineering, design, implementation, testing, and maintenance. It was stated that, in practice, one often uses more sophisticated process models. In this chapter, we continue this discussion. We introduce various alternative models for structuring the software development process.

Software development projects are often very large projects. A number of people work on such a project for a long time and therefore the whole process needs to be carefully planned and controlled: progress needs to be monitored, people and resources need to be allocated at the right point in time, etc. Earlier on, it was pointed out that progress of a software development project is particularly difficult to measure.

In order to control progress, we use a phased development process in which a number of clearly identifiable milestones are established between the start and finish of the project. We use a similar mechanism when constructing a house: foundations are laid, the first floor is reached, the house is weatherproofed, and so on. Often, installment payments are coupled to reaching those milestones.

Quite often, the milestones identified in a software development project correspond to the points in time at which certain documents become available:

- after requirements engineering, there is a requirements specification;

- after the design phase, there is a (technical) specification of the system;

- after implementation, there is a set of programs;

- after testing has been completed, there is a test report.

Traditional models for the phased development of software are, to a large extent, 'document-driven'. The pile of paper that is produced in the course of the project guides the development process. The development process is seen as a series of transformations. It starts with a clear requirements document and ends with running code. In the next section, we discuss the waterfall model, a well-known variation of the process model introduced in Chapter 1. In this variation, a check is performed after each transformation to determine whether we are still on the right track.

These document-driven methods are also known as *planning-driven* or *heavyweight* methods. They are planning-driven because of the emphasis on an upfront plan for the whole process and heavyweight because of the emphasis placed on the process.

In many a software development project, change is a fact of life. It may even be the case that the client has only a vague idea of the requirements for the system. In recent years, a number of *lightweight*, *agile* methods have been proposed that purportedly deal with these rapidly changing circumstances. These methods advocate not 'wasting' time on expensive planning and design activities early on, but delivering something valuable to the customer as quickly as possible. Based on feedback from the user, the next steps are then taken. Agile methods have evolved from approaches, such as prototyping and Rapid Application Development, that try to dispose of some or all of the drawbacks of the document-driven approach mentioned above. We discuss a number of lightweight approaches to software development in Section 3.2.

Evolutionary models take into account that much of what is called maintenance is really evolution. It would then seem natural to explicitly bear this anticipated evolution in mind from the very start. This is usually not the case. In both heavyweight and lightweight development approaches, the initial development of a software system is in general strictly separated from the subsequent maintenance phase. The major goal of a software development project then boils down to delivering a first version of the system to the user. This may result in excessive maintenance costs later on. In order to be able to properly assess costs and benefits, the total life cycle cost rather than just the development cost should be our primary focus. Going one step further, we may argue that management should concentrate on sets of similar products (known as 'product families') rather than individual products, thereby giving an incentive both to the building of reusable parts and the reuse of (parts of) existing products when developing new ones.

From all the possible life cycle models, we have to choose a particular one for any given project. By and large, heavyweight methods better fit (very) large projects and situations where the requirements can be decided upon at an early stage. Lightweight methods fit situations of rapid change, and projects that do not involve more than, say, 50 people. Different project characteristics, and appropriate ways to control them effectively, are discussed in Chapter 8.

The choice of a particular life cycle model also involves defining the individual steps and phases, their possible interaction, their deliverables, etc. By using an explicit process-modeling language (which may be supported by tools), we increase our understanding of the software process, we are provided with a handle to improve our control of software development, and we are given a baseline for process improvement. This type of process modeling is discussed in Section 3.7. Because of the much larger emphasis on planning, this type of modeling fits better with heavyweight methods.

3.1 THE WATERFALL MODEL

The waterfall model is essentially a slight variation of the model introduced in Chapter 1. The waterfall model is generally attributed to Royce (1970). However, a clearly phased approach to the development of software, including iteration and feedback, can be found in publications from the early 1960s.

The waterfall model particularly expresses the interaction between subsequent phases. Testing software is not an activity which strictly follows the implementation phase. In **each** phase of the software development process, we have to compare the results obtained against those that are required. In all phases, quality has to be assessed and controlled.

In Figure 3.1, V & V stands for Verification and Validation. Verification asks if the system meets its requirements (are we building the system right) and thus tries to assess the correctness of the transition to the next phase. Validation asks if the system meets the user's requirements (are we building the right system).

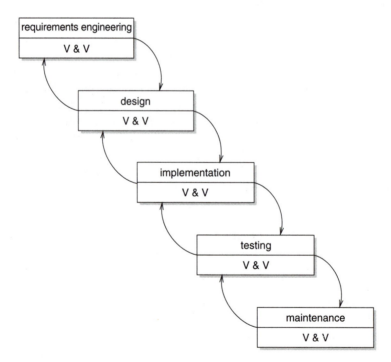

Figure 3.1 The waterfall model

Both the model introduced in Chapter 1 and the waterfall model place considerable emphasis on a careful analysis before the system is actually built. We want to prevent putting much energy into constructing a system which later turns out not to satisfy the user's requirements.

We therefore try to identify and tie down the user's requirements as early as possible. These requirements are documented in the requirements specification. On the basis of this document we may verify in subsequent phases whether or not these requirements are being met. Since it is difficult in practice, if not impossible, to completely specify the user's requirements, a regular test should also be carried out with the prospective user. These tests are termed validation. Through the validation steps, we may prevent the system under development diverging from the, possibly incompletely specified, user requirements.

Figure 3.2 depicts essentially the same process model as Figure 3.1. After its shape, it is known as the V-model. The V-model shows how different types of testing are related to the various development phases. For example, during acceptance testing, the complete system is tested against the requirements, under supervision of the user organization. The different test phases are discussed in Section 13.9.

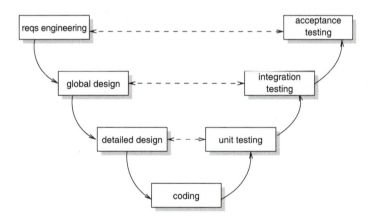

Figure 3.2 The V-model

McCracken and Jackson (1981) compare the waterfall model with a shop where the customer is obliged to give an order upon entering. There is no opportunity to look around, compare prices, change one's mind, or decide upon a different menu for today's dinner. Some things can be ordered by mail, but not all. The waterfall model of software development, like Escher's waterfall, is unrealistic.

There is ample quantitative evidence that the classic document-driven model has many shortcomings. In many a software development project, the strict sequencing of phases advocated by the waterfall model is not actually obeyed. Table 3.1 shows the average breakdown of activities across life cycle phases for a number of projects. In this, the label 'coding' refers to a phase which encompasses both implementation and unit testing.

Table 3.1 Breakdown of activities across life cycle phases, after (Zelkowitz, 1988)

Activity	Phase			
	Design	Coding	Integration testing	Acceptance testing
Integration testing	4.7	43.4	26.1	25.8
Coding	6.9	70.3	15.9	6.9
Design	49.2	34.1	10.3	6.4

So, for example, under 50% of the design effort was found to occur during the actual design phase: 34% of the design effort occurs during the coding period and, even worse, over 16% of the design effort takes place after the system is supposed to be finished.

The behavior of individual software designers may be characterized as an **opportunistic process** (Guindon and Curtis, 1988). Designers move back and forth across levels of abstraction ranging from application domain issues to coding issues. Milestone dates seem to be somewhat arbitrary and a significant part of the activities crosses phase boundaries.

3.2 AGILE METHODS

The American Kennel Club says 'The exciting sport of Agility has taken the world by storm. The Agility ring allows handler and dog to run full speed, while having to perform accurately and safely on A-Frames, Dog Walks, See-Saws and a wide variety of jumps and tunnels.' Software engineers are not dogs, but the analogy is clear.

When using a heavyweight development method, it is difficult to change direction. Once the contract has been signed, the development team's job is to deliver the functionality as laid down in the contract. If reality changes, or the user gets a different insight, the change is difficult to realize. It does not fit the architecture, it requires rework not accounted for, it lengthens the agreed schedule, and so on. Once started, software development is like an ocean steamer that does not easily change direction.

This phenomenon has been recognized over the years, and methods such as prototyping and evolutionary development ensued. But these methods still somehow carry an engineering flavor with them. Essentially, they still assume the world is ordered. It may be difficult to pinpoint the true requirements right away, but they will accrue over time.

True agile methods view the world as fundamentally chaotic. They assume change is inevitable. Their focus is to deliver value to the customer as quickly as possible, and not to bother about extensive plans and processes that will not be followed anyway. The essence of agile methods is laid down in the Manifesto for

Agile Software Development, published in 2001 by a group of well-known pioneers in this area (Beck *et al.*, 2001). The key values of the agile movement are:

- **Individuals and interactions** are more important than processes and tools.

- **Working software** is more important than comprehensive documentation.

- **Customer collaboration** is more important than contract negotiation.

- **Responding to change** is more important than following a plan.

Agile methods involve the users in every step taken. The development cycles are small and incremental. The series of development cycles is not extensively planned in advance, but the new situation is reviewed at the end of each cycle. This includes some, but not too much, planning for the next cycle.

At the end of each cycle, the system is up and running. That is, there is a working system, one that delivers value to its users. This strongly resembles evolutionary prototyping as discussed in Section 3.2.1. But the difference in wording reflects quite a different attitude. The term prototyping suggests something intermediate, not yet final, temporary. 'Working code' carries a more positive meaning. It denotes something of immediate value, even if not perfect yet.

Agile methods do not have an extensive architectural or design phase up front. After all, it does not make sense to spend much effort on design if you know this will quite likely be a waste of time. It is more effective to only do the design as far as needed for the immediate next step. Agile methods often have a separate activity, known as *refactoring*, to improve the design after each increment.

Agile methods are people-oriented, rather than process-oriented. They emphasize the human element in software development. Team spirit is considered very important. Team relationships are close. Often, an agile team occupies one big room. The users are on site as well. Agile methods have short communication cycles between developers and users, and among developers.

Finally, agile methods do not spend much energy on documentation. Why spend time on something that will soon be outdated? Rather, agile methods rely on the tacit knowledge of the people involved. If you have a question, ask one of your friends. Do not struggle with a large pile of paper that quite likely will not provide the answer anyway.

Some people contend that agile methods should be 'pure' and exhibit all of the characteristics mentioned above. Others believe that a mixture of planning-driven and agile methods can be productive as well. We concur with the latter view. For instance, in market-driven environments, where there is a strong pressure to deliver functionality in a timely manner, an organization may have a long-term vision of the functionality and a well-thought out architecture, and yet frequently build and deliver functionality. Cusumano and Yoffe (1999) refer to this development style as 'synchronize and stabilize'. Developers frequently synchronize their work, often at the end of each day, by building an executable version of the complete system and testing it. This is called the 'daily build'. Somewhat less frequently, the set of implemented features is stabilized, resulting in a new baseline from which further development takes place. In this style, the 'working software' value from the Agile Manifesto is emphasized most.

In the following subsections, we first discuss prototyping and incremental development, early methods that recognize that a planning-driven approach often does not fit the volatile situation at hand. Rapid application development (RAD) and the dynamic systems development method (DSDM) emphasize customer collaboration and the role of people in the process, and thus exhibit a number of key characteristics of agile methods. Finally, we discuss extreme programming (XP), a 'pure' agile method.

3.2.1 Prototyping

It is often difficult to get and maintain a sufficiently accurate perception of the requirements of the prospective user. This is not surprising. It is, in general, not sufficient to take the *existing* situation as the one and only starting point for setting up software requirements. An important reason for embarking on a software development project is that one is not pleased with the present situation. What is wanted instead of the present situation is often not easy to determine. This holds even more in cases where we are concerned with a new application and the customer does not know the full possibilities of automation. In such cases, the development of one or more prototypes may help.

Analogies with the development of other products are appealing here. When developing a new car or computer chip, one will also build one or more prototypes. These prototypes are tested intensively before a real production line is set up. For the development of the push-button telephone, about 2 000 prototypes were tested, with variations in form, size and positioning of the buttons, size and weight of the mouthpiece, etc.

It is possible to follow a similar road with software development. In this context, a prototype can be described as a working model of (possibly parts of) a software system, which emphasizes certain aspects. There is, however, one big difference between the development of software and the development of physical products such as cars, chips or telephones: in developing physical products, the highest costs are generally incurred during production, when multiple copies of the product are being produced. In software development, making multiple copies of the product is almost free. If we were to follow the hardware approach to prototyping in software development, and produce a prototype with the same functionality as the final product, we would in fact develop an operational system, with correspondingly high costs. It does not then seem plausible to start all over again and develop the 'real' system in a different way.

Using the definition given above and with the aim of developing a software prototype relatively cheaply, it is important that certain aspects are emphasized. This can be achieved through, for example:

- the use of very high-level languages, in which an executable version can be created quickly (this executable, but probably rather inefficient, version can be used to test the usability of the proposed system);

- the development of a system with less functionality, in particular as regards quality attributes such as speed and robustness.

One of the main difficulties for users is to express their requirements precisely. It is natural to try to clarify these through prototyping. This can be achieved by developing the user interface quickly. The prospective user may then work with a system that contains the interaction component but not, or to a much lesser extent, the software that actually processes the input. In this way, the user may get a good impression of what the future system will provide him with, **before** large investments are made to realize the system. Prototyping thus becomes a tool for requirements engineering.

This is illustrated graphically in Figure 3.3, which shows that the various phases are gone through in two ways. The left-hand side of the figure is concerned with the prototyping stages. The iteration corresponds to the user-validation process, whereby new or changed requirements trigger the next cycle. The right-hand side concerns the actual production of the operational system. The difference between the two

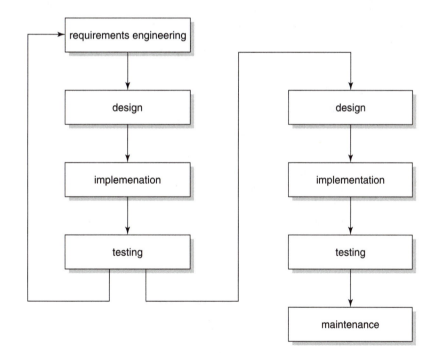

Figure 3.3 Prototyping as a tool for requirements engineering

branches is that, by using different techniques and tools, the left-hand side can be traversed much more quickly and with much lower costs.

In Figure 3.3, the prototyping phases and the later production phases have been clearly separated. This is appropriate, since we will use different techniques during the actual production phase, put much more emphasis on documentation, and so on. It is even feasible not to carry over the software product from the prototyping phases to the actual production phase, but to explicitly throw it away after the prototyping phases have come to an end. This is known as *throwaway prototyping*. It is not necessary to do so, though. The prototype may evolve into the final product. The user starts by formulating the raw requirements, on the basis of which a first version of the system is produced. The user starts to work with this system, which leads to new, or changed, requirements. The next version is then developed. After a number of such iterations, the user is satisfied and the last version developed is the product to be delivered. This is known as *evolutionary prototyping*. In practice, evolutionary prototyping is used much more often than throwaway prototyping. Discarding a (partly) working system is a hurdle that is not easily taken. In agile methods, the phrase 'working code' is often used instead of 'evolutionary prototype'.

Both throwaway and evolutionary prototyping have advantages and disadvantages. Table 3.2 summarizes the pros and cons that have emerged from case studies describing real-world experiences of applying a prototyping approach. Note that some properties can be influenced in both a positive and a negative way. Depending on circumstances, either or both may occur in an actual project. For example, the maintenance cost may go down because user needs are better satisfied or it may go up because development has been done in a quick and dirty way.

Table 3.2   Some observed pros and cons of prototyping

Advantages
−The resulting system is easier to use
−The resulting system has fewer features
−User needs are better accommodated
−The design is of higher quality
−Problems are detected earlier
−The resulting system is easier to maintain
−The development incurs less effort

Disadvantages
−The resulting system has more features
−The design is of lower quality
−The performance of the resulting system is worse
−The resulting system is harder to maintain
−Team members should be more experienced

Users and developers are generally more positive about systems developed using a prototyping approach than about systems developed in a waterfall process. This positive attitude concerns both the development process and the resulting product. Users feel more involved in the development process and have fewer conflicts with the designers. The extensive user involvement results in systems which better satisfy user needs.

Since users need not express all their requirements up front in a prototyping approach, there is less tendency to ask for bells and whistles (unnecessary extra features). As a consequence, the end result is a leaner system of which the functionality closer matches the real user requirements. If users are shown a working system at an early stage and are given the opportunity to try it out, chances are that problems are detected at an early stage as well. This prevents a waste of manpower which would otherwise be needed to redo part of the work. If users are in a position to influence and modify the design, the system features will better reflect their requirements and the system will be easier to use.

The use of special-purpose prototyping tools or languages makes it easy to add features. Since the time interval between successive versions of the prototype is small, users may think that it is easy to realize new features and may specify additional requirements. These aspects of prototyping may result in systems having more, rather than fewer, features.

Prototyping involves iterative design steps and, because of the repeated attention to the design, its quality may increase. Since it is known in advance that the design will evolve during subsequent prototyping steps, greater attention will be given to quality factors such as flexibility and modularity and, as a result, design quality may improve as well. In throwaway prototyping, the quality of the final design is often higher because of the learning experience of the prototyping steps. Also, this final design step is hardly, if at all, patched up because of rework actions. Because of these aspects, the resulting systems are often found to be easier to maintain.

On the other hand, prototyping generally does not enforce strict design and development standards. If we are concerned with a short development time, certain necessary activities will receive less attention. The chances are that documentation is sacrificed for speed. Because of additions resulting from frequent rework steps, the design quality of an evolutionary prototype may deteriorate. For that reason too, the resulting system may be less maintainable. Especially in evolutionary prototypes, the robustness of the system will often be less than is customary with a more traditional approach. In agile methods, refactoring is applied to counteract this phenomenon. Finally, performance tends to be worse because attention is focused on functionality and performance measures are either not taken at all or are taken at a point in time at which they have become too difficult to realize.

It is generally felt that prototyping projects require an experienced team. Prototyping involves making far-reaching design decisions, especially during early iterations. In each iteration, user requests have to be weighed against each other and against the ease and cost of their realization. Inexperienced team members are more likely to make poor choices, thereby seriously threatening the success of a prototyping effort.

From this discussion, we may gather the following recommendations for the use of prototyping techniques:

- prototyping is particularly useful in situations where the user requirements are unclear or ambiguous, when it can be a good way to clarify those requirements;

- prototyping is also particularly useful for systems with a considerable emphasis on the user interface and which need a high degree of user interaction;

- users and designers must be well aware of the prototyping approach and its pitfalls: users should realize that changing software is not all that easy and that a prototype is not a production-quality system; designers should be aware of the characteristics of prototyping projects and not become frustrated by frequent changes in user requirements;

- prototyping must be planned and controlled: limits must be imposed on the number of iterations; there must be explicit procedures for documenting and testing prototypes; the positive aspects of the traditional approach, which make the process manageable and controllable, should be applied to prototyping.

By taking appropriate counter-measures, the potential disadvantages of prototyping can be guarded against. Prototyping is, then, a viable alternative process model for many a software development project.

3.2.2 Incremental Development

In the preceding section, we discussed a way of using prototypes in which the final system is the last of a series of prototypes. Under careful management control, in order to ensure convergence, the next version is planned to accommodate new or changed user requirements. There is another way to work towards the final system in a number of iterations: we proceed incrementally. The functionality of the system is produced and delivered to the customer in small increments. Starting from the existing situation, we proceed towards the desired situation in a number of (small) steps. In each of these steps, the phased approach that we know from the waterfall model is employed.

Developing software in this way avoids the 'Big Bang' effect (in which nothing happens for a long time and then, suddenly, there is a completely new situation). Instead of building software, the software grows. With this incremental approach, the user is closely involved in planning the next step. Redirecting the project becomes easier since we may incorporate changed circumstances more quickly.

Incremental development can also be used to fight the 'overfunctionality' syndrome. Since users find it difficult to formulate their real needs, they tend to demand too much. Lacking the necessary knowledge of the malleability of software and its development process, they may be inclined to think that everything can be achieved. As a consequence, essential features appear next to bells and whistles in the list of requirements. Analysts are not able to distinguish one from the other, nor are they able to accurately estimate the effort required to implement individual features. Chances are, then, that much effort is spent on realizing features that are not really needed. As a result, many of today's systems offer rich functionality yet are, at the same time, ill-suited for the task at hand. For one thing, these systems are difficult to use simply because of the complexity incurred by their rich functionality.

With the incremental approach, attention is first focused on the essential features. Additional functionality is only included if and when it is needed. Systems thus developed tend to be leaner and yet provide sufficient support to their users. With the incremental approach, the most difficult parts or the parts that have the highest risk with respect to successful completion of the project are often tackled first.

Following this line of thought, Boehm (1988) suggests a spiral model of the software development process, in which each revolution of the spiral gives rise to the following activities:

- identify the subproblem which has the highest associated risk;

- find a solution for that problem.

The various process models already discussed can be coupled with Boehm's spiral model in a natural way (see Figure 3.4):

- If obtaining the proper set of user requirements is seen as the area with highest risk, follow the spiral a few times around to solve this subproblem (i.e., prototype).

- If the main issue is to obtain a robust and well-documented system from a precise requirements specification, follow the spiral once, using the traditional process model with its phases and corresponding milestones as intermediate steps.

- If developing software incrementally, track the spiral a number of times, once for each increment.

- During maintenance, the reported errors or changing requirements are triggers to track the spiral.

Viewed this way, the spiral model subsumes the other process models discussed so far.

Incremental development is strongly advocated by Gilb (1988). It is doubtful whether the time increment advocated by Gilb, up to a maximum of a few weeks, is always reasonable. But the advantages of incremental development are considerable, even with different time increments. Surprises that lurk within the traditional approach and that pose considerable difficulties on the management side of software development projects can be greatly diminished when software is developed and delivered incrementally.

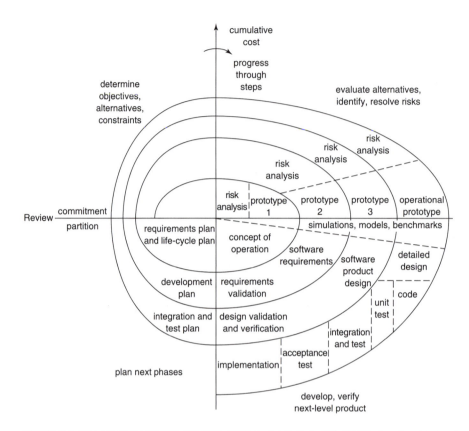

Figure 3.4 The spiral model (*Source*: B.W. Boehm, A spiral model of software development and enhancement, *IEEE Computer 21:5*, © 1988 IEEE. Reproduced with permission.)

3.2.3 Rapid Application Development and Dynamic Systems Development Method

Rapid Application Development (RAD) has a lot in common with other iterative development process models. It emphasizes user involvement, prototyping, reuse, the use of automated tools, and small development teams. In addition to that, it employs the notion of a *time box*, a fixed time frame within which activities are done. In most development models, a set of requirements is fixed and then the project attempts to fulfill these requirements within some estimated period of time. Within RAD, the time frame is decided upon first and then the project tries to realize the requested functionality within that time frame. If it turns out that not all of the functionality can be realized within the time frame, some of the functionality is sacrificed. The agreed deadline however is immovable.

The RAD life cycle consists of four phases:

- requirements planning,

- application design,

- construction,

- cutover.

The requirements planning and application design phases have much in common and may be combined for smaller projects. Together, they typically take less than two months. The main techniques used in these phases are known as joint requirements planning (JRP) and joint application design (JAD). Both these techniques make heavy use of workshops in which the developers and the prospective users work *together* (hence the adjective *joint*).

The goal of the JRP workshop is to get the requirements right the first time. For that reason, it is imperative that the key players, i.e. the end users of the system, are present. Requirements are prioritized, since it is likely that not all of them will be implemented in the first version of the system. This requirements prioritization is known as *triage*. Triage usually means a process used on the battlefield and in emergency rooms to sort injured people into groups based on their need for or likely benefit from immediate medical treatment. In RAD, the triage process is used to make sure that the most important requirements are addressed first. The result of this process is often a prioritization denoted by the acronym MoSCoW:

- **Must haves** are requirements that are definitely needed.

- **Should haves** are requirements that are important, but not absolutely needed for a usable system.

- **Could haves** are requirements that are only implemented if time allows.

- **Won't haves** are requirements that will be left for the next iteration.

As an example, consider the development of a Library Information System. The **Must have** category would include the ability to borrow and return an item and to enroll as a member. The **Should have** category might include facilities to reserve an item. The **Could have** category might include the ability to handle fines for items returned late. Finally, the **Won't have** category in the first iteration might include functions to profile users and notify them of newly arrived items.

It is customary to have two JAD workshops during the design phase. Again, the end users play an essential role in these workshops. The first JAD workshop yields an initial design of the system. The developers then construct a prototype, to be experimented with by the users. This prototype is evaluated during the second JAD workshop, improvements are decided upon, and the design is finalized.

The system is constructed by a highly skilled team of about four people, a 'Skilled With Advanced Tools' (SWAT) team (see also Section 5.2). The SWAT team becomes involved after the first JAD workshop. The team typically does its job in less than two months. In order to be able to do so, heavy use is made of tools, and existing components are reused whenever feasible. Within the time allotted (the time box), the SWAT team constructs a series of evolutionary prototypes. Developers and users work closely together during this process. Each prototype is reviewed by the users and the review sessions result in requests for enhanced or changed functionality. The agreed upon time frame is *not* exceeded. If necessary, some of the functionality is sacrificed instead.

For a SWAT team to operate successfully and deliver a good result in a very short time span, it has to feel a definite 'ownership' of the problem to be addressed. In such a situation, it is not very helpful if time estimates and deadlines are fixed by some manager. Instead, the SWAT team itself estimates the time, the SWAT team decides upon the number and length of the time boxes, and the SWAT team decides which functionality to implement in each iteration.

During the cutover phase, the final testing of the system takes place, users are trained, and the system is installed.

There are many variations on the RAD process model described above. For example, it is possible to have explicit time boxes for the construction of each of the intermediate prototypes. It is also possible to have JRP or JAD sessions after each prototyping cycle. The main ingredients, however, remain: prototyping, considerable user involvement, SWAT teams, and time boxes.

JRP and JAD have much in common with a design method known as participatory design (PD) or the Scandinavian school of software development. They both emphasize end-user involvement but they differ, however, in their goals. User involvement in JRP and JAD is primarily intended to speed up the process of producing the right system. User involvement in PD is motivated by a strong interest in the social context of the work environment.

The dynamic systems development method (DSDM) is a well-known framework that builds on RAD. DSDM is based on the nine principles depicted in Table 3.3. DSDM is a non-profit framework maintained by the DSDM Consortium (see www.dsdm.org). A high-level description of the framework is given in (Stapleton, 2003). The complete set of DSDM practices is only available to members of the DSDM Consortium.

The DSDM process has five phases (see Figure 3.5):

- In the **feasibility study**, the suitability of DSDM for the current project is assessed. This is different from a more traditional feasibility study, where the emphasis is on whether a solution is feasible at all. Next to questions such as 'Can we build this system at all?', the question 'Is DSDM appropriate for this project?' has to be answered as well. Characteristics that make DSDM a feasible approach reflect the principles of the method: it must be possible to identify the users of the system, the system should not be too large, and not all requirements should be known up front.

Table 3.3 The principles of DSDM

Principle	Description
Active user involvement is imperative.	Users support the team throughout the project, not just during requirements elicitation and acceptance testing. The communication channel between the development team and the users is kept short.
The team must be empowered to make decisions.	The team must be able to make quick decisions. Momentum is lost if the team has to wait for external approval of every small decision.
The focus is on frequent delivery of products.	Frequent delivery allows for frequent feedback from the user community and control of the decision-making process by managers.
Fitness for business purpose is the essential criterion for acceptance of deliverables.	The emphasis is on delivering the right product, not on gold-plating or conformance to specifications.
Iterative and incremental development is necessary to converge on an accurate business solution.	Requirements cannot be completely determined up front. Systems need to evolve and rework is a fact of life.
Changes during development are reversible.	A wrong path may be taken and backtracking is required to get to a safe point again.
Requirements are baselined at a high level.	The high-level requirements are determined during the business study phase and detailed requirements are determined during later iterative phases.
Testing is integrated throughout the life cycle.	Testing is not postponed until after coding has finished. It is done incrementally, after each component is written.
A collaborative and co-operative approach between stakeholders is essential.	Responsibilities are shared and developers need support from end-users to decide what to develop.

- The **business study** results in a high-level description of the business processes relevant to the system. These are determined using facilitated workshops (such as JRP) and result in a high-level baseline. In this phase, the high-level architecture is determined as well.

- The **functional model iteration** results in analysis models, prototypes, and implementation of the major functional components. Iteration is done in time boxes of typically two to six weeks. Each iteration consists of four activities: identify what you will do; agree on how you will do it; do it; and check that you have done it.

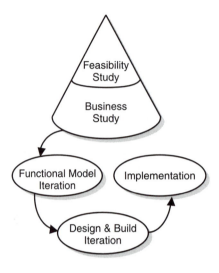

Figure 3.5 The DSDM process

- During the **design and build iteration**, the system is engineered to a sufficiently high standard. Here too, work is done in time boxes of typically two to six weeks, and the same four activities as in the functional model iteration are performed. Though the emphasis of functional model iterations is on deciding *what* to build, and that of design and build iterations is on building a properly engineered solution, the distinction between those two types of iteration is not always clearcut.

- In the **implementation** phase, the system is carried over to the customer environment. This phase also includes user training.

3.2.4 Extreme Programming

Extreme programming (XP for short) is a pure agile method. XP is based on a number of best practices that have been known for a long time. XP takes these practices to extreme levels.

For instance, we know that code reading by your colleagues, such as is done in walkthroughs and code inspections (see also Chapter 13) is a very effective test method. In XP, one does this all the time: two programmers work together at one computer screen. One of them does the coding, the other one looks over his shoulder, gives advice, notices small slips, asks questions, and so on. They act as pilot and co-pilot. At any point in time, the roles may shift. This practice is called *pair programming*.

The full set of XP practices is given in Table 3.4. Typically, an XP team is not too big and occupies one room. Planning meetings are very short and involve the immediate functionality to be delivered to the customer. Planning includes both

Table 3.4 Practices in extreme programming

XP practice	Description
The planning game	The scope of the next release is quickly determined. When necessary, the plan is updated.
Small releases	A simple system is first realized, then other versions are released in short cycles.
Metaphor	A simple metaphor is used for the whole system.
Simple design	The design is kept as simple as possible at any point in time. Complexity is removed as soon as possible.
Testing	Programmers continuously write unit tests and customers write acceptance tests.
Refactoring	The system is restructured without changing its behaviour, to improve quality.
Pair programming	All code is written by two programmers at one machine.
Collective ownership	Anyone can change any code, anywhere, at any time.
Continuous integration	The system is integrated and built many times a day.
40-hour week	As a rule, the team works only 40 hours per week. Working overtime should be the exception.
On-site customer	A real user should be on the team, full-time.
Coding standards	Coding standards are established, to ease communication.

the customer and the technical people. The customer has to set priorities, determine dates of releases, and so on. The customer describes desirable features of the system in stories and records them on index cards. The technical people estimate how long it will take to implement a story and decide on the order in which stories within one release will be implemented.

In XP, the design is kept as simple as possible. Since the future is, after all, unclear, there is no use designing a grand scheme that will not be followed anyhow. So the design only covers the current version of the system. After a task is accomplished, the system is checked to see how it can be improved (by removing duplicate code, making it simpler, making it more flexible). This is called *refactoring*. Refactoring need not be restricted to one's own code. Everyone is responsible for the whole system. To make this work, the team needs to set coding standards.

When a team works on implementing a story, at the same time it writes tests to check the implementation of that story. Before the new code is checked in, all these tests have to run successfully. After the code has been checked in, the full test suite is run and again all tests have to run successfully. If they do not, the new code is removed to fix it. This way, there always is a running system.

XP is based on five principles that drive its practices:

- **Rapid feedback** Feedback is obtained quickly, within hours, or at most a few days. As each small piece added is tested, developers immediately learn what works and what doesn't. As a running system is delivered frequently to the customer, the customer learns what value the system offers and what features are needed next.

- **Simplicity** Today's job is done today and tomorrow's job is left for tomorrow. Do not build in extra complexity so that a certain class becomes more flexible and may be reused if a certain feature is added. If and when this feature is needed, it will be added and code will be refactored to make it simpler.

- **Incremental change** In XP, things change in small increments. The plan changes a little at a time, the design changes a little at a time, the team changes a little at a time, etc.

- **Embracing change** By not planning, designing or coding more than is needed right now, most options for the future are kept. Only the most pressing problem is tackled today. The rest is left for tomorrow.

- **Quality work** Quality is a must. The team should find pride in delivering excellent quality.

As noted before in this chapter, agile methods are suited for certain projects, but not for all. This is certainly also true for XP, the most extreme agile approach. If requirements are unsure, the system is not too big, and the customer can be on site, XP deserves serious consideration. Early sources recommend using all of XP's practices, since they reinforce each other. But nowadays there also exist many approaches that adopt one or a few of XP's practices.

3.3 THE RATIONAL UNIFIED PROCESS (RUP)

The Rational Unified Process is an iterative development process, geared towards the development of object-oriented systems. It comes with a lot of tool support; there are sources and templates that a company can load onto an intranet; and there are sources and templates for various kinds of documents on the Internet. It complements the Unified Modeling Language (UML). RUP might be viewed as being between document-driven and agile methods. It has a well-defined process and includes reasonably extensive upfront requirements-engineering activities, yet it emphasizes stakeholder involvement through its use-case-driven nature. Its two-dimensional process structure is depicted in Figure 3.6.

RUP distinguishes four phases: inception, elaboration, construction, and transition. Within each phase, several iterations may occur. Along a second dimension,

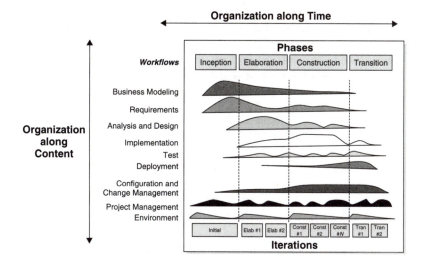

Figure 3.6 Process structure of RUP (*Source*: P. Kruchten, *The Rational Unified Process: An Introduction*, p. 23, © 2000 Pearson Education, Inc. Reproduced by permission of Pearson Education. All rights reserved.)

RUP distinguishes nine 'workflows', such as a requirements workflow and a test workflow. These workflows group logical activities and might extend over all phases, with varying levels of attention. For instance, the requirements workflow is likely to get a lot of attention during the early phases, while the deployment workflow is most relevant in the transition phase. This is illustrated by the undulating shapes next to each workflow in Figure 3.6, which allows us to differentiate between successive iterations and stress that different iterations have a different emphasis. It recognizes that requirements engineering, design, and other workflows are ongoing activities rather than phases with a strict start and end time.

The inception phase focuses on getting the objectives clear: what is the scope of this project, what are its boundaries, and what are the acceptance criteria that will be used when the system is delivered to its customers? During this phase too, the overall cost, schedule, and risks are estimated. Critical use cases are developed, as well as a candidate architecture. At the end of this phase, the business case for the system must be clear. This might be the input to a go/no-go decision (a decision whether or not to go ahead with the development).

The elaboration phase is mainly targeted at analyzing the problem domain and obtaining a sound architecture. At the end of this phase, most use cases will be identified and all major risks must be resolved.

The construction phase is a manufacturing, building process. The emphasis is on developing deployable products. Complete components are developed and thoroughly tested. User manuals are written. At the end of this phase, the first operational version of the system, the *beta release*, is ready.

In the transition phase, the system is released to the user community and beta-tested. During this phase, databases may have to be converted, users are trained and, in case of a replacement system, the legacy system being replaced is phased out.

RUP is based on a series of best practices (see Table 3.5) that have evolved over the years. Many of these best practices, of course, are also present in other development models. A strong point of RUP is that it provides a balanced integration

Table 3.5 Practices of RUP

Practice	Description
Iterative development	Systems are developed in an iterative way. This is not an uncontrolled process. Iterations are planned and progress is measured carefully.
Requirements management	RUP has a systematic approach to eliciting, capturing and managing requirements, including possible changes to these requirements.
Architecture and use of components	The early phases of RUP result in an architecture. This architecture is used in the remainder of the project. It is described in different views. RUP supports the development of component-based systems, in which each component is a nontrivial piece of software with well-defined boundaries.
Modeling and UML	Much of RUP is about developing models, such as a use-case model, a test model, etc. These models are described in UML.
Quality of process and product	Quality is not an add-on, but the responsibility of everyone involved. The testing workflow is aimed at verifying that the expected level of quality is met.
Configuration and change management	Iterative development projects deliver a vast amount of products, many of which are frequently modified. This asks for sound procedures to do so, and appropriate tool support.
Use-case-driven development	Use cases describe the behaviour of the system. They play a major role in various workflows, especially the requirements, design, test and management workflow.
Process configuration	One size does not fit all. Though RUP can be used 'as-is', it can also be modified and tailored to better fit specific circumstances.
Tool support	To be effective, a software development methodology needs tool support. RUP is supported by a wide variety of tools, especially in the area of visual modeling and configuration management.

of the best practices. Given its background, it is no surprise that RUP is geared towards the development of object-oriented systems. But RUP is suited for projects with widely different characteristics. The tuning of RUP to the situation at hand, however, is left to the user of the method.

3.4 MODEL-DRIVEN ARCHITECTURE

In traditional software development approaches, we build all kinds of models during requirements engineering and design. These models may be expressed more or less formally. Usually, the models are not all that formal. Typical examples include a list of requirements in natural language, a box-and-line diagram illustrating a global design, and UML diagrams; see also Chapter 10. The ultimate model is the source code, which is as formal as it can get.

The transitions between the various models are done manually. That is, we manually translate a requirements model into a design model. The design model is next manually translated into code. Any evolution is accomplished by changing the last model in the chain, i.e. the source code. Since we are usually pressed for time, the earlier requirements and design models are often not updated, so that they quickly become outdated.

In model-driven architecture (MDA)[1], the attention shifts from writing code to developing models. The design model is captured in a very precise formalism and is *automatically* translated into source code. Subsequent evolution then takes place at the modeling level. Once changes have been made there, the next version of the system is generated automatically. So maintenance is not done at the source code level, but at the model level. This paradigm shift is depicted in Figure 3.7.

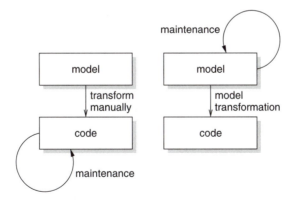

Figure 3.7 Code-based maintenance versus model-based maintenance

---

[1]The word 'architecture' in this phrase is somewhat of a misnomer. Model-driven development (MDD) better reflects what it is about.

In MDA, several models are distinguished. The main ones are the computation-independent model (CIM), the platform-independent model (PIM) and the platform-specific model (PSM). The CIM is the most abstract model; it captures the requirements. The CIM is transformed into the PIM, which describes the functionality of a system, without any platform-specific details. The PSM includes details of the target platforms, such as .NET or J2EE. Finally, the PSM is transformed into executable code.

The transformations from PIM to PSM, and from PSM to code, are automated. The transformation from CIM to PIM is not automated. Many discussions of MDA concentrate on the fully automated parts and leave out the CIM altogether. The model transformations from PIM to PSM and from PSM to code are defined in a specific language that defines how concepts from one level map onto concepts from another level. For each combination of PIM and PSM, such a model transformation must be defined. And likewise for each combination of PSM to code. However, once such a mapping is defined, it can be reused over and over again.

MDA is an initiative of the Object Management Group (OMG), a not-for-profit organization also responsible for UML (see Chapter 10). MDA's vision of developing software at the level of abstract models, and automating the actual generation of code, is not new. Earlier attempts include executable specifications, fourth-generation languages, and so on. These earlier attempts have largely failed. Some critics claim that MDA won't work either. But the argument is still open.

3.5 INTERMEZZO: MAINTENANCE OR EVOLUTION

> Old payroll programs never die;
> they just get fat around the middle.
> Robert Granholm (Datamation, 1971)

In Chapter 1, it was pointed out that a considerable maintenance effort is inevitable. Each maintenance task, whether it concerns repairing an error or adapting a system to new user requirements, in principle entails all aspects of the initial development cycle. During maintenance, we also have to analyze the problem and conceive a design which is subsequently implemented and tested.

The first big difference is that these changes are being made to an existing product. However, during initial development we often do not start from scratch either. If an existing organization decides to automate its order administration, the system may have to interface with already existing systems for, say, stock administration and bookkeeping. Thus, maintenance activities differ in degrees from initial development, rather than fundamentally. This relative difference is even more apparent when the system is prototyped or developed incrementally.

The second main difference, time pressure, has a much larger impact. Time pressure is most strongly felt when repairing errors, for then it is quite possible that certain parts of the organization have to shut down because the software is not operational. In such cases, we have to work against time to identify and repair the errors; we often skip a thorough analysis and design step and simply patch the code. The structure of the system tends to suffer from such patches. The system's entropy increases, which hampers later maintenance activities. Worse still, the system's documentation may not be updated. Software and the corresponding documentation then grow apart, which also hampers future maintenance activities. A more elaborate discussion of maintenance issues is given in Chapter 14.

Lehman and his co-workers have extensively studied the dynamics of software systems that need to be maintained and grow in size. Based on those quantitative studies, they formulated the following laws of software evolution:

1. **Continuing change** A system that is being used undergoes continuous change, until it is judged more cost-effective to restructure the system or replace it by a completely new version.

2. **Increasing complexity** A program that is changed becomes less and less structured (the entropy increases) and thus becomes more complex. One has to invest extra effort in order to avoid increasing complexity.

3. **Self-regulation** Software evolution processes are self-regulating and promote smooth growth of the software.

4. **Conservation of organizational stability (invariant work rate)** The overall progress in software development projects is statistically invariant.

5. **Conservation of familiarity** A system develops a constant growth increment to sustain the organization's familiarity with the system. When this increment is exceeded, problems concerning quality and usage will result.

6. **Continuing growth** The functionality of a system needs to continuously increase in order to maintain user satisfaction.

7. **Declining quality** The quality of a system declines unless it is actively maintained and adapted to its changing environment.

8. **Feedback system** Software evolution must be seen as a feedback system in order to achieve improvements.

In an early publication, Lehman (1974) compares the growth of software systems with that of cities and bureaucracies. He makes a distinction between progressive and anti-regressive activities in software development. Lehman considers this model also applicable to socio-economic systems. In a city, for instance, progressive activities contribute to an increase in the living standard or quality of life. Anti-regressive activities, such as garbage collection, serve to maintain the status quo. If insufficient attention is paid to those anti-regressive activities, decline will set in. Anti-regressive activities often are not interesting, politically speaking. It is an investment in the future, which had better be left to others. (The same phenomenon can be observed in the growth of the chemical industry and the resulting pollution problems.)

According to Lehman, the same kinds of activity occur within a software development project. Generating new code and changing existing code are progressive activities. These are interesting, challenging and rewarding activities. They provide the user with new or better functionality. Writing documentation, improving the structure of the code, and maintaining good communication between the people involved are anti-regressive activities. Neglecting these activities may not be harmful in the short term, but certainly will be in the long term. For each system, we have to look for a proper balance between these kinds of activity.

The law of self-regulation is illustrated by Figure 3.8 which depicts the growth pattern of system attributes over time. System attributes include the length (measured in lines of code), the number of modules, the number of user-callable functions, etc. The time axis may denote the release number, the number of months the system is operational, or a similar measure. (The actual data studied by Lehman concerned the relation between the number of modules and the release number of the OS360 operating system.)

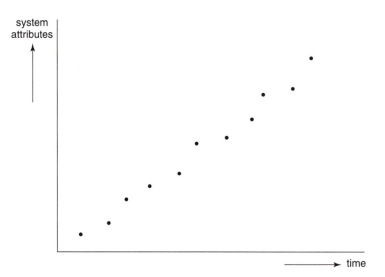

Figure 3.8 Growth of system attributes over time

The relation depicted in Figure 3.8 is almost linear. The ripples in the figure are very regular as well. Periods of more than linear growth alternate with periods of less than linear growth. Lehman explains the periods of more than linear growth by pointing to the pressure from users to get more functionality as fast as possible.

The developers or maintainers tend to bend under this pressure. As a consequence, they use tricks and shortcuts in the code, documentation lags behind, errors are introduced and the system is insufficiently tested. After a while, more attention is paid to anti-regressive activities: code needs to be refactored and documentation brought up to date before further growth is possible. The two kinds of activity stabilize over time.

The law of conservation of organizational stability seems rather surprising at first sight. Lehman and Belady (1985) found that such things as manpower and other resources do not correlate at all to the speed with which systems grow or change. Apparently, large systems are in some sort of saturated state. More people can be kept at work but, in the long run, they have no perceived impact on the evolution of the system.

More than average growth in some version of a system was, in Lehman and Belady's observations, almost always followed by a less than average growth in the next version (as expressed in the law of conservation of familiarity). In one of the systems they investigated, a substantially higher growth inevitably led to problems: lower reliability, higher costs, etc. Apparently, an organization has to sustain sufficient familiarity with its software. Here too, self-regulating feedback was observed.

From the preceding discussion, it follows that we have to be alert during maintenance. We have to preserve quality at each and every step. We may try to preclude the dangers sketched above by explicitly engaging ourselves in the various development phases during maintenance. The cyclic process followed during initial development then occurs during maintenance too. As with prototyping, the time needed to go through the complete cycle will, in general, be much shorter than during initial development. This way of looking at maintenance closely resembles the evolutionary view of software development. Realization of the first version of a software system is only the first step. True enough, this first step is more costly than most of the steps that follow, but it is not fundamentally different. In Chapter 1, we already noticed that putting maintenance on a par with development may also have positive effects on the social and organizational environment in which software development takes place.

The waterfall model gives us a *static* view of the system to be developed. Reality is different. In developing software, and in particular during maintenance, we are concerned with an evolving system. As we remarked before: software is not built, it grows.

3.6 SOFTWARE PRODUCT LINES

When similar products are developed, we may hope to reuse elements from earlier products during the development of new products. Such is not the habit in software development though. In many an organization there is no incentive to reuse elements (code, design, or any other artifact) from another system since that is not what we are being paid for. Similarly, there is no incentive to produce reusable elements, since the present project is all that counts.

As an alternative, we may conceive of the notion of a *software product line*, a set of software systems that share elements. In a software product line, reuse is planned, not accidental. To keep the scope within reasonable boundaries, the planned reuse is tied to a given domain.

Suppose we have developed a successful library system for our computer science faculty library. Chances are that we will be asked to develop a similar system for, say, the faculty of earth sciences. We reuse as much as possible from our first system but it is likely that some finetuning is needed to satisfy the other faculty. They may have maps that may be borrowed and that require some specific handling. Another faculty may come and ask for a third system. And so on. Rather than being reactive and reusing suitable elements from previous efforts, we may also be proactive and plan for the development of a series of systems in the domain of library automation right from the beginning. This involves two processes: domain engineering and application engineering.

In domain engineering, we analyze the domain for which we are going to develop. This process has a life cycle of its own. It results in a set of reusable components that form the basis for the products to be developed. Usually, a reference architecture for all products to be developed is produced as well. An important step in this process is to decide on the scope of the product line. Are we going to develop a product line for just university libraries, or for libraries in general? The former is simpler but has a more limited market. The latter potentially has a bigger market, but is likely to result in a more complex overall architecture and more complex products. Scoping for product lines is a difficult issue. It is influenced by the strategy of the organization and requires insight into the likely evolution of the domain. Finally, the domain engineering process yields a production plan, a guide to how to develop products within the product family.

Application engineering concerns the development of individual products. It usually follows a waterfall-like scheme. Its inputs are the outputs of the domain engineering process: the reference architecture, the production plan, and the set of reusable assets.

Product-line organizations often separate domain-engineering activities from application-engineering activities. Effectively, these activities then constitute separate projects. The development of an individual product may result in new or adapted components that lead to adaptations at the product-family level, which in turn affects the development of subsequent products. Consequently, there are feedback loops from the application-engineering process to the domain-engineering process and vice versa.

Software product lines are particularly suitable in domains where there is a lot of variation in quite similar products, such as mobile phones, television sets, or cameras. Companies operating in these domains have pioneered the product-line field. A more elaborate discussion of software product lines and other component-based approaches that involve separate development processes for components and applications is given in Chapter 18.

3.7 PROCESS MODELING

> Without a repeatable process, the only repeatable results you are likely
> to produce are errors.
> (Macala *et al.*, 1996)

In the 1980s, Osterweil launched the idea of describing software development processes as programs. These **process programs** are written in a **process programming language**. Like other programming languages, process programming languages have a rigorously defined syntax and semantics. As a simple example, consider the Pascal-like description of a review process in Figure 3.9.[2] It describes the consecutive steps of a review process. The process has two inputs: the document to be reviewed and some number which serves as a threshold. The routine returns a Boolean indicating whether or not another review is to be scheduled.

```
function review (document, threshold): Boolean;
begin prepare-review;
      hold-review(document, no-of-problems);
      make-report;
      return no-of-problems < threshold
end review;
```

Figure 3.9 A process program for the review process

In Figure 3.9, the review process is described in terms of the successive activities to be performed: first, the review is prepared, then the meeting is held, and finally a report is made. We may also describe the process in terms of the states it can be in. After the preparation activities (distribution of the document amongst participants, scheduling of a meeting, and so on), the document is ready to be reviewed. After the meeting has been held, a report can be written. After the report has been written, further steps can be taken. Figure 3.10 uses UML notation for state machine diagrams (see Section 10.3.2) to describe the review process in terms of states and transitions between states. The box labeled `review process` describes the review process proper. The inputs and outputs to the process are indicated by arrows leading into and out of the box.

---

[2] In a review, a document (such as piece of code or a design) is first studied individually by a couple of reviewers. The problems found are then discussed by the reviewers and the author of the document (see Section 13.4.2).

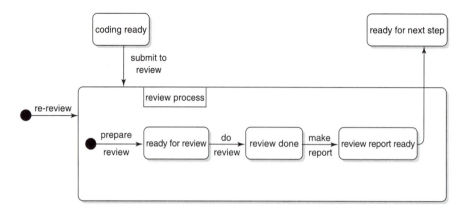

Figure 3.10 State transition diagram of the review process

Petri nets provide yet another formalism to describe process models. Figure 3.11 gives a Petri net view of the review process. A Petri net is a directed graph with two types of node: places and transitions. A place is depicted as a circle. It denotes a (partial) state of the system. A place is either marked or unmarked. In Figure 3.11, the place code ready is marked but review scheduled is not. A transition is depicted by a straight line. A transition receives input from one or more places, and delivers output to one or more places. The inputs and outputs are denoted by arrows leading to and from a transition. A transition denotes an activity which can be performed (in Petri net terminology, 'fired') if all of its input places are marked. Places can thus be thought of as preconditions for activities. In Figure 3.11, the review meeting cannot be held, since it has not been scheduled yet. Once it has been scheduled, the corresponding place is marked and the transition can be fired. The markings are then removed from all of the input places and all of the output places are marked instead.

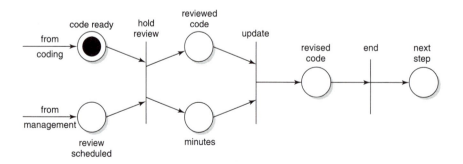

Figure 3.11 Petri net view of the review process

Petri nets are an attractive modeling technique for processes, since they allow a certain amount of nondeterminism and parallellism. For example, the process in Figure 3.11 does not specify the order in which coding and scheduling activities are to be performed. They may go on in parallel; synchronization takes place when both are finished.

A precise description of the software process, be it in a programming-language notation, a graphical notation, or otherwise, serves three main purposes:

- It facilitates understanding and communication. In a software development project, people have to work together. They thus need to have a shared view of the processes to be carried out and the roles they are to play in those processes. Either model of the review process given above can be used for this purpose.

- It supports process management and improvement. A precise description of activities to be performed can be used by project management to assign tasks and to keep track of who is doing what. If the software development process is to be improved, you first have to know what the current process is, i.e. it has to be modeled.

- It may serve as a basis for automated support. This automated support may guide or enforce the order in which tasks are carried out. For instance, a reviewer may automatically be sent a message indicating that a certain piece of code is ready for review as soon as its author releases that code. The automated support may also be used to monitor and track progress, collect process information and metrics, and so on.

The description of the review process in Figure 3.9 is very deterministic. It can be completely automated and executed without human intervention. In general, the work that is being modeled will be carried out by both humans and machines. The neutral term **enactment** is used to denote the execution of a process by either humans or machines. Support for process enactment is often combined with support for configuration management (see Section 4.1).

Though the precise modeling of the software process has definite advantages, the resulting process formality, or even rigidity, holds certain dangers and limitations as well:

- Many aspects of the software development process are heuristic or creative in nature and do not lend themselves to an algorithmic description. For example, the actual debugging or design processes will be quite difficult to capture in a process model.

- A process model is a model and, thus, a simplification of reality. For example, the above models of the review process do not specify what to do if the minutes of the meeting are not delivered or the review is not held because the author of the code is on sick leave, and so on.

- Process models often focus on the transformation of artifacts, such as code, a requirements specification, or a test plan. The progression of stages through which the artifact evolves can be confused with the organization of the processes through which people actually develop those artifacts. This argument was used earlier when we criticized the waterfall model. It is supported by the studies of Zelkowitz (1988) and Guindon and Curtis (1988), reported in Section 3.1. Parnas and Clements (1986) use similar arguments when they criticize the view that the software design process is a rational one.

- Processes that do not directly transform artifacts (for example, learning the application domain, handling requirements that fluctuate or conflict, and dealing with breakdowns in communication or coordination) tend to be ignored (Curtis *et al.*, 1988).

- Processes are treated as discrete rather than continuous in time (i.e. each project invokes a separate process). This view inhibits the transfer of knowledge between projects, as was discussed in the previous section.

Process modeling has received a lot of attention in the research literature. It is indicative of the need for more formal approaches to the description of the software process. The latest trend in process-modeling research is aimed at providing developers with computer guidance and assistance, rather than trying to fully automate the process. Such precise descriptions provide a basis for a range of support functions, ranging from the enactment of design steps to agenda management. This trend to support people rather than taking over fits in well with agile developments too.

3.8 SUMMARY

In this chapter we have addressed the software life cycle again. There are quite a few arguments against the strict sequential ordering of phases as discussed in Chapter 1. The traditional approach is, to a large extent, document-driven. On the way from start to finish a number of milestones are identified. Reaching those milestones is determined by the availability of certain documents. These documents then play a key role in controlling the development process. It is a heavyweight process, driven by planning.

Daily practice hardly fits this model. Change is inevitable, and we had better adopt a development method that accommodates change. In recent years, a number of agile, lightweight methods have been proposed that consciously deal with change. These have evolved from methods such as prototyping, incremental development, and Rapid Application Development. A very influential agile method is eXtreme Programming, or XP.

If a series of similar products is developed within a domain, it pays to plan reuse up front, rather than leaving it to individual projects to deliver reusable components.

This has led to the notion of software product lines, discussed in Section 3.6. In software product-line engineering, domain engineering takes care of developing reusable assets while application engineering produces individual products using those assets.

Finally, we introduced the notion of process modeling, which is aimed at describing the software development process in a precise and unambiguous way. Such descriptions are not intended to fully replace human activities, but rather to support them.

3.9 FURTHER READING

The waterfall model is generally attributed to Royce (1970) and became well-known through Boehm (1976). However, a clearly phased approach to the development of software, including iteration and feedback, can be found in earlier publications: (Benington, 1983) and (Hosier, 1961).

Advantages and disadvantages of prototyping, based on an analysis of 22 published case studies and 17 first-hand accounts, are given in (Gordon and Bieman, 1994). (Verner and Cerpa, 1997) addresses the different views held by analysts and managers of the pros and cons of prototyping.

For a very elaborate discussion of RAD, see (Martin, 1991). DSDM is discussed in (Stapleton, 2003). Participatory design is described in (Floyd *et al.*, 1989). (CACM, 1993a) is a special issue on participatory design. It contains articles describing experiences with participatory design, as well as a comparison of RAD and participatory design. Kruchten (2003) provides a good introduction to RUP. Robillard and Kruchten (2003) describe an academically adapted version of RUP.

There are many books about agile methods. The standard book on XP is by its inventor, Beck (2000). A good companion volume is (Jeffries *et al.*, 2001). Other agile methods include Scrum (Schwaber and Beedle, 2002) and the Crystal family of methodologies (Cockburn, 2002). For a comparison of a number of agile methods, see (Abrahamsson *et al.*, 2002). Boehm and Turner (2003) compare planning-driven and agile methods, and give advice on when to use which kind of method. Experiences with agile methods in large organizations are described in (Lindvall *et al.*, 2004). (McDowell *et al.*, 2006) discuss the advantages of pair programming.

A short introduction to model-driven architecture (MDA) is given in (Meservy and Fenstermacher, 2005). OMG's website (www.omg.org/mda) contains a lot of additional information on MDA.

Lehman and Belady (1985) give an overview of their early work on the laws of software evolution. (Lehman *et al.*, 1997) and (Cook *et al.*, 2006) provide an updated perspective. The formulation given in this chapter is based on (Lehman *et al.*, 1997).

A factory-like view of software development was suggested at the very first conference on Software Engineering (McIlroy, 1968). The term 'software factory' is also often associated with Japanese efforts to improve software development productivity (Cusumano, 1989). The notion of software product lines emerged in the 1980s as a way to increase economy of scale. Clements and Northrop (2002) and (Pohl *et al.*, 2005) provide an in-depth discussion of software product-line engineering.

Osterweil (1987) launched the idea of describing software development processes as programs. Critical appraisals of this view are given in (Lehman, 1987), (Curtis *et al.*, 1987) and (Curtis, 1989). Trends in software process modeling are described in (Fuggetta and Wolf, 1996) and (Cugola and Ghezzi, 1998).

Exercises

1. Describe the waterfall model of software development.

2. Describe the rapid application development (RAD) approach to software development.

3. Discuss the main differences between prototyping and incremental development.

4. Discuss the main differences between incremental development and RUP.

5. Discuss the law of continuing change.

6. How does the spiral model subsume prototyping, incremental development, and the waterfall model?

7. Explain the XP practices 'pair programming' and 'refactoring'.

8. What is MDA?

9. What is a software product line?

10. What is the main purpose of having an explicit description of the software development process in a process model?

11. What is process enactment?

12. Discuss the key values of the agile movement.

13. ♠ Suppose you are involved in a large project concerning the development of a patient planning system for a hospital. You may opt for one of two strategies. The first strategy is to start with a thorough analysis of user requirements, after which the system is built according to these requirements. The second strategy starts with a less complete requirements analysis phase, after which a pilot version is developed. This pilot version is installed in a few small departments. Further development of the system is guided by the experience gained in working with the pilot version. Discuss the pros and cons of both strategies. Which strategy do you favor?

14. ♡ Consider the patient planning system project mentioned in Exercise 13. Under what conditions would you opt for an agile approach for this project?

15. Discuss the relative merits of throwaway prototyping as a way of eliciting the 'true' user requirements and prototyping as an evolutionary development method.

16. In what ways may the notion of a software product line have an impact on the structure of the software development process?

17. ♡ Software maintenance increases system entropy. Discuss possible ways to counteract this effect.

18. ♡ One of the reasons for using planning-driven approaches in software development projects is that the plan provides some structure to measure project progress. Do you think this measure is adequate? Can you think of better ways to measure progress?

19. ♡ Discuss the differences between RAD and participatory design (see (Carmel *et al.*, 1993)).

20. ♠ Describe the requirements engineering process depicted in Figure 9.1 in a notation similar to a programming language. Be as precise as possible. Discuss the advantages and limitations of the resulting process description.

21. ♠ Describe the requirements engineering process depicted in Figure 9.1 in a state transition diagram. Discuss the advantages and limitations of the resulting process description.

4

Configuration Management

LEARNING OBJECTIVES

- To understand the main tasks and responsibilities of software configuration management

- To be aware of the contents of a configuration management plan

- To appreciate the interplay between the role of configuration management in software development and the capabilities of supporting tools

> Careful procedures are needed to manage the vast number of elements (source code components, documentation, change requests, etc.) that are created and updated over the lifetime of a large software system. This is especially true in distributed development projects. It is called configuration management.

In the course of a software development project, quite a few documents are produced. These documents are also changed from time to time. Errors have to be corrected, change requests have to be taken care of, etc. Thus, at each point in time during a project, different versions of the same document may exist in parallel.

Often too, a software system itself is not monolithic. Software systems exist in different versions or configurations. Different versions come about when changes are implemented after the system has been delivered to the customer. From time to time, the customer is then confronted with a new release. Different versions of components of a system may also exist during development. For instance, if a change request has been approved, a programmer may implement that change by rewriting one or more components. Another programmer, however, may still be using the previous version of those same components.

Different configurations also come about if a set of components may be assembled into a system in more than one way. The Amsterdam Compiler Kit (ACK) consists of a set of programs to develop compilers for ALGOL-like languages (Tanenbaum *et al.*, 1983). Important components of the ACK are:

- front ends for languages such as Pascal, C, or Modula-2 (a front end for a language translates programs in that language into the universal intermediate code, EM);

- different EM optimizers;

- back ends, which translate EM code to assembler-code for a variety of real machines.

A compiler is then obtained by selecting a front end for a specific language, a back end for a specific machine and, optionally, one or more optimizers. Each compiler is a configuration, a certain combination of elements from the ACK system. The ACK system is an example of a product line, from an era before that notion was used.

The key tasks of configuration management are discussed in Section 4.1. A configuration management plan lays down the procedures that describe how to approach configuration management. The contents of this document are discussed in Section 4.2. Configuration management is often supported by tools. The discussion of those tools is largely postponed until Chapter 15.

4.1 TASKS AND RESPONSIBILITIES

Configuration management is concerned with the management of all artifacts produced in the course of a software development project. Though configuration management also plays a role during the operational phase of a system, when different combinations of components can be assembled into one system and new releases of a system are generated, the discussion below centers around the role of configuration management during system development.

We will for the moment assume that, at any point in time, there is one official version of the complete set of documents related to the project. This is called the **baseline**. A baseline is 'a specification or product that has been formally reviewed and agreed upon, that thereafter serves as the basis for further development, and that can be changed only through formal change control procedures' (IEEE610, 1990). Thus, the baseline is the shared project database, containing all approved items. The baseline may or may not be stored in a real database and supported by tools to assist in retrieving and updating its elements. The items contained in the baseline are the **configuration items**. A configuration item is 'an aggregation of hardware, software, or both, that is designated for configuration management and treated as a single entity in the configuration management process' (IEEE610, 1990). Possible configuration items are:

- source code components,

- the requirements specification,

- the design documentation,

- the test plan,

- test cases,

- test results,

- the user manual.

At some point in time, the baseline will contain a requirements specification. As time goes on, elements will be added: design documents, source code components, test reports, etc. A major task of configuration management is to maintain the integrity of this set of artifacts.

This is especially important if changes are to be incorporated. Suppose that, during testing, a major flaw in some component is discovered. We then have to retrace our steps and correct not only that component but also the corresponding design documents, and possibly even the requirements specification. This may affect work being done by other people still using the old version. Worse still, someone else may wish to make changes to the same component at the same time. Configuration management takes care of controlling the release and change of these items throughout the software life cycle.

The way to go about this is to have one shared library or database that contains all approved items, the 'baseline'. Adding an item to this database, or changing an item, is subject to a formal approval scheme. For larger projects, this is the responsibility of a separate body, the configuration (or change) control board (CCB). The CCB ensures that any change to the baseline is properly authorized and executed. The CCB is staffed with people from the various parties involved in the project, such as development, testing, and quality assurance.

Any proposed change to the baseline is called a change request. A change request may concern an error found in some component, a discrepancy found between a design document and its implementation, an enhancement caused by changed user requirements, etc. A change request is handled as follows (see also Figure 4.1):

- The proposed change is submitted to the CCB. To be able to assess the proposed change, the CCB needs information as to how the change affects both the product and the development process. This includes information about the estimated amount of new or changed code, additional test requirements, the relationship to other changes, potential costs, complexity of the change, the severity of the defect

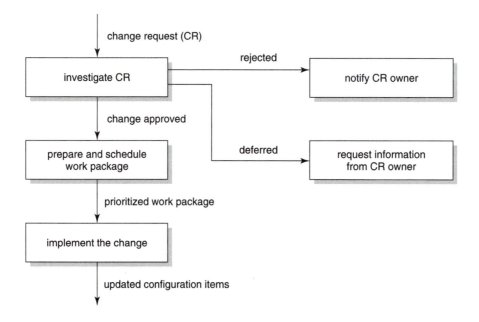

Figure 4.1 Workflow of a change request

(if it concerns one), resources needed, etc. Usually, a special change request form is provided to specify the information needed by the CCB.

- The CCB assesses the change request. The change request may be approved, rejected, or deferred if further information is required. If the request is approved, it eventually results in a work package which has to be scheduled.

- The CCB makes sure that all configuration items affected will eventually be updated accordingly. Configuration management provides a way of establishing the status of all items and, thereby, of the whole project.

Thus, configuration management is not only about keeping track of all the different versions of elements of a system; it also encompasses workflow management tasks. The process depicted in the state transition diagram in Figure 4.1, for example, describes what goes on in the life cycle of a change request. The process model thus defined exemplifies how the workflow of change requests can be managed.

In a similar vein, the state transition diagram in Figure 4.2 shows the workflow of developer tasks during the development of a system component. It shows the possible states of a system component and the transitions between them. For example, after a component has been coded, it is unit tested. If bugs are found during unit testing,

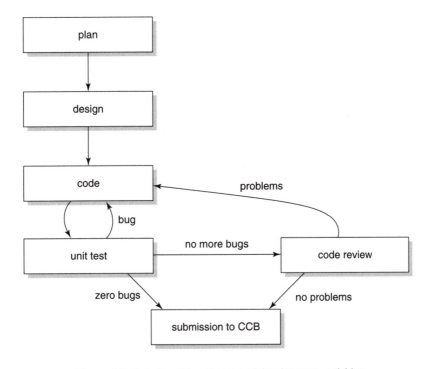

Figure 4.2 State transition diagram of development activities

further coding is necessary. Otherwise, the component enters the review stage. If the review reveals problems, the coding stage is re-entered. Otherwise, the component is submitted to the CCB for formal approval. Finally, if unit testing does not reveal any errors, the review stage is skipped.

If components are kept under configuration control, configuration management can be used to manage the workflow of development tasks as well. Changes in the status of a component then trigger subsequent activities, as indicated in the development workflow model.

We have to take care that the workflow schemes do not unnecessarily curtail the day-to-day working of the people involved in the project. New items should not be added to the baseline until they have been thoroughly reviewed and tested. Items from the shared database may be used freely by the participants. If an item has to be changed, the person responsible for implementing the change gets a copy of that item and the item is temporarily locked, so that others cannot simultaneously update the item. The person implementing the change is free to tinker with the copy. After the change has been thoroughly tested, it is submitted back to the CCB. Once the CCB has approved it, the revised item is included in the database, the change itself is documented with the item, and the item is unlocked again. A sequence of documented changes thus provides a revision history of that item.

When an item is changed, the old version is kept as well. The old version still has to be used by others until they have adapted to the change. Also, we may wish to go back to the old version if another change is requested. We thus have different versions of one and the same item, and must be able to distinguish them. This can be done through some numbering scheme, where each new version is identified by the next higher number. We then get, for a component X, versions X.0, X.1, X.2, and so on.

In a more sophisticated environment, we may even create different branches of revisions. Figure 4.3 gives an example of such a forked development. In the example, component X.2.1 may be the result of fixing a bug in component X.2. Component X.3 may concern an enhancement to X.2. It should be noted that merging those parallel development paths again can be difficult. Also, the numbering schemes soon tend to become incomprehensible.

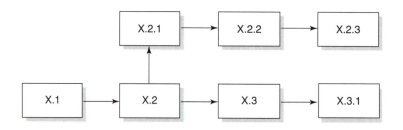

Figure 4.3 Parallel development paths

Configuration management is generally supported by powerful tools. Dart (1990) classifies the functionalities of software configuration management (SCM) tools as follows:

- **Components** SCM tools support storing, retrieving, and accessing of components. Several versions of a component may be stored, baselines can be established, and branches of revisions may be created.

- **Structure** SCM tools support the representation and use of the structure of a system made up of components and their interfaces. In terms of architectural viewpoints, this is the implementation viewpoint (see Section 11.3).

- **Construction** SCM tools support the construction of an executable version of the system. By default, the latest version of all configuration elements is used, but it is also possible to regenerate older versions of the system.

- **Auditing** SCM tools allow one to follow trails: which changes have been made to this component, who did those changes, and why. This way, a searchable archive of the system is maintained.

- **Accounting** The searchable archive allows one to gather statistics about the system and the development process. We may, for instance, search for components that have changed often and hypothesize about the quality of those components.

- **Controlling** SCM tools may be used for traceability purposes. If sufficient information is stored, we may trace defects to requirements, analyze the impact of changes, and so on.

- **Process** SCM tools may support users in selecting tasks and performing those tasks in the appropriate context. For instance, the tool may assist in assigning the handling of a change request to a certain developer and automatically provide the developer with a workspace containing the components that need to be changed.

- **Team** SCM tools may support collaboration, for example by generating a workspace for a group of collaborating developers, by noticing conflicts between developers, and so on.

Many SCM tools employ the **version-oriented** model of configurations. A physical change in a component then results in a new version, and different versions are thus characterized by their difference. Some tools use logical changes, rather than physical ones, as a basic unit of work in configuration management. This **change-oriented** model gives a more intuitive way of working and may prevent a lot of user errors when configuring a system. Rather than identifying a configuration by some arcane sequence of numbers, it is now identified by some baseline plus a set of changes. The set of changes may be empty. We thus specify

baseline X plus 'fix table size problem'

rather than

$$\{X.3.1, Y.2.7, Z.1.4, \ldots\}.$$

As noted, SCM tools also offer help in constructing ('building') an executable version of the system. One writes a 'program' that identifies the various components of the required system and their mutual dependencies. The system in question is then generated by executing this 'program': the components are retrieved automatically from the database containing the source code components, and all components are translated and linked together into an executable system. If the system is smart enough, only components that have changed are translated anew.

Early SCM tools emphasized the product-oriented tasks of configuration management. They provided functionality to lock and unlock elements, to automatically number revisions, and, by default, to provide users with the latest version of an item. If an item was changed, they prompted the user to document the change. Present-day SCM tools increasingly provide the other functionalities as well, and have become a key ingredient of managing modern, distributed and global, software development. Tools for configuration and version management are discussed more extensively in Chapter 15.

On one hand, configuration management entails procedures on how to handle changes to and versions of documents. On the other hand, it consists of tool support to maintain the version history and ensure an up-to-date version of the system. In planning-driven development, both aspects are important. In agile projects, the emphasis is on tool support. Agile projects favor continuous integration, where the individual work of one developer is rapidly integrated with other parts of the system and then tests are run to make sure everything still works as expected. Such a development cycle can take a few hours or, at most, one day. At the end of the day, one again has a running system that passes all tests. This process is known as the *daily build*.

4.2 CONFIGURATION MANAGEMENT PLAN

The procedures for configuration management are laid down in a document, the configuration management plan. For the contents of this plan, we follow the appropriate standard, IEEE828 (1998). This document describes methods to identify configuration items, to control change requests, and to document the implementation of those change requests. A sample table of contents for a configuration management plan is given in Table 4.1.

The SCM Management section describes how the project is being organized. Particular attention is paid to responsibilities that directly affect configuration management: how are change requests handled, how are development phases closed, how is the status of the system maintained, how are interfaces between components identified? The relationship with other functional organizations, such as software development and quality assurance, is also delineated.

The SCM Activities section describes how a configuration will be identified and controlled and how its status will be accounted and reported. A configuration is

Table 4.1 Contents of a software configuration management plan

Part	Description
1. Introduction	Purpose, scope, main terms and references
2. SCM Management	Organization, responsibilities and authorities
3. SCM Activities	Identification of configuration items, control, status accounting, and auditing process
4. SCM Schedules	Coordination with other activities
5. SCM Resources	Tools, human and computer resources
6. SCM Plan Maintenance	How the plan is kept up to date

identified by a baseline: a description of the constituents of that configuration. Such a configuration must be formally approved by the parties involved.

Clear and precise procedures are needed with respect to the processing of change requests if a software development project is to be controlled. A configuration control board (CCB) usually has the responsibility for evaluating and approving or rejecting proposed changes. The authority, responsibility, and membership of the CCB have to be stated. Since software components are usually incorporated in a library, procedures for controlling this library have to be established as well.

In order to be able to control a software development project, data has to be collected and processed. Information that is normally required includes: the present status of components, versions and change requests, as well as reports of approved changes and their implementation.

Changes to configuration items may affect items outside the scope of the plan, such as hardware items. These external items have to be identified and their interfaces controlled. In a similar vein, interfaces to items developed outside the project have to be identified and controlled.

4.3 SUMMARY

Configuration management is concerned with the management of all artifacts produced in the course of a software development project. It entails the following major activities:

- Configuration items must be identified and defined. A configuration item is a collection of elements that is treated as one unit for the purposes of configuration management. Examples of possible configuration items are the requirements specification, a software component, a test report, and the user documentation.

- The release and change of configuration items throughout the software life cycle must be controlled. This means that orderly procedures must be established as to whom is authorized to change or release configuration items.

- The status of configuration items and change requests must be recorded and reported. For example, the status of a change request may be proposed, approved, rejected, or incorporated.

For larger projects, a configuration control board (CCB) is usually established. The CCB is responsible for evaluating all change requests and maintaining the integrity of the complete set of documents that relate to a project. Its tasks and the further procedures for configuration management are laid down in a separate document, the configuration management plan.

The history and development of configuration management is closely tied to the history and development of configuration-management tools. In the early days, these tools emphasized the logging of physical file changes. There was little support for process aspects. Present-day configuration-management systems also address process aspects (workflow management) and many have adopted a change-oriented view of configurations as well as or instead of a version-oriented view. More and more, configuration-management tools function as document-management tools in that they support cooperation among a group of people, possibly distributed over multiple sites, working together on a collection of shared objects.

4.4 FURTHER READING

A readable introduction to the topic of configuration management is given in (Babich, 1986). A more recent source is (Jonassen Hass, 2002). (Estublier *et al.*, 2005) gives an excellent overview of the major developments in the field. Weber (1996) and Wiborg-Weber (1997) describe the change-oriented configuration management technology.

Further references for technical aspects of configuration management are given in Chapter 15.

Exercises

1. What are the main tasks of configuration management?

2. Describe the role of a configuration control board.

3. What is a configuration item?

4. What is a baseline?

5. Explain the difference between version-oriented and change-oriented configuration management.

6. Discuss the main contents of a configuration management plan.

7. ♡ Discuss differences and similarities between configuration management during the development and maintenance phases of a project.

8. ♡ Discuss possible differences between configuration management in a traditional waterfall development model and in an evolutionary development model (see also (Bersoff and Davis, 1991)).

9. ♡ Configuration management at the implementation level is often supported by tools. Can you think of ways in which such tools can also support the control of other artifacts (such as design documents and test reports)?

10. ♠ Devise a configuration management scheme for a small project (say, less than one person-year) and a large project (say, more than ten person-years). Give a rationale for the possible differences between those schemes.

11. ♠ To what extent could configuration-management tools support the gathering of quantitative project data? To what extent could such tools support project control?

5

People Management and Team Organization

LEARNING OBJECTIVES

- To be aware of the importance of people issues in software development
- To know of different ways to organize work
- To know of major types of management styles
- To appreciate different ways to organize a software development team

> Finding the right organizational framework and the right mix of skills for a development team is a difficult matter. Well-founded theory is not readily available for this. Yet, many stories of successful and less successful projects illustrate some of the intricacies of project team issues. This chapter sketches the major issues involved.

People are the organization's most important asset.

Humphrey (1997a)

In most organizations that develop software, programmers, analysts, and other professionals work together in a team. An adequate team structure depends on many factors, such as the number of people involved, their experience and involvement in the project, the kind of project, and individual differences and style. These factors also influence the way projects are managed. In this chapter, we discuss various aspects of people management, as well as some of the more common team organizations for software development projects.

The work to be done within the framework of a project, be it a software development project, building a house, or the design of a new car, involves a number of tasks. A critical part of management responsibility is to coordinate the tasks of all participants.

This coordination can be carried out in a number of ways. There are both external and internal influences on the coordination mechanism. Internal influences originate from characteristics of the project. External influences originate from the project's organizational environment. If these influences ask for conflicting coordination mechanisms, conflicts between the project and the environment are lurking around the corner.

Consider, as an example, a highly innovative software development project to be carried out within a government agency. The characteristics of the project may ask for a flexible, informal type of coordination mechanism, where the commitment of specialized individuals, rather than a strict adherence to formal procedures, is a critical success factor. On the other hand, the environment may be geared towards a bureaucracy with centralized control, which tries to impose formal procedures onto project management. These two mechanisms do not work harmoniously together. As a consequence, the project management may get crushed between those opposing forces.

Section 5.1 further elaborates the various internal and external factors that affect the way projects are managed, and emphasizes the need to pay ample attention to the human element in project management.

Software development involves teamwork. The members of the team have to coordinate their work, communicate their decisions, etc. For a small project, the team will consist of up to a few individuals. As the size of the project increases, so does the size of the team. Large teams are difficult to manage, however. Coordinating the work of a large team is difficult. Communication between team members tends to increase exponentially with the size of the team (see also Chapter 7). Therefore, large teams are usually split into smaller teams in a way that confines most of the coordination and communication within the sub-team.

Section 5.2 discusses several ways to organize a software development team. The hierarchical and matrix organizations can be found in other types of business too, while the chief programmer, SWAT and agile team are specific to software development. Though open source projects have no means to impose team structure, they usually converge to an onion-like organization as discussed in Section 5.2.6.

Because of outsourcing, networked companies, and globalization, software development has become a distributed activity. Teams in, say, Amsterdam, Boston, and Bangalore may have to cooperate on the development of the same system. How should we split up the tasks between these groups? How do we ensure that communication between these groups is effective? Cultural differences also play a role in multi-site development. For instance, people in Asia respect authority. In North America, it is more customary for team members to argue with their manager. Managers and team members should be aware of those differences and act accordingly. People issues that affect multi-site software development are discussed in Chapter 20.

5.1 PEOPLE MANAGEMENT

A team is made up of individuals, each of whom has personal goals. It is the task of project management to cast a team out of these individuals, whereby the individual goals are reconciled into one goal for the project as a whole.

Though the individual goals of people may differ, it is important to identify project goals at an early stage and unambiguously communicate these to the project members. Project members ought to know what is expected of them. If there is any uncertainty in this respect, team members will determine their own goals: one programmer may decide that efficiency has the highest priority, another may choose efficient use of memory, while yet a third will decide that writing a lot of code is what counts. Such widely diverging goals may lead to severe problems.

Once project goals are established and the project is under way, the performance of project members with respect to the project goals needs to be monitored and assessed. This can be difficult, since much of what is being done is invisible and progress is hard to measure.

Ideally, we would like to have an indication of the functionality delivered and define productivity as the amount of functionality delivered per unit of time. Productivity is mostly defined as the number of lines of code delivered per man-month. Everyone will agree that this measure is not optimal, but nothing better has been found. One of the big dangers of using this measure is that people tend to produce as much code as possible. This has a very detrimental effect. The most important cost driver in software development projects is the amount of code to be delivered (see also Chapter 7): writing less code is cheaper. Reuse of existing code is one way to save time and money; it should, therefore, be strongly advocated. Using the amount of code delivered per man-month as a productivity indicator creates no incentive for software reuse.

Another aspect of people assessment occurs in group processes such as peer reviews, inspections, and walkthroughs. These techniques are used during verification and validation activities, to discover errors or to assess the quality of the code or documentation. In order to make these processes effective it is necessary to clearly separate the documents to be assessed from their authors. Weinberg (1971) used the term 'egoless programming' in this context. An assessment of the product of someone's work should not imply an assessment of that person.

One of the major problems in software development is the coordination of activities of team members. As development projects grow bigger and become more complex, coordination problems quickly accumulate. To counteract these problems, management formalizes communication, for example by having formal project meetings, strictly monitored inspections, and an official configuration control board. However, informal, interpersonal communication is known to be a primary way in which information flows into and through a development organization. It is unwise to rule out this type of communication altogether.[1] Informal, interpersonal communication is most easily accomplished if people are physically at close quarters. Even worse, people are inclined to trade the ease with which information can be obtained against its quality. They will accept their neighbor's advice, even if they know that much better advice can be found on the next floor. To counteract this tendency, it is wise to bring together diverse stakeholders in controlled ways, for example by having domain experts in the design team, by having users involved in the testing of software, or through participatory design approaches. The collocation of all stakeholders is a main aspect of agile teams.

Successful software development teams exhibit a mix of qualities: technical competence, end-user empathy, and organizational awareness. Technical competency is, of course, required to deliver a high-quality system in the first place. End-user empathy and organizational awareness have to do with recognition of the individuals and the organization that have to cope with the system. A blend of these orientations in a team helps to ensure sufficient attention is given to each of the aspects (Klein *et al.*, 2002).

Team management entails a great many aspects, not the least important of which concern the care for the human element. Successes among software development projects can often be traced to a strong focus on cultural and sociological concerns, such as efforts to create a blame-free culture, or the solicitation of commitment and partnership. This chapter touches upon only a few aspects of this. Brooks (1995) and

---

[1] One shining example is in the following anecdote from (Weinberg, 1971). The manager of a university computing center got complaints about students and programmers chatting and laughing at the department's coffee machine. Being a real manager, concerned about productivity, he removed the coffee machine to some remote spot. Quickly thereafter, the load on the computing center consultants increased considerably. The crowd near the coffee machine was in fact an effective, informal communication channel, through which the majority of problems were solved.

DeMarco and Lister (1999) give many insightful observations regarding the human element of software project management.

In the remainder of this section, we confine ourselves to two rather general taxonomies of coordination mechanisms and management styles.

5.1.1 Coordination Mechanisms

In his classic text, Mintzberg (1983) distinguishes between five typical organizational configurations. Each configuration reflects an ideal environment and is associated with a specific coordination mechanism: a preferred mechanism for coordinating the tasks to be carried out within that configuration type. Mintzberg's configurations and associated coordination mechanisms are as follows:

- **Simple structure** In a simple structure, there may be one or a few managers and a core of people who do the work. The corresponding coordination mechanism is called *direct supervision*. This configuration is often found in new, relatively small organizations. There is little specialization, training and formalization. Coordination lies with separate people, who are responsible for the work of others.

- **Machine bureaucracy** When the content of the work is completely specified, it becomes possible to execute and assess tasks on the basis of precise instructions. Mass-production and assembly lines are typical examples of this configuration type. There is little training and much specialization and formalization. The coordination is achieved through *standardization of work processes*.

- **Divisionalized form** In this type of configuration, each division (or project) is granted considerable autonomy as to how the stated goals are to be reached. The operating details are left to the division itself. Coordination is achieved through *standardization of work outputs*. Control is executed by regularly measuring the performance of the division. This coordination mechanism is possible only when the end result is specified precisely.

- **Professional bureaucracy** If it is not possible to specify either the end result or the work contents, coordination can be achieved through *standardization of worker skills*. In a professional bureaucracy, skilled professionals are given considerable freedom as to how they carry out their jobs. Hospitals are typical examples of this type of configuration.

- **Adhocracy** In projects that are big or innovative in nature, work is divided amongst many specialists. We may not be able to tell exactly what each specialist should do, or how they should carry out the tasks allocated to them. The project's success depends on the ability of the group as a whole to reach a non-specified goal in a non-specified way. Coordination is achieved through *mutual adjustment*.

The coordination mechanisms distinguished by Mintzberg correspond to typical organizational configurations, such as a hospital or an assembly-line factory. In

Mintzberg's view, different organizations call for different coordination mechanisms. Organizations are not all alike. Following this line of thought, factors external to a software development project are likely to exert an influence on the coordination mechanisms for that project.

Note that most real organizations do not fit one single configuration type. Different parts of one organization may well be organized differently. Also, Mintzberg's configurations represent abstract ideals. In reality, organizations may tend towards one of these configurations, but carry aspects of others as well.

5.1.2 Management Styles

The development of a software system, the building of a house, and the planning of and participation in a family holiday are comparable in that each concerns a coordinated effort carried out by a group of people. Though these projects are likely to be dealt with in widely different ways, the basic assumptions that underlie their organizational structures and management styles have a lot in common. These basic assumptions can be highlighted by distinguishing between two dimensions in managing people:

- **Relation directedness** This concerns attention to an individual and his relationship to other individuals within the organization.

- **Task directedness** This concerns attention to the results to be achieved and the way in which these results must be achieved.

Both relation and task directedness may be high or low. This leads to four basic combinations, as depicted in Figure 5.1. Obviously, these combinations correspond to extreme orientations. For each dimension, there is a whole spectrum of possibilities.

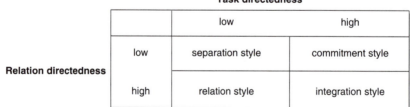

Task directedness

Relation directedness		low	high
	low	separation style	commitment style
	high	relation style	integration style

Figure 5.1 Four basic management styles, after (Reddin, 1970)

The style that is most appropriate for a given situation depends on the type of work to be done:

- **Separation style** This management style is usually most effective for routine work. Efficiency is the central theme. Management acts like a bureaucrat and applies rules and procedures. Work is coordinated hierarchically. Decision-making is top-down, formal, and based on authority. A major advantage of this style is that it results in a stable project organization. On the other hand, real innovations are difficult to accomplish. This style closely corresponds to Mintzberg's coordination through standardization of work processes.

- **Relation style** This style is usually most effective in situations where people have to be motivated, coordinated and trained. The tasks to be performed are bound to individuals. The work is not of a routine character, but innovative, complex, and specialized. Decision-making is a group process; it involves negotiation and consensus building. An obvious weak spot of this style is that it may result in endless chaotic meetings. The manager's ability to moderate efficient decision-making is a key success factor. This style best fits Mintzberg's mutual adjustment coordination mechanism.

- **Commitment style** This is most effective if work is done under pressure. For this style to be effective, the manager has to know how to achieve goals without arousing resentment. Decision making is not done in meetings. Rather, decisions are implied by the team's shared vision of the goals of the project. A potential weak spot of this style is that, once this vision has been agreed upon, the team is not responsive to changes in its environment, but blindly stumbles on along the road mapped out. This style best fits Mintzberg's professional bureaucracy.

- **Integration style** This fits situations where the result is uncertain. The work is explorative in nature and the various tasks are highly interdependent. It is the manager's task to stimulate and motivate. Decision-making is informal, bottom-up. This style promotes creativity and individuals are challenged to get the best out of themselves. A possible weak spot of this style is that the goals of individual team members become disconnected from those of the project and team members start to compete with one another. Again, Mintzberg's coordination through mutual adjustment fits this situation well.

Each of the coordination mechanisms and management styles identified may be used within software development projects. It is only reasonable to expect that projects with widely different characteristics ask for different mechanisms. An experienced team asked to develop a well-specified application in a familiar domain may achieve coordination through standardization of work processes. For a complex and innovative application, this mechanism is not likely to work, though.

In Chapter 8, we identify various types of software development project and indicate which type of coordination mechanism and management style best fits those projects. It should be noted that the coordination mechanisms suggested in Chapter 8 stem from internal factors, i.e. characteristics of the project on hand. As noted before, the project's environment will also influence its organization.

Notice that in the above discussion we looked from the manager to the team and its members. Alternatively, we may look at the relation and task *maturity* of individual team members. Relation maturity concerns the attitude of employees towards their job and management. Task maturity is concerned with technical competence. It is important that the manager aligns his dealings with team members with their respective relation and task maturity. For example, a recent graduate may have high task maturity and low relation maturity, and so his introduction into a skilled team may warrant some careful guidance.

5.2 TEAM ORGANIZATION

Within a team, different roles can be distinguished. There are managers, testers, designers, programmers, and so on. Depending on the size of the project, more than one role may be carried out by one person or different people may play the same role. The responsibilities and tasks of each of these roles have to be precisely defined in the project plan.

People cooperate within a team in order to achieve an optimal result. Yet it is advisable to strictly separate certain roles. It is a good idea to create a test team that is independent of the development team. Similarly, quality assurance should, in principle, be conducted by people not directly involved in the development process.

Large teams are difficult to manage and are therefore often split up into smaller teams. By clearly defining the tasks and responsibilities of the various sub-teams, communication can be largely confined to communication between members of the same sub-team. Quantifying the cost of interpersonal communication yields insights into the effect of team size on productivity and helps to structure large development teams effectively. Some simple formulae for doing so are derived in Chapter 7.

In the following subsections we discuss several organizational forms for software development teams.

5.2.1 Hierarchical Organization

In an environment which is completely dedicated to the production of software, we often encounter hierarchical team structures. Depending on the size of the organization or project, different levels of management can be distinguished.

Figure 5.2 gives an example of a hierarchical organization. The rectangles denote the various sub-teams in which the actual work is done. Circled nodes denote managers. In this example, two levels of management can be distinguished. At the lower level, different teams are responsible for different parts of the project. The managers at this level have a primary responsibility in coordinating the work within their respective teams. At the higher level, the work of the different teams is coordinated.

This type of hierarchical organization often reflects the global structure of the system to be developed. If the system has three major subsystems, there may be three teams, one for each subsystem, as in Figure 5.2. There may also be functional units associated with specific project-wide responsibilities, such as quality assurance and testing.

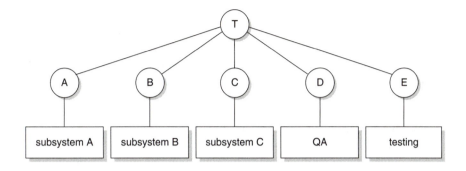

Figure 5.2 A hierarchical team organization

It is not possible to associate the hierarchical organization with only one of the coordination mechanisms introduced above. For each unit identified, any one of the coordination mechanisms mentioned earlier is possible. Also, one need not necessarily apply the same mechanism in each node of the hierarchy. Having different coordination mechanisms within one project is not without problems, however.

Based on an analysis of the characteristics of various subsystems, the respective managers may wish to choose a management style and coordination mechanism that best fits those characteristics. If one or more of the subsystems is highly innovative in nature, the management may opt for a mutual adjustment type of coordination. The higher levels within a hierarchy will usually tend towards a coordination mechanism based on some form of standardization, by imposing rules and procedures as in a machine bureaucracy, or measuring output as in a divisionalized configuration. In such cases, internal and external powers may well clash at one or more of the intermediate levels.

Another critical point in any hierarchical organization is the distance between the top and the bottom of the hierarchical pyramid. The 'real' work is generally done at the lower levels of this pyramid. The people at these lower levels generally possess the real knowledge of the application. The higher one rises in the hierarchy, the less specific the knowledge becomes (this is the main reason why management at these higher levels tends towards coordination through standardization). Yet, most decisions are taken at a fairly high level. In many cases, signals from the lower level somehow get subsumed at one of the intermediate levels.

As information seeps through the various levels in the hierarchy, it tends to become more and more rose-colored. The following scenario is not entirely fictitious:

- bottom: we have severe troubles in implementing module X;

- level 1: there are some problems with module X;

- level 2: progress is steady, I do not foresee any real problems;

- top: everything proceeds according to our plan.

These kinds of distortion are difficult to circumvent altogether. They are, however, reinforced by the fact that the organizational line along which progress is reported is also the line along which the performance of team members is measured and evaluated. Everyone is favored by a positive evaluation and is thus inclined to color the reports accordingly. If data on a project's progress is being collected and processed by people not directly involved in the assessment of team members, you have a much higher chance that the information collected is of sufficient reliability.

An equally problematic aspect of hierarchical organizations lies in the fact that one is judged, both socially and financially, according to the *level* at which one stands within the organization. It is thus natural to aspire to higher and higher levels within the hierarchy. It is, however, not at all clear that this is desirable. According to the Peter Principle, in a hierarchical organization each employee rises to the level of his incompetence (Peter and Hull, 1970). A good programmer need not be a good manager. A good programmer requires certain skills and a good manager requires different skills. In the long run, it seems wiser to keep people at a level at which they perform well and reward them accordingly.

5.2.2 Matrix Organization

In an environment where software is a mere byproduct, we often encounter some sort of matrix organization. People from different departments are then allocated to a software development project, possibly part-time. In this type of organization, it is sometimes difficult to control progress. An employee has to satisfy several bosses and may have the tendency to play off one boss against another.

We may also use a matrix organization in an environment completely dedicated to software development. The basic unit is a small, specialized group. There may be more than one unit with the same specialization. Possible specializations are, for instance, graphics programming, databases, user interfaces, and quality control. The units are organized according to their specialty. Projects, on the other hand, may involve units with different specialties. Individuals are thus organized along two axes, one representing the various specialist groups and one representing the projects to which they are assigned. This type of matrix organization is depicted in Table 5.1.

In such a situation, the project manager is responsible for the successful completion of the project. The manager in charge of one or more units with the same specialty has a longer-term mission, such as maintaining or enlarging the

Table 5.1 A matrix organization

	Real-time programming	Graphics	Databases	QA	Testing
Project C	X			X	X
Project B	X		X	X	X
Project A		X	X	X	X

knowledge and expertise of the members of his team. Phrased in terms of the basic management dimensions discussed earlier, the project manager is likely to emphasize task directedness, while the unit manager will emphasize relation directedness. Such an organization can be very effective, provided there is sufficient mutual trust and the willingness to cooperate and pursue the project's goals.

5.2.3 Chief Programmer Team

A team organization known as the 'chief programmer team' was proposed by Harlan Mills around 1970. The kernel of such a team consists of three people:

- The chief programmer is the team leader who takes care of the design and implements key parts of the system.

- The chief programmer's assistant can stand in for the chief programmer, if needed.

- The librarian takes care of the administration and documentation.

Besides these three people, an additional (small) number of experts may be added to the chief programmer team.

In this type of organization, fairly high demands are made upon the chief programmer. The chief programmer has to be very competent in the technical area, but he also has to have sufficient management capabilities. Are there enough people who can fulfill the chief programmer's role? Questions of competence may arise. The chief programmer plays a very central role: he takes all the decisions; other team members may well challenge some of his qualities.

The early notion of a chief programmer team seems somewhat elitist. It resembles a surgeon team in its emphasis on highly specialized tasks and charismatic leadership. However, the advantages of a team consisting of a small group of peers over a huge development team struggling to produce ever larger software systems may be regained in a modified form of the chief programmer team, in which the peer group aspects prevail. The development team consists of a small group of people collectively responsible for the task at hand. In particular, jobs are not structured around life cycle stages. There are no analysts, designers, or programmers, though the role of tester may be assigned to a specific person. Different levels of expertise may occur within the group. The most experienced people act as chief programmer and deputy chief programmer. At the other end of the scale, one or two trainees can be assimilated and get the necessary on-the-job training. A trainee may well act as the team's librarian.

5.2.4 SWAT Team

In projects with an evolutionary or iterative process model such as Rapid Application Development (RAD), a project organization known as the Skilled With Advanced Tools (SWAT) team is sometimes used. We may view the SWAT team as a software development version of a project team in which both task and relation directedness are high.

A SWAT team is relatively small. It typically has four or five members. Preferably, the team occupies one room. Communication channels are kept very short. The team does not have lengthy formal meetings with formal minutes. Rather, it uses workshops and brainstorming sessions of which little more than a snapshot of a white-board drawing is retained.

A SWAT team typically builds incremental versions of a software system. In order to do so effectively, it employs reusable components, very high-level languages, and powerful software generators. The work of team members is supported and coordinated through groupware or workflow management software.

As in the chief programmer team, the leader of a SWAT team is like a foreman in the building industry: he is both a manager and a co-worker. The members of a SWAT team are generalists. They may have certain specialties, but they must also be able to do a variety of tasks, such as participate in a workshop with customers, build a prototype, and test a piece of software.

Team motivation is very important in a SWAT team. A SWAT team often adopts a catchy name, motto or logo. This label then expresses their vision. Individuals derive pride and self-esteem from their membership of a SWAT team.

5.2.5 Agile Team

Agile approaches to software development grew out of, and have a lot in common with, the various iterative development approaches. In the same vein, an agile team has much in common with, e.g., a SWAT team: collocation, short communication channels, and a people-oriented attitude rather than a formalistic one. Often, people work in pairs, with a pilot and co-pilot, but without a hierarchy.

Because agile processes have little discipline enforced on them from the outside, they need discipline to come from within the team. Agile teams need self-discipline. If a pair of programmers develops some code and subsequent tests fail, they must take a step back and redo their work. After they have incorporated a piece of work, they must consider the system as a whole and refactor if needed.

For this to succeed, an agile team needs more-skilled people than a team that works according to a planning-driven approach. In a planning-driven approach, the plan is like a life-jacket that people can fall back upon. In an agile team, no such life-jacket is available, and people must be able to swim. In terms of the levels of understanding discussed in (Cockburn, 2002), an agile team requires people working at levels 2 or 3 and is deemed risky with people working at level 1 (see Table 5.2). In planning-driven environments, people working at levels 2 or 3 are only required during the definition stages of development. Thereafter, some people working at level 1 can be accommodated.

5.2.6 Open Source Software Development

One of the early books on open source software development is titled *The Cathedral and the Bazaar* (Raymond, 1999). The cathedral refers to traditional, heavyweight,

Table 5.2 Levels of understanding

Level	Description
Fluent – 3	People at this level move flexibly from one approach to another. As software developers, they can revise a method to fit an unprecedented new situation.
Detaching – 2	People at this level are proficient in a single approach and are ready to learn alternatives. They can adapt a method to a precedented new situation.
Following – 1	People at this level follow a single approach and are confused when confronted with something new. They can perform method steps, such as composing a pattern or running tests.

hierarchical software development as is common in closed source software development. Conversely, open source software development is like a bazaar: hordes of anarchist developers are casually organized in a virtual networked organization. The bazaar metaphor was chosen to reflect the babbling, chatting, seemingly unorganized form of the middle-Eastern marketplace. Though the bazaar metaphor may fit some open source development groups, many successful open source communities have adopted the more organized onion-like structure depicted in Figure 5.3.

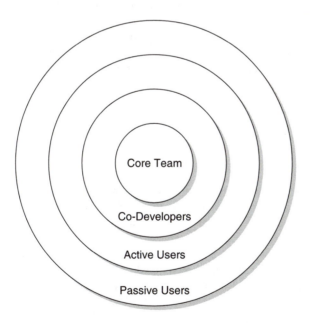

Figure 5.3 Onion-shaped structure of an open source community

In the onion-shaped structure of an open source community, four layers of participation are distinguished:

- The **core team** consists of a small team of experienced developers that also acts as the management team. Changes in kernel components of the software can only be made by members of the core team.

- The **co-developers** are a larger group of people surrounding the core team. Co-developers review code and do bug fixes.

- The **active users** are users of the most recent release of the system. They submit bug reports and feature requests, but do not themselves program the system.

- The **passive users** merely use stable releases of the software. They do not interact with the developers.

Usually, the outer layers contain more people than the inner layers. Often, the core team contains no more than 5–15 people. For example, (Mockus *et al.*, 2000) report that the 15-person core team of Apache did over 80% of functionality coding.

This type of open source project organization is a meritocracy; i.e., people fill roles based on talent and proven quality. People in one layer may move up to the next higher layer. Getting to the core is achieved by a process of earning trust, responsibility and status through competition and demonstrated talent. For example, an active user may become a co-developer by suggesting quality improvements over a period of time. Likewise, a longstanding record of quality fixes to the code may earn a co-developer a position in the core team.

The voluntary character of open source development gives rise to some specific challenges:

- Motivation to remain active

- Disagreement between developers

- Communication between developers

An open source community is 'a company without walls' (Fang and Neufeld, 2006). People may freely enter and leave the community. Developers participating in open source projects rarely do so selflessly. They expect something in return, such as the ability to learn new things, a higher status within their normal job, attention because they are part of a successful project, and so on. This should come as no surprise. Software professionals have high growth needs. Open source projects that challenge developer skills, have a well-modularized code base, and make use of advanced tools have a higher chance of attracting a sustainable community.

One of the worst things that may happen to an open source project is disagreement between developers. A common obstacle in open source projects is disagreement about development speed (Godfrey and Tu, 2000). Some developers may want to issue new releases frequently, while others may take a more cautious stance. Another potential source of disagreement is when users start to feel uncomfortable in the 'undemocratic democracy' of an open source project. Although many people may submit bug fixes or feature requests, the power to decide what actually happens usually lies with one or a few people in the core team. If the submissions of a developer are rejected time and again, he may get frustrated and leave the community or decide to create a fork (take a copy of the source code and start an independent development track).

Communication between developers is an issue in every distributed team. But in open source projects, the situation is worse because of the floating community membership and the lack of formal documentation. A clear modularization of the code is an important way to reduce the need for extensive communication. Open source communities further tend to use configuration control tools, bug-tracking systems, and mailing lists for communication.

5.2.7 General Principles for Organizing a Team

No matter how we try to organize a team, the key point is that it ought to be a *team*. From many tests regarding productivity in software development projects, it turns out again and again that factors concerning team capabilities have a far greater influence than anything else. Factors such as morale, group norms and management style play a more important role than such things as the use of high-level languages, product complexity, and so on (see, for instance, (Lawrence, 1981)).

Some general principles for team organization are given in (Koontz and O'Donnell, 1972). In particular, these general principles also apply to the organization of software development projects:

- **Use fewer, and better, people** The highest productivity is achieved by a relatively small group of people. This holds for novelists, soccer players and bricklayers. There is no reason to believe that it does not equally apply to programmers and other people working in the software field. Also, large groups require more communication, which has a negative effect on productivity and leads to more errors.

- **Try to fit tasks to the capabilities and motivation of the people available** In other words, take care that the Peter Principle does not apply in your situation. In many organizations, excellent programmers can be promoted only into managerial positions. It is far better to offer career possibilities in the more technical areas of software development and maintenance.

- **Help people to get the most from themselves** You should not pursue either of the following situations:

  - The reverse Peter Principle, in which people rise within an organization to the level at which they become indispensable. For instance, a programmer may become the only expert in a certain system. If he does not get a chance to work on anything else, it is not unlikely that this person, for want of a more interesting and challenging task, will leave your organization. At that point, you are in real trouble.

  - The Paul Principle, in which people rise within an organization to the level at which their expertise becomes obsolete within five years. Given the speed with which new developments enter the marketplace in software engineering, and computer science in general, it is very important that people get the opportunity to grow and stay abreast of new developments.

- **Select people to ensure a well-balanced and harmonious team** In general, this means that it is not sufficient only to have a few top experts. A soccer team needs regular players as well as stars. Selecting the proper mix of people is a complicated task. There are various good texts available that specifically address this question (for example, (Weinberg, 1971) and (Metzger, 1987)).

- **Remove people who do not fit the team** If it turns out that a team does not function as a coherent unit, we are often inclined to wait a little while, see how things develop, and hope for better times to come. In the long run, this is detrimental.

5.3 SUMMARY

Software is written by humans. Their productivity is partly determined by factors such as the programming language used, machine speed, and available tools. The organizational environment in which they are operating is equally important, however. Good team management distinguishes itself from bad team management above all by the degree to which attention is paid to these human factors. The human element in software project management was discussed in Section 5.1, together with well-known taxonomies of coordination mechanisms and management styles.

There are different ways to organize software developers in a team. These organizational forms and some of their caveats were discussed in Section 5.2. Hierarchical and matrix organizations are not specific to software development, while the chief programmer, SWAT and agile teams originated in the software field. Each of the latter somehow tries to reconcile the two types of management typically required in software development projects: an individualistic, personal approach where one tries to get the best out of team members, and a hierarchical, top-down management style to get things done in time and within budget. Successful open source projects usually have an onion-shaped organization.

5.4 FURTHER READING

A still very relevant source of information on psychological factors related to software development is (Weinberg, 1971). Brooks (1995) and DeMarco and Lister (1999) also contain a number of valuable observations. Coordination problems in software development are discussed in (Kraut and Streeter, 1995). (Software, 1996a) and (CACM, 1993b) are special journal issues on managing software projects.

Mintzberg (1983) is the classic text on the organization of management. The basic management styles discussed in Section 5.1.2 are based on (Reddin, 1970) and (Constantine, 1993).

(Couger and Zawacki, 1980) is an early source on the growth needs of software developers. (Procaccino *et al.*, 2006) also address this issue. Armour (2002) stresses the importance of social and communication aspects in software development projects.

The chief programmer team is described in (Baker, 1972). Its modified form is described in (Macro and Buxton, 1987). SWAT is discussed in (Martin, 1991). Agile teams are described in, amongst others, (Highsmith, 2004). The three levels of understanding are discussed in (Cockburn, 2002). (Software, 2005) contains a number of articles on how to adopt agile methods.

(SPIP, 2006) contains a collection of articles on open source development processes. Crowston and Howison (2006) discuss the health of open source communities. Aberdour (2007) discusses ways to achieve quality in open source software development.

Exercises

1. Explain Mintzberg's classification of organizational configurations and their associated coordination mechanisms.

2. Discuss Reddin's basic management styles.

3. What are the critical issues in a hierarchical team organization?

4. Highlight the differences between a chief programmer team, a SWAT team and an agile team.

5. Which of Reddin's management styles fits in best with an agile team?

6. What is the Peter Principle? Where does it crop up in software development?

7. Why would an agile team need better people than a team following a planning-based approach?

8. ♡ Consider a software development project you have been involved in. Which style of coordination mechanism or management style best fits this project? Do you consider the management to have been adequate or does the discussion in Section 5.1 point to possible improvements?

9. ♡ From a management point of view, discuss possible pros and cons of having a technical wizard on your development team.

10. ♠ Write an essay on the role of people issues in software development. To do so, you may consult some of the books that focus on people issues in software development, such as (Brooks, 1995), (Weinberg, 1971) and (DeMarco and Lister, 1999).

11. ♠ Discuss the pros and cons of an organization in which the primary departmentalization is vertical (i.e. by specialty, such as databases, human–computer interfaces, and graphics programming) as opposed to one in which the primary departmentalization is horizontal (i.e. by phase, such as design, implementation, and testing).

12. ♡ Write an essay on how open source software development projects are managed.

13. ♡ Discuss the pros and cons of letting people rotate between projects from different application domains as opposed to letting them become true experts in one particular application domain.

6

On Managing Software Quality

LEARNING OBJECTIVES

- To appreciate the need for sound measurements in determining software quality

- To critically assess various taxonomies of quality attributes

- To be able to contrast different views of software quality

- To be aware of international standards pertaining to software quality

- To know about the Capability Maturity Model

- To understand how an organization may set up its own measurement program

> Software quality is an important topic. With the increasing penetration of automation in everyday life, more and more people are coming into contact with software systems, and the quality of those systems is a major concern. Quality cannot be added as an afterthought. It has to be built in from the very beginning. This chapter discusses the many dimensions of quality of both the software product and the software process.

In their landmark book, *In Search of Excellence*, Peters and Waterman identify a number of key factors that set the very successful companies of the world apart from the less successful ones. One of those key factors is the commitment to quality of the very successful companies. Apparently, quality pays off.

Long-term profitability is not the only reason why attention to quality is important in software development. Because of the sheer complexity of software products and the often frequent changes that have to be incorporated during the development of software, continuous attention to, and assessment of, the quality of the product under development is needed if we ever want to realize satisfactory products. This need is aggravated by the increasing penetration of software technology into everyday life. Low-quality products will leave customers dissatisfied, will make users neglect the systems that are supposed to support their work, and may even cost lives.

One frightening example of what may happen if software contains bugs, has become known as 'Malfunction 54'. The Therac-25, a computerized radiation machine, was blamed in incidents that caused the deaths of two people and serious injuries to others. The deadly mystery was eventually traced back to a software bug, named 'Malfunction 54' after the message displayed at the console; see also Section 1.4.2. Commitment to quality in software development not only pays off, it is a sheer necessity.

This commitment calls for careful development processes. This attention to the development process is based on the premise that the quality of a product is largely based on the quality of the process that leads to that product, and that this process can indeed be defined, managed, measured, and improved.

Besides the product–process dichotomy, a dichotomy between conformance and improvement can also be distinguished. If we impose certain quality requirements on the product or process, we may devise techniques and procedures to ensure or test that the product or process does indeed *conform to* these objectives. Alternatively, schemes may be aimed at *improving* the quality of the product or process.

Table 6.1 gives examples of these four approaches to quality. Most of software engineering is concerned with improving the quality of the products we develop, and the label 'best practices' in this figure refers to all of the goodies mentioned elsewhere in this book. The other three approaches are discussed in this chapter.

Before we embark on a discussion of the different approaches to quality, we will first elaborate on the notion of software quality itself and how to measure it.

Table 6.1 Approaches to quality

	Conformance	Improvement
Product	ISO 9126	'best practices'
Process	ISO 9001 SQA	CMM SPICE Bootstrap

When talking about the height of a person, the phrase 'Jasper is 7 ft' conveys more information than 'Jasper is tall'. Likewise, we would like to express all kinds of quality attributes in numbers. We would prefer a statement of the form 'The availability of the system is 99%' to a mere 'The availability of the system is high'. Some of the caveats of the measurement issues involved are discussed in Section 6.1. In Section 6.2, we discuss various taxonomies of quality attributes, including ISO 9126. This is by no means the final word on software quality, but it is a good reference point to start from. This discussion also allows us to further illustrate some of the problems with measuring quality in quantitative terms.

'Software quality' is a rather elusive notion. Different people will have different perspectives on the quality of a software system. A system tester may view quality as 'compliance to requirements', whereas a user may view it as 'fitness for use'. Both viewpoints are valid, but they need not coincide. As a matter of fact, they probably won't. Part of the confusion about what the quality of a system entails and how it should be assessed is caused by mixing up these different perspectives. Rather than differentiating between various perspectives on quality, Total Quality Management (TQM) advocates an eclectic view: quality is the pursuit of excellence in everything. Section 6.3 elaborates on the different perspectives on quality.

The International Organization for Standardization (ISO) has established several standards that pertain to the management of quality. The one most applicable to our field, the development and maintenance of software, is ISO 9001. This standard is discussed in Section 6.4.

ISO 9001 can be augmented by procedures aimed specifically at quality assurance and control for software development. The IEEE Standard for Quality Assurance Plans is meant to provide such procedures. It is discussed in Section 6.5. Software quality assurance procedures provide the means to review and audit the software development process and its products. Quality assurance by itself does not guarantee quality products. Quality assurance merely sees to it that work is done the way it is supposed to be done.

The Capability Maturity Model (CMM)[1] is the best-known attempt at directions on how to improve the development process. It uses a five-point scale to rate organizations and indicates key areas of focus in order to progress to a higher

---

[1]Capability Maturity Model and CMM are registered in the U.S. Patent and Trademark Office.

maturity level. SPICE and Bootstrap are similar approaches to process improvement. CMM is discussed in Section 6.6.

Quality actions within software development organizations are aimed at finding opportunities to improve the development process. These improvements require an understanding of the development process, which can be obtained only through carefully collecting and interpreting data that pertain to quality aspects of the process and its products. Some hints on how to start such a quality improvement program are given in Section 6.7.

6.1 ON MEASURES AND NUMBERS

> When you can measure what you are speaking about, and express it in numbers, you know something about it; but when you cannot measure it, when you cannot express it in numbers, your knowledge is of a meagre and unsatisfactory kind; it may be the beginning of knowledge, but you have scarcely in your thoughts advanced to the stage of science.
> Lord Kelvin (1900)

> It is the mark of an instructed mind to rest satisfied with the degree of precision which the nature of a subject admits, and not to seek exactness when only an approximation of the truth is possible.
> Aristotle (330 BCE)

Suppose we want to express some quality attribute, say the complexity of a program text, in a single numeric value. Larger values are meant to denote more complex programs. If such a mapping C from programs to numbers can be found, we may next compare the values of $C(P_1)$ and $C(P_2)$ to decide whether program P_1 is more complex than program P_2. Since more complex programs are more difficult to comprehend and maintain, this type of information is very useful, e.g. for planning maintenance effort.

What then should this mapping be? Consider the program texts in Figure 6.1.

Most people will concur that text (a) looks less complex than text (b). Is this caused by:

- its length,

- the number of goto statements,

- the number of if statements,

- a combination of these attributes,

- something else?

Suppose we decide that the number of if statements is what counts. The result of the mapping is 0 for text (a) and 3 for text (b), and this agrees with our intuition.

```
1   procedure bubble
2       (var a: array [1..n] of integer; n: integer);
3   var i, j, temp: integer;
4   begin
5       for i:= 2 to n do
6           j:= i;
7           while j > 1 and a[j] < a[j-1] do
8               temp:= a[j];
9               a[j]:= a[j-1];
10              a[j-1]:= temp;
11              j:= j-1;
12          enddo
13      enddo
14  end;
```
(a)

```
1   procedure bubble
2       (var a: array [1..n] of integer; n: integer);
3   var i, j, temp: integer;
4   begin
5       for i:= 2 to n do
6           if a[i] ≥ a[i-1] then goto next endif;
7           j:= i;
8   loop: if j ≤ 1 then goto next endif;
9           if a[j] ≥ a[j-1] then goto next endif;
10          temp:= a[j];
11          a[j]:= a[j-1];
12          a[j-1]:= temp;
13          j:= j-1;
14          goto loop;
15  next: skip;
16      enddo
17  end;
```
(b)

Figure 6.1 Two versions of a sort routine (a) structured and (b) unstructured

However, if we take the sum of the number of if statements, goto statements, and loops, the result also agrees with our intuition. Which of these mappings is the one sought for? Is either of them 'valid' to begin with? What does 'valid' mean in this context?

A number of relevant aspects of measurement, such as attributes, units and scale types can be introduced and related to one another using the measurement framework depicted in Figure 6.2. This framework also allows us to indicate how metrics can be

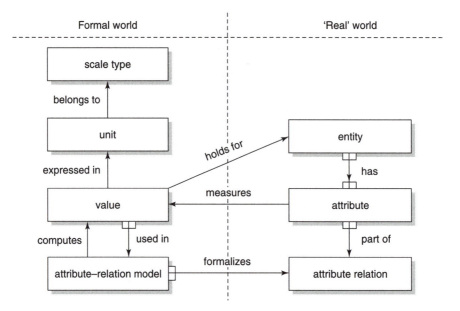

Figure 6.2 A measurement framework (*Source*: B. Kitchenham, S. Pfleeger and N. Fenton, Towards a Framework for Software Measurement Validation, *IEEE Transactions on Software Engineering 21:12*, © 1995 IEEE. Reproduced with permission.)

used to describe and predict properties of products and processes, and how to validate these predictions.

The model in Figure 6.2 has seven constituents:

- **Entity** An entity is an object in the 'real' world of which we want to know or predict certain properties. Entities need not denote material objects; projects and software are entities.

- **Attribute** Entities have certain properties which we call attributes. Different entities may have the same attribute: both people and cars have a weight. And, of course, a single entity can have more than one attribute. The forks that adorn the arrow labeled 'has' in Figure 6.2 indicate that this relationship is many to many.

- **Attribute relation** Different attributes of one or more entities can be related. For example, the attributes 'length' and 'weight' of an entity 'snake' are related. Similarly, the number of man-months spent on a project is related to the cost of that project. Also, an attribute of one entity can be related to an attribute of another entity. For example, the experience of a programmer may be related to the cost of a development project he is working on.

- **Value** We want to formally characterize the constituents of the model that reside in the 'real' world by *measuring* the attributes, i.e. assigning values to them.

- **Unit** Obviously, the value of an attribute is expressed in a certain unit, such as meters, seconds or lines of code.

- **Scale types** The unit in turn belongs to a certain scale type. Some common scale types are:

  - **Nominal** Attributes are merely classified: the color of my hair is gray, white or black.

  - **Ordinal** There is a (linear) ordering in the possible values of an attribute: one type of material is harder than another, one program is more complex than another.

  - **Interval** There is a (linear) ordering but the 'distance' between successive values of an attribute is the same, as in a calendar or temperature measured in degrees Fahrenheit.

  - **Ratio** There is a (linear) ordering with equal 'distance' between successive values, with the additional requirement that there exists a value 0, as in the age of a software system or the temperature measured in degrees Kelvin.

  - **Absolute** In this case we simply count the number of occurrences, as in the number of errors detected in a program.

  Note that we can sometimes measure an attribute in different units, where these units lie on different scales. For example, we can measure temperature on an ordinal scale: it either freezes or it doesn't. We can also measure it on an interval scale, in degrees Fahrenheit or Celsius, and we can measure it on a ratio scale, in degrees Kelvin.

- **Attribute–relation model** If there exists a relation between different attributes of, possibly different, entities in the 'real' world, we may express that relation in a formal model, the attribute–relation model. This model computes (predicts) the value of an attribute in which we are interested from the values of one or more other attributes of the model. The fork at the arrow labeled 'formalizes' in Figure 6.2 indicates that we can have more than one model for the same attribute relation.

Measurement is a mapping from the empirical, 'real' world to the formal, relational world. A **measure** is the number or symbol assigned to an attribute of an entity by this mapping. The value assigned obviously has a certain unit, e.g. lines of code. The unit in turn belongs to a certain scale, such as the ratio scale for lines of code or the ordinal scale for the severity of a failure.

In mathematics, the term **metric** has a very specific meaning: it describes how far apart two points are. In our field, the term is often used in a somewhat sloppy way.

Sometimes it denotes a measure, sometimes the unit of a measure. We use the term to denote the combination of:

- an attribute of an entity,

- the function which assigns a value to that attribute,

- the unit in which this value is expressed, and

- its scale type.

For each scale type, certain operations are allowed, while others are not. In particular, we cannot compute the average for an ordinal scale, but only its median (middle value). Suppose we classify a system as 'very complex', 'complex', 'average', 'simple' or 'very simple'. The assignment of numbers to these values is rather arbitrary. The only prerequisite is that a system that is classified as 'very complex' is assigned a larger value than a system classified as 'complex'. If we call this mapping W, the only requirement is: $W(\text{very complex}) > W(\text{complex}) > \cdots > W(\text{very simple})$. Table 6.2 gives an example of two valid assignments of values to this attribute.

Table 6.2 Example mappings for an ordinal scale

Very complex	Complex	Average	Simple	Very simple
5	4	3	2	1
100	10	5	2	1

Suppose we have a system with three components, which are characterized as 'very complex', 'average' and 'simple', respectively. By assigning the values from the first row, the average would be 3, so the whole system would be classified as of average complexity. Using the values from the second row, the average would be 35, something between 'complex' and 'very complex'. The problem is caused by the fact that, with an ordinal scale, we do not know whether successive values are *equidistant*. When computing an average, we tacitly assume they are.

We often cannot measure the value of an attribute *directly*. For example, the speed of a car can be determined from the values of two other attributes: a distance and the time it takes the car to travel that distance. The speed is then measured *indirectly*, by taking the quotient of two direct measures. In this case, the attribute–relation model formalizes the relation between the distance traveled, time, and speed.

We may distinguish between *internal* and *external* attributes. Internal attributes of an entity can be measured purely in terms of that entity itself. Modularity, size, defects encountered, and cost are typical examples of internal attributes. External attributes of an entity are those which can be measured only with respect to how that entity relates to its environment. Maintainability and usability are examples of external attributes. Most quality factors we discuss in this chapter are external attributes. External attributes can be measured only *indirectly*, since they involve the measurement of other attributes.

Empirical relations between objects in the real world should be preserved in the numerical relation system that we use. If we observe that car A drives faster than car B, then we would rather like our function S, which maps the speeds observed to some number, to be such that $S(A) > S(B)$. This is called the **representation condition**. If a measure satisfies the representation condition, it is said to be a **valid measure**.

The representation condition can sometimes be checked by a careful assessment of the attribute–relation model. For example, we earlier proposed to measure the complexity of a program text by counting the number of if statements. For this (indirect) measure to be valid we have to ascertain that:

- any two programs with the same number of if statements are equally complex, and

- if program A has more if statements than program B, then A is more complex than B.

Since neither of these statements is true in the real world, this complexity measure is not valid.

The validity of more complex indirect measures is usually ascertained through statistical means. Most of the cost estimation models discussed in Chapter 7, for example, are validated in this way.

Finally, the scale type of indirect measures merits some attention. If different measures are combined into a new measure, the scale type of the combined measure is the 'weakest' of the scale types of its constituents. Many cost-estimation formulae contain factors whose scale type is ordinal, such as the instability of the requirements or the experience of the design team. Strictly speaking, different values that result from applying such a cost-estimation formula should then be interpreted as indicating that certain projects require more effort than others. The intention though is to interpret them on a ratio scale, i.e. actual effort in man-months. From a measurement-theory point of view, this is not allowed.

6.2 A TAXONOMY OF QUALITY ATTRIBUTES

Some of the first elaborate studies ((McCall *et al.*, 1977) and (Boehm *et al.*, 1978)) on the notion of 'software quality' appeared in the late 1970s. In these studies, a number of aspects of software systems are investigated that somehow relate to the notion of software quality. In the ensuing years, a large number of people have tried to tackle this problem. Many taxonomies of quality factors have been published. The fundamental problems have not been solved satisfactorily, though. The various factors that relate to software quality are hard to define. It is even harder to measure them quantitatively. On the other hand, real quality can often be identified surprisingly easily.

In the *IEEE Glossary of Software Engineering Terminology*, quality is defined as 'the degree to which a system, component, or process meets customer or user needs or expectations'. Applied to software, then, quality should be measured primarily against the degree to which user requirements are met: correctness, reliability, usability, and so on. Software lasts a long time and is adapted from time to time in order to accommodate changed circumstances. It is important to the user that this is possible within reasonable costs. The customer is therefore also interested in quality factors which relate to the structure of the system, such as maintainability, testability and portability, rather than its use.

We will start our discussion of quality attributes with McCall's taxonomy, which distinguishes between two levels of quality attributes. Higher-level quality attributes, known as **quality factors**, are external attributes and can, therefore, be measured only indirectly. McCall introduced a second level of quality attributes, termed **quality criteria**. Quality criteria can be measured either subjectively or objectively. By combining the ratings for the individual quality criteria that affect a given quality factor, we obtain a measure of the extent to which that quality factor is being

Table 6.3 Quality factors (*Source*: J.A. McCall, P.K. Richards and G.F. Walters, Factors in Software Quality, RADC-TR-77-369, © 1977, US Department of Commerce.)

Correctness	The extent to which a program satisfies its specifications and fulfills the user's mission objectives.
Reliability	The extent to which a program can be expected to perform its intended function with required precision.
Efficiency	The amount of computing resources and code required by a program to perform a function.
Integrity	The extent to which access to software or data by unauthorized persons can be controlled.
Usability	The effort required to learn, operate, prepare input, and interpret output of a program.
Maintainability	The effort required to locate and fix an error in an operational program.
Testability	The effort required to test a program to ensure that it performs its intended function.
Flexibility	The effort required to modify an operational program.
Portability	The effort required to transfer a program from one hardware or software environment to another.
Reusability	The extent to which a program (or parts thereof) can be reused in other applications.
Interoperability	The effort required to couple one system with another.

satisfied. Users and managers tend to be interested in the higher-level, external, quality attributes.

For example, we cannot directly measure the reliability of a software system. We may however directly measure the number of defects encountered so far. This direct measure can be used to obtain insight into the reliability of the system. This involves a theory, which can be ascertained on good grounds, of how the number of defects relates to reliability. For most other aspects of quality though, the relation between the attributes that can be measured directly and the external attributes we are interested in is less obvious, to say the least.

Table 6.3 lists the quality factors and their definitions, as they are used in (McCall *et al.*, 1977). The definition of software reliability in Table 6.3 is rather narrow. A more complete definition is contained in the *IEEE Glossary of Software Engineering Terminology*: 'The ability of a system or component to perform its required functions under stated conditions for a specified period of time.' It is often expressed as a probability.

The quality factors can be broadly categorized into three classes. The first class contains those factors that pertain to the use of the software after it has become operational. The second class pertains to the maintainability of the system. The third class contains factors that reflect the ease with which a transition to a new environment can be made. These three categories are depicted in Table 6.4.

In ISO standard 9126, a similar effort has been made to define a set of quality characteristics and sub-characteristics (see Table 6.5). Their definitions are given in Tables 6.6 and 6.7. Whereas the quality factors and criteria as defined in (McCall *et al.*,

Table 6.4 Categories of software quality factors (*Source*: J.A. McCall, P.K. Richards and G.F. Walters, Factors in Software Quality, RADC-TR-77-369, © 1977, US Department of Commerce.)

Product operation:	
Correctness	Does it do what I want?
Reliability	Does it do it accurately all of the time?
Efficiency	Will it run on my hardware as well as it can?
Integrity	Is it secure?
Usability	Can I run it?
Product revision:	
Maintainability	Can I fix it?
Testability	Can I test it?
Flexibility	Can I change it?
Product transition:	
Portability	Will I be able to use it on another machine?
Reusability	Will I be able to reuse some of the software?
Interoperability	Will I be able to interface it with another system?

Table 6.5 Quality characteristics and sub-characteristics of ISO 9126

Characteristic	Sub-characteristics
Functionality	Suitability
	Accuracy
	Interoperability
	Security
	Functionality compliance
Reliability	Maturity
	Fault tolerance
	Recoverability
	Reliability compliance
Usability	Understandability
	Learnability
	Operability
	Attractiveness
	Usability compliance
Efficiency	Time behavior
	Resource utilization
	Efficiency compliance
Maintainability	Analyzability
	Changeability
	Stability
	Testability
	Maintainability compliance
Portability	Adaptability
	Installability
	Co-existence
	Replaceability
	Portability compliance

1977) are heavily interrelated, the ISO scheme is hierarchical: each sub-characteristic is related to exactly one characteristic.

The ISO quality characteristics strictly refer to a software *product*. Their definitions do not capture *process* quality issues. For example, security can be handled partly by provisions in the software and partly by proper procedures. Only the former is covered by the sub-characteristic 'security' of the ISO scheme. Furthermore, the sub-characteristics concern quality aspects that are *visible* to the user. Reusability, for example, is not included in the ISO scheme.

Table 6.6 Quality characteristics of the external and internal quality model of ISO 9126 (*Source*: ISO Standard 9126, *Software Quality Characteristics and Metrics*, © 2001. Reproduced by permission of Netherlands Normalisatie-instituut.)

Functionality	The capability of the software product to provide functions which meet stated and implied needs when the software is used under specified conditions.
Reliability	The capability of the software product to maintain a specified level of performance when used under specified conditions.
Usability	The capability of the software product to be understood, learned, used, and attractive to the user when used under specified conditions.
Efficiency	The capability of the software product to provide appropriate performance, relative to the amount of resources used, under stated conditions.
Maintainability	The capability of the software product to be modified. Modifications may include corrections, improvements or adaptation of the software to changes in the environment and in requirements and functional specifications.
Portability	The capability of the software product to be transferred from one environment to another.

The ISO characteristics and sub-characteristics, together with an extensive set of measures, make up ISO's *external and internal quality model*. Internal quality refers to the product itself, ultimately the source code. External quality refers to the quality when the software is executed. For example, the average number of statements in a method is a measure of internal quality, while the number of defects encountered during testing is a measure of external quality.

Ultimately, the user is interested in the *quality in use*, defined in (ISO 9126, 2001) as 'the user's view of the quality of the software product when it is executed in a specific environment and a specific context of use'. It measures the extent to which users can achieve their goals, rather than mere properties of the software (see also Section 6.3). Quality in use is modeled in four characteristics: effectiveness, productivity, safety, and satisfaction. The definitions of these quality-in-use characteristics are given in Table 6.8.

Theoretically, internal quality, external quality and quality in use are linked: internal quality indicates external quality which, in turn, indicates quality in use. In general, meeting criteria at one level is not sufficient for meeting criteria at the next level. For instance, satisfaction is partly determined by internal and external quality measures, but also includes the user's attitude towards the product. The latter has to be measured separately. Note that internal quality and external quality can be measured directly. Quality in use can in general only be measured indirectly.

Table 6.7 Quality sub-characteristics of the external and internal quality model of ISO 9126 (*Source*: ISO Standard 9126, *Software Quality Characteristics and Metrics*, © 2001. Reproduced by permission of Netherlands Normalisatie-instituut.)

Suitability	The capability of the software product to provide an appropriate set of functions for specified tasks and user objectives.
Accuracy	The capability of the software product to provide the right or agreed results or effects with the needed degree of precision.
Interoperability	The capability of the software product to interact with one or more specified systems.
Security	The capability of the software product to protect information and data so that unauthorized persons or systems cannot read or modify them and authorized persons or systems are not denied access to them.
Functionality compliance	The capability of the software product to adhere to standards, conventions or regulations in laws and similar prescriptions relating to functionality.
Maturity	The capability of the software product to avoid failure as a result of faults in the software.
Fault tolerance	The capability of the software product to maintain a specified level of performance in cases of software faults or of infringement of its specified interface.
Recoverability	The capability of the software product to re-establish a specified level of performance and recover the data directly affected in the case of a failure.
Reliability compliance	The capability of the software product to adhere to standards, conventions or regulations relating to reliability.
Understandability	The capability of the software product to enable the user to understand whether the software is suitable, and how it can be used for particular tasks and conditions of use.
Learnability	The capability of the software product to enable the user to learn its application.
Operability	The capability of the software product to enable the user to operate and control it.
Attractiveness	The capability of the software product to be attractive to the user.

Table 6.7   (*continued*)

Usability compliance	The capability of the software product to adhere to standards, conventions, style guides or regulations relating to usability.
Time behavior	The capability of the software product to provide appropriate response and processing times and throughput rates when performing its function, under stated conditions.
Resource utilization	The capability of the software product to use appropriate amounts and types of resources when the software performs its function under stated conditions.
Efficiency compliance	The capability of the software product to adhere to standards or conventions relating to efficiency.
Analyzability	The capability of the software product to be diagnosed for deficiencies or causes of failures in the software, or for the parts to be modified to be identified.
Changeability	The capability of the software product to enable a specified modification to be implemented.
Stability	The capability of the software product to avoid unexpected effects from modifications of the software.
Testability	The capability of the software product to enable modified software to be validated.
Maintainability compliance	The capability of the software product to adhere to standards or conventions relating to maintainability.
Adaptability	The capability of the software product to be adapted for different specified environments without applying actions or means other than those provided for this purpose for the software considered.
Installability	The capability of the software product to be installed in a specified environment.
Co-existence	The capability of the software product to co-exist with other independent software in a common environment sharing common resources.
Replaceability	The capability of the software product to be used in place of another specified software product for the same purpose in the same environment.
Portability compliance	The capability of the software product to adhere to standards or conventions relating to portability.

Table 6.8 Characteristics of the quality-in-use model of ISO 9126 (*Source*: ISO Standard 9126, *Software Quality Characteristics and Metrics*, © 2001. Reproduced by permission of ISO.)

Effectiveness	The capability of the software product to enable users to achieve specified goals with accuracy and completeness in a specified context of use.
Productivity	The capability of the software product to enable users to expend appropriate amounts of resources in relation to the effectiveness achieved in a specified context of use.
Safety	The capability of the software product to achieve acceptable levels of risk of harm to people, business, software, property or the environment in a specified context of use.
Satisfaction	The capability of the software product to satisfy users in a specified context of use.

Quality factors are not independent. Some factors will impact one another positively, while others will do so negatively. For example, a reliable program is more likely to be correct and vice versa. Efficiency, on the other hand, will generally have a negative impact on most other quality factors. This means that we will have to make tradeoffs between quality factors. If there is a strong requirement for one factor, we may have to relax other factors. These tradeoffs must be resolved at an early stage. An important objective of the software architecture phase is to bring these quality factors to the forefront and make the tradeoffs explicit, so that the stakeholders know what they are in for (see Chapter 11). By doing so, we are better able to build in the desired qualities, rather than merely assessing them after the fact.

6.3 PERSPECTIVES ON QUALITY

> What I (and everybody else) mean by the word quality cannot be broken down into subjects and predicates [...] If quality exists in an object, then you must explain why scientific instruments are unable to detect it [...] On the other hand, if quality is subjective, existing only [in the eye of] the observer, then this Quality is just a fancy name for whatever you'd like [...] Quality is not objective. It doesn't reside in the material world [...] Quality is not subjective. It doesn't reside merely in the mind.
> Robert Pirsig, *Zen and the Art of Motorcycle Maintenance* (1974)

Users will judge the quality of a software system by the degree to which it helps them accomplish tasks and by the sheer joy they have in using it. The manager of those users is likely to judge the quality of the same system by its benefits. These benefits can be expressed in cost savings or in a better and faster service to clients.

To a tester, the prevailing quality dimensions will be the number of defects found and removed, the reliability measured, or the conformance to specifications. To the maintenance programmer, quality will be related to the system's complexity, its technical documentation, and so on.

These different viewpoints are all valid. They are also difficult to reconcile. Garvin (1984) distinguishes five definitions of software quality:

- Transcendent definition

- User-based definition

- Product-based definition

- Manufacturing-based definition

- Value-based definition.

Transcendent quality concerns innate excellence. It is the type of quality assessment we usually apply to novels. We may consider *Zen and the Art of Motorcycle Maintenance* an excellent book; we may try to give words to our admiration but these words are usually inadequate. The practiced reader gradually develops a good feeling for this type of quality. Likewise, the software engineering expert may develop a good feeling for the transcendent qualities of software systems.

The user-based definition of quality concerns 'fitness for use' and relates to the degree in which a system addresses the user's needs. It is a subjective notion. Since different users may have different needs, they may assess a system's quality rather differently. The incidental user of a simple word-processing package may be quite happy with its functionality and possibilities while a computer scientist may be rather disappointed. The reverse situation may apply to a complex typesetting system such as LaTeX.

In the product-based definition, quality relates to attributes of the software. Differences in quality are caused by differences in the values of those attributes. Most of the research into software quality concerns this type of quality. It also underlies the various taxonomies of quality attributes discussed in Section 6.2.

The manufacturing-based definition of quality concerns conformance to specifications. It is the type of quality definition used during system testing, whereas the user-based definition is prevalent during acceptance testing.

The value-based definition deals with costs and profits. It concerns balancing time and cost on the one hand, and profit on the other hand. We may distinguish various kinds of benefit, not all of which can be phrased easily in monetary terms (Simmons, 1996):

- **Increased efficiency** Benefits are attributed to cost avoidance or reduction and their measures are economic.

- **Increased effectiveness** This is primarily reflected through better information for decision making. It can be measured in economic terms or through key performance indicators, such as a reduced time to market.

- **Added value** Benefits enhance the strategic position of the organization, e.g. through an increased market share. The contribution of the information technology component often cannot be isolated.

- **Marketable product** The system itself may be marketable or a marketable product may be identified as a by-product of system development.

- **Corporate IT infrastructure** Communication networks, database environments, and so on provide little benefit by themselves, but serve as a foundation for other systems.

Software developers tend to concentrate on the product-based and manufacturing-based definitions of quality. The resulting quality requirements can be expressed in quantifiable terms, such as the number of defects found per man-month or the number of branching points per module. The quality attributes discussed in the previous section fall into these categories. Such quality requirements however can not be directly mapped onto the, rather subjective, quality viewpoints of the users, such as 'fitness for use'. Nevertheless, users and software developers have to come to an agreement on the quality requirements to be met.

One way to try to bridge this gap is to define a common language between users and software developers in which quality requirements can be expressed. This approach is taken in (Bass *et al.*, 2003), where quality requirements are expressed in 'quality-attribute scenarios'. Figure 6.3 gives one example of how a quality attribute can be expressed in user terms. Quality-attribute scenarios have a role not only in specifying requirements, but also in testing whether these requirements are (going to be) met. For example, quality-attribute scenarios are heavily used in architecture assessments (see Chapter 11).

Quality is not only defined at the level of the whole system. In component-based development, quality is defined at the level of a component. For services, quality is defined at the level of an individual service. The environment of the component or service, i.e. some other component or service, will require certain qualities as well. So for components and services, there is a requires and a provides aspect to quality. Since a component or service generally does not know the context in which it is going to be embedded, it is difficult to decide on the 'right' quality level. One might then choose to offer different levels of quality. For example, a service that handles video streaming may be fast with low-quality images or slow with high-quality images. The user of that service then selects the appropriate quality of service (QoS) level. Quality aspects of components and services are touched upon in Chapters 18 and 19, respectively.

Developers tend to have a mechanistic, product-oriented view on quality, whereby quality is associated with features of the product. In this view, quality is

Quality attribute	Usability
Source	End user
Stimulus	Learn system features
Artifact	System
Environment	At run time
Response	Learn tasks supplied by the system for new employees
Response measure	Days on the job
Test	90% successful completion of assigned tasks in employee test for the system, within twice the average time of an experienced user
Worst	1 to 7 days
Plan	Less than 1 day (to passing of test)
Best	Less than 2 hours

Figure 6.3 A quality-attribute scenario that can be used by both users and developers

defined by looking from the program to the user (user friendliness, acceptability, etc.). To assess the quality of systems used in organizations, we have to adopt a process-oriented view on quality as well, where quality is defined by looking from the user to the program. This leads to notions such as 'adequacy' and 'relevance'. For example, a helpdesk staffed with skilled people may contribute considerably to the quality of a system as perceived by its users, but this quality attribute generally does not follow from a product-based view of quality.

A very eclectic view of quality is taken in Total Quality Management (TQM). In TQM, quality applies to every aspect of the organization and is pursued by every employee of that organization. TQM has three cornerstones:

- **Customer value strategy** Quality is a combination of benefits derived from a product and sacrifices required of the customer. The right balance between these benefits and sacrifices has to be sought. The key stakeholder in this balancing act is the customer, rather than the customer's boss. The attitude is not 'We know what is best for the customer', but 'Let's first determine what the customer needs'.

- **Organizational systems** Systems encompass more than software and hardware. Other materials, humans, and work practices belong to the system as well. Moreover, systems cross unit or department boundaries. In the TQM view, systems eliminate complexity rather than people. In TQM, culture is not dominated by power struggles. Rather, the organization takes advantage of the employees' pride in craftsmanship. Human resources are regarded as a critical resource rather than a mere cost factor.

- **Continuous improvement** A 'traditional' environment is reactive: improvement is triggered by a problem or the development of a new product. In TQM, quality is pursued proactively. Errors are not viewed as personal failures which require punishment, but as opportunities for learning. Performance is not evaluated in retrospect as either good or bad, but variation in performance is analyzed statistically to understand causes of poor performance. Authority is not imposed by position and rules, but is earned by communicating a vision.

TQM thus stresses improvement rather than conformance. CMM (see Section 6.6) builds on TQM and many of the requirements engineering techniques discussed in Chapter 9 owe a tribute to TQM as well.

6.4 THE QUALITY SYSTEM

The International Organization for Standardization (ISO) has developed ISO 9000, a series of standards for quality management systems (ISO 9000:2000, ISO 9001:2000, and ISO 9004:2000). ISO 9000 gives the fundamentals and vocabulary of the series of standards on quality systems. ISO 9001 integrates three earlier standards (labeled ISO 9001, ISO 9002 and ISO 9003) and specifies requirements for a quality system for any organization that needs to demonstrate its ability to deliver products that satisfy customer requirements. ISO 9004 contains guidelines for performance improvement. It is applicable after implementation of ISO 9001.

ISO 9001 is a generic standard that can be applied to any product. A useful complement for software is ISO/IEC 90003:2004, which contains guidelines for the application of ISO 9001 to computer software. It is a joint standard of ISO and the International Electrotechnical Commission (IEC). The scope of ISO/IEC 90003 is that it 'specifies requirements for a quality management system where an organization:

- needs to demonstrate its ability to consistently provide a product that meets customer and applicable regulatory requirements, and

- aims to enhance customer satisfaction through the effective application of the system, including processes for continual improvement of the system and the assurance of conformity to customer and applicable regulatory requirements.'

The standard is very comprehensive. It uses five perspectives from which to address the management of quality in software engineering:

- The systemic perspective deals with the establishment and documentation of the quality system itself. The quality system consists of a number of processes, such as those for software development, operation, and maintenance. These processes, and the quality system itself, have to be documented properly.

- The management perspective deals with the definition and management of the policies to support quality. The quality management system itself has to be developed, implemented, and regularly reviewed.

- The resource perspective deals with the resources needed to implement and improve the quality management system, as well as to meet customer and regulatory requirements. The resources include personnel, infrastructure, and the work environment.

- The product perspective deals with the processes to actually create quality products, such as those pertaining to requirements engineering, design, testing, production, and servicing. This perspective makes up over 60% of the standard.

- The improvement perspective deals with monitoring, measuring and analysis activities to maintain and improve quality.

Many organizations have tried to obtain ISO 9000 registration. The time and cost this takes depends on how much the current processes deviate from the ISO standards. If the current quality system is not already close to conforming, then ISO registration may take at least one year. ISO registration is granted when a third-party accredited body assesses the quality system and concludes that it does conform to the ISO standard. Reregistration is required every three years and surveillance audits are required every six months. ISO registration thus is a fairly drastic and costly affair, after which you certainly cannot sit back but have to keep the organization alert.

Since software development projects have some rather peculiar characteristics (frequent changes in requirements during the development process and the invisible nature of the product during its development), there is a need for quality assurance procedures which are tailored towards software development. This is the topic of Section 6.5.

6.5 SOFTWARE QUALITY ASSURANCE

The purpose of software quality assurance (SQA) is to make sure that work is done the way it is supposed to be done. More specifically, the goals of SQA (Humphrey, 1989) are:

- to improve software quality by appropriately monitoring the software and its development process;

- to ensure full compliance with the established standards and procedures for the software and the development process;

- to ensure that any inadequacies in the product, the process, or the standards are brought to management's attention so these inadequacies can be fixed.

Note that the SQA people themselves are not responsible for producing quality products. Their job is to review and audit, and to provide the project and management with the results of these reviews and audits.

There are potential conflicts of interest between the SQA organization and the development organization. The development organization may be facing deadlines and may want to ship a product, while the SQA people have revealed serious quality problems and wish to defer shipment. In such cases, the opinion of the SQA organization should prevail. For SQA to be effective, certain prerequisites must be fulfilled:

- It is essential that top management commitment is secured, so that suggestions made by the SQA organization can be enforced. If this is not the case, SQA soon becomes costly padding and a mere nuisance to the development organization.

- The SQA organization should be independent from the development organization. Its reporting line should also be independent.

- The SQA organization should be staffed with technically competent and judicious people. They need to cooperate with the development organization. If the two organizations operate as adversaries, SQA cannot be effective. We must realize that, in the long run, the aims of the SQA organization and the development organization are the same: the production of high-quality products.

The review and audit activities and the standards and procedures that must be followed are described in a software quality assurance plan.

IEEE Standard 730 offers a framework for the contents of a Quality Assurance Plan for software development (IEEE730, 1998). Table 6.9 lists the contents of such a document. IEEE Standard 730 applies to the development and maintenance of critical software. For non-critical software, a subset of the requirements may be used.

Table 6.9 Main components of IEEE Standard 730

1.	Purpose
2.	Reference documents
3.	Management
4.	Documentation
5.	Standards, practices, conventions, and metrics
6.	Reviews and audits
7.	Test
8.	Problem reporting and corrective action
9.	Tools, techniques, and methodologies
10.	Code control
11.	Media control
12.	Supplier control
13.	Records collection, maintenance, and retention
14.	Training
15.	Risk management

IEEE Standard 983 (IEEE983, 1986) is a useful complement to Standard 730. IEEE Standard 983 offers further guidelines as to the contents of a quality assurance plan and its implementation, evaluation, and modification.

A software quality assurance plan describes how the quality of the software is to be assessed. Some quality factors can be determined objectively. Most factors at present can be determined only subjectively. Most often then, we will try to assess the quality by reading documents, by inspections, by walkthroughs, and by peer reviews. In a number of cases, we may profitably employ tools during quality assurance, in particular, for static and dynamic analysis of program code. The actual techniques to be applied here are discussed in Chapter 13.

6.6 THE CAPABILITY MATURITY MODEL (CMM)

Consider the following course of events in a hypothetical software development project. An organization is to develop a distributed library automation system. A centralized computer hosts both the software and the database. A number of local libraries are connected to the central machine through a Web-based interface. The organization has some experience with library automation, albeit only with stand-alone systems.

In the course of the project, a number of problems manifest themselves. At first they seem to be disconnected and they do not alarm management. It turns out that the requirements analysis has not been all that thorough. Local requirements turn out to differ on some minor points. Though the first such deviations can be handled quite easily, keeping track of all the change requests becomes a real problem after a while. When part of the system has been realized, the team starts to test the Web interface but it turns out to be too complex and time-consuming.

The project gets into a crisis eventually. Management has no proper means to handle the situation. It tries to cut back on both functionality and quality in a somewhat haphazard way. In the end, a rather unsatisfactory system is delivered two months late. During the subsequent maintenance phase, a number of problems are solved, but the system never becomes a real success.

Though the above description is hypothetical, it is not all that unrealistic. Many an organization has insufficient control over its software development process. If a project gets into trouble, it is usually discovered quite late and the organization can only react in a somewhat chaotic way. More often than not, speed is confused with progress.

An important step in trying to address these problems is to realize that the software development process can indeed be controlled, measured, and improved. In order to gauge the process of improving the software development process, Watts Humphrey developed a software maturity framework which has evolved into the *Capability Maturity Model* (CMM). This framework owes tribute to Total Quality Management (TQM), which in turn is based on principles of statistical quality control as formulated by Walter Shewart in the 1930s and further developed by W. Edwards

Deming and Joseph Juran in the 1980s. Originally, there were separate CMM models for software engineering, systems engineering, and several others. These have now been integrated and carry the label CMMI.[2] CMM and CMMI were developed at the Software Engineering Institute (SEI) of Carnegie Mellon University. The version described here is CMMI version 1.2 for software engineering and systems engineering (CMMI Product Team, 2006).

In CMM (and CMMI), the software process is characterized as one of five **maturity levels**, evolutionary levels toward achieving a mature software process. To achieve a certain maturity level, a number of **process areas** must be in place. These process areas indicate important issues that have to be addressed in order to reach that level. Taken together, the process areas of a level achieve the set of goals for that level. Figure 6.4 lists the maturity levels and associated process areas of CMMI.

CMMI's maturity levels can be characterized as follows:

- **Initial level** At this level, the organization operates without formalized procedures, project plans, or cost estimates. Tools are not adequately integrated. Many problems are overlooked or forgotten, and maintenance poses real problems. Software development at this level can be characterized as being ad hoc. Performance can be improved by instituting basic project management controls:

  - **Requirements management** involves establishing and maintaining an agreement with the customer on the requirements of the system. Since requirements inevitably change, controlling and documenting these requirements is important.

  - **Project planning** involves making plans for executing and managing the project. To be able to do any planning, an approved statement of the work to be done is required. From this statement of work, estimates of the size of the project, the resources needed, and the schedule are determined, and risks to the project are identified. The results are documented in the project plan. This plan is used to manage the project; it is updated when necessary.

  - **Project monitoring and control** is concerned with the visibility of actual progress. Intermediate results have to be reviewed and tracked with respect to the project plan. When necessary, the project plan has to be realigned with reality.

  - **Supplier agreement management**. Where applicable, work done by suppliers has to be managed: plans for their part of the work have to be made and progress of their part of the job has to be monitored.

  - **Measurement and analysis** is concerned with making sure measurements are made and their results used. First, objectives for measurement and the way measures should be collected, stored, and analyzed are established. Next, the collection, storage, and analysis of data must be implemented. Finally, the results are used for decision making and corrective actions are taken where needed.

---

[2] CMMI is a service mark of Carnegie Mellon University.

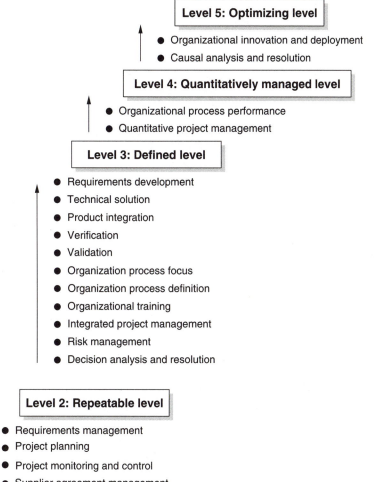

Figure 6.4 Maturity levels and associated process areas of CMMI

- **Process and product quality assurance** involves reviewing and auditing products and processes to validate that they comply with agreed upon standards and procedures.

- **Configuration management** is concerned with establishing and maintaining the integrity of all work items during the entire project life cycle. This involves the identification of configuration items and baselines and the establishment of procedures to control changes to them.

- **Repeatable** The main difference between the initial process level and the repeatable process level is that there is control over the way plans and commitments are established. Through prior experience in doing similar work, the organization has achieved control over costs, schedules, and change requests, and earlier successes can be repeated. The introduction of new tools, the development of a new type of product, and major organizational changes however still represent major risks at this level. The process areas needed to advance to the next level are aimed at standardizing the software process *across* the projects of the organization:

  - **Requirements development** involves the production and analysis of requirements. Requirements have to be elicited, analyzed, validated, and communicated to appropriate stakeholders. Requirements development is not a one-shot activity. Rather, requirements are identified and refined throughout the whole life cycle.

  - **Technical solution** is about design and implementation. Decisions concerning the architecture, custom development as opposed to an off-the-shelf solution, and modularization issues are typical ingredients of this process area.

  - **Product integration** concerns the assembling of a complete product from its components. This can be one stage after all components have been developed or it can proceed incrementally. An important element of product integration is the management of interfaces, to make sure that the components properly fit together.

  - **Verification** is concerned with ensuring that the product meets its requirements. Peer reviews are an effective means for early defect detection and removal. Peer reviews, such as walkthroughs and inspections, are practices in which peers try to identify errors and areas where changes are needed.

  - **Validation** is concerned with establishing that the product fulfills its intended use. As far as possible, validation activities should be done in the environment in which the product is intended to be used.

  - **Organization process focus** is concerned with organization process improvement. Measurements, lessons learned, project postmortems, and product evaluation reports are typical sources of information to guide improvement activities. The responsibility for guiding and implementing these activities is typically assigned to a process group. In this way, improvement of the organization's process capabilities is made a responsibility of the organization as a whole, rather than the individual project manager.

- **Organization process definition** is concerned with developing and maintaining a set of software process assets, such as process elements, life cycle models, and guidelines for tailoring a process model. Each project uses a process built out of these process assets.

- **Organizational training** is concerned with creating a training program that develops the necessary skills and knowledge of individuals to perform their roles. Training needs are identified at the level of the organization, the project, and the individual. The fulfillment of these needs is addressed as well.

- **Integrated project management** involves developing a project-specific software process from the organization's set of standard processes, as well as the actual management of the project using the tailored process. Since the software processes of different projects have a common ancestor, projects may now share data and lessons learned.

- **Risk management** concerns the identification of potential problems, so that timely actions can be taken to mitigate adverse effects.

- **Decision analysis and resolution** is concerned with establishing guidelines as to which issues should be subjected to formal evaluation processes, and the application of those formal processes. The selection of commercial off-the-shelf (COTS) components and architectural reviews are areas where formal evaluation processes might be applied.

- **Defined** At the defined process level, a set of standard processes for the development and maintenance of software is in place. The organization has achieved a solid foundation and may now start to examine its processes and decide how to improve them. There are major steps to advance to the next level:

  - **Organizational process performance** has the purpose of establishing and maintaining a quantitative understanding of the performance of the set of standard processes. Individual projects are measured and compared against expected results as documented in a baseline. The information is not only used to assess a project, but also to quantitatively manage it.

  - **Quantitative project management** involves the setting of performance goals, measuring process performance, analyzing these measurements, and making the appropriate adjustments to the process in order to bring it in line with the defined limits. There is, therefore, an organization-wide measurement program and the results of it are used to continuously improve the process. An example process measure is the number of lines of code reviewed per hour.

- **Quantitatively managed** At the quantitatively managed process level, quantitative data is gathered and analyzed on a routine basis. Everything is under control and attention may therefore shift from being reactive (what happens to the present project?) to being proactive (what can we do to improve future projects?). The focus shifts to opportunities for continuous improvement:

– **Organizational innovation and deployment** is concerned with the identification and deployment of improvements. Technical improvements relate to new technologies and their orderly transition into the organization. Process improvements relate to changing the process in order to improve the quality of the products and the productivity of the software development organization, and to reduce the time needed to develop products.

– **Causal analysis and resolution** is concerned with identifying common causes of defects, and preventing them from recurring.

• **Optimizing** At the final, optimizing, level, a stable base has been reached from which further improvements can be made. The step to the optimizing process level is a paradigm shift. Whereas attention at the other levels is focused on ways to improve the product, emphasis at the optimizing level has shifted from the product to the process. The data gathered can now be used to improve the software development process itself.

In 1989, Humphrey investigated the state of software engineering practice with respect to the CMM (Humphrey *et al.*, 1989). Although this study concerned the Department of Defense (DoD) software community, there is little reason to expect that the situation was much rosier in other environments. According to his findings, software engineering practice at that time was largely at the initial level. There were a few organizations operating at the repeatable level, and a few projects operating at the defined level. No organization or project operated at the managed or optimizing levels.

In the ensuing years, a lot has happened. Many organizations have initiated a software process improvement (SPI) program to achieve a higher maturity level. Most of these improvement programs concern a move to the repeatable or defined level. The number of organizations at these levels has significantly increased since 1989. There are still few organizations or projects at the managed or optimizing levels.

Reports from practical experience show that it takes about two years to move up a level. The cost ranges from $500 to $2000 per employee per year. The benefits, however, seem to easily outweigh the cost. Several companies have reported a return on investment of at least 5 to 1: every dollar invested in a process improvement program resulted in cost savings of at least five dollars.

6.6.1 Personal Software Process

To address the needs of small companies and small project teams, the Software Engineering Institute developed the Personal Software Process (PSP), a self-improvement process designed to help individuals to improve the way they work. Like the CMM, the PSP distinguishes between several maturity levels. The first step in PSP is to establish some basic measurements, such as development time and defects found, using simple forms to collect this data. At the next level, the data is used to estimate time and quality. At still higher levels, the personal data is used to *improve* the individual's performance.

The basic principles of the CMM and the PSP are thus very similar: know your process, measure your performance, and base your improvement actions on an analysis of the data gathered.

6.6.2 BOOTSTRAP and SPICE

BOOTSTRAP and SPICE are two other CMM-like maturity models. BOOTSTRAP uses a separate maturity rating for each of its practices. One of the interesting features of BOOTSTRAP is that all assessment results are collected in a database, thus allowing an organization to position itself by comparing its scores with those of similar organizations.

SPICE is an international initiative and has become an international standard (ISO/IEC 15504). SPICE stands for Software Process Improvement and Capability dEtermination. SPICE distinguishes different process categories, such as the management process, customer–supplier process, and engineering process. The capability (maturity) level is determined for each process category and each process. Like BOOTSTRAP, SPICE thus results in a maturity profile. The SPICE methodology places heavy emphasis on the way process assessments are performed.

6.6.3 Some Critical Notes

> Software development organizations exist to develop software rather than processes.
> Fayad (1997)

The massive attention of organizations to obtaining CMM or ISO 9000 certification holds the danger that focus shifts from developing software to developing processes. A certified organization does not guarantee the quality of the software developed under it. A mature development process is not a silver bullet; a framed certificate definitely is not.

CMM seems most appropriate for very big companies. It is doubtful whether small companies can afford the time and money required by a process improvement program as advocated by CMM. It is also doubtful whether they can afford to implement some of the process areas, such as the 'organization process focus' area, which requires the setting up of an organization process group. Though PSP may alleviate part of this criticism, the PSP does not have the same status as the CMM.

CMM is focused on discipline: structured work processes, strict plans, and standardization. This fits bigger companies better than small ones. It also better fits activities that lend themselves to a strict approach, such as configuration management and testing. Requirements analysis and design ask for a certain amount of creativity and a pure CMM approach may have a stifling effect. The dichotomy noted in Chapter 1 between the factory-like and craft-like aspects of software engineering also surfaces here.

CMM's original maturity levels constitute a rather crude five-point scale. If the assessment of a level 2 organization reveals that it fails the level 3 criteria on just one issue, the verdict is rather harsh: the organization simply remains at level 2. This may not improve morale after two years of hard labor and significant investment. For one thing, this implication of maturity assessments places high demands on their reliability. The rather crude assessment of organizations on a five-point scale may have other far-reaching consequences. The US government requires level 3 certification to qualify for contracts. Does this imply that level 1 and level 2 organizations are performing below standard? If level 3 certification is all that matters, is it worth while aiming for level 4 or 5?

CMM's original levels are like an instrument panel of an airplane with one gauge, which can display only a few discrete values; it provides the pilot with very little information. One may also envisage a software maturity 'instrument panel' with many gauges, each of which shows a lot of detail. BOOTSTRAP and SPICE are frameworks that result in a maturity profile rather than a single score. The same holds for CMMI, which comes in two variants: a **staged model** which, like the original CMM, has just five levels of maturity, and a **continuous model** in which process improvement is done on a per process-area basis.

CMM and software process improvement focus on operational excellence: the organization will deliver the best products if its processes are optimal. An organization may, however, also have other goals, such as more customer intimacy, a bigger market share, or product innovation. Such goals ask for SPI-goals different from the ones we are used to (Rifkin, 2001).

6.7 GETTING STARTED

In the preceding sections, we have discussed various ways to review the quality of a software product and the associated development process. The development organization itself should actively pursue the production of quality products, by setting quality goals, assessing its own performance and taking actions to improve the development process.

This requires an understanding of possible inadequacies in the development process and possible causes thereof. Such an understanding is to be obtained through the collection of data on both the process and the resulting products, and a proper interpretation of those numbers. It is rather easy to collect massive amounts of data and apply various kinds of curve-fitting techniques to them. In order to be able to properly interpret the trends observed, they should be backed by sound hypotheses.

An, admittedly ridiculous, example is given in Table 6.10. The numbers in this table indicate that black cows produce more milk than white cows. A rather naive

Table 6.10 Relation between the color of cows and average milk production

Color	Average production
White	10
Black	40

interpretation is that productivity can be improved significantly by repainting all the white cows.

Though the example itself is ridiculous, its counterpart in software engineering is not all that far-fetched. Many studies, for example, have tried to determine a relation between numbers indicating the complexity of software components and the quality of those components. Quite a few of those studies found a positive correlation between such complexity figures and, say, the number of defects found during testing. A straightforward interpretation of those findings then is to impose some upper bound on the complexity allowed for each component. However, there may be good reasons for certain components having a high complexity. For instance, Redmond and Ah-Chuen (1990) studied complexity metrics of a large number of modules from the MINIX operating system. Some of these, such as a module that handles escape character sequences from the keyboard, were considered justifiably complex. Experts judged a further decomposition of these modules not justified. Putting a simple upper bound on the allowable value of certain complexity metrics is too simplistic an approach.

An organization has to discover its opportunities for process improvements. The preferred way to do so is to follow a stepwise, evolutionary approach in which the following steps can be identified:

1. Formulate hypotheses.

2. Carefully select appropriate metrics.

3. Collect data.

4. Interpret the data.

5. Initiate actions for improvement.

These steps are repeated, so that the effect of the actions is validated, and further hypotheses are formulated. By following this approach, the quest for quality will permeate your organization, which will subsequently reap the benefits.

One example of this approach is discussed in (Genuchten, 1991). He describes an empirical study of reasons for delay in software development. The study covered six development projects from one department. Attention was focused on the collection of data relating to time and effort, such as differences between a plan and reality. A one-page data collection form was used for this purpose (see Table 6.11).

Table 6.11 Time sheet for an activity

	Planned	Actual	Difference	Reason
Effort	–	–	–	–
Starting date	–	–	–	–
Ending date	–	–	–	–
Duration	–	–	–	–

Some 30 reasons for delay were identified. These were classified into six categories after a discussion with the project leaders, and finalized after a pilot study. The reasons for delay were found to be specific to the environment.

A total of 160 activities were studied from mid 1988 to mid 1989. About 50% of the activities overran their plan by more than 10%. Comparison of planned and actual figures showed that the relative differences increased towards the end of the projects. It was found that one prime reason for the difference between plan and reality was 'more time spent on other work than planned'. The results were interpreted during a meeting with the project leaders and the department manager. The discussion confirmed and quantified some existing impressions. For some, the discussion provided new information. It showed that maintenance actions constantly interrupted development work. The meeting included a discussion on possible actions for improvement. It was decided to schedule maintenance as far as possible in 'maintenance weeks' and include those in quarterly plans. Another analysis study was started to gain further insights into maintenance activities.

This study provides a number of useful insights, some of which reinforce statements made earlier:

- The 'closed loop' principle states that information systems should be designed such that those who provide input to the system are also main users of its output. Application of this principle results in feedback to the supplier of data, who is thereby forced to provide accurate input. It also prevents users from asking for more than they need. In the above example, the data was both collected and analyzed by the project leaders. The outcome was reported back to those same project leaders and used as a starting point for further actions.

- Local data collection should be for local use. Data collected may vary considerably between departments. Data is best used to gain insight in the performance of the department where the data is collected. Use in another department makes little sense.

- The focus should be on continuous improvement. The data collection effort was aimed at locating perceived deficiencies in the software development process. It revealed causes for these deficiencies and provided an opportunity for improvement.

The question is not one of 'who is right and who is wrong', but rather 'how can we prevent this from happening again in future projects'.

- The study did not involve massive data collection. Simple data sheets were used, together with unambiguous definitions of the meaning of the various metrics. The approach is incremental, with the study giving an opportunity for small improvements and showing the way for the next study.

6.8 SUMMARY

In this chapter, we have paid ample attention to the notion of quality. Software quality does not come for free. It has to be actively pursued. The use of a well-defined model of the software development process and good analysis, design, and implementation techniques are a prerequisite. However, quality must also be controlled and managed. To be able to do so, it has to be defined rigorously. This is not without problems, as we saw in Sections 6.2 and 6.3. There exist numerous taxonomies of quality attributes. For each of these attributes, we need a precise definition, together with a metric that can be used to state quality goals, and to check that these quality goals are indeed being satisfied. Most quality attributes relate to aspects that are primarily of interest to the software developers. These engineer-oriented quality views are difficult to reconcile with the user-oriented 'fitness for use' aspects.

For most quality attributes, the relation between what is actually measured (module structure, defects encountered, etc.) and the attribute we are interested in is insufficiently supported by a sound hypothesis. For example, though programs with a large number of decision points are often complex, counterexamples exist which show that the number of decisions (essentially, McCabe's cyclomatic complexity) is not a good measure of program complexity. The issue of software metrics and the associated problems is further dealt with in Chapter 12.

Major standards for quality systems have been defined by ISO and IEEE. These standards give detailed guidelines as regards the management of quality. Quality assurance by itself does not guarantee quality products. It has to be supplemented by a quality program within the development organization. Section 6.7 advocates an evolutionary approach to establishing a quality program. Such an approach allows us to gradually build up expertise in the use of quantitative data to find opportunities for process improvements.

Finally, we sketched the software maturity framework developed by the Software Engineering Institute. This framework offers a means of assessing the state of software engineering practice, as well as a number of steps for improving the software development process. One of the major contributions of CMM and similar initiatives is their focus on *continuous improvement*. This line of thought has subsequently been successfully applied to other areas, resulting in, amongst others, a People-CMM, a Formal Specifications-CMM, and a Measurement-CMM.

6.9 FURTHER READING

Fenton and Pfleeger (1996) provide a very thorough overview of the field of software metrics. (Endres and Rombach, 2003) is a software engineering textbook focusing on empirical observations and measurements. The measurement framework discussed in Section 6.1 is based on (Kitchenham *et al.*, 1995). Kaner and Bond (2004) also give a framework for evaluating metrics. (Kitchenham *et al.*, 2007) discuss common errors made when applying software metrics. (Software, 1997b) and (JSS, 1995a) are special journal issues on software metrics. Many of the articles in these issues deal with the application of metrics in quality programs.

One of the first major publications on the topic of measurement programs is (Grady and Caswell, 1987). Success factors for measurement programs can be found in (Hall and Fenton, 1997) and (Gopal *et al.*, 2002). Pfleeger (1995) elaborates on the relation between metrics programs and maturity levels. Niessink and van Vliet (1998b) give a CMM-like framework for the measurement capability of software organizations.

The best known taxonomies of software quality attributes are given in (McCall *et al.*, 1977) and (Boehm *et al.*, 1978). The ISO quality attributes are described in (ISO 9126, 2001) and (Côté *et al.*, 2006). Critical discussions of these schemes are given in (Kitchenham and Pfleeger, 1996) and (Fenton and Pfleeger, 1996). (Suryn *et al.*, 2004) give an overview of ISO/IEC 90003.

Garvin (1984) gives quality definitions. Different kinds of benefit in a value-based definition of quality are discussed in (Simmons, 1996). For an elaborate discussion of Total Quality Management, see (Bounds *et al.*, 1994) and (Ishikawa, 1985).

The Capability Maturity Model (CMM) is based on the seminal work of (Humphrey, 1988) and (Humphrey, 1989). For a full description of the Capability Maturity Model Integrated (CMMI), see (CMMI Product Team, 2006). Practical experiences with software process improvement programs are discussed in (Wohlwend and Rosenbaum, 1994), (Diaz and Sligo, 1997), (Fitzgerald and O'Kane, 1999), (Conradi and Fuggetta, 2002) and (Dybå, 2005). Rainer and Hall (2003) discuss success factors and Baddoo and Hall (2003) discuss de-motivators for SPI. (Basili *et al.*, 2002) discuss lessons learned from 25 years of process improvement at NASA. A survey of benefits and costs of software process improvement programs is given in (Herbsleb *et al.*, 1997) and (Gartner, 2001). High-maturity, CMM level 5 organizations are discussed in (Software, 2000) and (Agrawal and Chari, 2007).

The Personal Software Process (PSP) is described in (Humphrey, 1996) and (Humphrey, 1997a). BOOTSTRAP is described in (Kuvaja *et al.*, 1994) and SPICE in (El Emam *et al.*, 1997).

Criticisms of CMM-like approaches are found in (Fayad, 1997) and (Fayad and Laitinen, 1997). El Emam and Madhavji (1995) discuss the reliability of process assessments.

Process improvement is the topic of several special journal issues; see (CACM, 1997) and (Software, 1994a). The journal *Software Process: Improvement and Practice* is wholly devoted to this topic.

Exercises

1. Define the following terms: measurement, measure, metric.

2. What is the difference between an internal and an external attribute?

3. Define the term *representation condition*. Why is it important that a measure satisfies the representation condition?

4. What is the main difference between an ordinal scale and an interval scale? And between an interval scale and a ratio scale?

5. What are the main differences between the user-based and product-based definitions of quality?

6. Which are the three categories of software quality factors distinguished by McCall?

7. Discuss the transcendent view of software quality.

8. Which of Garvin's definitions of quality is mostly used by the software developer? And which one is mostly used by the user?

9. Which quality viewpoint is stressed by ISO 9126?

10. Discuss the cornerstones of Total Quality Management.

11. What is the purpose of software quality assurance?

12. Why should the software quality assurance organization be independent of the development organization?

13. Why should project members get feedback on the use of quality data they submit to the quality assurance group?

14. Describe the maturity levels of the Capability Maturity Model.

15. What is the major difference between level 2 and level 3 of the Capability Maturity Model?

16. What is the difference between the staged and continuous versions of CMMI?

17. Why is it important to quantify quality requirements?

18. ♠ Consider a software development project you have been involved in. How was quality handled in this project? Were quality requirements defined at an early stage? Were these requirements defined such that they could be tested at a later stage?

19. ♡ Define measurable properties of a software product that make up the quality criteria Modularity and Operability. Do these properties constitute an objective measure of these criteria? If not, in what ways is subjectivity introduced?

20. ♡ Give a possible staffing for an SQA group, both for a small development organization (less than 25 people) and a large development organization (more than 100 people).

21. ♣ Draw up a quality assurance plan for a project you have been involved in.

22. ♠ One quality requirement often stated is that the system should be 'user-friendly'. Discuss possible differences between the developer's point of view and the user's point of view in defining this notion. Think of alternative ways to define system usability in measurable terms.

23. ♠ Using the classification of the Capability Maturity Model, determine the maturity level that best fits your organization. Which steps would you

propose to advance the organization to a higher maturity level? Are any actions being pursued to get from the current level to a more mature one?

24. ♠ Write a critical essay on software maturity assessment, as exemplified by the Capability Maturity Model. The further reading section provides ample pointers to the literature on this topic.

25. ♡ Discuss differences between SPI approaches for large and small companies (see also (Conradi and Fuggetta, 2002)).

26. ♡ In 1988 and 1998, surveys were conducted to assess the state of the art in software cost estimation in the Netherlands. One of the questions concerned the types of stakeholder involved in developing a cost estimate. The resulting percentages were as follows:

	1988	1998
Management	48.9	75.8
Staff department	22.8	37.4
Development team	22.6	23.6
Project manager	36.7	42.3
Customer	15.4	15.9
Other	8.9	8.2
Average # of parties involved	1.55	2.03

It was concluded that the state of the art with respect to cost estimation had improved. In 1998, the average number of parties involved had increased and this was felt to be a good sign. For each individual category, the percentage involved as a stakeholder had gone up as well.

Can you think of a possibly negative conclusion from this same set of data, i.e. that the situation has become *worse* since 1988?

7

Cost Estimation

LEARNING OBJECTIVES

- To appreciate the use of quantitative, objective approaches to software cost estimation

- To have insight into the factors that affect software development productivity

- To understand well-known techniques for estimating software cost and effort

- To understand techniques for relating effort to development time

Software development takes time and money. When commissioning a building project, you expect a reliable estimate of the cost and development time up front. Getting reliable cost and schedule estimates for software development projects is still largely a dream. Software development costs are notoriously difficult to estimate reliably at an early stage. Since progress is difficult to 'see' – just when is a piece of software 50% complete? – schedule slippages often go undetected for quite a while and schedule overruns are the rule, rather than the exception. In this chapter, we look at various ways to estimate software cost and schedule.

When commissioning someone to build a house, decorate a bathroom, or lay out a garden, we expect a precise estimate of the costs to be incurred before the operation is started. A gardener is capable of giving a rough indication of the cost on the basis of, say, the area of land, the desired size of the terrace or grass area, whether or not a pond is required, and similar information. The estimate can be made more precise in further dialog, before the first bit of earth is turned. If you expect similar accuracy as regards the cost estimate for a software development project, you are in for a surprise.

Estimating the cost of a software development project is a field in which one all too often relies on mere guesswork. There are exceptions to this procedure, though. There exist a number of algorithmic models that allow us to estimate total cost and development time of a software development project, based on estimates for a limited number of relevant cost drivers. Some of the important algorithmic cost estimation models are discussed in Section 7.1.

In most cost estimation models, a simple relation between cost and effort is assumed. The effort may be measured in man-months, for instance, and each man-month is taken to incur a fixed amount, say, of $5000. The total estimated cost is then obtained by simply multiplying the estimated number of man-months by this constant factor. In this chapter, we freely use the terms cost and effort as if they are synonymous.

The notion of total cost is usually taken to indicate the cost of the initial software development effort, i.e. the cost of the requirements engineering, design, implementation and testing phases. Thus, maintenance costs are not taken into account. Unless explicitly stated otherwise, this notion of cost will also be used by us. In the same vein, development time will be taken to mean the time between the start of the requirements engineering phase and the point in time when the software is delivered to the customer. The notion of cost as it is used here does not include possible hardware costs either. It concerns only personnel costs involved in software development.

Research in the area of cost estimation is far from crystallized. Different models use different measures and cost drivers, so that comparisons are very difficult. Suppose some model uses an equation of the form:

$$E = 2.7 KLOC^{1.05}$$

This equation shows a certain relation between effort needed (E) and the size of the product ($KLOC$ = Kilo Lines Of Code = Lines Of Code/1 000). The effort measure could be the number of man-months needed. Several questions come to mind immediately: What is a line of code? Do we count machine code or the source code in some high-level language? Do we count comment lines and blank lines that increase readability? Do we take into account holidays, sick-leave, and so on, in our notion of the man-month or does it concern a net measure? Different interpretations of these notions may lead to widely different results. Unfortunately, different models do use different definitions of these notions. Sometimes, it is not even known which definitions were used in the derivation of the model.

To determine the equations of an algorithmic cost estimation model, we may follow several approaches. We may base our equations on the results of experiments. In such an experiment, we vary one parameter, while keeping the other parameters constant. In this way, we may try to determine the influence of the parameter that is being varied. As a typical example, we may consider the question of whether or not comments help to build up our understanding of a program. Under careful control of the circumstances, we may pose a number of questions about the same program text to two groups of programmers. The first group gets program text without comments, the second group gets the same program text with comments. We may check our hypothesis using the results of the two groups. The, probably realistic, assumption in this experiment is that a better and faster understanding of the program text has a positive effect on the maintainability of that program. This type of laboratory experiment is often performed at universities, where students play the role of programmers. It is not self-evident that the results thus obtained also hold in industrial settings. In practice, there may be a rather complicated interaction between relevant factors. Also, the subjects may not be representative. Finally, the generalization from laboratory experiments that are (of necessity) limited in size to the big software development projects with which professionals are confronted is not possible. The general opinion is that results thus obtained have limited validity and certainly need further testing.

A second way to arrive at an algorithmic cost estimation model is based on an analysis of real project data, in combination with some theoretical underpinning. An organization may collect data about a number of software systems that have been developed. This data may concern the time spent on the various phases that are distinguished, the qualifications of the personnel involved, the points in time at which errors occurred, both during testing and after installation, the complexity, reliability and other relevant project factors, the size of the resulting code, etc. Based on a sound hypothesis of the relations between the various entities involved and a (statistical) analysis of this data, we may derive equations that numerically characterize these relations. An example of such a relation is the one given above, which relates E to $KLOC$. The usability and reliability of such equations is obviously very much dependent upon the reliability of the data on which they are based. Also, the hypothesis that underlies the form of the equation must be sound.

Findings obtained in this way reflect an average, a best possible approximation based on available data. We therefore have to be very careful in applying the results obtained. If the software to be developed in the course of a new project cannot be compared with earlier products because of the degree of innovation involved, we are in for a big surprise. For example, estimating the cost of the Space Shuttle project cannot be done through a simple extrapolation from earlier projects. We may hope, however, that the average software development project has a higher predictability as regards effort needed and the corresponding cost.

The way in which we obtain quantitative relations implies further constraints on the use of these models. The model used is based on an analysis of data from earlier projects. Application of the model to new projects is possible only insofar as those new projects resemble the projects on whose data the model is based. If we have collected data on projects of a certain kind and within a particular organization, a model based on this data cannot be used without amendment for different projects in a different organization. A model based on data about administrative projects in a government environment has little predictive value for the development of real-time software in the aerospace industry. This is one of the reasons why the models of, for example, Walston and Felix (1977) and Boehm (1981) (see Section 7.1 for more detailed discussions of these models) yield such different results for the same problem description.

The lesson to be learned is that blind application of the formulae from existing models will not solve your cost estimation problem. Each model needs tuning to the environment in which it is going to be used. This implies the need to continuously collect your own project data and to apply statistical techniques to calibrate model parameters.

Other reasons for the discrepancies between existing models are:

- Most models give a relation between man-months needed and size (in lines of code). As remarked before, widely different definitions of these notions are used.

- The notion 'effort' does not always mean the same thing. Sometimes, one only counts the activities starting from the design, i.e. after the requirements specification has been fixed. Sometimes one also includes maintenance effort.

Despite these discrepancies, the various cost estimation models do have a number of characteristics in common. These common characteristics reflect important factors that bear on development cost and effort. The increased understanding of software costs allows us to identify strategies for improving software productivity, the most important of which are:

- Writing less code. System size is one of the main determinants of effort and cost. Techniques that try to reduce size, such as software reuse and the use of high-level languages, can obtain significant savings.

- Getting the best from people. Individual and team capabilities have a large impact on productivity. The best people are usually a bargain. Better incentives, better work environments, training programs, and so on provide further productivity improvement opportunities.

- Avoiding rework. Studies have shown that considerable effort is spent redoing earlier work. The application of prototyping or evolutionary development process models and the use of modern programming practices (such as information hiding) can yield considerable savings.

- Developing and using integrated project support environments. Tools can help us eliminate steps or make steps more efficient.

In Section 7.1, we discuss and compare some of the well-known algorithmic models for cost estimation. In many organizations, software cost is estimated by human experts, who use their expertise and gut feeling, rather than a formula, to arrive at a cost estimate. Some of the dos and don'ts of expert-based cost estimation are discussed in Section 7.2.

Given an estimate of the size of a project, we are interested in the development time needed. We may conjecture that a project with an estimated effort of 100 man-months can be completed in one year with a team of 8.5 people or equally well in one month with a team of 100 people. This view is too naive. A project of a certain size corresponds to a certain nominal physical time period. If we try to shorten this nominal development time too much, we get into the 'impossible region' and the chance of failure sharply increases. This phenomenon is further discussed in Section 7.3.

The models discussed in Section 7.1 fit planning-driven development projects more than they do agile projects. And even for planning-driven projects, their value is disputed, since the size of the project is unknown when the estimate is needed. It is like the story about a man who has lost his keys in a dark place going to search for them under a lamp, since this is the only place with enough light for searching. These models do have value, though, for the insights they offer into which factors influence productivity. If we compare successive versions of models, such as COCOMO and COCOMO 2, we also get insight into how these productivity factors have changed over time.

In agile projects (see Chapter 3), iterations are usually fairly small and the increments correspond to one or a few user stories or scenarios. These user stories are estimated in terms of development weeks, dollars, or some artificial unit, such as 'Points'. Then it is determined which user stories will be realized in the current increment and development proceeds. Often, the agreed time box is sacrosanct: if some of the user stories cannot be realized within the agreed upon time frame, they are moved to a later iteration. Estimation accuracy is assumed to improve in the course of the project. Cost estimation for agile projects is discussed in Section 7.4.

7.1 ALGORITHMIC MODELS

To be able to get reliable estimates, we need to record historical data extensively. This historical data can be used to produce estimates for new projects. In doing so, we predict the expected cost due to *measurable* properties of the project at hand. Just as the cost of laying out a garden might be a weighted combination of a number of relevant attributes (size of the garden, size of the grass area, whether there is a pond), so we would like to estimate the cost of a software development project. In this section, we discuss efforts to get algorithmic models to estimate software cost.

In the introduction to this chapter, we noticed that programming effort is strongly correlated with program size. There exist various (non-linear) models which express this correlation. A general form is

$$E = (a + bKLOC^c)f(x_1, \ldots, x_n)$$

Here, KLOC again denotes the size of the software (lines of code/1 000), while E denotes the effort in man-months. a, b and c are constants, and $f(x_1, \ldots, x_n)$ is a correction which depends on the values of the entities $x_1, \ldots, x_n$. In general, the base formula

$$E = a + bKLOC^c$$

is obtained through regression analysis of available project data. Thus, the primary cost driver is software size, measured in lines of code. This nominal cost estimate is tuned by correcting it for a number of factors that influence productivity (so-called cost drivers). For instance, if one of the factors used is 'experience of the programming team', this could incur a correction to the nominal cost estimate of 1.50, 1.20, 1.00, 0.80 and 0.60 for very low, low, average, high and very high levels of expertise, respectively.

Table 7.1 contains some of the well-known base formulae for the relation between software size and effort. For reasons mentioned before, it is difficult to compare these models. It is interesting to note, though, that the value of c fluctuates around 1 in most models.

Table 7.1 Formulae for the relation between size and effort

Origin	Base formula	See section
Halstead	$E = 0.7KLOC^{1.50}$	12.1.4
Boehm	$E = 2.4KLOC^{1.05}$	7.1.2
Walston–Felix	$E = 5.2KLOC^{0.91}$	7.1.1

This phenomenon is well known from the theory of economics. In a so-called economy of scale, one assumes that it is cheaper to produce large quantities of the same product. The fixed costs are then distributed over a larger number of units, which decreases the cost per unit. We thus realize an increasing return on investment. In the opposite case, we find a diseconomy of scale: after a certain point the production of additional units incurs extra costs.

In the case of software, the lines of code are the product. If we assume that producing a lot of code will cost less per line of code, formulae such as that of Walston–Felix (where $c < 1$) result. This may occur, for example, because the cost of expensive tools such as program generators, programming environments and test tools can be distributed over a larger number of lines of code. Alternatively, we may reason that large software projects are more expensive, relatively speaking. There is a larger overhead because of the increased need for communication and management control, because of the problems and interfaces getting more complex, and so on. Thus, each additional line of code requires more effort. In such cases, we obtain formulae such as those of Boehm and Halstead (where $c > 1$). There is no really convincing argument for either type of relation, though the latter ($c > 1$) may seem more plausible. Certainly for large projects, the effort required does seem to increase more than linearly with size.

It is clear that the value of the exponent c strongly influences the computed value E, certainly for large values of $KLOC$. Table 7.2 gives the values for E, as they are computed for the models of Table 7.1 and some values for $KLOC$. The reader will notice large differences between the models. For small programs, Halstead's model yields the lowest cost estimates. For projects in the order of one million lines of code, this same model yields a cost estimate which is an order of magnitude higher than that of Walston–Felix.

Table 7.2   *E* versus *KLOC* for various base models

$KLOC$	$E = 0.7KLOC^{1.50}$	$E = 2.4KLOC^{1.05}$	$E = 5.2KLOC^{0.91}$
1	0.7	2.4	5.2
10	22.1	26.9	42.3
50	247.5	145.9	182.8
100	700.0	302.1	343.6
1 000	22 135.9	3 390.1	2 792.6

However, we should not immediately conclude that these models are useless. It is much more likely that there are big differences in the characteristics between the sets of projects on which the various models are based. Recall that the actual numbers used in those models result from an analysis of real project data. If this data reflects widely different project types or development environments, so will the models. We cannot simply copy those formulae. Each environment has its own specific characteristics and tuning the model parameters to the specific environment (a process called calibration) is necessary.

The most important problem with this type of model is to get a *reliable* estimate of the software size early on. How should we estimate the number of pages in a novel not yet written? Even if we know the number of characters, the number of locations and the time interval in which the story takes place, we should not expect a realistic size estimate up front. The further advanced we are with the project, the more accurate our size estimate will get. If the design is more or less finished, we may (possibly) form a reasonable impression of the size of the resulting software. Only if the system has been delivered, do we know the exact number.

The customer, however, needs a reliable cost estimate early on. In such a case, lines of code is a measure which is too inexact to act as a basis for a cost estimate. We therefore have to look for an alternative. In Section 7.1.4 we discuss a model based on quantities, which are known at an earlier stage.

We may also switch to another model during the execution of a project, since we may expect to get more reliable data as the project is making progress. We then get a cascade of increasingly detailed cost estimation models. COCOMO 2 is an example of this (see Section 7.1.5).

7.1.1 Walston–Felix

The base equation of the model derived by Walston and Felix (1977) is

$$E = 5.2KLOC^{0.91}$$

Some 60 projects from IBM were used in the derivation of this model. These projects differed widely in size and the software was written in a variety of programming languages. It therefore comes as no surprise that the model, applied to a subset of these 60 projects, yields unsatisfactory results.

In an effort to explain these wide-ranging results, Walston and Felix identified 29 variables that clearly influenced productivity. For each of these variables, three levels were distinguished: high, average and low. For 51 projects, Walston and Felix determined the level of each of these 29 variables and the productivity obtained (in terms of lines of code per man-month). These results are given in Table 7.3 for some of the most important variables. Thus, the average productivity turned out to be 500 lines of code per man-month for projects with a user interface of low complexity. With a user interface of average or high complexity, the productivity is 295 and 124 lines of code per man-month, respectively. The last column contains the productivity change PC, the absolute value of the difference between the high and low scores.

According to Walston and Felix, a productivity index I can now be determined for a new project, as follows:

$$I = \sum_{i=1}^{29} W_i X_i$$

The weights W_i are defined by

$$W_i = 0.5 \log(PC_i)$$

Here, PC_i is the productivity change of factor i. For the first factor from Table 7.3 (complexity of the user interface), the following holds: $PC_1 = 376$, so $W_1 = 1.29$. The variables X_i can take on values $+1$, 0 and -1, where the corresponding factor scores as low, average or high (and thus results in a high, average or low productivity, respectively). The productivity index obtained can be translated into an expected productivity (lines of code produced per man-month). Details of the latter are not given in (Walston and Felix, 1977).

The number of factors considered in this model is rather high (29 factors from 51 projects). It is not clear to what extent the various factors influence each other. Finally, the number of alternatives per factor is only three, which does not seem to offer enough choice in practical situations.

Nevertheless, the approach taken by Walston and Felix and their list of cost drivers have played a very important role in directing later research in this area.

Table 7.3 Productivity intervals (*Source*: C.E. Walston and C.P. Felix, A method for programming measurement and estimation, *IBM Systems Journal*, ©1977.)

Variable	Value of variable average productivity (LOC)			| high − low | (PC)
Complexity of user interface	<normal 500	normal 295	>normal 124	376
User participation during requirements specification	none 491	some 267	much 205	286
User-originated changes in design	few 297	−	many 196	101
User-experience with application area	none 318	some 340	much 206	112
Qualification, experience of personnel	low 132	average 257	high 410	278
Percentage programmers participating in design	<25% 153	25–50% 242	>50% 391	238
Previous experience with operational computer	minimal 146	average 270	extensive 312	166
Previous experience with programming languages	minimal 122	average 225	extensive 385	263
Previous experience with application of similar or greater size and complexity	minimal 146	average 221	extensive 410	264
Ratio of average team size to duration (people/month)	<0.5 305	0.5–0.9 310	>0.9 171	134

7.1.2 COCOMO

The COnstructive COst MOdel (COCOMO) is one of the best-documented algorithmic cost estimation models. In its simplest form, Basic COCOMO, the formula that relates effort to software size, reads

$$E = bKLOC^c$$

Here, b and c are constants that depend on the kind of project that is being executed. COCOMO distinguishes three classes of project:

- **Organic** A relatively small team develops software in a known environment. The people involved generally have a lot of experience with similar projects in their organization. They are thus able to contribute at an early stage, since there is no initial overhead. Projects of this type will seldom be very large projects.

- **Embedded** The product will be embedded in an environment which is very inflexible and poses severe constraints. An example of this type of project might be air traffic control or an embedded weapons system.

- **Semidetached** This is an intermediate form. The team may include a mixture of experienced and inexperienced people, the project may be fairly large, though not excessively large, etc.

For the various classes of project, the parameters of Basic COCOMO take on the following values:

$$
\begin{aligned}
\text{organic:} &\quad b = 2.4, c = 1.05 \\
\text{semidetached:} &\quad b = 3.0, c = 1.12 \\
\text{embedded:} &\quad b = 3.6, c = 1.20
\end{aligned}
$$

Table 7.4 gives the estimated effort for projects of each of those three modes, for different values of *KLOC* (though an 'organic' project of one million lines is not very

Table 7.4 Size versus effort in Basic COCOMO

KLOC	Organic $(E = 2.4KLOC^{1.05})$	Effort in man-months Semidetached $(E = 3.0KLOC^{1.12})$	Embedded $(E = 3.6KLOC^{1.20})$
1	2.4	3.0	3.6
10	26.9	39.6	57.1
50	145.9	239.4	392.9
100	302.1	521.3	904.2
1 000	3 390.0	6 872.0	14 333.0

realistic). Amongst other things, we may read from this table that the constant c soon starts to have a major impact on the estimate obtained.

Basic COCOMO yields a simple, and hence a crude, cost estimate based on a simple classification of projects into three types. Boehm (1981) also discusses two other, more complicated, models called Intermediate COCOMO and Detailed COCOMO. Both these models take into account 15 cost drivers – attributes that affect productivity, and hence costs.

All these cost drivers yield a multiplicative correction factor to the nominal estimate of the effort. (Both these models also use values for b which slightly differ from that of Basic COCOMO.) Suppose we find a nominal effort estimate of 40 man-months for a certain project. If the complexity of the resulting software is low, then the model tells us to correct this estimate by a factor of 0.85. A better estimate then would be 34 man-months. On the other hand, if the complexity is high, we get an estimate of $1.15 \times 40 = 46$ man-months.

The nominal value of each cost driver in Intermediate COCOMO is 1.00 (see also Table 7.10). So we may say that Basic COCOMO is based on nominal values for each of the cost drivers.

The COCOMO formulae are based on a combination of expert judgment, an analysis of available project data, other models, and so on. The basic model does not yield very accurate results for the projects on which the model has been based. The intermediate version yields good results and, if one extra cost driver (volatility of the requirements specification) is added, it even yields very good results. Further validation of the COCOMO models using other project data is not straightforward, since the necessary information to determine the ratings of the various cost drivers is, in general, not available. So we are left only with the ability to test the basic model. Here, we obtain fairly large discrepancies between the effort estimated and the actual effort needed.

An advantage of COCOMO is that we know all its details. A major update of the COCOMO model, better reflecting current and future software practices, is discussed in Section 7.1.5.

7.1.3 Putnam

Norden studied the distribution of manpower over time in a number of software development projects in the 1960s. He found that this distribution often had a very characteristic shape which is well-approximated by a Rayleigh distribution. Based upon this finding, Putnam (1978) developed a cost estimation model in which the manpower required (MR) at time t is given by

$$MR(t) = 2Kate^{-at^2}$$

where a is a speed-up factor which determines the initial slope of the curve, while K denotes the total manpower required, including in the maintenance phase. K equals the volume of the area delineated by the Rayleigh curve (see Figure 7.1).

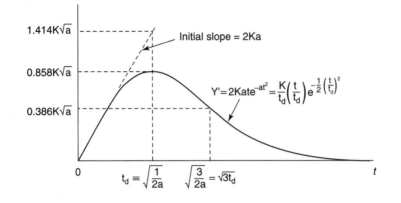

Figure 7.1 The Rayleigh curve for software schedules (*Source*: M.L. Shooman, Tutorial on software cost models, *IEEE Catalog nr TH0067-9*, ©1979 IEEE. Reproduced with permission.)

The shape of this curve can be explained theoretically as follows. Suppose a project consists of a number of problems for which a solution must be found. Let $W(t)$ be the fraction of problems for which a solution has been found at time t. Let $p(t)$ be the problem-solving capacity at time t. Progress at time t then is proportional to the product of the available problem-solving capacity and the fraction of problems yet unsolved. If the total amount of work to be done is set to 1, this yields:

$$\frac{dW}{dt} = p(t)(1 - W(t))$$

After integration, we get

$$W(t) = 1 - \exp\left(-\int^t p(\alpha)\,d\alpha\right)$$

If we next assume that the problem-solving capacity is well approximated by an equation of the form $p(t) = at$, i.e. the problem-solving capacity shows a linear increase over time, the progress is given by a Rayleigh distribution:

$$\frac{dW}{dt} = ate^{-(at^2)/2}$$

Integration of the equation for $MR(t)$ that was given earlier yields the cumulative effort I:

$$I(t) = K(1 - e^{-at^2})$$

In particular, we get $I(\infty) = K$. If we denote the point in time at which the Rayleigh curve assumes its maximum value by T, then $a = 1/(2T^2)$. This point T will be close to the point in time at which the software is being delivered to the customer. The volume of the area delineated by the Rayleigh curve between points 0 and T, then, is a good approximation of the initial development effort. For this, we get

$$E = I(T) = 0.3945K$$

This result is remarkably close to the often-used rule of thumb: 40% of the total effort is spent on the actual development, while 60% is spent on maintenance.

Various studies indicate that Putnam's model is well suited to estimating the cost of very large software development projects (projects that involve more than 15 man-years). The model seems to be less suitable for small projects.

A serious objection to Putnam's model, in our opinion, concerns the relation it assumes between effort and development time if the schedule is compressed relative to the nominal schedule estimate: $E = c/T^4$. Compressing a project's schedule in this model entails an extraordinarily large penalty (see also Section 7.3).

7.1.4 Function Point Analysis

Function point analysis (FPA) is a method of estimating costs in which the problems associated with determining the expected amount of code are circumvented. FPA is based on counting the number of data structures that are used. In the FPA method, it is assumed that the number of data structures is a good size indicator. FPA is particularly suitable for projects aimed at realizing business applications, in which the structure of the data plays a very dominant role. The method is less suited to projects in which the structure of the data plays a less prominent role and the emphasis is on algorithms (such as compilers and most real-time software).

The following five entities play a central role in the FPA model:

- Number of input types (I). The input types refer only to user input that results in changes in data structures. It does not refer to user input which is solely concerned with controlling the program's execution. Each input type that has a different format, or is treated differently, is counted. Although the records of a master file and those of a mutation file may have the same format, they are still counted separately.

- Number of output types (O). For the output types, the same counting scheme as for the input types is used.

- Number of inquiry types (E). Inquiry types concern input that controls the execution of the program and does not change internal data structures. Examples of inquiry types are menu selections and query criteria.

- Number of logical internal files (L). This concerns internal data generated by the system, and used and maintained by the system, such as, for example, an index file.

- Number of interfaces (F). This concerns data that is output to another application or is shared with some other application.

By trial and error, weights have been associated with each of these entities. The number of (unadjusted) function points, *UFP*, is a weighted sum of these five entities:

$$UFP = 4I + 5O + 4E + 10L + 7F$$

With FPA too, a further refinement is possible, by applying corrections to reflect differences in complexity of the data types. In that case, the constants used in the above formula depend on the estimated complexity of the data type in question. Table 7.5 gives the counting rules when three levels of complexity are distinguished. So, rather than having each input type count as four function points, we may count three, four or six function points, based on an assessment of the complexity of each input type.

Table 7.5   Counting rules for (unadjusted) function points

Type	Complexity level		
	Simple	Average	Complex
Input (I)	3	4	6
Output (O)	4	5	7
Inquiry (E)	3	4	6
Logical internal (L)	7	10	15
Interfaces (F)	5	7	10

Each input type has a number of data element types (attributes) and refers to zero or more other file types. The complexity of an input type increases as the number of its data element types or referenced file types increases. For input types, the mapping of these numbers to complexity levels is given in Table 7.6. For the other file types, these tables have the same format, with slightly different numbers along the axes.

Table 7.6   Complexity levels for input types

# of file types	# of data elements		
	1–4	5–15	>15
0 or 1	simple	simple	average
2–3	simple	average	complex
>3	average	complex	complex

As in other cost estimation models, the unadjusted function point measure is adjusted by taking into account a number of application characteristics that influence development effort. Table 7.7 contains the 14 characteristics used in the FPA model. The degree of influence of each of these characteristics is valued on a six-point scale, ranging from zero (no influence, not present) to five (strong influence). The total

Table 7.7 Application
characteristics in FPA

Data communications
Distributed functions
Performance
Heavily used configuration
Transaction rate
Online data entry
End-user efficiency
Online update
Complex processing
Re-usability
Installation ease
Operational ease
Multiple sites
Facilitate change

degree of influence DI is the sum of the scores for all characteristics. This number is then converted to a technical complexity factor (TCF) using the formula

$$TCF = 0.65 + 0.01DI$$

The (adjusted) function point measure, FP, is now obtained through

$$FP = UFP \times TCF$$

Finally, there is a direct mapping from the (adjusted) function points to lines of code. For instance, in (Albrecht, 1979) one function point corresponds to 65 lines of PL/I or 100 lines of COBOL, on average.

In FPA, it is not simple to decide exactly when two data types should be counted as separate. Also, the difference between, for example, input types, inquiry types, and interfaces remains somewhat vague. The International Function Point User Group (IFPUG) has published extensive guidelines on how to classify and count the various entities involved. This should overcome many of the difficulties that analysts have in counting function points in a uniform way.

Further problems with FPA have to do with its use of ordinal scales and the way complexity is handled. FPA distinguishes only three levels of component complexity. A component with 100 elements thus gets at most twice the number of function points as a component with one element. It has been suggested that a model which uses the raw complexity data, i.e. the number of data elements and file types referenced, might work as well as, or even better than, a model which uses an ordinal derivative thereof. In a sense, complexity is counted twice: both through the complexity level of the component and through one of the application characteristics. Yet it is felt that highly complex systems are not adequately dealt with, since FPA is predominantly concerned with counting externally visible inputs and outputs.

In applying the FPA cost estimation model, it still remains necessary to calibrate the various entities to your own environment. This holds even more for the corrections that reflect different application characteristics and the transition from function points to lines of code.

7.1.5 COCOMO 2: Variations on a Theme

COCOMO 2 is a revision of the 1981 COCOMO model, tuned to the life cycle practices of the 1990s and 2000s. It reflects our cumulative experience with and knowledge of cost estimation. By comparing its constituents with those of previous cost estimation models, it also offers us a way of learning about significant changes in our trade over the decades.

COCOMO 2 provides three increasingly detailed cost estimation models. These models can be used for different types of project, as well as during different stages of a single project:

- The **application composition** model is mainly intended for prototyping efforts, for instance to resolve user interface issues. (Its name suggests heavy use of existing components, presumably in the context of a powerful CASE environment.)

- The **early design** model is aimed at the architectural design stage.

- The **post-architecture** model deals with the actual development stage of a software project.

The post-architecture model can be considered an update of the original COCOMO model; the early design model is an FPA-like model; and the application composition model is based on counting system components of large granularity, known as object points. Object points have nothing to do with objects as in object-oriented development. In this context, objects are screens, reports, and 3GL modules.

The roots of this type of model can be traced back to several variations on FPA-type size measures. Function points as used in FPA are intended to be a user-oriented measure of system function. The user functions measured are the inputs, outputs, inquiries, etc. We may conjecture that these user-functions are technology-dependent and that FPA primarily reflects the batch-oriented world of the 1970s.

Present-day administrative systems are perhaps better characterized by their numbers of menus or screens. This line of thought has been pursued in various studies. (Banker *et al.*, 1991) compared object points with function points for a sample of software projects, and found that object points did almost as well as function points. Object points, however, are easier to determine and can be determined at an earlier point in time.

Total effort is estimated in the application composition model as follows:

1. Estimate the number of screens, reports, and 3GL components in the application.

2. Determine the complexity level of each screen and report (simple, medium or difficult). 3GL components are assumed to be always difficult. The complexity of a screen depends on the number of views and tables it contains. The complexity of a report depends on the number of sections and tables it contains. A classification table similar to those in FPA is used to determine the complexity level (see Table 7.8).

Table 7.8 Complexity levels for screens

# of views	# and source of data tables		
	total < 4 (<2 on server <3 on client)	total < 8 (2–3 on server 3–5 on client)	total ≥ 8 (>3 on server >5 on client)
<3	simple	simple	medium
3–7	simple	medium	difficult
>7	medium	difficult	difficult

3. Use the numbers given in Table 7.9 to determine the relative effort (in object points) to implement the object.

Table 7.9 Counting object points

Object type	Complexity		
	Simple	Medium	Difficult
Screen	1	2	3
Report	2	5	8
3GL component			10

4. The sum of the object points for the individual objects yields the number of object points for the whole system.

5. Estimate the reuse percentage, resulting in the number of new object points (NOP) as follows: $NOP = ObjectPoints \times (100 - \%Reuse)/100$.

6. Determine a productivity rate $PROD = NOP/man\text{-}month$. This productivity rate depends on the experience and capability of both the developers and the maturity of the CASE environment they use. It varies from 4 (very low) to 50 (very high).

7. Estimate the number of man-months needed for the project: $E = NOP/PROD$.

The early design model uses unadjusted function points (UFPs) as its basic size measure. These unadjusted function points are counted in the same way as they are counted in FPA. The unadjusted function points are then converted to source lines of code (SLOC), using a ratio SLOC/UFP which depends on the programming language used. In a typical environment, each UFP may correspond to, say, 91 lines of Pascal, 128 lines of C, 29 lines of C++, or 320 lines of assembly language. Obviously, these numbers are environment-specific.

The early design model does not use the FPA scheme to account for application characteristics. Instead, it uses a set of seven cost drivers, which are combinations of the full set of cost drivers of the post-architecture model (see Table 7.10). The intermediate, reduced set of cost drivers is:

- product reliability and complexity, a combination of required software reliability, database size, product complexity and documentation needs

- required reuse, which is equivalent to its post-architecture counterpart

- platform difficulty, a combination of execution time, main storage constraints, and platform volatility

- personnel experience, a combination of application, platform, and tool experience

- personnel capability, a combination of analyst and programmer capability and personnel continuity

- facilities, a combination of the use of software tools and multi-site development

- schedule, which is equivalent to its post-architecture counterpart.

These cost drivers are rated on a seven-point scale, ranging from extra low to extra high. The values assigned are similar to those in Table 7.10. Thus, the nominal values are always 1.00 and the values become larger or smaller as the cost driver is estimated to deviate further from the nominal rating. After the unadjusted function points have been converted to thousands of source lines of code ($KSLOC$), the cumulative effect of the cost drivers is accounted for by the formula

$$E = KSLOC \times \prod_i cost\ driver_i$$

The post-architecture is the most detailed model. Its basic effort equation is very similar to that of the original COCOMO model:

$$E = a \times KSLOC^b \times \prod_i cost\ driver_i$$

It differs from the original COCOMO model in its set of cost drivers, the use of lines of code as its base measure, and the range of values of the exponent b.

Table 7.10 Cost drivers and associated effort multipliers in COCOMO 2 (*Source*: B.W. Boehm *et al.*, *COCOMO II Model Definition Manual*, University of Southern California, 1997. Reproduced with permission.)

Cost drivers	Rating					
	Very low	Low	Nominal	High	Very high	Extra high
Product factors						
Reliability required	0.75	0.88	1.00	1.15	1.39	
Database size		0.93	1.00	1.09	1.19	
Product complexity	0.75	0.88	1.00	1.15	1.30	1.66
Required reusability		0.91	1.00	1.14	1.29	1.49
Documentation needs	0.89	0.95	1.00	1.06	1.13	
Platform factors						
Execution-time constraints			1.00	1.11	1.31	1.67
Main storage constraints			1.00	1.06	1.21	1.57
Platform volatility		0.87	1.00	1.15	1.30	
Personnel factors						
Analyst capability	1.50	1.22	1.00	0.83	0.67	
Programmer capability	1.37	1.16	1.00	0.87	0.74	
Application experience	1.22	1.10	1.00	0.89	0.81	
Platform experience	1.24	1.10	1.00	0.92	0.84	
Language and tool experience	1.25	1.12	1.00	0.88	0.81	
Personnel continuity	1.24	1.10	1.00	0.92	0.84	
Project factors						
Use of software tools	1.24	1.12	1.00	0.86	0.72	
Multi-site development	1.25	1.10	1.00	0.92	0.84	0.78
Required development schedule	1.29	1.10	1.00	1.00	1.00	

The differences between the COCOMO and COCOMO 2 cost drivers reflect major changes in the field. The COCOMO 2 cost drivers and the associated effort multipliers are given in Table 7.10. The values of the effort multipliers in this table are the result of calibration on a certain set of projects. The changes are as follows:

- Four new cost drivers have been introduced: required reusability, documentation needs, personnel continuity, and multi-site development. They reflect the growing influence of those aspects on development cost.

- Two cost drivers have been dropped: computer turnaround time and use of modern programming practices. Nowadays, developers use workstations, and (batch-processing) turnaround time is no longer an issue. Modern programming practices have evolved into the broader notion of mature software engineering practices, which are dealt with in the exponent *b* of the COCOMO 2 effort equation.

- The productivity influence, i.e. the ratio between the highest and lowest value, of some cost drivers has been increased (analyst capability, platform experience, and language and tools experience) or decreased (programmer capability).

In COCOMO 2, the user may use both *KSLOC* and *UFP* as base measures. It is also possible to use *UFP* for part of the system. The *UFP* counts are converted to *KSLOC* counts as in the early design model, after which the effort equation applies.

Rather than having three 'modes', with slightly different values for the exponent *b* in the effort equation, COCOMO 2 has a much more elaborate scaling model. This model uses five scale factors W_i, each of which is rated on a six-point scale from very low (5) to extra high (0). The exponent *b* for the effort equation is then determined by the formula:

$$b = 1.01 + 0.01 \times \sum_i W_i$$

So, *b* can take values in the range 1.01 to 1.26, thus giving a more flexible rating scheme than that used in the original COCOMO model.

The scale factors used in COCOMO 2 are:

- precedentedness, which indicates the novelty of the project to the development organization. Aspects such as experience with similar systems, the need for innovative architectures and algorithms, and the concurrent development of hardware and software are reflected in this factor.

- development flexibility, which reflects the need for conformance with pre-established and external interface requirements and puts a possible premium on early completion.

- architecture/risk resolution, which reflects the percentage of significant risks that have been eliminated. In many cases, this percentage will be correlated with the percentage of significant module interfaces specified, i.e. architectural choices made.

- team cohesion, which accounts for possible difficulties in stakeholder interactions. This factor reflects aspects such as the consistency of stakeholder objectives and cultures, and the experience of the stakeholders in acting as a team.

- process maturity, which reflects the maturity of the project organization according to the Capability Maturity Model (see Section 6.6).

Only the first two of these factors were, in a crude form, accounted for in the original COCOMO model.

The original COCOMO model allows us to handle reuse in the following way. The three main development phases, design, coding, and integration, are estimated to take 40%, 30%, and 30% of the average effort, respectively. Reuse can be catered for by separately considering the fractions of the system that require redesign (DM), recoding (CM), and re-integration (IM). An adjustment factor AAF is then given by the formula

$$AAF = 0.4DM + 0.3CM + 0.3IM$$

An adjusted value $AKLOC$, given by

$$AKLOC = KLOC \times AAF/100$$

is used in the COCOMO formulae, instead of the unadjusted value $KLOC$. In this way, a lower cost estimate is obtained if part of the system is reused.

By treating reuse this way, it is assumed that developing reusable components does not require any extra effort. You may simply reap the benefits when part of a system can be reused from an earlier effort. This assumption does not seem to be very realistic. Reuse does not come for free (see also Chapter 17).

COCOMO 2 uses a more elaborate scheme to handle reuse effects. This scheme reflects two additional factors that impact the cost of reuse: the quality of the code being reused and the amount of effort needed to test the applicability of the component to be reused.

If the software to be reused is strongly modular and strongly matches the application in which it is to be reused, and the code is well-organized and properly documented, then the extra effort needed to reuse this code is relatively low, estimated to be 10%. This penalty may be as high as 50% if the software exhibits low coupling and cohesion, is poorly documented, and so on. This extra effort is denoted by the software understanding increment SU.

The degree of assessment and assimilation (AA) denotes the effort needed to determine whether a component is appropriate for the present application. It ranges from 0% (no extra effort required) to 8% (extensive test, evaluation and documentation required).

Both these percentages are added to the adjustment factor AAF, yielding the equivalent kilo number of new lines of code ($EKLOC$):

$$EKLOC = KLOC \times (AAF + SU + AA)/100$$

7.1.6 Use-Case Points: Another Variation on a Theme

Function points, as discussed in Section 7.1.4, reflect transaction-oriented business applications from the 1970s. It may seem a bit odd to assume that the cost of modern, Web-based systems is determined by the number of input files, output files, and so on. On the other hand, it is an appealing idea to base the effort estimation on a small number of attributes of entities that are known at an early stage. The object points of COCOMO 2 are one example of this.

Another example is **use-case points**, which estimate effort based on a few characteristics of a set of use cases. The approach is very similar to that of FPA. First, the number of unadjusted use-case points (*UUCP*) is calculated. Next, this value is adjusted to cater for the complexity of the project (the technical complexity factor *TCF*) and the experience of the development team (the environmental complexity factor *ECF*). The formula thus reads

$$UCP = UUCP \times TCF \times ECF$$

The value of *UUCP* depends on the complexity of the use case itself and the complexity of the actors involved. The use-case categories and actor classifications and their associated weights are given in Tables 7.11 and 7.12. Note the similarity with the way complexities are computed in FPA (Table 7.6). A few simple and easy-to-count attributes determine the weight used.

Table 7.11 Use case categories

Category	Weight	Description
Simple	5	At most three steps in the success scenario; at most five classes in the implementation
Average	10	Four to seven steps in the success scenario; five to ten classes in the implementation
Complex	15	More than seven steps in the success scenario; more than ten classes in the implementation

Table 7.12 Actor classifications

Category	Weight	Description
Simple	1	Actor represents another system with a defined API
Average	2	Actor represents another system interacting through a protocol
Complex	3	Actor is a person interacting through an interface

The technical complexity factor, *TCF*, is very similar to that of FPA. A number of factors is distinguished that may influence productivity of a project. Examples are whether or not the project is for a distributed system, whether or not special security features are needed, and so on. Overall, these technical factors more reflect characteristics of modern systems than those of Table 7.7. Altogether, *TCF* may reduce or enlarge the nominal effort expressed by *UUCP* by about 40%.

Table 7.13 Environmental complexity factors

Description	Weight
Familiarity with UML	1.5
Part-time workers	−1
Analyst capability	0.5
Application experience	0.5
Object-oriented experience	1
Motivation	1
Difficult programming language	−1
Stable requirements	2

ECF works in a similar way. Table 7.13 lists the environmental complexity factors from (Clemmons, 2006). The factors 'Familiarity with UML' and 'Stable requirements' have a larger positive impact on effort than the others. Not surprisingly, 'Part-time workers' and 'Difficult programming language' have a negative impact. Again, a weight W_i and perceived value F_i is determined for each factor. The total impact is then given by

$$ECF = 1.4 - 0.03 \times \sum_i W_i \times F_i$$

The range of F_i is 0 to 5. So the value of *ECF* ranges from 1.4 ('Part-time workers' and 'Difficult programming language' have weight 0, while the others have weight 5) to 0.425 (all weights are 0). *ECF* thus has a somewhat larger impact on effort than *TCF*.

Finally, *UCP* is translated into actual hours by multiplying it with some constant denoting the development hours per use-case point. This value depends on the local situation. It may be computed using statistics from previous projects. Typically, the number of hours per use-case point is in the range 15 to 30. Experience indicates that use-case point estimates deviate by at most 20% from actual effort.

7.2 GUIDELINES FOR ESTIMATING COST

Many of the models discussed in Section 7.1 are based on data about past projects. One of the main problems in applying these models is the sheer *lack* of quantitative data about past projects. There simply is not enough data available. Though the importance of such a database is now widely recognized, we still do not routinely collect data on current projects. It seems as if we cannot spare the time to collect data; we have to write software. DeMarco (1982) makes a comparison with the medieval barber who also acted as a physician. He could have made the same objection: 'We cannot afford the time to take our patient's temperature, since we have to cut his hair.'

We thus have to shift to other methods to estimate costs. These other methods are based on the expertise of the estimators. In doing so, certain traps have to be circumvented. It is particularly important to prevent political arguments from entering the arena. Typical political lines of reasoning are:

- 'We were given 12 months to do the job, so it will take 12 months.' This might be seen as a variation of Parkinson's Law: work fills the time available.

- 'We know that our competitor put in a bid of $1M, so we need to schedule a bid of $0.9M.' This is sometimes referred to as 'pricing to win.'

- 'We want to show our product at the trade show next year, so the software needs to be written and tested within the next nine months, though we realize that this is rather tight.' This could be termed the 'budget' method of cost estimation.

- 'Actually, the project needs one year, but I can't sell that to my boss. We know that ten months is acceptable, so we'll settle for ten months.'

Politically colored estimates can have disastrous effects, as has been shown all too often during the short history of our field. Political arguments almost always play a role if estimates are being given by people directly involved in the project, such as the project manager or someone reporting to the project manager. Very soon, then, estimates will influence, or be influenced by, the future assessment of those persons. To quote DeMarco (1982), 'one chief villain is the policy that estimates shall be used to create incentives'.

Jørgensen (2005) gives the following guidelines for expert-based effort estimation:

- Do not mix estimation, planning, and bidding.

- Combine estimation methods.

- Ask for justification.

- Select experts with experience from similar projects.

- Accept and assess uncertainty.

- Provide learning opportunities.

- Consider postponing or avoiding effort estimation.

The politically colored lines of reasoning mentioned above all mix up estimation, planning, and bidding. However, they have different goals: estimation's only goal is accuracy; planning involves risk assessment and scheduling; and bidding is about winning a contract. Though these activities have different goals, they are of course related. A low bid, for instance, generally incurs a tight schedule and higher risks.

An interesting experiment on the effects of bidding on the remainder of a project is described in (Jørgensen and Grimstad, 2004). In this experiment, the authors study what is called *the winner's curse*, a phenomenon known from auctions, where players are uncertain of the value of an item when they bid. The highest bid wins, but the winner may be left with an item that's worth less than was paid for it. The term was first coined in the 1950s, when oil industries had no accurate way to estimate the value of their oil fields. In the software field, it has the following characteristics:

- Software providers differ in optimism in their estimates of most likely cost: some are over-optimistic, some are realistic, and some are pessimistic.

- Software providers with over-optimistic estimates tend to have the lowest bids.

- Software clients require a fixed-price contract.

- Software clients tend to select a provider with a low bid.

The result often is a Pyrrhic victory, a contract that results in low or negative profits to the bidder. But such a contract might also be risky for the client. Jørgensen and Grimstad (2004) describe an experiment in which they asked 35 companies for bids on a certain requirements specification. They then asked four companies to implement the system. They found that the companies with the lowest bids incurred the greatest risks.

Vacuuming a rug in two orthogonal directions is likely to pick up more dirt than vacuuming the rug twice in the same direction. Likewise, the combination of different estimation methods gives better estimates. So one may combine a COCOMO estimate with that of an expert, or estimates from experts with a different background. In this way, the bias that is inherent in a method or class of experts is mitigated.

Estimators should be held accountable for their estimates. Lederer and Prasad (2000) found that the use of estimates in performance evaluations of software managers and professionals is the only practice that leads to better estimates. In a slightly weaker form, one may at least ask for a justification of the estimate. Such a justification could refer to a calibrated model or a work breakdown structure in which cost estimates of components are derived from those in similar projects.

For lack of hard data, the cost of a software development project is often estimated through a comparison with earlier projects. If the estimator is very experienced, reasonable cost estimates may result. However, the learning effect of earlier experiences may lead to estimates that are too pessimistic in this case. Experience gained with a certain type of application may lead to higher productivity for subsequent projects. Similar applications thus give rise to lower costs.

McClure (1968) describes a situation in which a team was asked to develop a FORTRAN compiler for three different machines. The effort needed (in man-months) for these three projects is given in Table 7.14.

On the other hand, peculiar circumstances and particular characteristics of a specific project tend to get insufficient attention if cost is estimated through comparison with earlier projects. For example, a simple change of scale (automation of a local library with 25 000 volumes as opposed to a university library with over 1 000 000 volumes), slightly harsher performance requirements, a compressed schedule (which involves a larger team and thus incurs increased communication

Table 7.14   Learning effect of writing a FORTRAN compiler

Compiler	Number of man-months needed
1	72
2	36
3	14

overheads) may have a significant impact on the effort required in terms of man-months. Careless application of the comparison method of cost estimation leads to estimates such as 'the cost of this project is equal to the cost of the previous project'.

We may involve more than one expert in the estimation process. In doing so, each expert gives an estimate based on his own experience and expertise. Factors that are hard to quantify, such as personality characteristics and peculiar project characteristics, may thus be taken into account. Here too, the quality of the estimate cannot exceed the quality of the experts. The experts that participate in the estimate, then, should have experience in similar projects. It does not help all that much to ask an expert in office-automation systems to provide an estimate for an air-traffic-control system.

Estimates incur uncertainty. A cost estimate of, say, 100 man-months might mean that there is a 75% probability that the real cost of this project is between 80 and 120 man-months. It is *not* a point estimate. One method that aims to get a more reliable estimate is to have the expert produce more than one estimate. We all have the tendency to conceive an optimistic estimate as being realistic. (Have you ever heard of a software system being delivered ahead of time?) To obviate this tendency, we may employ a technique in which the expert is asked for three estimates: an optimistic estimate a, a realistic estimate m, and a pessimistic estimate b. Using a beta-distribution, the expected effort then is $E = (a + 4m + b)/6$. Though this estimate will probably be better than one based on the average of a and b, it seems justifiable to warn against too much optimism. Software has the tendency to grow and projects have the tendency to far exceed the estimated effort.

At the beginning of a project, the uncertainty is likely to be quite large. As a consequence, early cost estimates have a large range of uncertainty as well. As we progress to later phases, uncertainty decreases. For example, at the time of the feasibility study, the estimate may be 60% off, but the uncertainty may have decreased to 15% by the time the detailed design is ready (see Figure 7.2). After its shape, this is known as the 'cone of uncertainty'. In general, people considerably underestimate the size of the uncertainty interval (Jørgensen et al., 2004).

Training improves performance. This holds for skaters and it also applies to software cost estimators. Studies in other fields show that inexperienced people tend to overestimate their abilities and performance. There is no reason to expect the software field to be any different. The resulting cost and schedule overruns are all too

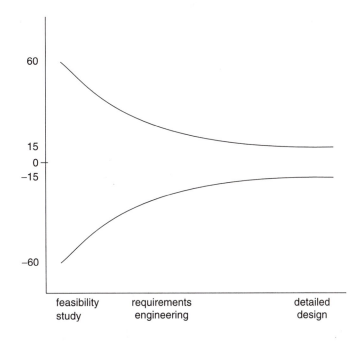

Figure 7.2 The cone of uncertainty

common. Harrison (2004) suggests that a prime reason for more mature organizations to have fewer cost overruns is not so much higher productivity or better processes, but greater self-knowledge. I concur the same is true for people estimating software costs.

While executing a task, people have to make a number of decisions. These decisions are strongly influenced by requirements set or proposed. The cost estimate is one such requirement which will have an impact on the end result. We may imagine a hypothetical case in which model A estimates the cost at 300 man-months. Now suppose the project actually takes 400 man-months. If model B would have estimated the project at 450 man-months, is model B better than model A? It is quite possible that, starting from the estimate given by model B, the eventual cost would have been 600 man-months. The project's behavior is influenced by the cost estimate. Choices made during the execution of a project are influenced by cost estimates derived earlier. If a cost estimate is not needed, it is wise not to make one.

7.3 DISTRIBUTION OF MANPOWER OVER TIME

Having obtained an estimate of the total number of man-months needed for a given project, we are still left with the question of how many calendar months it will take.

For a project estimated at 20 man-months, the kind of schedules you might think of, include:

- 20 people work on the project for 1 month;

- 4 people work on the project for 5 months;

- 1 person works on the project for 20 months.

These are not realistic schedules. We noticed earlier that the manpower needed is not evenly distributed over the time period of the project. From the shape of the Rayleigh curve, we find that we need to slowly increase manpower during the development stages of the project.

Cost estimation models generally also provide us with an estimate of the development time (schedule), T. Contrary to the effort equations, the various models show remarkable consistency when it comes to estimating the development time, as shown in Table 7.15.

Table 7.15   Relation between development time and effort

Walston–Felix	$T = 2.5E^{0.35}$
COCOMO (organic)	$T = 2.5E^{0.38}$
COCOMO 2 (nominal schedule)	$T = 3.0E^{0.33+0.2\times(b-1.01)}$
Putnam	$T = 2.4E^{1/3}$

The values T thus computed represent nominal development times. It is worth while studying ways to shorten these nominal schedules. Obviously, shortening the development time means an increase in the number of people involved in the project.

In terms of the Rayleigh curve model, shortening the development time amounts to an increase of the value a, the speed-up factor which determines the initial slope of the curve. The peak of the Rayleigh curve then shifts to the left and up. We thus get a faster increase of manpower required at the start of the project and a higher maximum workforce.

Such a shift does not go unpunished. Different studies show that individual productivity decreases as team size grows. There are two major causes of this phenomenon:

- As the team gets larger, the communication overhead increases, since more time will be needed for consultation with other team members, tuning of tasks, and so on.

- If manpower is added to a team during the execution of a project, the total team productivity decreases at first. New team members are not productive right from the start and they require time from the other team members during their learning process. Taken together, this causes a decrease in total productivity.

The combination of these two observations leads to the phenomenon that has become known as Brooks' Law: adding manpower to a late project only makes it later.

By analyzing a large amount of project data, (Conte *et al.*, 1986) found the following relation between average productivity L (measured in lines of code per man-month) and average team size P:

$$L = 777P^{-0.5}$$

In other words, individual productivity decreases exponentially with team size.

A theoretical underpinning of this is given on account of Brooks' observation regarding the number of communication links between the people involved in a project. This number is determined by the size and structure of the team. If, in a team of size P, each member has to coordinate his activities with those of all other members, the number of communication links is $P(P-1)/2$. If each member needs to communicate with one other member only, this number is $P-1$. Less communication than that seems unreasonable, since we would then have essentially independent teams. (If we draw team members as nodes of a graph and communication links as edges, we expect the graph to be connected.)

The number of communication links thus varies from roughly P to roughly $P^2/2$. In a true hierarchical organization, this leads to P^α communication paths, with $1 < \alpha < 2$. For an individual team member, the number of communication links varies from 1 to $P-1$. If the maximum individual productivity is L and each communication link results in a productivity loss l, the average productivity is

$$L_\gamma = L - l(P-1)^\gamma$$

where γ, with $0 < \gamma \leq 1$, is a measure of the number of communication links. (We assume that there is at least one person who communicates with more than one other person, so $\gamma > 0$.) For a team of size P, this leads to a total productivity

$$L_{tot} = P \times L_\gamma = P(L - l(P-1)^\gamma)$$

For a given set of values for L, l and γ, this is a function which, for increasing values of P, goes from 0 to some maximum and then decreases again. There is, thus, a certain optimum team size P_{opt} that leads to maximum team productivity. The team productivity for different values of P is given in Table 7.16. Here, we assume that individual productivity is $500\,LOC$/man-month ($L = 500$) and the productivity loss is 10% per communication link ($l = 50$). With full interaction between team members ($\gamma = 1$) this results in an optimum team size of 5.5 persons.

Everything takes time. We can not shorten a software development project indefinitely by trading off time against people. Boehm sets the limit at 75% of the nominal development time, on empirical grounds. A system that has to be delivered too fast gets into the 'impossible region' (see Figure 7.3). The chance of success becomes almost nil if the schedule is pressed too far.

In any case, a shorter development time induces higher costs. We may use the following rule of thumb: compressing the development time by X% results in a cost increase of X% relative to the nominal cost estimate (Boehm, 1984a).

Table 7.16 Impact of team size on productivity

Team size	Individual productivity	Total productivity
1	500	500
2	450	900
3	400	1 200
4	350	1 400
5	300	1 500
5.5	275	1 512
6	250	1 500
7	200	1 400
8	150	1 200

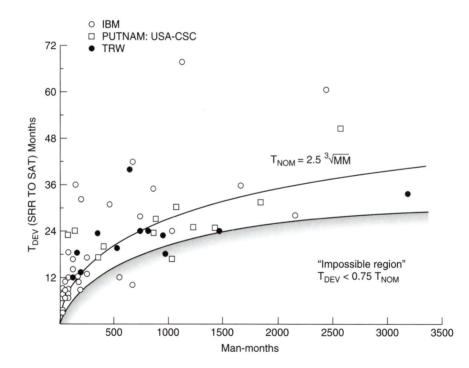

Figure 7.3 The impossible region (*Source*: B.W. Boehm, *Software Engineering Economics*, fig. 27-8, page 471, ©1981, reprinted by permission of Prentice Hall, Inc., Englewood Cliffs, NJ.)

7.4 AGILE COST ESTIMATION

One of the key values of agile development is that one should respond to change rather than follow a plan. This key value translates to a different attitude towards cost estimation as well. In agile development, there is no cost estimation for the whole project in advance. Since we assume things will change, such an upfront, overall cost estimation is considered useless. Usually, an agile development project delivers functionality in a number of iterations. Each iteration provides the user with a number of features. The number of features may be fixed and the next version is released when all features agreed upon have been implemented. Alternatively, the release date may be fixed and then the number of features is adjusted to fit the time box.

In either case, we are interested in estimating the cost and duration of a set of features. Doing this the agile way, the cost estimation proceeds in two steps:

1. Estimate the effort on a scale which is unitless.

2. Translate the effort estimation into a duration.

In Step 1, the effort required for each feature is estimated relative to the effort estimated for the other features. The unit in which the effort is expressed has no relation to actual time. Cohn (2006) calls them **story points**. One way to estimate the story points for a set of features is to first look for a feature that you think will require average effort. This feature, A, is assigned an average number of story points, say 5. Next, the other features are estimated relative to A. If you think feature B requires about half the effort of feature A, it is assigned 2 (or 3) story points. If B is estimated to require twice the effort of A, it is assigned ten story points. And so on, until all features have been assigned a story point size.

This process works best if the size of the features differs by at most one order of magnitude. It is difficult to accurately estimate the effort of a set of features if, say, some require 2 story points, while others require 100. One easy way to assign story points is to only use the values 1, 2, 4 and 8, say. A feature is then estimated to be double or half the size of another feature. Very small features may be estimated at 0 story points. Of course, you can't have too many features of size 0.

Agile development is a team effort and so is agile estimation. All team members may be involved in the estimation process. Cohn (2006) describes a poker-like game for doing this. For a given feature, all participants individually estimate the number of story points required and write their estimate on a card. All the cards are turned over at the same time. If you're lucky, the numbers on the cards are approximately the same. If the numbers vary widely, the participants explain why they estimated the effort the way they did. Once these explanations have been given, the poker game for that feature is repeated. Hopefully, the variation in the effort estimates will decrease. The process is repeated until the estimates are sufficiently similar. Note that this process is more than an entertaining estimation exercise. While explaining their estimates, tacit knowledge about the feature and its possible implementation is shared. The group effectively does part of the design while estimating.

After the effort for each feature has been estimated, the actual time needed per effort point is estimated. This is done by estimating the **velocity**. The velocity is the number of story points completed in one iteration. It is a measure of progress. For instance, the team might estimate it can implement eight story points in two weeks. This estimate is based on the team's experience with earlier projects. In maintenance, similar lines of thought are used when estimating the probability that components require changes, based on the change history of those components. It is commonly referred to as *yesterday's weather*: without any additional knowledge, we assume today's weather will be like yesterday's. As the project progresses, the team will accumulate knowledge about its performance and will estimate its velocity more accurately.

If the team does not manage to implement as many story points as it hoped to implement during the iteration, there is no immediate need to adjust the story points of features. Story points should *only* be adjusted if the relative size of a feature changes. The only thing that matters is that they are mutually consistent. If the schedule does not fit, it is more likely that the team overestimated the number of story points it can realize in a week.

Story points are a valid measure of effort only for the current project and the current team. Just as algorithmic models need to be calibrated for each organization, story points need to be determined anew for a new situation. For example, a feature that is estimated at 4 story points in one situation, may well be estimated at 8 story points in another. After all, it is an effort estimate *relative* to the effort required for the other features. If the other features change, so will the estimate. In the same vein, the velocity depends on the current project and the current team. In one project, a story point may amount to one week of work, while in another project a story point may take a month. A less experienced team might take two months for that same story point.

Story points are a pure measure of size. They only measure the size of features relative to one another. They have nothing to do with 'real' working days. People outside the team may have difficulty coping with the abstract nature of story points. As an alternative to story points, Cohn (2006) suggests using **ideal days**. An ideal day is a day in which you can work uninterrupted on a single feature. There are no phone calls from the customer, no meetings, no questions from the help desk that need an answer, no time lost because you are working on two things at the same time, etc. Similarly to the step from story points to real speed, in a second step the ideal days are translated into real days, taking into account all the factors that slow people down.

7.5 SUMMARY

It remains to be seen whether we will ever get one general cost estimation model. The number of parameters that impact productivity simply seems to be too large. Yet, each organization may develop a model which is well suited for projects to be undertaken within that organization. An organization may, and should, build a database with data on its own projects. Starting with a model such as COCOMO 2, the different parameters, i.e. applicable cost drivers and values for the associated effort multipliers, may then be determined. In the course of time, the model becomes more closely tuned to the organizational environment, resulting in better and better estimates. Reifer (2000), for example, describes how COCOMO 2 can be adapted to estimate for Web-based software development projects.

A word of caution: present-day algorithmic cost models are not all that good yet. At best, they yield estimates which are at most 25% off, 75% of the time, *for projects used to derive the model*. Expert-based cost estimates and the much simpler models that are based on counting a fairly small number of attributes, use-case points, or story points are a viable alternative.

Even when much better performance is realized, some problems remain when using the type of cost estimation model obtained in this way:

- Even though a model such as COCOMO 2 looks objective, a fair amount of subjectivity is introduced through the need to assign values to the various levels of a number of cost drivers. Based on an analysis of historical project data, Jones (1986) lists 20 factors which certainly influence productivity and another 25 for which it is probable. The set of COCOMO 2 cost drivers already allows for a variation of 1:800. A much smaller number of relevant cost drivers would reduce a model's vulnerability to the subjective assessment of project characteristics.

- The models are based on data from *old* projects and reflect the technology of those projects. In some cases, the project data may be quite old. The impact of more recent developments cannot easily be taken into account, since we do not have sufficient data on projects which exhibit those characteristics.

- Almost all models take into account attributes that impact the initial development of software. Attributes which specifically relate to maintenance activities are seldom taken into account. Also, factors such as the amount of documentation required or the number of business trips (in the case of a multi-site development) are often lacking. Yet, these factors may have a significant impact on the effort needed.

Algorithmic models usually result from applying statistical techniques such as regression analysis to a given set of project data. For a new project, the parameters of the model have to be determined and the model yields an estimate and, in some cases, a confidence interval.

In the introduction to this chapter, we compared cost estimation for software development with cost estimation for laying out a garden. When laying out a garden, we often follow a rather different line of thought, namely: given a budget of, say, $10 000, what possibilities are there? What happens if we trade off a pond against something else? Something similar is also possible with software. Given a budget of

$100 000 for library automation, what possibilities are there? Which user interface can we expect? What will the transaction speed be? How reliable will the system be? To be able to answer these types of question, we need to be able to analyze the sensitivity of an estimate to varying values of relevant attributes.

Finally, estimating the cost of a software development project is a highly dynamic activity. Not only may we switch from one model to another during the course of a project, estimates are also adjusted on the basis of experiences gained. Switching to another model during the execution of a project is possible, since we may expect to get more reliable data while the project is making progress. We may, for instance, imagine using the series of increasingly detailed COCOMO 2 models. When using some agile estimation approach, the estimates will improve over time as knowledge about one's performance increases.

We cannot, and should not, rely on a one-shot cost estimate. Controlling a software development project implies a regular check of progress, a regular check of estimates made, re-establishing priorities and weighing stakes, as the project progresses.

7.6 FURTHER READING

Early cost estimation models are described in (Nelson, 1966) and (Wolverton, 1974). The Walston–Felix model is described in (Walston and Felix, 1977). The model of Putnam and Norden is described in (Norden, 1970) and (Putnam, 1978). Boehm (1981) is the definitive source on the original COCOMO model. COCOMO 2 is described in (Boehm *et al.*, 1997) and (Boehm *et al.*, 2000).

Function point analysis (FPA) is developed by (Albrecht, 1979) and (Albrecht and Gaffney, 1983). Critical appraisals of FPA can be found in (Symons, 1988), (Kemerer, 1993), (Kemerer and Porter, 1992), (Abran and Robillard, 1992) and (Abran and Robillard, 1996). A detailed discussion of function points, its counting process and some case studies, is provided by (Garmus and Herron, 1996). (Costagliola *et al.*, 2005) describe a function-point type measure for object-oriented systems. Use case points were introduced in (Karner, 1993). Experiences with use case points are described in (Carroll, 2005) and (Mohagheghi *et al.*, 2005).

Cohn (2006) is a very good book on agile estimation. McConnell (2006) is a more general book on effort estimation.

The relation between project behavior and its cost estimate is discussed in (Abdel-Hamid *et al.*, 1993). Guidelines for cost estimation are given in (Boehm and Sullivan, 1999), (Fairley, 2002) and (Jørgensen, 2005). Jørgensen (2004) gives an overview of studies on expert estimation. Jørgensen (2005) gives useful guidelines for expert-based effort estimation. (Software, 2000) is a special issue devoted to software estimation.

Exercises

1. In which ways may political arguments influence cost estimates?

2. What does the Walston–Felix model look like?

3. How may the Rayleigh curve be related to software cost estimation?

4. Give a sketch of function point analysis (FPA).

5. Give a sketch of COCOMO 2.

6. Discuss the major differences between COCOMO 2 and FPA.

7. Give a rationale for Brooks' Law.

8. In which sense does function point analysis (FPA) reflect the batch-oriented world of the 1970s?

9. How may early cost estimates influence the way in which a project is executed?

10. Why is it difficult to compare different cost estimation models?

11. Discuss how to estimate feature size using story points.

12. Explain the cone of uncertainty.

13. Suppose you are involved in a project which is estimated to take 100 man-months. How would you estimate the nominal calendar time required for this project? Suppose the project is to be finished within six calendar months. Do you think such a schedule compression is feasible?

14. Why should software cost models be recalibrated from time to time?

15. ♠ How would you calibrate the COCOMO 2 model to fit software development in your organization?

16. ♡ Suppose you are managing a project which is getting behind schedule. Possible actions include renegotiating the time schedule, adding people to the project, and renegotiating quality requirements. In which ways can

these actions shorten the time schedule? Can you think of other ways to finish the project on time?

17. ♡ Suppose you have a LOC-based cost estimation model available whose parameters are based on projects from your own organization that used COBOL as the implementation language. Can you use this model to estimate the cost of a project whose implementation language is Pascal? What would change if the model were based on projects that used C?

18. ♡ Can you give an intuitive rationale for the values of the COCOMO 2 cost drivers (in Table 7.10) that relate to project attributes?

8

Project Planning and Control

LEARNING OBJECTIVES

- To appreciate looking at project control from a system point of view

- To be aware of typical project situations, and ways in which projects can be successfully dealt with in such situations

- To understand how risks can be prevented from becoming problems

- To know techniques for the day-to-day planning and control of software development projects

In this chapter, I try to reconcile the various approaches sketched in Chapters 3–7. A taxonomy of software development projects is given, together with recommended management practices for dealing with such projects. The chapter also deals with risk management and some well-known techniques for project planning and control.

Software development projects differ widely. These differences are reflected in the ways in which these projects are organized and managed. For some projects, the budget is fixed and the goal of the project is to maximize the quality of the end product. For others, quality constraints are fixed in advance, and the goal is to produce effectively a system that meets those quality constraints. If the developing organization has considerable experience with the application domain and the requirements are fixed and stable, a tightly structured approach may yield a satisfactory solution. In applications with fuzzy requirements and little previous experience in the development team, a more agile approach may be desirable.

It is important to identify those project characteristics early on, because they will influence the way a project is organized, planned and controlled. In Section 8.1, we will discuss project control from a systems point of view. This allows us to identify the major dimensions along which software development projects differ. These dimensions lead to a taxonomy of software development projects, which is discussed in Section 8.2. For each of the project categories distinguished, we will indicate how best to control the various entities identified in previous chapters. This type of assessment is to be done at the project planning stage.

This assessment links global risk categories to preferred control situations. Daily practice, however, is more complex. An actual project faces many risks, each of which has to be handled in turn. Even risks for which we hoped to have found an adequate solution may turn into problems later on. Risk factors therefore have to be monitored, and contingency plans have to be developed. The early identification of risks and the development and carrying out of strategies to mitigate these risks is known as **risk management**. Risk management is discussed in Section 8.3.

Software development projects consist of a number of interrelated tasks. Some of these will have to be handled sequentially (a module cannot be tested until it has been implemented), while others may be handled in parallel (different modules can be implemented concurrently). The dependencies between tasks can be depicted in a network from which a project schedule can be derived. These and similar tools for the micro-level planning and control of software development projects are discussed in Section 8.4.

8.1 A SYSTEMS VIEW OF PROJECT CONTROL

In the preceding chapters, we discussed several entities that need to be controlled. During the execution of a software development project, each of these entities needs to be monitored and assessed. From time to time, adjustments will have to be made. To be able to do so, we must know which entities can be varied, how they can be varied, and what the effect of adjustments is.

To this end, we will consider project control from a systems point of view. We now consider the software development project itself as a system. Project control may then be described in terms of:

- the system to be controlled, i.e. the software development project;

- the entity that controls the system, i.e. the project manager, his organization and the decision rules he uses;

- information which is used to guide the decision process. This information may come from two sources. It may come from the system being controlled (such as a notice of technical problems with a certain component) or it may have a source outside the system (such as a request to shorten development time).

The variables that play a role in controlling a system may be categorized into three classes: irregular variables, goal variables, and control variables.

Irregular variables are those variables that are input to the system being controlled. Irregular variables cannot be varied by the entity that controls the system. Their values are determined by the system's environment. Examples of irregular variables are the computer experience of the user or the project staffing level.

An important precondition for effective control is knowledge of the project's goals. In developing software, various conflicting goals can be distinguished. One possible goal is to *minimize development time*. Since time is often pressing, this goal is not unusual. Another goal might be to *maximize efficiency*, i.e. development should be done as cheaply as possible. Optimal use of resources (mostly manpower) is then needed. Yet a third possible goal is to *maximize quality*. Each of these goals is possible, but they can be achieved only if it is known which goals are being pursued. These goals collectively make up the set of goal variables.

The decision process is guided by the set of control variables. Control variables are entities which can be manipulated by the project manager in order to achieve the goals set forth. Examples of possible control variables are the tools to be used, project organization, efficiency of the resulting software, and features implemented.

It is not possible to make a rigid separation between the various sets of variables. It depends on the situation at hand whether a particular variable should be taken as an irregular variable, a goal variable, or a control variable. If the requirements are stable and fixed, one may for instance try to control the project by employing adequate personnel and using a proper set of tools. For another project, manpower may be fixed and one may try to control the project by extending the delivery date, relaxing quality constraints, etc.

However, in order to be able to control a project, the different sets of variables must be known. It must be known where control is, and is not, possible. This is only one prerequisite, though. In systems theory, the following conditions for effective control of a system are used:

- the controlling entity must know the goals of the system;

- the controlling entity must have sufficient control variety;

- the controlling entity must have information on the state, input, and output of the system;

- the controlling entity must have a conceptual control model. It must know how and to what extent the different variables depend on and influence each other.

When all these conditions are met, control can be rational, in which case there is no uncertainty, since the controlling entity is completely informed about every relevant aspect. The control problem can then be structured and formalized. Daily practice of software development is different, though. There may be insufficient room for control or the effect of control actions may not be known. Control then becomes much more intuitive or primitive. It is based on intuition, experience, and rules of thumb.

The degree to which a software development project can be controlled increases as the control variety increases. This control variety is determined by the number of control variables and the degree to which they can be varied. As noted before, the control variety is project dependent.

Controlling software development means that we must be able to measure both the project and the product. Measuring a project means that we must be able to assess progress. Measuring a product means that we must be able to determine the degree to which quality and functional requirements are being met.

Controlling software development projects implies that effective control actions are possible. Corrective actions may be required if progress is not sufficient or the software does not comply with its requirements. Effective control means that we know what the effect of control actions is. If progress is insufficient and we decide to allocate extra manpower, we must understand the impact of this extra manpower on the time schedule. If the quality of a certain component is less than required and we decide to allocate extra test time, we must know how much test time is required in order to achieve the desired quality.

In practice, controlling a software development project is not a rational process. The ideal systems theory situation is not met. There are a number of uncertainties which make managing such projects a challenging activity. Below, we will discuss a few idealized situations, based on the uncertainty of various relevant aspects.

8.2 A TAXONOMY OF SOFTWARE DEVELOPMENT PROJECTS

In Section 8.1, we identified several conditions that need to be satisfied in order to be able to control projects rationally. Since these conditions are often not met, we will have to rely on a different control mechanism in most cases. The control mechanism best suited to any given situation obviously depends on relevant characteristics of the project at hand.

Based on an analysis of software development project characteristics that are important for project control, we will distinguish several project situations, and indicate how projects can successfully be controlled in these situations.

We will group project characteristics into three classes: product characteristics, process characteristics, and resource characteristics. From the point of view of project control, we are interested in the degree of *certainty* of those characteristics. For example, if we have clear and stable user requirements, product certainty is high. If part of the problem is to identify user requirements or if the user requirements frequently change during the development project, product certainty is low.

If product certainty is high, control can be quite rational, insofar as it depends on product characteristics. Since we know what the product is supposed to accomplish, we may check compliance with the requirements and execute corrective actions if needed. If product certainty is low, this is not feasible. We either do not know what we are aiming at or the target is constantly moving. It is only reasonable to expect that control will be different in those cases.

For the present discussion, we are interested only in project characteristics that may differ between projects. Characteristics common to most or all software development projects, such as the fact that they involve teamwork, do not lead to different control paradigms.

We will furthermore combine the characteristics from each of the three categories identified above into one metric, the certainty of the corresponding category. This leaves us with three dimensions along which software development projects may differ:

- **Product certainty** is largely determined by two factors: whether or not user requirements are clearly specified, as regards both functionality and quality, and the volatility of those user requirements. Other product characteristics are felt to have a lesser impact on our understanding of what the end-product should accomplish.

- **Process certainty** is determined by such factors as: the possibility of redirecting the development process, the degree to which the process can be measured and the knowledge we have about the effect of control actions, and the degree to which new, unknown tools are being used.

- **Resource certainty** is largely determined by the availability of the appropriate qualified personnel.

If we allow each of these certainty factors to take one of two values (high and low), we get eight control situations, although some of them are not very realistic. If we have little or no certainty about the software to be developed, we can hardly expect to be certain about the process to be followed and the resources needed to accomplish our goals. Similarly, if we do not know how to carry out the development process, we also do not know which resources are needed. This leaves us with four archetypal situations, as depicted in Table 8.1.

Table 8.1 Archetypal control situations

	Realization	Allocation	Design	Exploration
Product certainty	high	high	high	low
Process certainty	high	high	low	low
Resource certainty	high	low	low	low

Below, we discuss each of these control situations in turn. In doing so, we pay attention to the following aspects of those control situations:

- the kind of control problem;

- the primary goals to be set in controlling the project;

- the coordination mechanism to be used;

- the development strategy, or process model, to be applied;

- the way and degree to which cost can be estimated.

8.2.1 Realization Control Situation

If the requirements are known and stable, it is known how the software is to be developed, there is sufficient control variety, the effect of control actions is known, and sufficient resources are available, we find ourselves in an ideal situation, a situation not often encountered in our field. The main emphasis will be on realization: how can we, given the requirements, achieve our goal in the most effective way? As for the development strategy, we may use some linear process model. Feedback to earlier phases, as in the waterfall model, is needed only for verification and validation activities.

To coordinate activities in a project of this type, we may use direct supervision. Work output can be standardized, since the end result is known. Similarly, the work processes and worker skills can be fixed in advance. There will thus be little need for control variety as far as these variables are concerned.

Management can be done effectively through a separation style. The work to be done is fixed through rules and procedures. Management can allocate tasks and check their proper execution.

As for cost estimation, we may successfully use one of the more formalized cost models. Alternatively, experts in the domain may give a reliable estimate. A cost estimation thus obtained can be used to guard the project's progress and yields a target to be achieved.

8.2.2 Allocation Control Situation

This situation differs from the realization control situation in that there is uncertainty as regards the resources. The major problem then becomes one of the availability of personnel. Controlling a project of this kind tends to become one of controlling capacity. The crucial questions become: How do we get the project staffed? How do we achieve the desired end-product with limited means?

According to (Mintzberg, 1983), one has to try to standardize the process as far as possible in this case. This makes it easier to move personnel between tasks. Guidelines and procedures may be used to describe how the various tasks have to be carried out.

As regards the development strategy, we may again opt for the waterfall model. We may either contract out the work to be done or try to acquire the right type and amount of qualified personnel.

As for cost estimation, either some cost estimation model or expert estimates can be used. Since there is uncertainty as regards resources, there is a need for sensitivity analyses in order to gain insight into such questions as: What will happen to the total cost and development time if we allocate three designers of level A rather than four designers of level B?

8.2.3 Design Control Situation

If the requirements are fixed and stable, but we do not know how to carry out the process, nor which resources to employ, the problem is one of design. Note that the adjective *design* refers to the design of the project, not the design of the software. We have to answer such questions as: Which milestones are to be identified? Which documents must be delivered and when? What personnel must be allocated? How will responsibilities be assigned?

In this situation, we have insufficient knowledge of the effect of allocating extra personnel, other tools, different methods and techniques. The main problem then becomes one of controlling the development process.

In Mintzberg's classification, this can best be pursued through standardization of work outputs. Since the output is fixed, control should be done through the process and the resources. The effect of such control actions is not sufficiently known, however.

In order to make a project of this kind manageable, one needs overcapacity. As far as the process is concerned, this necessitates margins in development time and budget. Keeping extra personnel is not feasible, in general.

In these situations, we will need frequently to measure progress towards the project's goals in order to allow for timely adjustments. Therefore, we may want to go from a linear development model to an incremental one in which the system is delivered in a series of releases. This preference will increase as the uncertainty increases.

Cost estimation will have to rely on past experience. We will usually not have enough data to use one of the more formalized cost estimation models. The need for sensitivity analyses will be more pressing than in the allocation control situation, since the uncertainty is greater. The project manager will be interested in the sensitivity of cost estimates to certain cost drivers. He might be interested in such questions as: What will happen to the development schedule if two extra analysts are assigned to this project? What will the effect be on the total cost if we shorten the development time by x days? By viewing cost estimation in this way, the manager will gain insight into, and increase his feeling for, possible solution strategies.

8.2.4 Exploration Control Situation

If the product certainty, process certainty, and resource certainty are all low, we have the most difficult control situation.

Because of these uncertainties, the work will be exploratory in nature. This situation does not fit a coordination mechanism based on standardization. In a situation as complex and uncertain as this one, coordination can best be achieved through mutual adjustment. The structure is one of 'adhocracy' (see Section 5.1.1). Experts from various disciplines work together to achieve some as yet unspecified goal.

A critical success factor in these cases is the commitment of all the people involved. Work cannot be split up into neat tasks. Flexibility in work patterns and work contents is important. Adherence to a strict budget cannot be enforced upon the team from above. The team members must commit themselves to the project. Management has to place emphasis on their relations with the team members.

Controlling a project of this kind is a difficult and challenging activity. To make a project of this kind manageable, our goal will be to maximize output, given the resources available to the project. This maximization may concern the quality of the product, or its functionality, or both.

Since requirements are not precisely known, some agile approach is appropriate as a process model. The larger the uncertainty, the more often we will have to check whether we are still on the right track. Thus, some development strategy involving many small steps and frequent user feedback is to be used. Cost estimation using some formalized model clearly is not feasible in these circumstances. The use of such models presupposes that we know enough of the project at hand to be able to compare it with previous projects. Such is not the case, though.

We may rely on expert judgments to achieve a rough cost estimate. Such a cost estimate, however, cannot and should not be used as a fixed anchor point as to when the project should be finished and how much it may cost. There are simply too many uncertainties involved. Rather, it provides us with some guidance as to the magnitude of the project. Based on this estimate, effort and time can be allocated for the project, for instance to produce a certain number of prototypes, a feasibility study, a pilot implementation of part of the product, or to start a certain number of time boxes. An agile effort estimation may be used to plan successive iterations. The hope is that in time the uncertainties will diminish sufficiently so that the project shifts to one of the other situations.

8.2.5 Summary of Control Situations

The four control situations discussed above are once more depicted in Table 8.2, together with a short characterization of the various control aspects discussed above. If we look at the columns of this table from another perspective, we may say that the waterfall model tries to remove all uncertainty at the very beginning but agile approaches allow uncertainty to decrease gradually as the project moves on.

For big projects, it may be effective to use different control mechanisms at the macro and micro levels (Karlström and Runeson, 2005). At the macro level,

Table 8.2 Control situations (*After*: F.J. Heemstra, *How much does software cost?* ©1989, Kluwer Bedrijfswetenschappen. Reproduced with permission.)

	Realization	Allocation	Design	Exploration
Product certainty	high	high	high	low
Process certainty	high	high	low	low
Resource certainty	high	low	low	low
Primary goal in control	Optimize resource usage Efficiency and schedule	Acquisition, training of personnel	Control of the process	Maximize result Lower risks
Coordination, Management style	Standardization of product, process, and resources Hierarchy, separation style	Standardization of product and process	Standardization of process	Mutual adjustment Commitment Relation style
Development strategy	Waterfall	Waterfall	Incremental	Incremental Prototyping Agile
Cost estimation	Models Guard process	Models Sensitivity analysis	Expert estimate Sensitivity analysis	Agile estimate Risk analysis Provide guidance

management may have to coordinate the work of different teams and report to higher management. This may require an approach in which explicit stages and corresponding milestones are distinguished. At the level of a small subteam, though, one may still apply agile methods to control the day-to-day work.

By taking the different control aspects into account during the planning stage of a software development project, we can tailor the project's management to the situation at hand. In doing so, we recognize that software development projects are not all alike. Neglecting project-specific characteristics is likely to result in project failures, such as those that have often been reported upon in the literature but equally often remain hidden from the public.

8.3 RISK MANAGEMENT

> Risk management is project management for adults.
> Tim Lister

In Section 8.2, we identified global risk categories and tied them to preferred control situations. In this section, the emphasis is on individual risks and their management *during* project execution. In some sense too, the discussion below takes a more realistic point of view, in that we also consider adverse situations such as unrealistically tight schedules and design gold plating.

The potential risks of a project must be identified as early as possible. It is rather naive to suppose that a software project will run smoothly from start to finish. It won't. We should identify the risks of a software project early on and provide measures to deal with them. Doing so is not a sign of unwarranted pessimism. Rather, it is a sign of wisdom.

In software development, we tend to ignore risks. We assume an optimistic scenario under all circumstances and we do not reserve funds for dealing with risks. We rely on heroics when chaos sets in. If risks are identified at all, their severity is often underestimated, especially by observers higher in the hierarchy. A designer may have noticed that a certain subsystem poses serious performance problems. His manager assumes that the problem can be solved. His manager's manager assumes the problem *has* been solved.

A risk is a possible future negative event that may affect the success of an effort. So, a risk is not a problem, yet. It may become one, though, and risk management is concerned with *preventing* risks from becoming problems. Some common examples of risks and ways to deal with them, are:

- Requirements may be unstable, immature, unrealistic, or excessive. If we merely list the requirements and start to realize the system in a linear development mode, it is likely that a lot of rework will be needed. This results in schedule and budget overruns, since this rework was not planned. If the requirements volatility is identified as a major risk, an evolutionary development strategy can be chosen. This situation fits the exploration control situation identified in Section 8.2.4.

- If there is little or no user involvement during the early development stages, a real danger is that the system will not meet user needs. If this is identified as a risk, it can be mitigated, e.g. by having users participate in design reviews.

- If the project involves different or complex domains, the spread of application knowledge within the project team may be an issue. Recognizing this risk may result in timely attention and resources being applied to a training program for team members.

- If the project involves more than one development site, communication problems may arise. A common way to deal with this is to pay attention to socialization issues, for instance by scheduling site visits. Global software development is discussed in Chapter 20.

At the project planning stage, risks are identified and handled. A risk management strategy involves the following steps:

1. Identify the risk factors. There are many possible risk factors. Each organization may develop its own checklist of such factors. The top ten risk factors from (Boehm, 1989) are listed in Table 8.3.

2. Determine the risk exposure. For each risk, we have to determine the probability p that it will actually occur and the effect E (e.g. in dollars or loss of man-months) that it will have on the project. The risk exposure then equals $p \times E$.

3. Develop strategies to mitigate the risks. Usually, this will only be done for the N risks that have the highest risk exposure or for those risks whose exposure exceeds some threshold α.

   There are three general strategies for mitigating risks: avoidance, transfer, and acceptance. We may avoid risks by taking precautions so that they do not occur: buying more memory, assigning more people, providing a training program for team members, and so on. We may transfer risks by looking for another solution, such as a prototyping approach to handle unstable requirements. Finally, we may accept risks. In the latter case, we have to provide a contingency plan, to be invoked when the risk does become a problem.

4. Handle risks. Risk factors must be monitored. For some risks, the avoidance or transfer actions may succeed, and those risks will never become a problem. We may be less lucky for those risks that we decided up front not to handle. Also, some of our actions may turn out to be less successful, and risks that we hoped to have handled adequately may become a problem after all. Finally, project characteristics change over time and so do the risks. Risk management thus is a cyclic process, and occasionally risks must be handled by re-assessing the project, invoking a contingency plan, or even a transfer to crisis mode.

Table 8.3 Top ten risk factors

Risk	Description
Personnel shortfall	May manifest itself in a variety of ways, such as inexperience with the domain, tools or development techniques to be used; personnel turnover; loss of critical team members; or simply the size of the team.
Unrealistic schedule/budget	Estimates may be unrealistic with respect to the requirements.
Wrong functionality	May have a variety of causes, such as an imperfect understanding of the customer needs, the complexity of communication with the client, insufficient domain knowledge of the developers and designers.
Wrong user interface	In certain situations, the user-friendliness of the interface is critical to its success.
Gold plating	Developers may wish to develop 'nice' features not asked for by the customer.
Requirements volatility	If many requirements change during development, the amount of rework increases.
Bad external components	The quality or functionality of externally supplied components may be below what is required for this project.
Bad external tasks	Subcontractors may deliver inadequate products, or the skills obtained from outside the team may be inadequate.
Real-time shortfalls	The real-time performance of (parts of) the system may be inadequate.
Capability shortfalls	An unstable environment or new or untried technology pose a risk to the development schedule.

Wallace and Keil (2004) give a useful categorization of risk factors. They distinguish four types of risk (see also Figure 8.1):

- C1: Risks related to customers and users, including a lack of user participation, conflicts between users, or a user organization resisting change. Part of this can be mitigated through an agile approach. But equally often, such risks are beyond the project manager's control.

- C2: Risks that have to do with the scope of the project and its requirements. Various factors from Table 8.3 fall into this category: wrong functionality, gold plating, requirements volatility. Project managers should be able to control this type of risk.

- C3: Risks that concern the execution of the project: staffing, methodology, planning, control. Factors such as personnel shortfall and an unrealistic schedule or budget belong to this category. Again, project managers should be able to control these risks.

- C4: Risks that result from changes in the environment, such as changes in the organization in which the system is to be embedded, or dependencies on outsourcing partners. Project managers often have few means to control these risks.

Level of control

		low	high
relative importance	low	customers and users (C1)	scope and requirements (C2)
	high	environment (C4)	execution (C3)

Figure 8.1 Risk categories

From a study of a large number of projects, Wallace and Keil (2004) found that risk categories C2 and C3 affect project outcomes most. They also found that execution risks (C3) are much more important in explaining process outcome than scope or requirements risks. This would suggest an ordering amongst the types of risks that managers had better pay attention to: first C3, then C2, and finally C4 and C1.

When you return to Table 8.3 after having studied the remainder of this book, you will note that many of the risk factors listed are extensively addressed in various chapters. These risk factors present themselves as cost drivers in cost estimation models, as drivers for user involvement in requirements engineering and design, as the focus of process models, such as prototyping and XP, and so on. As Tom Gilb says: 'If you don't actively attack the risks, they will actively attack you' (Gilb, 1988, p. 72).

8.4 TECHNIQUES FOR PROJECT PLANNING AND CONTROL

A project consists of a series of activities. We may graphically depict the project and its constituent activities by a **work breakdown structure** (WBS). The WBS reflects the decomposition of a project into subtasks down to a level needed for effective planning and control. Figure 8.2 contains a very simple example of a work breakdown structure for a software development project. The activities depicted at the leaf nodes of the work breakdown structure correspond to unit tasks, while the higher-level nodes constitute composite tasks. We will assume that each activity has a well-defined beginning and end that is indicated by a milestone, a scheduled event for which some person is held accountable and which is used to measure and control progress. The end of an activity is often a deliverable, such as a design document, while the start of an activity is often triggered by the end of some other activity.

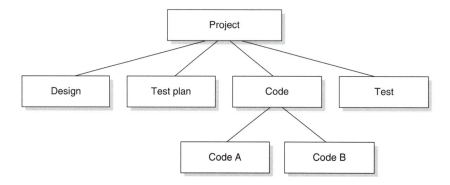

Figure 8.2 Simple work breakdown structure for a software development project

Activities usually consume resources, such as people or computer time, and always have a certain duration. Activities must often be executed in a specific order. For example, we can not test a module before it is coded. This type of relation between tasks can be expressed as constraints. Usually, the constraints concern temporal relations between activities. Such constraints are also called precedence relations. Project planning involves the scheduling of all activities such that the constraints are satisfied and the resource limits are not exceeded. Several techniques are available to support this scheduling task.

The activities from the simple work breakdown structure of a software development project, together with their duration and temporal constraints, are given in Table 8.4. Note that Table 8.4 contains more information on temporal relations than is given in Figure 8.2. Though the left-to-right reading of the work breakdown structure suggests a certain time ordering, it does not give the precise precedence relations between activities.

Table 8.4 Activities, their duration, and temporal constraints

Activity	Duration	Constraints
Design	10	—
Test plan	5	Design finished
Code A	10	Design finished
Code B	5	Design finished
Test	10	Code finished, Test plan finished

The set of activities and their constraints can also be depicted in a network. For our example, this network is given in Figure 8.3. The nodes in the network denote activities. This type of network is therefore known as an 'activity-on-node' network. Each node also carries a weight, the duration of the corresponding activity. An arrow from node A to node B indicates that activity A has to be finished before activity B can start. These network diagrams are often termed Program Evaluation and Review Technique (PERT) charts. PERT charts were developed and first used successfully in the management of the Polaris missile program in the 1950s. While the original PERT technique was concerned solely with the time span of activities and their interrelations, subsequent developments have led to a variety of techniques that accommodate an increasing number of project factors.

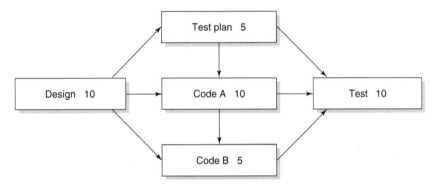

Figure 8.3 PERT chart

From the PERT chart we may compute the earliest possible point in time at which the project can be completed. Let us assume that the network has a unique start node B and end node E. If there is more than one node with in-degree 0 (i.e. having no predecessors in the network), a new start node B is created with outgoing edges to all nodes having in-degree 0. This new node B gets a zero weight (duration). A similar procedure is followed to create the end node E if there is more than one node having out-degree 0.

We next label each node i in the network with an ordered pair of numbers (S_i, the earliest possible time at which activity i can start, and F_i), the earliest possible time at which activity i can finish. The algorithm for doing so involves a breadth-first search of the network (cf. (Boehm, 1981)):

1. The start node B is labeled $(0, D_B)$, where D_B is the duration of activity B.

2. For all unlabeled nodes whose predecessors are all labeled nodes, the earliest possible starting time is the latest finishing time of all the predecessor nodes:

$$S_N = \max_{i \in P(N)} F_i$$

where $P(N)$ is the set of predecessor nodes of N.

The corresponding finishing time is $F_N = S_N + D_N$, where D_N is the duration of activity N.

Node N is labeled as (S_N, F_N).

3. Repeat Step 2 until all nodes have been labeled.

The earliest possible finishing time of the whole project now equals F_E, E being the end node of the network. We may subsequently compute the latest point in time at which activity L should finish: for each node N,

$$L_N = \min_{i \in Q(N)} S_i$$

where $Q(N)$ is the set of successor nodes of N.

The results of this computation can be presented graphically in a **Gantt chart** (these charts are named after their inventor). In a Gantt chart, the time span of each activity is depicted by the length of a segment drawn on a calendar. The Gantt chart of our software development example is given in Figure 8.4. The gray areas show slack (or float) times of activities. It indicates that the corresponding activity may consume more than its estimated time, or start later than the earliest possible starting time, without affecting the total duration of the project. For each activity N, the corresponding segment in the Gantt chart starts at time S_N and ends at L_N.

Activities without slack time are on a **critical path**. If activities on a critical path are delayed, the total project is delayed. Note that there is always at least one sequence of activities that constitutes a critical path.

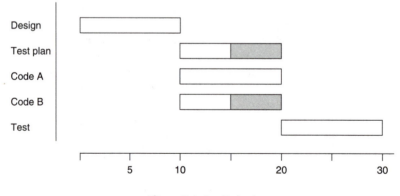

Figure 8.4 Gantt chart

In an 'activity-on-node' network, the activities are depicted as nodes, while the arrows denote precedence relations between activities. Alternatively, we may depict a set of interrelated activities in an 'activity-on-arrow' network. In an activity-on-arrow network, the arrows denote activities, while the nodes represent the completion of milestone events. Figure 8.5 depicts the example as an activity-on-arrow network. The latter representation is intuitively appealing, especially if the length of an arrow reflects the duration of the corresponding activity. Note that this type of network may have to contain dummy activities which are not needed in the activity-on-node network. These dummy activities represent synchronization of interrelated activities. In our example, dummy activities (arrows) are needed to make sure that the *test* activity is not started until the *test plan*, *code A* and *code B* activities have all been completed.

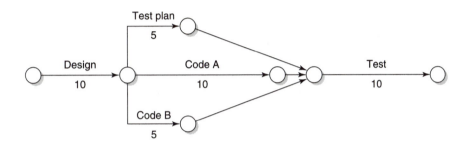

Figure 8.5 An activity-on-arrow network

The PERT technique has evolved considerably since its inception 50 years ago. For example, as well as expressing a constraint that activity B may start only after an activity A has ended, we may also specify that activity B may only start after activity C has started. We may also extend the technique so that it handles resource constraints. For instance, if we have only one programmer available, the Gantt chart of Figure 8.4 would not work, since it assumes that coding of modules A and B is done in parallel. The PERT technique may even be extended further to allow for sensitivity analysis. By allowing so-called 'what-if' questions ('what if we allocate three designers rather than four?', 'what if coding of module A takes two months rather than one?'), we get a feeling for the sensitivity of a schedule to certain variations in resource levels, schedule overruns, and so on.

The Critical Path Method (CPM) is, as the name suggests, a technique very similar to PERT and developed at around the same time.

In our discussion, we presented a Gantt chart as a graphical visualization of a schedule that results from network analysis. Actually, we may use a Gantt chart as a scheduling mechanism in its own right. We may simply list all activities and indicate their earliest starting time and latest ending time on the calendar. Gantt charts by themselves, however, do not carry information on dependencies between activities. This makes it hard to adjust schedules, for instance when a certain activity slips. As far as planning goes, we therefore prefer to use Gantt charts as a way of visualizing the result of network analysis.

Using the information contained in the Gantt chart and knowledge of personnel resources required for each activity, we may establish a personnel plan indicating how many people are required in each unit of time. Since personnel costs are a major part of project expenditures, this personnel plan provides a direct means for planning project expenditures.

When the project is under way, its control is based on monitoring the project's progress and expenditure. Time spent per activity per project member can be recorded on time cards. These time cards are the basis for determining cumulative effort and expenditure. The cumulative data can be compared with the planned levels of effort and expenditure. In order to judge properly whether the project is still on track, management needs progress information as well. The most common way to provide this is via milestone reports: activities cannot be considered completed until a proper report has been produced and accepted.

The Gantt chart provides a very direct means of comparing actual project status with the project schedule. Schedule slippage shows itself immediately. Slippage of activities on a critical path then necessitates prompt management action to renegotiate the schedule, the project's deliverables, or both. Note that schedule slippage is a sneaky affair; projects get behind one day at a time. Note also that project schedules should at any point in time reflect the true project. An accepted change necessitates reconsideration of the schedule.

Gantt charts, work breakdown structures and similar planning instruments focus on the tasks needed to create a product. Cohn (2006) mentions several reasons why such a task-oriented approach to planning is problematic:

- Activities never finish early. Parkinson's Law says 'Work expands to fill the time available.' If a developer gets ten days to develop some component, it will take ten days, not nine or eight. If needed, the time allocated can always be filled with gold-plating activities.

- Lateness is passed down the schedule. Consider the Gantt chart in Figure 8.4. In order to be able to start testing earlier than planned, *both* the design task and the coding of component A must finish earlier than planned. However, if *either* of these tasks is late, then the testing task will start late as well.

- Tasks are not independent. If the design task of Figure 8.4 turns out to take longer than expected, most likely the coding and testing tasks will also take longer than expected.

Agile planning focuses on the features in the product, not on the tasks to realize those features. Agile planning is very much tied to the incremental approach, where each iteration starts with prioritizing the features to be implemented. The following factors play a role in the agile planning process (Cohn, 2006):

- The value of the features. This can be expressed in monetary terms, considering for example the expected number of copies sold, the return on investment (how quickly money invested will increase in value) or the discounted payback period (how long does it take to earn back the investment, taking into account that money received in the future is worth less than money received today) (Tockey, 2004).

Since it may be difficult to express the return in monetary terms, an alternative is to have a sorted MoSCoW list or to consider the desirability of features derived from a Kano model (see Section 9.1.4, where we discuss prioritizing requirements).

- The cost of implementing the features. As a first approximation, this simply amounts to calculating money expended now to implement the feature now. But it is often worth while to look a bit further. Implementing a feature now may incur higher costs for other features implemented later on. Conversely, implementing a feature at a later stage may be cheaper, for instance because we can use some technology developed or available by that time.

- New knowledge acquired by implementing the features. This knowledge concerns both the product and the process. More knowledge about the product allows for better decision making as to what to implement and how. Better knowledge about the process increases insight in the effectiveness of the team, skills of developers, and so on. Both decrease uncertainty, and it is wise to give priority to implementing those features that bring a lot of new knowledge.

- The risk removed by implementing the features. Suppose we categorize features as high risk or low risk and high value or low value. Then the preferred order is to first implement the high-risk–high-value features. These features give the most value *and* they eliminate significant risk. Next, preference should be given to implementing the high-value–low-risk features followed by the low-risk–low-value features. For obvious reasons, high-risk–low-value features had better be avoided altogether.

Of these four factors, the one expressing the value of a set of features is the main selection criterion.

8.5 SUMMARY

In this chapter, we looked at project control from a systems point of view and gained insight into how different kinds of projects can be managed and controlled. We identified four archetypal situations, which demand different process models, coordination mechanisms and management styles.

Real projects face many risks and it is a wise project manager who pays attention to them early on. A risk is a possible future negative event that may affect success. It is not a problem yet, but it may become one. Risk management is concerned with *preventing* risks from becoming problems. It involves the following steps:

1. Identify the risk factors.

2. Determine the risk exposure, i.e. the probability that a risk will happen, multiplied by its cost.

3. Develop strategies to mitigate risks, especially those with a high risk exposure. Risks may be avoided, transferred, or accepted.

4. Handle the risks: monitor risk factors and take action when needed.

In Section 8.4, we focused on the planning and control of activities within a project. By depicting the set of activities and their temporal relations in a graph, techniques such as PERT offer a simple yet powerful means to schedule and control these activities (see, for example, (Boehm, 1981)). PERT and similar techniques focus on the tasks required to create a product. They may work well if the product is known, but they are not very well suited to handle all of the uncertainties inherent in many a software development project. Agile planning focuses on the features that make up a product and allows for better adjustments as we go along.

8.6 FURTHER READING

Some general software project management sources are: (Boehm, 1981), (Brooks, 1995), (Humphrey, 1997b) and (Royce, 1998). Highsmith (2004) and Cohn (2006) focus on agile project management, while Boehm and Turner (2003) and Karlström and Runeson (2005) discuss how to combine agile and plan-based approaches. Boehm and Turner (2005) discuss how to implement agile processes in a traditional environment. Software (2005) is a special journal issue on adapting agility.

The discussion in Section 8.2 is based on (Heemstra, 1989).

Boehm (1989) gives a good overview of software risk management. Risk management experiences are reported on in (Software, 1997a). The risk categories discussed in Section 8.3 stem from (Wallace and Keil, 2004). Pfleeger (2000) compares software risk management with risk management in other disciplines.

Exercises

1. List the conditions for effective systems control.

2. Is the waterfall approach suitable for a realization-type problem? If so, why?

3. Is the waterfall approach suitable for an exploration-type problem? If so, why?

4. What is risk management?

5. How can risks be mitigated?

6. Rephrase the cost drivers of the COCOMO cost-estimation model as risk factors.

7. What is a work breakdown structure?

8. What is a PERT chart?

9. What is a Gantt chart?

10. Describe the factors taken into account in agile planning.

11. ♠ Classify a project you have been involved in with respect to product certainty, process certainty, and resource certainty. Which of the archetypal situations sketched in Section 8.2 best fits this project? In what ways did the actual project control differ from that suggested for the situation identified? Can you explain possible differences?

12. ♡ Consider the patient planning system mentioned in Exercise 3.13. Suppose the project team consists of several analysts and two members of the hospital staff. The analysts have a lot of experience in the design of planning systems, though not for hospitals. As a manager of this team, which coordination mechanism and management style would you opt for?

13. ♡ Discuss the pros and cons of a hierarchical and a matrix team organization for the patient-planning project.

14. ♠ Consider a project you have been involved in. Identify the major irregular, control, and goal variables for this project. In what ways did the control variables influence project control?

15. ♡ Suppose one of your team members is dissatisfied with his situation. He has been involved in similar projects for several years now. You have assigned him these jobs because he was performing so well. Discuss possible actions to prevent this employee from leaving the organization.

16. ♡ Why is planning (i.e., the activity) more important than the plan (the document)?

17. ♡ Suppose you are the manager of a project that is getting seriously behind schedule. Your team is having severe problems with testing a particular subsystem. Your client is pressing you to deliver the system on time. How would you handle this situation? How would you handle the situation if you were a member of the team and your manager was not paying serious attention to your signals?

Part II

The Software Life Cycle

CONTENTS

When designing a garden, you begin by formulating your requirements – how large should the grass area be? should you leave a corner to raise potatoes? where should the sand-bin be put? do the requirements interfere with future maintenance work on the house (!)? etc. After that, a design is drawn up, which is carefully documented in a blueprint. Only then will the gardener cut the first sod.

A similar approach is followed when developing software. In a number of phases – requirements engineering, design, implementation, and testing – the software system will take shape. After the software is delivered to the client, it must be maintained. Reiteration of phases occurs because changes have to be incorporated and errors must be corrected. The result is a highly cyclical process, the 'software life cycle'.

The various phases of the initial development cycle are the topics of Chapters 9–13, and Chapter 14 is devoted to software maintenance. In each phase, modeling techniques are used to represent the results of that phase. A sample of well-known modeling techniques is discussed in Chapter 10. In each phase, also, tools are employed. The main classes of tools and their role in the software development process are discussed in Chapter 15.

9

Requirements Engineering

LEARNING OBJECTIVES

- To understand that requirements engineering is a cyclical process involving four types of activity: elicitation, specification, validation, and negotiation

- To appreciate the role of social and cognitive issues in requirements engineering

- To be able to distinguish a number of requirements elicitation techniques

- To be aware of the contents of a requirements specification document

- To know various techniques and notations for specifying requirements

- To know different ways to structure a set of requirements

This chapter covers requirements engineering, the first major phase in a software development project. The most challenging and difficult aspect of requirements engineering is to get a complete description of the problem to be solved. We discuss a number of techniques for eliciting requirements from the user. Following elicitation, these requirements must be negotiated, validated, and documented.

> The hardest single part of building a system is deciding what to build.
>
> Brooks (1987)

The requirements engineering phase is the first major step towards the solution of a data-processing problem. During this phase, the user's requirements with respect to the future system are carefully identified and documented. These requirements concern both the functions to be provided and a number of additional requirements, such as performance, reliability, user documentation, user training, cost, and so on. During the requirements engineering phase, we do not yet address the question of *how* to achieve these user requirements in terms of system components and their interaction. This is postponed until the design phase.

A requirement is 'a condition or capability needed by a user to solve a problem or achieve an objective' (IEEE610, 1990). The 'user' alluded to in this definition may be an end user of the system, a person behind the screen. However, it may also denote several classes of indirect users, such as people who do not themselves turn the knobs but rather use the information that the system delivers. It may also denote the client (customer) who pays the bill. During requirements engineering, different types of user may be the source of different types of requirements. Hopefully, the end users will be the main source of information regarding the functional, task-related requirements. Other requirements, e.g. those that relate to security issues, may well be phrased by other stakeholders.

The word 'requirement' suggests that, once stated, it **has** to be met. In reality, this is hardly ever the case. Most requirements are negotiable. Time to market, cost, conflicting quality requirements, and conflicting needs of stakeholders all lead to a situation where tradeoffs may have to be made.

The result of the requirements engineering phase is documented in the **requirements specification**. The requirements specification reflects the mutual understanding of the problem to be solved between the analyst and the client. It is the basis for a contract, be it formal or informal, between the client of the system and the development organization. Eventually, the system delivered will be assessed by testing its compliance with the requirements specification.

The requirements specification serves as a starting point for the design phase. In the design phase, the architecture of the system is devised in terms of system components and interfaces between those components. The design phase results in a specification as well: a precise description – preferably in some formal language – of the architecture, its components, and its interfaces.

The notion 'specification' thus has several meanings. To prevent confusion, we will always use the prefix 'requirements' if it denotes the result of the requirements engineering phase. To make matters worse, the phase in which the user's requirements are analyzed and documented is also sometimes called the 'specification' phase. We feel this to be somewhat of a misnomer and will not use the term in this way.

We use the term **requirements engineering** rather than the narrower notion of **requirements analysis** to emphasize that it is an iterative and cooperative process of analyzing a problem, documenting the resulting observations, and checking the accuracy of the understanding gained. Requirements engineering not only involves technical concerns of how to represent the requirements. Social and cognitive aspects play a dominant role as well.

Requirements engineering and design generally cannot be strictly separated in time. In some cases, the requirements specification is very formal and can be viewed as a high-level design specification of the system to be built. Often, a preliminary design is done after an initial set of requirements has been determined. Based on the result of this design effort, the requirements specification may be changed and refined. This type of iteration also occurs when prototyping techniques are being used. In pure agile development projects, requirements emerge concurrently with an up-and-running system. Well-known techniques such as data flow diagrams and UML class diagrams are used to structure and document both requirements specifications and designs.

It is only for ease of presentation that the requirements engineering and design phases are strictly separated and treated consecutively in this book.

During requirements engineering, a number of quite different matters are being addressed. Let us look at an example and consider the (hypothetical) case of a university's library automating its operation. We start with the library containing a number of cabinets. These cabinets hold a huge number of cards, one per book. Each card contains the names of the authors, the book title, ISBN, publication year, and other useful data. The cards are ordered alphabetically by the name of the first author of each book.

This ordering system in fact presents major problems as it only works well if we know the first author's name. If we only know the title, or if we are interested in books on a certain topic, the author catalog is of little or no help.

A software solution seems obvious. If we store the data for each book once in a database, we may subsequently sort the entries in many different ways. Appropriate tools can enable the user to search the database interactively. By providing Internet access to the database, service can be greatly enhanced.

During the requirements engineering phase, a number of user requirements will be raised. Some of those requirements will concern updating the database: that is, adding, deleting, and changing records. Others will concern functions to be provided to ordinary members of the library, such as:

- giving a list of all books written by X;

- giving a list of all books whose title contains Y;

- giving a list of all books on topic Z;

- giving a list of all books that arrived after date D.

It is expedient to try to group user requirements into a few categories, ranging from 'essential requirements' to 'nice features'. As noted in Chapter 3, users tend to have difficulties in articulating their real needs. Chances are, then, that much effort is spent on realizing features which later turn out to be mere bells and whistles. By using a layered scheme in both the formulation of user requirements and their subsequent realization, some of the problems that beset software development projects can be circumvented. In our library system example, for instance, the requirement 'Give a list of all books that arrived after date D' could be classified as a nice feature. Service is not seriously degraded if this function is not provided, since we may temporarily place the acquisitions on a dedicated shelf.

It is also possible to try to predict a number of future requirements, which will not be implemented in the present project. It is, however, sensible to pay attention to these matters at an early stage, so that they can be accommodated during the design of the system. Possible future requirements of our library system could include such things as:

- storing information about books that have been ordered but have not been received;

- storing information about library members, such as their name and address, and the dates on which books are lent to them, which can then be used to generate a reminder notice for books not returned on time.

The above functions concern the use of the software by library members and library personnel. There are other stakeholders as well, though. For example, library management may wish to use the system to get information on member profiles in order to improve the title acquisition process.

Besides these requirements, which directly relate to the functions of the software to be delivered, a number of other matters should be addressed during the requirements engineering phase. For our library example, as a minimum, the following points have to be addressed:

- On which machine will the system be implemented and which operating system will be used? If the data is to be stored in a DBMS, which (type of) DBMS is to be used? What type of access is to be used and how many access points will be supported?

- Which classes of users can be distinguished? In our example, both library personnel and library members will have to be served. What kind of knowledge do these users have? Will certain functions of the system be restricted to certain classes of user? Normal library members will probably not be allowed to update the database or print the contents of the database.

- What is the size of the database and how is it expected to grow in the course of time? These factors influence both storage capacity needed and algorithms to be used. For a database containing several thousands of books, some not very efficient searching algorithm might suffice. For the Library of Congress, the situation is quite different, though.

- What response time should the system offer? A search request for a certain book will have to be answered fairly quickly. If the user has to wait too long for an answer, he will become dissatisfied and search the shelves directly. Related questions concern the interaction between response time and the expected number of question sessions per unit of time.

- How much will a system of this kind cost? In our library example, we should not only pay attention to the direct costs incurred by the software development effort. The cost of converting the information contained in the present file cabinets to a suitable database format should not be neglected. These, less visible, indirect costs may well outweigh the direct cost of designing and implementing the new system.

This relatively simple example already shows that it is not sufficient to merely list the functional requirements of the new system.

The system's envisioned environment and its interaction with that environment should be analyzed as well. In our example, this concerns the library itself, to start with. The consequences of introducing a system like this one can be much greater than it seems at first sight. Working procedures may change, necessitating retraining of personnel, changes in personnel functions and changes in the overall organizational structure. Some members of staff may even become redundant. Checking whether membership fees have been paid might involve interfacing with the financial system, owned by another department.

In general, the setting up of an automated system may have more than just technical repercussions. Often, not enough attention is paid to these other repercussions. The lack of success of many software development projects can be traced back to a neglect of non-technical aspects.

In practice, the requirements engineering process is often more complex than sketched above:

- Ordinary library automation is a relatively well-known domain, where we may expect users to be able to articulate their requirements. But suppose our library system also has to support elderly people in their dealings with the world around them, including daily news, relevant government regulations, information about healthcare, and the like. For the latter type of support, a more agile approach seems more appropriate, where the requirements emerge as we go along, rather than being elicited up front.

- Much software developed today is *market-driven* rather than *customer-driven*. For example, rather than developing a system for one specific library, we could develop a 'generic' library application. Requirements for this generic library application are created by exploring the library domain, while tradeoffs between requirements are based on market considerations, product fit, and so on. We may decide that our system need not address the concerns of the Library of Congress (too small a market), but that it should definitely interface with accounting system Y, since that system is widely used in university departments, and this is perceived to be an important market for our library application.

- For various reasons (cost, time to market, and quality), we may want to employ commercial off-the-shelf (COTS) components in our library system. We then have to trade off our requirements against the possibilities offered by those COTS components.

Following Sommerville (2005), we distinguish four processes in requirements engineering:

- **Requirements elicitation** In general, the requirements analyst is not an expert in the domain being modeled. Through interaction with domain specialists, such as professional librarians, he has to build himself a sufficiently rich model of that domain. Thus, requirements elicitation is about *understanding* the problem. The fact that different disciplines are involved in this process complicates matters. In many cases, the analyst is not a mere outside observer of the domain to be modeled, simply eliciting facts from domain specialists. He may have to take a stand in a power struggle or decide between conflicting requirements, thereby actively participating in the construction of the domain of interest. Section 9.1 discusses various issues related to, and a number of techniques used in, requirements elicitation.

- **Requirements specification** Once the problem is understood, it has to be *described*. In Section 9.2, we give guidelines for the contents of a requirements specification document. This document describes the product to be delivered, not the process of how it is developed. Project requirements are described in the project plan, discussed in Chapter 2. The collection of requirements not only has to be documented, it also has to be managed during the course of a project. Quite a number of techniques exist for specifying requirements, ranging from very informal (natural language) to very formal (mathematical). Throughout this book, a number of such modeling techniques are discussed, such as those of UML in Chapter 10 and techniques for specifying quality requirements in Chapter 6. The design techniques discussed in Chapter 12 are often also used for specifying requirements. Section 9.3 is confined to a discussion of some global techniques for modeling requirements.

- **Requirements validation and verification** Once the problem is described, the different parties involved have to *agree upon* its nature. We have to ascertain that the correct requirements are stated (validation) and that these requirements are stated correctly (verification). Some verification and validation techniques that can be applied at this early stage are sketched in Section 9.4.

- **Requirements negotiation** Usually, requirements have to be negotiated. Because of time constraints or other factors, a selection may have to be made from the list of requirements put forth. Or stakeholders may have conflicts that need to be resolved. Often, stakeholders have conflicting quality requirements whose impact can only be determined by looking at the software architecture. This is further dealt with in Chapter 11.

Obviously, these processes involve iteration and feedback. In document-driven approaches, these iterations precede design and implementation. In agile processes, design and implementation are part of the iteration and feedback loop. In either case, there is a central repository in which the requirements are documented. The major interactions are shown in Figure 9.1.

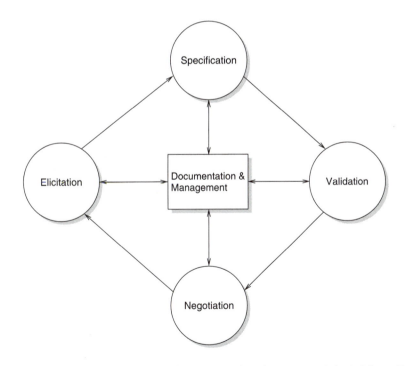

Figure 9.1 A framework for the requirements engineering process (adapted from (Sommerville, 2005))

The emphasis in our discussion of requirements engineering will be on modeling the external behavior of the system, i.e. all those parts and aspects of the system that *end users* consider important. Other views are relevant as well, for instance, a model which highlights the way the system supports the business or which indicates how a system is deployed on a collection of hardware devices. Some of these other views are discussed in Chapter 11.

9.1 REQUIREMENTS ELICITATION

In Chapter 1, the first part of the software life cycle was depicted as shown in Figure 9.2. The fact that the text 'requirements specification' is placed in a rectangle suggests, not unjustly, that it concerns something very concrete and explicit. The 'problem' is less well defined, less clear, even fuzzy in many cases. The primary goal of the requirements engineering phase is to elicit the contours and constituents of this fuzzy problem. This process is also known as **conceptual modeling**.

During requirements engineering we are modeling part of reality. The part of reality in which we are interested is referred to as the **universe of discourse** (UoD). Example universes of discourse are a library system, a factory automation system, an assembly line, and an elevator system.

The model constructed during the requirements engineering phase is an **explicit conceptual model** of the UoD. The adjective 'explicit' indicates that the model must be able to be communicated to the relevant people (such as analysts and users). To this end, it should contain all relevant information from the UoD. One of the persistent problems of requirements analysis and, for that matter, analysis in general, is to account for all of the relevant influences and leave out irrelevant details.

In our library example, we could easily have overlooked the fact that in a number of cases the author's name as it appears on the cover of a book is not the 'canonical' author's name. This phenomenon occurs in particular with authors from countries that use non-Latin scripts. The transcription of the Russian name чехов reads 'Chekhov' in English and 'Tsjechow' in Dutch. In such cases, librarians want to include the author's name twice: once as it is spelled on the book and once as it is spelled in the various

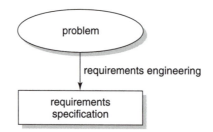

Figure 9.2 The first part of the software life cycle

search processes. An answer to a question such as 'which books by Chekhov does our library possess?' should also inform us about the non-English titles.

Subtle mismatches between the analyst's notion of terms and concepts and their proper meaning within the domain being modeled can have profound effects. Such mismatches can most easily occur in domains we already 'know', such as a library. An illuminating discussion of potential problems in (formally) specifying the requirements of a library system can be found in (Wing, 1988). Problems noted include:

- A library employee may also be a member of the library, so the two sets of system users are not disjoint.

- There is a difference between a book (identified by its ISBN) and the (physical) copies of a book owned by the library.

- It is not sufficient to simply denote the status of a book by a Boolean value (present or not present, i.e. lent out). For instance, a book or, more properly, a copy of a book, may be lost, stolen, or in repair.

People involved in a UoD have an **implicit conceptual model** of that UoD. An implicit conceptual model consists of the background knowledge shared by people in the UoD. The fact that this knowledge is shared gives rise to 'of course' statements by people from within the UoD, because this knowledge is taken for granted. ('Of course, a copy of a book is not the same as a book.') Part of the implicit conceptual model is not verbalized. It contains tacit knowledge, knowledge that is skillfully applied and functions in the background. Finally, an implicit conceptual model contains habits, customs, prejudices, and even inconsistencies.

During conceptual modeling, an implicit conceptual model is turned into an explicit one. In doing so, the analyst is confronted with two types of problem: analysis problems and negotiation problems. Analysis problems arise from the fact that part of the implicit conceptual model is not verbalized, that the implicit conceptual model evolves with time, that the user and analyst talk a different language, and that the implicit conceptual model cannot be completely codified. Negotiation problems arise because people in the UoD may counteract the analysis process, because the implicit conceptual models of people in the UoD may differ, or because of opposing interests of the people involved (such as library personnel versus their managers). Both types of problems are discussed below.

The problem to be addressed by the automated system arises from the user, a human. This person must be able to describe the problem in both a correct and complete way. It must be communicated to a person who in general has a rather different background. The analyst often lacks a sufficiently profound knowledge of the application domain in which the problem originated. He has to learn the language of the application domain and become acquainted with its terminology, concepts and procedures. Especially in large projects, the application knowledge tends to be thinly spread amongst the specialists involved, which easily leads to integration and coordination difficulties.

In many cases, it makes sense to distinguish between properties that denote some objective truth about the domain being modeled and properties one would like to hold in the system to be developed. Jackson (2001) uses the terms **indicative** for domain properties and **optative** for user requirements. Indicative properties simply have to be dealt with. Optative properties are subject to debate and negotiation. The library example already shows that the distinction between these two types of properties is not always easy to make.

In our earlier example, the librarian has to express his wishes. It is possible that the inclusion of two author names ('Tsjechow' and 'Chekhov') is seen as an obvious detail which need not be brought forward explicitly. The analyst at the other side of the table may still get the impression that he has a complete picture of the system. This type of omission may have severe consequences.

> A number of years back, a large automated air defense system was being developed in the US. During one of the final tests of this system, an alarm signal was issued. One of the computers detected an unknown missile. It turned out to be the moon. This possibility had not been thought of.

Eliciting correct and complete information is an important prerequisite for success. This turns out to be rather problematic in practice. Asking the prospective user what is wanted does not generally work. More often than not we get a rather incomplete and inaccurate picture of the situation. Important reasons for this are human limitations for processing information, selecting information, and solving problems. These limited human capabilities are aggravated by such factors as:

- the complexity and variation in requirements that can be imposed upon software;

- the differences in background between the client, or user, and the software specialist.

In research on human information processing, one often uses a model in which human memory consists of two components: short-term memory in which information is processed and long-term memory in which permanent knowledge is stored. Short-term memory has a limited capacity: one often says that it has about seven slots. Long-term memory on the other hand has a very large capacity. So, information is processed in a relatively small part of human memory. Long-term memory is thus accessed in an indirect way. In addition, humans also employ external memories when information is processed: a blackboard, a piece of paper, etc.

If a person being interviewed during requirements engineering uses only his short-term memory, the limitations of it may have an impact on the results. This may easily occur if no use is made of external memories. Things can be forgotten, simply because our short-term memory has limited capacity.

Humans are also inclined to be prejudiced about selecting and using information. We are, in particular, inclined to let recent events prevail. In making up a requirements specification, this leads to requirements bearing on the present situation, presently available information, recent events, etc.

Humans are not very capable of rational thinking. They will simplify things and use a model which does not really fit reality. Other limitations that influence our model of reality are determined by such factors as education, prejudice, practice, etc. This same kind of simplification occurs when software requirements are drawn up, and the result will be limited by the same factors.

We cannot always expect the user to be able to precisely state his requirements at an early stage. One reason for investigating the opportunities of automation is often because of a certain dissatisfaction with the present situation. People are not satisfied with the present situation and have the impression that automation will help. Whether this is true or not – many data processing problems are organizational problems – simply automating the present situation is not always the solution. Something different is wanted, though it is not clear what. Only when insight into the possibilities of automation is gained will real requirements show themselves. This is one of the reasons for the sheer size of the maintenance problem. About half of the maintenance effort concerns adapting software to (new) requirements of the user. To counteract this trend, software development process models that acknowledge this learning process, such as prototyping, incremental development, and agile methods are to be preferred over those that do not, i.e. the waterfall model and its variants. The most extreme form is to have no requirements engineering phase at all, but to pick up what emerges from the collaborative effort of a large group of people, as happens in Wikipedia. This is discussed in Section 9.1.6.

Through a careful analysis, we may hope to build a sound perspective of user requirements and anticipate future changes. However, no matter how much time is spent in a dialog with the prospective users, future changes remain hard to foresee. We may go a step further and stipulate that requirements will *never* be complete. In this respect, specifying requirements has much in common with forecasting the weather: there is a limit to how far the future can be predicted.

In a situation where the goal of a software development project is to improve an existing 'system', be it a manual process or a (partly) automated one, it is generally helpful to explicitly distinguish two modeling steps. In the first step, the current situation is modeled. Based on an analysis of the strengths and weaknesses of the current situation, the situation-to-be is next modeled. Business process redesign (BPR), in particular, stresses the distinction between these two modeling steps.

For the requirements engineering phase to be successful, we need methods and techniques that try to bypass the difficulties sketched above. The degree to which powerful techniques are required depends on the experience of the people involved in the requirements engineering phase (both users and analysts) and the expertise of the analyst with the application domain. Section 9.1.2 discusses a number of techniques for requirements elicitation.

But before we discuss these techniques, we first elaborate in Section 9.1.1 how different world views result in different approaches to requirements engineering.

In Section 9.1.3, we discuss how requirements relate to higher-level goals and how different viewpoints may result in different, and sometimes conflicting, sets of requirements. In Sections 9.1.4 and 9.1.5, we discuss how to prioritize requirements and how requirements relate to the selection of COTS components.

9.1.1 Requirements Engineering Paradigms

Most requirements engineering methods, and software development methods in general, are Taylorian in nature. Around the turn of the 20th century, Taylor introduced the notion of 'scientific management', in which tasks are recursively decomposed into simpler tasks and each task has one 'best way' to accomplish it. By careful observations and experiments this one best way can be found and formalized into procedures and rules. Scientific management has been successfully applied in many a factory operation. The equivalent in requirements engineering is to interview domain experts and observe end users at work in order to obtain the 'real' user requirements. After this, the experts go to work and implement these requirements. During the latter process, there is no further need to interact with the user community. This view of software development is a functional, and rational, one. Its underlying assumption is that there is one objective truth, which merely needs to be discovered during the analysis process.

Though this view has its merits in drawing up requirements in purely *technical* realms, many universes of discourse involve people as well – people whose model of the world is incomplete, subjective, irrational, and may conflict with the world view of others. In such cases, the analyst is not a passive outside observer of the UoD. Rather, he actively participates in the *shaping* of the UoD.

It is increasingly being recognized that the Taylorian, functional, approach is not the only, and need not be the most appropriate, approach to the requirements engineering process.

Analysts have a set of assumptions about the nature of the subject of study. Such a set of assumptions is commonly called a 'paradigm'. In our field, these assumptions concern the way in which analysts acquire knowledge (epistemological assumptions) and their view of the social and technical world (ontological assumptions).

The assumptions about knowledge result in an objectivist–subjectivist dimension. If the analyst takes the objectivist point of view, he applies models and methods derived from the natural sciences to arrive at the one and only truth. In the subjectivist position, the analyst's principal concern is to understand how the individual creates, modifies, and interprets the world he is in.

The assumptions about the world result in an order–conflict dimension. The order point of view emphasizes order, stability, integration, and consensus. On the other hand, the conflict view stresses change, conflict, and disintegration. These two dimensions and their associated extreme positions yield four paradigms for requirements engineering and, more generally, information systems development:

- **Functionalism** (objective–order). In the functionalist paradigm, the developer is the system expert who searches for measurable cause–effect relationships. An empirical organizational reality is believed to exist, independent of the observer. Systems are developed to support rational organizational operation. Their effectiveness and efficiency can be tested objectively, by tests similar to those used in other engineering disciplines.

- **Social-relativism** (subjective–order). In this paradigm, the analyst operates as a facilitator. Reality is not something immutable 'out there' but is constructed in the human mind. The analyst is a change agent. He seeks to facilitate the learning of all people involved.

- **Radical-structuralism** (objective–conflict). In the radical paradigm the key assumption is that system development intervenes in the conflict between two or more social classes for power, prestige, and resources. Systems are often developed to support the interests of the owners, at the expense of the interests of the labor force. In order to redress the power balance, this paradigm suggests that the analyst should act as a labor partisan. System requirements should evolve from a cooperation between the labor force and the analyst. This approach is thought to lead to systems that enhance craftsmanship and working conditions.

- **Neohumanism** (subjective–conflict). The central theme in this paradigm is emancipation. Systems are developed to remove distorting influences and other barriers to rational discourse. The system developer acts as a social therapist in an attempt to draw together, in an open discussion, a diverse group of individuals, including customers, the labor force, and various levels of management.

Admittedly, these paradigms reflect extreme orientations. In practice, some mixture of assumptions will usually guide the requirements engineering process. Yet it is fair to say that most system development techniques emphasize the functionalist view.

In the subjectivist–objectivist dimension, it is important to realize that a good deal of subjectivism may be involved in the shaping of the UoD. If we have to develop a system to control a copying machine, we may safely take a functional stand. We may expect such a machine to operate purely rationally. In the analysis process, we list the functions of the machine, its internal signals, conditions, and so on, in order to get a satisfactory picture of the system to be developed. Once these requirements are identified, they can be frozen and some waterfall-like process model can be employed to realize the system. If, however, our task is to develop a system to support people in doing their job, such as some office automation system, a purely functional view of the world may easily lead to ill-conceived systems. In such cases, end-user participation in the shaping of the UoD is of paramount importance. Through an open dialog with the people concerned, we may encourage the prospective users to influence the system to be developed. Part of the analyst's job in this case is to reconcile the views of the participants in the analysis process. Continuous feedback during the actual construction phases with possibilities for redirection may further enhance the chance of success. It is the future users who are going to work with the system. It is of no avail to confront them with a system that does not satisfy their needs.

Automation transforms organizations and, thus, affects the organization's employees. It may raise fears and other emotions with the employees affected. For instance, our library system potentially gives people access to a lot more information than they previously had. Some people may prefer to have access only to information related to their tasks and responsibilities. During requirements engineering, we have to be conscious of these effects. The pure functionalist paradigm then is of no avail.

A dissatisfied user will try to neglect the system or, at best, express additional requirements immediately. The net result is that the envisaged gain in efficiency or effectiveness is not reaped.

An illuminating and well-documented example of possible effects of following a fairly radical paradigm is given in (Page *et al.*, 1993); see also Section 1.4.3. Although the computer-aided despatch system for the London Ambulance Service would significantly impact the way ambulance crews carried out their jobs, there was little consultation with them. Some of the consequences of this approach were the following (Page *et al.*, 1993, pp. 40–41):

- The system allocated the nearest available resource regardless of originating station, so crews often had to operate further and further from their home base. This resulted in them operating in unfamiliar territory with further to go to reach their home station at the end of a shift.

- The new system took away the flexibility crews previously had for the station to decide which resource to allocate. This inevitably led to problems when a different resource was used to the one that was allocated.

- A lack of voice contact made the whole process more impersonal and exacerbated the 'them and us' situation.

If the conceptual models of the participants differ, we may either look for a compromise or opt for one of the views expressed. It is impossible to give general guidelines on how to handle such cases. Looking for a compromise can be a tedious affair and may lead to a system that no one is really happy with. Opting for one particular view of the world will make one party happy, but may result in others completely neglecting the system developed. Worse yet, they may decide to develop a competing system.

9.1.2 Requirements Elicitation Techniques

The two main sources of information for the requirements elicitation process are the users and the (application) domain. These sources both presuppose that there exists something 'out there' to start with, from which requirements can be elicited. In market-driven software development though, this is often not the case; requirements elicitation in such projects is more like requirements invention or problem formulation, guided by marketing and sales considerations.

Figure 9.3 lists a number of elicitation techniques, which are elaborated upon below. The figure also tells us that the user is the major source of information in some techniques, while the domain is predominant in others. Furthermore, the figure indicates whether each technique is particularly useful for modeling the current or the anticipated future situation.

You should generally vacuum a rug in two directions rather than one; likewise, you should use multiple requirements elicitation techniques.

Technique	Main info source		Strong on	
	Domain	User	Current	Future
Interview		X	X	
Delphi technique		X	X	
Brainstorming session		X		X
Task analysis		X	X	
Scenario (use-case) analysis		X	X	X
Ethnography	X		X	
Form analysis	X		X	
Analysis of natural language descriptions	X		X	
Synthesis of reqs from an existing system	X		X	
Domain analysis	X		X	
Use of reference models	X		X	
Business process redesign (BPR)	X		X	X
Prototyping		X		X

Figure 9.3 Requirements elicitation techniques

Asking: We may simply ask the users what they expect from the system. A presupposition then is that the user is able to bypass his own limitations and prejudices. Asking may take the form of an interview, a brainstorm, or a questionnaire. In an open-ended interview, the user freely talks about his tasks. This is the easiest form of requirements elicitation but it suffers from all of the drawbacks mentioned before. In a structured interview, the analyst tries to overcome them by leading the user, for example through closed or probing questions.

In discussion sessions with a group of users, we often find that some users are far more articulate than others and thus have a greater influence on the outcome. The consensus thus reached need not be well-balanced. To overcome this problem, a Delphi technique may be employed. The Delphi technique is an iterative technique in which information is exchanged in written form until a consensus is reached. For example, participants may write down their requirements, sorted in order of importance. The sets of requirements thus obtained are distributed to all participants, who reflect on them to obtain a revised set of requirements. This procedure is repeated several times until sufficient consensus is reached.

For consumer products, such as word-processing packages, antivirus software or software for your personal administration, users often have the option to give feedback, raise questions, report bugs, and so on, electronically. This type of information is also regularly gathered and stored by sales and marketing people in the course of their contacts with customers. These logs can be mined and in this way provide a valuable source of information when looking for requirements for the next release of that software.

Task analysis: Employees working in some domain perform a number of tasks, such as handling requests to borrow a book, cataloging new books, ordering books, etc. Higher-level tasks may be decomposed into subtasks. For example, the task 'handle request to borrow a book' may lead to the following subtasks:

- check member identification,

- check for limit on the number of books that may be borrowed,

- register book as being borrowed by the library member,

- issue a slip indicating the due back date.

Task analysis is a technique to obtain a hierarchy of tasks and subtasks to be carried out by people working in the domain. Any of the other techniques discussed may be used to get the necessary information to draw this hierarchy. There are no clear-cut rules as to when to stop decomposing tasks. A major heuristic is that at some point users tend to 'refuse' to decompose tasks any further. For instance, when being asked how the member identification is checked, the library employee may say 'Well, I simply check his id.' At this point, further decomposition is meaningless.

Task analysis is often applied at the stage when (details about) the human–computer interaction component are being decided upon. This underestimates its potency as a general requirements elicitation technique. It also gives the (wrong) impression that users are only concerned with the 'look and feel' of the interface.

Scenario-based analysis: Instead of looking for generic plans, as in interviews or task analysis, the analyst may study **instances** of tasks. A scenario is a story which tells us how a specific task instance is executed. The scenario can be real or artificial. An example of a real scenario is that the analyst observes how a library employee handles an actual user request. We may ask the library employee to verbalize what he is doing and make an audio or video recording of it. This **think-aloud** method is a fairly unobtrusive technique to study people at work. It is often used to assess prototypes or existing information systems.

Alternatively, we may construct artificial scenarios and discuss them with the user. As a first shot, we may for example draw up the following scenario for returning a book:

1. The due date for the book is checked. If the book is overdue, the member is asked to pay the appropriate fine.

2. The book is recorded as being eligible for checking-out.

3. The book is put back in its proper place.

When this scenario is discussed with the library employee, a number of related issues may crop up, either through probing questions from the analyst or because the user contrasts the scenario with daily practice. Example questions that could be raised include such things as:

- What happens when the person returning the book is not a registered member of the library?

- What happens when the book returned is damaged?

- What happens if the member returning this book has other books that are overdue or an outstanding reservation for another book?

In essence, this type of story-telling provides the user with an artificial mock-up version of the software eventually to be delivered. It serves as a paper-based prototype to gain a better understanding of the requirements. If tied to UML-type modeling, scenario-based analysis is often called **use-case analysis**; see Section 10.3.6. Scenarios and use cases are the elicitation methods most often used.

Scenario-based analysis is often done in a somewhat haphazard way. In that case, there is no way of telling whether enough scenarios have been drawn up and a sufficiently accurate and complete picture of the requirements is obtained. Writing good scenarios is by no means easy. Though it may look trivial to 'just record user episodes', a fair amount of domain expertise is needed to get a good and reliable set of scenarios.

Scenarios can be looked at from different perspectives. In the above example scenario for returning a book, the scenario lists a series of actions or events that together make up some episode. The focus then is on the process aspect, showing how the system proceeds through successive states. Alternatively, the same scenario may be looked at from a user perspective: How does the user interact with the system? What functionalities is she offered? Yet another perspective is that the scenario leads to discussions about alternatives from which a certain choice has to be made, as in the questions that the example scenario above raised.

Ethnography: A major disadvantage of eliciting requirements through, for example, interviews is that the analyst imposes his view of how the world is ordered onto the user. Such methods may fail if the analyst and user do not share a category system. The analyst may, for example, ask the following question: 'If a member wants to borrow a book but has an outstanding fine, do you:

a) Refuse the request, or

b) Handle the request anyway.'

This binary choice need not map actual practice. The library employee may, for example, grant the request provided part of the outstanding fine is settled or if he knows the member to be trustworthy.

Thinking-aloud protocols are based on the idea that users have well-defined goals and subgoals, and that they traverse such goal trees in a neat top-down manner. People however often do not have preconceived plans, but rather proceed in somewhat opportunistic ways.

A disadvantage of task analysis is that it considers the individual tasks of individual people, without taking into account the social and organizational environment in which these tasks are executed.

Ethnographic methods are claimed not to have such shortcomings. In ethnography, groups of people are studied in their natural settings. It is well-known from sociology where, for example, Polynesian tribes are studied by living with them for an extended period of time. Likewise, user requirements can be studied by participating in their daily work for a period of time, for example by becoming a library employee. The analyst becomes an apprentice, recognizing that the future users of the system are the real experts in their work. Ethnographic methods are more likely to uncover tacit knowledge than most other elicitation techniques.

Form analysis: A lot of information about the domain being modeled can often be found in various forms being used. For example, to request some conference proceedings from another library, the user might have to fill in a form such as the one in Figure 9.4.

Forms provide us with information about the data objects of the domain, their properties, and their interrelations. They are particularly useful as an input to modeling the data aspect of the system; see also Section 10.1.1.

Library users often have incomplete knowledge of the information sources they are interested in. For example, someone might be looking for the proceedings of the *International Conference on Software Engineering* that took place in Berlin. Only if the

Proceedings Request Form	
Member name	....
Member address	....
	....
Title	....
Series no	....
Editor	....
Place	....
Publisher	....
Year	....
Signature	....

Figure 9.4 A sample form

various entries from the above form are used as entities in the underlying data model can such a query be answered easily. In this case, the form directly points at a useful requirement which might otherwise go unnoticed.

Natural language descriptions Like forms, natural language descriptions provide a lot of useful information about the domain to be modeled. The operating instructions for library employees might for instance contain a paragraph like the one given in Figure 9.5. This text gives us such information as:

- There are (at least) two accounts that orders can be charged to.

- There is a list of staff members authorized to sign off such requests.

- There is the possibility of ordering multiple copies of a title on behalf of students.

Title acquisition

Before a request to acquire a title can be complied with, form B has to be filled in completely. A request cannot be handled if it is not signed by an authorized staff member or the account to be charged ('Student' or 'Staff') is not indicated. A request is not to be granted if the title requested is already present in the title catalog, unless it is marked 'Stolen' or 'Lost', or the account is 'Student'.

Figure 9.5 A sample instruction for library employees

Often, natural language descriptions (and forms) provide the analyst with background information to be used in conjunction with other elicitation techniques such as interviews. Natural language descriptions in particular tend to assume a lot of tacit knowledge by the reader. For example, if form B contains an ISBN, this saves the library employee some work, but the request will probably still be handled if this information is not provided. A practical problem with natural language descriptions is that they are often not kept up to date. Like software documentation, their validity tends to deteriorate with time.

Derivation from an existing system: Starting from an existing system, for instance a similar system in some other organization or a description in a text book, we may formulate the requirements of the new system. Obviously, we have to be careful and take the peculiar circumstances of the present situation into account.

Rather than looking at one particular system, we may also study a number of systems in some application domain. This meta-requirements analysis process is known as **domain analysis**. Its goal generally is to identify reusable components, concepts, structures, and so on. It is dangerous to look for reusable requirements in immature domains. Requirements may then be reused simply because they are available, not because they fit the situation at hand. They become 'dead wood'. In the context of requirements analysis, domain analysis can be viewed as a technique for deriving a 'reference' model for systems within a given domain. Such a reference model provides a skeleton (architecture) that can be augmented and adapted to fit the specific situation at hand.

Domain analysis is further discussed in Chapter 17, in the context of software reuse.

Business process redesign (BPR): In many software development projects, the people involved jump to conclusions rather quickly: automation is the answer. Even worse, their conclusion might be that automating the current situation is the answer. In business process redesign (or business process reengineering), a rather different strategy is followed. It is an organizational activity to radically redesign business processes to achieve competitive breakthroughs in, e.g. quality, cost, or user satisfaction. In BPR, we depart completely from the existing ways of doing things. BPR involves the following steps:

1. Identify processes for innovation. Two major approaches for doing so are the exhaustive and high-impact approach. In the exhaustive approach, an attempt is made to identify all processes, which are then prioritized for their redesign urgency. The high-impact approach attempts to identify the most important processes only, or the ones that conflict with the business vision.

2. Identify change levers. In this step, opportunities to facilitate process improvement are identified. Three types of lever can be recognized: organizational enablers (such as empowering teams), human resource enablers (such as task enrichment) and information technology enablers.

3. Develop a process vision. For redesign to be successful, the organization needs to know which goals it wants to reach. This is described in the process vision. The main components of a process vision are: process objectives (measurable targets of the future performance of the system), process attributes (qualitative and descriptive properties of the future process), critical success factors, and constraints (organizational, cultural, and technological).

4. Understand the existing process. This includes documenting the existing process, measuring it, and identifying problematic aspects. It allows us to assess the health of the existing process and brings problems to the surface.

5. Design and prototype the new process. This is the final step. Prototyping makes it possible to try out new structures, thereby reducing the risk of failure.

BPR is not really a requirements elicitation technique proper. It is mentioned here because it emphasizes an essential issue to be addressed during the requirements engineering phase. Business processes should not be driven by information technology. Rather, information technology should enable them. Though a complete BPR effort is not necessary or feasible in many situations, rethinking the existing processes and procedures is a step which is all too often thoughtlessly skipped in software development projects.

As an example, consider our library automation project once again. Careful inspection of the current situation might reveal that things aren't all that bad. However, the impression is that the number of requests that could not be granted has steadily risen in the past years. This is perceived to be the main cause of the increasing number of dissatisfied users. Since service to its customers has high priority, one of the objectives is to decrease the number of requests that cannot be satisfied by 50% within two years. For this to be possible, the library should be allowed to spend the available budget at its own discretion, rather than being triggered by signals from researchers only (this sounds radical, doesn't it). It is therefore decided to augment the existing automated system with modules to keep track of both successful and unsuccessful requests. Based on the insights gained from this measurement process during a period of three months, a decision will be taken as to how large a percentage of the annual budget will be reallocated.

Prototyping Given the fact that it is difficult, if not impossible, to build the right system from the start, we may decide to use prototypes. Starting from a first set of requirements, a prototype of the system is constructed. This prototype is used for experiments, which lead to new requirements and more insight into the possible uses of the system. In one or more ensuing steps, a more definite set of requirements is developed. Prototyping is discussed in Section 3.2.1. Other agile processes follow a similar strategy in which requirements are quickly translated into a running system to be assessed by its users.

Of these requirements elicitation techniques, 'asking' is the least certain strategy, while 'prototyping' is the least uncertain. Besides the experience of both users and analysts, the uncertainty of the process is also influenced by the stability of the environment, the complexity of the product to be developed, and the familiarity with the problem area in question. We may try to estimate the impact of those factors on the vulnerability of the resulting requirements specification, and then decide on a primary method for requirements elicitation based on this estimate.

For a well-understood problem, with very experienced analysts, interviewing the prospective users may suffice. However, if it concerns an advanced and ill-understood problem from within a rapidly changing environment and the analysts have little or no experience in the domain in question, it seems wise to follow an agile process.

Requirements uncertainty is not the only problem project managers have to cope with, and a different process is not the only solution they opt for. Political aspects (such as hidden agendas and conflicts between stakeholders) are often seen as larger risks than mere requirements uncertainty (Moynihan, 2000). Of course, these are related. In both cases, the chances are high that requirements will change. Project managers often follow a formal route to handle disagreements between stakeholders and let the customers sign off the requirements document. Whether this is the answer in the long run is questionable, though.

As the uncertainty decreases, the beneficial effects of user participation in requirements engineering diminish. With greater uncertainty, however, greater user participation does have a positive effect on the quality of requirements engineering.

It is generally wise to have multiple customer–developer links in a software development project, and during requirements engineering in particular. Keil and Carmel (1995) studied the relation between project success and the number and type of such customer–developer links. The authors observed a strong correlation between the number of links and project success: more links implied more successful projects. The relative contribution to project success diminishes as the number of links grows; there is no need to have more than, say, half a dozen links. A further interesting observation from this study is that links with *direct* users have more impact on project success than links with *indirect* users such as user representatives or sales people. Finally, it was noted that customer-driven development projects tend to use and prefer different types of link to market-driven development projects. For example, the favorite link for custom development – facilitated teams – was not used by package developers, while the favorite link for package developers – support lines – was seldom used for custom projects.

We should be very careful in our assessment of which requirements elicitation technique to choose. It is all too common to be too optimistic about our ability to properly assess software requirements.

As an example, consider the following anecdote from a Dutch newspaper. A firm in the business of farm automation had developed a system in which microchips were put in cows' ears. Subsequently, each individual cow could be tracked: food and water supply was regulated and adjusted, the amount and quality of the milk automatically recorded and analyzed, etc. Quite naturally, this same technique was next successfully applied to pigs. Thereafter, it was tried on goats. A million-dollar, fully automated goat farm was built. But alas, things did not work out that well for goats. Unlike cows and pigs, goats eat everything, including their companions' chips.

9.1.3 Goals and Viewpoints

In this section, we discuss two ways to structure a set of requirements. One way to do so is in a hierarchical structure: higher-level requirements are decomposed into lower-level ones. The high-level requirements are often termed goals. The other structuring method links requirements to specific stakeholders. Management may have one set of requirements and the end users may have another set of requirements. These different sets of requirements are called viewpoints. In both cases, elicitation and structuring go hand in hand.

For example, one of the requirements elicited for our library system could be that the system should allow users to search the database for a particular book. By asking ourselves or the stakeholders *why* this requirement is needed, a higher-level requirement is detected, that is, the necessity of having search facilities. Again asking 'why', a high-level goal of serving the customers is arrived at. Going the other way, by asking *how* the library system may help serve the customers, a requirement to learn about user preferences and use this knowledge while interacting with the user might emerge. In this way, by asking *why* and *how* questions, a hierarchical structure of goals and requirements develops. Figure 9.6 contains an example of such a hierarchical structure.

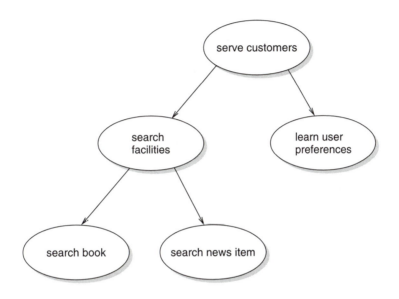

Figure 9.6 Hierarchy of requirements

Figure 9.6 depicts a refinement structure, in which each requirement is refined (decomposed) into a set of subrequirements that together satisfy the parent requirement. The subrequirements are AND-related: 'search book' and 'search news item' together make up the 'search facilities' requirement.

We may also include other types of relationship. For instance, we may have certain options for a particular requirement and, to that end, have OR-relations next to AND-relations. We may also include other types of link. If we have a requirement to impose fines on customers who return items late, we may conceive this as conflicting with our goal of serving customers and connect these two requirements by a link of type 'conflicts with'.

This so-called **goal-driven requirements engineering** results in a graph connecting high-level goals to lower-level requirements. This graph can be reasoned about, e.g. to validate that certain goals are indeed reached or to detect conflicts (Lamsweerde, 2001).

It is often useful to collect and organize requirements from different perspectives or **viewpoints**. Different stakeholders may have different sets of requirements.

Different quality concerns may also lead to different sets of requirements, leading for instance to a security viewpoint. The latter type of perspective is usually dealt with during software architecture design, and is discussed in Chapter 11. The techniques discussed in Chapter 10 implicitly denote different viewpoints as well, such as a data viewpoint in the entity–relationship models. Here, we focus on different viewpoints caused by different stakeholders. These different viewpoints may be in conflict, and these conflicts need to be recognized and dealt with during requirements engineering. The computer-aided dispatch system for the London Ambulance Service again provides a clear case of conflicting viewpoints: management wants an effective system; crew members want to get home within a reasonable time after their shift has ended (see also Sections 1.4.3 and 9.1.1). For our library system, conflicts between stakeholders may likewise occur.

Consider, for example, the following issue which may crop up during the requirements elicitation phase for our library system. The system has to offer certain features to register and handle fines. An item not returned in time incurs a fine of, say, $0.25 per day. John, one of the library employees involved in the specification process, takes the following position (denoted 'Pos A' in Figure 9.7): members should be warned about outstanding fines at the earliest possible moment. His argument ('Arg A') is that service is degraded if a member cannot borrow an item because some other member has not returned that item on time. Mary, the library manager, takes a rather different position ('Pos B'): members should *not* be warned about outstanding fines until the due date has expired one month. Her argument ('Arg B') is that fines are a most welcome addition to the library budget, which is under severe pressure because of the continuing price increase of journal subscriptions.

This situation is depicted in the graph in Figure 9.7. The graph contains nodes of types 'issue', 'position' and 'argument', and directed links of type 'response-to', 'taken-by' and 'supports'. Capturing this type of information in an automated system offers possibilities for storing, tracing and manipulating the very diverse types of information gathered during the requirements engineering phase. An early system along these lines is gIBIS, a system designed to capture design decisions early in the process.

Two viewpoints in particular are important during requirements engineering: the business viewpoint and the personal viewpoint. The business viewpoint is usually propagated by management stakeholders, while the personal viewpoint is usually propagated by end users. However, end users tend to also ascribe to business requirements, at least at an early stage. For instance, when John is asked whether fines are a welcome addition to the subsidy the library gets from the government, a likely answer is 'yes'. This requirement is viewed as a requirement of the business, not a personal requirement of John. Only when he is confronted with the consequences does he realize that this is, after all, not what he wants. And a request to change the system will follow.

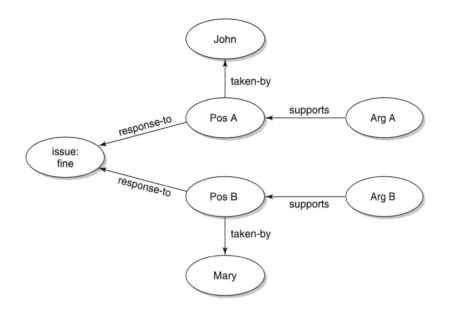

Figure 9.7 Representation of conflicting viewpoints

9.1.4 Prioritizing Requirements

> Our task is not to provide every button and pull-down menu enhancement
> that our customers ask for, but to invent a completely new way of
> working – one that will thrill and amaze them.
> Robertson (2002)

In most cases, not all requirements can be realized, so we have to make a selection. In
Section 3.2.3 we mentioned a very simple form of requirements prioritization called
triage. A variant often used is known as MoSCoW (the Os are just there to be able to
pronounce the word). Using MoSCoW, we distinguish four types of requirement:

- **Must haves**: these are the top-priority requirements, the ones that definitely
  have to be realized in order to make the system acceptable to the customer.

- **Should haves**: these requirements are not strictly mandatory, but they are
  highly desirable.

- **Could haves**: if time allows, these requirements will be realized as well. In
  practice, they usually won't.

- **Won't haves**: these requirements will not be realized in the present version.
  They are recorded though. They will be considered again for a future version
  of the system.

The MoSCoW scheme assumes that requirements can be ordered along a single axis and that realizing more requirements yields more satisfied customers. The reality is often more complex. In the **Kano model** of (Kano, 1993), user preferences are classified into five categories, as listed in Table 9.1. The way customers value the Attractive, Must-be and One-dimensional categories of requirements is depicted in Figure 9.8. This figure shows that offering attractive, so-called killer features is what will really excite your customers. The above quote from Robertson (2002) points in the same direction: amaze your customer by giving him something he never even dreamt of.

Table 9.1 Kano's requirements categories

Attractive	The customer is more satisfied if the requirement (for example, issuing an automatic alert when new books by a beloved author arrive) is met but not less satisfied if it is not.
Must-be	The customer is dissatisfied if the requirement (for example, the ability to search the library catalog) is not met but satisfied if it is does not rise above neutral.
One-dimensional	Satisfaction is proportional to how many of the requirements (for example, alternative ways to search the library catalog) are met.
Indifferent	The customer does not really care about the requirement (for example, whether different categories of library items are displayed in a different color on the screen).
Reverse	The customer's judgement of the requirement is the opposite of what the analyst expected. For example, the analyst may have thought the library customer would want the system to remember her search patterns so as to be able to serve her better next time, while the customer wants to start afresh each time.
Questionable	The customer's preferences are not clear. She both seems to like and dislike a certain feature.

In market-driven software development, the product often has a series of releases. The list of requirements for such products is usually derived from sales information, user logs from earlier versions of the system, and other sources of indirect information. One then has to decide which requirements to include in the current version, and which ones to postpone to a future one. Business-case analysis, return on investment estimations, and similar economics-driven argumentations are used to set priorities. This priority setting is to be repeated for each version, since user preferences may change, the market reacts, and so on.

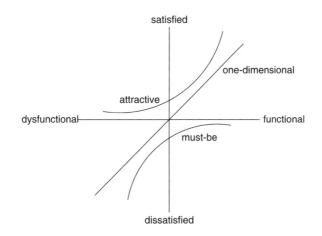

Figure 9.8 The Kano diagram

Finally, the prioritization of requirements is related to the notion of *scoping* in software product lines. If we want to develop a series of similar library systems, we have to delimit the domain we intend to handle. A smaller domain, say only scientific libraries, is easier to realize, but has a smaller market. A set of products covering a larger domain is more difficult to realize, yet has the promise of larger sales and profits.

9.1.5 COTS selection

Up till now, we have dealt with a situation where the customer phrases requirements, after which a system that satisfies these requirements is developed. With commercial off-the-shelf (COTS) software, the customer has to choose from what is available. In practice, the situation is not always that clear cut and a COTS system may be extended or adapted to suit the customer's needs. For our discussion, we assume it is a pure selection process.

COTS selection is an iterative process comprising the following steps:

1. Define requirements. As in ordinary requirements elicitation processes, a list of requirements for the product is derived. Any of the elicitation techniques discussed in Section 9.1.2 may be used in this process.

2. Select components. A set of components that can handle the requirements posed is determined. This selection process may involve market research, Internet browsing, and a variety of other techniques.

3. Rank the components. The components are ranked in the order in which they satisfy the requirements.

4. Select the most appropriate component or repeat the process.

Often, the set of components and requirements is too large to make a complete analysis and ranking in one step feasible. An iterative process is then followed, whereby the most important requirements are used to make a first selection from the set of available components. In a next step, a larger list of requirements is assessed against a smaller set of components. And so on.

There are different ways to rank components. A straightforward method is the weighted scoring method (WSM). Each requirement is given a weight and the alternatives are given a score for each requirement, say on a scale from 1 to 5. In Table 9.2, three components labeled A, B, and C are scored on three criteria: performance, supplier reputation, and functionality. In the example, components B and C score highest, and these might next be scrutinized further.

A major drawback of WSM is that every criterion can be compensated for by any other criterion. In the example from Table 9.2, component C makes it to the next round even though it scores very low on functionality. More complex ranking schemes, such as the analytic hierarchy process (AHP) overcome this drawback (Saaty, 1990).

Table 9.2   Weighted scoring method

Criterion	Weight	A	B	C
Performance	2	1	3	5
Supplier	1	2	2	5
Functionality	3	4	5	1
Total		16	23	18

9.1.6 Crowdsourcing

Many years ago, I used to visit a toy store with my son Jasper to browse the shelves with LEGO boxes and pick one we liked, to build a castle, fire engine or aeroplane. Nowadays, children (and probably their fathers too) visit the LEGO website. This site provides a CAD tool, so that you can design your own customized model of your favorite building or car. Once done, you press a button to generate a bill of materials, after which the components needed are gathered, put in a box, and shipped. You may leave the model created in a gallery. Rather than creating a model from scratch, you may browse the gallery and pick a model from there. The models that are most often selected are prepackaged and shipped to the toy stores.

This way, LEGO does not need any 'requirements engineers', people who develop new models and hope that their customers will be thrilled by them. Rather, the requirements engineering process is outsourced to a large community of volunteers: the children (and their fathers). It is called **crowdsourcing**.

Crowdsourcing as a business model is not uncommon. Wikipedia works that way. Companies may create a portal where users can suggest and vote for product improvements to guide innovation. In the area of software, companies sometimes rely on open source communities for innovations. The open source community then acts as a filter: the requirements that matter seep through and become part of the open source product. Next, the commercial company incorporates the open source software as part of its own product.

Rather than passively waiting for something interesting to happen, we may also try to induce a crowd to collaborate. This is usually done by providing a kernel or platform from which users can develop ideas and products. A user does not have to 'invent' what an online encyclopedia looks like, but can immediately contribute to the existing Wikipedia framework. Likewise, many open source projects start from a kernel developed by a very small community.

9.2 REQUIREMENTS DOCUMENTATION AND MANAGEMENT

The end product of the requirements engineering phase in a document-driven development project is a requirements specification. The requirements specification is an a posteriori reconstruction of the results of the analysis phase.

The requirements specification changes during and after the requirements phase. These changes need to be managed.

9.2.1 Requirements Specification

The purpose of the requirements specification is to communicate the results of the analysis phase to others. It serves as an anchor point against which subsequent steps can be justified.

The requirements specification is also the starting point for the next phase: design. Consequently, a very precise, even mathematical, description is preferable. On the other hand, the specification must also be understandable to the user. This often means a readable document, using natural language and pictures. In practice, one has to look for a compromise. Alternatively, the requirements specification may be presented in different, but consistent, forms to the different audiences involved.

Besides readability and understandability, various other requirements for this document can be stated (IEEE830, 1998):

- It should be *correct*. There is no procedure to guarantee correctness. The requirements specification should be validated against other (superior) documents and the actual needs of the users to assess its correctness.

- It should be *unambiguous*, both to those who create it and to those who use it. We must be able to uniquely interpret requirements. Because of its very nature, this is difficult to realize in a natural language.

- It should be *complete*. It should document all significant matters relating to functionality, performance, constraints, and so on. The responses to both correct and incorrect input should be specified; phrases such as 'to be determined' are particularly insidious. Unfortunately, it is not always feasible to complete the specification at an early stage. If certain requirements can only be made specific at a later stage, the requirements specification should at least document the ultimate point in time at which this should have happened.

- It should be (internally) *consistent*, i.e. different parts of it should not be in conflict with each other. Conflicting requirements can be both logical and temporal. Using different terms for one and the same object may also lead to conflicts.

- It should rank requirements for *importance* or *stability*. Typically, some requirements are more important than others. In some cases, a simple ranking scheme (such as 'essential', 'worthwhile', and 'optional') will suffice; in other cases, a more sophisticated classification scheme may be needed (see also Section 9.1.4). We may indicate the stability of requirements by indicating the likelihood, or the expected number, of changes. Through the explicit incorporation of this type of information in the requirements document, users are stimulated to give more consideration to each requirement. It also gives developers the opportunity to better direct their attention.

- It should be *verifiable*. This means that there must be a finite process to determine whether or not the requirements have been met. Phrases such as 'the system should be user-friendly' are not verifiable. Likewise, the use of quantities that cannot be measured, as in 'the system's response time should usually be less than two seconds', should be avoided. A requirement such as 'for requests of type X, the system's response time is less than two seconds in 80% of cases, with a maximum machine load of Y', is verifiable.

- It should be *modifiable*. Software models a part of reality. Therefore it changes. The corresponding requirements specification has to evolve with the reality being modeled. Thus, the document must be organized in such a way that changes can be accommodated readily (a tabular or database format, for example). Redundancy must be prevented as much as possible, for otherwise there is the danger that changes lead to inconsistencies.

- It should be *traceable*. The origin and rationale of every requirement must be traceable. A clear and consistent numbering scheme makes it possible for other documents to uniquely refer to parts of the requirements specification.

As a guideline for the contents of a requirements specification we will follow IEEE Standard 830. This standard does not give a rigid form for the requirements specification. In our opinion, the precise ordering and contents of the elements of this document are less than essential. The important point is to choose a structure which adheres to the above constraints. (IEEE830, 1998) uses a global structure such as that depicted in Table 9.3.

Table 9.3 Global structure of the requirements specification (*Source*: *IEEE Recommended Practice for Software Requirements Specifications*, IEEE Standard 830, ©1998. Reproduced by permission of IEEE.)

1. *Introduction*
      1.1 Purpose
      1.2 Scope
      1.3 Definitions, acronyms and abbreviations
      1.4 References
      1.5 Overview
2. *Overall description*
      2.1 Product perspective
      2.2 Product functions
      2.3 User characteristics
      2.4 Constraints
      2.5 Assumptions and dependencies
3. *Specific requirements*

For any nontrivial system, the detailed requirements will constitute by far the largest part of the requirements document. It is therefore helpful to somehow categorize these detailed requirements. This can be done along different dimensions, such as:

- **Mode**: Systems may behave differently depending on the mode of operation, such as training or operational. For example, performance or interface requirements may differ between modes.

- **User class**: Different functionality may be offered to different classes of users, such as library members and library personnel.

- **Objects**: Requirements may be classified according to the objects (real-world entities) concerned. This classification scheme is a natural one when used in conjunction with an object-oriented analysis technique (see Section 12.3).

- **Response**: Some systems are best described by placing together functions in support of the generation of a response, for example functions associated with catalog queries or library member status information.

- **Functional hierarchy**: When no other classification fits, some functional hierarchy, for example organized by common inputs, may be used.

As an example, Table 9.4 gives a refinement of the section on specific requirements along the dimension of user classes. Figure 9.9 contains (part of) a possible requirements specification for the library example, following the IEEE guidelines.

Table 9.4 Outline of the Specific Requirements section (*Source*: *IEEE Recommended Practice for Software Requirements Specifications*, IEEE Standard 830, ©1998. Reproduced by permission of IEEE.)

3. *Specific requirements*
3.1 External interface requirements
3.1.1 User interfaces
3.1.2 Hardware interfaces
3.1.3 Software interfaces
3.1.4 Communications interfaces
3.2 Functional requirements
3.2.1 User class 1
3.2.1.1 Functional requirement 1.1
3.2.1.2 Functional requirement 1.2
. . .
3.2.2 User class 2
. . .
3.3 Performance requirements
3.4 Design constraints
3.5 Software system attributes
3.6 Other requirements

The IEEE framework for the requirements specification is especially appropriate in document-driven models for the software development process: the waterfall model and its variants. When a prototyping technique is used to determine the user interface, the IEEE framework can be used to describe the outcome of that prototyping process. The framework assumes a model in which the result of the requirements engineering process is unambiguous and complete. Though it is stated that requirements should be ranked for importance and that requirements that may be delayed until future versions may be included as subsets, this does not imply that a layered view of the system can be readily derived from a requirements document drawn up this way.

Irrespective of the format chosen for representing requirements, the success of a product strongly depends upon the degree to which the desired system is properly described during the requirements engineering phase. Small slips in the requirements specification may necessitate large changes in the final software. In Chapter 1, we described this by saying that software is not continuous.

1. *Introduction.*

  1.1 *Purpose.* This document states the requirements of an automated library system for a medium-sized library of a research institute. The requirements stated serve as a basis for the acceptance procedure of this system. The document is also intended as a starting point for the design phase.

  1.2 *Scope.* The intended product automates the library functions described in DOC1. Its purpose is to provide a more effective service to the library users, in particular through the online search facilities offered. More details of the performance requirements are given in section 3.3 of this document. Once this system is installed, the incorporation of new titles will go from an average of 15 minutes down to an average of 5 minutes.

  1.3 *Definitions, acronyms and abbreviations.* Library member: . . . , Library personnel: . . . , User: The term user may refer to both library members and library personnel, and is used to denote either class of user. Title catalog: . . . , PICA: . . . , etc.

  1.4 *References.* DOC1: . . . , DOC2: . . . , etc.

  1.5 *Overview.* Section 2 of this document gives a general overview of the system. Section 3 gives more specific requirements for functions offered. These functions are categorized according to the class of users they support: (external) members of the library and library personnel, respectively.

2. *Overall description.*

  2.1 *Product perspective.* The already installed database system X will be used to store the various catalogs as well as the library member administration. There are no interfaces to other systems. The system will be realized on the Y configuration. The maximum external storage capacity for the catalogs of the system is 1500 MB. Library personnel will use a bar-code reader to enter member, book and journal identifications. The interface protocol to the bar-code reader is described in DOC4.

  2.2 *Product functions.* The system provides two types of function:

    – Functions by which users may search the catalogs of books and journal articles. A list of these functions is given in DOC1. A more detailed description is given in Section 3.2.1.

    – Functions by which library personnel may update the administration of borrowed titles and the system's catalogs; see section 3.2.2.

  The user of the system selects one of the functions offered through the main menu (section 3.2.1.1 and 3.2.2.1).

  2.3 *User characteristics.* The library members are incidental users of the system and have little knowledge of automated systems of this kind. The system therefore has to be self-instructing. Specific requirements are formulated in sections 3.1.1 and 3.3. The library personnel will be trained in the use of the system; see section 3.1.1.

Figure 9.9 Partial requirements specification for the library example

2.4 *Constraints.* Library members may only search the catalogs of books and journal articles. They are not allowed to update a catalog or access the user administration. The latter functionality is to be offered only through a dedicated, password-protected interface.

2.5 *Assumptions and dependencies.* . . .

3. *Specific requirements.*

3.1 *External interface requirements.*

3.1.1 *User interfaces.* The screen formats for the different features are specified in Appendix A. Appendix B lists the mapping of commands to function keys. The user can get online help at any point by giving the appropriate command. Appendix C contains a list of typical usage scenarios. These usage scenarios will be used as acceptance criteria: 80% of the users must be able to go through them within 10 minutes. An instruction session for library personnel should take at most two hours.

3.1.2 *Hardware interfaces.* The user interface is screen-oriented. The system uses up to ten function keys.

3.1.3 *Software interfaces.* The interface with database system X is described in DOC2.

3.1.4 *Communications interfaces.* Not applicable.

3.2 *Functional requirements.*

3.2.1 *Library member functions.*

3.2.2.1 *Select member feature.* The user selects one of the options from the main menu. Subsequent actions are described in sections 3.2.1.2 and 3.2.1.3. At any point, the user has an option to return to the main menu (see Appendix B).

3.2.1.2 *Search book catalog.* Given (part of) a book title or author name, the user may search the book catalog for titles that match the input given. The user is offered a screen with two fill-in-the-blank areas (one for the title and one for the author), one of which is to be filled in.

Input. The input may contain both upper- and lower-case letters. Special symbols allowed are listed in DOC1. Any other glyphs entered are discarded and are not shown on the screen. The input is considered complete when the processing command is issued.

Processing. All lower-case letters are turned into upper-case letters. The string thus obtained is used when querying the database. A database entry matches the title string given if the transformed input is a substring of the title field of the entry. The same holds for the author field if (part of) an author name is input.

Output. A list of titles that match the input is displayed. Up to four titles are shown on the screen. The user may traverse the list of titles found using the screen-scrolling commands provided. A warning is issued if no title matches the input given.

3.2.1.3 *Search article catalog.* . . .

Figure 9.9 *(continued)*

3.2.2 *Library personnel functions.*

> 3.2.2.1   *Select personnel feature.* Through a dedicated, password-protected interface, library personnel are offered an extended main menu, listing the options available to all users and the options available only to library personnel. The latter are described in sections 3.2.2.2 and 3.2.2.3.

> 3.2.2.2   *Borrow title.* . . . .

> 3.2.2.3   *Modify catalog.* . . . .

3.3 *Performance requirements.* The system will initially support 32 concurrent access points. Its maximum capacity is 128 concurrent access points.

The present database holds 25 000 book titles and 500 journal subscriptions. The storage capacity needed for data is 300 MB. On average 1 000 books and 2 000 journal issues enter the library per year. The average journal issue has six articles. This requires a storage capacity of 15 MB per year.

The system must be able to serve 20 users simultaneously. With this maximum load and a database size of 450 MB, user queries as listed in sections 3.2.1 and 3.2.2 must be answered within five seconds in 80% of the cases.

3.4 *Design constraints.*

> 3.4.1 *Standards compliance.* Title descriptions must be stored in PICA format. This format is described in DOC3.

> 3.4.2 *Hardware limitations.* See section 2.1.

3.5 *Software system attributes.*

> 3.5.1 *Availability.* During normal office hours (9 am–5 pm) the system must be available 95% of the time. A backup of the system is made every day at 5 pm.

> 3.5.2 *Security.* The functions described in Section 3.2.2 are restricted to library employees and are password-protected. . . . .

> 3.5.3 *Maintainability.* . . . .

3.6 *Other requirements.* . . . .

Figure 9.9 *(continued)*

The importance of a solid requirements specification cannot be stressed often enough. In some cases, up to 95% of the code of large systems has had to be rewritten in order to adhere to the ultimate user requirements.

9.2.2 Requirements Management

A fundamental problem with the IEEE framework discussed in Section 9.2.1 is that it describes only the end product. Before this final stage is reached, the 'current' set of requirements is in a constant state of flux. And even after the requirements phase is ended, requirements will change and new requirements will be put forth. The latter phenomenon is known as **requirements creep**, and is the cause for many run-away projects.

Changes in requirements cannot be circumvented. In many cases, it is not wise to aim for an early freeze of the requirements either. In general, the preferred situation is as depicted in Figure 9.10: over the course of time, the set of requirements becomes more and more stable.

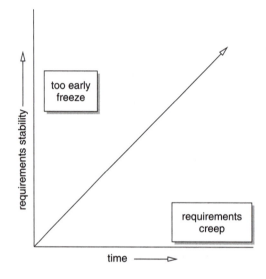

Figure 9.10 Requirements stability over time

Obviously, this evolving set of requirements has to be managed. Requirements management involves three activities:

- requirements identification,

- requirements change management, and

- requirements traceability.

Each requirement has to have a unique means of identification. The simplest method is to number them. If there is a hierarchical organization, as in a goal-hierarchy, it can be reflected in the numbering scheme. Since requirements are often changed and updated, it is expedient to include versioning information as well. Finally, we may add some attributes to each requirement, such as its status, priority, the main stakeholder involved, and so on. Requirements engineering tools usually have a way of storing requirements in a structured repository.

Changes to requirements have to be managed properly. By viewing each requirement as a configuration item, the rules and procedures of configuration management (Chapter 4) can be applied.

We may connect requirements to solution elements such as design elements or even software components that realize those requirements. In this way, we establish **traceability** from requirements to code and vice versa. This allows us to trace where requirements are realized (forward traceability), and why certain solutions are chosen (backward traceability). Traceability information is important in all development phases. It can be used to answer a variety of questions, such as:

- Where is this requirement implemented?

- Do we need this requirement?

- Are all requirements linked to solution elements?

- Which requirement does this test case cover?

- What is the impact of this requirement?

- Do we need this design element (piece of code)?

This way of making explicit the relationship between requirements and solutions is closely related to **design space analysis**. In design space analysis, the aim is to explicitly model all possible combinations of requirements and solutions. Design space analysis originated in the field of human–computer interaction. A well-known notation for design space analysis is known as 'questions, options, and criteria' (QOC). Questions correspond to requirements; options are the possible answers to those requirements; and criteria refer to the reasons for choosing a particular option. For instance, we may display the result of a news query by a library customer (the question) sorted either by date of publication or by author name (the options). The criterion for using a specific ordering could be the source of the news item; for example, newspaper articles could be sorted by date and journal articles by author name.

On one hand, design space analysis results in a rich structure in which an extensive record is built up of the rationale for a specific solution. Why is this system built the way it is? Which alternatives did we consider but reject? Which requirements survived the tradeoffs we had to make? On the other hand, capturing all this information is expensive and the immediate benefits are difficult, if not impossible, to prove. This is a main reason why design rationale has, by and large, failed to transfer to practice.

9.3 REQUIREMENTS SPECIFICATION TECHNIQUES

The document that is produced during requirements engineering – the requirements specification – serves two groups of people. For the user, the requirements specification is a clear and precise description of the functionality that the system has to offer. For the designer, it is the starting point for the design. It is not easy to serve both groups with one document.

9.3.1 Choosing a Notation

The user is, in general, best served by a document which speaks his language, the language that is used within the application domain. In the library example, this would result in using terms such as 'title description' and 'catalog'.

The designer, on the other hand, is best served by a language in which concepts from his world are used. In terms of the library example, he may prefer concepts such as 'record' (an instance of which might be termed 'title description') or 'file'. In one sense, this boils down to a difference in language. However, this difference is of fundamental importance with respect to the later use of the system's description.

If the system is described in the user's language, the requirements specification is mostly phrased in some natural language. If we try to somewhat formalize this description, we may end up with a technique in which certain forms have to be filled in or certain drawing techniques have to be applied.

If, on the other hand, the expert language of the software engineer plays a central role, we often use some formal language. A requirements specification phrased in such a formal language may be checked using formal techniques, for instance with regard to consistency and completeness.

In practice, a strong prevalence of the user's expert language shows itself. We may then use existing concepts from the environment in which the system is going to be used. Admittedly, these concepts are not sharply defined, but in general there are no misconceptions between the experts in the application domain as regards the meaning of those concepts. A description in terms of those concepts can thus still be very *precise*. Since the first goal of the requirements specification is to get a *complete* description of the problem to be solved, the user's expert language may be the best language for the requirements specification.

However, there are certain drawbacks attached to the use of natural language. Meyer (1985) gives an example which illustrates very well what may go wrong when natural language is used in a requirements specification. Meyer lists seven sins which may beset the analyst when using natural language:

- **Noise**: This refers to the presence of text elements that do not contain information relevant to the problem. Variants of noise are redundancy and regret. *Redundancy* occurs when things are repeated. Since natural language is very flexible, related matters can easily be phrased in completely different ways. When this happens the cohesion between matters gets blurred. *Regret* occurs when statements are reversed or shaded. In the library example, for instance, we could have used the phrase 'a list of all books written by author D' several times and only then realize that this list may be empty, necessitating some special reaction from the system.

- **Silence**: Silence occurs when aspects that are of importance for a proper solution of the problem, are not mentioned. An example of this may be that the need for two variants of an author's name was not stated explicitly.

- **Over-specification**: This occurs when elements of a requirements specification correspond to aspects of a possible solution, rather than to aspects of the problem. As an example, we could have specified that books be kept sorted by the first author's name. Over-specification limits the solution space for the designer.

- **Contradictions**: If the description of one aspect is given more than once, in different words, contradictions may occur. This risk is especially threatening when one tries to be too literary. A requirements specification is not meant to be a novel.

- **Ambiguity**: Natural language allows for more than one meaning for any phrase. Ambiguity can easily occur when terms are used that belong to the jargon of one or both parties. A 'book' may denote both a physical object and a more abstract entity of which several instantiations (copies) may exist.

- **Forward references**: A forward reference refers to aspects of the problem that are only defined later in the text. This especially occurs in large documents that lack a clear structure. Natural language in itself does not enforce a clear structure.

- **Wishful thinking**: Some descriptions of aspects of the system are such that a realistic solution will be hard to find.

A possible alternative given by Meyer is to first describe and analyze the problem using some formal notation and then translate it back into natural language. The natural language description thus obtained will, in general, represent a more precise notion of the problem that is readable to the user. Obviously, both these models must be kept up to date.

Quite a number of techniques and accompanying notations have evolved to support the requirements engineering process. Most often, the representation generated is a set of semantic networks. Each such representation has various types of nodes and links between nodes, distinguished by visual clues such as their shape or natural language labels. Nodes typically represent things like processes, stores, objects, and attributes. Nodes are joined by arrows representing relationships such as data flow, control flow, abstraction, part–whole, or is-part-of.

Typical examples of such techniques and their representations are discussed in Chapter 10. Entity–relationship modeling (Section 10.1.1) is a widely known technique to model the data aspect of an information system. Finite state machines (Section 10.1.2) can be viewed as a technique to model the functional aspect. They have much wider applicability though and constitute a basic underlying mechanism for many modeling techniques. In particular, the Unified Modeling Language (UML) owes tribute to them. UML diagrams (Section 10.3) are widely used to model the result of both requirements engineering and design.

9.3.2 Specifying Non-Functional Requirements

The IEEE framework depicted in Table 9.4 lists four types of non-functional requirements: external interface requirements, performance requirements, design constraints
and software system attributes. These non-functional requirements can be viewed as
constraints placed upon the development process or the products to be delivered.

External interface requirements and design constraints are generally phrased in
terms of (non-negotiable) obligations to be met. They are dictated at the start of the
project and often concern matters which surpass an individual development project.
Examples of such requirements include:

- hardware, software and communications interfaces to be complied with;

- user interfaces that have to obey company standards;

- report formats to be adhered to;

- process constraints such as ISO 9000 compliance or a prescribed development
  method;

- hardware limitations caused by the available infrastructure.

The remaining non-functional requirements are also known as quality requirements.
Quality requirements are notoriously difficult to specify and verify. This topic is dealt
with extensively in Chapter 6. At this point, we merely wish to re-emphasize two
essential issues: quality requirements should be expressed in objective, measurable
terms and perfection incurs infinite cost. Like all other requirements, quality requirements should be verifiable. Requirements such as 'the system should be flexible', 'the
system should be user-friendly', or 'response times should be fast', can never be verified
and should not therefore appear in the requirements specification. Other phraseology
can be used such as 'for activities of type A, the system should have a maximum
response time of one second in 80% of the cases, while a maximum response time of
three seconds is allowed in the remaining 20% of the cases.'

Conversely, extreme levels of quality requirements, such as zero defects or
response times of less than 1 second in 100% of the cases, generally incur extremely
high costs or are not feasible at all. Given the fact that users find it difficult to
express their true requirements, they may be inclined to ask for too much where
quality requirements are concerned, 'just to be on the safe side'. To the analyst and
developers, it is likewise difficult to assess the feasibility of those requirements. How
can we be sure about response times before even one line of code has been written?

Consider the following example of what may and may not be technically
feasible. Suppose we have an application in which two kinds of transactions may
occur. Those transactions are characterized by their frequency, CPU-time needed,
and the number of physical I/O transports. The average I/O access time is also
given. Using a statistical distribution describing the dynamics of these systems, one

may then answer questions such as, 'how much capacity should the CPU have in order to achieve a response time of at most 2 seconds in X% of cases?' Some given configuration may satisfy the constraints for the case X = 80. A somewhat more stringent requirement (X = 90) may require doubling of the CPU capacity. An even more severe requirement (X = 95) might well not be achievable by the range of machines available.

At first sight, the differences between these requirements seem marginal. They turn out to have a tremendous effect, though. An early and careful analysis of the technical feasibility may yield surprising answers to a number of important questions. Usually, this type of analysis is done at software architecture time. There are many examples of projects in which lots of money was spent on software development efforts which turned out to be not practically feasible (Baber, 1982).

9.4 VERIFICATION AND VALIDATION

In Chapter 1, we argued that a careful study of the correctness of the decisions made at each stage is a critical success factor. This means that during requirements engineering we should already start verifying and validating the decisions laid down in the requirements specification.

The requirements specification should reflect the mutual understanding of the problem to be solved by the prospective users and the development organization: has everything been described and has it been described properly? Validating the requirements thus means checking them for properties such as correctness, completeness, ambiguity, and internal and external consistency. Of necessity, this involves user participation in the validation process. They are the owners of the problem and they are the only ones who can decide whether the requirements specification adequately describes their problem.

If the requirements specification itself is expressed in a formal language, the syntax and semantics of that representation can be verified through formal means. However, the requirements specification can never be completely validated in a formal way, simply because the point of departure of requirements engineering is informal. Most of the testing techniques applied at this stage are therefore informal as well. They are meant to ascertain that the parties involved have the same, proper understanding of the problem. A major stumbling block at this stage is ensuring the user understands the contents of the requirements specification. The techniques applied at this stage often resolve to a translation of the requirements into a form palatable to user inspection: natural-language paraphrasing, the discussion of possible usage scenarios, prototyping, and animation.

Besides testing the requirements specification itself, we also generate at this stage the test plan to be used during system or acceptance testing. A test plan is a document prescribing the scope, approach, resources, and schedule of the testing activities. It identifies the items and features to be tested, the testing tasks to be performed, and the personnel responsible for these tasks. We may at this point develop such a plan for the system testing stage, i.e. the stage at which the development organization tests the complete system against its requirements. Acceptance testing is similar, but is performed under supervision of the user organization. Acceptance testing is meant to determine whether or not the users accept the system.

A more elaborate treatment of the various verification and validation techniques is given in Chapter 13.

9.5 SUMMARY

During the requirements engineering phase, we try to get a complete and clear description of the problem to be solved and the constraints that must be satisfied by any solution to that problem. During this phase, we not only consider the functions to be delivered but we also pay attention to requirements imposed by the environment. The requirements engineering phase results in a series of models concentrating on different aspects of the system (such as its functionality, user interface, and communication structure) and different perspectives (audiences). The result of this process is documented in a requirements specification. A good framework for the contents of the requirements specification is given in (IEEE830, 1998). It should be kept in mind that this document contains an a posteriori reconstruction of an as yet ill-understood iterative process.

This iterative process involves four types of activity:

- requirements elicitation, which is about *understanding* the problem,

- requirements specification, which is about *describing* the problem,

- requirements validation, which is about *agreeing upon* the problem, and

- requirements negotiation, which is about *fitting* the problem to the situation at hand.

In many cases, it is not feasible to fully complete requirements engineering before starting design and construction. In agile development processes, requirements engineering is an iterative process intertwined with design and construction.

During requirements engineering we are modeling part of reality. The part of reality we are interested in is referred to as the universe of discourse (UoD). The modeling process is termed conceptual modeling.

People involved in a UoD have an implicit conceptual model of that UoD. During conceptual modeling, an implicit model is turned into an explicit one. The explicit conceptual model is used to communicate with other people, such as users and designers, and to assess the validity of the system under development during all subsequent phases. During the modeling process, the analyst is confronted by analysis problems and negotiation problems. Analysis problems have to do with getting the requirements right. Negotiation problems arise because different people involved may have different views on the UoD to be modeled, opposing interests, and so on.

Existing approaches to requirements engineering are largely Taylorian in nature. They fit a functional view of software development in which the requirements engineering phase serves to elicit the 'real' user requirements. It is increasingly being recognized that the Taylorian approach need not be the most appropriate approach to requirements engineering. Many universes of discourse involve people whose world model is incomplete, irrational, or in conflict with the world view of others. In such cases, the analyst is not a passive outside observer of the UoD, but actively participates in shaping the UoD. The analyst gets involved in negotiation problems and has to choose the view of some party involved or assist in obtaining some compromise.

The following description techniques are often used for the requirements specification:

- natural language,

- pictures, and

- formal language.

An advantage of using natural language is that the specification is very readable and understandable to the user and other non-professionals involved. Pictures may have an advantage in putting across the functional architecture of the system. A formal language allows us to use tools in analyzing the requirements. Because of its precision, it is a good starting point for the design phase. We may also argue that both formal and informal notations should be used, since they augment and complement each other. For each of the parties involved, a notation should be chosen that is appropriate to the task at hand.

9.6 FURTHER READING

There are many text books fully devoted to requirements engineering. Davis (1993) provides a fairly complete coverage of 'classic' requirements specification techniques. Davis (2005) focuses on requirements engineering in the face of tight schedule constraints. Wieringa (1996) discusses a number of requirements specification techniques in quite some depth and makes the distinction between implicit and explicit conceptual models. Loucopoulos and Karakostas (1995) and Kotonya and Sommerville (1997) have a stronger emphasis on the full requirements engineering process. (Juristo *et al.*, 2002) discuss the state of the practice in requirements engineering. Hofman and Lehner (2001) focus on successful requirements practices. Sommerville (2005) discusses recent developments in the field.

Pohl (1993) and Goguen and Jirotka (1994) emphasize the role of social and cognitive issues in requirements engineering. (Ramos *et al.*, 2005) argue that emotion is relevant in requirements engineering. The thin spread of application knowledge amongst the specialists involved is discussed in (Curtis *et al.*, 1988). Difficulties of requirements engineering for market-driven software development are addressed in (Potts, 1993). Moynihan (2000) discusses how managers cope with requirements uncertainty.

The objectivist–subjectivist and order–conflict dimensions and the resulting four paradigms for requirements engineering are discussed in (Hirschheim and Klein, 1989). Various socio-technical, subjectivist approaches to requirements elicitation are discussed in (Atkinson, 2000).

Task analysis is discussed in (Sebillotte, 1988). Scenario-based requirements engineering techniques are discussed in (Weidenhaupt *et al.*, 1998) and (TrSE, 1998). (Sutcliffe *et al.*, 1998) describe how to create and document scenarios during requirements engineering. Business process redesign is described in (Keen, 1991) and (Tapscott and Caston, 1993). A framework for BPR is given in (Davenport, 1993).

Research in requirements elicitation is aimed at developing techniques which overcome our limitations as humans in conveying information. An early overview of this type of problem is given in (Davis, 1982). A more recent survey and evaluation of elicitation techniques is given in (Goguen and Linde, 1993). Example experience reports are given in (Sommerville *et al.*, 1994); Coakes and Coakes (2000) take an ethnographic approach; and Beyer and Holtzblatt (1995) view the analyst as an apprentice to the user.

Lamsweerde (2001) gives a very good overview of goal-oriented requirements engineering. (Mylopoulos *et al.*, 2001) is another article by pioneers in this area. Darke and Shanks (1996) and Sommerville and Sawyer (1997) provide a good overview of viewpoints in the context of requirements engineering.

(Leffingwell and Widrig, 2000) is fully devoted to requirements management. One of the first discussions of requirements traceability is (Gotel and Finkelstein, 1994). Design space analysis is discussed in (Moran and Carroll, 1994). The Questions, Options, Criteria (QOC) approach stems from (MacLean *et al.*, 1991). gIBIS, a hypertext system designed to capture early design decisions, is described in (Conklin and Begeman, 1988).

Kano's model is discussed in (Kano, 1993). The quest for creativity in requirements engineering is further stressed in (Robertson, 2002), (Austin and Devin, 2003) and (Maiden *et al.*, 2004).

(Morisio *et al.*, 2002b) give a taxonomy of COTS products. COTS selection procedures are discussed in (Maiden and Ncube, 1998).

Exercises

1. What are the four major types of activity in requirements engineering?

2. What is requirements elicitation?

3. What is the difference between an implicit and an explicit conceptual model?

4. In what sense are most requirements engineering techniques Taylorian in nature?

5. Describe the requirements elicitation technique called 'task analysis'.

6. Describe the requirements elicitation technique called 'scenario-based analysis'.

7. In which circumstances is ethnography a viable requirements elicitation technique?

8. What is goal-oriented requirements engineering?

9. How can conflicting requirements be represented in viewpoints?

10. What does MoSCoW stand for?

11. Why is the distinction between the Attractive, Must-be and One-dimensional categories of requirements in Kano's model relevant?

12. How does the presence of COTS components affect requirements engineering?

13. Why is requirements traceability important?

14. List and discuss the major quality requirements for a requirements document.

15. List and discuss the major drawbacks of using natural language for specifying requirements.

16. ♠ Draw up a requirements specification for a system whose development you have been involved with, following IEEE Standard 830. Discuss the major differences between the original specification and the one you wrote.

17. ♡ What are major differences in the external environment of an office automation system and that of an embedded system, such as an elevator control system. What impact will these differences have on the requirements elicitation techniques to be employed?

18. ♡ For an office information system, identify different types of stakeholder. Can you think of ways in which the requirements of these stakeholders might conflict?

19. ♡ Refine the framework in Figure 9.1 such that it reflects the situation in which we have to explicitly model both the current and the new work situation.

20. ♡ Discuss the pros and cons of the following descriptive means for a requirements specification: full natural language, constrained natural language, and a pictorial language (such as UML).

21. ♡ Which of the descriptive means mentioned in Exercise 20 would you favor for describing the requirements of an office automation system? And which one for an elevator control system?

22. ♠ Take the requirements specification document from a project you have been involved in and assess it with respect to the requirements for such a document as listed in Section 9.2 (unambiguity, completeness, etc.).

23. ♡ How would you test the requirements stated in the document from Exercise 22? Are the requirements testable to start with?

24. ♠ How would you go about determining the requirements for a hypertext-like browsing system for a technical library. Both users and staff of the library only have experience with keyword-based retrieval systems.

25. ♡ As an analyst involved in the development of this hypertext browsing system, discuss possible stands in the subjectivist–objectivist and order–conflict dimensions. What are the arguments for and against these stands?

26. ♠ Write a requirements specification for a hypertext browsing system.

27. ♡ Study the following specification for a simple line formatter:

The program's input is a stream of characters whose end is signaled by a special end-of-text character, ET. There is exactly one ET character in each input stream. Characters are classified as:

- break characters – BL (blank) and NL (new line);
- the end-of-text indicator – ET;
- nonbreak characters – all others.

A *word* is a non-empty sequence of nonbreak characters. A *break* is a sequence of one or more break characters. Thus, the input can be viewed as a sequence of words separated by breaks, with possible leading and trailing breaks, and ending with ET.

The program's output should be the same sequence of words as in the input, with the exception that an oversized word (i.e. a word containing more than MAXPOS characters, where MAXPOS is a positive integer) should cause an error exit from the program (i.e. a variable, Alarm, should have the value TRUE). Up to the point of an error, the program's output should have the following properties:

- A new line should start only between words and at the beginning of the output text, if any.
- A break in the input is reduced to a single break character in the output.
- As many words as possible should be placed on each line (i.e. between successive NL characters).
- No line may contain more than MAXPOS characters (words and BLs).

Identify as many trouble spots as you can in this specification. Compare your findings with those in (Meyer, 1985).

28. ♡ What are the major uses of a requirements specification. In what ways do these different uses affect the style and contents of a requirements document?

10

Modeling

LEARNING OBJECTIVES

- To know about various classic modeling techniques

- To know about the Unified Modeling Language (UML) and its main diagram types

- To know the terminology of object orientation

In the course of a software development project, and most notably during requirements engineering and design, many modeling notations are used. These range from very informal sketches of system functions or screen layouts, to highly formal descriptions of system behavior. The most common notations used are box-and-line diagrams with semiformal semantics. In this chapter, we discuss a number of these diagrammatic notations.

During software development, a lot of communication takes place. This communication is supported by all kinds of notations to convey its message. A sketch of a screen layout may support the communication between a user and a requirements engineer. A much more formal description of class interfaces may support the communication between a designer and a developer.

The most common notations used to support communication between the various stakeholders involved in software development involve some sort of box-and-line diagrams. Sometimes, these diagrams have very informal semantics. For instance, the boxes may denote parts of the system, where it is not clear what exactly a part is. One box may denote a major subsystem, another box may denote the set of security measures taken. Likewise, lines may denote a parts-of relation, a calling relation, a uses relation, and so on. While being drawn, these loose semantics may not be a problem. But the next day, confusion will arise.

An alternative is to use diagrams that have a more precise semantics. If the readers know these semantics, there need not be any confusion over what exactly is meant. If the semantics are precise enough, the diagrams can be subjected to all kinds of consistency checks. Tools may generate the diagrams, read them, and possibly even generate executable code from the diagrams. Finally, we may link the diagrams to the methods that generate them, thereby giving some operationalization to their construction process. For instance, the steps in a design method can be linked to the steps for generating the corresponding diagram. The latter kinds of diagrams are discussed in Chapter 12, together with a discussion of the corresponding design methods.

In this chapter, we discuss a number of semiformal modeling notations. Most of them use some sort of box-and-line diagram. Some use a more textual layout. The diagrams and schema are usually drawn during requirements engineering and design. Some primarily serve requirements engineering. For instance, use-case diagrams are usually drawn during requirements engineering. Jackson structure diagrams, on the other hand, are mostly used during design. Many modeling notations serve both.

Currently, the mainstream modeling notations stem from the Unified Modeling Language (UML). Many diagrams from UML, though, are based on or derived from earlier ones. And, certainly in legacy applications, you may come across many of these older notations. Therefore, a sample of both is provided in this chapter.

UML evolved from some of the mainstream object-oriented analysis and design methods. The concept of object orientation, in turn, has its roots in the development of programming languages, most notably SIMULA-67 and Smalltalk. With respect to analysis and design (and requirements analysis), object orientation is best viewed by highlighting the differences with more traditional design methods such as functional decomposition and dataflow design. Whereas traditional techniques focus on identifying the *functions* that the system is to perform, object-oriented methods focus on identifying and interrelating the *objects* that play a role in the system. Section 10.2 introduces a number of relevant concepts, such as object, attribute, class, relationship. In one way or another, these concepts show up in many UML diagram types.

10.1 CLASSIC MODELING TECHNIQUES

We discuss four classic modeling techniques that have been around for quite a while:

- Entity–relationship modeling (ERM) is a data modeling technique, pioneered by Chen (1976). UML class diagrams are based on ERM.

- Finite state machines (FSMs) are used to model states and state transitions. In the early days, certain types of formal language, such as those used in compilers, were modeled as finite state machines. UML state machine diagrams are based on finite state machines.

- Data flow diagrams (DFDs) model a system as a set of processes and data flows that connect these processes. It is the notation used in data flow design. UML sequence diagrams resemble DFDs.

- CRC cards are a simple requirements elicitation tool. Much of the information collected on CRC cards can also be represented as UML communication diagrams.

Many other classic modeling notations are tied to a certain analysis or design method. We discuss some of them in Chapter 12 in the context of a discussion of design methods. The ones discussed here are relatively method-independent.

10.1.1 Entity–Relationship Modeling

In data-intensive systems, modeling the (structure of) the data is an important concern. Until the 1970s, data modeling techniques very much mixed up implementation concerns with concerns arising from the logical structure of the universe of discourse (UoD). For example, the book catalog would be modeled as a 'table' containing 'tuples' ('records') with alphanumeric fields containing the title and author and numeric fields containing the publication year and number of pages.

Entity–relationship modeling (ERM), as pioneered by Chen, is directed at modeling the logical, semantic structure of the UoD, rather than its realization in

Table 10.1   ERM concepts and their meaning

Entity	distinguishable object of some type
Entity type	type of a set of entities
Attribute value	piece of information (partially) describing an entity
Attribute	type of a set of attribute values
Relationship	association between two or more entities

some database system. Entity–relationship models are depicted in **entity–relationship diagrams** (ERDs). There are many variants of ERM, which differ in their graphical notations and extensions to Chen's original approach. The basic ingredients of ERM are given in Table 10.1.

An entity is a 'thing' that can be uniquely identified. Entities are usually depicted in an ERD as rectangles. Example entities are:

- tangible objects, such as copies of a book, identified by some number;

- intangible objects, such as books identified by their ISBN, or members of some organizational construct, such as library employees identified by their employee number.

Entities have properties known as attributes. For example, some library employee may have the name 'Jones'. Here, 'Jones' is the value of the attribute called 'name'. Attributes are usually depicted as circles or ellipses.

Both entities and attribute values have a **type**. As modelers, we tend to view a type as a set of properties shared by its instances. As implementors, we tend to view a type as a set of values with a number of associated operations. For the attribute 'number of books on loan', the set of values could be 0..10 with operations such as increment and decrement. For the entity type 'book copy', candidate operations would be 'borrow', 'return', and so on.

Entities are linked through relationships. For example, the relationship 'borrow' involves the entities 'book copy' and 'library member'. Most often, a relationship is binary, i.e. it links two entities. A relationship is denoted by a diamond linked to the entities involved.

Entity–relationship models impose restrictions on the cardinality of relationships. In its simplest form, the relationships are 1–1, 1–N, or N–M. The relationship 'borrow' is 1–N: a copy of a book can be borrowed by one member only, while a member may have borrowed more than one book copy. In an ERD, these cardinality constraints are often indicated by small adornments of the arrows linking the entities.

An example entity–relationship diagram is given in Figure 10.1. Cardinality constraints have been indicated by explicitly indicating the set of possibilities. Thus, this ERD states that a book copy can be borrowed by at most one member, and a member may borrow up to ten book copies.

An entity–relationship model can be obtained using any of the elicitation techniques discussed in Chapter 9. In particular, form analysis and analysis of natural

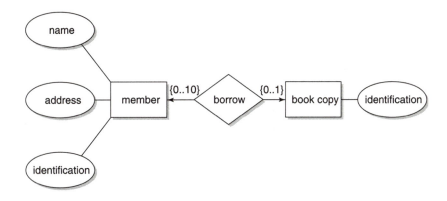

Figure 10.1 An entity–relationship diagram

language descriptions are often used. Since ERMs tell only part of the story, additional techniques have to be employed to model other aspects. Many structured analysis techniques, for example, incorporate ERM to model the data aspect.

Entity–relationship modeling is a natural outgrowth of database modeling. Originally, ERM was intended to model the logical structure of data, rather than the logical structure of the UoD. In heuristics on how to obtain a 'good' entity–relationship model, these roots are still visible. For example, some of these heuristics resemble normalization constraints from database theory. This may explain why some do not commend entity–relationship modeling as a requirements specification technique (see, e.g., (Davis, 1993)).

Present-day ERM has a lot in common with object-oriented analysis techniques. For example, subtype–supertype relations between entity types are included in many ERM-techniques. Conversely, the class diagram of UML (see Section 10.3.1) includes many elements from ERM.

10.1.2 Finite State Machines

At any one point in time, our library system is in one of a (vast) number of possible states. The state of the library can be expressed in terms of:

- the collection of titles available,

- the collection of titles ordered but not yet received,

- the collection of library members,

- the balance of the account from which acquisitions are paid.

Any action occurring in the library, be it the return of a book or the appointment of a new employee, transforms the current state s into a new state s'.

Requirements specification techniques which model a system in terms of states and transitions between states are called **state-based** modeling techniques. A simple yet powerful formalism for specifying states and state transitions is the **finite state machine** (FSM). An FSM consists of a finite number of states and a set of transitions from one state to another that occur on input signals from a finite set of possible stimuli. The initial state is a specially designated state from which the machine starts. Usually, one or more states are designated as final states. Pictorially, FSMs are represented as **state transition diagrams** (STDs). In a state transition diagram, states are represented as bubbles, with a label identifying the state, and transitions are indicated as labeled arcs from one state to another, where the label denotes the stimulus which triggers the transition. Figure 10.2 gives an FSM depicting the possible states of a book copy and the transitions between those states. The final state is the one labeled 'written off'. Any of the others could be designated as the initial state.

Figure 10.2 models only a tiny part of the library system. It does not describe the complete state of the system in any one bubble, nor does it depict all possible state transitions. Modeling a system in one, large, monolithic STD is not to be recommended. Such a structure soon becomes unwieldy and difficult to understand. Though we could model the system in a series of FSMs, we would still have the problem of how to integrate them into one model.

A possible way out is to allow for a hierarchical decomposition of FSMs. This is the essence of a notation known as **statecharts**. In statecharts, groups of states can be viewed as a single entity at one level, to be refined at the next level of abstraction. In UML, FSMs are modeled as state machine diagrams (Section 10.3.2).

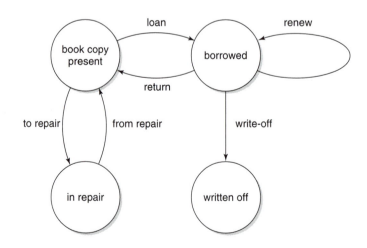

Figure 10.2 A state transition diagram

10.1.3 Data Flow Diagrams

The data flow design method originated in the early 1970s with Yourdon and Constantine. In its simplest form, data flow design is but a functional decomposition with respect to the flow of data. A component (module) is a black box which transforms some input stream into some output stream. The main notation used is that of data flow diagrams (DFDs).

Four types of data entity are distinguished in a data flow diagram:

- **External entities** are the source or destination of a transaction. These entities are located outside the domain considered in the data flow diagram. External entities are indicated as squares.

- **Processes** transform data. Processes are denoted by circles.

- **Data stores** lie between two processes and are places where data structures are stored until needed. They are indicated by the name of the data store between two parallel lines.

- **Data flows** between processes, external entities and data stores are paths along which data structures travel. A data flow is indicated by an arrow.

Data flow diagrams result from a top-down decomposition process. The diagram at the highest level has one process only, denoting 'the system'. This top-level diagram is then further decomposed. For our library example, this could lead to the data flow diagram of Figure 10.3. A client request is first analyzed in a process labeled 'preliminary processing'. As a result, one of 'borrow title' or 'return title' is activated. Both these processes update a data store labeled 'catalog administration'. Client requests are logged in a data store 'log file'. This data store is used to produce management reports.

The design method mostly used in conjunction with data flow diagrams is discussed in Section 12.2.2. There, we also give more example data flow diagrams.

10.1.4 CRC Cards

CRC stands for Class–Responsibility–Collaborators. A CRC card is simply a $4'' \times 6''$ or $5'' \times 7''$ index card with three fields labeled Class, Responsibility and Collaborators. CRC cards were developed in response to a need to document collaborative design decisions. CRC cards are especially helpful in the early phases of software development, to help identify components, discuss design issues in multi-disciplinary teams, and specify components informally. CRC cards may be termed a low-tech tool, as opposed to the high-tech tools we commonly use. Yet they are highly useful. They are also fun to work with in our all-too-serious business meetings.

CRC cards are not only used in collaborative design sessions. Within the design pattern community, for instance, they are used to document the elements that participate in a pattern.

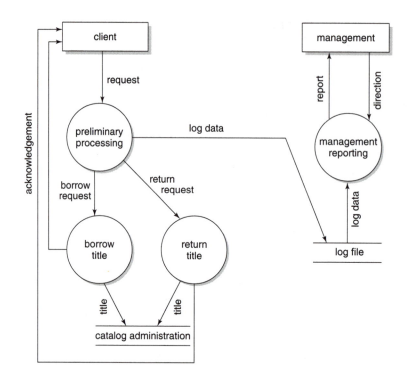

Figure 10.3 Data flow diagram for library automation

The word 'class' in CRC is a historical relic. CRC cards can be used to describe any design element. We will stick to the original terminology, however. The class name appears in the upper-left corner of the card. A bulleted list of responsibilities appears under the class name and a list of collaborators appears on the right part of the card. Figure 10.4 gives an example of a CRC card for a `Reservations` component in our library system.

The main responsibilities of this component are to keep an up-to-date list of reservations and to handle reservations on a FIFO basis. Its collaborators are the `Catalog` and `User session` components. The types of interaction with these components are shown in Figure 10.13.

10.2 ON OBJECTS AND RELATED STUFF

What matters is not how closely we model today's reality but how extensible and reusable our software is.
Meyer (1996)

The world around us is full of objects, animate and inanimate, concrete and abstract: trees and tables, cars and legal cases. According to some, analysis and design is

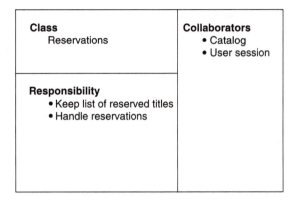

Figure 10.4 A CRC card

about modeling those real-world objects. By and large, this view has its origins in the Scandinavian school of programming language design (SIMULA-67) and software development. It may be termed the European view. According to others, analysis and design is about identifying reusable components and building their inheritance hierarchy. This latter view, which may be termed the American view, clearly shows itself in the above quotation.

What then *is* an object? As might be expected, there are different views of what the notion of object entails. We may distinguish the following points of view:

- The modeling viewpoint: an object is a conceptual model of some part of a real or imaginary world. From this point of view, important characteristics are:

  - each object has an identity, which distinguishes it from all other objects;
  - objects have substance: properties that hold and can be discovered by investigating an object.

From a practical point of view, object identity is an immutable tag, or address, which uniquely identifies that object. Different objects occupy different regions of memory. Pragmatically also, objects may be regarded as implementations of abstract data types (ADTs). An object then consists of a mutable state, i.e. the set of variables of the ADT, and operations to modify or inspect the state. Typically, the only way to access an object is through these operations. The operations thus act as an interface to the object. An object then is a collection of three aspects:

```
object = identity + variables + operations
```

or

```
object = identity + state + behavior
```

- The philosophical viewpoint: objects are existential abstractions, as opposed to universal abstractions. In some circles (notably the Smalltalk world), 'everything is an object'. In this view, objects act as a unifying notion underlying all computation. However, one may also argue that there are two rather distinct types of abstraction. Some kinds of entity have a natural beginning and end. They are created at some point in time, exist for a while, and are destroyed. The kinds of entity modeled as objects during analysis and design typically belong to this class. Other kinds of entity, such as numbers, dates, and colors, have 'eternal' existence. They are not instantiated; they cannot be changed; they 'live' forever. These entities are usually referred to as values.

- The software engineering viewpoint: objects are data abstractions, encapsulating data as well as operations on those data. This viewpoint stresses locality of information and representation independence; see also Sections 12.1.1 and 12.1.3. However, not all programming languages enforce data abstraction, and objects need not always encapsulate an abstract data type. We might claim that data abstraction and objects are somewhat orthogonal, independent dimensions.

  A programming language that merely allows us to encapsulate abstract data types in modules is often termed **object-based**. The adjective 'object-oriented', then, is reserved for languages that also support **inheritance** (discussed below).

- The implementation viewpoint: an object is a contiguous structure in memory. Technically, an object may be regarded as a record of data and code elements. An object may be composite or aggregate (possessing other objects). Sub-objects may, in turn, possess even 'smaller' sub-objects, and so on. The lowest-level objects in this hierarchy are atomic objects, typically denoting integers, real numbers or Booleans.

  The implementation of this 'possessed-by' relation appears to be intricate. On the one hand, objects may be contained in other objects. In this representation, all references are dispensed with. There is no concept of sharing. This scheme is known as **value semantics**. Value semantics is inadequate for object-oriented systems, since such systems require sharable objects. The opposite scheme is **reference semantics**: data is represented as either an atomic object or as an aggregate of references to other objects. Pure reference semantics is inefficient in the case of primitive objects such as integers or characters. A combination in which aggregate objects may contain other objects, refer to other objects, or do both at the same time, is commonly used as a storage scheme. The choice of a particular storage model is, to some extent, reflected in the high-level language semantics (for example, where it concerns copying or comparing objects).

- The formal viewpoint: an object is a state machine with a finite set of states and a finite set of state functions. These state functions map old states and inputs to new states and outputs.

Formalization of the concepts and constructions of object-oriented languages is difficult. Mathematical formalisms tend to be value-based. Imperative concepts, such as state and sharing, that are central to object-oriented languages do not fit easily within such schemes.

During analysis, the conceptual viewpoint is usually stressed. Those who are of the opinion that analysis and design blend smoothly into one another tend to keep this view during design. Others, however, are of the opinion that analysis and design are different, irrespective of whether they are object-oriented or not. They are likely to stress other viewpoints during design. The definition of an object as given in (Coad and Yourdon, 1991) also reflects the tension between a problem-oriented and a solution-oriented viewpoint: an object is 'an *abstraction* of something in a problem domain, reflecting the capabilities of a system to keep information about it, interact with it, or both; an *encapsulation* of Attribute values and their exclusive Services'. We will come back to this dichotomy when discussing object-oriented methods in Section 12.3.

As noted above, objects are characterized by a set of attributes (properties). A table has legs, a table top, size, color, etc. The **attribute** concept originates with entity–relationship modeling; see Section 10.1.1. In ERM, attributes represent *intrinsic properties* of entities, properties whose value does not depend on other entities. Attributes denote identifying and descriptive properties, such as name or weight. *Relationships* on the other hand denote *mutual* properties, such as an employee being assigned to a project or a book being borrowed by a member. In UML, these relationships are called associations. In UML, the distinction between attributes and relationships formally does not exist. Both are properties of a class. It is considered good practice in UML to model simple properties as attributes and more complex properties as associations.

In the context of object-oriented modeling, the term attribute is sometimes used to denote any field in the underlying data structure. In that case, the object's identity is an attribute, the state denotes the set of 'structural' attributes, and the operations denote the 'behavioral' attributes. We use the term 'attribute' to denote a structural attribute. Collectively, the set of attributes of an object thus constitutes its state. It includes the intrinsic properties, usually represented as values, as well as the mutual properties, usually represented as references to other objects.

At the programming-language level, objects that have the same set of attributes are said to belong to the same *class*. Individual objects of a class are called *instances* of that class. So we may have a class `Table`, with instances `MyTable` and `YourTable`. These instances have the same attributes, with possibly different values.

An object not only encapsulates its *state*, but also its *behavior*, i.e. the way in which it acts upon other objects and is acted upon by other objects. The behavior of an object is described in terms of *services* provided by that object. These services are invoked by *sending messages* from the object that requests the service to the object that is acted upon.

In order for a collection of objects to operate together as intended, each of the objects must be able to rely on the proper operation of the objects with which it interacts. In a *client–server* view, one object, the client, requests some service from another object, the server. This mutual dependency may be viewed as a contract between the objects involved. The client will not ask more than what is stated in the contract, while the server promises to deliver what is stated in the contract. In this perspective, services are also referred to as *responsibilities*.

The major behavioral aspect of an object concerns state changes. The state of an object instance is not static, but changes over time: the object instance is created, updated, and eventually destroyed. Also, certain information may be requested from an object. This information may concern the state of the object instance, but it may also involve a computation of some sort.

For example, a customer of a library may have attributes such as `Name`, `Address`, and `BooksOnLoan`. It must be possible to create an instance of the object type `Customer`. When doing so, suitable values for its attributes must be provided. Once the instance has been created, state changes are possible: books are loaned and returned, the customer changes address, etc. Finally, the instance is destroyed when the customer ceases to be a member. Information requested may concern such things as a list of books on loan or the number of books on loan. The former is part of the state that describes a particular customer and can be retrieved directly from that state. `NumberOfBooksOnLoan` is a service that requires a computation of some sort, for example counting the number of elements in `BooksOnLoan`.

We are generally not concerned with individual objects. Our goal is to identify and relate the object types (i.e. classes). We will often use the term object to denote an object type. One of our major concerns during analysis and design is to identify this set of objects, together with their attributes (state) and services (behavior).

Relations between objects can be expressed in a classification structure. The major types of relation depicted in such structures are listed in Table 10.2. If we have objects `Table` and `Chair`, we may also define a more general object `Furniture`. `Table` and `Chair` are said to be *specializations* of `Furniture`, while `Furniture` is a *generalization* of `Table` and `Chair`. These relations are also known as 'is-a' relations. The is-a relation is a well-known concept from entity–relationship modeling.

Table 10.2   Major types of relations between objects

Relation	Example
Specialization–generalization, is-a	`Table` *is-a* `Furniture`
Whole–part, has	`Table` *has* `TableTop`
Member-of, has	`Library` *has* `Member`

The specialization–generalization relations can be expressed in a hierarchical structure such as the one in Figure 10.5. In its most general form, the classification

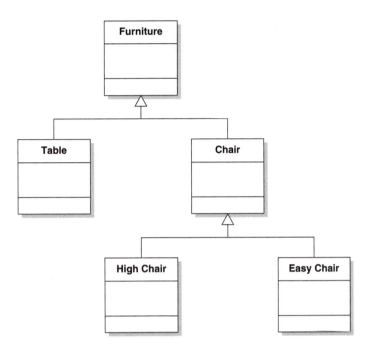

Figure 10.5 Object hierarchy

structure is a directed acyclic graph (DAG). Many classification structures can be depicted as a tree, in which each object is a direct descendant of exactly one other object. At the programming-language level, **single inheritance** corresponds to a tree structure, while **multiple inheritance** corresponds to a DAG.

Different objects may share some attributes. Both tables and chairs have a height, for instance. Rather than defining the full set of attributes for each object, we may define common attributes at a higher level in the object hierarchy and let descendants *inherit* those attributes. We may therefore define the attribute Height at the level of Furniture rather than at the level of each of its descendants. Obviously, this is just another way of looking at the object hierarchy. The fact that Chair and Table are both descendants of Furniture already suggests that they share certain properties, properties that are common to the various types of furniture. The fact that they are different descendants of Furniture also suggests that they each have unique properties.

Alternatively, we may view the object hierarchy as a *type hierarchy*. Chair and Table are *subtypes* of Furniture, in the same way as Cardinal is a subtype of Integer. In this view, an object is a restriction of the objects of which it is a specialization. Each chair is a piece of furniture but the reverse is not true.

By explicitly relating objects in the object hierarchy, a much tighter semantic binding between related objects is realized than is possible in more traditional design approaches. In a functional decomposition of our library automation problem for example, there is virtually no way to make the similarities between books and journals explicit in the design. In an object-oriented design, objects `Book` and `Journal` can be made descendants of a more general object `Publication` and attributes such as `Publisher` can be inherited from this more general type of object.

The is-a relation is one way to organize (object) types into a hierarchy. The part-of relation is another major organizational property of object types. A `Table` 'has' a `TableTop` and `Legs`. A `Publication` 'has' a `TitleDescription` and a `Publisher`. This part-of relation *aggregates* components into a 'whole'. It describes how compound things are made up of simpler things. By definition, the compound is at a higher level of abstraction than its components.

An object such as `TableTop` is made up of attributes, for example `Color`, `Width` and `Length`. At the next level, objects such as `TableTop` and `Legs` are assembled into a higher-level object, viz. `Table`. At that level, we may introduce additional attributes, such as `Size`, so that `Table` may also be seen as an aggregate of the first kind. In general, a compound object consists of a number of (references to) other objects and a number of 'simple' attributes, i.e. values.

In the case of `Table`, the part-of relation is a real-world part-of relation. In the case of `Publication`, `Publisher` does not correspond to some part of the underlying real-world object. It merely is part of the *representation* of the object `Publication`. Sometimes, an explicit distinction is made between the real-world part-of relation and the representational part-of (or component-of) relation. In UML, they are called *composition* and *aggregation*, respectively.

In many modeling methods, the part-of relation subsumes the *member-of* relation. The member-of relation is used to model the relationship between a set and its members. It is, however, sometimes useful to be able to distinguish between these organizational properties. For example, the part-of relation is generally considered to be transitive, whereas the member-of relation is not. If `Book` is a member of `Library` and `Library` is a member of `PublicInstitutions`, we do not want to infer that `Book` is a member of `PublicInstitutions`.

10.3 THE UNIFIED MODELING LANGUAGE

The Unified Modeling Language has its roots in the object-oriented analysis and design methods of the 1980s. Several key players in this field (Grady Booch, John Rumbaugh and Ivar Jacobson) joined Rational and started to unify their methods and notations. This resulted in the first versions of UML. At a later stage, the Object Management Group (OMG), an open consortium of companies, took over. OMG now controls the activities around UML and has adopted it as one of its standards. UML is by far the most widely used notation for both requirements engineering and design. The current version is known as UML 2.

The 13 diagrams of UML 2 are listed in Table 10.3. Some diagrams, such as the class diagram and the state machine diagram, have been there since the beginning

Table 10.3 UML 2 diagram types

Diagram	Description
Activity (D)	To model business processes, workflow, procedural logic. Similar to a flowchart but supports parallelism, as in a Petri net
Class (S)	To model classes, their features and relationships (see Section 10.3.1)
Communication (D)	To model the flow of messages between instances of classes. Very similar to the sequence diagram (see Section 10.3.4)
Component (S)	To model a set of components and their interrelationships, through interfaces (see Section 10.3.5)
Composite structure (D)	To model the internal dynamic structure of a class
Deployment (S)	To model the physical layout, i.e. the assignment of system elements to hardware elements
Interaction overview (S)	Combines activity diagrams and sequence diagrams
Object (S)	To model objects and their relationships at some point in time; also known as instance diagram
Package (S)	To model the grouping of elements into packages
Sequence (D)	To model the order in which messages are exchanged between instances of classes (see Section 10.3.3)
State machine (D)	To model the states in which an object can be and the transition between states (see Section 10.3.2)
Timing (D)	To model state changes of an object over time
Use case (D)	To model use cases (see Section 10.3.6)

of object orientation. Others are more recent. For example, the composite structure diagram and the timing diagram were introduced in UML 2. The class diagram is the diagram most often used (75%), followed by the use-case diagram and the communication diagram (50%) (Dobing and Parsons, 2006). People usually do not adhere all that strictly to the semantics of the language (Lange *et al.*, 2006). Some of the diagrams give a static view. For instance, a class diagram shows the static structure of a system. Other diagrams give a dynamic, or behavioral view, i.e. they show what happens when the system is executed. For instance, a sequence diagram shows which messages are exchanged between instances of classes. In Table 10.3, static diagrams are marked with an S and dynamic diagrams are marked with a D. In the following subsections, we discuss the most important UML diagrams.

10.3.1 The Class Diagram

Class diagrams depict the static structure of a system. A class diagram is a graph in which the nodes are objects (classes) and the edges are relationships between objects. By decorating the edges, many kinds of relationship can be modeled. These relationships fall into two groups: *generalizations* and *associations*.

The most common example of a generalization class diagram depicts the subclass–superclass hierarchy. Figure 10.5 is an example of such a class diagram. The classes are denoted by rectangles that have three compartments. These compartments contain, from top to bottom:

- the name of the class,

- the list of attributes of the class, and

- the list of operations of the class.

UML allows for quite some variety in its notation. We may for instance depict a class as a rectangle with one compartment only, just giving the name of the class. Adding slightly more detail, we may depict a class as a rectangle having two compartments, where the second one characterizes the responsibilities of that class, i.e., what it is supposed to do, as kind of an inline comment. Figure 10.6 gives the three-compartment representation in which a number of analysis-level details have been added. We may even extend the notation further and add implementation-level details, such as whether attributes and operations are public or private. We may think of these different representations as different views of the same model element. We

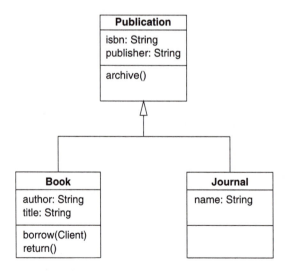

Figure 10.6 UML class diagram: generalization

may envision tool support that allows the user to switch from one representation to another, suppressing or adding detail as the need arises.

The hollow triangle in Figure 10.6 indicates that the structure is a specialization–generalization structure. Generalization is shown as a solid path from the more specific element (such as Book) to the more general element (Publication), with a large hollow triangle at the end of the path. A group of generalization paths may be shown as a tree with a shared segment, as in Figure 10.6.

The *attributes* of a class denote *properties* of that class. For example, publisher is a property of Publication. Next to attributes, UML has another way of denoting properties of a class, viz. *associations*. A UML association is depicted as a solid line connecting two classes. This line may be adorned with a variety of glyphs and textual information to provide further specifics of the relationship. A simple association between a library and its clients is depicted in Figure 10.7a. The (optional) name of

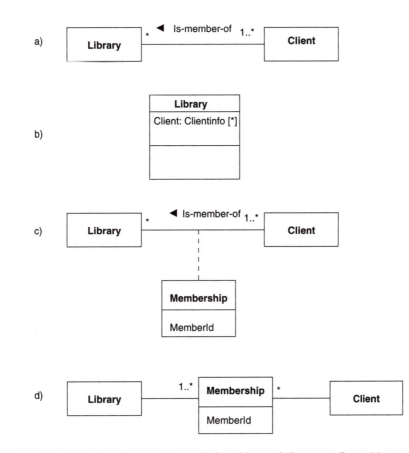

Figure 10.7 UML class diagram: (a) association, (b) association as attribute, (c) association class, (d) association class as a full class

the association is printed near the path. The solid triangle indicates the direction in which the verb is to be read. Note that associations are bi-directional: a client is a member of a library and a library has members. Further adornments can be added to indicate properties of the association. In Figure 10.7a we have added multiplicity information: a client can be a member of one or more libraries, while a library may have zero or more clients.

Strictly speaking, there is no difference between an attribute and an association. In Figure 10.7b, we have depicted `Client` as an attribute of `Library`. Usually, simple properties such as numbers and dates are modeled as attributes, while more significant concepts are modeled as associations.

An association such as `Member-of` also has class properties. For example, this association has attributes, e.g. `MemberId`, and operations, such as `BecomeMember` and `CeaseToBeMember`. Alternatively, we may say that class `Membership` has association properties. In UML, this model element is termed an **association class**. It can be depicted as a class symbol attached by a dashed line to an association path, as in Figure 10.7c. We may even promote an association class to a full class, as in Figure 10.7d. Notice that the multiplicities have moved. A membership (of a client) can be to one or more libraries, whereas the membership (of the library) relates to zero or more clients.

The part-of relationship is called **aggregation** or **composition** in UML. In an aggregation, objects can be part of more than one other object. For example, if our library maintains lists of required reading for certain courses, then a given book may be a part of more than one required reading list. Aggregation is denoted by an open diamond as an association role adornment. Composition is a strong notion of aggregation, in which the part object may belong to only one whole object. With composition, the parts are expected to live and die with the whole. If a table is composed of four legs and a tabletop, the table *owns* these parts. They cannot be part of another table at the same time. Composition is denoted by a solid filled diamond as an association role adornment, as in Figure 10.8a, which shows a `Book` with parts `title`, `author`, and `isbn`. A book has one title and one ISBN, so these parts have multiplicity 1. We assume here that a book may have up to three authors, so that part has multiplicity of 1..3. At the whole end of composition, the multiplicity is either 1 or 0..1. This part-of relationship is a relationship between a class and the classes of its attributes. An alternative notation for this part-of relation therefore consists of the top two compartments of the diagram for a class, as in Figure 10.8b.

Next to generalization and association, there are many other ways in which elements of a class diagram may depend on each other. For example, one class may call operations from another class, create instances of another class, and so on. Such dependencies are depicted with a dashed arrow, labeled with the type of dependency. If all dependencies are included in a class diagram, it soon becomes very cluttered. So it is wise to include only important dependencies. Many types of dependency need not be modeled by hand, but can be derived from the source code, and tools exist to do so.

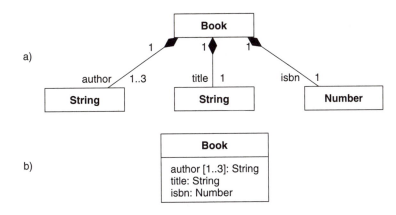

Figure 10.8 UML class diagram: composition as (a) association role adornment and (b) a simple class diagram

An *abstract class* is a class that cannot be instantiated directly. Only its (concrete) clients can. Abstract classes typically occur in hierarchies of data types. For instance, we may have an abstract class List, with subclasses such as LinkedList and ArrayList. The abstract class List may have abstract operations, such as get, that can only be made concrete at the subclass level. At the level of List, we then merely state that each of its subclasses will provide an implementation of get. In our library example, we could have designated Publication as an abstract class. Abstract classes are indicated by printing their name in italics.

An *interface* is a class all of whose features are abstract. It has no implementation. Interfaces are a useful means of splitting the set of properties of a class into subsets, in case other classes only need access to subsets of those properties. For instance, class Publication may have properties that are accessible to customers of the library, as well as properties that are for internal use only, such as its price, who authorized acquisition, and so on. We may then define two interfaces to Publication that are made available to other classes in the system. Publication then *provides* different interfaces to different client classes, who in turn *require* the interface. Interfaces are marked with the keyword «interface», as in Figure 10.9. Interfaces are often used to increase the robustness of a model, by restricting access to only the properties really needed.

10.3.2 The State Machine Diagram

A major class of services provided by an object relates to the object's life cycle: an object instance is created, updated zero or more times, and finally destroyed. State transition diagrams, which depict the possible states of an object and the transitions between those states, are a good help in modeling this life cycle.

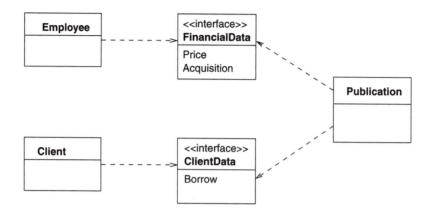

Figure 10.9 UML class diagram: interface

Usually, the finite state machine model and its associated state transition diagram (see Section 10.1.2) are extended in several ways when used in modeling the behavior of objects over time:

- In the classical finite state machine model, states do not have local variables. All necessary information is coded in the state. This easily leads to unwieldy models. For instance, suppose we want to model an object `LibraryMember` as follows: a person may become a member of the library, borrow up to ten books, and cease to be a member of the library. This leads to a finite state machine with states such as `has-borrowed-0-books`, `has-borrowed-1-book`, `has-borrowed-2-books`, ..., `has-borrowed-10-books`. If the number of books on loan are modeled as a local variable, the number of states in the model would be reduced from 12 to 2.

  For this reason, the finite state machine is usually extended by adding local variables to the model. A state in this extended finite state machine then comprises both the explicit state represented by a node in the state transition diagram and the value of the model's variables.

  These local variables are not only used to decrease the number of states. State transitions may now also change the values of variables; the variables may be tested to determine the next state and transitions may be guarded by the value of the variables. In Figure 10.10, the number of books on loan is kept in the local variable N. This variable is initialized to zero, updated when a book is borrowed or returned, and tested when a person terminates his membership.

- The components being modeled interact with the environment: there are input events and output actions. In all modeling methods that we know of, input events trigger transitions. When a person becomes a member of the library, this triggers

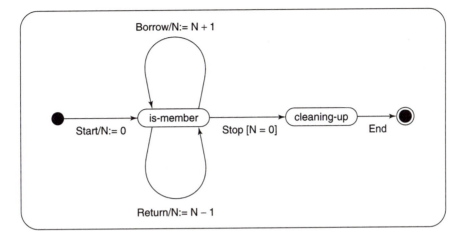

Figure 10.10 UML state machine diagram: object Member

the initial transition; when she borrows a book, it triggers a transition from a state, say, has-borrowed-7-books to a state has-borrowed-8-books. If the model has local variables, the latter state transition may result in a change in the value of such a local variable. In Figure 10.10, the input events are denoted as strings that label state transitions (such as Start and Borrow).

Different modeling methods have different ways to handle output actions. Sometimes, output actions are associated with a transition (this is known as a Mealy machine), sometimes output actions are associated with a state (a Moore machine). In the latter case, the output action is carried out as soon as the state is entered. In a formal sense, Mealy machines and Moore machines have the same expressive power.

- Finite state diagrams may become unwieldy. Therefore, one may add some structure, through a hierarchy. Part of the model may be compressed into one state. If we are interested in the details of a state, we may 'zoom in' on that state.

Many modeling methods, including UML, depict the sequence of states that an object goes through in a variant of the **statechart**. Statecharts are extended finite state machines (i.e. they have local variables) in which output actions may be associated with both transitions and states and in which states can be arranged hierarchically. In UML, this type of diagram is called a **state machine diagram**. As with class diagrams, UML has a rich notation for state machine diagrams. We will illustrate the major ingredients through a few examples (see also Figures 10.10 and 10.11).

A state is some condition in the life of an object. It is shown as a rectangle with rounded corners. An initial (pseudo) state is shown as a small filled circle. This initial state is a mere notational device; an object can not be in such a state. It indicates the

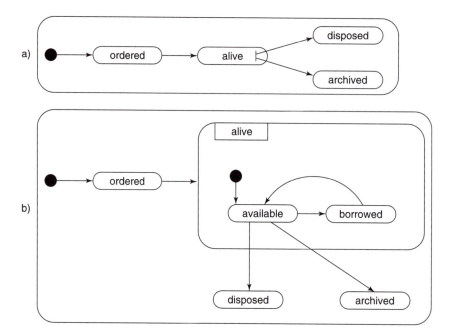

Figure 10.11 UML state machine diagram: object Book, (a) global view and (b) expanded view

transition to the first 'real' state. A final (pseudo) state is shown as a circle surrounding a small filled circle. This final state is also a notational device. A transition is shown as a solid arrow from one state to another. When a change of state occurs, that transition is said to 'fire'. A transition has a label that comes in three parts. The general form is *trigger-signature [guard]/activity*. All three parts are optional. The trigger-signature denotes the event which triggers the transaction, such as the borrowing of a book. The event may be guarded by a Boolean expression. For example, the transition from state is-member to cleaning-up in Figure 10.10 is guarded by the expression '$N = 0$': it can only occur if the number of books on loan is zero. When an event occurs, only one transition can be taken. So if multiple transitions occur with the same event, the guards must be mutually exclusive. The transition label may include a procedural expression after the symbol '/'. This procedural expression is executed when the transition fires.

Figure 10.11 gives an example of nested states. Figure 10.11a gives a global view of the life cycle of an object Book: a book is ordered, stays alive for a while, and is eventually either disposed of or archived. In Figure 10.11b, state alive is expanded to show its finer structure. In this example, the state is refined into mutually exclusive disjoint substates: a book is *either* available *or* borrowed.[1] The transition from

---

[1] UML also allows you to refine a state into concurrent substates. For example, when a book is returned, several things have to be done. It has to be checked whether the book is returned within the fixed time. If

state `ordered` to state `alive` is drawn to the boundary of state `alive`. This is equivalent to a transition to the initial state within the graphics region of `alive`. The transition from the nested state `available` to states `disposed` and `archived` is made directly. To indicate this transition from a suppressed internal state of `alive` to `disposed` and `archived` in Figure 10.11a, the transitions are not drawn from the boundary of `alive`, but from a so-called **stub**, shown as a small vertical line drawn inside its boundary.

10.3.3 The Sequence Diagram

Objects communicate by sending messages. To carry out a certain task, a particular sequence of messages may have to be exchanged between two or more objects. The time ordering in which this sequence of messages has to occur may be depicted in a **sequence diagram**. A sequence diagram is one type of **interaction diagram**. A second type of interaction diagram is the **communication diagram**, discussed in Section 10.3.4. In the telecommunications domain, sequence diagrams are known as message sequence charts; they provide a standard notation for designing and specifying protocols. The sequence diagram is also used in the design pattern community, to graphically depict the interaction between two or more objects participating in a design pattern.

In a sequence diagram, the horizontal dimension shows the various objects that participate in the interaction. An object is shown as a vertical dashed line, its 'lifeline'. The period in which the object is active (within the particular sequence of messages depicted) is shown as a thin rectangle. If the distinction between active and inactive is not important, the entire lifeline may be shown as an activation, as in Figure 10.12. The ordering in which the objects are shown carries no meaning.

The vertical dimension denotes the time sequencing of messages. Usually, only the *order* in which messages are displayed carries meaning. For real-time applications, the time axis may show actual numerical values.

Messages are shown as labeled arcs from one object to another. The vertical arrangement of messages indicates their order. The labels may also contain sequence numbers, which are particularly useful to indicate concurrency. A message may also be labeled with a guard, a Boolean expression that states the condition which must hold for the message to be sent.

Figure 10.12 shows a possible sequence of interactions between a user, a catalog of available books, and an object which handles reservations. The first message comes from an outside, unknown source. This message is called the **found message**. The user then sends a request to the catalog to look up a certain title. The catalog reacts by sending data about that title to the user. If the title is not available (this is indicated by a Boolean expression, the guard, within square brackets), a request to reserve that title

not, some fine may be due. Possible outstanding reservations need to be checked as well and, if so, one of these reservations must be handled. These subprocesses can be handled concurrently. There can be a state `returning book` which, when refined, results in two or more concurrent, and-related substates. This is shown by tiling the graphics region of the state using dashed lines to separate subregions.

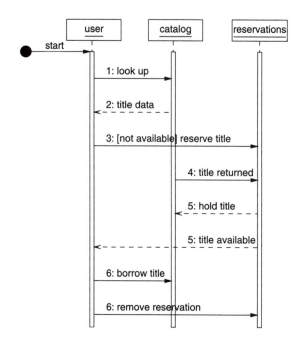

Figure 10.12 UML sequence diagram: reserving a title

is sent to the object that handles reservations. Some time later, that title will become available again and reservations will be notified. The object reservations will then send a message to the catalog to hold that book and will notify the user that the title is now available. The ordering of those two messages is irrelevant, so they carry the same sequence number. The user may now borrow the title and the corresponding reservation will be removed.

Again, UML has a rich notational vocabulary for sequence diagrams. It is possible to distinguish asynchronous message-passing from synchronous message-passing, to indicate iteration, to show the creation and destruction of objects, and so on. The main purpose of the sequence diagram however remains the same: an easy-to-read overview of the passing of messages in a particular interaction sequence.

10.3.4 The Communication Diagram

The communication diagram is another way to show one possible scenario for the interaction between a number of related objects. A communication diagram is a directed graph where the nodes denote entities and the edges denote communication between those entities.

Figure 10.13 shows the same sequence of interactions as the scenario depicted in the sequence diagram in Figure 10.12. Communication diagrams emphasize the

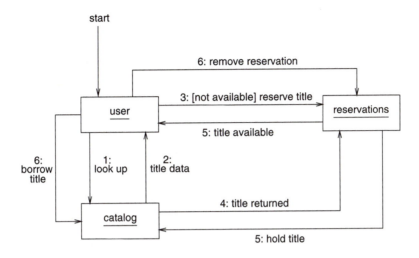

Figure 10.13 UML communication diagram: reserving a title

objects and their relationships relevant to a particular interaction. To provide more detail about the interaction, relevant attributes may be shown inside the nodes (by adding another compartment, as in a class diagram) and these attributes may also be incorporated in the labels of the edges.

Sequence diagrams emphasize the ordering of messages and sequence numbers are optional; in a communication diagram, sequence numbers are mandatory since the ordering does not show itself graphically.

10.3.5 The Component Diagram

When designing larger systems, it may be useful to be able to identify entities larger than a single class. This can be done in a **component diagram**. In software architecture descriptions, for instance, the component diagram is a good way to depict a module view of a system (see Section 11.3).

In essence, a component diagram is a class diagram with the stereotype ≪component≫. In UML 1, the component diagram had a special form. In UML 2, this form is often depicted as a small component icon inside the component, as in Figure 10.14. Other than this icon, the component diagram does not introduce any new notation.

Components contain classes or other components. In Figure 10.14 we have modeled Publication as a component containing two classes, called Searching and Storage. Components are connected by interfaces. Figure 10.14 uses the 'ball-and-socket' notation to depict interfaces. Both this notation and the one used in Figure 10.9 are allowed in both class diagrams and component diagrams.

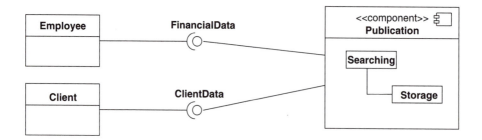

Figure 10.14 UML component diagram

10.3.6 The Use Case

One possible requirements elicitation technique is scenario-based analysis; see also Chapter 9. A scenario is a story which tells how a specific task instance is executed. Often, different scenarios are variations on the same theme. For instance, one scenario may describe the ordinary borrowing of a book, another one may describe borrowing a book when there are still outstanding fines, and so on. A set of scenarios having the same user goal, in this case borrowing, is called a **use case**.

A use case can be documented in various ways: as narrative text, formally using pre- and postconditions, for example, or graphically as in a state transition diagram. The **use-case diagram** provides an overview of a set of use cases. Each use case is shown as an ellipse with the name of the use case. The use cases are enclosed by a rectangle denoting the system boundary. An actor that initiates or participates in a scenario is shown as a stick figure with the name of the actor below. Figure 10.15

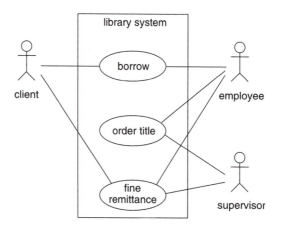

Figure 10.15 UML use case diagram

shows part of the use-case diagram for our library system. Borrowing a book involves two actors: a client and an employee of the library. Many other use cases will involve those two actors as well. The ordering of a new book needs approval of a supervisor, as does the remittance of a fine.

10.4 SUMMARY

During requirements engineering and design, a variety of modeling notations are applied. Most of these use some sort of box-and-line diagram. The mainstream modeling notations of today stem from the Unified Modeling Language (UML). Many UML diagrams are based on or derived from earlier types of diagram. In this chapter, we discussed a selection of classic modeling notations as well as the major UML diagram types.

The classic modeling notations discussed are:

- entity–relationship modeling (ERM), used to model the structure of data,

- finite state machines (FSMs), used to model states and state transitions of a system,

- data flow diagrams (DFDs), used to model functional decomposition with respect to data,

- CRC Cards, a simple notation to document collaborative design decisions.

UML evolved from earlier object-oriented analysis and design methods. Concepts used in UML, such as object, attribute, class, and relationship, originate in the field of object orientation. UML 2 offers 13 diagram types that fall into two classes. Some diagrams give a static view of the system. For instance, a class diagram shows how a system is statically organized into classes. Other diagrams give a dynamic view. For instance, a sequence diagram shows the time ordering of message exchanges between instance of classes.

10.5 FURTHER READING

Entity–relationship modeling was pioneered by Chen (1976). Many texts on database modeling include an elaborate discussion of ERM; see, for example, (Batini *et al.*, 1992). Statecharts are described in (Harel, 1988). CRC cards are described in (Beck and Cunningham, 1989).

The different views of the notion of object are discussed in (Taivalsaari, 1993). The various meanings of attribute and related notions such as aggregate, part and member are discussed in (Motschnig-Pitrik, 1996). Wegner (1992) is a classic paper on the various dimensions of object-oriented modeling.

Fowler (2004) provides a good introduction to UML. UML is extensively discussed in two books by its creators, (Booch *et al.*, 1999) and (Rumbaugh *et al.*, 1999). Actual usage of UML is reported in (Dobing and Parsons, 2006), (Lange *et al.*, 2006) and (Grossman *et al.*, 2005).

Exercises

1. Explain the following concepts from entity–relationship modeling: entity, entity type, attribute value, attribute, relationship.

2. Define the following terms: object, state, attribute, message, and inheritance.

3. Explain the difference between the specialization–generalization relation and the whole–part relation.

4. Explain the difference between a class diagram and a state machine diagram.

5. Explain the difference between a sequence diagram and a communication diagram.

6. Explain the difference between a class diagram and a component diagram.

7. What are CRC cards and use-case scenarios used for in object-oriented analysis and design?

8. In what respects does a UML state diagram differ from a state transition diagram?

9. ♡ In what sense can the interface to a class be considered a contract? What are the repercussions of this for subtyping relations? (See (Meyer, 1992).)

11

Software Architecture

LEARNING OBJECTIVES

- To appreciate the role of software architecture in software development
- To understand the relation between software architecture and design decisions
- To be able to document a software architecture in different views
- To be able to characterize some important software architectural styles
- To understand the role and purpose of software architecture assessments

> Software architecture concerns the large-scale structure of software systems. This large-scale structure reflects the early, essential design decisions. The decision process involves negotiating and balancing functional and quality requirements on the one hand and possible solutions on the other hand. Software architecture is not a phase strictly following requirements engineering, but the two are intertwined. In this chapter, we discuss how to design, document, and evaluate software architectures.

A good design is the key to a successful product. Almost 2 000 years ago, the Roman architect Vitruvius recorded what makes a design good: durability (*firmitas*), utility (*utilitas*), and charm (*venustas*). These quality requirements still hold, for buildings as well as software systems. A well-designed system is easy to implement, is understandable and reliable, and allows for smooth evolution. Badly designed systems may work at first, but they are hard to maintain, difficult to test, and unreliable.

During the design phase, the system is decomposed into a number of interacting components. The top-level decomposition of a system into major components together with a characterization of how these components interact, is called its **software architecture**. Viewed this way, software architecture is synonymous with global design. There is, however, more to software architecture than mere global design.

Software architecture serves three main purposes:

- It is a vehicle for communication among stakeholders. A software architecture is a global, often graphic, description that can be communicated to the customers, end users, designers, and so on. By developing scenarios of anticipated use, relevant quality aspects can be analyzed and discussed with various stakeholders. The software architecture also supports communication during development. It can be used to develop a *skeletal* version of the system. This skeletal version contains all of the architecture's components in a rudimentary form. The skeletal system can be used as an environment for the incremental implementation of the system. It can also be used as an environment (test harness) for testing the system.

- It captures early design decisions. In a software architecture, the global structure of the system has been decided upon, through the explicit assignment of functionality to components of the architecture. These early design decisions are important since their ramifications are felt in all subsequent phases. It is therefore paramount to assess their quality at the earliest possible moment. By evaluating the architecture, a first and global insight into important quality aspects can be obtained. The global structure decided upon at this stage also structures development: the work-breakdown structure may be based on the decomposition chosen at this stage, testing may be organized around this same decomposition, and so on.

- It is a transferable abstraction of a system. The architecture is a basis for reuse. Design decisions are often ordered, from essential to nice features. The essential decisions are captured in the architecture, while the nice features can be decided upon at a later stage. The software architecture thus provides a basis for a family of similar systems, a **product line**; see also Chapter 18. The global description captured in the architecture may also serve as a basis for training, e.g. to introduce new team members.

The traditional view holds that the requirements fully determine the structure of a system. Traditional design methods as discussed in Chapter 12 work that way. Their aim is to systematically bridge the gap between the requirements and some blueprint of an operational system in which all of the requirements are met. It is increasingly being recognized that other forces influence the architecture (and, for that matter, the design) as well:

- Architecture is influenced by the development organization. In our library example, for example, the hardware and software for reading bar codes might be subcontracted to some organization having special expertise in that area. There will then be one or more system components with externally dictated functionality and interfaces to deal with this part of the problem. If an organization deploys one or more systems with a certain architecture, (maintenance) expertise will be structured according to the decomposition chosen in that architecture and there will be a pressure to have future systems follow that same architecture.

- Architecture is influenced by the background and expertise of the architect. If an architect has a positive experience with, say, a layered architecture, he is likely to use that same approach on his next project.

- Architecture is influenced by its technical and organizational environment. In financial applications, for instance, government rules may require a certain division of functionality between system components. In embedded systems, the functionality of hardware components may influence the functionality of and interaction between software components. Finally, the software engineering techniques prevalent in the development organization will exert influence on the architecture.

This mutual influencing between an architecture and its environment is a cyclical process, known as the architecture business cycle (ABC) (Bass *et al.*, 2003). For example, an architecture yields certain units of work, corresponding to the components distinguished in the architecture. If the same components occur over and over again, expertise will be organized according to the functionality embedded in these components. The development organization may then become expert in certain areas. This expertise then becomes an asset which may affect the goals of the development organization. The organization may try to develop and market a series of similar products in which this expertise is exploited.

Traditional design is inward-looking: given a set of requirements, how can we derive a system that meets those requirements. Software architecture has an outward focus as well: it takes into account how the system fits into its environment. Software architecting includes negotiating and balancing of functional and quality requirements on one hand, and possible solutions on the other hand. This is further elaborated in Section 11.1. Balancing requirements also requires that the candidate software architecture is assessed. This is a form of testing, discussed in Section 11.5.

One of the early definitions of software architecture is (Shaw *et al.*, 1995):

> The architecture of a software system defines that system in terms of computational components and interactions among those components.

A more recent definition is (Bass *et al.*, 2003):

> The software architecture of a program or computing system is the structure or structures of the system, which comprise software elements, the externally visible properties of those elements, and the relationships among them.

The latter definition reflects, among others, the insight that there may be more than one structure that is of interest. In house construction, we use different drawings: one for the electrical wiring, one for the water supply, etc. These drawings reflect different structures which are all part of the same overall architecture. We generally observe the architecture through one of these more specific views. The same holds for software architecture. This is further elaborated in Section 11.3.

In the software architecture, the global structure of the system has been decided upon. This global structure captures the early, major design decisions. Whether a design decision is major or not really can only be ascertained with hindsight, when we try to change the system. Only then will it show which decisions were really important. A priori, it is often not at all clear if and why one design decision is more important than another (Fowler, 2003). For instance, we may decide to separate the user interface from the processing part and store data about books in a flat file in our library system. Both decisions could be important but they need not be. Separating the user interface from the processing part is generally considered good design. If, at a later stage, changes occur in either part, we will be glad to have made this decision. If no such changes occur, the decision was not all that important, after all. Deciding to use flat files to store data in our library system may turn out to have been important if our library grows and we are forced to switch to database storage of data. But again, if no such change occurs, the decision wasn't that important either.

Viewed this way, the architectural design process is about making the important design decisions. Next, these important design decisions need to be documented. Both the process of making architectural decisions and their documentation for later use are discussed in Section 11.2.

A very active field of research these days is aimed at identifying and describing components at a higher level of abstraction, i.e. above the level of a module or abstract data type. These higher-level abstractions are known as **design patterns** and **software architectural styles** (or **architectural patterns**).

Part of the work in software architecture is aimed at characterizing and classifying these software architectural styles, as well as developing appropriate notations and supporting tools. The ultimate goal is that the resulting abstractions become part of the vocabulary of software engineers, in much the same way as abstract data types are already part of that vocabulary. Section 11.4 gives an overview of the major issues involved in software architectural styles. Design patterns are further discussed in Chapter 12.

Today's work in software architecture is broad in scope. Almost any topic in software engineering is being rethought in architectural terms. The discussion in this chapter is focused on how to design, name, document, and assess software architectures.

11.1 SOFTWARE ARCHITECTURE AND THE SOFTWARE LIFE CYCLE

If software architecture is just global design, we would be selling old wine in new bottles. The design phase then is simply split into two subphases: architectural, global design and detailed design. The methods used in these two subphases might be different, but both essentially boil down to a decomposition process, taking a set of requirements as their starting point. Both design phases then are inward-looking: starting from a set of requirements, derive a system that meets those requirements.

A 'proper' software architecture phase however has an outward focus as well. It includes the negotiating and balancing of functional and quality requirements with possible solutions. This means requirements engineering and software architecture are not consecutive phases that are more or less strictly separated, but instead they are heavily intertwined. An initial set of functional and quality requirements is the starting point for developing an initial architecture. This initial architecture results in a number of issues that require further discussion with stakeholders. For instance, the envisaged solution may be too costly, integration with existing systems may be complex, maintenance may be an issue because of a lack of staff with certain expertise, or performance requirements cannot be met. These insights lead to further discussions with stakeholders, a revised set of requirements, and a revised architecture. This iterative process continues until an agreement is reached. Only then will detailed design and implementation proceed. The difference between these two paradigms is illustrated in Figure 11.1.

We thus see important differences between traditional process models that do not pay specific attention to software architecture and process models that do pay attention to software architecture:

- In traditional models, iteration only concerns functional requirements. Once the functional requirements are agreed upon, design starts. In process models that include a software architecture phase, iteration involves both functional and quality

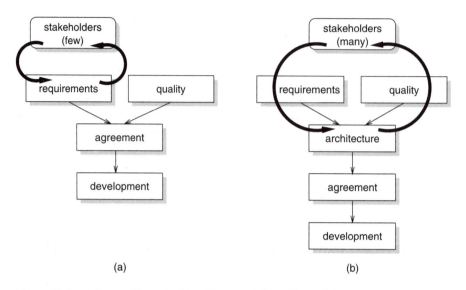

Figure 11.1 Software life cycle (a) without and (b) with explicit attention to software architecture

requirements. Only when the combined set of functional and quality requirements is agreed upon will development proceed.

- Traditional models involve negotiation with a few stakeholders only. Usually, only the client and end users are involved. Negotiations about architectural solutions may involve a much larger variety of stakeholders and include, for instance, the future maintenance organization for the system to be developed and owners of other systems that this system has to interact with.

- In traditional models there is no balancing of functional and quality requirements. Once the functional requirements are agreed upon, development proceeds and it is assumed that quality requirements can be met. If it turns out that the quality requirements cannot be met, the project gets into trouble. Deadlines slip, functionality is skipped, more hardware is bought, etc. In process models that include a software architecture phase, there is a balancing of functional and quality requirements at an early stage.

11.2 ARCHITECTURE DESIGN

Design is a problem-solving activity and, as such, is very much a matter of trial and error. In the presentation of a mathematical proof, subsequent steps dovetail well into each other and everything drops into place at the end. The actual discovery of the proof probably went quite differently. The same holds for the design of software. We should not confuse the outcome of the design process with the process itself. The outcome of the design process is a 'rational reconstruction' of that process. (Note that we made precisely the same remark with respect to the outcome of the requirements engineering process.)

During design, the system is decomposed into parts that each have a lower complexity than the system as a whole, while the parts together solve the user's problem. The design problem can now be formulated as follows: how to determine this decomposition. There really is no universal method for this. The design process is a creative one, and the quality and expertise of the designers is a critical determinant for its success. Yet, during the course of the years, a number of ideas and guidelines have emerged which may serve us in designing software. These have resulted in a large number of design methods, which are the topic of Chapter 12.

In a similar vein, architectural design methods have been developed. A good example is attribute-driven design (ADD), described in (Bass *et al.*, 2003). The input to the ADD process are the requirements, formulated as a set of prioritized quality attribute scenarios. A quality attribute scenario is a scenario as known from requirements engineering, but whose description explicitly captures quality information; see also Section 6.3.

ADD is described as a top-down decomposition process. In each iteration, one or a few components are selected for further decomposition. In the first iteration, there is only one component, 'the system'. From the set of quality attribute scenarios, an important quality attribute is selected that will be handled in the current refinement step. For instance, in our library system, we may have decided on a first decomposition of the system into three layers: a presentation layer, a business logic layer, and a data layer. In a further ADD step, we may decide to decompose the presentation layer, and select usability as the quality attribute that drives this decomposition. A pattern is then selected that satisfies the quality attribute. For instance, a data validation pattern (Folmer *et al.*, 2003) may be applied to verify whether data items have been entered correctly. Finally, the set of quality attribute scenarios is verified and refined to prepare for the next iteration.

ADD gives little guidance for the precise order and kind of refinement steps. This is very much a matter of the architect's expertise. The same rather global support is given by other architecture design methods, as discussed by (Hofmeister *et al.*, 2007). The global workflow common to these methods is depicted in Figure 11.2. At the centre, is the *backlog*, which contains a list of issues to be tackled, open problems, ideas that still have to be investigated, and so on. The name derives from Scrum, an agile method (Schwaber and Beedle, 2002). There, the backlog drives the project. In (architecture) design projects, the notion of a backlog is usually not represented explicitly. Yet, it is always there, if only in the head of the architect. There are three inputs to the backlog: context, requirements, and evaluation results. The context refers to such things as ideas the architect may have, available assets that can be used, constraints set, and so on. Obviously, the requirements constitute another important input. In each step of the architecting process, one or a few items from the backlog are taken and used to transform the architecture developed so far. The result of this

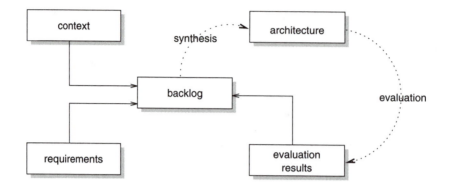

Figure 11.2 Global workflow in architecture design

transformation is evaluated (usually rather informally) and this evaluation may in turn change the contents of the backlog. New items (for instance, new problems) may be added, items may disappear or become obsolete, and the priorities of backlog items may change.

Figures 11.1b and 11.2 describe the same iterative process. Whereas the former emphasizes interactions with external parties, the latter emphasizes the architectural design process itself. The latter process model is also more finegrained. Many of the iterations involving one or more items of the backlog, a synthesis step, evaluation of the result, and updating the backlog, will be done by the architect and not involve communication with other stakeholders. But once in a while, communication with other stakeholders takes place, and this is the level at which Figure 11.1b applies.

The architecture design process is very much driven by the architect's experience, much more so than by any of the 'architecture design' methods. An experienced architect *knows* how to handle a given issue, rather than some method telling him how to perform a design iteration. This is also true for the design methods discussed in Chapter 12 that are applied at the more detailed levels of design. Their descriptions usually give much more guidance than those for architecture design methods but this guidance is mostly used by inexperienced designers. Since architecture design is usually done by experienced designers, the amount of guidance given, and needed, is less. Attention then shifts to techniques for documenting the *result* of the design process: the decisions, their rationale, and the resulting design.

If architecture is the set of design decisions, then documenting the architecture boils down to documenting the set of design decisions. This is usually not done fully, though. We can usually get at the *result* of the design decisions, the solutions chosen, but not at the reasoning behind them. Much of the *rationale* behind the solutions is lost forever or resides only in the heads of the few people associated with them, if they are still around.

So the reasoning behind a design decision is not explicitly captured. This is tacit knowledge, essential for the solution chosen, but not documented. At a later stage, it then becomes difficult to trace the reasons of certain design decisions. In particular, during evolution one may stumble upon these design decisions, try to undo them or work around them, and get into trouble when this turns out to be costly if not impossible.

There are different types of undocumented design decisions:

- The design decision is implicit: the architect is unaware of the decision or it concerns 'of course' knowledge. Examples include prior experience, implicit company policies to use certain approaches, standards, and so on.

- The design decision is explicit but undocumented: the architect takes a decision for a very specific reason (e.g. using a certain user-interface policy because of time constraints). The reasoning is not documented and thus is likely to vaporize over time.

- The design decision is explicit and explicitly undocumented: the reasoning is hidden. There may be tactical company reasons to do so or the architect may have personal reasons (e.g. to protect his position).

It is a fantasy to want to document all design decisions. There are far too many of them and not all of them are that important. Documenting design decisions takes time and effort from the architect, a very busy person. But we may try to document the really important decisions.

A design decision addresses one or more issues that are relevant to the problem at hand. There may be more than one way to resolve these issues, so that the decision is a choice from amongst a number of alternatives. The particular alternative selected preferably is chosen because it has some favorable characteristics. That is, there is a rationale for our particular choice. Finally, the particular choice made may have implications for subsequent decision making. Table 11.1 gives a template for the types of information that is important to capture for each design decision.

Table 11.1 Elements of a design decision

Element	Description
Issues	Design issues being addressed by this decision
Decision	The decision taken
Status	The status of the decision, e.g. pending, approved
Assumptions	The underlying assumptions about the environment in which the decision is taken
Alternatives	Alternatives considered for this decision
Rationale	An explanation of why the decision was chosen
Implications	Implications of this decision, such as the need for further decisions or requirements
Notes	Any additional information one might want to capture

Table 11.2 gives an example of a design decision for our library application. It concerns the choice of a three-tier architecture, consisting of a presentation layer, a business logic layer, and a data management layer.

Table 11.2   Example of a design decision

Element	Description
Issues	The system has to be structured so that it is maintainable, reusable, and robust.
Decision	A three-tier architecture, consisting of a presentation layer, a business logic layer, and a data management layer.
Status	Approved.
Assumptions	The system has no hard real-time requirements.
Alternatives	A service-oriented architecture (SOA) or a different type of X-tier architecture (e.g. one with a fat client including both presentation and business logic, and a data management tier).
Rationale	Maintenance is supported and extensions are easy to realize because of the loose coupling between layers. Both the presentation layer and the data management layer can be reused in other applications. Robustness is supported because the different layers can easily be split over different media and well-defined layer interfaces allow for smoother testing.
Implications	Performance is hampered since all layers have to be gone through for most user actions.
Notes	None.

Design decisions are often related. A given design decision may constrain further decisions, exclude or enable them, override them, be in conflict with them, and so on. These relationships between design decisions resemble the kind of relationships that may exist between requirements, as discussed in Section 9.1.3. And likewise, the notations and tools used to capture this information are very similar as well. A simple way to structure design decisions hierarchically is in the form of a decision tree (see Figure 11.3).

11.3 ARCHITECTURAL VIEWS

A software architecture serves as a vehicle for communication among stakeholders. Example stakeholders are: end users of the anticipated system, security experts, representatives from the maintenance department, owners of other systems that this system has to interface with, software developers, and of course the architect himself. These stakeholders all have a stake, but the stakes may differ. End users will be interested to see that the system will provide them with the functionality asked for.

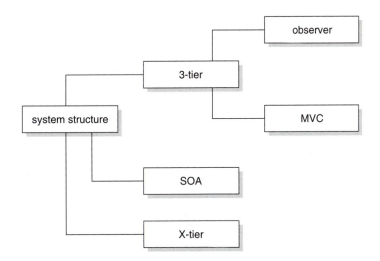

Figure 11.3 Tree of design decisions

Software developers will be interested to know where to implement this functionality. Maintainers want to assure themselves that components are as independent as possible.

In some cases, it may be possible to devise one single architecture representation that serves all these stakeholders. In general, this will not work, though. A specific stakeholder is best served by a representation of the software architecture that highlights his concerns. Just think of civil engineering, where one representation may highlight the outer appearance of a structure while another highlights construction aspects.

IEEE Standard 1471 (IEEE1471, 2000) gives a general structure for software architecture representations. The main elements from this standard are:

- **stakeholder**: an individual, team, or organization (or classes hereof) with interests in, or concerns relative to, a system;

- **view**: a representation of a whole system from the perspective of a related set of concerns;

- **viewpoint**: the purposes and audience for a view and the techniques or methods employed in constructing a view.

So the stakeholder concerns determine which representations (views) are appropriate for a specific software architecture. Each view has a corresponding viewpoint which gives the 'syntax' of the view, much like a construction drawing has an accompanying description telling what all the glyphs in the drawing mean.

(IEEE1471, 2000) does not tell you *which* viewpoints to use. In essence, it suggests we develop an appropriate set of viewpoints for each separate software architecture. It does have the notion of a library viewpoint, though, a viewpoint that might be useful across different software architectures. (Bass *et al.*, 2003) give a collection of viewpoints that is useful across a wide variety of software architectures. These viewpoints fall into three classes:

- **Module viewpoints** give a *static* view of the system. They are usually depicted in the form of box-and-line diagrams where the boxes denote system components and the lines denote some relation between those components. Table 11.3 describes typical module viewpoints.

- **Component-and-connector viewpoints** give a *dynamic* view of the system, i.e. they describe the system in execution. Again, they are usually depicted as box-and-line diagrams. Table 11.4 describes typical component-and-connector viewpoints.

- **Allocation viewpoints** give a relation between the system and its environment, such as who is responsible for which part of the system. Table 11.5 gives typical allocation viewpoints.

Of course, you do not use all these viewpoints for a single software architecture. Usually, one from each category will suffice. You may for instance choose the

Table 11.3 Module viewpoints

Viewpoint	Description
Decomposition	Elements are related by the 'is a submodule of' relation. Larger elements are composed of smaller ones. It is the result of a top-down refinement process. The decomposition viewpoint often forms the basis for the project organization and the system's documentation. It is the viewpoint we are most used to in software design.
Uses	The relation between elements is 'uses' (A calls B, A passes information to B, etc.). The uses relation goes back to Parnas (1972); see also Chapter 12. The uses relation is important when we want to assess modifiability: if an element is changed, all elements it is used by potentially have to be changed as well. It is also useful to determine incremental subsets of a system: if an element is in a given subset, all elements it uses must also be in that subset.
Layered	This is a special case of the uses viewpoint. It is useful if we want to view the system as a series of layers, where elements from layer n can only use elements from layers $< n$. Layers can often be interpreted as virtual machines.
Class	Elements are described as a generalization of other elements. The relation between elements is 'inherits from'. It is obviously most applicable for object-oriented systems.

Table 11.4 Component-and-connector viewpoints

Viewpoint	Description
Process	The system is described as a series of processes, connected by communication or synchronization links. It is useful if we want to reason about the performance or the availability of the system.
Concurrency	To determine opportunities for parallelism, a sequence of computations that can be allocated to a separate physical thread later in the design process is collected in a 'logical thread'. It is used to manage issues related to concurrent execution.
Shared data	Describes how persistent data is produced, stored, and consumed. It is particularly useful if the system centers around the manipulation of large amounts of data. It can be used to assess qualities such as performance and data integrity.
Client–server	Describes a system that consists of cooperating clients and servers. The connectors are the protocols and messages that clients and servers exchange. This viewpoint expresses separation of concerns and physical distribution of processing elements.

Table 11.5 Allocation viewpoints

Viewpoint	Description
Deployment	Shows how software is assigned to hardware elements and which communication paths are used. It allows one to reason about, e.g., performance, security, and availability.
Implementation	Indicates how software is mapped onto file structures. It is used in the management of development activities and for build processes.
Work assignment	Shows who is doing what and helps to determine which knowledge is needed where. For instance, one may decide to assign functional commonality to a single team.

decomposition, deployment, and work-assignment viewpoints. It is also possible to combine viewpoints. In Figure 11.4 we have combined the decomposition viewpoint and the client–server viewpoint to create a view of our library system. In specific cases, additional architectural views may be helpful or needed. In systems for which the user interface is of critical importance, a separate user-interface view may be developed; in electronic commerce applications, a view highlighting security aspects may come in handy; and so on.

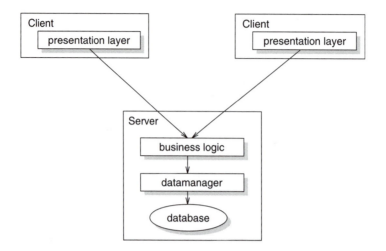

Figure 11.4 A three-tier architecture

Many organizations have developed their own set of library viewpoints. A well-known set of library viewpoints is known as the '4 + 1 model' (Kruchten, 1995). It consists of the following viewpoints:[1]

- a **conceptual**, or **logical**, **viewpoint** that describes the system in terms of major design elements and their interactions;

- an **implementation viewpoint** that gives a view of the system in terms of modules or packages and layers;

- a **process viewpoint** that describes the dynamic structure of the system in terms of tasks, processes, their communication, and the allocation of functionality to run-time elements; this view is only needed if the system has a significant degree of concurrency;

- a **deployment viewpoint** that contains the allocation of tasks to physical nodes; this view is only needed if the system is distributed.

The '+1' viewpoint is a set of important use cases. This set of use cases drives the architectural design and serves as glue to connect the other four viewpoints. The '4 + 1 model' is part of the RUP development methodology (Kruchten, 2003).

The above viewpoints are all technical in nature. Often, it is also useful to construct one or more viewpoints which emphasize business concerns. Figure 11.5 gives a business-oriented view of our library system. It addresses three aspects of

---

[1] We use the terminology from RUP (Kruchten, 2003). In (Kruchten, 1995), slightly different terminology is used.

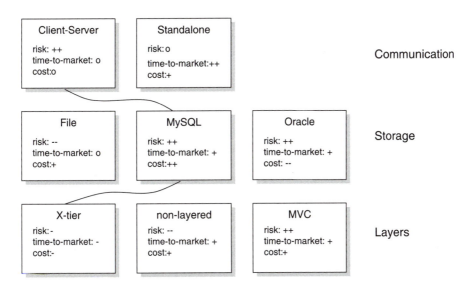

Figure 11.5 A business view

the architecture: communication, storage, and layers. For each, several alternatives are given and, for each alternative, the risk, time to market, and cost are indicated. One alternative for each aspect is chosen. These alternatives are connected by curved lines. In this way, a quick overview is obtained. The view is easy to grasp, especially so for non-technical stakeholders.[2]

11.4 ARCHITECTURAL STYLES

One interesting theory of problem-solving in the programming domain states that programmers solve such problems using **programming plans**, program fragments that correspond to stereotypical actions, and rules that describe programming conventions. For example, to compute the sum of a series of numbers, a programmer uses the 'running total loop plan'. In this plan, some counter is initialized to zero and is incremented with the next value of a series in the body of a loop. Experts tend to recall program fragments that correspond to plan structures before they recall other elements of the program. This nicely maps onto the idea that knowledge is stored in human memory in meaningful units (chunks).

An expert programmer has at his disposal a much larger number of knowledge chunks than a novice programmer. This concerns both programming knowledge and knowledge about the application domain. Both during the search for a solution and during program comprehension, the programmer tries to link to knowledge already

---

[2]This business view was created by Cuno de Boer, Raymond Backus, Youri op 't Roodt, and Reinier L'Abée, students in my 2005 Software Architecture course.

present. As a corollary, part of our education as a programmer or software engineer should consist of acquiring a set of useful knowledge chunks.

At the level of algorithms and abstract data types, such a body of knowledge has been accumulated over the years and has been codified in text books and libraries of reusable components. As a result, abstractions, such as `QuickSort`, embodied in procedures, and abstract data types, such as `Stack` and `BinaryTree`, have become part of our vocabulary and are routinely used in our daily work.

The concepts embodied in these abstractions are useful during the design, implementation, and maintenance of software for the following reasons:

- They can be used in a variety of settings and can be given unique names. The names are used in communicating the concepts and serve as labels when retrieving and storing them in human memory. The label `QuickSort` rings the same bell for all people working in our field.

- We have notations and mechanisms to support their use and reuse, such as procedure calls and the module concept.

- We have organized related concepts into (semantic) networks that can be searched for an item that fits the problem at hand. For example, we know the time and space tradeoffs between `QuickSort` and `BubbleSort` or between a standard binary search tree and an AVL-tree, and we know the grounds on which to make a choice.

Design patterns are collections of a few modules (or, in object-oriented circles, classes) that are often used in combination, and which together provide a useful abstraction. A design pattern is a recurring solution to a standard problem. The prototypical example of a pattern is the Model–View–Controller (MVC) pattern from Smalltalk. We may view design patterns as micro-architectures. Design patterns are further discussed in Section 12.5.

Two further notions often used in this context are (**application**) **framework** and **idiom**. An application framework is a partially complete system which needs to be instantiated to obtain a complete system. It describes the architecture of a family of similar systems. It is thus tied to a particular application domain. The best-known examples are frameworks for building user interfaces. An idiom is a low-level pattern, specific to some programming language. For example, the *counted-pointer* idiom (Buschmann *et al.*, 1996, pp. 353–8) can be used to handle references to objects created dynamically in C++. It keeps a reference counter which is incremented or decremented when references to an object are added or removed. Memory occupied by an object is freed if no references to that object remain, i.e. when the counter becomes zero. Frameworks and idioms thus offer solutions that are more concrete and language-specific than the architectural styles and design patterns we will discuss.

Work in the area of software architecture and design patterns has been strongly influenced by the ideas of the architect Christopher Alexander, as formulated in (Alexander, 1979) and (Alexander *et al.*, 1977). The term 'pattern' derives from Alexander's work and the format used to describe software architectural styles and design patterns is shaped after the format Alexander used to describe his patterns, such as 'alcove', 'office connection' or 'public outdoor room'. In software engineering, we often draw a parallel with other engineering disciplines, in particular civil engineering. This comparison is made to highlight both the similarities, such as the virtues of a phased approach, and the differences, such as the observation that software is logical rather than physical, which hampers the control of progress. The comparison with the field of architecture is often made to illustrate the role of different views, as expressed in the different types of blueprint produced. Each of these blueprints emphasizes a particular aspect.

The classical field of architecture provides some further interesting insights for software architecture. These insights concern:

- the notion of architectural style,

- the relationship between style and engineering, and

- the relationship between style and materials.

Architecture is a (formal) arrangement of architectural elements. An architectural style abstracts from the specifics of an architecture. The decomposition of our library system might, for instance, result in an architecture consisting of one main program and four subroutines, sharing three data stores. If we abstract from these specifics, we obtain its architectural style, in which we concentrate on the types of its elements and their interconnections.

Viewed in this way, an architectural style describes a certain codification of elements and their arrangement. Conversely, an architectural style *constrains* both the elements and their interrelationships. For example, the Tudor style *describes* how a certain type of house looks and also *prescribes* how its design should look. In a similar vein, we may characterize a software architectural style such as, say, the pipes-and-filter style.

Different engineering principles apply to different architectural styles. This often goes hand in hand with the types of materials used. Cottage-style houses and high-rise apartment buildings differ in the materials used and the engineering principles applied. A software design based on abstract data types (the material) emphasizes separation of concerns by encapsulating secrets (the engineering principle). A design based on pipes and filters emphasizes bundling of functionality in independent processes.

When selecting a certain architectural style with its corresponding engineering principles and materials, we are guided by the problem to be solved as well as the larger context in which the problem occurs. We cannot build a skyscraper from wooden posts. Environmental regulations may prohibit us erecting high-rise buildings in rural areas. And, the narrow frontages of many houses on the Amsterdam canals are partly due to the fact that local taxes were based on the number of street-facing windows. Similar problem- and context-specific elements guide us in the selection of a software architectural style.

These similarities between classical architecture and software architecture provide us with clues as to what constitutes a software architectural style and what its description should look like.

(Alexander *et al.*, 1977) presents 253 'patterns', ranging in scale from how a city should look down to rules for the construction of a porch. Perhaps his most famous pattern is about the height of buildings:

> There is abundant evidence to show that high buildings make people crazy.
>
> . . .
>
> High buildings have no genuine advantage, except in speculative gains to banks and land owners. They are not cheaper, they do not help create open space, they make life difficult for children, they are expensive to maintain, they wreck the open spaces near them, and they damage the light and air and view. But quite apart from this, empirical evidence shows that they can actually damage people's minds and feelings.
>
> . . .
>
> In any urban area, no matter how dense, keep the majority of buildings four stories high or less. It is possible that certain buildings should exceed this limit, but they should never be buildings for human habitation.

An Alexandrian pattern is not a cookbook, black-box recipe for architects, any more than a dictionary is a toolkit for a novelist. Rather, a pattern is a flexible generic scheme providing a solution to a problem in a given context. In a narrative form, its application looks like this:

> IF you find yourself in <context>, for example <examples>, with <problem>,
>
> THEN for some <reasons>, apply <pattern> to construct a solution leading to a <new context> and <other patterns>.

The 'Four-Story Limit' pattern may, for example, be applied in a context where one has to design a suburb. The citation gives some of the reasons for applying this pattern. If it is followed, it will give rise to the application of other patterns, such as those for planning parking lots, the layout of roads, or the design of individual houses.[3]

---

[3] Here, we may note another similarity between classical architecture and software architecture. In the 1950s and 1960s, housing was a major problem in Western Europe and beyond. There were far too few houses available, most of those were of a bad quality (damp, no bathroom, too small). In the post-war economic boom, many suburbs were constructed with lots of spacious apartments, each one a container made of steel and concrete. These new suburbs solved one problem – the housing of a large number of people – but at the same time created other problems which only showed themselves much later, e.g. lack of community feeling and social ties, high crime rates. As a result, massive renovation projects have started and many a high-rise apartment building has been demolished.

In software development, we developed company-wide systems in the 1970s and 1980s with an emphasis on performance, uniformity, and standardized ways of working. Many of these systems are unable to cope satisfactorily with today's requirements of flexibility and adaptability, and are therefore being renovated.

Shaw (1996) characterizes a number of well-known software architectural styles in a framework that resembles a popular way of describing design patterns. Both the characterization and the framework are shaped after Alexander's way of describing patterns. We will use this framework to describe a number of well-known and classic architectural styles. The framework has the following entries:

- **Problem**: A description of the type of problem this style addresses. Certain characteristics of the requirements will guide the designer in his choice of a particular style. For example, if the problem consists of a series of independent transformations, a pipes-and-filter type of architecture suggests itself.

- **Context**: A designer will be constrained in the use of a style by certain characteristics of the environment. Or, to put it the other way round, a style imposes certain requirements on the environment. For example, the pipes-and-filter style usually relies on operating system support for data transfer between filters.

- **Solution**: A description of the solution chosen. The major elements of a software architecture are **components** and **connectors**. Components are the building blocks of a software architecture. They usually embody a computational element of some sort (such as a procedure), but a component can also be a data store (such

Table 11.6 Some component types (*Source*: M. Shaw and D. Garlan, *Software Architecture: Perspectives on an emerging discipline*, p. 149, © 1996. Reprinted by permission of Prentice Hall.)

Type	Description
Computational	The component performs a computation of some sort. Usually, the input and output to the component are fairly simple, e.g. procedure parameters. The component may have a local state, but this state disappears after the component has done its job. Example components of this type are (mathematical) functions and filters.
Memory	A memory component maintains a collection of persistent, structured data, to be shared by a number of other components. Examples are a database, a file system, or a symbol table.
Manager	A manager component contains a state and a number of associated operations. When invoked, these operations use or update the state, and this state is retained between successive invocations of the manager's operations. Abstract data types and servers are example components of this type.
Controller	A controller component governs the time sequence of other events. A top-level control module and a scheduler are examples hereof.

as a database). The connectors describe how components interact.[4] The order
of execution of components is governed by the **control structure**. The control
structure captures how control is transferred during execution. Some typical
components and connectors are given in Tables 11.6 and 11.7.

Table 11.7 Some connector types (*Source*: M. Shaw and D. Garlan, *Software Architecture:
Perspectives on an emerging discipline*, pp. 149–50, © 1996. Reprinted by permission of
Prentice Hall.)

Type	Description
Procedure call	With this type of connector, there is a single thread of control between the caller and the called component. Control is transferred to the component being called, and this component remains in control until its work has ended. Only then is control transferred back to the calling component. The traditional procedure call and the remote procedure call are examples of this type of connector.
Data flow	With a data flow connector, processes interact through a stream of data, as in pipes. The components themselves are independent. Once input data to a component is available, it may continue its work.
Implicit invocation	With implicit invocation, a computation is invoked when a certain event occurs, rather than by explicit interaction (as in a procedure call). Components raising events do not know which component is going to react and invoked components do not know which component raised the event to which they are reacting.
Message passing	Message passing occurs when we have independent processes that interact through explicit, discrete transfer of data, as in TCP/IP. Message passing can be synchronous (in which case the sending/receiving process is blocked until the message has been completely sent/received) or asynchronous (in which case the processes continue their work independently).
Shared data	When using shared data connectors, components operate concurrently on the same data space, as in blackboard systems or multiuser databases. Usually, some blocking scheme prevents concurrent writes to the same data.
Instantiation	With instantiation, one component (the instantiator) provides space for the state required by another component (the instantiated), as in abstract data types.

---

[4]These notions of component and connector are not related to the component-and-connector
viewpoints discussed in Section 11.3.

The choice of components and connectors is not independent. Usually, a style is characterized by a combination of certain types of component and connector, as well as a certain control structure. The **system model** captures the intuition behind such a combination. It describes the general flavor of the system.

- **Variants**: Architectural styles give a rather general description. Often, certain variants or specializations may be identified, which differ from the general style.

- **Examples**: One should include references to real examples of a style. Architectural styles do not stem from theoretical investigations, but result from identifying and characterizing best practice.

Figures 11.6 to 11.11 contain descriptions of six well-known architectural styles: a main program with subroutines, an abstract data type, implicit invocation, pipes and filters, repository, and layered.

In the main-program-with-subroutines architectural style, the main tasks of the system are allocated to different components, which are called, in the appropriate order, from a control component. The decomposition is strongly geared towards an ordering of the various actions to be performed with respect to time. The top-level component controls this ordering.

Components in the main-program-with-subroutines type of decomposition often use shared data storage. Decisions about data representations, then, are a mutual property of the components that use the data. We may also try to make those decisions locally rather than globally. In that case, the user does not get direct access to the data structures, but is offered an interface. The data can only be accessed through appropriate procedure or method calls. This is the essence of the abstract-data-type architectural style.

A major advantage of abstract data types over shared data is that changes in data representation and algorithms can be accomplished relatively easily. Changes in functionality, however, may be much harder to realize. This is because method invocations are explicit, hard-coded in the implementation. An alternative is to use the implicit invocation style. In implicit invocation, a component is not invoked explicitly. Instead, an **event** is generated. Other components in the system may express their interest in this event by associating a method with it; this method is automatically invoked each time the event is raised. Functional changes can be realized easily by changing the list of events that components are interested in.

Some applications consist of a series of components in which component i produces output which is read and processed by component $i + 1$, in the same order in which it is written by component i. In such cases, we need not explicitly create these intermediate data structures. Rather, we may use the pipe-and-filter mode of operation that is well-known from UNIX, and directly feed the output of one transformation into the next one. The components are called filters and the FIFO connectors are called pipes. An important characteristic of this scheme is that any structure imposed

---

Style: Main program with subroutines

Problem The system can be described as a hierarchy of procedure definitions. This style is a natural outcome of a functional decomposition of a system (see Chapter 12). The top-level module acts as the main program. Its main task is to invoke the other modules in the right order. As a consequence, there is usually a single thread of control.

Context This style naturally fits in with programming languages that allow for nested definitions of procedures and modules.

Solution

    System model Procedures and modules are defined in a hierarchy. Higher-level modules call lower-level modules. The hierarchy may be strict, in which case modules at level n can only call modules at level $n - 1$, or it may be weak, in which case modules at level n may call modules at level $n - i$, with $i \geq 1$. Procedures are grouped into modules following such criteria as coupling and cohesion (see Chapter 12).

    Components (Groups of) procedures, which may have their own local data, and global data which may be viewed as residing in the main program.

    Connectors Procedure call and shared access to global data.

    Control structure There is a single, centralized thread of control; the main program pulls the strings.

Variants This style is usually applied to systems running on one CPU. Abstractly, the model is preserved in systems running on multiple CPUs and using the Remote Procedure Call (RPC) mechanism to invoke processes.

Examples Parnas (1972)

Figure 11.6 Main-program-with-subroutines architectural style (*Source*: M. Shaw, Some Patterns for Software Architectures, in (Vlissides *et al.*, 1996, pp. 255–269). Reproduced by permission of M. Shaw.)

---

on the data to be passed between adjacent filters has to be explicitly encoded in the datastream that connects these filters. This encoding scheme involves decisions which must be known to both filters. The data has to be unparsed by one filter while the next filter must parse its input in order to rebuild that structure. The Achilles' heel of the pipes-and-filters scheme is error handling. If one filter detects an error, it is cumbersome to pass the resulting error message through intermediate filters all the way to the final output. Filters must also be able to resynchronize after an error has been detected and filters further downstream must be able to tolerate incomplete input.

Style: Abstract data type

Problem A central issue is to identify and protect related bodies of information. The style is especially suited for cases where the data representation is likely to change during the lifetime of the system. When the design matches the structure of the data in the problem domain, the resulting components encapsulate problem-domain entities and their operations.

Context Many design methods, most notably the object-oriented ones, provide heuristics to identify real-world objects. These objects are then encapsulated in components of the system. Object-oriented programming languages provide the class concept, which allows us to relate similar objects and reuse code through the inheritance mechanism.

Solution

System model Each component maintains its own local data. Components hide a secret, viz. the representation of their data.

Components The components of this style are managers, such as servers, objects, and abstract data types.

Connectors Operations are invoked through procedure calls (messages).

Control structure There is usually a single thread of control. Control is decentralized, however; a component may invoke any component whose services it requires.

Variants Methods or languages that are not object-oriented only allow us to hide data representations in modules. Object-oriented methods or languages differ as regards their facilities for relating similar objects (single or multiple inheritance) and their binding of messages to operations (compile time or run time); see also Chapter 12.

Examples Parnas (1972); Booch (1994) for worked examples

Figure 11.7 Abstract-data-type architectural style (*Source*: M. Shaw, Some Patterns for Software Architectures, in (Vlissides *et al.*, 1996, pp. 255–269). Reproduced by permission of M. Shaw.)

The repository style fits situations where the main issue is to manage a richly structured body of information. In our library example in Chapter 9, the data concerns things such as the stock of available books and the collection of members of the library. This data is persistent and it is important that it always reflects the true state of affairs. A natural approach to this problem is to devise database schemas for the various types of data in the application (books, journals, library clients, reservations, and so on) and store the data in one or more databases. The functionality of the system

Style: Implicit invocation

Problem We have a loosely coupled collection of components, each of which carries out some task and may enable other operations. The major characteristic of this style is that it does not bind recipients of signals to their originators. It is especially useful for applications that need to be able to be reconfigured, by changing a service provider or by enabling and disabling operations.

Context This style usually requires an event handler that registers components' interests and notifies others. Because of the intrinsically decentralized nature of systems designed this way, correctness arguments are difficult. For the same reason, building a mental model of such systems during program comprehension is difficult too.

Solution

System model Processes are independent and reactive. Processes are not invoked explicitly, but implicitly through the raising of an event.

Components Components are processes that signal events without knowing which component is going to react to them. Conversely, processes react to events raised somewhere in the system.

Connectors Components are connected through the automatic invocation of processes that have registered interest in certain events.

Control structure Control is decentralized. Individual components are not aware of the recipients of signals.

Variants There are two major categories of systems exploiting implicit invocation. The first category comprises the so-called tool-integration frameworks as exemplified by many software development support environments. They consist of a number of 'toolies' running as separate processes. Events are handled by a separate dispatcher process which uses some underlying operating system support such as UNIX sockets; see, for example, (Reiss, 1990). The second category consists of languages with specialized notations and support for implicit invocation, such as the 'when-updated' features of some object-oriented languages; see for example (Sutton *et al.*, 1990).

Examples (Garlan *et al.*, 1992); Reiss (1990); (Sutton *et al.*, 1990)

Figure 11.8 Implicit-invocation architectural style (*Source*: M. Shaw, Some Patterns for Software Architectures, in (Vlissides *et al.*, 1996, pp. 255–269). Reproduced by permission of M. Shaw.)

Style: Pipes and filters

Problem A series of independent, sequential transformations on ordered data. Usually, the transformations are incremental. Often, the structure of the datastreams is very simple: a sequence of ASCII characters. If the data has a rich structure, this will imply quite some overhead for the parsing and unparsing of the data.

Context This style requires that the system can be decomposed into a series of computations, *filters*, that incrementally transform one or more input streams. It usually relies on operating system operations to transfer the data from one process to another (*pipes*). Error handling is difficult to deal with uniformly in a collection of filters.

Solution

> **System model** The resulting systems are characterized by continuous data flow between components, where the components incrementally transform datastreams.
>
> **Components** The components are filters that perform local processing; i.e. they read part of their input data, transform the data, and produce part of their output. They have little internal state.
>
> **Connectors** Datastreams (usually plain ASCII, as in UNIX).
>
> **Control structure** Data flow between components. Each component usually has its own thread of control.

Variants Pure filters have little internal state and process their input locally. In the degenerate case, they consume all of their input before producing any output. In that case, the result boils down to a batch-processing type of system.

Examples Delisle and Garlan (1990)

Figure 11.9 Pipes-and-filters architectural style (*Source*: M. Shaw, Some Patterns for Software Architectures, in (Vlissides *et al.*, 1996, pp. 255–269). Reproduced by permission of M. Shaw.)

---

is incorporated in a number of, relatively independent, computational elements. The result is a repository architectural style.

Modern compilers are often structured in a similar way. Such a compiler maintains a central representation of the program to be translated. A rudimentary version of that representation results from the first, lexical, phase: a sequence of tokens rather than a sequence of character glyphs. Subsequent phases, such as syntax and semantic analysis, further enrich this structure into, for example, an abstract syntax tree. In the end, code is generated from this representation. Other tools, such as symbolic

Style: Repository

Problem The central issue is managing and maintaining a richly structured body of information. The information must typically be manipulated in many different ways. The data is long-lived and its integrity is important.

Context This style often requires considerable support, in the form of a run-time system augmented with a database. Data definitions may have to be processed to generate support to maintain the correct structure of the data.

Solution

   System model The major characteristic of this model is its centralized, richly structured body of information. The computational elements acting upon the repository are often independent.

   Components There is one memory component and many computational processes.

   Connectors Computational units interact with the memory component by direct access or procedure call.

   Control structure The control structure varies. In traditional database systems, for example, control depends on the input to the database functions. In a modern compiler, control is fixed: processes are sequential and incremental. In blackboard systems, control depends on the state of the computation.

Variants Traditional database systems are characterized by their transaction-oriented nature. The computational processes are independent and triggered by incoming requests. Modern compilers, and software development support environments, are systems that increment the information contained in the repository. Blackboard systems have their origin in AI. They have been used for complex applications such as speech recognition, in which different computational elements each solve part of the problem and update the information on the blackboard.

Examples (Barstow *et al.*, 1984) for software development environments; Corkill (1997) for blackboard architectures

Figure 11.10 Repository architectural style (*Source*: M. Shaw, Some Patterns for Software Architectures, in (Vlissides *et al.*, 1996, pp. 255–269). Reproduced by permission of M. Shaw.)

Style: Layered

Problem We can identify distinct classes of services that can be arranged hierarchically. The system can be depicted as a series of concentric circles, where services in one layer depend on (call) services from inner layers. Quite often, such a system is split into three layers: one for basic services, one for general utilities, and one for application-specific utilities.

Context Each class of service has to be assigned to a specific layer. It may occasionally be difficult to properly identify the function of a layer succinctly and, as a consequence, to assign a given function to the most appropriate layer. This holds the more if we restrict visibility to just one layer.

Solution

> **System model** The resulting system consists of a hierarchy of layers. Usually, visibility of inner layers is restricted.
>
> **Components** The components in each layer usually consist of collections of procedures.
>
> **Connectors** Components generally interact through procedure calls. Because of the limited visibility, the interaction is limited.
>
> **Control structure** The system has a single thread of control.

Variants A layer may be viewed as a virtual machine, offering a set of 'instructions' to the next layer. Viewed thus, the peripheral layers get more and more abstract. Layering may also result from a wish to separate functionality, e.g. into a user-interface layer and an application-logic layer. Variants of the layered scheme may differ as regards the visibility of components to outer layers. In the most constrained case, visibility is limited to the next layer up.

Examples Linden and Müller (1995); Ho and Olsson (1996); (Bohrer *et al.*, 1998)

Figure 11.11 Layered architectural style (*Source*: M. Shaw, Some Patterns for Software Architectures, in (Vlissides *et al.*, 1996, pp. 255–269). Reproduced by permission of M. Shaw.)

debuggers, pretty-printing programs, or static analysis tools, may also employ the internal representation built by the compiler. The resulting architectural style again is that of a repository: one memory component and a number of computational elements that act on the repository. Unlike the database variant, the order of invocation of the elements matters in the case of a compiler. Also, different computational elements enrich the internal representation, rather than merely update it.

The repository architectural style can also be found in certain AI applications. In computationally complex applications, such as speech recognition, an internal representation is built and acted upon by different computational elements. For example, one computational element may filter noise, another one builds up phonemes, etc. The internal representation in this type of system is called a **blackboard** and the architecture is sometimes referred to as a blackboard architecture. A major difference with traditional database systems is that the invocation of computational elements in a blackboard architecture is triggered by the current state of the blackboard, rather than by (external) inputs. Elements from a blackboard architecture enrich and refine the state representation until a solution to the problem is found.

Our final example of an architectural style is the layered architectural style. A prototypical instance is the ISO Open System Interconnection Model for network communication. It has seven layers: physical, data, network, transport, session, presentation, and application. The bottom layer provides basic functionality. Higher layers use the functionality of lower layers. The different layers can be viewed as virtual machines whose 'instructions' become more powerful and abstract as we go from lower layers to higher layers.

In a layered scheme, by definition, lower levels cannot use the functionality offered by higher levels. The other way round, the situation is more varied. We may choose to allow layer n to use the functionality of each layer m, with $m < n$. We may also choose to limit the visibility of functionality offered by each layer and, for example, restrict layer n to use only the functionality offered by layer $n - 1$. A design issue in each case is how to assign functionality to the different layers of the architecture, i.e. how to characterize the virtual machine it embodies. If visibility is not restricted, some of the elegance of the layered architecture gets lost. This situation resembles that of programming languages containing low-level, bit-manipulation operations alongside `while` statements and procedure calls. If visibility is restricted, we may end up copying functionality to higher levels without increasing the level of abstraction.

Linden and Müller (1995) give an example of a layered architectural style for use in telecommunications. In this example, layers do not correspond to different levels of abstraction. Rather, the functionality of the system has been separated. Two main guidelines drive the assignment of functionality to layers in this architecture:

- Hardware-dependent functionality should be placed in lower layers than application-dependent functionality.

- Generic functionality should be placed in lower layers than specific functionality.

The resulting architecture has four layers:

- *Operating system* This layer comprises the run-time system, database, memory management, and so on.

- *Equipment maintenance* This layer houses the control for peripheral devices and its interconnection structure. It deals with such things as data distribution and fault-handling of peripheral hardware. The bottom two layers together constitute the distributed operating infrastructure upon which applications run.

- *Logical-resource management* Logical resources come in two flavors. The first class contains abstractions from hardware objects. The second class consists of software-related logical objects, such as those for call-forwarding in telephony.

- *Service management* This layer contains the application functionality.

A similar line of thought can be followed in other domains. For instance, it is hard to predict how future household electronic equipment will be assembled into hardware boxes. Will the PC and the television be in the same box? Will the television and the DVD player be combined or will they remain as separate boxes? No one seems to know. Since the life of many of these products is about six months, industry is forced to use a building-block approach, emphasizing reuse and the development of product families rather than products. A division of functionality into a hardware-related inner layer, a generic signal processing layer, and a user-oriented service layer suggests itself. The above architecture for telecommunications applications can be understood along the same lines.

In practice, we usually encounter a mixture of architectural styles. For example, many software development environments can be characterized as a combination of the repository and layered architectural styles; see also Chapter 15. The core of the system is a repository in which the various objects, ranging from program texts to work-breakdown structures, reside. Access to these objects as well as basic mechanisms for the execution and communication of tools are contained in a layer on top of this repository. The tools themselves are configured in one or more layers on top of these basic layers. Interaction between tools may yet follow another paradigm, such as implicit invocation.

11.5 SOFTWARE ARCHITECTURE ASSESSMENT

The software architecture captures early design decisions. Since these early decisions have a large impact, it is important to start testing even at this early stage. Testing software architectures is commonly referred to as **software architecture assessment**: the software architecture is assessed with respect to quality attributes such as maintainability, flexibility, and so on.

It is important to keep in mind that in this process the architecture is assessed, while one hopes the results will hold for a system yet to be built. As a result, conclusions will often be at quite a general level. Also, there is some uncertainty about whether these results will actually be realized. Suppose the architecture is assessed for maintainability. Even if the outcome is quite positive, a sloppy implementation process may yet spoil the rosy picture. Figure 11.12 illustrates this issue. Architecture assessment takes place at the left-hand side of the figure, while one assumes the results will be valid for the right-hand side.

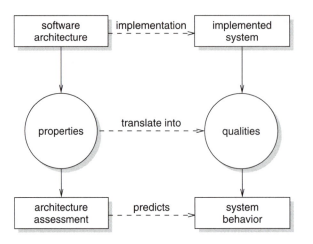

Figure 11.12 The relation between a software architecture assessment and actual system behavior

There are two broad classes of techniques for evaluating a software architecture. The first class comprises measuring techniques that rely on quantitative information. Examples include architecture metrics and simulation. The second class comprises questioning techniques, in which one investigates how the architecture reacts to certain situations. This is often done with the help of scenarios. In the following text, we concentrate on the latter.

There are different types of scenario one may use in architecture assessments. Common types are:

- **Use cases**: these are often already available or can be derived from the requirements.

- **Change cases**: change cases describe possible or likely future situations. They describe 'what if' situations, such as 'what if our library has to be able to handle DVDs as well as books and journals?'.

- **Stress situations**: these describe extreme conditions under which the system has to operate, such as limits with respect to performance or the number of concurrent users of the system.

- **Far-into-the-future scenarios**: these are like change cases, but farther away. For instance, we may envision a future in which a library changes from a document archive to a memory archive. We may want to retain how an old-fashioned bakery smells or the sound of an Amsterdam tram.

One of the best known architecture assessment methods is the Architecture Tradeoff Analysis Method (ATAM). As the name says, an important goal of ATAM is to determine how quality attributes interact. If we decide to include an authorization component to increase security, it is likely to degrade performance. By making the consequences of design decisions explicit, it becomes possible for stakeholders to trade off the different possibilities and make informed decisions, with clear insight into the consequences thereof.

The main steps of ATAM are listed in Table 11.8. There may be a preparatory phase in which participants meet to discuss the whole exercise, and a follow-up phase at the end in which a written report is delivered. The early steps are meant to make the participants familiar with the major quality drivers for the system (step 2), the solution chosen (step 3), and the approaches and patterns used in this solution (step 4). In step 5, the quality requirements are articulated in more detail. The project's decision makers are key in this process. The end result of this exercise is a tree. The root node is termed 'utility'. It expresses the overall quality of the architecture. The next level contains the quality attributes that will be evaluated. These are again broken down into more detailed constituents. The leaf nodes are concrete scenarios. Figure 11.13 gives part of a possible utility tree for assessing our library system.

Table 11.8 Steps of ATAM

1. Present method to stakeholders
2. Present business drivers (by project manager)
3. Present architecture (by lead architect)
4. Identify architectural approaches
5. Generate quality attribute tree
6. Analyze architectural approaches
7. Brainstorm and prioritize scenarios
8. Analyze architectural approaches
9. Present results

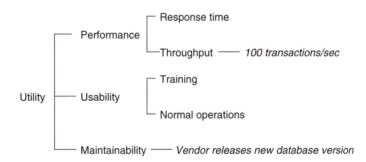

Figure 11.13 An example utility tree

The leaf nodes in Figure 11.13 are printed in italic. This description is incomplete. The full representation has to contain more information, for example the type of information contained in a quality attribute scenario (see Section 6.3).

A complete utility tree may contain more scenarios than can be analyzed during the assessment. It is then useful to prioritize scenarios. ATAM suggests two criteria for doing so. Using the first criterion, the stakeholders indicate how important the scenarios are (e.g. using a simple three-point scale: High, Medium, Low). Using the second criterion, the architect ranks the scenarios according to how difficult he believes it will be to satisfy the scenario, using the same three-point scale. In the remainder of the assessment, one may then, for instance, concentrate on the scenarios that score High on both scales.

In step 6, the scenarios are discussed one at a time. For each scenario, the architect walks the stakeholders through the architecture, explaining how the architecture supports that scenario. This may trigger a further discussion of the architectural approaches chosen. The end result is a documented list of sensitivity points, tradeoff points, risks, and nonrisks, relating the architectural decisions made to the relevant quality attributes.

A **sensitivity point** is a property of the architecture that is critical for a certain quality attribute. For example, the possibility of undoing user actions critically affects the usability of our library system, and this property therefore is a sensitivity point with respect to usability. At the same time, this decision also is a sensitivity point with respect to performance. If a decision is a sensitivity point for more than one quality attribute, it is called a **tradeoff point**. If performance is of utmost importance, the decision to include an undo facility may be a **risk**. If this decision is not critical, it is a **nonrisk**.

The utility tree is based on the main drivers used during the design of the architecture. Its construction is done in consultation with the main decision makers. There are other stakeholders, such as a maintenance manager or security expert, that can also be polled for additional scenarios. This is done in step 7. In a similar way to step 5, these scenarios are prioritized and a selection is made for further study. In a similar way to step 6, these additional scenarios are analyzed in step 8. Finally, the collected information is summarized and presented to all stakeholders in step 9.

The result of an architecture assessment goes way beyond a list of sensitivity points, tradeoff points, risks, and nonrisks. Stakeholders, including the architect, often construct a much deeper understanding of the architecture, its underlying decisions, and the ramifications thereof. Also, better documentation is often delivered as a byproduct of the assessment. This is similar to the extra benefits of software inspections and walkthroughs besides the identification of software errors (see Section 13.4.2).

In practice, organizations often perform software architecture assessments in a less rigid sense than suggested by the above description of ATAM. Usually, a cafeteria-like approach is followed, whereby elements from ATAM and similar methods are chosen that best fit the situation at hand (Kazman *et al.*, 2006).

11.6 SUMMARY

Software architecture is concerned with the description of elements from which systems are built, the interaction among those elements, patterns that guide their composition, and constraints on those patterns. The design of a software architecture is driven by quality concerns. The resulting software architecture is described in different views, each of which addresses specific concerns on behalf of specific stakeholders. This resembles the way different drawings of a building emphasize different aspects on behalf of its different stakeholders.

It is important to document not only the resulting solution but also the decisions that led to that solution, its rationale, and other information that is helpful to guide its further evolution.

Software architecture is an important notion, for more than one reason:

- The comparison with traditional architecture reveals commonalities which help us to get a better grip on the software design process and its products. Software architecture is not only concerned with the blueprint that is the outcome of the design process. The notion of an architectural style has merits of its own and the relationship between style on the one hand and engineering and materials on the other hand provide additional insights into what software design entails (Perry and Wolf, 1992).

- The field may eventually yield a repertoire of concepts that software architects can use in their search for solutions. Expert designers in any field build on a vast collection of reusable concepts. These concepts are given unique names, which are used to communicate them, and serve as labels when retrieving and storing them in human memory. Software architecture is concerned with identifying, describing and categorizing components at a high level of abstraction. The resulting abstractions are to become part of the vocabulary of software engineers, much as abstract data types are already part of that vocabulary.

- Phrasing a software design in software architectural terms promotes consistency during development and maintenance. Phrasing the global design in terms of an architecture forces us to think about its general flavor, in terms of types of component and connector, as well as a certain control structure. By making this intuition explicit, it both *describes* and *prescribes* how the system should look and how it may evolve over time.

- A software architecture captures early design decisions. The architecture can be used to evaluate those decisions. It also provides a way to discuss those decisions and their ramifications with the various stakeholders.

11.7 FURTHER READING

Shaw and Garlan (1996) is an early influential source that discusses the emerging field of software architecture, in particular software architectural styles. (Bass *et al.*, 2003) give a broad overview of the field, including the various forces that influence software architecture and the purposes of a software architecture, and ADD. It includes a number of case studies to illustrate these issues. (Clements *et al.*, 2003) is wholly devoted to architecture documentation and architectural views. The state of the art in software architecture is reflected in (Software, 2006b). A comparison between the classical field of architecture and software architecture is made in (Perry and Wolf, 1992). Different architectural views of the same system are the topic of (Kruchten, 1995) and (Soni *et al.*, 1995). Rozanski and Woods (2005) give a very good catalog of useful architectural viewpoints. Architecture as a set of design decisions is the topic of (Tyree and Akerman, 2005). Architectural mismatches as a consequence of implicit assumptions are discussed in (Garlan *et al.*, 1995).

Software architecture and design patterns have been strongly influenced by the works of the architect Christopher Alexander. It is certainly worthwhile to have a look at (Alexander *et al.*, 1977) and (Alexander, 1979). Lea (1994) gives an introduction to his work for software engineers. Alexander (1999) explains the origins of pattern theory. (Buschmann *et al.*, 1996) is an excellent source for architectural patterns. The theory of programming plans stems from (Soloway, 1986).

(Clements *et al.*, 2002) discuss software architecture evaluation in great depth. (Maranzano *et al.*, 2005) discuss experiences with architecture reviews. A survey of architecture assessment methods is given in (Dobrica and Niemelä, 2002).

Many issues related to software architecture have not been touched upon in this chapter. These include efforts to classify software architectural styles along different dimensions (Shaw and Clements, 1996), architecture description languages and supporting tools (Shaw *et al.*, 1995), architecture description languages (Medvidovic and Taylor, 2000), architecture reconstruction (Deursen *et al.*, 2004), and the role of the software architect (Kruchten, 1999), (Mustapic *et al.*, 2004).

Exercises

1. Give a definition of the term 'software architecture'. Explain the different elements in this definition.

2. What is the difference between software architecture and top-level design?

3. What is the main purpose of a software architecture?

4. What is the relation between design decisions and software architecture?

5. Explain the architecture design method called Attribute-Driven Design (ADD).

6. What is the role of the backlog in design?

7. What is the difference between the notions of software architecture and design pattern?

8. What is the difference between the conceptual or logical viewpoint and the implementation viewpoint?

9. Explain the difference between module, component-and-connector, and allocation viewpoints.

10. Describe in your own words the essence of the implicit-invocation architectural style.

11. In what sense does the abstract-data-type architectural style constrain the designer?

12. Why is error-handling difficult in the pipes-and-filter architectural style?

13. Why is language so important in software design?

14. Define the following component types: computational, memory, and manager.

15. Define the following connector types: data flow, message passing, and shared data.

16. In what sense may the layers in a layered architecture be viewed as virtual machines?

17. What is a software architecture assessment?

18. Explain the steps of ATAM.

19. ♠ To what extent may the development organization, background and expertise of the designer, and the technical environment have influenced the architecture of the Web? See also (Bass *et al.*, 2003, Chapter 13).

20. ♡ Take a software system you have been involved in. Identify and document three important design decisions for that system.

21. ♡ For the same system, develop a module view. Indicate the concerns this view addresses.

22. ♡ For the same system, develop a business-oriented view. Indicate the concerns this view addresses.

23. ♡ What are the possible roles of software architecture and design patterns during software comprehension?

24. ♠ Write an essay on the influence of social and organizational issues on software architecture. See, for example, (Cockburn, 1996).

25. ♠ Write an essay on the role of the software architect. See, for example, (Kruchten, 1999).

12

Software Design

LEARNING OBJECTIVES

- To be able to discern desirable properties of a software design

- To understand different notions of complexity, at both the component and system level

- To be aware of some object-oriented metrics

- To be aware of some widely known classical design methods

- To understand the general flavor of object-oriented analysis and design methods

- To be aware of a global classification scheme for design methods

- To understand the role of design patterns and be able to illustrate their properties

- To be aware of guidelines for the design documentation

Software design concerns the decomposition of a system into its constituent parts. A good design is the key to the successful implementation and evolution of a system. A number of guiding principles for this decomposition help to achieve quality designs. These guiding principles underlie the main design methods discussed in this chapter. Unlike more classical design fields, there is no visual link between the design representation of a software system and the ultimate product. This complicates the communication of design knowledge and raises the importance of proper design representations.

During software development, we should adhere to a planned approach. If we want to travel from point A to point B, we will (probably) consult a map first. According to some criterion, we will then plan our route. The time-loss caused by the planning activity is bound to outweigh the misery that occurs if we do not plan our trip at all but just take the first turn left, hoping that this will bring us somewhat closer to our destination. In designing a garden, we also follow some plan. We do not start by planting a few bulbs in one corner, an apple tree in another, and a poplar next to the front door.

The above examples sound ridiculous. They are. Yet, many a software development project is undertaken in this way. Somewhat exaggeratedly, we may call it the 'programmer's approach' to software development. Much software is still being developed without a clear design phase. The reasons for this 'code first, design later' attitude are many:

- We do not want to, or are not allowed to, 'waste our time' on design activities.

- We have to, or want to, quickly show something to our customer.

- We are judged by the amount of code written per man-month.

- We are, or expect to be, pressed for time.

For many types of system (just think of an airline reservation system), such an approach grossly underestimates the complexity of software and its development. Just as with the furnishing of a house or the undertaking of a long trip, it is paramount to put thought into a plan, resulting in a blueprint that is then followed during actual construction. The outcome of this process (the blueprint) will be termed the **design** or, if the emphasis is on its notation, the (**technical**) **specification**. The process of making this blueprint is also called design. To a large extent, the quality of the design determines the quality of the resulting product. Errors made during the design phase often go undetected until the system is operational. At that time, they can be repaired only by incurring very high costs.

Software design is a 'wicked problem'. The term originated in research into the nature of design issues in social planning problems. Properties of wicked problems in this area are remarkably similar to properties of software design:

- A wicked problem has no definite formulation. The design process can hardly be separated from either the preceding requirements engineering phase or the subsequent documentation of the design in a specification. These activities will, in practice, overlap and influence each other. At the more global (architectural) stages of system design, the designer will interact with the user to assess fitness-for-use aspects of the design. This may lead to adaptations in the requirements specification. The more detailed stages of design often cannot be separated from the specification method used. One corollary of this is that the waterfall model does not fit the type of problem it is meant to address.

- A wicked problem has no stopping rule. There is no criterion that tells us when *the* solution has been reached. Though we do have a number of quality measures for software designs, there does not exist a single scale against which to measure the quality of a design. There probably never will be such a scale.

- The solution to a wicked problem is not true or false. At best, it is good or bad. The software design process is not analytic. It does not consist of a sequence of decisions each of which brings us somewhat closer to that one, optimal solution. Software design involves making a large number of tradeoffs, such as those between speed and robustness. As a consequence, there is a number of *acceptable* solutions, rather than one best solution.

- Every wicked problem is a symptom of another problem. Resolving one problem may very well result in an entirely different problem elsewhere. For example, the choice of a particular dynamic data structure may solve the problem of an unknown input size and at the same time introduce an efficiency problem. A corollary of this is that small changes in requirements may have large consequences in the design or implementation. In Chapter 1, we described this by saying that software is not continuous.

During design we may opt for a Taylorian, functionality-centered view and consider the design problem as a purely technical issue. Alternatively, we may realize that design involves user issues as well and therefore needs some form of user involvement. The role of the user during design need not be restricted to that of a guinea-pig in shaping the actual user interface. It may also involve much deeper issues.

Rather than approaching system design from the point of view that human weaknesses need to be compensated for, we may take a different stand and consider computerized systems as a way of supporting human strengths. Likewise, systems need not reflect the interests of system owners only. In a democratic world, systems can be designed so that all those involved benefit. This less technocratic attitude leads to extensive user involvement during all stages of system development. Agile development methods advocate this type of approach.

Whereas traditional system development has a *production* view in which the technical aspects are optimized, the 'Scandinavian school' pays equal attention to the human system and holds the view that technology must be compatible with organizational and social needs. The various possible modes of interaction between the designer or analyst on the one hand and the user on the other hand are also discussed in Section 9.1.

Pure agile approaches **do** suggest starting by planting just a few bulbs in one corner of the garden. If we happen to move into our new house in late fall and want some color when spring sets in, this sounds like the best thing we can do. If we change our mind at some later point in time, we can always move the bulbs and do some additional garden design. It thus depends on the situation at hand how much upfront design is feasible (see also Chapter 8). In this chapter, we assume enough context and requirements are known to warrant an explicit design step. Of course, there may be successive design steps in successive iterations.

From the technical point of view, the design problem can be formulated as follows: how can we decompose a system into parts such that each part has a lower complexity than the system as a whole, while the parts together solve the user's problem? Since the complexity of the individual components should be reasonable, it is important that the interaction between components is not too complicated.

Design has both a *product* aspect and a *process* aspect. The product aspect refers to the result, while the process aspect is about how we get there. At the very global, architectural levels of design, there is little process guidance, and the result is very much determined by the experience of the designer. For that reason, Chapter 11 largely focuses on the characterization of the result of the global design process, the software architecture. In this chapter, we focus on the more detailed stages of design, where more process guidance has been accumulated in a number of software design methods. But for the more detailed stages of software design too, the representational aspect is the more important one. This representation is the main communication vehicle between the designer and the other stakeholders. Unlike more classical design fields, there is no visual link between the design representations of a software system and the ultimate product. The blueprint of a bridge gives us lots of visual clues as to how that bridge will eventually look. This is not the case for software and we have to seek other ways to communicate design knowledge to our stakeholders.

There really is no universal design method. The design process is a creative one, and the quality and expertise of the designers are a critical determinant for its success. However, over the years a number of ideas and guidelines have emerged which may serve us in designing software.

The single most important principle of software design is **information hiding**. It exemplifies how to apply **abstraction** in software design. Abstraction means that we concentrate on the essential issues and ignore, abstract from, details that are irrelevant at this stage. Considering the complexity of the problems we are to solve, applying some sort of abstraction is a sheer necessity. It is simply impossible to take in all the details at once.

Section 12.1 discusses desirable design properties that bear on quality issues, most notably maintainability and reusability. Five properties are identified that have a strong impact on the quality of a design: abstraction, modularity, information hiding, complexity, and system structure. Assessment of a design with respect to these properties allows us to get an impression of design quality, albeit not a very quantitative one yet. Efforts to quantify such heuristics have resulted in a number of metrics specifically aimed at object-oriented systems.

A vast number of design methods exist, many of which are strongly tied to a certain notation. These methods give strategies and heuristics to guide the design process. Most methods use a graphical notation to depict the design. Though the details of those methods and notations differ widely, it is possible to provide broad characterizations in a few classes. The essential characteristics of those classes are elaborated upon in Sections 12.2 and 12.3.

Design patterns are collections of a few components (or, in object-oriented circles, classes) which are often used in combination and which together provide a useful abstraction. A design pattern is a recurring solution to a standard problem. The opposite of a pattern is an antipattern: a mistake often made. The prototypical example of a pattern is the Model–View–Controller (MVC) pattern from Smalltalk. A well-known antipattern is the Swiss Army Knife: an overly complex class interface. Design patterns and antipatterns are discussed in Section 12.5.

During the design process, quite a lot of documentation is generated. This documentation serves various users, such as project managers, designers, testers, and programmers. Section 12.6 discusses IEEE Standard 1016. This standard contains useful guidelines for describing software designs. The standard identifies a number of roles and indicates, for each role, the type of design documentation needed.

Finally, Section 12.7 discusses some verification and validation techniques that may fruitfully be applied at the design stage.

12.1 DESIGN CONSIDERATIONS

Up till now we have used the notion of 'component' in a rather intuitive way. It is not easy to give an accurate definition of that notion. Obviously, a component does not denote some random piece of software. We apply certain criteria when decomposing a system into components.

At the programming-language level, a component usually refers to an identifiable unit with respect to compilation. We will use a similar definition of the term 'component' with respect to design: a component is an identifiable unit in the design. It may consist of a single method, a class, or even a set of classes. It preferably has a clean interface to the outside world and the functionality of the component then is only approached through that interface.

There are, in principle, many ways to decompose a system into components. Obviously, not every decomposition is equally desirable. In this section, we are interested in desirable properties of a decomposition, irrespective of the type of system or the design method used. These properties can in some sense be used as a measure of the quality of the design. Designs that have those properties are considered superior to those that do not have them.

The design properties we are most interested in are those that facilitate maintenance and reuse: simplicity, a clear separation of concepts into different components, and restricted visibility (i.e. locality) of information.[1] Systems that have those properties are easier to maintain since we may concentrate our attention on those parts that are directly affected by a change. These properties also bear on reusability, because the resulting components tend to have a well-defined functionality that fits concepts from the application domain. Such components are likely candidates for inclusion in other systems that address problems from the same domain.

In the following subsections, we discuss five interrelated issues that have a strong impact on the above properties:

- abstraction,

- modularity,

- information hiding,

- complexity, and

- system structure.

For object-oriented systems, a specific set of quality heuristics and associated metrics has been defined. The main object-oriented metrics are discussed in Section 12.1.6.

12.1.1 Abstraction

Abstraction means that we concentrate on the essential properties and ignore, *abstract from*, details that are not relevant at the level we are currently working. Consider, for example, a typical sorting component. From the outside we cannot (and need not be able to) discern exactly how the sorting process takes place. We need only know that the output is indeed sorted. At a later stage, when the details of the sorting component are decided upon, then we can rack our brains about the most suitable sorting algorithm.

The complexity of most software problems makes applying abstraction a sheer necessity. In the ensuing discussion, we distinguish two types of abstraction: *procedural abstraction* and *data abstraction*.

---

[1]Obviously, an even more important property of a design is that the corresponding system should perform the required tasks in the specified way. To this end, the design should be validated against the requirements.

The notion of procedural abstraction is fairly traditional. A programming language offers `if` constructs, loop constructs, assignment statements, and so on. The transition from a problem to be solved to these primitive language constructs is a large one in many cases. To this end, a problem is first decomposed into subproblems, each of which is handled in turn. These subproblems correspond to major tasks to be accomplished. They can be recognized by their description, in which some verb plays a central role (for example, *read* the input, *sort* all records, *process* the next user request, *compute* the net salary). If needed, subproblems are further decomposed into even simpler subproblems. Eventually we get at subproblems for which a standard solution is available. This type of (top-down) decomposition is the essence of the main-program-with-subroutines architectural style (see Section 11.4).

The result of this type of stepwise decomposition is a hierarchical structure. The top node of the structure denotes the problem to be solved. The next level shows its first decomposition into subproblems. The leaf nodes denote primitive problems. This is schematically depicted in Figure 12.1.

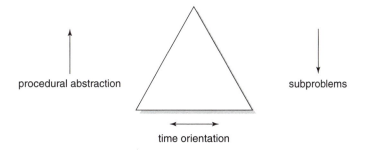

procedural abstraction   subproblems

time orientation

Figure 12.1 The idea of procedural abstraction

The procedure concept offers us a notation for the subproblems that result from this decomposition process. The application of this concept is known as procedural abstraction. With procedural abstraction, the name of a procedure (or method, in object-oriented languages) is used to denote the corresponding sequence of actions. When that name is used, we need not bother ourselves about the exact way in which its effect is realized. The important thing is that, after the call, certain prestated requirements are fulfilled.

This way of going about the process closely matches the way in which humans are inclined to solve problems. Humans too are inclined to the stepwise handling of problems. Procedural abstraction thus offers an important means of tackling software problems.

When designing software, we are inclined to decompose the problem so that the result has a strong time orientation. A problem is decomposed into subproblems that follow each other in time. In its simplest form, this approach results in input – process – output schemes: a program first has to read and store its data, next some process computes the required output from this data, and the result finally is output. Application of this technique may result in programs that are difficult to adapt and hard to comprehend. Applying data abstraction results in a decomposition which shows this affliction to a far lesser degree.

Procedural abstraction is aimed at finding a hierarchy in the program's control structure: which steps have to be executed and in which order. Data abstraction is aimed at finding a hierarchy in the program's data. Programming languages offer primitive data structures for integers, real numbers, truth values, characters and possibly a few more. Using these building blocks, we may construct more complicated data structures, such as stacks and binary trees. Such structures are of general use in application software. They occur at a fairly low level in the hierarchy of data structures. Application-oriented objects, such as 'paragraph' in text-processing software or 'book' in our library system, are found at higher levels of the data structure hierarchy. This is schematically depicted in Figure 12.2.

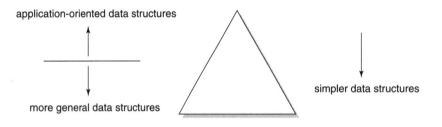

Figure 12.2 The idea of data abstraction

For the data, too, we wish to abstract from details that are not relevant at a certain level. In fact, we already do so when using the primitive data structures offered by our programming language. In using these, we abstract from details such as the internal representation of numbers and the way in which the addition of two numbers is realized. At the programming language level we may view the integers as a set of objects $(0, 1, -1, 2, -2, \ldots)$ and a set of operations on these objects $(+, -, \times, /, \ldots)$. These two sets together determine the data type `integer`. To be able to use this data type, we need only name the set of objects and specify its operations.

We may proceed along the same lines for the data structures not directly supported by the programming language. A data type `binary-tree` is characterized by a set of objects (all conceivable binary trees) and a set of operations on those objects. When using binary trees, their representation and the implementation of the corresponding operations need not concern us. We need only ascertain the intended effect of the operations.

Applying data abstraction during design is sometimes called **object-oriented design**, since the type of object and the associated operations are encapsulated in one component. The buzzword 'object-oriented' however also has a subtly different meaning in the context of design. We will further elaborate upon this notion in Section 12.3.

Languages such as Ada, Java and C++ offer a language construct (called **package**, **class**, and **struct**, respectively) that allows us to maintain a syntactic separation between the implementation and specification of data types. Note that it is also possible to apply data abstraction during design when the ultimate language does not offer the concept. However, it then becomes more cumbersome to move from design to code.

We noticed before that procedural abstraction fits in nicely with the way humans tend to tackle problems. To most people, data abstraction is a bit more complicated.

When searching for a solution to a software problem we will find that the solution needs certain data structures. At some point we will also have to choose a representation for these data structures. Rather than making those decisions at an early stage and imposing the result on all other components, you are better off if you create a separate subproblem and make only the procedural, implementation-independent, interfaces public. Data abstraction thus is a prime example of information hiding.

The development of these abstraction techniques went hand-in-hand with other developments, particularly those in the realm of programming languages. Procedures were originally introduced to avoid the repetition of sequences of instructions. At a later stage, we viewed the name of a procedure as an abstraction of the corresponding instruction sequence. Only then did the notion of procedural abstraction get its present connotation. In a similar vein, developments in the field of formal data type specifications and language notions for components (starting with the **class** concept of SIMULA-67) strongly contributed to our present notion of data abstraction.

As a final note, we remark that we may identify yet a third type of abstraction, **control abstraction**. In control abstraction, we abstract from the precise order in which a sequence of events is to be handled. Though control abstraction is often implicit when procedural abstraction is used, it is sometimes convenient to be able to explicitly model this type of nondeterminacy, for instance when specifying concurrent systems. This topic falls outside the scope of this book.

12.1.2 Modularity

During design, the system is decomposed into a number of components and the relationships between those components are indicated. In another design of the same system, different components may show up and there may be different relationships between the components. We may try to compare those designs by considering both a typology for the individual components and the type of connections between them. This leads us to two structural design criteria: **cohesion** and **coupling**.

Cohesion may be viewed as the glue that keeps the component together. It is a measure of the mutual affinity of the elements of a component. In general we will wish to make the cohesion as strong as possible. In their classic text, Yourdon and Constantine (1975) identify the following seven levels of cohesion of increasing strength:

- **Coincidental cohesion**: Elements are grouped into components in a haphazard way. There is no significant relation between the elements.

- **Logical cohesion**: Elements realize tasks that are logically related. One example is a component that contains all input routines. These routines do not call one another and they do not pass information to each other. Their function is just very similar.

- **Temporal cohesion**: The elements are independent but they are activated at about the same point in time. A typical example of this type of cohesion is an initialization component.

- **Procedural cohesion**: The elements have to be executed in a given order. For instance, a component may have to first read some data, then search a table, and finally print a result.

- **Communicational cohesion**: The elements of a component operate on the same (external) data. For instance, a component may read some data from a disk, perform certain computations on the data, and print the result.

- **Sequential cohesion**: The component consists of a sequence of elements where the output of one element serves as input to the next element.

- **Functional cohesion**: All elements contribute to a single function. Such a component often transforms a single input into a single output. The well-known mathematical subroutines are a typical example of this. Less trivial examples are components such as 'execute the next edit command' and 'translate the program given'.

In a classic paper on structured design, (Stevens *et al.*, 1974) provide some simple heuristics that may be of help in establishing the degree of cohesion of a component. They suggest writing down a sentence that describes the function (purpose) of the component and examining that sentence. Properties to look for include the following:

- If the sentence is compound, has a connective (such as a comma or the word 'and'), or contains more than one verb, then that component is probably performing more than one function. It is likely to have sequential or communicational cohesion.

- If the sentence contains words that relate to time (such as 'first', 'next', 'after', and 'then'), then the component probably has sequential or temporal cohesion.

- If the sentence contains words such as 'initialize', the component probably has temporal cohesion.

The levels of cohesion identified above reflect the cohesion between the *functions* that a component provides. Abstract data types cannot easily be accommodated in this scheme. Macro and Buxton (1987) therefore propose adding an extra level, **data cohesion**, to identify components that encapsulate an abstract data type. Data cohesion is even stronger than functional cohesion.

It goes without saying that it is not always an easy task to obtain the strongest possible cohesion between the elements of a component. Though functional cohesion may be attainable at the top levels and data cohesion at the bottom levels, we often have to settle for less at the intermediate levels of the component hierarchy. The tradeoffs to be made here are what makes design such a difficult, and yet challenging, activity.

The second structural criterion is **coupling**. Coupling is a measure of the strength of the intercomponent connections. A high degree of coupling indicates a strong dependence between components. A high degree of coupling between components means that we can only fully comprehend this set of components as a whole and may result in ripple effects when a component has to be changed, because such a change is likely to incur changes in the dependent components as well. Loosely coupled components, on the other hand, are relatively independent and are easier to comprehend and adapt. Loose coupling therefore is a desirable property of a design (and its subsequent realization). The following types of coupling can be identified (from tightest to loosest):

- **Content coupling**: One component directly affects the working of another component. Content coupling occurs when a component changes another component's data or when control is passed from one component to the middle of another (as in a jump). This type of coupling can, and should, always be avoided.

- **Common coupling**: Two components have shared data. The name originates from the use of COMMON blocks in FORTRAN. Its equivalent in block-structured languages is the use of global variables.

- **External coupling**: Components communicate through an external medium, such as a file.

- **Control coupling**: One component directs the execution of another component by passing the necessary control information. This is usually accomplished by means of flags that are set by one component and reacted upon by the dependent component.

- **Stamp coupling**: Complete data structures are passed from one component to another. With stamp coupling, the precise format of the data structures is a common property of those components.

- **Data coupling**: Only simple data is passed between components.

The various types of coupling emerged in the 1970s and reflect the data type concepts of programming languages in use at that time. For example, programming languages of that time had simple scalar data types such as real and integer. They allowed arrays of scalar values and records were used to store values of different types. Components were considered data-coupled if they passed scalars or arrays. They were considered stamp-coupled if they passed record data. When two components are control-coupled, the assumption is that the control is passed through a scalar value.

Nowadays, programming languages have much more flexible means of passing information from one component to another, and this requires a more detailed set of coupling levels. For example, components may pass control data through records (as opposed to scalars only). Components may allow some components access to their data and deny it to others. As a result, there are many levels of visibility. The coupling between components need not be commutative. When component A passes a scalar value to B and B returns a value which is used to control the further execution of A, then A is data-coupled to B, while B is control-coupled to A. As a result, people have extended and refined the definitions of cohesion and coupling levels.

Coupling and cohesion are dual characteristics. If the various components exhibit strong internal cohesion, the intercomponent coupling tends to be minimal, and vice versa.

Simple interfaces – weak coupling between components and strong cohesion among a component's elements – are of crucial importance for a variety of reasons:

- Communication between programmers becomes simpler. When different people are working on the same system, it helps if decisions can be made locally and do not interfere with the working of other components.

- Correctness proofs become easier to derive.

- It is less likely that changes will propagate to other components, which reduces maintenance costs.

- The reusability of components is increased. The fewer assumptions that are made about an element's environment, the greater the chance of fitting another environment.

- The comprehensibility of components is increased. Humans have limited memory capacity for information processing. Simple component interfaces allow for an understanding of a component independent of the context in which it is used.

- Empirical studies show that interfaces exhibiting weak coupling and strong cohesion are less error-prone than those that do not have these properties.

12.1.3 Information Hiding

The concept of information hiding originates from a seminal paper (Parnas, 1972). The principle of information hiding is that each component has a secret which it hides from other components.

Design involves a sequence of decisions, such as how to represent certain information, or in which order to accomplish tasks. For each such decision we should ask ourselves which other parts of the system need to know about the decision and how it should be hidden from parts that do not need to know.

Information hiding is closely related to the notions of abstraction, cohesion, and coupling. If a component hides some design decision, the user of that component may abstract from (ignore) the outcome of that decision. Since the outcome is hidden, it cannot possibly interfere with the use of that component. If a component hides some secret, that secret does not penetrate the component's boundary, thereby decreasing the coupling between that component and its environment. Information hiding increases cohesion, since the component's secret is what binds the component's constituents together. Note that, in order to maximize its cohesion, a component should hide *one* secret only.

It depends on the programming language used whether the separation of concerns obtained during the design stage will be identifiable in the ultimate code. To some extent, this is of secondary concern. The design decomposition will be reflected, if only implicitly, in the code and should be explicitly recorded (for traceability purposes) in the technical documentation. It is of great importance for the later evolution of the system. A confirmation of the impact of such techniques as information hiding on the maintainability of software can be found in (Boehm, 1983).

12.1.4 Complexity

> Like all good inventions, readability yardsticks can cause harm in misuse.
> They are handy statistical tools to measure complexity in prose. They
> are useful to determine whether writing is gauged to its audience. But
> they are not formulae for writing. ... Writing remains an art governed
> by many principles. By no means all factors that create interest and affect
> clarity can be measured objectively.
> Gunning (1968)

In a very general sense, the complexity of a problem refers to the amount of resources required for its solution. We may try to determine complexity in this way by measuring, say, the time needed to solve a problem. This is called an *external* attribute: we are not looking at the entity itself (the problem), but at how it behaves.

In the present context, complexity refers to attributes of the software that affect the effort needed to construct or change a piece of software. These are *internal* attributes: they can be measured purely in terms of the software itself. For example, we need not execute the software to determine their values.

Both these notions are very different from the complexity of the computation performed (with respect to time or memory needed). The latter is a well-established field in which many results have been obtained. This is much less true for the type of complexity in which we are interested. Software complexity in this sense is still a rather elusive notion.

Serious efforts have been made to measure software complexity in quantitative terms. The resulting metrics are intended to be used as anchor points for the decomposition of a system, to assess the quality of a design or program, to guide reengineering efforts, etc. We then measure certain attributes of a software system, such as its length, the number of `if` statements, or the information flow between components, and try to relate the numbers thus obtained to the system's complexity. The type of software attributes considered can be broadly categorized into two classes:

- **intracomponent attributes** are attributes of individual components, and

- **intercomponent attributes** are attributes of a system viewed as a collection of components with dependencies.

In this subsection, we are dealing with intracomponent attributes. Intercomponent attributes are discussed in Section 12.1.5. We may distinguish two classes of complexity metrics:

- **Size-based** complexity metrics. The size of a piece of software, such as the number of lines of code, is fairly easy to measure. It also gives a fair indication of the effort needed to develop that piece of software (see also Chapter 7). As a consequence, it could also be used as a complexity metric.

- **Structure-based** complexity metrics. The structure of a piece of software is a good indicator of its design quality, because a program that has a complicated control structure or uses complicated data structures is likely to be difficult to comprehend and maintain, and thus more complex.

The easiest way to measure software size is to count the number of lines of code. We may then impose limits on the number of lines of code per component. In (Weinberg, 1971), for instance, the ideal size of a component is said to be 30 lines of code. In a variant, limits are imposed on the number of elements per component. Some people claim that a component should contain at most seven elements. This number seven can be traced back to research in psychology, which suggests that human memory is hierarchically organized with a short-term memory of about seven slots, while there is a more permanent memory of almost unlimited capacity. If there are more than seven pieces of information, they cannot all be stored in short-term memory and information gets lost.

There are serious objections to the direct use of the number of lines of code as a complexity metric. Some programmers write more verbose programs than others. We should at least normalize the counting to counteract these effects and be able to compare different pieces of software.

A second objection is that this technique makes it hard to compare programs written in different languages. If the same problem is solved in different languages, the results may differ considerably in length. For example, APL is more compact than COBOL.

Finally, some lines are more complex than others. An assignment statement such as:

```
a = b
```

looks simpler than a loop:

```
while (current = null) {current = current.next;}
```

although they each occupy one line.

Halstead (1977) uses a refinement of counting lines of code. This refinement is meant to overcome the problems associated with metrics based on a direct count of lines of code.

Halstead's method, also known as 'software science', uses the number of operators and operands in a piece of software. The set of operators includes the arithmetic and Boolean operators, as well as separators (such as a semicolon between adjacent instructions) and (pairs of) reserved words. The set of operands contains the variables and constants used. Halstead then defines four basic entities:

- n_1 is the number of unique (i.e. different) operators in the component;

- n_2 is the number of unique (i.e. different) operands in the component;

- N_1 is the total number of occurrences of operators;

- N_2 is the total number of occurrences of operands.

Figure 12.3 contains a simple sorting routine. Table 12.1 lists the operators and operands of this routine together with their frequencies. Note that there is no generally agreed definition of what exactly an operator or operand is, so the numbers given have no absolute meaning. This is part of the criticism of this theory.

```
1        public static void sort(int x []) {
2            for (int i = 0; i < x.length - 1; i++) {
3                for (int j = i+1; j < x.length; j++) {
4                    if (x[i] > x[j]) {
5                        int save = x[i];
6                        x[i] = x[j];
7                        x[j] = save;
8                    }
9                }
10           }
11       }
```

Figure 12.3 A simple sorting routine

Table 12.1 Counting the number of operators and operands in the `sort` routine

Operator	Number of occurrences	Operand	Number of occurrences
public	1	x	9
static	1	length	2
void	1	i	7
sort()	1	j	6
int	4	save	2
[ ]	7	0	1
{ }	4	1	2
for (; ;)	2		
=	5		
<	2		
.	2		
−	1		
++	2		
+	1		
if (...)	1		
>	1		
;	3		
$n_1 = 17$	$N_1 = 39$	$n_2 = 7$	$N_2 = 29$

Using the primitive entities defined above, Halstead defines a number of derived entities, such as:

- Size of the vocabulary: $n = n_1 + n_2$.

- Program length: $N = N_1 + N_2$.

- Program volume: $V = N \log_2 n$.

  This is the minimal number of bits needed to store N elements from a set of cardinality n.

- Program level: $L = V^*/V$.

  Here V^* is the most compact representation of the algorithm in question. For the example in Figure 12.3 this is `sort (x) ;`, so $n = N = 3$, and $V^* = 3 \log_2 3$. From the formula, it follows that L is at most 1. Halstead postulates that the program level increases if the number of different operands increases, while it decreases if the number of different operators or the total number of operands increases. As an approximation of L, he therefore suggests: $\hat{L} = (2/n_1)(n_2/N_2)$.

- Programming effort: $E = V/L$.

The effort needed increases with volume and decreases as the program level increases. E represents the number of mental discriminations (decisions) to be taken while implementing the problem solution.

- Estimated programming time in seconds: $\hat{T} = E/18$.

  The constant 18 is determined empirically. Halstead explains this number by referring to (Stroud, 1967), which discusses the speed with which human memory processes sensory input. This speed is said to be 5–20 units per second. In Halstead's theory, the number 18 is chosen. This number is also referred to as *Stroud's number*.

The above entities can only be determined after the program has been written. It is, however, possible to estimate a number of these entities. When doing so, the values for n_1 and n_2 are assumed to be known. This may be the case, for instance, after the detailed design step. Halstead then estimates program length as:

$$\hat{N} = n_1 \log_2 n_1 + n_2 \log_2 n_2$$

An explanation for this formula can be given as follows. There are $n_1 2^{n_1} \times n_2 2^{n_2}$ ways to combine the n given symbols such that operators and operands alternate. However, the program is organized and organization generally gives a logarithmic reduction in the number of possibilities. Doing so yields the above formula for $\hat{N}$. Table 12.2 lists the values for a number of entities from Halstead's theory for the example routine in Figure 12.3.

Table 12.2 Values for 'software science' entities for the routine in Figure 12.3

Entity	Value
Size vocabulary	24
Program length	68
Estimated program length	89
Program volume	312
Level of abstraction	0.015
Estimated level of abstraction	0.028
Programming effort	20 800
Estimated programming time	1 155

A number of empirical studies have addressed the predictive value of Halstead's formulae. These studies often give positive evidence of the validity of the theory.

The theory has also been heavily criticized. The underpinning of Halstead's formulae is not convincing. Results from cognitive psychology, such as Stroud's number, are badly used, which weakens the theoretical foundation. Halstead concentrates on the coding phase and assumes that programmers are 100% devoted to a programming task for an uninterrupted period of time. Practice is likely to be quite different. Different people use quite different definitions of the notions of operator and operand, which may lead to widely different outcomes for the values of entities. Yet, Halstead's work has been very influential. It was the first major body of work to point out the potential of metrics for software development.

The second class of intracomponent complexity metrics concerns metrics based on the structure of the software. If we try to derive a complexity metric from the structure of a piece of software, we may focus on the control structure, the data structures, or a combination of these.

If we base the complexity metric on the use of data structures, we may do so by considering, for instance, the number of instructions between successive references to one object. If this number is large, information about these variables must be retained for a long period of time when we try to comprehend that program text. Following this line of thought, complexity can be related to the average number of variables for which information must be kept by the reader.

The best-known structure-based complexity metric is McCabe's *cyclomatic complexity* (McCabe, 1976). McCabe bases his complexity metric on a (directed) graph depicting the control flow of a component. He assumes that the graph of a single component has a unique start and end node, that each node is reachable from the start node, and that the end node can be reached from each node. In that case, the graph is connected. If the component is a class consisting of one or more methods, then the control graph has a number of connected subgraphs, one for each of its methods.

The cyclomatic complexity, CV, equals the number of predicates (decisions) plus 1 in the component that corresponds to this control graph. Its formula reads

$$CV = e - n + p + 1$$

where e, n and p denote the number of edges, nodes, and connected subgraphs in the control graph, respectively.

Figure 12.4 shows the control flow graph for the example routine from Figure 12.3. The numbers inside the nodes correspond to the line numbers from Figure 12.3. The cyclomatic complexity of this graph is $13 - 11 + 1 + 1 = 4$. The decisions in the component from Figure 12.3 occur in lines 2, 3 and 4. In both `for` loops, the decision is to either exit the loop or iterate it. In the `if` statement, the choice is between the `then` part and the `else` part.

McCabe suggests imposing an upper limit of ten for the cyclomatic complexity of a component. McCabe's complexity metric is also applied to testing. One criterion used during testing is to get a good coverage of the possible paths through the component. Applying McCabe's cyclomatic complexity leads to a structured testing strategy involving the execution of all linearly independent paths (see also Chapter 13).[2]

Complexity metrics such as those of Halstead, McCabe, and many others all measure attributes which are in some sense related to the size of the task to

---

[2]The number of linearly independent paths is related to the cyclomatic number of a graph, which is why this is called the 'cyclomatic complexity'.

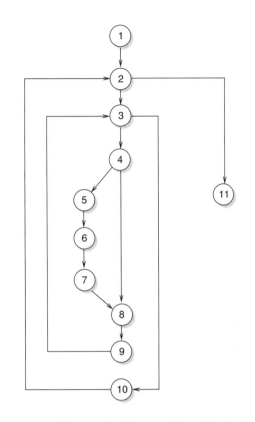

Figure 12.4 Control flow graph of the example routine from Figure 12.3

be accomplished, be it the time in man-months, the number of lines of code, or something else. As such, they may serve various purposes: determining the optimal size of a component, estimating the number of errors in a component, or estimating the cost of a piece of software.

All known complexity metrics suffer from some serious shortcomings, though:

- They are not very context-sensitive. For example, any component with five if statements has the same cyclomatic complexity. Yet we may expect that different organizations of those if statements (consecutive versus deeply nested, say) have an effect on the perceived complexity of those components. In terms of measurement theory, this means that cyclomatic complexity does not fulfill the 'representation condition', which says that the empirical relations should be preserved in the numerical relation system. If we empirically observe that component A is more complex than component B, then any complexity metric F should be such that $F_A > F_B$.

- They measure only a few facets. Halstead's method does not take into account the control flow complexity, for instance.

We may formulate these shortcomings as follows: complexity metrics tell us something about the complexity of a component (i.e. a higher value of the metric is likely to represent greater complexity), but a more complex component does not necessarily result in a higher value for a complexity metric. Complexity is made up of many specific attributes. It is unlikely that there will ever be one 'general' complexity metric.

We should thus be very careful in the use of complexity metrics. Since they seem to measure along different dimensions of what is perceived as complexity, the use of multiple metrics is likely to yield better insights. But even then the results must be interpreted with care. Redmond and Ah-Chuen (1990), for instance, evaluated various complexity metrics for a few systems, including the MINIX operating system. Of the 277 components in MINIX, 34 have a cyclomatic complexity greater than ten. The highest value (58) was observed for a component that handles a number of ASCII escape character sequences from the keyboard. This component, and most others with a large cyclomatic complexity, was considered 'justifiably complex'. An attempt to reduce the complexity by splitting those components would increase the difficulty of understanding them while artificially reducing its complexity value. Complexity yardsticks too can cause harm in misuse.

Finally, we may note that various validations of both software science and cyclomatic complexity indicate that they are not substantially better indicators of coding effort, maintainability, or reliability than the length of a component (number of lines of code). The latter is much easier to determine, though.

The high correlation that is often observed between a size-related complexity metric and a control-related complexity metric such as McCabe's cyclomatic complexity should not come as a surprise. Large components tend to have more `if` statements than small components. What counts, however, is the *density* with which those `if` statements occur. This suggests a complexity metric of the form CV/LOC rather than CV.

12.1.5 System Structure

We may depict the outcome of the design process, a set of components and their mutual dependencies, in a graph. The nodes of this graph correspond to components and the edges denote relations between components. We may think of many types of intercomponent relations, such as:

- component A contains component B;

- component A follows component B;

- component A delivers data to component B;

- component A uses component B.

The type of dependencies we are interested in are those that determine the complexity of the relations between components. The amount of knowledge that components have of each other should be kept to a minimum. To be able to assess this, it is important to know, for each component, which other components it *uses*, since that tells us which knowledge of each other they (potentially) use. In a proper design, the information flow between components is restricted to flow that comes about through method calls. The graph depicting the 'uses' relation is therefore often termed a **call graph**.

The call graph may have different shapes. In its most general form it is a directed graph (see Figure 12.5a).[3] If the graph is acyclic, i.e. it does not contain a path of the form $M_1, M_2, \ldots, M_n, M_1$, the uses relation forms a hierarchy. We may then decompose the graph into a number of distinct layers such that a component at one layer uses only components from lower layers (Figure 12.5b). Going one step further, we get a scheme such as the one in Figure 12.5c, where components from level *i* use

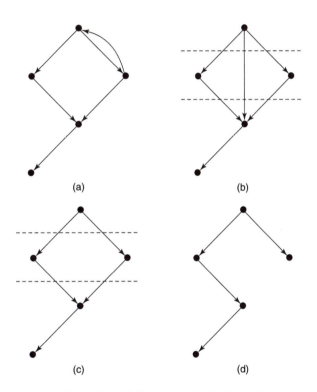

Figure 12.5 Component hierarchies: (a) directed graph, (b) directed acyclic graph, (c) layered graph, (d) tree

---

[3] We assume that the graph is connected, i.e. that there is a path between each pair of nodes if we ignore the direction of the arrows that link nodes. This assumption is reasonable, since otherwise the graph can be split into two or more disjoint graphs between which there is no information flow. These disjoint graphs then correspond to independent components.

only components from level $i + 1$. Finally, if each component is used by only one other component, the graph reduces to a tree (Figure 12.5d).

There are various aspects of the call graph that can be measured. Directly measurable attributes that relate to the 'shape' of the call graph include:

- its *size*, measured in terms of the number of nodes, the number of edges, or the sum of these;

- its *depth*, the length of the longest path from the root to some leaf node (in an acyclic directed graph);

- its *width*, the maximum number of nodes at some level (in an acyclic directed graph).

We do not know of studies that try to quantitatively relate those measures to other complexity-related aspects such as debugging time, maintainability, etc. They may be used, though, as one of the parameters in a qualitative assessment of a design.

It is often stated that a good design should have a tree-like call graph. It is therefore worthwhile to consider the **tree impurity** of a call graph, i.e. the extent to which the graph deviates from a pure tree. Suppose we start with a connected (undirected) graph (such as the ones in Figure 12.5b–d, if we ignore the direction of the arrows). If the graph is not a tree, it has at least one cycle, i.e. a path from some node A via one or more other nodes back to A again. We may then remove one of the edges from this cycle and the result will still be a connected graph. We may continue removing edges from cycles until the result is a tree, as we did in the transition from Figure 12.5b to Figure 12.5c to Figure 12.5d. The final result is called the graph's **spanning tree**. The number of edges removed in this process is an indication of the graph's tree impurity.

In order to obtain a proper measure of tree impurity we proceed as follows. The complete graph K_n is the graph with n nodes and the maximum number of edges. This maximum number of edges is $n(n - 1)/2$. A tree with n nodes has $(n - 1)$ edges. Given a connected graph G with n nodes and e edges, we define its tree impurity $m(G)$ as the number of extra edges divided by the maximum number of extra edges:

$$m(G) = 2(e - n + 1)/(n - 1)(n - 2)$$

This measure of tree impurity fits our intuitive notion of that concept. The value of $m(G)$ lies between 0 and 1. It is 0 if G is a tree and 1 if it is a complete graph. If we add an edge to G, the value of $m(G)$ increases. Moreover, the 'penalty' of extra edges is proportional to the size of the spanning tree.

It is not always easy, or even meaningful, to strive for a neat hierarchical decomposition. We will often have to settle for a compromise. It may for instance be appropriate to decompose a system into a number of clusters, each of which contains a number of components. The clusters may then be organized hierarchically, while the components within a given cluster show a more complicated interaction pattern. Also, tree-like call graphs do not allow for reuse (if a component is reused within the same system, its node in the call graph has at least two ancestors).

The call graph allows us to assess the *structure* of a design. In deriving the measures above, each edge in the call graph is treated alike. Yet, the complexity of the information flow that is represented by the edges is likely to vary. As noted in the earlier discussion on coupling, we would like the intercomponent connections to be 'thin'. Therefore, we would like a measure which does not merely count the edges, but which also considers the amount of information that flows through them.

The best-known attempt to measure the total level of information flow between the components of a system is due to Henri and Kafura (1981). Their measures were able to identify change-prone UNIX procedures and evaluate potential design changes. Shepperd (1990) studied the information flow measure extensively and proposed several refinements, thus obtaining a 'purer' metric. Using Shepperd's definitions, the information flow measure is based on the following notions of local and global data flow:

- A **local flow** from component A to component B exists if

  a) A invokes B and passes it a parameter, or

  b) B invokes A and A returns a value.

- A **global flow** from component A to component B exists if A updates some global data structure and B retrieves from that structure.

Using these notions of local and global data flow, Shepperd defines the 'complexity' of a component M as

$$complexity(M) = (fan\text{-}in(M) \times fan\text{-}out(M))^2$$

where

- $fan\text{-}in(M)$ is the number of (local and global) flows whose sink is M, and

- $fan\text{-}out(M)$ is the number of (local and global) flows whose source is M.

A weak point of the information flow metric is that all flows have equal weight. Passing a simple integer as a parameter contributes equally to this measure of complexity as invoking a complex global data structure. The abstract-data-type architectural style easily results in components with a high fan-in and fan-out. If the same system is built using global data structures, its information flow metric is likely to have a smaller value. Yet, the information flow to and from the components in the abstract-data-type style generally concern simple scalar values only and are therefore considered simpler.

In a more qualitative sense, the information flow metric may indicate spots in the design that deserve our attention. If some component has a high fan-in, this may indicate that the component has little cohesion. Also, if we consider the information flow per level in a layered architecture, an excessive increase from one level to the next might indicate a missing level of abstraction.

During design, we (pre)tend to follow a top-down decomposition strategy. We may take a completely different stand and try to *compose* a hierarchical system structure from a flat collection of system elements. Elements that are in some sense 'closest' to one another are grouped together. We then have to define some measure for the distance between elements and a mathematical technique known as cluster analysis can be used to do the actual grouping. Elements in the same group are more like other elements within the same group and less like elements in other groups. If the measure is based on the number of data types that elements have in common, this clustering results in abstract data types or, more generally, components having high cohesion. If the measure is based on the number of data bindings between elements, the result is likely to have a low value for the information-flow metric.

The measure chosen, in a sense, determines how we define 'friendship' between elements. Close friends should be grouped in the same component while distant relatives may reside in different components. The various qualitative and quantitative design criteria that we have discussed above have different, but in essence very similar, definitions of friendship.

Though much work remains to be done, a judicious use of available design metrics is already a valuable tool in the design and quality assurance of software systems.

12.1.6 Object-Oriented Metrics

At the level of individual methods of an object-oriented system, we may assess quality characteristics of components by familiar metrics such as: length, cyclomatic complexity, and so on. At higher levels of abstraction, object-oriented systems consist of a collection of classes that interact by sending messages. Familiar intercomponent metrics which focus on the relationships between components do not account for the specifics of object-oriented systems. In this section, we discuss a few metrics specifically aimed at characteristics of object-oriented systems. These metrics are listed in Table 12.3.

WMC is a measure of the size of a class. The assumption is that larger classes are in general less desirable. They take more time to develop and maintain and they are likely to be less reusable. The formula is: $WMC = \sum_{i=1}^{n} c_i$, where c_i is the complexity

Table 12.3 A suite of object-oriented metrics

WMC	Weighted methods per class
DIT	Depth of class in inheritance tree
NOC	Number of children
CBO	Coupling between object classes
RFC	Response for a class
LCOM	Lack of cohesion of a method

of method i. For the complexity of an individual method we may choose its length, cyclomatic complexity, and so on. Most often, c_i is set at 1. In that case, we simply count the number of methods. Besides being simple, this has the advantage that the metric can be applied during design, once the class interface has been decided upon. Note that each entry in the class interface counts as one method, the principle being that each method which requires additional design effort should be counted. For example, different constructors for the same operation, as is customary in C++, count as different methods.

Classes in an object-oriented design are related through a subtype – supertype hierarchy. If the class hierarchy is deep and narrow, a proper understanding of a class may require knowledge of many of its superclasses. On the other hand, a wide and shallow inheritance structure occurs when classes are more loosely coupled. The latter situation may indicate that commonality between elements is not sufficiently exploited. DIT is the distance of a class to the root of its inheritance tree. Note that the value of DIT is somewhat language-dependent. In Smalltalk, for example, every class is a subclass of `Object`, and this increases the value of DIT. A widely accepted heuristic is to strive for a forest of classes, i.e. a collection of inheritance trees of medium height.

NOC counts the number of immediate descendants of a class. If a class has a large number of descendants, this may indicate an improper abstraction of the parent class. A large number of descendants also suggests that the class is to be used in a variety of settings, which will make it more error-prone. The idea thus is that higher values of NOC suggest a higher complexity of the class.

CBO is the main coupling metric for object-oriented systems. Two classes are coupled if a method of one class uses a method or state variable of the other class. The CBO is a count of the number of other classes with which it is coupled. As with the traditional coupling metric, high values of CBO suggest tight bindings with other components and this is undesirable.

In the definition of CBO, all couplings are considered equal. However, if we look at the different ways in which classes may be coupled, it is reasonable to say that:

- access to state variables is worse than mere parameter passing;
- access to elements of a foreign class is worse than access to elements of a superclass;
- passing many complex parameters is worse than passing a few simple parameters;
- messages that conform to Demeter's Law[4] are better than those which do not.

---

[4]The Law of Demeter is a generally accepted design heuristic for object-oriented systems. It says that the methods of a class should depend only on the top-level structure of their own class. More specifically, in the context of a class C with method M, M should only send messages to:

- the parameters of C, or
- the state variables of C, or
- C itself.

If we view the methods as bubbles and the couplings as connections between bubbles, CBO simply counts the number of connections for each bubble. In reality, we consider some types of couplings worse than others: some connections are 'thicker' than others and some connections are to bubbles 'further away'. For the *representation condition* of measurement theory to hold, these empirical relations should be reflected in the numerical relation system.

Martin (2002) defines coupling measures at the package level:

- The **afferent coupling** (C_a) of a package P is the number of other packages that depend upon classes within P (through inheritance or associations). It indicates the dependence of a package on its environment.

- The **efferent coupling** (C_e) of a package P is the number of packages that classes within P depend upon. It indicates the dependence of the environment on a package.

Adding these numbers together results in a total coupling measure of a package P. The ratio $I = C_e/(C_e + C_a)$ indicates the relative dependence of the environment to P with respect to the total number of dependencies between P and its environment. If C_e equals zero, P does not depend at all on other packages and $I = 0$ as well. If on the other hand C_a equals zero, P only depends on other packages and no other package depends on P. In that case, $I = 1$. I thus can be seen as an instability measure for P. Larger values of I denote a larger instability of the package.

RFC measures the 'immediate surroundings' of a class. Suppose a class C has a collection of methods M. Each method from M may in turn call other methods, from C or any other class. Let $\{R_i\}$ be the set of methods called from method M_i. Then the **response set** of this class is defined as: $\{M\} \cup_i \{R_i\}$, i.e. the set of messages that may potentially be executed if a message is sent to an object of class C. RFC is defined as the number of elements in the response set. Note that we only count method calls up to one level deep. Larger values of RFC means that the immediate surroundings of a class is larger in size. There is, then, a lot of communication with other methods or classes. This makes comprehension of a class more difficult and increases test time and complexity.

The final object-oriented metric to be discussed is the lack of cohesion of a method. The traditional levels of cohesion express the degree of mutual affinity of the elements of a component. It is a measure of the glue that keeps the component together. If all methods of a class use the same state variables, these state variables serve as the glue which ties the methods together. If some methods use one subset of the state variables and other methods use another subset of the state variables, the class lacks cohesion. This may indicate a flaw in the design and it may be better to split it into two or more subclasses. LCOM is the number of disjoint sets of methods of a class. Any two methods in the same set share at least one local state variable. The preferred value for LCOM is 0.

There are obviously many more metrics that aim to address the specifics of object-oriented systems. Most of these have not been validated extensively, though. Several experiments have shown that the above set does have some merit. Overall, WMC, CBO, RFC and LCOM have been found to be the more useful quality indicators.

These metrics for example were able to predict fault-proneness of classes during design, and were found to have a strong relationship to the maintenance effort. The merits of DIT and NCO remain somewhat unclear.

Note that many of these metrics correlate with class size. One may expect that larger classes have more methods, more descendants, more couplings with other classes, etc. (El Emam *et al.*, 2001) indeed found that class size has a confounding effect on the values of the above metrics. It thus remains questionable whether these metrics tell more than a plain LOC count.

12.2 CLASSICAL DESIGN METHODS

Having discussed the properties of a good system decomposition, we now come to a question which is at least as important: how do you get a good decomposition to start with?

There exist a vast number of design methods, a sample of which are given in Table 12.4. These design methods generally consist of a set of guidelines, heuristics, and procedures on how to go about designing a system. They also offer a notation for expressing the result of the design process. Together they provide a *systematic* way of organizing and structuring the design process and its products.

For some methods, such as FSM or Petri nets, emphasis is on the notation, while the guidelines on how to tackle design are not very well developed. Methods such as JSD, on the other hand, offer extensive prescriptive guidelines as well. Most notations are graphical and somewhat informal, but OBJ uses a very formal mathematical language. Some methods concentrate on the design stage proper, while others, such as SSADM and JSD, are part of a wider methodology covering other life cycle phases as well. Finally, some methods offer features that make them especially useful for the design of certain types of application, such as SA/RT (for real-time systems) or Petri nets (for concurrent systems).

In the following subsections, we discuss three classical design methods:

- functional decomposition, which is a rather general approach to system design, not tied to any specific method listed in Table 12.4; many different notations can be used to depict the resulting design, ranging from flowcharts or pseudocode to algebraic specifications;

- data flow design, as exemplified by SA/SD;

- design based on data structures, as is done in JSP and JSD.

Table 12.4   A sample of design methods

Decision tables	Matrix representation of complex decision logic at the detailed design level.
E–R	Entity–relationship model. Family of graphical techniques for expressing data relationships; see also Chapter 10.
Flowcharts	Simple diagram technique to show control flow at the detailed design level. Exists in many flavors; see (Tripp, 1988) for an overview.
FSM	Finite state machine. A way to describe a system as a set of states and possible transitions between those states; the resulting diagrams are called state transition diagrams; see also Chapter 10.
JSD	Jackson System Development; see Section 12.2.3. Successor to, and more elaborate than, JSP; has an object-oriented flavor.
JSP	Jackson Structured Programming. Data-structure-oriented method; see Section 12.2.3.
NoteCards	Example hypertext system. Hypertext systems make it possible to create and navigate through a complex organization of unstructured pieces of text (Conklin, 1987).
OBJ	Algebraic specification method; highly mathematical (Goguen, 1986).
OOD	Object-oriented design; exists in many flavors; see Section 12.3.
Petri nets	Graphical design representation, well-suited for concurrent systems. A system is described as a set of states and possible transitions between those states. States are associated with tokens and transitions are described by firing rules. In this way, concurrent activities can be synchronized (Peterson, 1981).
SA/SD	Structured analysis/structured design; data flow design technique; see also Section 12.2.2.
SA/RT	Extension to structured analysis so that real-time aspects can be described (Hatley and Pirbhai, 1988).
SSADM	Structured systems analysis and design method. A highly prescriptive method for performing the analysis and design stages; UK standard (Downs et al., 1992).

A fourth design method, object-oriented design, is discussed in Section 12.3. Whereas the above three methods concentrate on identifying the *functions* of the system, object-oriented design focuses on the *data* on which the system is to operate. Object-oriented design is the most popular design approach today, not the least because of the omnipresence of UML as a notational device for the outcome of both requirements engineering and design.

12.2.1 Functional Decomposition

In a functional decomposition, the intended function is decomposed into a number of subfunctions that each solve part of the problem. These subfunctions themselves may be further decomposed into yet more primitive functions, and so on. Functional decomposition is a design philosophy rather than a design method. It denotes an overall approach to problem decomposition which underlies many a design method.

With functional decomposition, we apply **divide-and-conquer** tactics. These tactics are analogous to, but not the same as, the technique of **stepwise refinement** as it is applied in 'programming in the small'. Using stepwise refinement, the refinements tend to be context-dependent. As an example, consider the following pseudo-code algorithm to insert an element into a sorted list:

```
procedure insert(a, n, x);
begin insert x at the end of the list;
    k:= n + 1;
    while element_k is not at its proper place
    do swap element_k and element_k - 1;
        k:= k-1
    enddo;
end insert;
```

The refinement of a pseudo-code instruction such as $element_k$ is not at its proper place is done within the context of exactly the above routine, using knowledge of other parts of this routine. In the decomposition of a large system, it is precisely this type of dependency that we try to avoid. The previous section addressed this issue at great length.

During requirements engineering, the base machine has been decided upon. This base machine need not be a 'real' machine. It can be a programming language or some other set of primitives that constitutes the bottom layer of the design. During this phase too, the functions to be provided to the user have been fixed. These are the two ends of a rope. During the design phase we try to get from one end of this rope to the other. If we start from the user function end and take successively more detailed design decisions, the process is called top-down design. The reverse is called bottom-up design.

- **Top-down design:** Starting from the main user functions at the top, we work down decomposing functions into subfunctions. Assuming we do not make any mistakes on the way down, we can be sure to construct the specified system. With top-down design, each step is characterized by the design decisions it embodies. To be able to apply a pure top-down technique, the system has to be fully described. This is hardly ever the case. Working top-down also means that the earliest decisions are the most important ones. Undoing those decisions can be very costly.

- **Bottom-up design:** Using bottom-up design, we start from a set of available base functions. From there we proceed towards the requirements specification through abstraction. This technique is potentially more flexible, especially since the lower layers of the design could be independent of the application and thus have wider applicability. This is especially important if the requirements have not been formulated very precisely yet or if a family of systems has to be developed. A real danger of the bottom-up technique is that we may miss the target.

In their pure form, neither the top-down nor the bottom-up technique is likely to be used all that often. Both techniques are feasible only if the design process is a pure and rational one. And this is an idealization of reality. There are many reasons why the design process cannot be rational. Some of these have to do with the intangibles of design processes per se, some originate from accidents that befall many a software project. Parnas and Clements (1986) list the following reasons, amongst others:

- Mostly, users do not know exactly what they want and they are not able to tell all they know.

- Even if the requirements are fully known, a lot of additional information is needed. This information is discovered only when the project is under way.

- Almost all projects are subject to change. Changes influence earlier decisions.

- People make errors.

- During design, people use the knowledge they already have, experiences from earlier projects, and so on.

- In many projects, we do not start from scratch – we build from existing software.

Design exhibits a 'yo-yo' character: something is devised, tried, rejected again, new ideas crop up, etc. Designers frequently go about in rather opportunistic ways. They frequently switch from high-level, application domain issues to coding and detailed design matters, and use a variety of means to gather insight into the problem to be solved. At most, we may present the result of the design process as if it came about through a rational process.

A general problem with any form of functional decomposition is that it is often not immediately clear along which dimension the system is decomposed. If we decompose along the time axis, the result is often a main program that controls the order in which a number of subordinate components is called. In Yourdon's classification, the resulting cohesion type is temporal. If we decompose with respect to the grouping of data, we obtain the type of data cohesion exhibited in abstract data types. Both these functional decompositions can be viewed as an instance of some architectural style. Rather than worrying about which dimension to focus on during functional decomposition, you had better opt for a particular architectural style and let that style guide the decomposition.

At some intermediate level, the set of interrelated components comprises the software architecture as discussed in Chapter 11. This software architecture is a product which serves various purposes: it can be used to discuss the design with different stakeholders; it can be used to evaluate the quality of the design; it can be the basis for the work-breakdown structure; it can be used to guide the testing process, etc. If a software architecture is required, it necessitates a design approach in which, at quite an early stage, every component and connection is present. A bottom-up or top-down approach does not meet this requirement, since in both these approaches only part of the solution is available at intermediate points in time.

Parnas (1978) offers the following useful guidelines for a sound functional decomposition:

1. Try to identify subsystems. Start with a *minimal* subset and define minimal extensions to this subset.

   The idea behind this guideline is that it is extremely difficult, if not impossible, to get a complete picture of the system during requirements engineering. People ask too much or they ask the wrong things. Starting from a minimal subsystem, we may add functionality incrementally, using the experience gained with the actual use of the system. The idea is very similar to that of agile approaches, discussed in Chapter 3.

2. Apply the information-hiding principle.

3. Try to define extensions to the base machine step by step.

   This holds for both the minimal machine and its extensions. Such incremental extensions lead to the concept of a **virtual machine**. Each layer in the system hierarchy can be viewed as a machine. The primitive operations of this machine are implemented by the lower layers of the hierarchy. This machine view of the component hierarchy nicely maps onto a layered architectural style. It also adds a further dimension to the system structuring guidelines offered in Section 12.1.5.

4. Apply the uses relation and try to place the dependencies thus obtained in a hierarchical structure.

Obviously, the above guidelines are strongly interrelated. It has been said before that a strictly hierarchical tree structure of system components is often not feasible. A compromise that often is feasible is a layered system structure as depicted in Figure 12.6.

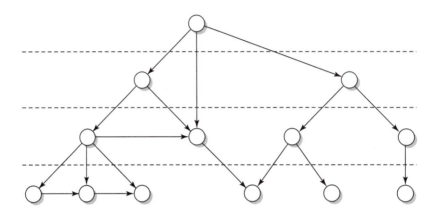

Figure 12.6 A layered system structure

The arrows between the various nodes in the graph indicate the uses relation. Various levels can be distinguished in the structure depicted. Components at a given level only use components from the same, or lower, levels. The layers distinguished in Figure 12.6 are not the same as those induced by the acyclicity of the graph (as discussed in Section 12.1.5) but are rather the result of viewing a distinct set of components as an abstract, virtual machine. Deciding how to group components into layers in this way involves considering the semantics of those components. Lower levels in this hierarchy bring us closer to the 'real' machine on which the system is going to be executed. Higher levels are more application-oriented. The choice of the number of levels in such an architecture is a (problem-dependent) design decision.

This work of Parnas heralds some of the notions that were later recognized as important guiding principles in the field of software architecture. The idea of a minimal subset to which extensions are defined is very similar to the notion of a product-line architecture: a basic architecture from which a family of similar systems can be derived. The layered approach is one of the basic architectural styles discussed in Section 11.4.

12.2.2 Data Flow Design (SA/SD)

The data flow design method originated in the early 1970s with Yourdon and Constantine. In its simplest form, data flow design is but a functional decomposition with respect to the flow of data. A component is a black box which transforms some input stream into some output stream. In data flow design, heavy use is made of graphical representations known as data flow diagrams (DFDs) and structure charts. Data flow diagrams were introduced as a modeling notation in Section 10.1.3.

Data flow design is usually seen as a two-step process. First, a logical design is derived in the form of a set of data flow diagrams. This step is referred to as *structured analysis* (SA). Next, the logical design is transformed into a program structure represented as a set of structure charts. The latter step is called *structured design* (SD). The combination is referred to as SA/SD.

Structured analysis can be viewed as a proper requirements engineering method insofar as it addresses the modeling of some universe of discourse (UoD). It should be noted that, as data flow diagrams are refined, the analyst performs an implicit (top-down) functional decomposition of the system as well. At the same time, the diagram refinements result in corresponding data refinements. The analysis process thus has design aspects as well.

Structured design, being a strategy to map the information flow contained in data flow diagrams into a program structure, is a genuine component of the (detailed) design phase.

The main result of structured analysis is a series of data flow diagrams. Four types of data entity are distinguished in these diagrams:

- **External entities** are the source or destination of a transaction. These entities are located outside the domain considered in the data flow diagram. External entities are indicated as squares.

- **Processes** transform data. Processes are denoted by circles.

- **Data flows** between processes, external entities, and data stores. A data flow is indicated by an arrow. Data flows are paths along which data structures travel.

- **Data stores** lie between two processes. This is indicated by the name of the data store between two parallel lines. Data stores are places where data structures are stored until needed.

We illustrate the various process steps of SA/SD by analyzing and designing a simple library automation system. The system allows library clients to borrow and return books. It also reports to library management about how the library is used by its clients (for example, the average number of books on loan and authors much in demand).

At the highest level, we draw a **context diagram**, a data flow diagram with one process, denoting 'the system'. Its main purpose is to depict the interaction of the system with the environment (the collection of external entities). For our simple library system, this is done in Figure 12.7. This diagram has yet to be supplemented by a description of the structure of both the input and output to the central process.

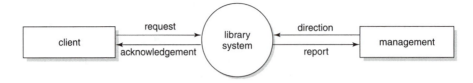

Figure 12.7 Context diagram for library automation

Next, this top-level diagram is further decomposed. For our example, this could lead to the data flow diagram of Figure 12.8 (which is the same as Figure 10.3). In this diagram, we have expanded the central process node of the context diagram. A client request is first analyzed in a process labeled 'preliminary processing'. As a result, one of 'borrow title' or 'return title' is activated. Both these processes update a data store labeled 'catalog administration'. Client requests are logged in a data store 'log file'. This data store is used to produce management reports.

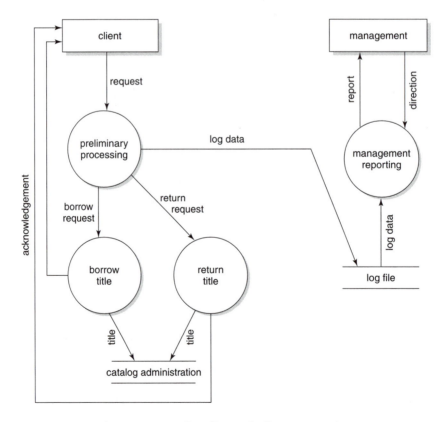

Figure 12.8 Data flow diagram for library automation

For more complicated applications, various diagrams could be drawn, one for each subsystem identified. These subsystems in turn are further decomposed into diagrams at yet lower levels. We thus get a hierarchy of diagrams. As an example, a possible refinement of the 'preliminary processing' node is given in Figure 12.9. In lower-level diagrams, the external entities are usually omitted.

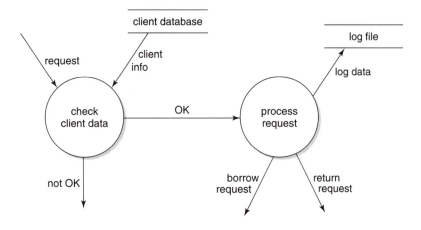

Figure 12.9 Data flow diagram for 'preliminary processing'

The top-down decomposition stops when a process becomes sufficiently straightforward and does not warrant further expansion. These primitive processes are described in *minispecs*. A minispec serves to communicate the algorithm of the process to relevant parties. It may use notations such as structured natural language, pseudocode, or decision tables. Example screen layouts can be added to illustrate how the input and output will look. An example minispec for 'process request' is given in Figure 12.10.

The contents of the data flows in a DFD are recorded in a data dictionary. Though this name suggests something grand, it is nothing more than a precise description of the structure of the data. This is often done in the form of regular expressions, such as the example in Figure 12.11. Nowadays, the static aspects of the data tend to be modeled in ER diagrams; see Chapter 10.

The result of structured analysis is a logical model of the system. It consists of a set of DFDs, augmented by descriptions of its constituents in the form of minispecs, formats of data stores, and so on. In the subsequent structured design step, the data flow diagrams are transformed into a collection of components (subprograms) that call one another and pass data. The result of the structured design step is expressed in a hierarchical set of **structure charts**. There are no strict rules for this step. Text-books on the data flow technique give guidelines, and sometimes even well-defined strategies, for how to get from a set of data flow diagrams to a hierarchical model

```
Identification: Process request
Description:
    1.  Enter type of request
        1.1 If invalid, issue a warning and repeat step 1
        1.2 If step 1 has been repeated five times, terminate the
            transaction
    2.  Enter book identification
        2.1 If invalid, issue a warning and repeat step 2
        2.2 If step 2 has been repeated five times, terminate the
            transaction
    3.  Log the client identification, request type and book
        identification
    4.  ...
```

Figure 12.10 Example minispec for 'process request'

```
borrow-request = client-id + book-id
return-request = client-id + book-id
log-data = client-id + [borrow | return] + book-id
book-id = author-name + title + (isbn) + [proc | series | other]
```

Conventions: [ ] means include one of the enclosed options; + means AND; () means enclosed items are optional; options are separated by |

Figure 12.11 Example data dictionary entries

for the implementation. These guidelines are strongly inspired by the various notions discussed in Section 12.1, most notably cohesion and coupling.

The major heuristic involves the choice of the top-level structure chart. Many data-processing systems are essentially transform-centered: input is read and possibly edited, a major transformation is done, and the result is output. One way to decide upon the central transformation is to trace the input through the data flow diagram until it can no longer be considered input. The same is done, in the other direction, for the output. The bubble in between is as the *central transform*. If we view the bubbles in a DFD as beads, and the data flows as threads, we obtain the corresponding structure chart by picking the bead that corresponds to the central transformation and shaking the DFD.[5] The processes in the data flow diagram become the components of the corresponding structure chart and the data flows become component invocations. Note that the arrows in a structure chart denote component invocations, whereas the arrows in a data flow diagram denote flows of data. These arrows often point in opposite directions; a flow of data from A to B is often realized through an invocation

---

[5] We do the same when turning a free tree into an oriented tree. A free tree has no root. By selecting one node of the tree as the root, the parent–child relations are brought about.

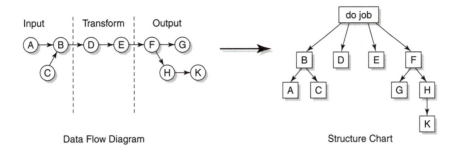

Figure 12.12 From data flow diagram to structure chart

of A by B. Sometimes it is difficult to select one central transformation. In that case, a dummy root element is added and the resulting input–process–output scheme is of the form depicted in Figure 12.12.

Because of the transformation orientation of the structure chart, the relations between components in the graph have a producer–consumer character. One component produces a stream of data which is then consumed by another component. The control flow is one whereby components invoke subordinate components so as to realize the required transformation. There is a potentially complex stream of information between components, corresponding to the data flow that is passed between producer and consumer.

The major contribution of structured design is found in the guidelines that aim to reduce the complexity of the interaction between components. These guidelines concern the cohesion and coupling criteria discussed in Section 12.1.

12.2.3 Design Based on Data Structures

The best-known technique for design based on data structures originated with Jackson (1975). The technique is known as Jackson Structured Programming (JSP). Essentials of JSP have been carried over to Jackson System Development (JSD). JSP is a technique for programming-in-the-small and JSD is a technique for programming-in-the-large. We discuss both techniques in turn.

The basic idea of JSP is that a good program reflects the structure of both the input and the output in all its facets. Given a correct model of the data structures, we may straightforwardly derive the corresponding program from the model. It is often postulated that the structure of the data is much less volatile than the transformations applied to the data. As a consequence, designs that take the data as their starting point should be 'better' too. This same argument is also used in the context of object-oriented analysis and design.

JSP distinguishes elementary and compound components. Elementary components are not further decomposed. There are three types of compound component: sequence, iteration and selection. Compound components are represented by diagrams (also called **Jackson diagrams** or **structure diagrams**) or some sort of pseudocode (called **structure text** or **schematic logic**). The base form of both representations are given in Figure 12.13. In the structure text, 'seq' denotes sequencing, 'itr' denotes iteration, 'sel' denotes selection, and 'alt' denotes alternatives.

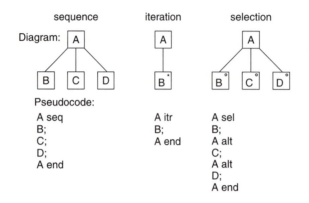

Figure 12.13 Compound components in Jackson's notation

Most modern programming languages have structures (loops, if statements and sequential composition) for each of these diagrammatic notations or, for that matter, the corresponding pseudocode for the structure of data. The essence of Jackson's technique is that the structure diagrams of the input and output can be merged, thus yielding the global structure of the program.

To illustrate this line of thought, consider a fragment from a library system. The system keeps track of which books from which authors are being borrowed (and returned). From this log, we want to produce a report that lists how often each title is borrowed. Using Jackson's notation, the input for this function could be as specified in Figure 12.14.[6] A possible structure for the output is given in Figure 12.15.

The program diagram to transform the log into a report is obtained by merging the two diagrams; see Figure 12.16. The structure of the resulting program can be derived straightforwardly from this diagram (see Figure 12.17).

This merging of diagrams does not work for the lower levels of our problem, 'process mutation' and its subordinate nodes. The cause is something called a **structure clash**: the input and output data structures do not really match. The reason is that the input consists of a sequence of mutations. In the output, all mutations for a given book are taken together. So, the mutations have to be sorted first. We have to restructure the system, for instance as depicted in Figure 12.18.

A clear disadvantage of the structure thus obtained is that there is now an intermediate file. Closer inspection shows that we do not really need this file. This is immediately clear if we depict the structure as in Figure 12.19.

---

[6]For simplicity's sake, we have assumed that the input is already sorted by author.

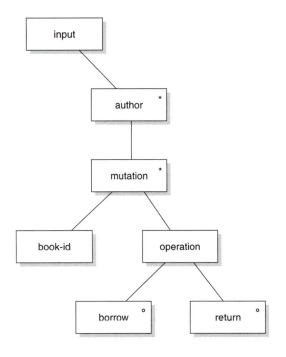

Figure 12.14 Log of books borrowed and returned, in JSP notation

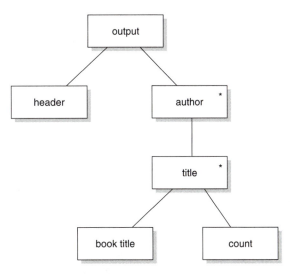

Figure 12.15 Report of books borrowed, in JSP notation

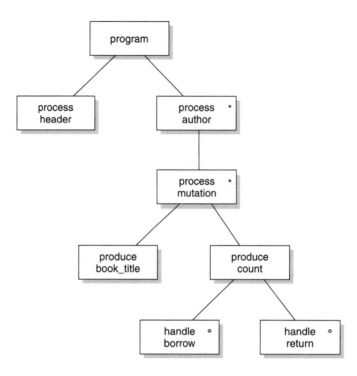

Figure 12.16 Result of merging the input and output diagrams

```
make header
until EOF loop
    process author:
        until end_of_author loop
            process_mutation:
                  ...
        endloop
endloop.
```

Figure 12.17 Top-level structure of the program to produce a report

Here, we may *invert* component A1 and code it such that it serves as a replacement of component B2. Alternatively (and in this case more likely), we may invert B1 and substitute the result for component A2. In either case, the first-in–first-out (FIFO) type of intermediate file between the two components is removed by making one of the components a subordinate of the other.

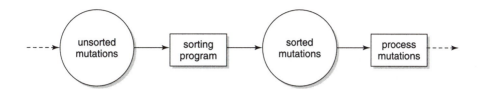

Figure 12.18 Restructuring of the system

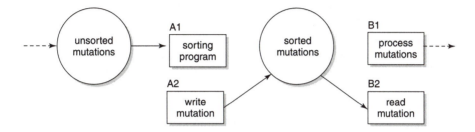

Figure 12.19 A different view of the system

This example shows the fundamental issues involved in the use of JSP:

- modeling input and output using structure diagrams,

- merging the diagrams to create the program structure, meanwhile

- resolving possible structure clashes, and finally

- optimizing the result through program inversion.

If we choose a linear notation for the structure diagrams, the result falls into the class of 'regular expressions'. Thus, the expressive power of these diagrams is that of a finite automaton. Some of the structure clashes crop up if the problem cannot be solved by a finite automaton.

Both in the functional decomposition and in the data flow design methods, the problem structure is mapped onto a functional structure. This functional structure is next mapped onto a program structure. In contrast, JSP maps the problem structure onto a data structure and the program structure is derived from this data structure. JSP is not much concerned with the question of how the mapping from problem structure to data structure is obtained.

Jackson System Development (JSD) tries to fill this gap. JSD distinguishes three stages in the software development process:

- A **modeling stage** in which a description is made of the real-world problem through the identification of entities and actions;

- A **network stage** in which the system is modeled as a network of communicating concurrent processes;

- An **implementation stage** in which the network of processes is transformed into a sequential design.

The first step in JSD is to model the part of reality we are interested in, the UoD. JSD models the UoD as a set of entities, objects in the real world that participate in a time-ordered sequence of actions. For each entity, a process is created which models the life cycle of that entity. Actions are events that happen to an entity. For instance, in a library the life cycle of an entity Book could be as depicted in Figure 12.20. The life cycle of a book starts when it is acquired. After that it may be borrowed and returned any number of times. The life cycle ends when the book is either archived or disposed of. The life cycle is depicted using **process structure diagrams** (PSDs). PSDs are hierarchical diagrams that resemble the structure diagrams of JSP, with its primitives to denote concatenation (ordering in time), repetition, and selection. PSDs have a pseudocode equivalent called **structure text** which looks like the schematic logic of JSP.

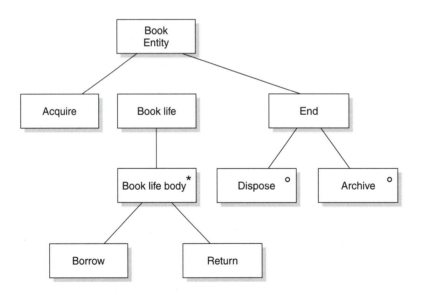

Figure 12.20 Process structure diagram for the entity Book

Process structure diagrams are finite state diagrams. In traditional finite state diagrams, the bubbles (nodes) represent possible states of the entity being modeled while the arrows denote possible transitions between states. The opposite is true for PSDs. In a PSD, nodes denote state transitions and arrows denote states.

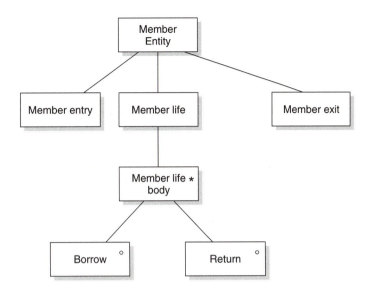

Figure 12.21 Process structure diagram for the entity Member

Following this line of thought, an entity Member can be described as in Figure 12.21: members enter the library system, after which they may borrow and return books until they cease to be a member.

The modeling stage is concerned with identifying entities and the events (actions) that happen to them. These actions collectively constitute the life cycle of an entity. As with other design methods, there is no simple recipe to determine the set of entities and actions. The approach generally taken has a linguistic stance. From notes, documentation, interviews and the like, we may draw up a preliminary list of actions and entities. One heuristic is to look for real-world objects with which the system is to interact. Since a library is all about books, an entity Book immediately suggests itself. From statements such as 'members borrow books', we may infer that an event Borrow occurs in the life cycle of both books and members. Once such a preliminary list is made up, further reflection should lead to a precisely demarcated life cycle of the entities identified.

Entities are made up of actions. These actions are atomic, i.e. they cannot be further decomposed into subactions. Actions respond to events in the real world. The action Acquire that is part of the life cycle of the entity Book is triggered when a real-world event, the actual acquisition of a book, takes place. In the process structure diagram, actions show up as leaf nodes.

Events are communicated to the system through data messages, called **attributes**. In a procedural sense, these attributes constitute the parameters of the action. For the action Acquire, we may have such attributes as ISBN, date-of-acquisition, title and authors.

Entities have attributes as well: local variables that keep information from the past and collectively determine its state. The entity Book for example may retain some or all of the information that was provided upon acquisition (for example, ISBN, title). Entities also have two special attributes. First, the *identifier attribute* uniquely identifies the entity. Second, each entity has an attribute that indicates its status. This attribute can be viewed as a pointer to some leaf node of the process structure diagram.

Each entity can be viewed as a separate, long-running, process. In the library example, each book and each member has its own life cycle. The processes though are not completely independent. During the network stage, the system is modeled as a network of interconnected processes. This network is depicted in a **system specification diagram** (SSD). JSD has two basic mechanisms for interprocess communication:

- An entity may inspect the *state vector* of another entity. This state vector describes the local state of an entity at some point in time.

- An entity may asynchronously pass information to another entity through a *datastream*.

Recall that the actions Borrow and Return occur in the life cycle of both Book and Member (see Figures 12.20 and 12.21). Such common actions create a link between these entities. As a consequence, the life cycles of these entities are synchronized with respect to these events.

If a member wants to borrow a book, certain information about that book is required. A Member entity may obtain that information by inspecting the state vector of the appropriate Book entity. This type of communication is indicated by the diamond in Figure 12.22. In an implementation, state vector communication is usually handled through database access.

Figure 12.22 State vector (SV) communication between Member and Book

If our system is to log information on books being borrowed, we may model this by means of a datastream from an entity Book to an entity Log. A datastream is handled on a FIFO basis; it behaves like the UNIX filter. The notation for the datastream type of communication is given in Figure 12.23.

The final stage of JSD is the implementation stage, in which the concurrent model that is the result of the network stage is transformed into an executable system. One of the key concepts for this stage is program inversion: the

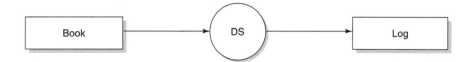

Figure 12.23 Datastream (DS) communication between `Book` and `Log`

communication between processes is replaced by a procedure call, so that one process becomes a subordinate of another process. This is very similar to the notion of program inversion as present in JSP.

12.3 OBJECT-ORIENTED ANALYSIS AND DESIGN METHODS

The key concepts that play a role in the object-oriented approach to analysis and design have been mentioned already in Chapter 10: objects, their attributes and services, and the relationships between objects. It follows quite naturally from the above that the object-oriented approach to systems analysis and design involves three major steps:

1. Identify the objects;

2. Determine their attributes and services;

3. Determine the relationships between objects.

Obviously, these steps are highly interrelated and some form of iteration will be needed before the final design is obtained. The resulting picture of the system as a collection of objects and their interrelationships describes the **static** structure (decomposition) of the system. This static model is graphically depicted in some variant of the class diagram as described in Section 10.3.1.

An object instance is created, updated zero or more times, and finally destroyed. Finite state diagrams depicting the possible states of an object and the transitions between those states are a good help in modeling this life cycle. Object-oriented methods generally use some variant of the state machine diagram of UML to show this **dynamic** model of the behavior of system components; see Section 10.3.2.

Components of the system communicate by sending messages. These messages are part of a task that the system has to perform. We may find out which messages are needed, and in which order they have to be exchanged, by considering typical usage scenarios. Scenario analysis is a requirements elicitation technique. In object-oriented circles, this technique is known as **use-case analysis**. The resulting model of the communication between system components is depicted in a sequence or communication diagram; see Sections 10.3.3 and 10.3.4. These views are also part of the dynamic model.

The guidelines for finding objects and their attributes and services are mostly linguistic in nature, much like the ones mentioned in our discussion of JSD in

Section 12.2.3. Indeed, the modeling stage of JSD is object-oriented too. The guidelines presented below are loosely based on (Coad and Yourdon, 1991) and (Rumbaugh *et al.*, 1991). Their general flavor is similar to that found in other object-oriented approaches. The global process models of some well-known object-oriented methods are discussed in Sections 12.3.1 and 12.3.2.

The problem statement for a library automation system given in Figure 12.24 will serve as an example to illustrate the major steps in object-oriented analysis and design. We will elaborate part of this problem in the text, and leave a number of detailed issues as exercises.

Problem statement

Design the software to support the operation of a public library. The system has a number of stations for customer transactions. These stations are operated by library employees. When a book is borrowed, the identification card of the client is read. Next, the station's bar code reader reads the book's code. When a book is returned, the identification card is not needed – only the book's code needs to be read.
Clients may search the library catalog from any of a number of PCs located in the library. When doing so, the user is first asked to indicate how the search is to be done: by author, by title, or by keyword.
. . .

Special functionality of the system concerns changing the contents of the catalog and the handling of fines. This functionality is restricted to library personnel. A password is required for these functions.
. . .

Figure 12.24 Problem statement for library automation system

A major guiding principle for identifying objects is to look for important concepts from the application domain. Objects to be found in a library include `Books`, `FileCabinets`, `Customers`, etc. In an office environment, we may have `Folders`, `Letters`, `Clerks`, etc. These domain-specific entities are our prime candidates for objects. They may be real-world objects, such as a book; roles played, such as the customer of a library; organizational units, such as a department; locations, such as an office; or devices, such as a printer. Potential objects can also be found by considering existing classification or assembly (whole–part) structures. From interviews, documentation, and so on, a first inventory of objects can be made.

From the first paragraph of the problem description in Figure 12.24, the following list of candidate objects can be deduced, simply by listing all the nouns:

```
software
library
```

```
system
station
customer
transaction
book
library employee
identification card
client
bar code reader
book's code
```

Some objects on this candidate list should be eliminated:

- `Software`, for example, is an implementation construct which should not be included in the model at this point in time. A similar fate should befall terms such as `algorithm` and `linked list`. At the detailed design stage, there may be reasons to introduce (or reintroduce) them as solution-oriented objects.

- Vague terms should be replaced by more concrete terms or eliminated. `System` is a vague term in our candidate list. The stations and PCs will be connected to the same host computer, so we might as well use the notion `computer` instead of `system`.

- `Customer` and `client` are synonymous terms in the problem statement. Only one of them is therefore retained. We must be careful in how we model `client` and `library employee`. One physical person may assume both roles. Whether it is useful to model these as distinct objects or as different roles of one object is difficult to decide at this point. We will treat them as separate objects for now, but keep in mind that this may change when the model is refined.

- The term `transaction` refers to an operation applied to objects, rather than an object in itself. It involves a sequence of actions such as handing an identification card and a book copy to the employee, inserting the identification card into the station, reading the book's bar code, and so on. Only if transactions themselves have features which are important to the system should they be modeled as objects. For instance, if the system has to produce profile information about client preferences, it may be useful to have an object `transaction`.

- The term `book` is a bit tricky in this context. A book in a library system may denote both a physical copy and an abstract key denoting a particular {author, title} combination. The former meaning is intended when we speak about the borrowing of a book, while the latter is intended where it concerns entries in the library catalog. Inexperienced designers may equate these interpretations and end up with the wrong system. We are interested (in this part of the system) in modeling book *copies*.

- The book's code describes an individual object rather than a class of objects. It should be restated as an attribute of the object book copy.

Figure 12.25 lists the relationships between objects that can be inferred from the problem statement in Figure 12.24. These relationships are directly copied from the problem statement or are part of the tacit knowledge we have of the domain.

From the problem statement:

---

employee operates station
station has bar code reader
bar code reader reads book copy
bar code reader reads identification card

Tacit knowledge:

---

library owns computer
library owns stations
computer communicates with station
library employs employee
client is member of library
client has identification card

Figure 12.25 Relationships inferred from the problem statement

The resulting objects and relationships are included in the initial class diagram of Figure 12.26. We have only included the names of the relationships in this diagram. Further adornments, such as cardinality constraints and specialization–generalization information, may be included when the model is refined.

We next identify the attributes of objects. Attributes describe an instance of an object. Collectively, the attributes constitute the state of the object. Attributes are identified by considering the characteristics that distinguish individual instances, yet are common properties of the instances of an object type. We thus look for atomic attributes rather than composite ones. For our library customer, we would for example obtain attributes Name and Address rather than a composite attribute NameAnd-Address. At this stage, we also try to prevent redundancies in the set of attributes. So rather than having attributes BooksOnLoan and NumberOfBooksOnLoan, we settle for the former only, since the latter can be computed from that attribute.

The major services provided by an object are those that relate to its life cycle. For example, a copy of a book is acquired, is borrowed and returned zero or more times, and finally goes out of circulation. A person becomes a member of the library

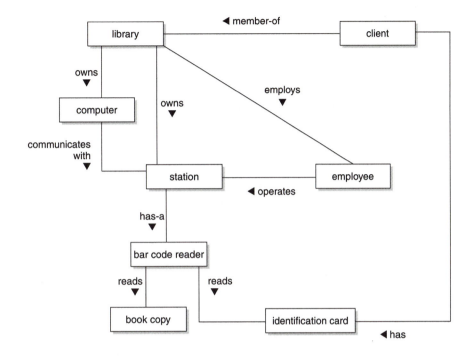

Figure 12.26 (Part of) the initial object model for a library system

and may borrow and return books, reserve titles, change address, pay fines, and so on, until he finally ceases to be a member.

These services concern the state of an object: they read and write the object's attributes. Services that provide information about the state of an object may or may not involve some type of computation. Note that it is always possible to optimize the actual implementation by keeping redundant information in the state as it is maintained by the object. For example, we may decide to include the number of books on loan in the state as implemented, rather than computing it when required. This need not concern us at this stage though. Whether services are actually implemented by computational means or by a simple lookup procedure is invisible to the object that requests the information.

Further insight into which services are required can be obtained by investigating usage scenarios. We may prepare typical dialogs between components of the system in both normal and exceptional situations. For example, we may consider the situation in which a client successfully borrows a book, one in which the client's identification card is no longer valid, one in which he still has to pay an outstanding fine, and so on. A sequence diagram for the normal situation of borrowing a book is shown in

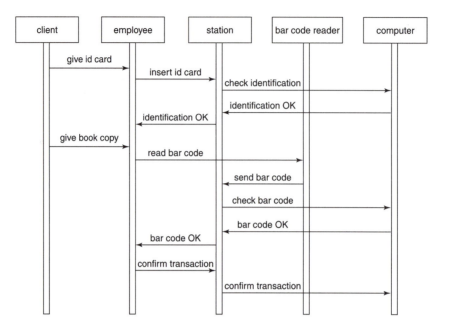

Figure 12.27 Sequence diagram for borrowing a book

Figure 12.27. A number of events take place when this interaction takes place. These events will be handled by operations of the objects involved.

Services are but one way through which objects may be related. The relations which give systems a truly object-oriented flavor are those which result from whole–part and specialization–generalization classifications.

Part of the classification of objects may result from the pre-existing real-world classifications that the system is to deal with. Further classification of objects into an object hierarchy involves a search for relations between objects. To start with, we may consider an object as a generalization of other possible objects. For instance, the object Book may be viewed as a generalization of the objects Novel, Poetry and ReferenceBook. Whether these specializations are meaningful depends on the problem at hand. If the system does not need to distinguish between novels and poetry, we should not define separate objects for them. The distinction between novels and poetry on the one hand and reference books on the other is sensible, though, if novels and poetry can be borrowed, but reference books cannot.

In a similar way, we may consider similarities between objects, thus viewing them as specializations of a more general object. If our library system calls for objects Book and Journal that have a number of attributes in common, we may introduce a new object Publication as a generalization of these objects. The common attributes are lifted to the object `Publication`; `Book` and `Journal` then inherit these attributes. Note that generalizations should still reflect meaningful real-world entities. There is no point in introducing a generalization of `Book` and `FileCabinet` simply because they have a common attribute of `Location`.

The object `Publication` is an *abstract object*. It is an object for which there are no instances. The library only contains instances of objects that are a specialization of `Publication`, such as `Book` and `Journal`. Its function in the object hierarchy is to relate these other objects and to provide an interface description to its users. The attributes and services defined at the level of `Publication` together constitute the common interface for all its descendants.

The specialization–generalization hierarchy also makes it possible to lift services to higher levels of the hierarchy. Doing so often gives rise to so-called **virtual functions**. Virtual functions are services of an object for which a (default) implementation is provided which can be redefined by specializations of that object. The notion of virtual functions greatly enhances reusability, since a variant of some object can now be obtained by constructing a specialization of that object in which some services are redefined.

Decisions as to which objects and attributes to include in a design, and how to relate them in the object hierarchy, are highly intertwined. For instance, if an object has only one attribute, it is generally better to include it as an attribute in other objects. Also, the instances of an object should have common attributes. If some attributes are only meaningful for a subset of all instances, then we really have a classification structure. If some books can be borrowed, but others cannot, this is an indication of a classification structure where the object `Book` has specializations such as `Novel` and `ReferenceBook`.

Note also that, over time, the set of attributes of and services provided by an object tends to evolve, while the object hierarchy remains relatively stable. If our library decides to offer an extra service to its customers, say borrowing records, we may simply adapt the set of attributes and extend the set of services for the object `Customer`.

Object-oriented design can be classified as a **middle-out** design method. The set of objects identified during the first modeling stages constitutes the middle level of the system. In order to implement these domain-specific entities, lower-level objects are used. These lower-level objects can often be taken from a class library. For the various object-oriented programming languages, quite extensive class libraries already exist. The higher levels of the design constitute the application-dependent interaction of the domain-specific entities.

In the following subsections, we discuss three design methods that typify the evolution of object-oriented analysis and design:

- the Booch method, an early object-oriented analysis and design method, with an emphasis on employing a new and rich set of notations;

- Fusion, developed at HP, with a much larger emphasis on the various process steps of the method;

- the Rational Unified Process (RUP), a full life cycle model associated with UML.

12.3.1 The Booch Method

The global process model of the method described in (Booch, 1994) is shown in Figure 12.28. It consists of four steps, to be carried out in roughly the order shown. The process is iterative, so each of the steps may have to be done more than once. The first cycles are analysis-oriented, while later ones are design-oriented. The blurring of activities in this process model is intentional. Analysis and design activities are assumed to be under opportunistic control. It is therefore not deemed realistic to prescribe a purely rational order for the activities to be carried out.

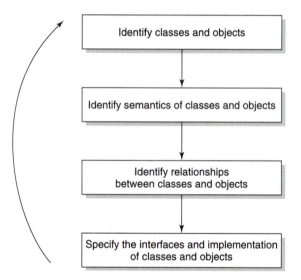

Figure 12.28 The process model of Booch (*Source*: G. Booch, *Object-Oriented Analysis and Design*, ©1994, Benjamin Cummings Publishing Company. Reproduced by permission of Addison Wesley Longman.)

The first step is aimed at identifying classes and objects. The purpose of this step is to establish the boundaries of the problem and to obtain a first decomposition. During analysis, the emphasis is on finding meaningful abstractions from the application domain. During design, objects from the solution domain may be added. The major outcome of this step is a data dictionary containing a precise description of the abstractions identified.

The second step is concerned with determining the behavior and attributes of each abstraction, and the distribution of responsibilities over components of the system. Attributes and desired behavior are identified by analyzing typical usage scenarios. As this process proceeds, responsibilities may be reallocated to get a more balanced design, or be able to reuse (scavenge) existing designs. The outcome of this step is a reasonably complete set of responsibilities and operations for each abstraction. The results are documented in the data dictionary and, at a later stage, in interface specifications for each abstraction. The semantics of usage scenarios are captured in sequence and communication diagrams (termed **interaction diagrams** and **object diagrams**, respectively, in (Booch, 1994)).

The third step is concerned with finding relationships between objects. During analysis, the emphasis is on finding relationships between abstractions. During design, tactical decisions about inheritance, instantiation, and so on are made. The results are shown in class diagrams, communication diagrams, and 'module diagrams', which show the modular structure of a system.

Finally, the abstractions are refined to a detailed level. A decision is made about the representation of each abstraction, algorithms are selected, and solution-oriented classes are added where needed.

The most notable characteristics of Booch's method are:

- A rich set of notations: it uses six types of diagram, each with a fairly elaborate vocabulary; as a result, many aspects of a system can be modeled

- A poor process model: it is difficult to decide when to iterate, and what to do in a specific iteration.

12.3.2 Fusion

The Fusion method for object-oriented analysis and design has two major phases: analysis and design. Its global process model is shown in Figure 12.29.

The analysis phase is aimed at determining the system's objects and their interactions. The static structure is shown in a class diagram (called an **object model** in Fusion) and documented in a data dictionary. The dynamics are shown in the interface model. The interface model consists of a life cycle model for each object, denoted by a regular expression (i.e., a flat representation of a state machine diagram) and a specification of the semantics of each operation in a pre- and postcondition style. The analysis process is assumed to be an iterative process. This iteration stops when the models are complete and consistent.

Fusion's design phase results in four models, which are essentially derived in the order indicated in Figure 12.29. Object interaction graphs resemble communication graphs. They describe how objects interact at run time: what objects are involved in a computation and how they are combined to realize a given specification. Visibility graphs describe how the communications between objects are realized. For each object, it is determined which other objects must be referenced and how. Different

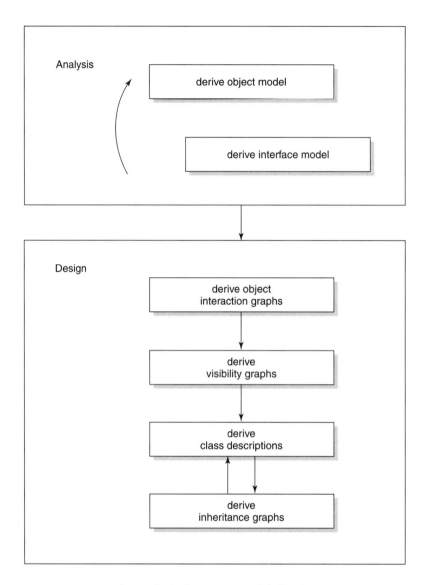

Figure 12.29 The process model of Fusion

kinds of references are distinguished, taking into account aspects such as the lifetime of the reference and whether references can be shared. Next, the object model, interaction graphs, and visibility graphs are used to derive a description of each class. The operations and the initial set of attributes for each object are established at this stage. Finally, the inheritance relations are decided upon and depicted in the inheritance graph, which is a class diagram. The class descriptions are then updated to reflect this inheritance structure.

The most notable characteristics of Fusion are:

- A large amount of attention is paid to the design phase. Fusion defines four models for the design phase and gives detailed guidelines for the kind of things that have to be incorporated in these models.

- The version of the method as published in (Coleman *et al.*, 1994) hinges on the availability of a good requirements document. Extensions to this version include the absorption of use cases to drive the analysis process.

- As a method, Fusion is very prescriptive. The contrast with the opportunistic approach of Booch is striking. Fusion's prescriptiveness might be considered both a strength and a weakness.

12.3.3 RUP Revisited

The Rational Unified Process (RUP) is a full process model; see also Section 3.3. RUP has a number of workflows, such as a requirements workflow, analysis and design workflow, and test workflow, and four phases: inception, elaboration, construction, and transition. Workflows describe the activities to be carried out, while the phases indicate the organization along the time axis. Most workflows extend over most phases.

Here, we discuss the analysis and design workflow, in which the requirements are transformed into a design. RUP is an iterative process, so this transformation is carried out in a number of iterations as well. The first iterations take place in the elaboration phase of RUP. In that phase, the architecture of the system is determined. The RUP way of doing architectural design reasonably fits the global workflow model discussed in Section 11.2. In subsequent iterations, concerning the lower-level design, the main activities are *analyze behavior* and *design components*.

The purpose of the *analyze behavior* step is to transform the use cases into a set of design elements that together serve as a model of the problem domain. It is about *what* the system is to deliver. It produces a black-box model of the solution. The purpose of the *design elements* step is to refine the definitions of the design elements into classes, relationships, interfaces, and so on. In this activity, the black-box, *what* model is turned into a white-box, *how* model.

During both activities, the design is reviewed and the results are fed back into the next iteration.

Notable characteristics of RUP are:

- It is a very complete, iterative model that goes much further than mere analysis and design.

- It makes heavy use of UML to represent artifacts and views.

- Use cases play a central role. They provide thread information from one workflow to another. For example, the analysis and design workflow produces *use-case realizations*, which describe how use cases are actually realized by a collection of interacting objects and classes.

12.4 HOW TO SELECT A DESIGN METHOD

It is not easy to compare the many design methods that exist. They all have their pros and cons. None of them gives us a straightforward recipe as to how to proceed from a list of requirements to a successfully implemented system. We always need some sort of magic in order to get a specific decomposition. The expertise and quality of the people involved have a major impact on the end result of the design process.

Problem solving is based on experience. It is estimated that an expert has over 50 000 chunks of domain-specific knowledge at his disposal. When solving a problem, we try to map the problem at hand onto the knowledge available. The greater this knowledge is, and the more accessible it is, the more successful this process will be.

The prescriptiveness of the design methods differs considerably. The variants of functional decomposition and the object-oriented design methods rely heavily on the heuristic knowledge of the designers. Jackson's techniques seem to suffer less from this need. Especially if structure clashes do not occur, JSP provides a well-defined framework for tackling design. The prescriptive nature of JSP possibly explains to some extent its success in the past, especially in the realm of administrative data processing. JSD offers similar advantages. Its strict view of describing data structures as a list of events may lead to problems, however, if the data structures do not fit this model. JSP has a static view of the data. More importantly, it does not tell us *how* to organize the data. As such, this technique seems most suited to problems where the structure of the data has been fixed beforehand. JSD and object-oriented methods offer better support as regards the structuring of data. Though these methods give useful heuristics for the identification of objects, obtaining a well-balanced set of objects is still very much dependent on the skills of the designer.

The data flow technique has a more dynamic view of the datastreams that are the base of the system to be constructed. We may often view the bubbles from a data flow diagram as clerks that perform certain transformations on incoming data to produce data for other clerks. The technique seems well-suited for circumstances where an existing manual system is to be replaced by a computerized one. A real danger, though, is that the existing system is just copied, while additional requirements are overlooked.

If we take into account that a substantial part of the cost of software is spent in *maintaining* that software, it is clear that such factors as flexibility, comprehensibility, and modularity should play a crucial role when selecting a specific design technique. The ideas and guidelines of Parnas are particularly relevant in this respect. The object-oriented philosophy incorporates these ideas and is well-matched to current programming languages, which allow for a smoother transition between the different development phases.

12.4.1 Design Method Classification

Quite a few attempts have been made to classify design methods along various dimensions, such as the products they deliver, the kind of representations used, or their level of formality. A simple but useful framework is proposed in (Blum, 1994). It has two dimensions: an orientation dimension and a model dimension.

In the orientation dimension, a distinction is made between problem-oriented techniques and product-oriented techniques. Problem-oriented techniques concentrate on producing a better understanding of the problem and its solution. Problem-oriented techniques are human-oriented. Their aim is to describe, communicate, and document decisions. Problem-oriented techniques usually have one foot in the requirements engineering domain. Conversely, product-oriented techniques focus on a correct transformation from a specification to an implementation. The second dimension relates to the products, i.e. models, that are the result of the design process. In this dimension, a distinction is made between conceptual models and formal models. Conceptual models are descriptive. They describe an external reality, the universe of discourse. Their appropriateness is established through validation. Formal models on the other hand are prescriptive. They prescribe the behavior of the system to be developed. Formal models can be verified.

Using this framework, we may classify a number of techniques discussed in this book as in Table 12.5. The four quadrants of this matrix have the following characteristics:

  I **Understand the problem** These techniques are concerned with understanding the problem and expressing a solution in a form that can be discussed with domain specialists (i.e. the users).

 II **Transform to implementation** Techniques in this category help to transform a collection of UoD-related concepts into an implementation structure.

III **Represent properties** These techniques facilitate reasoning about the problem and its solution.

IV **Create implementation units** This category contains techniques specifically aimed at creating implementation units such as packages or classes.

The above arguments relate to characteristics of the problem to be solved. There are several other environmental factors that may impact the choice of a particular design technique and, as a consequence, the resulting design (similar arguments hold for the software architecture; see Chapter 11):

• Familiarity with the problem domain: If the designers are well-acquainted with the type of problem to be solved, a top-down technique or a technique based on data structures may be very effective. If the design is experimental, one will go about it in a more cautious way, and a bottom-up design technique then seems more appropriate.

Table 12.5 Classification of design techniques

	Problem-oriented	Product-oriented
Conceptual	I ER Modeling Structured Analysis OO Analysis	II Structured Design OO Design
Formal	III JSD	IV Functional Decomposition JSP

- Designer's experience: Designers that have a lot of experience with a given method will, in general, be more successful in applying that method. They are aware of the constraints and limitations of the method and will be able to successfully bypass the potential problems.

- Available tools: If tools are available to support a given design method, it is only natural to make use of them. In general, this also implies that the organization has chosen that design method.

- Overall development philosophy: Many design methods are embedded in a wider philosophy which also addresses other aspects of system development, ranging from ways to conduct interviews or reviews to full-scale models of the software life cycle. The organized and disciplined overall approach endorsed by such a development philosophy is an extra incentive for using the design method that goes with it.

12.4.2 Object Orientation: Hype or the Answer?

Moving from OOA to OOD is a progressive expansion of the model.
Coad and Yourdon (1991, p. 178)

The transition from OOA to OOD is difficult.
Davis (1995)

Strict modeling of the real world leads to a system that reflects today's reality but not necessarily tomorrow's. The abstractions that emerge during design are key to making a design flexible.
(Gamma et al., 1995)

The above quotes hint at some important questions still left unanswered in our discussion of object-oriented methods:

- Do object-oriented methods adequately capture the requirements engineering phase?

- Do object-oriented methods adequately capture the design phase?

- Do object-oriented methods adequately bridge the gap between these phases, if such a gap exists?

- Are object-oriented methods really an improvement over more traditional methods?

The goal of requirements engineering is to model relevant aspects of the real world, the world in which the application has to operate. Requirements engineering activities concern both capturing knowledge of this world and modeling it. The language and methods for doing so should be problem-oriented (domain-oriented). They should ease communication with users as well as validation of the requirements by users. Most object-oriented methods assume that the requirements have been established before the analysis starts. Of the four processes distinguished in Chapter 9 (elicitation, specification, validation, and negotiation), object-oriented methods by and large only cover the requirements *specification* subprocess. Though many object-oriented methods have incorporated use-case analysis, the purpose of it is primarily to model the functional behavior of the system rather than to elicit user requirements.

A rather common view of proponents of object orientation is that object-oriented analysis (OOA) and object-oriented design (OOD) are very much the same. OOD simply adds implementation-specific classes to the analysis model. This view, however, can be disputed. OOA should be problem-oriented; its goal is to increase our understanding of the problem. The purpose of design, whether object-oriented or otherwise, is to decide on the parts of a solution, their interaction, and the specification of each of these parts. This difference in scope places OOA and OOD at a different relative 'distance' from a problem and its solution, as shown in Figure 12.30.

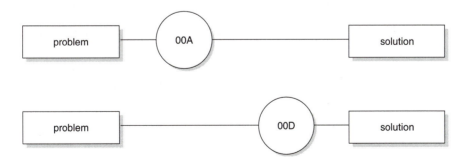

Figure 12.30 The 'distance' between OOA, OOD and a problem and its solution

There are good reasons to distinguish OOA-type activities and OOD-type activities, as is done in Fusion, for example. During design, attention is focused on specifying how to create and destroy objects, on identifying generalizations (abstract, if necessary) of objects in order to promote reuse or maintainability, and so on. An object `Publication` as a generalization of `Book` and `Journal` need not be considered during analysis, since it does not increase our understanding of the domain. On the other hand, an object such as `identification card` may well disappear from the model during design.

Most software development organizations have accumulated a lot of experience in developing software following the traditional, function- or process-oriented style. A lot of legacy software has been developed and documented that way. As a consequence, knowledge of these methods is still required in many an organization.

Many organizations have switched to some kind of object-oriented analysis and design approach. Hard evidence of increased productivity or quality has not been determined, though. Several experiments have been done to test the effectiveness of the object-oriented paradigm, and the results do seem to indicate some deeper problems. For example, in one experiment it was tested how effective object-oriented models are as the main vehicle of communication between the typical customer and the developer (Moynihan, 1996). It was found that the traditional, functional models were easier to understand, provoked more questions and comments, gave a more holistic understanding of the business, and better helped to evaluate likely implementations. In another experiment, it was tested whether novice analysts are able to develop requirements more easily with certain methods than with others, and whether they learn to use certain methods more readily than others (Vessey and Conger, 1994). Again, the results were negative for object orientation: novice analysts were better able to apply the process-oriented method and significant learning only occurred for the process-oriented method.

In a similar vein, Arisholm and Sjøberg (2004) found that novice users have fewer problems maintaining systems that have centralized control compared to systems having delegated control. In a centralized control style, one or a few large classes are in control. These large classes coordinate the work of a lot of smaller classes. This resembles the hierarchical main-program-with-subroutines architectural style. In a delegated style, responsibilities are distributed over a larger set of classes. Proponents of object orientation usually advocate a delegated control style. It seems one needs a certain maturity to be effective with this style.

The inheritance mechanism of object orientation needs to be handled with care too, as noted in Section 12.1.6. Deep hierarchies require one to comprehend design or implementation units that may be far apart. Such designs tend to be error prone (Bieman *et al.*, 2001) and more difficult to inspect (Dunsmore *et al.*, 2002), because of the delocalized nature of information in them.

There may well be some truth in the observation that users do not think in objects; they think in tasks. From that point of view, use-case analysis may be seen as one way to introduce a functional view into an otherwise object-oriented approach.

12.5 DESIGN PATTERNS

A design pattern is a recurring structure of communicating components that solves a general design problem within a particular context. A design pattern differs from an architectural style in that it does not address the structure of a complete system, but only that of a few (interacting) components. Design patterns may thus be termed micro-architectures. On the other hand, a design pattern encompasses more than a single component, method or class.

The archetypal example of a design pattern is the Model–View–Controller (MVC) pattern. Interactive systems consist of computational elements as well as elements to display data and handle user input. It is considered good design practice to separate the computational elements from those that handle I/O. This separation of concerns is achieved by the MVC pattern.

MVC involves three components: the Model, the View, and the Controller. The model component encapsulates the system's data as well as the operations on those data. The model component is independent of how the data is represented or how input is done. A view component displays the data that it obtains from the model component. There can be more than one view component. Finally, each view has an associated controller component. A controller handles input actions. Such an input action may cause the controller to send a request to the model, for example to update its data, or to its view, for example to scroll.

For any given situation, the above description has to be considerably refined and made more precise. For instance, a controller may or may not depend on the state of the model. If the controller does not depend on the state of the model, there is a one-way flow of information: the controller signals an input event and notifies the model. If the controller does depend on the state of the model, information flows in the other direction as well. The latter type of dependence can be observed in most word-processing systems, for example, where menu entries are made active or inactive depending on the state of the model.

MVC was first used in the Smalltalk environment. Since then it has been applied in many applications. In various graphical user interface platforms, a variant has been applied in which the distinction between the view and the controller has been relaxed. This variant is called the Document–View pattern; see (Kruglinski, 1996).

Design patterns have a number of properties which explain what they offer, as well as why and how they do so:

- A pattern addresses a recurring design problem that arises in specific design situations and presents a solution to it. Many software systems include computational elements as well as user-interface elements. For reasons of flexibility, we may wish to separate these as much as possible. MVC offers a solution to precisely this recurring problem.

- A pattern must balance a set of opposing forces, i.e. characteristics of the problem that have to be dealt with in its solution. For example, in interactive applications we want to be able to present information in different ways, changes to the data must be reflected immediately in all views affected by these changes, and different 'look and feel' interfaces should not affect the application code. MVC seeks to balance all these forces.

- Patterns document existing, well-proven design experience. Patterns are not invented; they evolve with experience. They reflect best practices. MVC, for example, is used in various application frameworks as well as in scores of interactive systems.

- Patterns identify and specify abstractions above the level of single components. MVC has three interacting components which *together* solve a given problem.

- Patterns provide a common vocabulary and understanding for design principles. By now, MVC has become a widely known label for a certain solution to a certain problem. We may use the term in conversation and writing much as we use terms such as 'quicksort' or 'Gauss interpolation'. Patterns thus become part of our language for describing software designs.

- Patterns are a means of documentation. As with software architectures, patterns both describe and prescribe things. Descriptively, patterns offer a way to document your software, for example by simply using the pattern names in documentation. Prescriptively, pattern names give users hints as to how to extend and modify software without violating the pattern's vision. If your system employs MVC, computational aspects are strictly separated from representational aspects, and you know that this separation must be maintained during the system's evolution.

- Patterns support the construction of software with defined properties. On the one hand, MVC offers a skeleton for the construction of interactive systems. MVC however also addresses certain non-functional requirements, such as flexibility and changeability of user interfaces. These non-functional requirements often constitute the major problem directly addressed by the pattern.

When describing patterns it is customary to use a schema similar to that used for describing architectural styles. The main entries of such a schema therefore are:

- *context*: the situation giving rise to a design problem,

- *problem*: a recurring problem arising in that situation, and

- *solution*: a proven solution to that problem.

We illustrate this by sketching a possible application of two design patterns in a library automation system. Suppose our library system involves a central database and a number of users, some of which are based at remote sites. We wish to optimize these remote accesses, for example by using a cache. However, we do not wish to clutter the application code with code that handles such optimizations. The *Proxy* pattern addresses this problem. In the Proxy pattern, a client does not directly address an original. Rather, the client addresses a proxy, a representative of that original. This proxy shields the non-application specific aspects, such as optimization through a cache. The Proxy pattern can be described as in Figure 12.31.[7]

Context A client needs services from another component. Though direct access is possible, this may not be the best approach.

Problem We do not want to hard-code access to a component into a client. Sometimes, such direct access is inefficient; in other cases it may be unsafe. This inefficiency or insecurity is to be handled by additional control mechanisms, which should be kept separate from both the client and the component to which it needs access.

Solution The client communicates with a representative rather than with the component itself. This representative, the *proxy*, also does any additional pre- and postprocessing that is needed.

Figure 12.31 The *Proxy* pattern

The Proxy pattern exists in many variants. The variant discussed above could be termed a *Cache Proxy*: emphasis is on sharing results from remote components. Other variants are the *Remote Proxy* (which shields network access, inter-process communication, and so on), the *Protection Proxy* (protection from unauthorized access) and the *Firewall Proxy* (protection of local clients from the outside world). Web servers typically use a Firewall Proxy pattern to protect users from the outside world.

Most users of the library system are incidental users for whom we want a friendly interface, including powerful undo facilities. On the other hand, experienced library employees want a user interface with keyboard shortcuts for most commands. Furthermore, we want to be able to log user requests for later analysis, for example to find out which authors are in demand. We want to separate these 'extras' from the actual application code. The *Command Processor* pattern addresses this issue. Example uses of the Command Processor pattern can, for instance, be found in user-interface toolkits. Its characteristics are given in Figure 12.32.[8]

Applications typically involve a mixture of details that pertain to different realms, such as the application domain, the representation of data to the user, the access to a remote server, and so on. If these details are mixed up in the software, the result will be difficult to comprehend and maintain.

Expert designers have learned to separate such aspects so as to increase the maintainability, flexibility, and adaptability (in short, the quality) of the systems they

---

[7] See (Buschmann *et al.*, 1996, pp. 263–75) for a more elaborate description.
[8] see (Buschmann *et al.*, 1996, pp. 277–90) for a more elaborate description.

Context User interfaces which must be flexible or provide functionality that goes beyond the direct handling of user functions. Examples are undo facilities or logging functions.

Problem We want a well-structured solution for mapping an interface to the internal functionality of a system. All 'extras' which have to do with the way user commands are input, additional commands such as undo or redo, and any non-application-specific processing of user commands, such as logging, should be kept separate from the interface to the internal functionality.

Solution A separate component, the *command processor*, takes care of all commands. The command processor component schedules the execution of commands, stores them for undo, logs them for analysis, and so on. The actual execution of the command is delegated to a supplier component within the application.

Figure 12.32 The *Command Processor* pattern

design. If needed, they introduce some intermediate abstract entity to bridge aspects of a solution they wish to keep separate. The Proxy and Command Processor patterns, as well as many other design patterns found in (Gamma *et al.*, 1995) and (Buschmann *et al.*, 1996), offer elegant and flexible solutions to precisely these divide-and-conquer type design situations.

Patterns describe common practices that have proven useful. Antipatterns describe recurring practices that have been proven to generate problems. Next to collections of patterns, people have developed collections of mistakes often made and described them as antipatterns. Knowledge of antipatterns is useful during design to prevent common pitfalls, and during evolution to improve an evolving design. In the latter case, one actually searches for antipatterns and applies a technique called *refactoring* to improve the design; see also Chapter 14. Descriptions of antipatterns usually include the refactoring remedy. Some well-known antipatterns are:

- The God Class. In this situation, there is one central class that is in control and holds most responsibilities. It is linked to a lot of other classes that execute relatively simple tasks. It is also known as The Blob. When such a design is refactored, responsibilities are more evenly distributed. Note though that we previously observed that centralized designs are often more easily comprehended by novices.

- Lava flow. At the code level, this amounts to dead code. Following the slogan 'If it ain't broken, don't touch it', obsolete code and obsolete design elements may be dragged along indefinitely.

- Poltergeists. These are classes that have limited responsibilities and usually live for a short time. Their role is often just to start up other processes.

- Golden Hammer. This occurs when an available solution is applied to a problem that it does not really fit ('if the only available tool is a hammer, every problem is a nail'). This antipattern is common practice when organizations feel they have to use database package X or interface toolkit Y, simply because they have a license or because their employees have deep knowledge of that technology. At the level of an individual designer, it shows up as the obsessive use of a small set of patterns.

- Stovepipe. This phenomenon occurs if multiple systems are developed independently and each one uses its own set of technologies for the user interface, database, platform, and so on. Integration and cooperation then becomes difficult. Such a situation is often encountered when organizations merge or different organizations link their information systems in a chain. At a more local level, it occurs if developers or design teams reinvent the wheel.

- Swiss Army Knife. This is an excessively complex class interface. It occurs when a designer wants to make a class as general and reusable as possible.

12.6 DESIGN DOCUMENTATION

A requirements specification is developed during requirements engineering. That document serves a number of purposes. It specifies the users' requirements and as such it often has legal meaning. It is also the starting point for the design and thus serves another class of user.

The same applies to the design documentation. The description of the design serves different users, who have different needs. A proper organization of the design documentation is therefore very important.

IEEE1016 (1987) discusses guidelines for the description of a design. This standard mainly addresses the kind of information needed and its organization. For the actual description of its constituent parts, any existing design notation can be used.

(Barnard *et al.*, 1986) distinguishes between seven user roles for the design documentation:

1. The **project manager** needs information to plan, control, and manage the project. He must be able to identify each system component and understand its purpose and function. He also needs information to make cost estimates and define work packages.

2. The **configuration manager** needs information to be able to assemble the various components into one system and to control changes.

3. The **designer** needs information about the function and use of each component and its interfaces to other components.

4. The **programmer** must know about algorithms to be used, data structures, and the kinds of interaction with other components.

5. The **unit tester** must have detailed information about components, such as algorithms used, required initialization, and data needed.

6. The **integration tester** must know about relations between components, and the function and use of the components involved.

7. The **maintenance programmer** must have an overview of the relations between components. He must know how the user requirements are realized by the various components. When changes are to be realized, he assumes the role of the designer.

In IEEE Standard 1016, the project documentation is described as an information model. The entities in this model are the components identified during the design stage. Each of these components has a number of relevant attributes, such as its name, function, and dependencies.

IEEE Standard 1016 distinguishes ten attributes. These attributes are minimally required in each project. The documentation about the design *process* is strongly related to the design documentation. The design process documentation includes information pertaining to, among others, the design status, alternatives that have been rejected, and revisions that have been made. It is part of configuration control, as discussed in Chapter 4. The attributes from IEEE Standard 1016 are:

- **Identification**: the unique name of the component, for reference purposes

- **Type**: the kind of component, such as subsystem, procedure, class, or file

- **Purpose**: the specific purpose of the component (this will refer to the requirements specification)

- **Function**: what the component accomplishes (for a number of components, this information occurs in the requirements specification)

- **Subordinates**: the components of which the present entity is composed (it identifies a static is-composed-of relation between entities)

- **Dependencies**: a description of the relationships with other components

  It concerns the uses relation, see Section 12.1.5, and includes more detailed information on the nature of the interaction (including common data structures, order of execution, parameter interfaces, and so on).

- **Interface**: a description of the interaction with other components

  This concerns both the method of interaction (how to invoke an entity, how communication is achieved through parameters) and rules for the actual interaction (encompassing things such as data formats, constraints on values and the meaning of values).

- **Resources**: the resources needed

  Resources are entities external to the design, such as memory, printers, or a statistical library. This includes a discussion of how to solve possible race or deadlock situations.

- **Processing**: a refinement of the function attribute that describes the algorithms used, initialization, and the handling of exceptions

- **Data**: a description of the representation, use, format, and meaning of internal data.

Different users have different needs as regards design documentation. A sound organization of this documentation is needed so that each user may quickly find the information he is looking for. We may construct a matrix in which it is indicated which attributes are needed for which user role. This matrix is depicted in Table 12.6.

Table 12.6 User roles and attributes (*Source*: H.J. Barnard *et al.*, A recommended practice for describing software designs: IEEE Standards Project 1016, *IEEE Transactions on Software Engineering*, 12(2), ©1986, IEEE.)

Attributes	User roles						
	1	2	3	4	5	6	7
Identification	×	×	×	×	×	×	×
Type	×	×				×	×
Purpose	×	×					×
Function	×		×			×	
Subordinates	×						
Dependencies		×				×	×
Interface			×	×	×	×	
Resources	×	×				×	×
Processing				×	×		
Data				×	×		

It is not necessarily advantageous to incorporate all attributes into one document: each user gets much more than the information needed to play his role. However, it is not necessarily advantageous to provide separate documentation for each user role: in that case, some items will occur three or four times, which is difficult to handle and complicates the maintenance of the documentation.

Table 12.7 Views on the design (*Source*: H.J. Barnard *et al.*, A recommended practice for describing software designs: IEEE Standards Project 1016, *IEEE Transactions on Software Engineering*, 12(2), © 1986, IEEE.)

Design view	Description	Attributes	User roles
Decomposition	Decomposition of the system into components	Identification, type, purpose, function, subcomponents	Project manager
Dependencies	Relations between components and between resources	Identification, type, purpose, dependencies, resources	Configuration manager, maintenance programmer, integration tester
Interface	How to use components	Identification, function, interfaces	Designer, integration tester
Detail	Internal details of components	Identification, computation, data	Component tester, programmer

In IEEE Standard 1016, the attributes are grouped into four clusters. The decomposition is made such that most users need information from only one cluster, while these clusters contain a minimum amount of superfluous information for that user. This decomposition is given in Table 12.7. It is interesting to note that each cluster has its own view on the design. Each such view gives a complete description, thereby concentrating on certain aspects of the design. This may be considered an application of the IEEE recommended practice for architectural descriptions (IEEE1471, 2000) long before that standard was developed.

- The **decomposition description** describes the decomposition of the system into components. Using this description we may follow the hierarchical decomposition and describe the various abstraction levels.

- The **dependencies description** gives the coupling between components. It also sums up the resources needed. We may then derive how parameters are passed and which common data is used. This information is helpful when planning changes to the system and when isolating errors or problems in resource usage.

- The **interface description** tells us how functions are to be used. This information constitutes a contract between different designers and between designers and programmers. Precise agreements about this are especially needed in multi-person projects.

- The **detail description** gives internal details of each component. Programmers need these details. This information is also useful when composing component tests.

12.7 VERIFICATION AND VALIDATION

Errors made at an early stage are difficult to repair and incur high costs if they are not discovered until a late stage of development. It is therefore necessary to pay extensive attention to testing and validation issues during the design stage.

The way in which the outcome of the design process can be subjected to testing strongly depends upon the way in which the design is recorded. If some formal specification technique is used (as in model-driven architecture), the resulting specification can be tested formally. It may also be possible to do static tests, such as checks for consistency. Formal specifications may sometimes be executed, which offers additional ways to test the system. Such prototypes are especially suited to testing the user interface. Users often have little idea of the possibilities to be expected and a specification-based prototype offers good opportunities for aligning users' requirements and designers' ideas.

Often, the design is stated in less formal ways, limiting the possibilities for testing to forms of reading and critiquing text, such as inspections and walkthroughs. However, such design reviews provide an extremely powerful means for assessing designs.

During the design process the system is decomposed into a number of components. We may develop test cases based on this process. These test cases may be used at a later stage, during functional testing. Conversely, the software architecture can be used to guide the testing process. A set of scenarios of typical or anticipated future usage can be used to test the quality of the software architecture.

A more comprehensive discussion of the various test techniques is given in Chapter 13.

12.8 SUMMARY

Just like designing a house, designing software is an activity which demands creativity and a fair dose of craftsmanship. The quality of the designer is of paramount importance in this process. Mediocre designers will not deliver excellent designs.

The essence of the design process is that the system is decomposed into parts that each have less complexity than the whole. Some form of abstraction is always used in this process. We have identified several guiding principles for the decomposition of a system into components. These principles result in the following desirable properties for the outcome of the design process, a set of components with mutual dependencies:

- Components should be internally cohesive, i.e. the constituents of a component should 'belong together' and 'be friends'. By identifying different levels of *cohesion*, a qualitative notion of component cohesion is obtained.

- The interfaces between components should be as 'thin' as possible. Again, various levels of component *coupling* have been identified, allowing for an assessment of mutual dependencies between components.

- Each component should hide one secret. *Information hiding* is a powerful design principle, whereby each component is characterized by a secret which it hides from its environment. Abstract data types are a prime example of the application of this principle.

- The structure of the system, depicted as a graph whose nodes and edges denote components and dependencies between components, respectively, should have a simple and regular shape. The most-constrained form of this graph is a tree. In a less-constrained form the graph is acyclic, in which case the set of components can be split into a number of distinct layers of abstraction.

Abstraction is central to all of these features. In a properly designed system, we should be able to concentrate on the relevant issues and ignore the irrelevant ones. This is an essential prerequisite for comprehending a system, for implementing parts of it successfully without having to consider design decisions made elsewhere, and for implementing changes locally, thus allowing for a smooth evolution of the system.

The above features are highly interrelated and reinforce one another. Information hiding results in components with high cohesion and low coupling. Cohesion and coupling are dual characteristics. A clear separation of concerns results in a neat design structure.

We have discussed several measures for quantifying properties of a design. The most extensive research in this area concerns complexity metrics. These complexity metrics concern both attributes of individual components (called intra-component attributes) and attributes of a set of components (called intercomponent attributes).

A word of caution is needed, though. Software complexity is a very illusive notion, which cannot be captured in a few simple numbers. Different complexity metrics measure along different dimensions of what is perceived as complexity. Also, large values for any such metric do not necessarily imply a bad design. There may be good reasons to incorporate certain complex matters into one component.

A judicious and knowledgeable use of multiple design metrics is a powerful tool in the hands of the craftsman. Thoughtless application, however, will not help. To paraphrase Gunning, the inventor of the fog index (a popular readability measure for natural language prose): design metrics can cause harm in misuse.

There exist a great many design methods. They consist of a number of guidelines, heuristics, and procedures on how to approach designing a system, and notations to express the result of that process. Design methods differ considerably in their prescriptiveness, formality of notation, scope of application, and extent of incorporation in a more general development paradigm. Several tentative efforts have been made to compare design methods along different dimensions.

We discussed four design methods in this chapter:

- functional decomposition,

- data flow design,

- data structure design, and

- object-oriented design.

The first three design methods have been around longest. Object-oriented analysis and design came later, and this is now the most widely used approach, partly caused also by the popularity of the notations of UML and its associated tools and full-scale development methods, such as RUP.

Proponents of object-oriented methods have claimed a number of advantages of the object-oriented approach over the more traditional, function-oriented, approaches to design:

- The object-oriented approach is more natural. It fits the way we view the world around us. The concepts that show up in the analysis model have a direct counterpart in the UoD being modeled, thus providing a direct link between the model and the world being modeled. This makes it easier for the client to comprehend the model and discuss it with the analyst.

- The object-oriented approach focuses on structuring the problem rather than any particular solution to it. This point is closely related to the previous one. In designs based on the functional paradigm, the components tend to correspond to parts of a solution to the problem. It may not be easy to relate these components to the original problem. The result of an object-oriented analysis and design is a hierarchy of objects with their associated attributes which still resembles the structure of the problem space.

- The object-oriented approach provides for a smoother transition from requirements analysis to design to code. In our discussion of the object-oriented approach, it is often difficult to strictly separate UoD modeling aspects from design aspects. The object hierarchy that results from this process can be directly mapped onto the class hierarchy of the implementation (provided the implementation language is also object-oriented). The attributes of objects become encapsulated by services provided by the objects in the implementation.

- The object-oriented approach leads to more flexible systems that are easier to adapt and change. Because the real-world objects have a direct counterpart in the implementation, it becomes easy to link change requests to the corresponding program components. Through the inheritance mechanism, changes can often be realized by adding another specialized object rather than through tinkering with the code. For example, if we wish to extend our system dealing with furniture by adding another type of chair, say armchair, we do so by defining a new object `ArmChair`, together with its own set of attributes, as another specialization of `Chair`.

- The object-oriented approach promotes reuse by focusing on the identification of real-world objects from the application domain. In contrast, more traditional approaches focus on identifying functions. In an evolving world, objects tend to be stable, while functions tend to change. For instance, in an office environment the functions performed are likely to change with time, but there will always be letters, folders, and so on. Thus, an object-oriented design is less susceptible to changes in the world being modeled.

- The inheritance mechanism adds to reusability. New objects can be created as specializations of existing objects, inheriting attributes from the existing objects. At the implementation level, this kind of reuse is accomplished through code sharing. The availability of extensive class libraries contributes to this type of code reuse.

- Objects in an object-oriented design encapsulate abstract data types. As such, an object-oriented design potentially has all the right properties (such as information hiding, abstraction, high cohesion, and low coupling).

The object-oriented approach, however, does not by definition result in a good design. It is a bit too naive to expect that the identification of domain-specific entities is all there is to good design. The following issues must be kept in mind:

- There are other objects besides the ones induced by domain concepts. Objects that have to do with system issues such as memory management or error recovery do not naturally evolve from the modeling of the UoD. Likewise, 'hypothetical' objects that capture implicit knowledge from the application domain may be difficult to identify.

- The separation of concerns that results from the encapsulation of both state and behavior into one component need not be the one that is most desirable. For example, for many an object it might be necessary to be able to present some image of that object to the user. In a straightforward application of the object-oriented method, this would result in each object defining its own ways for doing so. This, however, is against good practices of system design, where we generally try to isolate the user interface from the computational parts. A clearly identifiable user interface component adds to consistency and flexibility.

- With objects, we also have to consider the uses relation. An object uses another object if it requests a service from that other object. It does so by sending a message. The bottom-up construction of a collection of objects may result in a rather loosely-coupled set, in which objects freely send messages to other objects. With a nod at the term 'spaghetti code' (denoting overly complex control patterns in programs), this is known as the *ravioli* problem (or antipattern). If objects have a complicated usage pattern, it is difficult to view one object without having to consider many others as well.

A design pattern is a structure of communicating components that solves a general design problem within a particular context. A design pattern thus encompasses more than a single component. It involves some, usually 2–5, communicating components which *together* solve a problem. The problem that the pattern solves is a general, recurring one, which can be characterized by the context in which it arises. A design pattern differs from an architectural style in that it does not address the structure of a complete system, but only that of a few (interacting) components. Design patterns may thus be termed micro-architectures. Not surprisingly, the good things about design patterns are essentially the same as those listed for software architectures in Chapter 11.

Design patterns describe best practice. They represent the collective experience of some of the most experienced and successful software designers. Likewise, antipatterns describe widely shared bad practices. The description of both patterns and antipatterns, as found in textbooks, is the result of endless carving and smoothing. Some are the outcome of writers' workshops, a format commonly used to review literature, suggesting that we should review software literature with a profoundness like that used to review poetry (as a consequence, these writers' workshops are also known as workers' write shops).

The distinction between the notions of 'software architecture' and 'design pattern' is by no means sharp. Some authors for example use the term 'architectural pattern' to denote the architectural styles we discussed in Section 11.4. The notions of 'application framework' and 'idiom' are generally used to denote a software architecture and a design pattern, respectively, at a more concrete, implementation-specific level. But again, the distinction is not sharp.

Finally, the design itself must be documented. IEEE Standard 1016 may serve as a guideline for this documentation. It lists a number of attributes for each component of the design. These attributes may be clustered into four groups, each of which represents a certain view of the design. This resembles the way IEEE Standard 1471 advocates documenting a software architecture.

Unfortunately, the design documentation typically describes only the design *result* and not the process that led to that particular result. Yet, information about choices made, alternatives rejected, and deliberations on the design decisions is a valuable additional source of information when a design is to be implemented, assessed, or changed.

12.9 FURTHER READING

(Budgen, 2003) is a good textbook on software design. I found the 'software as a wicked problem' analogy in that text. (Bergland and Gordon, 1981) and (Freeman and Wasserman, 1983) are compilations of seminal articles on software design. For an interesting discussion on the 'Scandinavian' approach to system development, see (Floyd *et al.*, 1989) or (CACM, 1993a). Wieringa (1998) provides an extensive survey of both classical and object-oriented design methods and their notations.

The classic text on structured analysis and design is (Yourdon and Constantine, 1975). Other names associated with the development of SA/SD are DeMarco (1979) and Gane and Sarson (1979).

For a full exposition of JSP, the reader is referred to (Jackson, 1975) or (King, 1988). JSP is very similar to a method developed by J.-D. Warnier in France at about the same time (Warnier, 1974). The latter is known as Logical Construction of Programs (LCP) or the Warnier–Orr method, after Ken Orr who was instrumental in the translation of Warnier's work. For a full exposition of JSD, see (Jackson, 1983), (Cameron, 1989) or (Sutcliffe, 1988). The graphical notations used in this chapter are those of (Sutcliffe, 1988).

Booch's method for object-oriented analysis and design is discussed in (Booch, 1994). Fusion is described in (Coleman *et al.*, 1994). Updates to this 1994 version can be found in (Coleman, 1996). RUP is discussed in (Kruchten, 2003). A critical discussion of the differences and similarities between object-oriented analysis and object-oriented design is given in (Davis, 1995) and (Hødalsvik and Sindre, 1993).

Fenton and Pfleeger (1996) present a rigorous approach to the topic of software metrics. The authors explain the essentials of measurement theory and illustrate them using a number of proposed metrics (including those for complexity, quality assessment, and cost estimation).

Cohesion and coupling were introduced in (Yourdon and Constantine, 1975). Efforts to objectify these notions can be found in (Offutt *et al.*, 1993), (Patel *et al.*, 1992) and (Xia, 2000). Darcy (2005) describes empirical studies to validate the importance of weak coupling and strong cohesion.

Halstead's method, 'software science', is described in (Halstead, 1977) and (Fitzsimmons and Love, 1978). Positive evidence of its validity is reported in (Curtis *et al.*, 1979) and (Elshoff, 1976). A good overview of the criticism of this method (as well as McCabe's cyclomatic complexity and Henri and Kafura's information flow metric) is given in (Shepperd and Ince, 1993). McCabe's cyclomatic complexity is introduced in (McCabe, 1976). In most discussions of this metric, the wrong formula is used; see Exercise 24 or (Henderson Sellers,

1992). Discussions in favor of using a (cyclomatic) complexity *density* metric can be found in (Mata-Toledo and Gustafson, 1992) and (Hops and Sherif, 1995).

Definitions of the object-oriented metrics introduced in Section 12.1.6 can be found in (Chidamber and Kemerer, 1994). A critical assessment of these metrics is given in (Hitz and Montazeri, 1996) and (Churcher and Shepperd, 1995). To meet some of this criticism, we have adopted the definition of LCOM suggested in (Li and Henry, 1993). Experiments to validate the Chidamber–Kemerer metrics suite are reported in (Succi *et al.*, 2003), (Darcy and Kemerer, 2005) and (Gyimóthy *et al.*, 2005).

Design patterns have their origin in the work of Cunningham and Beck, who developed patterns for user interfaces in Smalltalk, such as 'no more than three panes per window' (Power and Weiss, 1987, p. 16). MVC was first used in the Smalltalk environment (Krasner and Pope, 1988). Since that time, the topic has drawn a lot of attention, especially in object-oriented circles. A major collection of design patterns was published by the 'Gang of Four' (Gamma *et al.*, 1995). Another good collection of design patterns can be found in (Buschmann *et al.*, 1996). The latter text has a somewhat less object-oriented perspective than (Gamma *et al.*, 1995). (Brown *et al.*, 1998) describe a collection of well-known antipatterns. Since 1994, there has been an annual conference on pattern languages of programming (PLOP). The format for describing patterns has not only been used for design patterns; there are also collections of analysis patterns, process patterns, test patterns, etc.

Exercises

1. What is the difference between procedural abstraction and data abstraction?

2. List and explain Yourdon and Constantine's seven levels of cohesion.

3. Explain the notions cohesion and coupling.

4. In what sense are the various notions of coupling technology-dependent?

5. What is the essence of information hiding?

6. Give an outline of Halstead's software science.

7. Determine the cyclomatic complexity of the following program:

```
no_6 = true; sum = 0;
for (i = 1; i < no_of_courses; i++) {
    if (grade[i] < 7) no_6 = false;
    sum = sum + grade[i];
};
average = sum / no_of_courses;
if ((average ≥ 8) && (no_6))
    System.out.println("with distinction");
```

8. Would the cyclomatic complexity be any different if the last if statement were written as follows:

```
if (average ≥ 8) {
    if (no_6)
        System.out.println("with distinction");
}
```

Does this concur with your own ideas of a control complexity measure, i.e. does it fulfill the representation condition?

9. Give the formula and a rationale for the information flow complexity metric.

10. Is cyclomatic complexity a good indicator of system complexity?

11. Draw the call graphs for a nontrivial program you have written and determine its tree impurity. Does the number obtained agree with our intuitive idea about the 'quality' of the decomposition?

12. Compute Henri and Kafura's information flow metric for the design of two systems you have been involved in. Do these numbers agree with our intuitive understanding?

13. Why is the depth of a class in the inheritance tree (DIT) a useful metric to consider when assessing the quality of an object-oriented system?

14. What does response for a class (RFC) measure?

15. How does the Law of Demeter relate to the maintainability of object-oriented systems?

16. Discuss the relative merits and drawbacks of deep and narrow versus wide and shallow inheritance trees.

17. What is functional decomposition?

18. Give a global sketch of the data flow design method.

19. Explain what a structure clash is in JSP.

20. What is the main difference between problem-oriented and product-oriented design methods?

21. Discuss the general flavor of RUP's analysis and design workflow.

22. What are the differences between object-oriented design and the simple application of the information-hiding principle?

23. What are the properties of a design pattern?

24. ♡ Make it plausible that the formula for the cyclomatic complexity should read $CV = e - n + p + 1$ rather than $CV = e - n + 2p$.

    Hint: consider the following program:

    ```
    begin
        if A then B else C endif;
        call P;
        print("done")
    end;

    procedure P;
        begin
            if X then Y else Z endif
        end P;
    ```

    Draw the flow graph for this program as well as for the program obtained by substituting the body of procedure P inline. Determine the cyclomatic complexity of both variants, using both formulae. See also (Henderson Sellers, 1992).

25. ♠ Write the design documentation for a project you have been involved in, following IEEE Standard 1016.

26. ♠ Discuss the pros and cons of:

- functional decomposition,
- data flow design,
- design based on data structures, and
- object-oriented design

for the design of each of:

- a compiler,
- a patient-monitoring system, and
- a stock-control system.

27. ♠ Discuss the possible merits of the design techniques in Exercise 26 with respect to reusability.

28. ♠ Augment IEEE Standard 1016 such that it also describes the design rationale. Which user roles are in need of this type of information?

29. ♡ According to (Fenton and Pfleeger, 1996), any tree impurity metric m should have the following properties:

a) $m(G) = 0$ if and only if G is a tree;

b) $m(G_1) > m(G_2)$ if G_1 differs from G_2 only by the insertion of an extra arc;

c) For $i = 1, 2$ let A_i denote the number of arcs in G_i and N_i the number of nodes in G_i. Then if $N_1 > N_2$ and $A_1 - N_1 + 1 = A_2 - N_2 + 1$, then $m(G_1) < m(G_2)$.

d) For all graphs G, $m(G) \leq m(K_N) = 1$ where N = number of nodes of G and K_N is the (undirected) complete graph of N nodes.

Give an intuitive rationale for these properties. Show that the tree impurity metric discussed in Section 12.1.5 has these properties.

30. ♡ Extend the object model of Figure 12.26 such that it also models user queries to the catalog.

31. ♡ Extend the model from Exercise 30 such that it also includes the attributes and services of objects.

32. ♠ Write an essay on the differences and similarities of analysis and design activities in object-oriented analysis and design.

33. ♡ Why would object-oriented design be more 'natural' than, say, data flow design?

34. ♠ Discuss the assertion 'The view that object-oriented methods make change easy is far too simplistic'. Consult (Lubars *et al.*, 1992), who found that changes to object models were fairly localized whereas changes to behavior models had more far-reaching consequences.

35. ♡ The Document–View pattern relaxes the separation of view and controller in MVC. Describe the Document–View pattern in terms of the context in which it arises, the problem addressed, and its solution. Compare your solution with the Observer pattern in (Gamma *et al.*, 1995, p. 293).

36. ♡ How do design patterns impact the quality of a design?

13

Software Testing

LEARNING OBJECTIVES

- To be aware of the major software testing techniques

- To see how different test objectives lead to the selection of different testing techniques

- To appreciate a classification of testing techniques, based on the objectives they try to reach

- To be able to compare testing techniques with respect to their theoretical power as well as their practical value

- To understand the role and contents of testing activities in different life cycle phases

- To be aware of the contents and structure of the test documentation

- To be able to distinguish different test stages

- To be aware of some mathematical models to estimate the reliability of software

> Testing should not be confined to merely executing a system to see whether a given input yields the correct output. During earlier phases, intermediate products can, and should, be tested as well. Good testing is difficult. It requires careful planning and documentation. There exist a large number of test techniques. We discuss the major classes of test techniques with their characteristics.

Suppose you are asked to answer the kind of questions posed in (Baber, 1982):

- Would you trust a completely automated nuclear power plant?

- Would you trust a completely automated pilot whose software was written by yourself? What if it was written by one of your colleagues?

- Would you dare to write an expert system to diagnose cancer? What if you are personally held liable in a case where a patient dies because of a malfunction of the software?

You will (probably) have difficulties answering all these questions in the affirmative. Why? The hardware of an airplane probably is as complex as the software for an automatic pilot. Yet, most of us board an airplane without any second thoughts.

As our society's dependence on automation increases, the quality of the systems we deliver increasingly determines the quality of our existence. We cannot hide from this responsibility. The role of automation in critical applications and the threats these applications pose should make us ponder. *ACM Software Engineering Notes* runs a column 'Risks to the public in computer systems' in which we are told of numerous (near-)accidents caused by software failures. The discussion on software reliability provoked by the Strategic Defense Initiative is a case in point (Parnas, 1985; Myers, 1986; Parnas, 1987). Discussions, such as those about the Therac-25 accidents or the maiden flight of the Ariane 5 (see Section 1.4), should be compulsory reading for every software engineer.

Software engineering is engineering. Engineers aim for the perfect solution, but know this goal is generally unattainable. During software construction, errors are made. To locate and fix those errors through excessive testing is a laborious affair and mostly not all the errors are found. Good testing is at least as difficult as good design.

With the current state of the art we are not able to deliver fault-free software. Different studies indicate that 30–85 errors per 1000 lines of source code are made. These figures seem not to improve over time. During testing, quite a few of those errors are found and subsequently fixed. Yet, some errors do remain undetected. Myers (1986) gives examples of extensively tested software that still contains 0.5–3 errors per 1000 lines of code. A fault in the seat-reservation system of a major airline company incurred a loss of $50 million in one quarter. The computerized system reported that cheap seats were sold out when this was, in fact, not the case. As a consequence, clients were referred to other companies. The problems were not discovered until quarterly results were found to lag considerably behind those of their competitors.

Testing is often taken to mean executing a program to see whether it produces the correct output for a given input. This involves testing the end-product, the software itself. As a consequence, the testing activity often does not get the attention it deserves. By the time the software has been written, we are often pressed for time, which does not encourage thorough testing.

Postponing test activities for too long is one of the most severe mistakes often made in software development projects. This postponement makes testing a rather costly affair. Figure 13.1 shows the results of a 1980 study by Boehm about the cost of error correction relative to the phase in which the error is discovered. This picture shows that errors which are not discovered until after the software has become

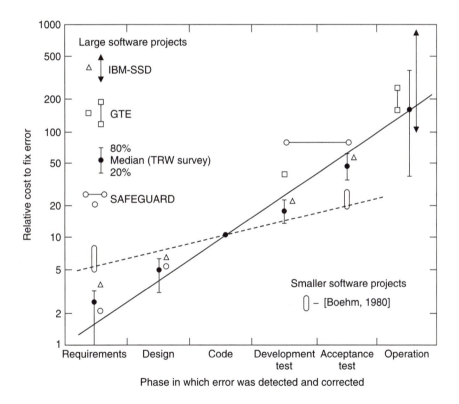

Figure 13.1 Relative cost of error correction (*Source*: Barry B. Boehm, *Software Engineering Economics*, Figure 4.2, p. 40, ©1981, Reprinted by permission of Prentice Hall, Inc. Englewood Cliffs, NJ.)

operational incur costs that are 10 to 90 times higher than those of errors that are discovered during the design phase. This ratio still holds for big and critical systems (Boehm and Basili, 2001). For small, noncritical systems, the ratio may be more like 1 to 5.

The development methods and techniques that are applied in the phases prior to implementation are least developed, relatively. It is therefore not surprising that most of the errors are made in those early phases. An early study by Boehm showed that over 60% of the errors were introduced during the design phase, as opposed to 40% during implementation (Boehm, 1975). Worse still, two-thirds of the errors introduced at the design phase were not discovered until after the software had become operational.

It is therefore incumbent on us to carefully plan our testing activities as early as possible. We should also start the actual testing activities at an early stage. An extreme form of this is test-driven development, one of the practices of XP, in which development *starts* with writing tests. If we do not start testing until after the implementation stage, we are really far too late. The requirements specification, design, and design specification may also be tested. The rigor with which this can be done depends on the form in which these documents are expressed. This has already been hinted at in previous chapters. In Section 13.2, we will again highlight the various verification and validation activities that may be applied at the different phases of the software life cycle. The planning and documentation of these activities is discussed in Section 13.3.

Before we decide upon a certain approach to testing, we have to determine our test objectives. If the objective is to find as many errors as possible, we will opt for a strategy which is aimed at revealing errors. If the objective is to increase our confidence in the proper functioning of the software, we may well opt for a completely different strategy. So the objective will have an impact on the test approach chosen, since the results have to be interpreted with respect to the objectives set forth. Different test objectives and the degree to which test approaches fit these objectives are the topic of Section 13.1.

Testing software shows only the presence of errors, not their absence. As such, it yields a rather negative result: up to now, only n ($n \geq 0$) errors have been found. Only when the software is tested exhaustively are we certain about its functioning correctly. In practice this seldom happens. A simple program such as:

```
for (i = 1; i < 100; i++) {
    if (a[i]) System.out.println("1");
    else System.out.println("0");
};
```

has 2^{100} different outcomes. Even on a very fast machine – say a machine which executes 10 million print instructions per second – exhaustively testing this program would take 3×10^{14} years.

An alternative to this brute force approach to testing is to prove the correctness of the software. Proving the correctness of software very soon becomes a tiresome activity, however. It furthermore applies only in circumstances where software requirements are stated formally. Whether these formal requirements are themselves correct has to be decided upon in a different way.

We are thus forced to make a choice. It is of paramount importance to choose a sufficiently small, yet adequate, set of test cases. Test techniques may be classified according to the criterion used to measure the adequacy of a set of test cases:

- **Coverage-based testing** Testing requirements are specified in terms of the coverage of the product (program, requirements document, etc.) to be tested. For example, we may specify that all statements of the program should be executed at least once if we run the complete test set, or that all elementary requirements from the requirements specification should be exercised at least once.

- **Fault-based testing** Testing requirements focus on detecting faults. The fault-detecting ability of the test set then determines its adequacy. For example, we may artificially seed a number of faults in a program, and then require that a test set reveal at least, say, 95% of these artificial faults.

- **Error-based testing** Testing requirements focus on error-prone points, based on knowledge of the typical errors that people make. For example, off-by-1 errors are often made at boundary values such as 0 or the maximum number of elements in a list, and we may specifically aim our testing effort at these boundary points.

Alternatively, we may classify test techniques based on the source of information used to derive test cases:

- **Black-box testing**, also called **functional** or **specification-based testing**: test cases are derived from the specification of the software, i.e. we do not consider implementation details.

- **White-box testing**, also called **structural** or **program-based testing**: a complementary approach, in which we *do* consider the internal logical structure of the software in the derivation of test cases.

We will use the first classification and discuss different techniques for coverage-based, fault-based, and error-based testing in Sections 13.5 to 13.7. These techniques involve the actual execution of a program. Manual techniques which do not involve program execution, such as code reading and inspections, are discussed in Section 13.4. In Section 13.8 we assess some empirical and theoretical studies that aim to put these different test techniques in perspective.

The above techniques are applied mainly at the component level. This level of testing is often done concurrently with the implementation phase. It is also called **unit testing**. Besides the component level, we also have to test the integration of a set of components into a system. Possibly also, the final system will be tested once more under direct supervision of the prospective user. In Section 13.9, we will sketch these different test phases.

At the system level, the goal pursued often shifts from detecting faults to building trust, by quantitatively assessing reliability. Software reliability is discussed in Section 13.10.

13.1 TEST OBJECTIVES

Until now, we have not been very precise in our use of the notion of an 'error'. In order to appreciate the following discussion, it is important to make a careful distinction between the notions *error*, *fault*, and *failure*. An error is a human action that produces an incorrect result. The consequence of an error is software containing a fault. A fault thus is the manifestation of an error. If encountered, a fault may result in a failure.[1]

So, what we observe during testing are failures. These failures are caused by faults, which are in turn the result of human errors. A failure may be caused by more than one fault and a fault may cause different failures. Similarly, the relation between errors and faults need not be 1–1.

One possible aim of testing is to find faults in the software. Tests are then intended to expose failures. It is not easy to give a precise, unique, definition of the notion of failure. A programmer may take the system's specification as reference point. In this view, a failure occurs if the software does not meet the specifications. The user, however, may consider the software erroneous if it does not match expectations. 'Failure' thus is a relative notion. If software fails, it does so with respect to something else (a specification, user manual, etc). While testing software, we must always be aware of what the software is being tested against.

In this respect, a distinction is often made between 'verification' and 'validation'. The *IEEE Glossary* defines verification as the process of evaluating a system or component to determine whether the products of a given development phase satisfy the conditions imposed at the start of that phase. Verification thus tries to answer the question: Have we built the system right?

The term 'validation' is defined in the *IEEE Glossary* as the process of evaluating a system or component during or at the end of the development process to determine whether it satisfies specified requirements. Validation then boils down to the question: Have we built the right system?

Even with this subtle distinction in mind, the situation is not all that clear-cut. Generally, a program is considered correct if it consistently produces the right output.

---

[1] The *IEEE Standard Glossary of Software Engineering Terminology* (IEEE610, 1990) gives four definitions of the word 'error'. To distinguish between these definitions, the words 'error', 'fault', 'failure' and 'mistake' are used. The word 'error' in the *Glossary* is used to denote a measurement error, while 'mistake' is used to denote a human error. Though 'mistake' has the advantage of being less condemning, we follow the accepted software engineering literature in this respect. Our definitions of 'fault' and 'failure' are the same as those in the *Glossary*.

We may, though, easily conceive of situations where the programmer's intention is not properly reflected in the program but the errors simply do not manifest themselves. An early empirical study showed that many faults are never activated during the lifetime of a system (Adams, 1984). Is it worth fixing those faults? For example, some entry in a case statement may be wrong, but this fault never shows up because it happens to be subsumed by a previous entry. Is this program correct, or should it rather be classified as a program with a 'latent' fault? Even if it is considered correct within the context at hand, chances are that we get into trouble if the program is changed or parts of it are reused in a different environment.

As an example, consider the maiden flight of the Ariane 5. Within 40 seconds after take-off, at an altitude of 3 700 meters, the launcher exploded. This was ultimately caused by an overflow in a conversion of a variable from a 64-bit, floating-point number to a 16-bit, signed integer. The piece of software containing this error was reused from the Ariane 4 and had *never* caused a problem in any of the Ariane 4 flights. This is explained by the fact that the Ariane 5 builds up speed much faster than the Ariane 4, which in turn resulted in excessive values for the parameter in question; see also Section 1.4.1.

With the above definitions of error and fault, such programs must be considered faulty, even if we cannot devise test cases that reveal the faults. This still leaves open the question of how to define errors. Since we cannot but guess what the programmer's real intentions were, this can only be decided upon by an oracle.

Given the fact that exhaustive testing is not feasible, the test process can be thought of as depicted in Figure 13.2. The box labeled P denotes the object (program, design document, etc.) to be tested. The test strategy involves the selection of a subset of the input domain. For each element of this subset, P is used to 'compute' the corresponding output. The expected output is determined by an 'oracle', something outside the test activity. Finally, the two answers are compared.

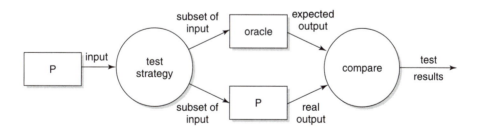

Figure 13.2 Global view of the test process

The most crucial step in this process is the selection of the subset of the input domain which will serve as the test set. This test set must be adequate with respect to some chosen test criterion. In Section 13.1.1, we elaborate upon the notion of test adequacy.

Test techniques generally use some systematic means of deriving test cases. These test cases are meant to provoke failures. Thus, the main objective is fault detection. Alternatively, our test objective could be to increase our confidence in failure-free behavior. These quite different test objectives, and their impact on the test selection problem, are the topic of Section 13.1.2.

To test whether the objectives are reached, test cases are tried in order that faults manifest themselves. A quite different approach is to view testing as fault prevention. This leads us to another dimension of test objectives, which to a large extent parallels the evolution of testing strategies over the years. This evolution is discussed in Section 13.1.3.

Finally, the picture so far considers each fault equally hazardous. In reality, there are different types of fault, and some faults are more harmful than others. All techniques to be discussed in this chapter can easily be generalized to cover multiple classes of faults, each with its own acceptance criteria.

Some faults are critical and we will have to exert ourselves in order to find those critical faults. Special techniques, such as fault-tree analysis, have been developed to this end. Using fault-tree analysis, we try to derive a contradiction by reasoning backwards from a given, undesirable, end situation. If such a contradiction can be derived, we have shown that that particular situation can never be reached.

13.1.1 Test Adequacy Criteria

Consider the program text in Figure 13.3 and a test set S containing just one test case:

```
n = 2, A[0] = 10, A[1] = 5
```

If we execute the program using S, then all statements are executed at least once. If our criterion to judge the adequacy of a test set is that 100% of the statements are executed, then S is adequate. If our criterion is that 100% of the branches are executed, then S is not adequate, since the (empty) else branch of the if statement is not executed by S.

```
public static void selection_sort (int a, int n) {
    int i, j, small, temp;
    for (i = 0; i < n-2; i++) {
        small = i;
        for (j = i+1; j < n-1; j++)
            if (Math.abs(a[j]) < Math.abs(a[small])) small = j;
        temp = a[i]; a[i] = a[small]; a[small] = temp;
    }
}
```

Figure 13.3 Erroneous selection sort procedure

A **test adequacy criterion** thus specifies requirements for testing. It can be used in different ways: as stopping rule, as measurement, or as test case generator. If a test adequacy criterion is used as a stopping rule, it tells us when sufficient testing has been done. If statement coverage is the criterion, we may stop testing if all statements have been executed by the tests done so far. In this view, a test set is either good or bad; the criterion is either met, or it isn't. If we relax this requirement a bit and use, say, the percentage of statements executed as a test quality criterion, then the test adequacy criterion is used as a measurement. Formally, it is a mapping from the test set to the interval [0, 1]. Note that the stopping-rule view is in fact a special case of the measurement view. Finally, the test adequacy criterion can be used in the test selection process. If 100% statement coverage has not been achieved yet, an additional test case is selected that covers one or more untested statements. This generative view is used in many test tools.

Test adequacy criteria are closely linked to test techniques. For example, coverage-based test techniques keep track of which statements, branches, and so on, are executed, and this gives us an easy handle to determine whether a coverage-based adequacy criterion has been met or not. The same test technique, however, does not help us in assessing whether all error-prone points in a program have been tested. In a sense, a given test adequacy criterion and the corresponding test technique are opposite sides of the same coin.

13.1.2 Fault Detection Versus Confidence Building

> Failures are needles in the haystack of the input domain.
> Hamlet and Taylor (1990)

Suppose we wish to test some component P which sorts an array A[0 .. n-1] of integers, $1 \leq n \leq 1\,000$. Since exhaustive testing is not feasible, we are looking for a strategy in which only a small number of tests are exercised. One possible set of test cases is the following:

Let n assume values 0, 1, 17 and 1 000. For each of n = 17 and n = 1 000, choose three values for the array A:

- A consists of randomly selected integers;
- A is sorted in ascending order;
- A is sorted in descending order.

In following this type of constructive approach, the input domain is partitioned into a finite, small number of subdomains. The underlying assumption is that these subdomains are **equivalence classes**, i.e. from a testing point of view each member from a given subdomain is as good as any other. For example, we have tacitly assumed that one random array of length 17 is as good a test as any other random array of length i with $1 < i < 1000$.

Suppose the actual sorting algorithm used is the one from Figure 13.3. If the tests use positive integers only, the output will be correct. The output will not be correct if a test input happens to contain negative integers.

The test set using positive integers only does not reveal the fault because the inputs in the subdomains are not really interchangeable (instead of comparing the values of array entries, the algorithm compares their absolute values). Any form of testing which partitions the input domain works perfectly if the right subdomains are chosen. In practice however, we generally do not know where the needles are hidden, and the partition of the input domain is likely to be imperfect.

Both functional and structural testing schemes use a systematic means to determine subdomains. They often use peculiar inputs to test peculiar cases. Their intention is to provoke failure behavior. Their success hinges on the assumption that we can indeed identify subdomains with a high failure probability. Though this is a good strategy for fault detection, it does not necessarily inspire confidence.

The user of a system is interested in the probability of failure-free behavior. Following this line of thought, we are not so much interested in the faults themselves, but rather in their manifestations. A fault which frequently manifests itself will, in general, cause more damage than a fault which seldom shows up. This is precisely what we hinted at above when we discussed fault detection and confidence building as possible test objectives.

If failures are more important than faults, the goal pursued during the test phase may also change. In that case, we will not pursue the discovery of as many faults as possible but will strive for high reliability. Random testing does not work all that well if we want to find as many faults as possible – hence the development of different test techniques. When pursuing high reliability, however, it is possible to use random input.

In order to obtain confidence in the daily operation of a software system, we have to mimic that situation. This requires the execution of a large number of test cases that represent typical usage scenarios. Random testing does at least as good a job in this respect as any form of testing based on partitioning the input domain.

This approach has been applied in the Cleanroom development method. In this method, the development of individual components is done by programmers who are not allowed to actually execute their code. The programmer must then convince himself of the correctness of his components using manual techniques such as stepwise abstraction (see also Section 13.4).

In the next step, these components are integrated and tested by someone else. The input for this process is generated according to a distribution which follows the expected operational use of the system. During this integration phase, one tries to reach a certain required reliability level. Experiences with this approach are positive.

The quantitative assessment of failure probability brings us into the area of software reliability. Section 13.10 is devoted to this topic.

13.1.3 From Fault Detection to Fault Prevention

In the early days of computing, programs were written and then debugged to make sure that they ran properly. Testing and debugging were largely synonymous terms. Both referred to an activity near the end of the development process when the software had been written, but still needed to be 'checked out'.

Today's situation is rather different. Testing activities occur in every phase of the development process. They are carefully planned and documented. The execution of software to compare actual behavior with expected behavior is only one aspect out of many.

Gelperin and Hetzel (1988) identify four major testing models. These roughly parallel the historical development of test practices. The models and their primary goals are given in Table 13.1.

Table 13.1 Major testing models (*Source*: D. Gelperin and B. Hetzel, The growth of software testing, *Communications of the ACM* 31(6), pp. 687–95, ©1988. Reproduced by permission of the Association for Computing Machinery, Inc.)

Model	Primary goal
Phase models	
Demonstration	Make sure that the software satisfies its specification
Destruction	Detect implementation faults
Life cycle models	
Evaluation	Detect requirements, design, and implementation faults
Prevention	Prevent requirements, design, and implementation faults

The primary goal of the demonstration model is to make sure that the program runs and solves the problem. The strategy is like that of a constructive mathematical proof. If the software passes all tests from the test set, it is claimed to satisfy the requirements. The strategy gives no guidelines as to how to obtain such a test set. A poorly chosen test set may mask poor software quality. Most programmers will be familiar with the process of testing their own programs by carefully reading them or executing them with selected input data. If this is done very carefully, it can be beneficial. This method also holds some dangers, however. We may be inclined to consider this form of testing as a method to convince ourselves or someone else that the software does *not* contain errors. We will then, partly unconsciously, look for test cases which support this hypothesis. This type of demonstration-oriented approach to testing is not to be advocated.

Proper testing is a very destructive process. A program should be tested with the purpose of finding as many faults as possible. A test can only be considered successful if it leads to the discovery of at least one fault. (In a similar way, a visit to your physician is only successful if he finds a 'fault' and we generally consider such a visit unsatisfactory if we are sent home with the message that nothing wrong could be found.) In order to improve the chances of producing a high quality system, we should reverse the strategy and start looking for test cases that *do* reveal faults. This may be termed a proof by contradiction. The test set is then judged by its ability to detect faults.

Since we do not know whether any residual faults are left, it is difficult to decide when to stop testing in either of these models. In the demonstration-oriented model, the criteria most often used to determine this point in time seem to be the following:

- stop if the test budget has run out;

- stop if all test cases have been executed without any failures occurring.

The first criterion is pointless, since it does not tell us anything about the quality of the test effort. If there is no money at all, this criterion is most easily satisfied. The second criterion is pointless as well, since it does not tell us anything about the quality of the test cases.

The destruction-oriented model usually entails some systematic way of deriving test cases. We may then base our stop criterion on the test adequacy criterion that corresponds to the test technique used. An example of this might be: 'We stop testing if 100% of the branches are covered by the set of test cases and all test cases yield an unsuccessful result'.

Both these models view testing as one phase in the software development process. As noted before, this is not a very good strategy. The life-cycle-testing models extend testing activities to earlier phases. In the evaluation-oriented model, the emphasis is on analysis and review techniques to detect faults in requirements and design documents. In the prevention model, emphasis is on the careful planning and design of test activities. For example, the early design of test cases may reveal that certain requirements cannot be tested and thus such an activity helps to prevent errors from being made in the first place. Test-driven development falls into this category as well.

We may observe a gradual shift of emphasis in test practice, from a demonstration-like approach to prevention-oriented methods. Though many organizations still concentrate their test effort late in the development life cycle, various organizations have shown that upstream testing activities can be most effective. Quantitative evidence of this is provided in Section 13.8.3.

Testing need not only result in software with fewer errors. Testing also results in valuable knowledge (error-prone constructs and so on) which can be fed back into the development process. In this view, testing is a learning process, which can be given its proper place in an improvement process.

13.2 TESTING AND THE SOFTWARE LIFE CYCLE

In the following subsections we discuss the various verification and validation activities which can be performed during the requirements engineering, design, implementation, and maintenance phases. In doing so, we also indicate the techniques and tools that may be applied. These techniques and tools are further discussed in subsequent sections. A summary is given in Table 13.2.

Table 13.2 Activities in the various phases of the software life cycle (*Adapted from*: W.R. Adrion, M.A. Branstad, and J.C. Cherniavski, Validation, verification, and testing of computer software, *ACM Computing Surveys* 14(2), ©1982. Reproduced by permission of the Association for Computing Machinery, Inc.)

Phase	Activities
Requirements engineering	— determine test strategy
	— test requirements specification
	— generate functional test data
Design	— check consistency between design and requirements specification
	— evaluate the software architecture
	— test the design
	— generate structural and functional test data
Implementation	— check consistency between design and implementation
	— test implementation
	— generate structural and functional test data
	— execute tests
Maintenance	— repeat the above tests in accordance with the degree of redevelopment

Software developers aim for clean code that works. We try to accomplish that by first focusing on the 'clean code' part, and next on the 'that works' part. The clean code part is about proper analysis and design, writing elegant and robust code, and so on. Only after we're done with that, do we start testing to make sure the software works properly. Test-driven development (TDD) takes the opposite approach: we first make sure the software works and then tackle the clean code part. We discuss test-driven development in Section 13.2.5.

13.2.1 Requirements Engineering

The verification and validation techniques applied during this phase are strongly dependent upon the way in which the requirements specification has been laid down. Something which should be done at the very least is to conduct a careful review or inspection in order to check whether all aspects of the system have been properly described. As we saw earlier, errors made at this stage are very costly to repair if they go unnoticed until late in the development process. (Boehm, 1984b) gives four essential criteria for a requirements specification:

- completeness;

- consistency;

- feasibility;

- testability.

Testing a requirements specification should primarily be aimed at testing these criteria.

The aim of testing the completeness criterion is to determine whether all components are present and described completely. A requirements specification is incomplete if it contains such phrases as 'to be determined' or if it contains references to undefined elements. We should also watch for the omission of functions or products, such as back-up or restart procedures and test tools to be delivered to the customer.

A requirements specification is consistent if its components do not contradict each other and the specification does not conflict with external specifications. We thus need both internal and external consistency. Moreover, each element in the requirements specification must be traceable. It must, for instance, be possible to decide whether a natural language interface is really needed.

According to Boehm, feasibility has to do with more than functional and performance requirements. The benefits of a computerized system should outweigh the associated costs. This must be established at an early stage and necessitates timely attention to user requirements, maintainability, reliability, and so on. In some cases, the project's success is very sensitive to certain key factors, such as safety, speed, availability of certain types of personnel; these risks must be analyzed at an early stage.

Lastly, a requirements specification must be testable. In the end, we must be able to decide whether or not a system fulfills its requirements. So requirements must be specific, unambiguous, and quantitative. The quality-attribute scenario framework from (Bass *et al.*, 2003) is an example of how to specify such requirements; see also Section 6.3.

Many of these points are raised by (Poston, 1987). According to Poston, the most likely errors in a requirements specification can be grouped into the following categories:

- missing information (about functions, interfaces, performance, constraints, reliability, and so on);

- wrong information (not traceable, not testable, ambiguous, and so forth);

- extra information (bells and whistles).

Using a standard format for documenting the requirements specification, such as IEEE Standard 830 (discussed in Chapter 9), may help enormously in preventing these types of errors occurring in the first place.

Useful techniques for testing the degree to which criteria have been met are mostly manual (reading documents, inspections, reviews). Scenarios for the expected use of the system can be devised with the prospective users of the system. If requirements are already expressed in use cases, such scenarios are readily available. In this way, a set of functional tests is generated.

At this stage also, a general test strategy for subsequent phases must be formulated. It should encompass the choice of particular test techniques; evaluation criteria; a test plan; a test scheme; and test documentation requirements. A test team may also be formed at this stage. These planning activities are dealt with in Section 13.3.

13.2.2 Design

The criteria mentioned previously (completeness, consistency, feasibility, and testability) are also essential for the design. The most likely errors in design resemble the kind of errors one is inclined to make in a requirements specification: missing, wrong, and extraneous information. For the design too, a precise documentation standard is of great help in preventing these types of errors. IEEE Standards 1471 and 1016, discussed in Chapters 11 and 12, respectively, are examples of such standards.

During the architectural design phase, a high-level conceptual model of the system is developed in terms of components and their interaction. This architecture can be assessed, for example by generating scenarios which express quality concerns, such as maintainability and flexibility, in very concrete terms and evaluating how the architecture handles these scenarios; see also Section 11.5.

During the design phase, we decompose the total system into subsystems and components, starting from the requirements specification. We may then develop tests based on this decomposition process. Design is not a one-shot process. During the design process a number of successive refinements will be made, resulting in layers showing increasing detail. Following this design process, more detailed tests can be developed as the lower layers of the design are decided upon.

We may also test the design itself. This includes tracing elements from the requirements specification to the corresponding elements in the design description, and vice versa. Well-known techniques for doing so are, amongst others, simulation, design walkthroughs, and design inspections.

In the requirements engineering phase, the possibilities for formally documenting the resulting specification are limited. Most requirements specifications make excessive use of natural language descriptions. For the design phase, there are ample opportunities to formally document the resulting specification. The more formally the design is specified, the more possibilities we have for applying verification techniques, as well as formal checks for consistency and completeness.

13.2.3 Implementation

During the implementation phase, we do the 'real' testing. One of the most effective techniques to find errors in a program text is to carefully read that text, or have it read. This technique has been successfully applied for a long time. Somewhat formalized variants are known as 'code inspection' and 'code walkthrough'. We may also apply the technique of stepwise abstraction: the function of the code is determined in a number of abstraction steps, starting from the code itself. We may try to prove the correctness of the code using formal verification techniques. The various manual test techniques are discussed in Section 13.4.

There are many tools to support the testing of code. We may distinguish between tools for static analysis and tools for dynamic analysis. Static analysis tools inspect the program code without executing it. They include tests such as: are all variables declared and given a value before they are used? Dynamic analysis tools are used in conjunction with the actual execution of the code, for example tools that keep track of which portions of the code have been covered by the tests so far.

All of the above techniques are aimed at evaluating the quality of the source code as well as its compliance with design specifications and code documentation.

It is crucial to control the test information properly while testing the code. Tools may help us to do so, for example, test drivers generate the test environment for a component to be tested, test stubs simulate the function of a component not yet available, and test data generators provide us with data. In bottom-up testing, we will, in general, make much use of test drivers, while top-down testing implies the use of test stubs. The test strategy (top-down versus bottom-up) may be partly influenced by the design technique used. If the high level, architectural design is implemented as a skeletal system whose holes yet have to be filled in, that skeletal system can be used as a test driver.

Tools (test harnesses and test systems) may also be profitable while executing the tests. A simple and yet effective tool is one which compares test results with expected results. The eye is a very unreliable medium. After a short time, all results look OK. An additional advantage of this type of tool support is that it helps to achieve a standard test format. This, in turn, helps with regression testing.

13.2.4 Maintenance

On average, more than 50% of total life-cycle costs is spent on maintenance. If we modify the software after a system has become operational (because an error is found late on, or because the system must be adapted to changed requirements), we will have to test the system anew. This is called regression testing. To have this proceed smoothly, the quality of the documentation and the possibilities for tool support, are crucial factors.

In a *retest-all* approach, all tests are rerun. Since this may consume a lot of time and effort, we may also opt for a *selective retest*, in which only some of the tests are rerun. A regression test selection technique is then used to decide which subset should be rerun. We would like this technique to include all tests in which the modified and the original program produce different results, while omitting tests that produce the same results.

13.2.5 Test-Driven Development (TDD)

Suppose our library system needs to be able to prevent borrowing of items by members that are on a black list. We could start by redesigning part of the system and implementing the necessary changes: a new table, BlackList, and appropriate checks in method Borrow. We also have to decide when members are put on the black list, and how to get them off that list. After having done all the necessary analysis and design, and implemented the changes accordingly, we devise test cases to test for the new functionality.

This order of events is completely reversed in **test-driven development** (TDD). In test-driven development, we first write a few tests for the new functionality. We may start very simple, and add a test in the start-up method to ensure that the black list is initially empty:

```
assertEquals(0, BlackList)
```

Of course, this test will fail. To make it succeed, we have to introduce BlackList, and set it equal to 0. At the same time, we make a list of things still to be done, such as devising a proper type for BlackList, including operations to add and remove members to that list, an update of Borrow to check whether a person borrowing an item is on the black list, and so on. This list of things to be done is similar to the backlog used by architects while architecting a system (see Section 11.2).

After we have made the simple test work, the new version of the system is inspected to see whether it can be improved. Another small change is contemplated. We may for example decide to make BlackList into a proper list, and write some simple tests to see that after adding an item to the list, that item is indeed in the list. Again, the test will fail and we update the system accordingly. Possibly, improvements can be made now since the library system probably contains other list-type classes that we can inherit from and some duplicate code can be removed. And so on.

Test-driven development is one of the practices of eXtreme Programming (see Section 3.2.4). As such, it is part of the agile approach to system development which favors small increments and redesign (refactoring) where needed rather than big design efforts. The practice is usually supported by an automated unit testing framework, such as JUnit for Java, that keeps track of the test set and reports back readable error messages for tests that fail (Hunt and Thomas, 2003). The assertEquals method used above is one of the methods provided by the JUnit framework. The framework allows for a smooth integration of coding and unit testing. On the fly, a test set is built that forms a reusable asset during the further evolution of the system. JUnit and similar frameworks have greatly contributed to the success of test-driven development.

The way of working in each iteration of test-driven development consists of the following steps:

1. Add a test.

2. Run all tests and observe that the one added fails.

3. Make a small change to the system to make the test work.

4. Run all tests again and observe that they run properly.

5. Refactor the system to remove duplicate code and improve its design.

In pure eXtreme Programming, iterations are very small, and may take from a few minutes up to, say, an hour. But test-driven development can also be done in bigger leaps and can be combined with more traditional approaches.

Test-driven development is much more than a test method. It is a different way of developing software. The effort put into the upfront development of test cases forces one to think more carefully of what it means for the current iteration to succeed or fail. Writing down explicit test cases subsumes part of the analysis and design work. Rather than producing UML diagrams during requirements analysis, we produce tests. And these tests are used immediately, by the same person that implemented the functionality that the test exercises. Testing then is not an afterthought, but becomes an integral part of the development process. Another benefit is that we have a test set and a test criterion to decide on the success of the iteration. Experiments with test-driven development indicate that it increases productivity and reduces defect rates.

13.3 VERIFICATION AND VALIDATION PLANNING AND DOCUMENTATION

Like the other phases and activities of the software development process, the testing activities need to be carefully planned and documented. Since test activities start early in the development life cycle and span all subsequent phases, timely attention to the planning of these activities is of paramount importance. A precise description of the various activities, responsibilities and procedures must be drawn up at an early stage.

The planning of test activities is described in a document called the software verification and validation plan. We base our discussion of its contents on IEEE Standard 1012. (IEEE1012, 2004) describes verification and validation activities for a waterfall-like life cycle in which the following phases are identified:

- concept phase

- requirements phase

- design phase

- implementation phase

- test phase

- installation and checkout phase

- operation and maintenance phase

The first of these, the concept phase, is not discussed in the present text. Its aim is to describe and evaluate user needs. It produces documentation which contains, for example, a statement of user needs, results of feasibility studies, and policies relevant to the project. The verification and validation plan is also prepared during this phase. In our approach, these activities are included in the requirements engineering phase.

The sections to be included in the verification and validation (V&V) plan are listed in Table 13.3. The structure of this plan resembles that of other standards discussed earlier. The plan starts with an overview and gives detailed information on every aspect of the topic being covered.

More detailed information on the many V&V tasks covered by this plan can be found in (IEEE1012, 2004). Following the organization proposed in this standard, the bulk of the test documentation can be structured along the lines identified in Table 13.4. The Test Plan is a document describing the scope, approach, resources, and schedule of intended test activities. It can be viewed as a further refinement of the verification and validation plan and describes in detail the test items, features to be tested, testing tasks, who will do each task, and any risks that require contingency planning.

The Test Design Specification defines, for each software feature or combination of such features, the details of the test approach and identifies the associated tests. The Test Case Specification defines inputs, predicted outputs, and execution conditions for each test item. The Test Procedure Specification defines the sequence of actions for the execution of each test. Together with the Test Plan, these documents describe the input to the test execution.

The Test Item Transmittal Report specifies which items are going to be tested. It lists the items, specifies where to find them, and gives the status of each item. It constitutes the release information for a given test execution.

The final three reports are the output of the test execution. The Test Log gives a chronological record of events. The Test Incident Report documents all events observed that require further investigation. In particular, this includes tests from which the outputs were not as expected. Finally, the Test Summary Report gives an overview and evaluation of the findings. A detailed description of the contents of these various documents is given in (IEEE829, 1998).

Table 13.3 Sample contents of the Verification and Validation Plan (*Source: IEEE Standard for Software Verification and Validation Plans, IEEE Standard 1012*, ©2004. Reproduced by permission of IEEE.)

1. Purpose
2. Referenced documents
3. Definitions
4. Verification and validation overview
    - 4.1. Organization
    - 4.2. Master schedule
    - 4.3. Software Integrity Level Scheme
    - 4.4. Resources summary
    - 4.5. Responsibilities
    - 4.6. Tools, techniques, and methodologies
5. V&V Processes
    - 5.1. Management
    - 5.2. Acquisition
    - 5.3. Supply
    - 5.4. Development
    - 5.5. Operation
    - 5.6. Management
6. V&V reporting requirements
7. V&V administrative requirements
    - 7.1. Anomaly reporting and resolution
    - 7.2. Task iteration policy
    - 7.3. Deviation policy
    - 7.4. Control procedures
    - 7.5. Standards, practices, and conventions

Table 13.4 Main constituents of test documentation, after (IEEE829, 1998)

Test Plan
Test Design Specification
Test Case Specification
Test Procedure Specification
Test Item Transmittal Report
Test Log
Test Incident Report
Test Summary Report

13.4 MANUAL TEST TECHNIQUES

A lot of research effort is spent on finding techniques and tools to support testing. Yet, a plethora of heuristic test techniques have been applied since the beginning of the programming era. These heuristic techniques, such as walkthroughs and inspections, often work quite well, although it is not always clear why.

Test techniques can be separated into **static** and **dynamic** analysis techniques. During dynamic analysis, the program is executed. With this form of testing, the program is given some input and the results of the execution are compared with the expected results. During static analysis, the software is generally not executed. Many static test techniques can also be applied to non-executable artifacts such as a design document or user manual. It should be noted, though, that the borderline between static and dynamic analysis is not very sharp.

A large part of the static analysis is nowadays done by the language compiler. The compiler checks whether all variables have been declared, whether each method call has the proper number of actual parameters, and so on. These constraints are part of the language definition. We may also apply a more strict analysis of the program text, such as a check for initialization of variables, or a check on the use of non-standard, or error-prone, language constructs. In a number of cases, the call to a compiler is parameterized to indicate the checks one wants to be performed. Sometimes, separate tools are provided for these checks.

The techniques to be discussed in the following subsections are best classified as static techniques. The techniques for coverage-based, fault-based, and error-based testing, to be discussed in Sections 13.5 to 13.7, are mostly dynamic in nature.

13.4.1 Reading

We all read, and reread, and reread our program texts. It is the most traditional test technique we know of. It is also a very successful technique for finding faults in a program text (or a specification or a design).

In general, it is better to have someone else read your texts. The author of a text knows all too well what the program (or any other type of document) ought to convey. For this reason, the author may be inclined to overlook things, suffering from some sort of trade blindness.

A second reason why reading by the author himself might be less fruitful, is that it is difficult to adopt a destructive attitude towards one's own work. Yet such an attitude is needed for successful testing.

A somewhat institutionalized form of reading each other's programs is known as **peer review**. This is a technique for anonymously assessing programs for quality, readability, usability, and so on.

Each person partaking in a peer review is asked to hand in two programs: a 'best' program and one of lesser quality. These programs are then randomly distributed amongst the participants. Each participant assesses four programs: two 'best' programs and two programs of lesser quality. After all the results have been collected, each participant gets the (anonymous) evaluations of their programs, as well as the statistics of the whole test.

The primary goal of this test is to give the programmer insight into his own capabilities. The practice of peer reviews shows that programmers are quite capable of assessing the quality of their peers' software.

A necessary precondition for successfully reading someone else's code is a business-like attitude. Weinberg (1971) coined the term **egoless programming** for this. Many programmers view their code as something personal, like a diary. Derogatory remarks ('how could you be so stupid as to forget that initialization') can disastrously impair the effectiveness of such assessments. The opportunity for such an antisocial attitude to occur seems to be somewhat smaller with the more formalized manual techniques.

13.4.2 Walkthroughs and Inspections

Walkthroughs and inspections are both manual techniques that spring from the traditional desk-checking of program code. In both cases, it concerns teamwork and the product to be inspected is evaluated in a formal session, following precise procedures.

Inspections are sometimes called **Fagan inspections**, after their originator (Fagan, 1976, 1986). In an inspection, the code to be assessed is gone through, statement by statement. The members of the inspection team (usually four people) get the code, its specification, and the associated documents a few days before the session takes place.

Each member of the inspection team has a well-defined role. The *moderator* is responsible for the organization of inspection meetings. He chairs the meeting and ascertains that follow-up actions agreed upon during the meeting are indeed performed. The moderator must ensure that the meeting is conducted in a businesslike, constructive way and that the participants follow the correct procedures and act as a team. The team usually has two *inspectors* or *readers*, knowledgeable peers that paraphrase the code. Finally, the *code author* is a largely silent observer. He knows the code to be inspected all too well and is easily inclined to express what he intended rather than what is actually written down. He may, though, be consulted by the inspectors.

During the formal session, the inspectors paraphrase the code, usually a few lines at a time. They express the meaning of the text at a higher level of abstraction than what is actually written down. This gives rise to questions and discussions which may lead to the discovery of faults. At the same time, the code is analyzed using a checklist of faults that often occur. Examples of possible entries in this checklist are:

- wrongful use of data: variables not initialized, array index out of bounds, dangling pointers;

- faults in declarations: the use of undeclared variables or the declaration of the same name in nested blocks;

- faults in computations: division by zero, overflow (possible in intermediate results too), wrong use of variables of different types in the same expression, faults caused by an erroneous understanding of operator priorities;

- faults in relational expressions: using an incorrect operator ($>$ instead of $\geq$, $=$ instead of $==$) or an erroneous understanding of priorities of Boolean operators;

- faults in control flow: infinite loops or a loop that is executed $n + 1$ or $n - 1$ times rather than n times;

- faults in interfaces: an incorrect number of parameters, parameters of the wrong type, or an inconsistent use of global variables.

The result of the session is a list of problems identified.

These problems are not resolved during the formal session itself. This might easily lead to quick fixes and distract the team from its primary goal. After the meeting, the code author resolves all the issues raised and the revised code is verified once again. Depending on the number of problems identified and their severity, this second inspection may be done by the moderator only or by the complete inspection team.

Since the goal of an inspection is to identify as many problems as possible in order to improve the quality of the software to be developed, it is important to maintain a constructive attitude towards the developer whose code is being assessed.[2] The results of an inspection therefore are often marked confidential. These results should certainly *not* play a role in the formal assessment of the developer in question.

In a walkthrough, the team is guided through the code using test data. The test data is mostly of a fairly simple kind, otherwise tracing the program logic soon becomes too complicated. The test data serves as a way of starting a discussion, rather than as a serious test of the program. In each step of this process, the developer may be questioned regarding the rationale of the decisions. In many cases, a walkthrough boils down to some sort of manual simulation.

Both walkthroughs and inspections may profitably be applied at all stages of the software life cycle. The only precondition is that there is a clear, testable document. It is estimated that these review methods detect 50–90% of defects (Boehm and Basili, 2001). Both techniques serve not only to find faults: if properly applied, these techniques may help to promote team spirit and morale. At the technical level, the people involved may learn from each other and enrich their knowledge of algorithms, programming style, programming techniques, error-prone constructions, and so on. Thus, these techniques also serve as a vehicle for process improvement. Under the general umbrella of 'peer reviews', they are part of the CMM level 3 key process area **Verification** (see Section 6.6).

A potential danger of this type of review is that it remains too shallow. The people involved may become overwhelmed with information; they may have

---

[2]One way of creating a non-threatening atmosphere is to always talk about 'problems' rather than 'faults'.

insufficient knowledge of the problem domain; their responsibilities may not have been clearly delineated. As a result, the review process does not pay off sufficiently.

Parnas and Weiss (1987) describe a type of review process in which the people involved have to play a more active role. They distinguish between different types of specialized design review. Each of these reviews concentrates on certain desirable properties of the design. As a consequence, the responsibilities of the people involved are clear. The reviewers have to answer a list of questions ('under which conditions may this function be called?', 'what is the effect of this function on the behavior of other functions?', and so on). In this way, the reviewers are forced to study carefully the design information received. Problems with the questionnaire and documentation can be posed to the developers, and the completed questionnaires are discussed by the developers and reviewers. Experiments suggest that inspections with specialized review roles are more effective than inspections in which review roles are not specialized.

A very important component of Fagan inspections is the meeting in which the document is discussed. Since meetings may incur considerable costs or time-lags, one may try to do without them. Experiments suggest that the added value of group meetings, in terms of the number of problems identified, is quite small.

13.4.3 Correctness Proofs

The most complete static analysis technique is the proof of correctness. In a proof of correctness we try to prove that a program meets its specification. In order to be able to do so, the specification must be expressed formally. We mostly do this by expressing the specification in terms of two assertions which hold before and after the program's execution, respectively. Next, we prove that the program transforms one assertion (the precondition) into the other (the postcondition). This is generally denoted as:

{P} S {Q}

Here, S is the program, P is the precondition, and Q is the postcondition. Termination of the program is usually proved separately. The above notation should thus be read as: if P holds before the execution of S and S terminates, then Q holds after the execution of S.

Formally verifying the correctness of a not-too-trivial program is a very complex affair. Some sort of tool support is helpful, therefore. Tools in this area are often based on heuristics and proceed interactively.

Correctness proofs are very formal and, for that reason, they are often difficult for the average programmer to construct. The value of formal correctness proofs is sometimes disputed. We may state that the thrust in software is more important than some formal correctness criterion. Also, we cannot formally prove every desirable property of software. Whether we built the right system can only be decided upon through testing (validation).

On the other hand, it seems justified to state that a thorough knowledge of this type of formal technique will result in better software.

13.4.4 Stepwise Abstraction

In the top-down development of software components, we often employ stepwise refinement. At a certain level of abstraction, the function to be executed will be denoted by a description of that function. At the next level, this description is decomposed into more basic units.

Stepwise abstraction is just the opposite. Starting from the instructions of the source code, the function of the component is built up in a number of steps. The function thus derived should comply with the function as described in the design or requirements specification.

To illustrate this technique, consider the search routine of Figure 13.4. We know, from the accompanying documentation for instance, that the elements in array a (from index 1 up to index a.length) are sorted when this routine is called.

```
1    public static int binsearch (int [ ] a, int x) {
2        int low, high, mid; Boolean found;
3        low = 1; high = a.length; mid = 0; found = false;
4        while ((low ≤ high) && (!found)) {
5            mid = (low + high) / 2;
6            if (x < a[mid])
7                high = mid - 1;
8            else {
9                if (x > a[mid])
10                   low = mid + 1;
11               else
12                   found = true;
13           }
14       }
15       if (found) return mid;
16       else return 0;
17   }
```

Figure 13.4 A search routine

We start the stepwise abstraction with the instructions of the `if` statement on lines 6–13. `x` is compared with `a[mid]`. Depending on the result of this comparison, one of `high`, `low`, and `found` is given a new value. If we take into account the assignments on lines 3 and 5, the function of this `if` statement can be summarized as

> stop searching (`found` = **true**) if `x == a[mid]`, or
> shorten the interval [`low .. high`] that might contain `x`, to an interval
> [`low' .. high'`], where `high' - low' < high - low`

Alternatively, this may be described as a postcondition to the `if` statement:

> (`found ==` **true and** `x == a[mid]`) **or**
> (`found ==` **false and** `x ∉ a[1 .. low' - 1]` **and**
>   `x ∉ a[high' + 1 .. a.length]` **and** `high' - low' < high - low`)

Next, we consider the loop in lines 4–14, together with the initialization on line 3. As regards termination of the loop, we may observe the following. If `1 ≤ a.length` upon calling the routine, then `low ≤ high` at the first execution of lines 4–14. From this, it follows that `low ≤ mid ≤ high`. If the element searched for is found, the loop stops and the position of that element is returned. Otherwise, either `high` is assigned a smaller value, or `low` is assigned a higher value. Thus, the interval [`low .. high`] gets smaller. At some point in time, the interval will have length of 1, i.e. `low = high` (assuming the element still is not found). Then, `mid` will be assigned that same value. If `x` still does not occur at position `mid`, either `high` will be assigned the value `low - 1`, or `low` will be assigned the value `high + 1`. In both cases, `low > high` and the loop terminates. Together with the postcondition given earlier, it then follows that `x` does not occur in the array `a`. The function of the complete routine can then be described as:

> result = 0 ↔ x ∉ a[1 .. a.length]
> 1 ≤ result ≤ a.length ↔ x = a[result]

So, stepwise abstraction is a bottom-up process to deduce the function of a piece of program text from that text.

13.5 COVERAGE-BASED TEST TECHNIQUES

> Question: What do you do when you see a graph?
> *Answer: Cover it!*
> Beizer (1995)

In coverage-based test techniques, the adequacy of testing is expressed in terms of the coverage of the product to be tested, for example, the percentage of statements executed or the percentage of functional requirements tested.

Coverage-based testing is often based on the number of instructions, branches or paths visited during the execution of a program. It is helpful to base the discussion of this type of coverage-based testing on the notion of a control graph. In this control graph, nodes denote actions, while the (directed) edges connect actions with subsequent actions (in time). A path is a sequence of nodes connected by edges. The graph may contain cycles, i.e. paths $p_1, \ldots, p_n$ such that $p_1 = p_n$. These cycles correspond to loops in the program (or gotos). A cycle is 'simple' if its inner nodes are distinct and do not include p_1 (or p_n, for that matter). Note that a sequence of actions (statements) that has the property that whenever the first action is executed, the other actions are executed in the given order may be collapsed into a single, compound, action. So when we draw the control graph for the program in Figure 13.5, we may put the statements on lines 7–10 in different nodes, but we may also put them all in a single node.

In Sections 13.5.1 and 13.5.2 we discuss a number of test techniques which are based on coverage of the control graph of the program. Section 13.5.3 illustrates how these coverage-based techniques can be applied at the requirements specification level.

```
1    public static void sort(int [ ] a) {
2        int j, temp; Boolean flag = true;
3        while (flag) {
4            flag = false;
5            for (j = 0; j < a.length-1; j++) {
6                if (a[j] > a[j+1]) {
7                    temp = a[j];
8                    a[j] = a[j+1];
9                    a[j+1] = temp;
10                   flag = true;
11               }
12           }
13       }
14   }
```

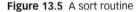

Figure 13.5 A sort routine

13.5.1 Control-Flow Coverage

During the execution of a program, we follow a certain path through its control graph. If some node has multiple outgoing edges, we choose one of those (which is also called a **branch**). In the ideal case, the tests collectively traverse all possible paths. This **all-paths coverage** is equivalent to exhaustively testing the program.

In general, this is not possible. A loop often results in an infinite number of possible paths. If we do not have loops, but only branch instructions, the number of possible paths increases exponentially with the number of branching points. There may also be paths that are never executed (quite likely, the program contains a fault in that case). We therefore search for a criterion which expresses the degree to which the test data approximates the ideal coverage.

Many such criteria can be devised. The most obvious is the criterion which counts the number of statements (nodes in the graph) executed. It is called the **all-nodes coverage**, or **statement coverage**. This criterion is rather weak because it is relatively simple to construct examples in which 100% statement coverage is achieved, while the program is nevertheless incorrect.

Consider as an example the program given in Figure 13.5. It is easy to see that a single test, with n = 2, a[1] = 5, a[2] = 3, results in each statement being executed at least once. So, this one test achieves 100% statement coverage. However, if we change, for example, the test a[i] ≥ a[i - 1] in line 6 to a[i] = a[i - 1], we still obtain a 100% statement coverage with this test. Although this test also yields the correct answer, the changed program is incorrect.

We get a stronger criterion if we require that, at each branching node in the control graph, all possible branches are chosen at least once. This is known as **all-edges coverage** or **branch coverage**. Here too, 100% coverage is no guarantee of program correctness.

Nodes that contain a condition, such as the Boolean expression in an `if` statement, can be a combination of elementary predicates connected by logical operators. A condition of the form

    i > 0 **or** j > 0

requires at least two tests to guarantee that both branches are taken. For example,

    i = 1, j = 1

and

    i = 0, j = 1

will do. Other possible combinations of truth values of the atomic predicates (i = 1, j = 0 and i = 0, j = 0) need not be considered to achieve branch coverage. **Multiple condition coverage** requires that all possible combinations of elementary predicates in conditions be covered by the test set. This criterion is also known as **extended branch coverage**.

Finally, McCabe's cyclomatic complexity metric (McCabe, 1976) has also been applied to testing. This criterion is also based on the control graph representation of a program. A basis set is a maximal linearly independent set of paths through a graph. The cyclomatic complexity (CV) equals this number of linearly independent paths (see also Section 12.1.4). Its formula is

$$CV(G) = V(G) + 1$$

Here, $V(G)$ is the graph's cyclomatic number:

$$V(G) = e - n + p,$$

where

e = the number of edges in the graph

n = the number of nodes

p = the number of maximal connected subgraphs, i.e. subgraphs for which each pair of nodes is connected by some path

As an example, consider the program text of Figure 13.6. The corresponding control graph is given in Figure 13.7. For this graph, $e = 15$, $n = 13$, and $p = 1$. So $V(G) = 3$ and $CV(G) = 4$. A possible set of linearly independent paths for this graph is: $\{1-2-3-4-5-6-7-8-9-12-4, 5-7, 8-10-11, 4-13\}$.

```
1   public static void freq_count(int [ ] a, int [ ] b, n, x) {
2       Boolean found = false;
3       int i = -1; int n = a.length;
4       while ((!found) && (i < n-1)) {
5           if (a[i++] == x)
6               found = true;
7       }
8       if (found)
9           b[i] = b[i] + 1;
10      else {
11          addElement(a, x); addElement(b, 1);
12      }
13  }
```

Figure 13.6 An insertion routine

A possible test strategy is to construct a test set such that all linearly independent paths are covered. This adequacy criterion is known as the **cyclomatic-number criterion**.

13.5.2 Data Flow Coverage

Starting from the control graph of a program, we may also consider how variables are treated along the various paths. This is termed data flow analysis. With data flow analysis too, we may define test adequacy criteria and use these criteria to guide testing.

In data flow analysis, we consider the definitions and uses of variables along execution paths. A variable is *defined* in a certain statement if it is assigned a (new) value because of the execution of that statement. After that, the new value is used in subsequent statements. A definition in statement X is *alive* in statement Y if there

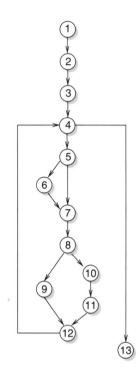

Figure 13.7 Control-flow graph of the insert routine from Figure 13.6

exists a path from X to Y in which that variable is not assigned a new value at some intermediate node. In the example in Figure 13.5, for instance, the definition of `flag` at line 4 is still alive at line 9 but not at line 10. A path such as the one from line 4 to 9 is called **definition-clear** (with respect to `flag`). Algorithms to determine such facts are commonly used in compilers in order to allocate variables optimally to machine registers.

We distinguish between two types of variable use: **P-uses** and **C-uses**. P-uses are predicate uses, such as those in the conditional part of an `if` statement. All other uses are C-uses. Examples of the latter are uses in computations or I/O statements.

A possible test strategy is to construct tests which traverse a definition-clear path between each definition of a variable to each (P- or C-) use of that definition and each successor of that use. (We have to include each successor of a use to force all branches following a P-use to be taken.) We are then sure that each possible use of a definition is being tested. This strategy is known as **all-uses coverage**. A slightly stronger criterion requires that each definition-clear path is either cycle-free or a simple cycle. This is known as **all-DU-paths** coverage. Several weaker data flow criteria can be defined as well:

- **All-defs coverage** simply requires the test set to be such that each definition is used at least once.

- **All-C-uses/Some-P-uses coverage** requires definition-clear paths from each definition to each computational use. If a definition is used only in predicates, at least one definition-clear path to a predicate use must be exercised.

- **All-P-uses/Some-C-uses coverage** requires definition-clear paths from each definition to each predicate use. If a definition is used only in computations, at least one definition-clear path to a computational use must be exercised.

- **All-P-uses coverage** requires definition-clear paths from each definition to each predicate use.

13.5.3 Coverage-Based Testing of Requirements Specifications

Program code can be easily transformed into a graph model, thus allowing for all kinds of test adequacy criteria based on graphs. Requirements specifications, however, may also be transformed into a graph model. As a consequence, the various coverage-based adequacy criteria can be used in both black-box and white-box testing techniques.

Consider the example fragment of a requirements specification document for our library system in Figure 13.8. We may rephrase these requirements a bit and present them in the form of elementary requirements and relations between them. The result can be depicted as a graph, where the nodes denote elementary requirements and the edges denote relations between elementary requirements; see Figure 13.9. We may use this graph model to derive test cases and apply any of the control-flow coverage criteria to assess their adequacy.

Function `Order` allows the user to order new books. The user is shown a fill-in-the-blanks screen with fields such as `Author`, `Title`, `Publisher`, `Price` and `Department`. The `Title`, `Price` and `Department` fields are mandatory. The `Department` field is used to check whether the department's budget is large enough to purchase this book. If so, the book is ordered and the department's budget is reduced accordingly.

Figure 13.8 A requirements specification fragment

A very similar route can be followed if the requirement is expressed in the form of a use case. Figure 13.10 gives a possible rewording of the fragment from Figure 13.8. It uses the format from (Cockburn, 2001). The use case describes both the normal case, called the Main Success Scenario, as well as extensions that cover situations that branch off the normal path because of some condition. For each extension, both

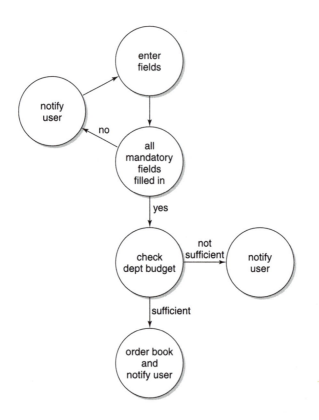

Figure 13.9 Graph model of Figure 13.8

the condition and the steps taken are listed. Note that Figure 13.9 directly mimics the use case description from Figure 13.10. The use case description also allows us to straightforwardly derive test cases and apply control-flow coverage criteria.

Generally speaking, a major problem in determining a set of test cases is to partition the program domain into a (small) number of equivalence classes. We try to do so in such a way that testing a representative element from a class suffices for the whole class. Using control-flow coverage criteria, for example, we assume that any test of some node or branch is as good as any other such test. In the above example, for instance, we assume that *any* execution of the node labeled 'check dept. budget' will do.

The weak point in this procedure is the underlying assumption that the program behaves equivalently on all data from a given class. If this assumption is true, the partition is perfect and so is the test set. This assumption will not hold, in general (see also Section 13.1.2).

Use Case: Order new Book

Primary Actor: Library user
Scope: Library
Level: User goal
Stakeholders and Interests:
>   User – wants to acquire new books
>   Department – wants to guard its budget
Precondition: User is logged on
Minimum Guarantee: User id has been validated
Success Guarantee: Order is accepted
Main Success Scenario:
>   1. User fills in form
>   2. Book information is checked
>   3. Department budget is checked
>   4. Order is placed
>   5. User is informed about placed order
Extensions:
>   2a. Book information is not valid
>   2a1. User is asked to correct information
>   3a. Department budget is inadequate
>   3a1. Order is rejected, user is notified

Figure 13.10 Use case description of Figure 13.8

13.6 FAULT-BASED TEST TECHNIQUES

In coverage-based testing techniques, we consider the structure of the problem or its solution, and the assumption is that a more comprehensive covering is better. In fault-based testing strategies, we do not *directly* consider the artifact being tested when assessing the test adequacy. We only take into account the test set. Fault-based techniques are aimed at finding a test set with a high ability to detect faults.

We will discuss two fault-based testing techniques: error seeding and mutation testing.

13.6.1 Error Seeding

Text books on statistics often contain examples along the following lines:

> If we want to estimate the number of pikes in Lake Soft, we proceed as follows:

> 1. Catch a number of pikes, N, in Lake Seed;

2. Mark them and throw them into Lake Soft;

3. Catch a number of pikes, M, in Lake Soft.

Supposing that M' out of the M pikes are found to be marked, the total number of pikes originally present in Lake Soft is then estimated as $(M - M') \times N/M'$.

A somewhat unsophisticated technique is to try to estimate the number of faults in a program in a similar way. The easiest way to do this is to artificially seed a number of faults in the program. When the program is tested, we discover both seeded faults and new ones. The total number of faults is then estimated from the ratio of those two numbers.

We must be aware of the fact that a number of assumptions underlie this method – amongst others, the assumption that both real and seeded faults have the same distribution.

There are various ways of determining which faults to seed in the program. A not very satisfactory technique is to construct them by hand. It is unlikely that we will be able to construct very realistic faults in this way. Faults thought up by one person have a fair chance of having been thought up already by the person that wrote the software.

Another technique is to have the program independently tested by two groups. The faults found by the first group can then be considered seeded faults for the second group. In using this technique, though, we must realize that there is a chance that both groups detect (the same type of) simple faults. As a result, the picture might well be distorted.

A useful rule of thumb for this technique is the following: if we find many seeded faults and relatively few others, the result can be trusted. The opposite is not true. This rule of thumb is more generally applicable: if, during testing of a certain component, many faults are found, it should not be taken as a positive sign. Quite the contrary, it is an indication that the component is probably of low quality. As Myers (1979) observed: 'The probability of the existence of more errors in a section of a program is proportional to the number of errors already found in that section.' The same phenomenon has been observed in some experiments, where a strong linear relationship was found between the number of defects discovered during early phases of development and the number of defects discovered later.

13.6.2 Mutation Testing

Suppose we have some program P which produces the correct results for some tests T_1 and T_2. We generate some variant P' of P. P' differs from P in just one place. For instance, a $+$ is replaced by a $-$, or the value v_1 in a loop of the form

```
for (var = v₁; var < v₂; var++)
```

is changed into $v_1 + 1$ or $v_1 - 1$. Next, P' is tested using tests T_1 and T_2. Let us assume that T_1 produces the same result in both cases, whereas T_2 produces different results. Then T_1 is the more interesting test case, since it does not discriminate between two variants of a program, one of which is certainly wrong.

In **mutation testing**, we generate a (large) number of variants of a program. Each of those variants, or mutants, slightly differs from the original version. Usually, mutants are obtained by mechanically applying a set of simple transformations called mutation operators (see Table 13.5).

Table 13.5 A sample of mutation operators

Replace a constant by another constant
Replace a variable by another variable
Replace a constant by a variable
Replace an arithmetic operator by another arithmetic operator
Replace a logical operator by another logical operator
Insert a unary operator
Delete a statement

Next, all these mutants are executed using a given test set. As soon as a test produces a different result for one of the mutants, that mutant is said to be dead. Mutants that produce the same results for all of the tests are said to be alive. As an example, consider the erroneous sort procedure in Figure 13.3 and the correct variant thereof which compares array elements rather than their absolute values. Tests with an array which happens to contain positive numbers only will leave both variants alive. If a test set leaves us with many live mutants, then that test set is of low quality, since it is not able to discriminate between all kinds of variant of a given program.

If we assume that the number of mutants that is equivalent to the original program is 0 (normally, this number will certainly be very small), then the **mutation adequacy score** of a test set equals D/M, where D is the number of dead mutants and M is the total number of mutants.

There are two major variants of mutation testing: **strong mutation testing** and **weak mutation testing**. Suppose we have a program P with a component T. In strong mutation testing, we require that tests produce different results for program P and a mutant P'. In weak mutation testing, we only require that component T and its mutant T' produce different results. At the level of P, this difference need not crop up. Weak mutation adequacy is often easier to establish. Consider a component T of the form

```
if (x < 4.5) ...
```

We may then compute a series of mutants of T, such as

```
if (x > 4.5) ...
if (x = 4.5) ...
if (x > 4.6) ...
```

```
if (x < 4.4) ...
   ...
```

Next, we have to devise a test set that produces different results for the original component T and at least one of its variants. This test set is then adequate for T.

Mutation testing is based on two assumptions: the *competent programmer hypothesis* and the *coupling effect hypothesis*. The competent programmer hypothesis states that competent programmers write programs that are 'close' to being correct. So the program written may be incorrect but it differs from a correct version by relatively minor faults. If this hypothesis is true, we should be able to detect these faults by testing variants that differ slightly from the correct program, i.e. mutants. The coupling effect hypothesis states that tests that can reveal simple faults can also reveal complex faults. Experiments give some empirical evidence for these hypotheses.

13.7 ERROR-BASED TEST TECHNIQUES

Suppose our library system maintains a list of 'hot' books. Each newly acquired book is automatically added to the list. After six months, it is removed again. Also, if a book is more than four months old and is being borrowed less than five times a month or is more than two months old and is being borrowed at most twice a month, it is removed from the list.

This rather complex requirement can be graphically depicted as in Figure 13.11. It shows that the two-dimensional (age, average number of loans) domain can be

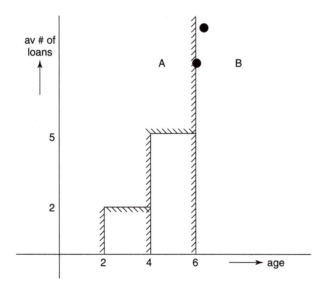

Figure 13.11 Partitioning of the input space

partitioned into four subdomains. These subdomains relate directly to the requirements as stated above. The subdomains are separated by borders such as the line $age = 6$. For each border, it is indicated which of the adjacent subdomains is closed at that border by placing a hachure at that side of the border. A subdomain S is *closed* at a border if that border belongs to S; otherwise, it is *open* at that border.

An obvious test technique for this requirement is to use an input from each of these subdomains. If the program follows the logic of the requirement, then test adequacy for that requirement equals path coverage for the corresponding program. However, in error-based testing, we focus on error-prone points and these are often found near the borders of subdomains.

One such test strategy concentrates on ON and OFF points. An ON point is a point on the border of a subdomain. If a subdomain is open with respect to some border, then an OFF point of a border is a point just inside that border. If a subdomain is closed with respect to some border, then an OFF point lies just outside that border. Two adjacent subdomains share the same ON point; they may share the same OFF point. In Figure 13.11, the solid circle on the line $age = 6$ is an ON point of both A and B, while the circle just off this line is an OFF point of both these subdomains.

Suppose we have subdomains $D_i, i = 1, \ldots, n$. We may then construct a test set which contains N test cases for ON points of each border B of each subdomain D_i, and at least one test case for an OFF point of each border. The resulting test set is called $N \times 1$ **domain adequate**.

Above, we illustrated this error-based technique in its black-box, specification-based form. The same technique can be applied to program text, though. If a program contains code of the form:

```
if (x > 6) ...
else {
    if (x > 4) && (y < 5) ...
    else {
        if (x > 2) && (y ≤ 2) ...
        else ...
        }
    }
```

then we may identify the same four subdomains and use the same technique to test for boundary cases. In fact, this technique is just a systematic way to do what experienced programmers have done for a long time: test for boundary values, such as 0, *nil*, lists with 0 or 1 element, and so on.

13.8 COMPARISON OF TEST TECHNIQUES

Most test techniques are heuristic in nature and lack a sound theoretical basis. Manual test techniques rely heavily on the qualities of the participants in the test process. But even the systematic approaches taken in functional and structural test techniques have a rather weak underpinning and are based on assumptions that are generally not true.

Experiments show that it is sometimes deceptively simple to make a system produce faults or even let it crash. (Miller *et al.*, 1990) describe one such experiment, in which they were able to crash or hang approximately 30% of the UNIX utilities on seven versions of the UNIX operating system. The utilities tested included commonly used text editors and text formatters.

Similar results have been obtained in mutation analysis experiments. In one such experiment (Knight and Ammann, 1985), 17 programs developed by different programmers from one specification were used. These programs had all been thoroughly tested. Some of them had successfully withstood one million tests. For each of those programs, 24 mutants were created, each mutant containing one seeded fault. The programs thus obtained were each tested 25 000 times. The results can be summarized as follows:

- Some seeded faults were found quickly, some needed quite a few tests, and some remained undetected even after 25 000 tests. This pattern was found for each of the 17 programs.

- In some cases, the original program failed, while the modified program yielded the right result.

Several attempts have been made to obtain more insights into the theoretical aspects of test techniques. An example is the research that is aimed at relating different test adequacy criteria. Test adequacy criteria serve as rules used to determine whether or not testing can be terminated. An important issue then is to decide whether one such criterion is 'better' than another. In Section 13.8.1, we compare the strength of a number of test adequacy criteria discussed in previous sections. In Section 13.8.2, we investigate a number of fundamental properties of test adequacy criteria. This type of research is aimed at gaining a deeper insight into properties of different test techniques.

Several experiments have been done to compare different test techniques. Real data on the fault-detection capabilities of test techniques used in a number of projects is also available. In Section 13.8.3, we discuss several of these findings, which may provide some practical insight into the virtues of a number of test techniques.

13.8.1 Comparison of Test Adequacy Criteria

A question that may be raised is whether, say, the all-uses adequacy criterion is stronger or weaker than the all-nodes or all-edges adequacy criteria. We may define the notion 'stronger' as follows: criterion X is stronger than criterion Y if, for all programs P and all test sets T, X adequacy implies Y adequacy. In the testing literature, this relation is known as 'subsume'. In this sense, the all-edges criterion is stronger than (subsumes) the all-nodes criterion. The all-uses criterion, however, is not stronger than the all-nodes criterion. This is caused by the fact that programs may contain statements which only refer to constants. For the following program:

```
if (a < b)
    System.out.println("0");
    else System.out.println("1");
```

the all-uses criterion will be satisfied by any non-empty test set, since this criterion does not require that each statement be executed. If we ignore references to constants, the all-uses criterion is stronger than the all-nodes criterion. With the same exception, the all-uses criterion is also stronger than the all-edges criterion.

A problem with any graph-based adequacy criterion is that it can only deal with paths that can be executed (feasible paths). Paths which cannot be executed are known as 'infeasible paths'. Infeasible paths result if parts of the graph are unreachable, as in

```
if (true)
    x = 1;
else
    x = 2;
```

The else branch is never executed, yet most adequacy criteria require this branch to be taken. Paths that are infeasible also result from loops. If a loop is of the form

```
for (i = 1; i < 10; i++)
    body
```

all feasible paths that traverse the resulting cycle in the graph will do so exactly ten times.

There does not exist a simple linear scale along which the strength of all program-based adequacy criteria can be depicted. For the criteria discussed in Sections 13.5 to 13.7, the subsume hierarchy is depicted in Figure 13.12, as far as it is known. An arrow $A \rightarrow B$ indicates that A is stronger than (subsumes) B. In most cases, the subsume relation holds for both the feasible and not feasible versions of the criteria. Arrows adorned with an asterisk denote relations which hold only for the not feasible version.

The subsume relation compares the thoroughness of test techniques, not their ability to detect faults. If an adequacy criterion is used to generate the next test case, the subsume relations of Figure 13.12 do not necessarily imply better fault detection. However, if some other tool is used to generate test cases, and the criterion is only used to decide when to stop testing, a stronger adequacy criterion implies better fault detection as well.

The theoretical upper bounds for the number of test cases needed to satisfy most of the coverage-based adequacy criteria are quadratic or exponential. Empirical studies, however, show that, in practice, these criteria are usually linear in the number of conditional statements.

13.8.2 Properties of Test Adequacy Criteria

A major problem with any test technique is to decide when to stop testing. As noted, functional and structural test techniques provide only weak means for doing

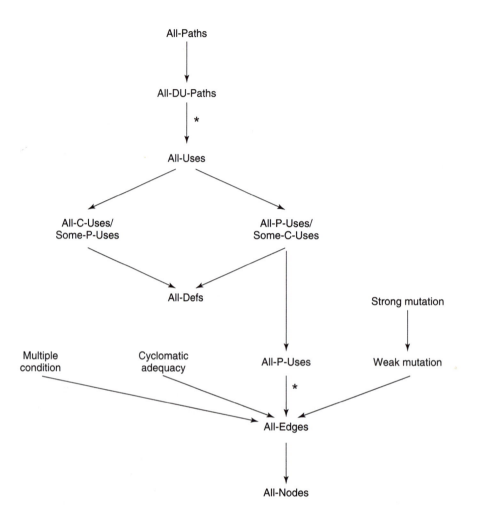

Figure 13.12 Subsume hierarchy for program-based adequacy criteria

so. Weyuker (1988) provides an interesting set of properties of test adequacy criteria. Although it is intuitively clear that any test adequacy criterion should satisfy all of the properties listed, it turns out that even some of the well-known test techniques such as all-nodes coverage and all-edges coverage fail to satisfy several of them.

The characteristics identified relate to program-based adequacy criteria, i.e. criteria that involve the program's structure. The first four criteria, however, are fairly general and should apply to any test adequacy criterion. The following 11 properties are identified in (Weyuker, 1988):[3]

---

[3]Reproduced by permission of the Association for Computing Machinery, Inc.

- **Applicability property** For every program, there exists an adequate test set. Exhaustive testing obviously satisfies this criterion but, in general, we will look for a reasonably sized test set. Both all-nodes and all-edges coverage criteria do not fulfill this property. If the program contains unexecutable code, there are no tests to cover those parts of the program.

- **Non-exhaustive applicability property** This property says that, even if exhaustive testing may be required in some cases, a criterion should certainly not require exhaustive testing in all circumstances.

- **Monotonicity property** This property states that once a program has been adequately tested, running some additional tests can do no harm. Obviously, the additional tests may reveal further faults, but this does not deem the original test set inadequate. It merely improves the quality of the test process.

- **Inadequate empty set property** The empty test set is not an adequate test set for any program. A test adequacy criterion should measure how well the testing process has been conducted. If a program has not been tested at all, it certainly has not been adequately tested.

- **Antiextensionality property** This property states that semantic equivalence is not sufficient to imply that the programs are to be tested in the same way. For instance, routines BubbleSort and QuickSort are likely to require different test sets. This property is specific for program-based adequacy criteria, which depend on the implementation rather than the function being implemented. In a specification-based approach, this property need not hold.

- **General multiple change property** Whereas the previous property states that semantic 'closeness' is not sufficient to imply that two programs can be tested in the same way, this property states that syntactic closeness is not sufficient either. Programs are said to be syntactically close if they have the same structure and the same data flow characteristics. This is the case, for instance, when some of the relational or arithmetic operators in those programs differ. Though the shape of these programs is the same, testing them on the same data may well cause different paths through the flow graph being executed.

- **Antidecomposition property** This property states that if a component is adequately tested in one environment, this does not imply that it is adequately tested for some other environment. Put in other words: if some assembly of components is adequately tested, this does not imply that the individual components have been adequately tested as well. For example, a sorting routine may well be adequately tested in an environment where the size of the array is always less than ten. If we move that routine to an environment which requires much larger arrays to be sorted, it must be tested anew in that environment.

- **Anticomposition property** This property reflects just the opposite: even if components have been adequately tested in isolation, we still have to test their composition in order to ascertain that their interfaces and interactions work properly.

- **Renaming property** If two programs differ only in inessential ways, as is the case when different variable names are used, then an adequate test set for one of these programs also suffices for the other.

- **Complexity property** Intuitively, more complex programs require more testing. This property reflects this intuition by stating that for every program there exist other programs that require more testing.

- **Statement coverage property** One central property of program-based adequacy criteria is that they should at least cause every executable statement of the program to be executed.

As noted, the all-nodes and all-edges coverage metrics fail to satisfy the applicability criterion. This is rather unsatisfactory, since it implies that we may not be able to decide whether testing has been adequate. If 50% coverage has been obtained using either of these criteria, we do not know whether additional tests will help. It may be that the other 50% of the statements or branches is not executed by any input.

Both the all-nodes and all-edges criteria do not satisfy the antidecomposition and anticomposition criteria either. For example, if all statements of individual components are executed using some given test set, then this same test set is likely to satisfy that criterion on their composition. Further research along these lines is expected to deepen our insight into what test techniques may or may not accomplish.

13.8.3 Experimental Results

> When one vacuums a rug in one direction only, one is likely to pick up
> less dirt than if the vacuuming occurs in two directions.
> (Cha *et al.*, 1988, p. 386)

The most common techniques for unit testing have been discussed in the previous sections. The effectiveness of those techniques is discussed by Basili and Selby (1987). They describe an experiment in which both professional programmers and students participated. Three techniques were compared:

- stepwise abstraction;

- functional testing based on equivalence classes and boundary value analysis (see Section 13.7);

- structural testing with 100% statement coverage.

Basili and Selby compared the effectiveness of these techniques as regards detecting faults, the associated costs, and the kinds of faults found. Some of the results of this experiment were:

- The professional programmers detected more faults with stepwise abstraction. Also, they did so faster than with the other techniques. They discovered more faults with functional testing than with structural testing. The speed with which they did so did not differ.

- In one group of students, the various test techniques yielded the same results as regards the number of faults found. In a second group, structural testing turned out to be inferior to the other techniques. The speed with which faults were detected did not differ.

- The number of faults found, the speed of fault detection, and the total effort needed depended upon the kind of program being tested.

- More interface faults were found with stepwise abstraction.

- More faults in the control structure were found with functional testing.

Other experiments also indicate that there is no uniform 'best' test technique. Different test techniques tend to reveal different types of fault. The use of multiple test techniques certainly results in the discovery of *more* faults. It is difficult though to ascribe the discovery of faults to the use of a specific technique. It may well be that the mere fact that test techniques force us to pay systematic attention to the software is largely responsible for their success.

Several studies have reported on the fault-detection capabilities of (Fagan) inspections. Myers (1988) reports that about 85% of the major errors in the Space Shuttle software were found during early inspections. Inspections have been found to be superior to other manual techniques such as walkthroughs. Inspections were also found to have the additional benefit of improving both quality and productivity. There is some controversy about the added value of group meetings.

Finally, there is ample empirical evidence that early attention to fault detection and removal really pays off. Boehm's data, presented in the introduction to this chapter, can be augmented by other results, such as those of Collofello and Woodfield (1989). His data stems from a large real-time software project, consisting of about 700 000 lines of code developed by over 400 people. Some of his findings are reproduced in Table 13.6. For example, of the 676 design faults that could have been caught, 365 were caught during the design review (= 54%). The overall design review efficiency was not much different from code review efficiency, while the testing phase was somewhat less efficient. The latter is not all that surprising, since the design and code reviews are likely to have removed many of the faults that were easy to detect. These results again suggest that the use of multiple techniques is preferable to the use of a single technique.

Table 13.6   Fault-detection efficiency

	% design faults found	% coding faults found	Combined efficiency
Design review	54	–	54
Code review	33	84	64
Testing	38	38	38

The results become much more skewed if we take into account the cost-effectiveness of the different test techniques. The cost-effectiveness metric used is the ratio of 'costs saved by the process' to 'costs consumed by the process'. The costs saved by the process are the costs that would have been spent if the process had not been performed and faults had to be corrected later. The cost-effectiveness results found in this study are given in Table 13.7. These results indicate that, for every hour spent in design reviews and correcting design faults, more than eight hours of work are saved. The cost-effectiveness of the testing phase itself is remarkably low. This is not really surprising, since much time is wasted during the actual testing phase in performing tests that do not reveal any faults. These findings once more confirm the statement that early testing really pays off.

Table 13.7   Cost-effectiveness results found in (Collofello and Woodfield, 1989)

Design review	Code review	Testing
8.44	1.38	0.17

13.9 TEST STAGES

During the design phase, the system to be built has been decomposed into components. Generally, these components form some hierarchical structure. During testing, we often let ourselves be led by this structure. We do not immediately start to test the system as a whole but start by testing the individual components (called **unit testing**). These components are incrementally integrated into a system. Testing the composition of components is called **integration testing**.

In doing this, we may take one of two approaches. In the first approach, we start by testing the low-level components, which are then integrated and coupled with components at the next higher level. The subsystem thus obtained is tested next. Then gradually we move towards the highest-level components. This is known as bottom-up testing. The alternative approach is top-down testing. In top-down testing, the top-level components are tested first and are gradually integrated with lower-level components.

In bottom-up testing, we often have to simulate the environment in which the component being tested is to be integrated. Such an environment is called a test driver. In top-down testing the opposite is true: we have to simulate lower-level components through test stubs.

Both methods have advantages and disadvantages. For instance, in bottom-up testing it may be difficult to get a sound impression of the final system during the early stages of testing because whilst the top-level components are not integrated, there is no system, only bits and pieces. With top-down testing, on the other hand, writing the stubs can be rather laborious. If the implementation strategy is one whereby a skeletal system is built first and then populated with components, this skeletal system can be used as a test driver and the order of testing then becomes much less of an issue.

In practice, it is often useful to combine both methods. It is not necessarily the case that some given design or implementation technique drives us in selecting a particular test technique. If the testing is to partly parallel the implementation, ordering constraints induced by the order of implementation have to be obeyed, though.

The program-based adequacy criteria make use of an underlying language model. Subtle differences in this underlying model may lead to subtle differences in the resulting flow graphs as used in coverage-based criteria, for instance. Roughly speaking, the results reported hold at the level of a procedure or subroutine in languages such as FORTRAN, Pascal, and so on.

As a consequence, the corresponding test techniques apply at the level of individual methods in object-oriented programs. Testing larger components of object-oriented programs, such as parameterized classes or classes that inherit part of their functionality from other classes, resembles regression testing as done during maintenance. We then have to decide how much retesting should be done if methods are redefined in a subclass or a class is instantiated with another type as a parameter.

Other forms of testing exist besides unit testing and integration testing. One possibility is to test the whole system against the user documentation and requirements specification after integration testing has finished. This is called the **system test**. A similar type of testing is often performed under supervision of the user organization and is then called **acceptance testing**. During acceptance testing, emphasis is on testing the usability of the system, rather than compliance of the code against some specification. Acceptance testing is a major criterion upon which the decision to accept or reject a system is based. In order to ensure proper delivery of all necessary artifacts of a software development project, it is useful to let the future maintenance organization have a right of veto in the acceptance-testing process.

If the system has to become operational in an environment different from the one in which it has been developed, a separate **installation test** is usually performed.

The test techniques discussed in the previous sections are often applied during unit and integration testing. When testing the system as a whole, the tests often use random input, albeit that the input is chosen such that it is representative of the system's operational use. Such tests can also be used to quantitatively assess the system's reliability. Software reliability is the topic of Section 13.10.

The use of random input as test data has proven to be successful in the Cleanroom development method. In several experiments, it was found that aselect testing resulted in a high degree of statement and branch coverage. If a branch was not executed, it often concerned the treatment of an exceptional case.

13.10 ESTIMATING SOFTWARE RELIABILITY

In much of this book the reader will find references to the fact that most software does not function perfectly. Faults are found in almost every run-of-the-mill software system: the software is not 100% reliable. In this section we concentrate on quantitative, statistical notions of software reliability.

One benefit of such information is that it can be put to use in planning our maintenance effort. Another reason for collecting reliability information could be contractual obligations regarding a required reliability level. Software for telephone-switching systems, for instance, requires such quantitative knowledge of the system's expected availability. We need to know the probability of wrong connections being due to faults in the software.

A second application of reliability data is found in testing. A major problem with testing is deciding when to stop. One possibility is to base this decision on reaching a certain reliability level. If the required reliability level is not reached, we need an estimate of the time it will take to reach that level.

In order to be able to answer this type of question, a number of **software reliability models** have been developed which strongly resemble the well-known hardware reliability models. These are statistical models where the starting point is a certain probability distribution for expected failures. The precise distribution is not known in advance. We must measure the points in time at which the first n failures occur and look for a probability distribution that fits those data. We can then make predictions using the probability distribution just obtained.

In this section, we concentrate on two models which are not too complicated and yet yield fairly good results: the **basic execution time model** and the **logarithmic Poisson execution time model**.

The goal of many test techniques discussed in this chapter is to find as many faults as possible. What we in fact observe are *manifestations* of faults, i.e. failures. The system fails if the output does not meet the specification. Faults in a program are static in nature, failures are dynamic. A program can fail only when it is executed. From the user's point of view, failures are much more important than faults. For example, a fault in a piece of software that is never, or hardly ever, used is, in general, less important than a fault which manifests itself frequently. Also, one fault may show up in different ways and a failure may be caused by more than one fault.

In the following discussion on reliability, we are not concerned with the expected number of faults in a program. Rather, the emphasis is on the expected number of failures. The notion of time plays an essential role. For the moment, we define reliability as the probability that the program will not fail during a certain period of time.

The notion of time deserves further attention. Ultimately, we are interested in statements regarding calendar time. For example, we might want to know the probability that a given system will not fail in a one-week period or we might be interested in the number of weeks of system testing still needed to reach a certain reliability level.

Both models discussed below use the notion of execution time. Execution time is the time spent by the machine actually executing the software. Reliability models based on execution time yield better results than those based on calendar time. In many cases, an a posteriori translation of execution time to calendar time is possible. To emphasize this distinction, execution time is denoted by τ and calendar time by t.

The failure behavior of a program depends on many factors: quality of the designers, complexity of the system, development techniques used, etc. Most of these cannot adequately be dealt with as variables in a reliability model and therefore are assumed to be fixed. For this reason, reliability, when discussed in this section, always concerns a specific project.

Some factors affecting failure behavior can be dealt with, though. As remarked, the models discussed are based on the notion of execution time. This is simple to measure if we run one application on a stand-alone computer. Translation between machines that differ in speed can be taken care of relatively easily. Even if the machine is used in multiprogramming mode, translation from the time measured to proper execution time may be possible. This is the case, for instance, if time is relatively uniformly distributed over the applications being executed.

The input to a program is also variable. Since we estimate the model's parameters on the basis of failures observed, the predictions made only hold insofar as future input resembles the input which led to the observed failure behavior. The future has to resemble the past. In order to get reliable predictions, the tests must be representative of the later operational use of the system. If we are able to allocate the possible inputs to different equivalence classes, simple readjustments are possible here too.

We may summarize this discussion by including the environment in the definition of our notion of software reliability. Reliability then is defined as the probability that a system will not fail during a certain period of time in a certain environment.

Finally, software systems are not static entities. Software is often implemented and tested incrementally. Reliability of an evolving system is difficult to express. In the ensuing discussion, we therefore assume that our systems are stable over time.

We may characterize the failure behavior of software in different ways. For example, we may consider the expected time to the next failure, the expected time interval between successive failures, or the expected number of failures in a certain time interval. In all cases, we are concerned with random variables, since we do not know exactly when the software will fail. There are at least two reasons for this uncertainty. Firstly, we do not know where the programmer made errors. Secondly, the relation between a certain input and the order in which the corresponding set of instructions is being executed is not usually known. We may therefore model subsequent failures as a stochastic process. Such a stochastic process is characterized by, amongst other things, the form and probability distribution of the random variables.

When the software fails, we try to locate and repair the fault that caused this failure. In particular, this situation arises during the test phase of the software life cycle. Since we assume a stable situation, the application of reliability models is particularly appropriate during system testing, when the individual components have been integrated into one system. This system-test situation, in particular, is discussed below.

In this situation, the failure behavior does not follow a constant pattern but changes over time, since faults detected are subsequently repaired. A stochastic process whose probability distribution changes over time is called *non-homogeneous*. The variation in time between successive failures can be described in terms of a function $\mu(\tau)$ which denotes the average number of failures until time τ. Alternatively, we may consider the failure intensity function $\lambda(\tau)$, the average number of failures per unit of time at time τ. $\lambda(\tau)$, then, is the derivative of $\mu(\tau)$. If the reliability of a program increases through fault correction, the failure intensity will decrease.

The relationship between $\lambda(\tau)$, $\mu(\tau)$ and τ is graphically depicted in Figure 13.13. The models to be discussed below, the basic execution time model (BM) and the logarithmic Poisson execution time model (LPM), differ in the form of the failure intensity function $\lambda(\tau)$.

Both BM and LPM assume that failures occur according to a non-homogeneous Poisson process. Poisson processes are often used to describe the stochastic behavior of real-world events. Examples of Poisson processes are: the number of telephone calls expected in a given period of time or the expected number of car accidents in a given period of time. In our case, the processes are non-homogeneous, since the failure intensity changes as a function of time, assuming a (partly) successful effort to repair the underlying errors.

In BM, the decrease in failure intensity, as a function of the number of failures observed, is constant. The contribution to the decrease in failure intensity thus is the same for each failure observed. In terms of the mean number of failures observed (μ), we obtain:

$$\lambda(\mu) = \lambda_0(1 - \mu/\nu_0)$$

Here, λ_0 denotes the initial failure intensity, i.e. the failure intensity at time 0. ν_0 denotes the number of failures observed if the program is executed for an infinite time period. Note that, since λ is the derivative of μ and both are functions of τ, λ in fact only depends on τ. We return to this later.

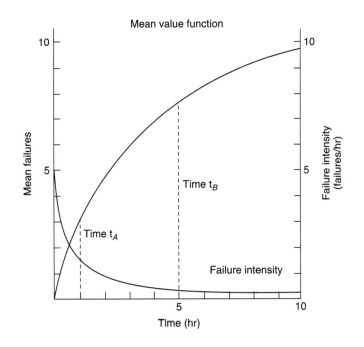

Mean value function

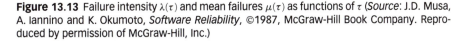

Figure 13.13 Failure intensity $\lambda(\tau)$ and mean failures $\mu(\tau)$ as functions of τ (*Source*: J.D. Musa, A. Iannino and K. Okumoto, *Software Reliability*, ©1987, McGraw-Hill Book Company. Reproduced by permission of McGraw-Hill, Inc.)

In LPM, the first failure contributes more to the decrease in failure intensity than any subsequent failures. More precisely, the failure intensity is exponential in the number of failures observed. We then get:

$$\lambda(\mu) = \lambda_0 \exp^{-\theta\mu}$$

In this model, θ denotes the decrease in failure intensity. For both models, the relation between λ and μ is depicted in Figure 13.14. (Note that the two curves intersect in this picture. This need not necessarily be the case. It depends on the actual values of the model parameters.)

Both models have two parameters: λ_0 and ν_0 for BM; and λ_0 and θ for LPM. These parameters have yet to be determined, for instance from the observed failure behavior during a certain period of time.

We can explain the shape of these functions as follows: given a certain input, the program in question will execute a certain sequence of instructions. A completely different input may result in a completely different sequence of instructions to be executed. We may partition all possible inputs into a number of classes such that input from any one class results in the execution of the same sequence of instructions.

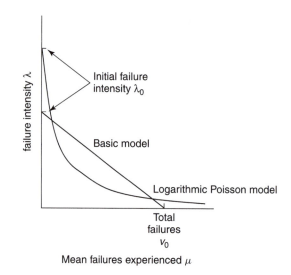

Figure 13.14 Failure intensity λ as a function of μ (*Source*: J.D. Musa, A. Iannino and K. Okumoto, *Software Reliability*, ©1987, McGraw-Hill Book Company. Reproduced by permission of McGraw-Hill, Inc.)

Some example classes could be a certain type of command in an operating system or a certain type of transaction in a database system.

The user selects input from the various possible classes according to some probability distribution. We define the **operational profile** as the set of possible input classes together with the probabilities that input from those classes is selected.

The basic execution time model implies a uniform operational profile. If all input classes are selected equally often, the various faults have an equal probability of manifesting themselves. Correction of any of those faults then contributes the same amount to the decrease in failure intensity. It has been found that BM still models the situation fairly well in the case of a fairly non-uniform operational profile.

With a strong non-uniform operational profile, the failure intensity curve has a convex shape, as in LPM. Some input classes are, then, selected relatively often. As a consequence, certain faults show up earlier and are corrected sooner. These corrections have a larger impact on the decrease in failure intensity.

In both models, λ and μ are functions of τ (execution time). Furthermore, failure intensity λ is the derivative of mean failures μ. For BM, we may therefore write

$$\lambda(\mu) = \lambda_0(1 - \mu/v_0)$$

as

$$\frac{\mathrm{d}\mu(\tau)}{\mathrm{d}\tau} = \lambda_0(1 - \mu(\tau)/v_0)$$

Solving this differential equation yields

$$\mu(\tau) = \nu_0(1 - \exp^{-\lambda_0\tau/\nu_0})$$

and

$$\lambda(\tau) = \lambda_0 \exp^{-\lambda_0\tau/\nu_0}$$

In a similar way, we obtain for LPM:

$$\mu(\tau) = \ln(\lambda_0\theta\tau + 1)/\theta$$

and

$$\lambda(\tau) = \lambda_0/(\lambda_0\theta\tau + 1)$$

For LPM, the expected number of failures in infinite time is infinite. Obviously, the number of failures observed during testing is finite.

Both models allow that fault correction is not perfect. In BM the effectiveness of fault correction is constant, though not necessarily 100%. This again shows up in the linearity of the failure intensity function. In LPM, the effectiveness of fault correction decreases with time. Possible reasons could be that it becomes increasingly more difficult to locate the faults, for example because the software becomes less structured or the personnel less motivated.

If the software is operational and faults are not being corrected, the failure intensity remains constant. Both models then reduce to a homogeneous Poisson process with failure intensity λ as the parameter. The number of failures expected in a certain time period follows a Poisson distribution. The probability of exactly n failures being observed in a time period of length τ is then given by

$$P_n(\tau) = (\lambda\tau)^n \times \exp^{-\lambda\tau}/n!$$

The probability of 0 failures in a time frame of length τ then is $P_0(\tau) = \exp(-\lambda\tau)$. This is precisely what we earlier denoted by the term software reliability.

Given a choice of either of the models BM or LPM, we are next faced with the question of how to estimate the model's parameters. We may do so by measuring the points in time at which the first N failures occur. This gives us points $T_1, \ldots, T_n$. These points can be translated into pairs $(\tau, \mu(\tau))$. We may then determine the model's parameters so that the resulting curve fits the set of measuring points. Techniques such as Maximum Likelihood or Least Squares are suited for this.

Once these parameters have been determined, predictions can be made. For example, suppose the measured data results in a present failure intensity λ_P and the required failure intensity is λ_F. If we denote the additional test time required to reach failure intensity λ_F by $\Delta\tau$, then we obtain for BM:

$$\Delta\tau = (\nu_0/\lambda_0)\ln(\lambda_P/\lambda_F)$$

And for LPM we get:

$$\Delta\tau = (1/\theta)(1/\lambda_F - 1/\lambda_P)$$

Obviously, we may also start from the equations for μ. We then obtain estimates for the number of failures that have yet to be observed before the required failure intensity level is reached.

For BM, this extrapolation is graphically depicted in Figure 13.15. Since estimating the model's parameters is a statistical process, we do not actually obtain one solution. Rather, we get reliability intervals. Such a reliability interval denotes the interval which contains a parameter with a certain probability. For example, λ_0 may be in the interval $[80,100]$ with probability 0.75. So the curve in Figure 13.15 is actually a band. The narrower this band is, the more accurately the parameters have been estimated for the same reliability of the interval. In general, the estimates are more accurate if they are based on more data.

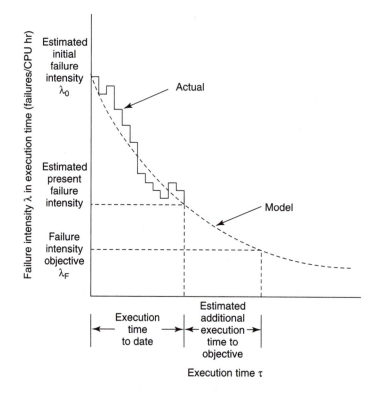

Figure 13.15 A conceptual view of the parameter-estimating process (*Source*: J.D. Musa, A. Iannino and K. Okumoto, *Software Reliability*, ©1987, McGraw-Hill Book Company. Reproduced by permission of McGraw-Hill, Inc.)

In the above discussion, we used the notion of execution time. That calendar time is a less useful notion on which to base our model can be seen as follows: suppose the points in time at which the first N failures occurred were expressed in terms of calendar time. Suppose also that we try to correct a fault as soon as it manifests itself. If the manpower available for fault correction is limited and is capable of solving a fixed number of problems per day, the failure intensity will be constant if it is based on calendar time. We do not, then, observe any progress.

Quite a few reliability models have been proposed in the literature. The major differences concern the total number of failures (finite or infinite) that can be experienced in infinite time and the distribution of the failures experienced at a given point in time (for example, Poisson, and binomial).

An important question then arises as to which model to choose. By studying a number of failure data sets, it has been observed that no one model is consistently the best. We therefore have to look for the model that gives the best prediction on a project-by-project basis. Since we do not know in advance which model will perform best, it is wise to adopt an eclectic approach, and use a number of different models simultaneously.

13.11 SUMMARY

In this chapter, we discussed a great number of test techniques. We emphasized the importance of early fault detection. It is important to pay attention to testing during the early stages of the software development process. Early testing activities are the ones that are most cost effective. Early testing activities provide opportunities to prevent errors from being made in the first place. An extreme form of this is test-driven development, where writing tests is the very first thing we do.

In practice, the various manual test techniques seem to be used most often. They turn out to be at least as successful as the various structural and functional techniques. Inspections in particular have been found to be a very cost-effective test technique. Next to the test techniques used, a major element in software fault detection and removal is the choice of personnel – some people are significantly better at finding and removing faults than others.

Since exhaustive testing is generally not feasible, we have to select an adequate set of test cases. Test techniques can be classified according to the criterion used to measure the adequacy of a test set. Three broad categories of test adequacy criteria can be distinguished:

- **coverage-based testing**, in which testing requirements are specified in terms of the coverage of the product to be tested, for example, the percentage of statements executed;

- **fault-based testing**, in which the focus is on detecting faults, for example, the percentage of seeded faults detected;

- **error-based testing**, which focuses on testing error-prone points, such as 0, 1, or the upper bound of an array.

A test adequacy criterion can be used as a stopping rule, a measurement instrument, or a generator of test cases. Test adequacy criteria and the corresponding test techniques can be viewed as two sides of the same coin. A coverage-based test technique makes it easy to measure coverage-based criteria, but does not help us in assessing whether all error-prone points have been tested.

Experimental evaluations show that there is no uniform best test technique. Different techniques tend to reveal different types of error. It is therefore wise to 'vacuum the carpet in more than one direction'.

One line of research addresses the relative power of test adequacy criteria. A well-known measure for comparing program-based test adequacy criteria is the subsume relation: criterion X subsumes Y if, for all programs P and all test sets T, X adequacy implies Y adequacy. Many of the well-known adequacy criteria have been related to one another in a subsume hierarchy.

As with any other life cycle activity, testing has to be carefully planned, controlled, and documented. Some of the IEEE Standards provide useful guidelines for doing this (IEEE829, 1998; IEEE1012, 2004).

Section 13.10 was devoted to a discussion of how to quantitatively estimate the reliability of a piece of software. The currently available software reliability models are limited in their immediate practical value. In particular, no model consistently performs best.

13.12 FURTHER READING

Well-known textbooks on testing are (Myers, 1979) (and its updated version (Myers, 2004)), (Beizer, 1995) and (Copeland, 2003). Whittaker (2000) gives a concise overview of the field. For a further discussion of safety issues, see (Leveson, 1991). Fault-tree analysis is discussed in (Leveson, 1986). (Zhu *et al.*, 1997) give a very good overview of the types of test strategy discussed in Sections 13.5 to 13.7 and the associated adequacy criteria. Rothermel and Harrold (1996) and Harrold (1999) give a very good overview of regression test techniques. Testing object-oriented software is addressed in (Binder, 2000).

The first attempts at developing some theory on testing date back to the 1970s and 80s (Goodenough and Gerhart, 1975), (Howden, 1982), and (Howden, 1985). Thereafter, much of that research has been directed towards finding and relating test adequacy criteria (Weyuker, 1988), (Clarke *et al.*, 1989), (Weyuker, 1990), (Frankl and Weyuker, 1993a), (Frankl and Weyuker, 1993b), (Parrish and Zweben, 1995), and (Zhu, 1996). Experimental evaluations of test adequacy criteria can be found in (Frankl and Weiss, 1993), (Weyuker, 1993), (Offutt and Lee, 1994), (Harrold *et al.*, 1997), and (Frankl *et al.*, 1997). Experiments that compare manual and functional or structural test techniques are reported upon in (Basili and Selby, 1987), (Kamsties and Lott, 1995), and (Wood *et al.*, 1997). (Juristo *et al.*, 2004) give an overview of 25 years of testing technique experiments.

The Cleanroom development method is described in (Selby *et al.*, 1987) and (Mills *et al.*, 1987). Experiences with Cleanroom are discussed in (Currit *et al.*, 1986) and (Trammell *et al.*, 1992). Stepwise abstraction is described in (Linger *et al.*, 1979).

Beck (2003) describes test-driven development. Janzen and Saiedian (2005) give a somewhat wider perspective on its potential. Hunt and Thomas (2003) is one of the many textbooks describing JUnit. Effects of test-driven development on productivity and errors are reported in (Maximilien and Williams, 2003) and (Erdogmus *et al.*, 2005).

Inspections were introduced by Fagan in the 1970s (Fagan, 1976, 1986). Gilb and Graham (1993) is a textbook on inspections; Wiegers (2002) is a textbook on peer reviews. There have been many experimental evaluations of inspections; see for instance (Knight and Myers, 1993), (Weller, 1993), (Grady and van Slack, 1994), (Porter *et al.*, 1995), (Porter *et al.*, 1997), (Porter *et al.*, 1998), and (Biffl and Halling, 2002). Parnas and Lawford (2003a) and Parnas and Lawford (2003b) are introductions to two companion special journal issues on software inspections. (Ciolkowski *et al.*, 2003) discuss the state of the art in software reviews.

The basic execution time model and the logarithmic Poisson execution time model are extensively discussed, and compared with a number of other models, in (Musa *et al.*, 1987). (Lyu, 1995) is a very comprehensive source on software reliability. Experiences with software reliability modeling are reported in (Jeske and Zhang, 2005). Whittaker and Voas (2000) give criteria other than time and operational profile that affect reliability.

Exercises

1. What is a test adequacy criterion? What uses does it have?

2. Describe the following categories of test technique: coverage-based testing, fault-based testing, and error-based testing.

3. What assumptions underlie the mutation testing strategy?

4. What is the difference between black-box testing and white-box testing?

5. Define the following terms: error, fault, and failure.

6. What is a Fagan inspection?

7. What is test-driven development?

8. Define the following categories of control-flow coverage: all-paths coverage, all-edges coverage, all-statements coverage.

9. Consider the following routine (in Modula-2):

```
procedure SiftDown(var A: array of integer; k, n: integer);
var parent, child, insert, Ak: integer;
begin
    parent:= k; child:= k + k;
    Ak:= A[k]; insert:= Ak;
    loop
        if child > n then exit end;
        if child < n then
            if A[child] > A[child+1] then child:= child+1 end
        end;
        if insert <= A[child]
            then exit
            else A[parent]:= A[child];
                parent:= child; child:= child + child
        end
    end;
    A[parent]:= Ak
end SiftDown;
```

(This operation performs the sift-down operation for heaps; if necessary, you may consult any text on data structures to learn more about heaps.) The routine is tested using the following input:

```
n = 5, k = 2,
A[1] = 80, A[2] = 60, A[3] = 90, A[4] = 70, A[5] = 10.
```

Will the above test yield 100% statement coverage? If not, provide one or more additional test cases such that 100% statement coverage is obtained.

10. For the example routine from Exercise 9, construct a test set that yields 100% branch coverage.

11. For the example routine from Exercise 9, construct a test set that achieves all-uses coverage.

12. Consider the following two program fragments:

```
Fragment 1:
found = false; counter = 1;
while ((counter < n) && (!found)) {
    if (table[counter] == element) found:= true;
    counter = counter + 1;
};
if (found) System.out.println("found");
else System.out.println("not found");

Fragment 2:
found = false; counter = 1;
while ((counter < n) && (!found)) {
    found = table[counter] == element;
    counter = counter + 1
};
if (found) System.out.println("found");
else System.out.println("not found");
```

Can the same test set be used if we wish to achieve 100% branch coverage for both fragments?

13. What is mutation testing?

14. Which assumptions underlie mutation testing? What does that say about the strengths and weaknesses of this testing technique?

15. When is one testing technique stronger than another?

16. What is the difference between a system test and an acceptance test?

17. Contrast top-down and bottom-up integration testing.

18. What is the major difference between the basic execution time model and the logarithmic Poisson execution time model of software reliability?

19. Give a definition of software reliability. Give a rationale for the various parts of this definition.

20. Why is it important to consider the operational profile of a system while assessing its reliability?

21. Can you think of reasons why reliability models based on execution time yield better results than those based on calendar time?

22. Can software reliability be determined objectively?

23. ♠ Read (DeMillo *et al.*, 1979), and (Fetzer, 1988) and the reactions to it (cited in the bibliography entry for that article). Write a position paper on the role of correctness proofs in software development.

24. ♠ For a (medium-sized) system you have developed, write a software verification and validation plan (SVVP) following IEEE Standard 1012. Which of the issues addressed by this standard were not dealt with during the actual development? Could a more thorough SVVP have improved the development and testing process?

25. ♡ Consider the following sort routine:

```
public static void selection_sort (int a, int n) {
    int i, j, small, temp;
    for (i = 0; i < n-2; i++) {
        small = i;
        for (j = i+1; j < n-1; j++)
            if (a[j] < a[small]) small = j;
        temp = a[i]; a[i] = a[small]; a[small] = temp;
    }
}
```

Determine the function (by means of pre- and postconditions) of this routine using stepwise abstraction.

26. ♡ Generate ten mutants of the procedure in Exercise 25. Next, test these mutants using the following set of test cases:

   - an empty array;
   - an array of length 1;
   - a sorted array of length 10;
   - an array of 10 elements that all have the same value;
   - an array of length 10 with random elements.

   Which of these mutants stay alive? What does this tell you about the quality of these tests?

27. ♡ Construct an example showing that the antidecomposition and anti-composition axioms from Section 13.8.2 do not hold for the all-nodes and all-edges testing criteria. Why are these axioms important?

28. ♠ With one or two fellow students or colleagues, inspect a requirements or design document not produced by yourself. Is the documentation sufficient to do a proper inspection? Discuss the findings of the process with the author of the document. Repeat the process with a document of which you are the author.

29. ♡ Assess the strengths and weaknesses of:

   - functional or structural testing,
   - correctness proofs,
   - random testing, and
   - inspections

   for fault finding and confidence building.

30. ♡ One way of testing a high-level document such as a requirements specification is to devise and discuss possible usage scenarios with prospective users of the system to be developed. What additional merits can this technique have over other types of review?

31. ♡ How do you personally feel about a Cleanroom-like approach to software development?

32. ♡ Discuss the following claim: 'Reliability assessment is more important than testing.' Can you think of reasons why both are needed?

14

Software Maintenance

LEARNING OBJECTIVES

- To know about well-known categories of maintenance tasks and data on their distribution

- To be able to discern major causes of maintenance problems

- To be aware of reverse engineering, its limitations, and tools to support it

- To appreciate different ways in which maintenance activities can be organized

- To understand major differences between development and maintenance and the consequences of them

> Software maintenance is not limited to the correction of faults. A large part of maintenance deals with accommodating new or changed user requirements and adapting software to a changed environment. It is about evolution, rather than just maintenance. We discuss the various types of maintenance task and how to organize them.

Like living organisms and most natural phenomena, software projects follow a life cycle that starts from emptiness, is followed by rapid growth during infancy, enters a long period of maturity, and then begins a cycle of decay that almost resembles senility.
Jones (1989)

Software, unlike a child, does not grow smarter and more capable; unfortunately, it does seem to grow old and cranky.
Lyons (1981)

Consider UBank, a multinational bank, a typical large organization that is heavily dependent upon automation for its daily operation. UBank is the result of a number of mergers and takeovers.

UBank has hundreds of offices spread all over the world. It has a number of mainframes at a central site, as well as thousands of workstations and printers connected. It has Internet connectivity, all over the world, and strives for $24 * 7$ availability. The workload is an enormous number of transactions per hour. The bank has hundreds of application systems averaging over 500 000 lines of code. Programs are written in a variety of languages, most notably COBOL, various 4GLs and JCL. The systems make use of huge databases implemented under IDMS, INGRES, and so on. Some of the basic information is shared by many systems.

Quite likely, the bank has no complete overview of its application portfolio. Because of the mergers and acquisitions, integration of applications is a big issue. There are many wrappers, bridges, and other temporary ways to glue systems together. There are more people involved in maintaining UBank's information systems than there are people involved in developing new systems for UBank.

There are many organizations like UBank, organizations whose portfolio of information systems is vital for their day-to-day operation. At the same time, these information systems are ageing and it becomes increasingly difficult to keep them 'up and running'. An increasing percentage of the annual budget of these organizations is spent on keeping installed systems functioning properly.

It is estimated that there are more than 100 billion lines of code in production in the world. As much as 80% of it is unstructured, patched, and badly documented. It is a gargantuan task to keep these software systems operational: errors must be corrected and systems must be adapted to changing environments and user needs.

This is what software maintenance is about. Software maintenance is defined as (IEEE610, 1990):

> The process of modifying a software system or component after delivery to correct faults, improve performance or other attributes, or adapt to a changed environment.

So software maintenance is, in particular, *not* limited to the correction of latent faults. The distinction between development and maintenance is fuzzy, to say the least. This makes it hard to be very bold about percentages and types of maintenance category. In Section 14.1, we revisit the discussion about types of maintenance activity from Chapter 1 and provide a more balanced view.

Changes in both the system's environment and user requirements are inevitable. Software models part of reality, and reality changes, whether we like it or not. So the software has to change too. It has to evolve. A large percentage of what we are used to calling maintenance, is actually evolution.

When looking for ways to reduce the maintenance problem, it is worth bearing in mind the classification of maintenance activities given in Chapter 1:

- Higher-quality code, better test procedures, better documentation, and adherence to standards and conventions may help to save on corrective maintenance.

- By anticipating changes during requirements engineering and design and by taking them into account during realization, future perfective and adaptive maintenance can be realized more easily. In particular, the explicit evaluation of a software architecture with respect to ease of change is to be recommended. Through its inheritance and virtual typing capabilities, the object-oriented development paradigm in particular offers opportunities for isolating parts that are susceptible to changes from those that are less so. Many design patterns are aimed at encapsulating change-prone elements.

- Finer tuning to user needs may lead to savings in perfective maintenance. This may, for example, be achieved through prototyping techniques, a more intensive user participation during the requirements engineering and design phase, or another agile approach to development.

- Less maintenance is needed when less code is written. The sheer length of the source code is the main determinant of total cost, both during initial development and during maintenance. In particular, a 10% change in a component of 200 LOC is more expensive than a 20% change in a component of 100 LOC. The reuse of existing software in particular has a very direct impact on maintenance costs.

These possible actions are all concerned with initial software development. This is not surprising, since the key to better maintainable software is to be found there. All these issues have been discussed at great length in previous chapters.

Better initial development though will not automatically result in lower maintenance costs. Worse, Dekleva (1992) found exactly the opposite. He found that development projects with analysis and design phases that produce a logical representation of the system's function incur *higher* maintenance cost than projects that did not produce such a representation. The explanation is that the users eventually learn what can reasonably be asked during maintenance. If they know a structured approach has been followed, they expect enhancements can be asked for and will be realized. So they ask for enhancements. If they know no structured approach has been followed, they expect that only necessary bug fixing is feasible and maintenance requests will remain moderate. So higher quality may well incur higher maintenance cost.

Maintenance problems are here to stay. Some of these problems are inherent – systems degrade when they are changed over and over again – while others are caused by simple facts of life: real development and maintenance activities are carried out in less than perfect ways. The major causes of the resulting maintenance problems are addressed in Section 14.2.

This discussion of maintenance problems suggests two approaches to improve the situation. Section 14.3 discusses various ways to rediscover lost facts (such as 'what does this routine accomplish?' and 'which design underlies a given system?') and restructure existing software systems in order to improve their maintainability.

The second approach, discussed in Section 14.5, entails a number of organizational and managerial actions to improve software maintenance.

14.1 MAINTENANCE CATEGORIES REVISITED

Let us recall part of the discussion from Chapter 1. Following Lientz and Swanson (1980), we distinguished four types of maintenance activity:[1]

- **Corrective maintenance** deals with the repair of faults found.

- **Adaptive maintenance** deals with adapting software to changes in the environment, such as new hardware or the next release of an operating system. Adaptive maintenance does not lead to changes in the system's functionality.

- **Perfective maintenance** mainly deals with accommodating new or changed user requirements. It concerns functional enhancements to the system. Perfective maintenance also includes activities to increase the system's performance or to enhance its user interface.

- **Preventive maintenance** concerns activities aimed at increasing the system's maintainability, such as updating documentation, adding comments, and improving the modular structure of the system.

---

[1]The IEEE uses slightly different definitions. In particular, it combines Lientz and Swanson's adaptive and perfective categories, and calls the combination adaptive maintenance. The reader should be aware of these different definitions of maintenance categories, especially when interpreting percentages spent on the different categories.

Notice that 'real' maintenance activities – the correction of faults – accounts for about 25% of the total maintenance effort only. Half of the maintenance effort concerns changes to accommodate changing user needs, while the remaining 25% largely concerns adapting software to changes in the external environment (see Figure 14.1).

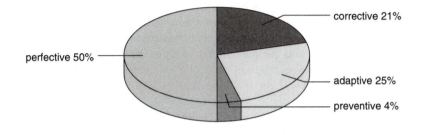

Figure 14.1 Distribution of maintenance activities

Recall also that the total cost of system maintenance is estimated to comprise at least 50% of total life cycle costs. Similar figures hold for the personnel involved. Table 14.1 gives an estimate of the number of people working in software development compared to software maintenance, according to (Jones, 2006).

Table 14.1 Distribution of developers and maintainers in the US

Year	Development	Maintenance	Maintenance percentage
1975	350 000	75 000	17.65
1990	900 000	800 000	47.06
2005	775 000	2 500 000	76.34

The data in Figure 14.1 are based on (Lientz and Swanson, 1980) and reflect the state of the practice in the 1970s. Later studies have shown that the situation has not changed for the better. Nosek and Palvia (1990) raised the major maintenance issues once again and came to the disturbing conclusion that maintenance problems have remained pretty much the same, notwithstanding advances in structured development methodologies and techniques. Other studies, such as (Basili *et al.*, 1996) give roughly the same results. The relative distribution of maintenance activities is about the same as it was 20 years ago. Systems though have become larger, maintenance staff has grown, there are more systems, and there is a definite trend to an increase in maintenance effort relative to development effort.

Some studies give results that are quite different from the general picture sketched above. (Schach *et al.*, 2003), for instance, investigated maintenance effort in three systems and found corrective maintenance percentages of 50% and more, and very low percentages for adaptive maintenance. There is no convincing argument for these differences.

In many organizations, the definition of software maintenance does not follow the IEEE definition. Some organizations for instance define change efforts larger than, say, three months, as development rather than maintenance. This blurs the picture even further. In practice also, people find it difficult to distinguish between adaptive and perfective maintenance (Hatton, 2007). What remains then is a distinction between correcting faults and 'the rest'. The latter mostly caters for 75% or more of the maintenance effort.

The maintenance categories from (Lientz and Swanson, 1980) refer to the software only. Keeping software alive incurs other costs too, though. For instance, new users must be trained and the helpdesk needs to be staffed. Nowadays, it is not uncommon that these supporting costs account for around 25% of the cost of keeping a system deployed.

Another way to look at the distribution of maintenance cost and prevailing types of maintenance tasks is along the time dimension. We may distinguish the following maintenance life cycle stages:

- During the **introductory** stage of a new system, most of the effort is spent on user support. Users have to be trained and they often contact the helpdesk for clarification.

- Next follows a **growth** stage, in which more and more users start to explore the system's possibilities. As far as maintenance is concerned, emphasis during this stage is on correcting faults.

- The growth stage is followed by a period of **maturity**. Users know what the system can and cannot do, and ask for enhancements.

- Finally, a period of **decline** sets in. Technology replacement, such as another platform or user interface kit, constitutes a major category of maintenance tasks during this period.

Successful maintenance requires knowledge of the application. After initial delivery, this knowledge is usually available. Either knowledge of the application is explicitly transferred to the maintenance organization via documentation, training, and so on, or the developers become maintainers of the application. But over time, this knowledge vaporizes and, at some point in time, it has become scant. This point in time more or less coincides with the transition from the mature stage to the declining stage. The 'if it ain't broken, don't fix it' adage then becomes prevalent. Bennett and Rajlich (2000) use the terms **evolution stage** and **servicing stage** to distinguish between the period in which the system can successfully evolve and the subsequent period where this is no longer the case. In the latter stage, changes become tactical. For example, necessary changes are realized through patches and wrappers.

Finally, we may consider the distribution of effort over the activities of a single maintenance task. For code-related tasks, the main activities are:

- **Isolation** The first activity is concerned with determining the part of the system (components, classes) that needs to be changed.

- **Modification** This concerns the actual changes. One or more components are adapted to accommodate the change.

- **Testing** After the changes have been made, the system has to be tested anew (regression testing).

As a rule of thumb, isolation takes about 40% of effort, while the other two activities each take about 30%. This distribution is not the same for all types of maintenance. For corrective maintenance, isolation often takes an even larger share, while for adaptive maintenance tasks, the actual modification takes longer. During corrective maintenance, the fault that caused the failure has to be found, and this may take a lot of effort. Once it is found, the actual modification is often fairly small. For adaptive maintenance tasks, the reverse holds.

14.2 MAJOR CAUSES OF MAINTENANCE PROBLEMS

The following story reveals many of the problems that befall a typical software maintenance organization. It is based on an anecdote once told by David Parnas and concerns the re-engineering of software for fighter planes.

The plane in question has two altimeters. The onboard software tries to read either meter and displays the result. The software for doing so is depicted in Figure 14.2. The code is unstructured and does not contain any comments. With a little effort, though, its functioning can be discerned. A structured version of the same code is given in Figure 14.3. What puzzles us is the meaning of the default value 3000.

```
IF not-read1 (V1) GOTO DEF1;
display (V1);
GOTO C;
DEF1: IF not-read2 (V2) GOTO DEF2;
display (V2);
GOTO C;
DEF2: display (3000);
C:
```

Figure 14.2 Unstructured code to read altimeters

```
if read-meter1 (V1) then display (V1) else
if read-meter2 (V2) then display (V2) else
    display (3000)
endif;
```

Figure 14.3 Structured code to read altimeters

Why on earth does the system display the value 3000 (which, at first sight is not very peculiar) when both altimeters cannot be read?

The rationale for the default value could not be discerned from the (scarce or nonexistent) documentation. Eventually, the programmer who had written this code was traced. He said that, when writing this piece of code, he did not know what to display in case both altimeters were unreadable. So he asked one of the fighter pilots what their average flying altitude was. The pilot made a back-of-the-envelope calculation and came up with the above value: the average flying altitude is 3 000 feet. Hence this fragment.

The person reengineering the software rightfully thought that this was not the proper way to react to malfunctioning hardware. Fighter planes either fly at a very high altitude or very close to the ground. They do not fly in the middle. So he contacted the officials in charge and asked permission to display a clear warning message instead, such as a flashing 'PULL UP'.

The permission to change the value displayed was denied. Generations of fighter pilots were by now trained to react appropriately to the current default message. Their training manual even stated a warning phrase like 'If the altimeter reader displays the value 3000 for more than a second, PULL UP'.

This story can't be true. Or can it? It does illustrate some of the major causes of maintenance problems:

- unstructured code,

- maintenance programmers having insufficient knowledge of the system or application domain; understanding the rationale behind code is one of the most serious problems maintainers face,

- documentation being absent, out of date, or at best insufficient.

Another maintenance problem (not illustrated by the anecdote) is that software maintenance has a bad image.

Unstructured code is used here as a generic term for systems that are badly designed or coded. It manifests itself in a variety of ways: the use of gotos, long procedures, poor and inconsistent naming, high component complexity, weak cohesion and strong coupling, unreachable code, deeply nested if statements, and so on.

Even if systems were originally designed and built well, they may have become harder to maintain in the course of time. Much software that is to be maintained was developed in the pre-structured programming era. The software was designed and written for machines with limited processing and memory capacities. It may have been moved to different hardware or software platforms more than once without its basic structure having changed.

This is not the whole story either. The bad structure of many present-day systems at both the design and code level is not solely caused by their age. As a result of their studies of the dynamics of software systems, Lehman and Belady formulated a series of Laws of Software Evolution (see also Chapter 3). The ones that bear most on software maintenance are:

- **Law of continuing change**: A system that is being used undergoes continuing change, until it is judged more cost-effective to restructure the system or replace it by a completely new version.

- **Law of increasing complexity**: A program that is changed, becomes less and less structured (the entropy increases) and thus becomes more complex. One has to invest extra effort in order to avoid increasing complexity.

Large software systems tend to stay in production for a long time. After being put into production, enhancements are inevitable. As a consequence of the implementation of these enhancements, the entropy of software systems increases over time. The initial structure degrades and complexity increases. This in turn complicates future changes to the system. Such software systems show signs of arthritis. Preventive maintenance may delay the onset of entropy but, usually, only a limited amount of preventive maintenance is carried out.

Eventually, systems cannot be properly maintained any more. In practice, it is often impossible to completely replace old systems by new ones. Developing completely new systems from scratch is too expensive, the system contains too many residual errors to start with, or it is impossible to re-articulate the original requirements. Usually, a combination of these factors applies. Increasing attention is therefore given to ways to 'rejuvenate' or 'recycle' existing software systems and ways to create structured versions of existing operational systems in order that they become easier to maintain.

Entropy is not only caused by maintenance. In agile methods, such as XP, it is an accepted intermediate stage. These methods have an explicit step to improve the code. This is known as **refactoring**. Refactoring is based on identifying 'bad smells' and reworking the code to improve its design (see also Section 14.3.1).

At a low level, the code improvement process can be supported by tools such as code restructures and reformatters. To get higher-level abstractions generally requires human guidance and a sufficient understanding of the system.

This leads us to the second maintenance problem: the scant knowledge maintenance programmers have of the system or application domain. Note that the lack of application domain knowledge pertains to software development in general (Curtis *et al.*, 1988). The situation with respect to software maintenance is aggravated by the fact that there are usually scarce sources that can be used to build such an understanding. In many cases, the source code is the only reliable source. A major issue in software maintenance then is to gain a sufficient understanding of a system from its source code. The more spaghetti-like this code is, the less easy it becomes to disentangle it. An insufficient understanding results in changes that may have unforeseen ripple effects which in turn incur further maintenance tasks.

Maintenance is also hampered if documentation is absent, insufficient, or out-of-date. Experienced programmers have learnt to distrust documentation: a disappointing observation in itself, albeit realistic. During initial development, documentation often comes off badly because of deadlines and other time constraints. Maintenance itself often occurs in a 'quick-fix' mode whereby the code is patched to accommodate changes. Technical documentation and other higher-level descriptions of the software then do not get updated. Maintenance programmers having to deal with these systems have become part historian, part detective, and part clairvoyant (Corby, 1989).

Careful working procedures and management attention could prevent such a situation from occurring. But even then we are not sure that the right type of documentation will result. Two issues deserve our attention in this respect:

- A design rationale is often missing. Programmers and designers tend to document their final decisions, not the rationale for those decisions and the alternatives rejected. Maintenance programmers have to reconstruct this rationale and may easily make the wrong decisions.

- In trying to comprehend a piece of software, programmers often operate in an opportunistic mode. Based on their programming knowledge, in terms of programming plans and other stereotyped solutions to problems, they hypothesize a reasonable structure. Problems arise if the code does not meet these assumptions.

Finally, the noun 'maintenance' in itself has a negative connotation. Maintaining software is considered a second-rate job. Maintenance work is viewed as unchallenging and unrewarding. Preferably, new and inexperienced programmers are assigned to the maintenance group, possibly under the guidance of an experienced person. The more experienced people are to be found working on initial software development. In the structure of the organization, maintenance personnel rank lower, both financially and organizationally, than programmers working on the development of new systems.

This tends to affect morale. Maintenance programmers are often not happy with their circumstances and try to change jobs as fast as possible. The high turnover of maintenance programmers precludes them from becoming sufficiently familiar with the software to be maintained which in turn hampers future maintenance.

It would be far better to have a more positive attitude towards maintenance. Maintaining software is a very difficult job. The job content of a maintenance programmer is more demanding than the job content of a development programmer. The programs are usually written by other people, people who often cannot be consulted because they have left the firm or are entangled in the development of new systems. When making changes in an existing system, one is bound by the very structure of that system. There is generally a strong time pressure on maintenance personnel. Maintenance work requires more skills and knowledge than development does. It is simply more difficult (Chapin, 1987).

The maintenance group is of vital importance. It is they who keep things going. It is their job to ensure that the software keeps pace with the ever-changing reality. Compared to software development, software maintenance has more impact on the well-being of an organization.

14.3 REVERSE ENGINEERING AND REFACTORING

> What we're doing now with reverse engineering is Archeology. We're trying to gain an understanding of existing systems by examining ancient artifacts and piecing together the software equivalent of broken clay pots. Then we look to restructuring and reengineering to save the clay.
> Chikofsky (1990)

It is fashionable in our trade to coin new terms once in a while and offer them as a panacea to the software crisis. One of the magical terms is **reverse engineering**. It comes under different guises and means altogether different things to different people. In the discussion below, we use the terminology from (Chikofsky and Cross II, 1990). The different terms are illustrated in Figure 14.4.

Chikofsky defines reverse engineering as 'the process of analyzing a subject system to

- identify the system's components and their interrelationships and

- create representations of the system in another form or at a higher level of abstraction.'

According to this definition, reverse engineering only concerns inspection of a system. Adaptations of a system and any form of restructuring, such as changing gotos into structured control constructs, do not fall within the strict definition of reverse engineering. Reverse engineering is akin to the reconstruction of a lost blueprint. Retiling the bathroom or the addition of a new bedroom is an altogether different affair. If this distinction is not carefully made, the meaning of the term reverse engineering dilutes too much and it reduces to a fancy synonym for maintenance.

The above definition still leaves open the question whether or not the resulting description is at a higher level of abstraction. To emphasize the distinction, Chikofsky uses the notions of **design recovery** and **redocumentation**, respectively.

Redocumentation concerns the derivation of a semantically equivalent description at the same level of abstraction. Examples of redocumentation are the transformation of a badly indented program into one having a neat lay-out or the construction of a set of flowcharts for a given program.

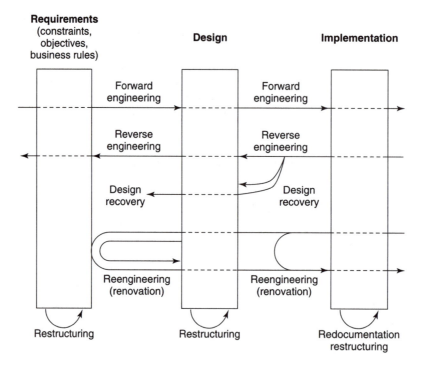

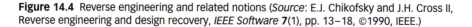

Figure 14.4 Reverse engineering and related notions (*Source*: E.J. Chikofsky and J.H. Cross II, Reverse engineering and design recovery, *IEEE Software* **7**(1), pp. 13–18, ©1990, IEEE.)

Design recovery concerns the derivation of a semantically equivalent description at a higher level of abstraction. Some people limit the term 'reverse engineering' to efforts that result in higher-level descriptions and thus equate the term to what we have termed design recovery.

Note that 100% functional equivalence is difficult to achieve in reverse engineering. The person carrying out the process (the reengineer) may encounter errors in the original system and may want to correct them. Such errors may be deeply hidden in the original system and become much more troublesome in the reverse engineered system. The programming language may be incompletely defined and its implementation may depend on certain machine characteristics. Data equivalence may be difficult to achieve because of typing issues, approximations, data conversions, etc. In practice, it seems sensible to solve this issue by agreeing on some acceptance test for the reengineered system, thereby relaxing the 100% functional equivalence requirement.

Obviously, reverse engineering is often done in circumstances where the target system is adapted as well. Two important subclasses are **restructuring** and **reengineering**.

Restructuring concerns the transformation of a system from one representation to another, at the same level of abstraction. The functionality of the system does not change. The transformation of spaghetti code to structured code is a form of restructuring. The redesign of a system (possibly after a design recovery step) is another example of restructuring. In agile methods, restructuring the code to improve its design is an explicit process step. There, it is known as **refactoring**. Refactoring is discussed in Section 14.3.1.

Refactoring is a white-box method, in that it involves inspection of and changes to the code. It is also possible to modernize a system without touching the code. For example, a legacy system may be given a modern user interface. The old, text-based interface is then wrapped to yield, for example, a graphical user interface or a client running in a Web browser. This is a black-box method. The code of the old system is not inspected: the input and output are simply redirected to the wrapper. Usability is increased, although the capabilities of the new type of interface are often not fully exploited. A similar black-box technique can be used to switch to another database, or integrate systems through intermediate XML documents. A third black-box wrapping technique is applied at the level of components, where both business logic and data are wrapped and accessed through an interface as if it were, say, a JavaBean.

These wrapping techniques do not change the platform on which the software is running. If a platform change is involved in the restructuring effort of a legacy system, this is known as **migration**. Migration to another platform is often done in conjunction with value-adding activities such as a change of interface or code improvements.

Restructuring is sometimes done in conjunction with efforts to convert existing software into reusable building blocks. Such reclamation efforts may well have higher (indirect) payoffs than mere savings in maintenance expenditure for the particular system being restructured, especially if the effort concerns a family of similar systems. The latter is often done in combination with domain engineering and the development of a (reusable) architecture or framework.

With reengineering, also called **renovation**, real changes are made to the system. The reverse-engineering step is followed by a traditional forward-engineering step in which the required changes are incorporated.

Each of the above transformations starts from a given description of the system to be transformed. In most cases this is the program code, which may or may not be adequately documented. However, it is also possible to restructure an existing design or reconstruct a requirements specification for a given design. For these transformations too, the term reverse engineering applies.

Both reverse engineering and restructuring can be done manually, but it is a rather tiresome affair. Quite a number of tools have been developed to support these processes. These tools are discussed in Section 14.3.3. There are, however, some inherent limitations as to how much can be achieved automatically. These limitations are discussed in Section 14.3.2.

14.3.1 Refactoring

The modern name for restructuring is **refactoring**. Refactoring has become popular as one of the practices from XP (see Section 3.2.4). Of course, programmers have applied the technique in some form since the beginning of programming.[2] Quite often, refactoring activities are not explicitly planned; they occur somewhat unnoticed in the daily work of software developers. In XP and other agile methods, they are an explicit method step.

There are arguments both for and against refactoring. The classic engineering rule 'if it ain't broken, don't fix it' is a compelling argument against refactoring. On the other hand, the second law of software evolution tells us that software becomes increasingly complex over time. So we are forced to apply refactoring to keep the software maintainable. These arguments are both valid. It depends on the phase the software is in which argument is the decisive one. During the evolution stage, when knowledge about the system is still around, refactoring is a viable option. During the servicing stage, knowledge will have vaporized to some extent and refactoring then may well introduce more problems than it solves. During that stage, one may decide, for example, to add a wrapper and not to touch the software any more.

Refactoring is applied when the structure of the software is of substandard quality. Fowler used the term **bad smells** to indicate occurrences of substandard code quality. Fowler (1999) lists the following 22 bad smells:[3]

- **Long Method** A method that is too long

- **Large Class** A class that is too big, in terms of instance variables or methods

- **Primitive Obsession** The use of primitives, such as numbers, instead of small classes such as `Dollar`

- **Long Parameter List** A parameter list that is too long

- **Data Clumps** Groups of data items that are often used together, such as the height, width, and color of a graphical object; if you remove one of the items, the rest doesn't make sense any more

- **Switch Statements** The use of type codes instead of polymorphism. This results in case statements all over the code

- **Temporary Field** A class variable that is only used in some circumstances

---

[2] My earliest recall of a refactoring activity goes back to 1970. I was at that time fulfilling my compulsory military service. I couldn't properly fire a gun, so I was assigned to the army's computer center as a programmer. A couple of weeks before I was demobilized, I finished my last FORTRAN program. To fill up the time, I decided to improve it a bit: improve the structure, remove redundant gotos, and so on. Configuration control was unheard of at the time and I only retained the last copy of the source code. By the time I left the army, I had introduced some faults and I could not make the program work any more. They were probably glad I left, but not this way.

[3] Fowler also gives detailed instructions on how to improve the bad code.

- **Refused Bequest** A subclass that does not support all of the methods or data it inherits

- **Alternative Classes with Different Interfaces** Methods that do the same things but have different interfaces; for example, methods `DisplayRectangle` and `DisplayCircle`.

- **Parallel Inheritance Hierarchies** Two class hierarchies with the relation that if one of them has to be extended, so has the other

- **Lazy Class** A class that isn't doing all that much; this might be the result of a previous refactoring operation

- **Data Class** A class that holds data but little else

- **Duplicate Code** According to Fowler (1999), this is 'number one in the stink parade'

- **Speculative Generality** Code for which the programmer *anticipated* some future need, but this future is unknown

- **Message Chains** When an object asks for an object from another object, which in turn asks for an object from yet another object, and so on

- **Middle Man** A class that delegates most of its tasks to other classes; delegation is OK, too much delegation is not

- **Feature Envy** A method that is more tightly coupled to, i.e. interested in, other classes than the class where it is located

- **Inappropriate Intimacy** Two classes that are coupled too tightly

- **Divergent Change** A class that needs to be changed for different reasons, e.g. each time a new database is added and each time the user interface changes

- **Shotgun Surgery** The opposite of the Divergent Change smell: for every change, many classes have to be changed

- **Incomplete Library Class** A library that doesn't offer all the functionality needed for the task at hand

- **Comments** Comments are bad if they compensate for low-quality code.

This is quite a long list, and somewhat hard to go through manually in each and every refactoring situation. (Mäntylä *et al.*, 2003) give a useful categorization of these bad smells into seven broad categories (see Table 14.2). These categories give handles as to the kind of situation one should look for when refactoring code.

The first category, the **Bloaters**, denote situations in which something has grown too large to handle effectively. The Primitive Obsession is placed there, because the

Table 14.2   Categories of 'bad smell'

Category	Bad smells
Bloaters	Long Method, Large Class, Primitive Obsession, Long Parameter List, Data Clumps
Object-Oriented Abusers	Switch Statements, Temporary Field, Refused Bequest, Alternative Classes with Different Interfaces, Parallel Inheritance Hierarchies
Change Preventers	Divergent Change, Shotgun Surgery
Dispensables	Lazy Class, Data Class, Duplicate Code, Speculative Generality
Encapsulators	Message Chains, Middle Man
Couplers	Feature Envy, Inappropriate Intimacy
Others	Incomplete Library Class, Comments

functionality to handle the primitives has to be placed in some other class, which may then grow too large. The **Object-Oriented Abusers** denote situations where the possibilities of object orientation are not fully exploited. The **Change Preventers** hinder further evolution of the software. The **Dispensables** represent things that can be removed. The **Encapsulators** deal with data communication. The two smells in this category are opposite: decreasing one will increase the other. The **Couplers** represent situations where coupling is too high. The **Others** category, finally, contains the smells that do not fit another category.

Bad smells occur not only at the code level. At the design level, the evolution of systems through successive releases may provide valuable information about bad smells. For example, if certain classes often change or classes are introduced in one version, disappear in the next, and then reappear again, they merit closer inspection.

Fowler (1999) states that 'no set of metrics rivals informed human intuition'. On the other hand, several of the metrics defined in Section 12.1 do relate to a number of the bad smells listed above. For example, a high value for McCabe's cyclomatic complexity could indicate the Switch Statement bad smell, while a high value for the Coupling Between Object Classes (CBO) metric could indicate a Feature Envy bad smell. Metrics thus may augment human intuition in the search for bad smells.

14.3.2 Inherent Limitations

> If you pass an unstructured, unmodular mess through one of these restructuring systems, you end up with at best, a structured, unmodular mess.
> Wendel (1986)

Reverse engineering is mostly not limited to redocumentation in a narrow sense. We are often inclined to ask why certain things are being done the way they are done, what the meaning is of a certain code fragment, and so on. We must therefore investigate how programmers go about studying program text. The relevance of these issues shows from results of a study into maintenance activities (Fjelstad and Hamlen, 1979), confirmed by (Yu and Chen, 2006):

- Maintenance programmers study the original program code about one and a half times as long as its documentation.

- Maintenance programmers spend as much time reading the code as they do implementing a change.

Insights into the discovery process which takes place during maintenance activities will give us the necessary insight to put various developments regarding reverse engineering and refactoring into perspective.

In forward-engineering activities, we usually proceed from high-level abstractions to low-level implementations. Information gets lost in the successive steps involved in this process. If we want to reverse the route, this information must be reconstructed. The object we start with, a piece of source code, in general, usually offers insufficient clues for a full reconstruction.

The programmer uses various sources of information in his discovery process. For example, if the design documentation is available, that documentation will reveal something about the structure of the system. A characteristic situation in practice is that the source code is the only reliable source of information. So this source code has to be studied in order to discover the underlying abstractions. The question is how the programmer goes about doing this.

Several theories have been developed to describe this comprehension process. Common to these theories is that expert programmers may draw on a vast number of knowledge chunks. These knowledge chunks are called in when software is developed.

Within the realm of programming, it is postulated that experts know of programming plans or beacons. A **programming plan** is a program fragment that corresponds to a stereotypical action. For example, to compute the sum of a series of numbers, a programmer uses the 'running total loop plan'. In this plan, some counter is initialized to zero and is incremented with the next value of a series in the body of a loop. A **beacon** is a key feature that typically indicates the presence of a particular structure or operation. Beacons seem to be very diagnostic of program meaning. For example, the kernel idea or central operation in a sorting program is a swap operation. If we are presented with a program that contains a swap operation, our immediate reaction would then be that it concerns some sorting program.

This type of program comprehension process occurs when studying existing software. Meaningful units are isolated from the 'flat' source text. Knowledge from human memory is called in during this process. The more knowledge the reader has about programming or the application domain, the more successful this process will be. The better the source code maps onto knowledge already available to the reader, the more effective this process will be.

During the comprehension process, the reader forms hypotheses and checks these hypotheses with the actual text. Well-structured programs and proper documentation ease this process. If application-domain concepts map onto well-delineated program units then the program text is more easily understood. If the structure of a program shows no relation to the structure of the application domain, or the reader cannot discern this structure, then understanding of the program text is seriously hampered.

As a side remark we note that there are two extreme strategies for studying program text:

- the as-needed strategy, and

- the systematic strategy.

In the as-needed strategy, program text is read from beginning to end like a piece of prose and hypotheses are formulated on the basis of local information. Inexperienced programmers in particular tend to fall back onto this strategy. In the systematic strategy, an overall understanding of the system is formed by a systematic top-down study of the program text. The systematic approach gives a better insight into causal relations between program components.

These causal relations play an important role when implementing changes. So-called delocalized plans, in which conceptually related pieces of code are located in program parts that are physically wide apart, may seriously hamper maintenance activities. Excessive use of inheritance increases the use of delocalized plans. If our understanding is based on local clues only, modifications may easily result in 'ripple effects', i.e. changes that are locally correct but lead to new problems at different, unforeseen places. Use of the as-needed strategy increases the probability of ripple effects.

During the comprehension process the programmer uses knowledge that has its origin outside the program text proper. To illustrate this phenomenon, consider the program text from Figure 14.5.

```
for (i = 1; i < n; i++) {
    for (j = 1; j < n; j++) {
        if (A[j, i]) {
            for (k = 1; k < n; k++) {
                if (A[i, k]) A[j, k] = true;
            }
        }
    }
}
```

Figure 14.5 Warshall's algorithm to compute the transitive closure of a graph

The program fragment of Figure 14.5 manipulates a Boolean matrix A. Before this fragment is executed, the matrix has a certain value. The matrix is traversed in a rather complicated way (potentially, each element is visited n^3 times) and once in a while an element of the array is set to $true$. But what does this fragment *mean*? What does it *do*?

An expert will 'recognize' Warshall's algorithm. Warshall's algorithm computes the transitive closure of a relation (graph). The notions 'transitive closure', 'relation' and 'graph' have a precise meaning within a certain knowledge domain. If you do not know the meaning of these notions, you have not made any progress in understanding the algorithm either.

At yet another level of abstraction, the meaning of this fragment could be described as follows. Suppose we start with a collection of cities. The relation A states, for each pair of cities i and j, whether there is a direct rail connection between cities i and j. The code fragment of Figure 14.5 computes whether there is a connection at all (either direct or indirect) between each pair of cities. Warshall's algorithm has many applications. If you know the algorithm, you will recognize the fragment reproduced in Figure 14.5. If you do not know the algorithm, you will not discover the meaning of this fragment either.

As a second example, consider the code fragment of Figure 14.6, adapted from (Biggerstaff, 1989). The fragment will not mean much to you. Procedure and variable names are meaningless. A meaningful interpretation of this fragment is next to impossible. The same code fragment is given in Figure 14.7, though with meaningful names.

```
public static void A(w x) {
    b(y, n1);
    b(x, n2);
    m(w[x]);
    y = x;
    r(p[x]);
};
```

Figure 14.6 An incomprehensible code fragment

```
public static void change_window(window nw) {
    border(current_window, no_highlight);
    border(nw, highlight);
    move_cursor(w[nw]);
    current_window = nw;
    resume(process[nw]);
};
```

Figure 14.7 Code fragment with meaningful names

From Figure 14.7, you may grasp that the routine has something to do with window management. The border of the current window is depicted in a lighter shade while the border of another window is highlighted. The cursor is positioned in the now highlighted window and the process of that window is restarted. If we add a few comments to the routine, its text becomes fairly easy to interpret. Meaningful names and comments together provide for an informal semantics of this code which suffice for a proper understanding.

This informal semantics goes much further than building local knowledge of the meaning of a component. Developers use naming conventions also to find their way around in a large system. Organizations often prescribe naming conventions precisely for this reason. When design and architecture documentation is not updated, these naming conventions serve as a proxy for that documentation.

Common to these two examples and the altimeter anecdote from Section 14.2 is that we need *outside* information for a proper interpretation of the code fragments. The outside information concerns concepts from a certain knowledge domain or a design rationale that was only present in the head of the programmer.

The window management example is illustrative for yet another reason. Tools manipulate sequences of symbols. In principle, tools do not have knowledge of the (external) meaning of the symbols being manipulated. In particular, a reverse-engineering tool has no knowledge of 'windows', 'cursor' and so on. These notions derive their meaning from the application domain, not from the program text itself. From the tool point of view, the texts of Figures 14.6 and 14.7 are equally meaningful.

The above observations have repercussions for the degree to which tools can support the reverse engineering and restructuring process. Such tools cannot turn a badly designed system into a good one. They cannot infer knowledge from a source text which is not already contained in that text without calling in external knowledge as an aid. In particular, completely automatic design recovery is not feasible. You can't make a pig out of a sausage.

14.3.3 Tools

During the reverse engineering process, the programmer builds an understanding of what the software is trying to accomplish and why things are done the way they are done. Several classes of tool may support the task of program understanding:

- Tools to ease perceptual processes involved in program understanding (reformatters)

  Tools may, for example, produce a neat lay-out in which nested instructions are indented and blank lines are put between successive methods. More advanced tools print procedure names in a larger font or generate page headers which contain the name of the component, its version number, creation date, and so on.

- Tools to gain insight into the static structure of programs

  For example, tools that generate tables of contents and cross-reference listings help to trace the use of program elements. Browsers provide powerful interactive capabilities for inspecting the static structure of programs. Hypertext systems provide mechanisms to extend the traditional flat organization of text by their capabilities for linking non-sequential chunks of information. If system-related information is kept in a hypertext form, this opens up new possibilities for interactive, dynamic inspection of that information. Code analyzers may be used to identify potential trouble spots by computing software complexity metrics, highlighting 'dead code', or indicating questionable coding practices or bad smells. Finally, tools may generate a graphical image of a program text in the form of a control graph or a calling hierarchy. Tools may analyze the surface structure of large systems, e.g. by considering variable names, and cluster parts that seem to be highly related. The result of this clustering provides a first guess at a restructuring for the system.

- Tools that inspect the version history of a system (see also Section 14.4)

  These tools may, for example, highlight components that have been changed very often, indicating candidates for reengineering. Tools that identify pairs of components that have often changed together but are not logically related may indicate weak spots in the software architecture.

- Tools to gain insight into the dynamic behavior of programs

  Next to traditional text-oriented debugging systems there are systems which provide graphical capabilities to monitor program execution, e.g. to animate data structures or the execution flow.

Note that these tools provide support for maintenance tasks in general (alongside tools such as test coverage monitors, which keep track of program paths executed by a given set of test data, and source comparators, which identify changes between program versions). With respect to reverse engineering, the above tools may be classified as redocumentation tools. By far the majority of reverse engineering tools fall into this category.

Tools which result in a description at a higher level of abstraction (design-recovery tools) have some inherent limitations, as argued in the previous section. Tools for design recovery need a model of the application domain in which concepts from that domain are modeled in an explicit way, together with their mutual dependencies and interrelations. Completely automatic design recovery is not feasible in the foreseeable future. Concepts from an application domain usually carry an informal semantics. Tools for design recovery may, in a dialog with the human user, search for patterns, make suggestions, indicate relations between components, etc. Such a tool may be termed a 'maintenance apprentice'.

Many tools exist for restructuring program code. The history of these restructuring tools goes all the way back to the late 1960s. Böhm and Jacopini (1966) published a seminal paper in which it was shown that gotos are not necessary for creating programs. The roots of restructuring tools, such as Recoder (Bush, 1985), can be traced to the constructive proof given in Böhm and Jacopini's paper. Recoder structures the control flow of COBOL programs.

Restructuring tools can be very valuable – a well-structured program is usually easier to read and understand. A study reported by Gibson and Senn (1989) provides evidence that structural differences do affect maintenance performance. Specifically, it was found that eliminating gotos and redundancy appears to decrease both the time required to perform maintenance and the frequency of ripple effects.

Yet, the merit of restructuring tools is limited. They will not transform a flawed design into a good one.

14.4 SOFTWARE EVOLUTION REVISITED

Lehman and Belady studied the evolution of software systems and formulated their well-known laws of software evolution. Empirical studies have given general support for these laws.

Apparently, there is quite a bit of regularity in the evolution of software. We can use this insight and try to predict the *future* evolution of a specific system by looking at the *actual* evolution of that system till now. We then base our next action on information from the past. We may, for example, decide which components to reengineer by looking at components that changed a lot in the recent past. The assumption then is that components that changed a lot in the recent past are likely to change in the near future too. Gîrba *et al.* (2004) used the term *yesterday's weather* to characterize this idea: if we have no further information, we may guess that today's weather will be like yesterday's.

Gîrba and Ducasse (2006) distinguish two types of analysis of evolutionary data: **version-centered analysis** and **history-centered analysis**. In version-centered analysis, differences between successive versions of a system are studied. The results are typically depicted in a figure with time (i.e. successive versions) along one axis and the relevant aspects of the system on another. For example, we may consider the relative size of the different components of a system over time, as illustrated in Figure 14.8 (adapted from (Gîrba and Ducasse, 2006)).

Each rectangle in Figure 14.8 denotes a component. The width and height of a rectangle each stand for an attribute of that component. The width may for instance denote the number of classes of a component, while the height denotes its number of interfaces. Figure 14.8 tells us that component A is stable and small, while component D is stable and big. Component C shows a steady growth from one version to the next and component B exhibits some ripple effects in versions 2 and 3, but has been stable since then.

In a history-centered analysis, a particular viewpoint is chosen, and the evolution of a system is depicted with respect to that viewpoint. For example, Figure 14.9 shows how often different components are changed together. Each node denotes a component, and the thickness of the edges denotes how often two connected components are changed together (co-changes). A thicker edge between components

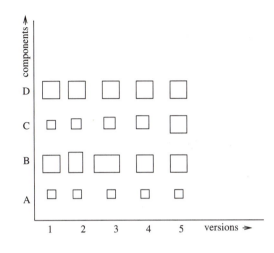

Figure 14.8 Size versus version

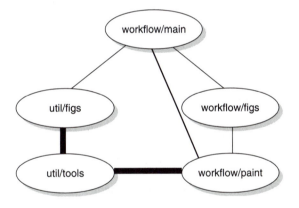

Figure 14.9 Components that change together

indicates more frequent co-changes. This information may, for instance, be derived from the versioning database.

From Figure 14.9 we learn that components util/figs and util/tools are changed together frequently. The same holds for components util/tools and workflow/paint. The names of the components suggest that components util/figs and util/tools are structurally related, while util/tools and workflow/paint are structurally unrelated. From this additional information, we might infer that the interaction between components util/tools and workflow/paint deserves our attention. Alternatively, we may label the components with the (external) features they participate in and the view then shows whether changes frequently affect different features.

A version-centered analysis depicts the version information as-is. It is up to the user to detect any pattern. In Figure 14.8, it is the user who has to detect growing or shrinking components; the picture just presents the facts. In a history-centered analysis, some hypothesis guides the representation and the patterns are then encoded in the representation, as in Figure 14.9.

14.5 ORGANIZATIONAL AND MANAGERIAL ISSUES

The duties of maintenance management are not different from those of other organizational functions, and software development in particular. In Chapter 2 we identified five entities that require continuous attention of management:

- time, i.e. progress towards goals;

- information, in particular the integrity of the complete set of documents, including change requests;

- organization of the team, including coordination of activities;

- quality of the product and process;

- money, i.e. cost of the project.

In this section, we address these issues from a maintenance perspective. We pay particular attention to issues that pose specific problems and challenges to maintenance: the organization of maintenance activities, major differences between development and maintenance, the control of maintenance tasks, and quality assessment.

14.5.1 Organization of Maintenance Activities

The primary question to be addressed here is whether or not software maintenance should be assigned to a separate organizational unit. The following discussion is largely based on an insightful study of different forms of systems staff departmentalization presented in (Swanson and Beath, 1990). The authors of this article explore the strengths and weaknesses of three alternative bases for staff departmentalization. The three organizational forms with their focal strengths and weaknesses are listed in Table 14.3. We will sketch out the W- and A-Type organizations and discuss the L-Type organization with its pros and cons more elaborately.

Traditionally, departmentalization in software development tended to be according to work type (a W-Type scheme). In such a scheme, people analyze user needs, or design systems, or implement them, or test them, etc. Even though they cooperate in a team, each team member has quite separate responsibilities and roles.

In a W-Type scheme, work assignments may originate from both development and maintenance projects. For example, a designer may be involved in the design of a

Table 14.3 Tradeoffs between alternative organizational forms (*Source*: E.B. Swanson and C.M. Beath, Departmentalization in software development and maintenance, *Communications of the ACM* **33**(6), pp. 658–67. Reproduced by permission of the Association for Computing Machinery, Inc.)

W-Type	Departmentalization by work type (analysis versus programming)
	Focal strength: development and specialization of programming knowledge and skills
	Focal weakness: costs of coordination between systems analysts and programmers
A-Type	Departmentalization by application domain (application group A versus application group B)
	Focal strength: development and specialization of application knowledge
	Focal weakness: costs of coordination and integration among application groups
L-Type	Departmentalization by life-cycle phase (development versus maintenance)
	Focal strength: development and specialization of service orientation and maintenance skills
	Focal weakness: costs of coordination between development and maintenance units

(sub)system in the context of some development project or in the design of a change to an existing system. Likewise, a programmer may implement an algorithm for a new system or realize changes in an operational program.

Note that the development of new systems does not occur in a vacuum. Designers of new systems reuse existing designs and must take into account constraints imposed by existing systems. Programmers involved in development projects have to deal with interfaces to existing software, existing databases, etc. In the W-Type scheme, the distinction between development and maintenance work is primarily a distinction between the different *origins* of the work assignment.

A second form of departmentalization is one according to application areas, the A-Type scheme. Nowadays, computerized applications have extended to almost all corners of the enterprise. Systems have become more diversified. Application domain expertise has become increasingly important for successful implementation of information systems. Deep knowledge of an application domain is a valuable but scarce resource. Nurturing of this expertise amongst staff is one way to increase quality and productivity in both development and maintenance. In larger organizations, we may therefore find units with particular expertise in certain application domains, such as financial systems, office automation, or real-time process control.

Finally, we may departmentalize according to life-cycle phases, as is done in the L-Type scheme. In particular, we may distinguish between development and maintenance. With an increasing portfolio of systems to be maintained and the increasing business need of keeping the growing base of information systems working satisfactorily, the division of development and maintenance into separate organizational units is found more often.

Separating development and maintenance has both advantages and disadvantages. The major advantages are:

- Clear accountability as we can clearly separate the cost and effort involved in maintenance activities from investments in new developments. If personnel are involved in both types of work, they have some freedom in charging their time. It is then more difficult to measure and predict the 'real' cost of software maintenance.

- Intermittent maintenance tasks make it difficult to predict and control the progress of new system development. If people do both maintenance work and development, some control can be exercised by specifically allocating certain periods of time as maintenance periods. For instance, the first week of each calendar month may be set aside for maintenance. But even then, maintenance problems are unpredictable and some need immediate attention. Many a schedule slippage is due to the drain of maintenance.

- A separation of maintenance and development facilitates and motivates the maintenance organization to conduct a meaningful acceptance test before the system is taken into production. If such an acceptance test is not conducted explicitly, maintenance may be confronted with low-quality software or systems which still need a 'finishing touch' that the development team has left undone for lack of time.

- By specializing on maintenance tasks, a higher quality of user service can be realized. By their very nature, development groups are focused on system delivery, whereas maintenance people are service-oriented and find pride in satisfying user requests. We further elaborate upon this issue in Section 14.5.2.

- By concentrating on the systems to be maintained, a higher level of productivity is achieved. Maintenance work requires specific skills of which a more optimal use can be made in a separate organization. If people are involved in both development and maintenance, more staff have to be allocated to maintenance and the familiarity with any particular system is spread more thinly.

On the other hand, the strict separation of development and maintenance has certain disadvantages as well:

- Demotivation of personnel because of status differences, with consequential degradation of quality and productivity

  Managerial attitudes and traditional career paths are the main causes for these motivational problems. Conversely, proper managerial attention to maintenance work goes a large way towards alleviating the morale problem. For example, an organization may decide to hire new people into development only and explicitly consider a transfer to maintenance as a promotion. (Most organizations do exactly the opposite.)

- Loss of knowledge about the system (with respect to both its design and the application domain knowledge incorporated) when the system is transferred from development to maintenance

  Various strategies can mitigate against this loss. For example, a future maintainer of a system may spend some time with the development team, a developer may stay with maintenance until the maintainers have become sufficiently acquainted with the system, or a designer may instruct the maintainers about the design of a system.

- Coordination costs between development and maintenance, especially when the new system replaces an existing one

- Increased cost of system acceptance by the maintenance organization

  If the system is explicitly carried over from development, certain quality and documentation criteria must be met. Within an A-type organization, these requirements can often be relaxed a bit or their fulfillment is postponed. It is by no means clear though that this really incurs an increase in cost. In the long run, it may well be cheaper to accept only systems which pass a proper maintenance acceptance test.

- Possible duplication of communication channels to the user organization.

Based on an analysis of existing departmentalizations and the resulting list of strengths and weaknesses, Swanson and Beath express a slight preference for having development and maintenance as separate organizational units. We concur with that. Careful procedures could be devised that overcome some or all of the disadvantages listed. We should stress that personnel demotivation is a real issue in many organizations. It deserves serious management attention.

Combinations of departmentalization types are also possible. In particular, combinations of A-Type and L-Type departmentalizations are quite common. So, within the maintenance organization, smaller groups may specialize in some application domain, i.e. a specific collection of information systems. This may be termed the L-A-scheme. Conversely, in an A-L-scheme, a small maintenance unit is found within a group that specializes in a certain application area. The L-A-scheme is more likely to exhibit the advantages of the L-scheme than the A-L-scheme does.

Too much specialization is a lurking danger though. A system should never become someone's private property. A variation of the reverse Peter principle applies here: people rise within an organization to a level at which they become indispensable. Job rotation is one way to avoid people becoming too entrenched in the peculiarities of a system. There is a tradeoff though, since such a step also means that in-depth knowledge of a system is sacrificed.

14.5.2 Software Maintenance from a Service Perspective

> Software maintenance organizations need to realize that they are in the
> customer service business.
> Pigoski (1996)

Software development results in a product, a piece of software. Software maintenance
can be seen as providing a service. There are notable differences between products and
services, which mean that the quality of products and services is judged differently.
As a consequence, the quality of software development and software maintenance
is also judged differently and maintenance organizations should pay attention to
service-specific quality aspects.

Apparently, this is not widely recognized yet. Within the software maintenance
domain, the focus is still on product aspects. The final phases of software development
supposedly concern the delivery of an operations manual, installing the software,
handling change requests, and fixing bugs. In practice, the role of an IT department
is much broader during the deployment stage, as is illustrated by the ubiquitous help
desk.

This is confirmed by (Stålhane et al., 1997) who report on a survey to find those
aspects of software quality that customers consider most important. The main insight
to be gained from their study is the strong emphasis customers place on service
quality. The top five factors found in their study are: service responsiveness, service
capacity, product reliability, service efficiency, and product functionality. They also
quote an interesting result from a quality study in the telecommunications domain.
To the question 'Would you recommend others to buy from this company?', 100% of
users that had complained and got a satisfactory result answered 'yes'. Of users that
had not complained, only 87% answered 'yes'. Apparently, it is more important to get
a satisfactory service than to have no problems at all.

The main differences between products and services are as follows:

- Services are **intangible**; products are tangible. This is considered the most basic
  difference between products and services. Services – being benefits or activities – cannot be seen, felt, tasted, or touched, unlike products. Consequently,
  services cannot be counted, stored, patented, readily displayed, or communicated,
  and pricing is more difficult.

- Because services are created by activities, and activities are performed by humans,
  services tend to be more **heterogeneous** than products. Customer satisfaction
  depends on employee actions during the service delivery. Service quality depends
  on factors which are difficult to control, such as the ability of customers to articulate
  their needs, the ability and willingness of personnel to satisfy those needs, the
  presence or absence of other customers, and the level of demand for the service.
  These complicating factors make it hard to know whether the service was delivered
  according to plan or specification.

- Services are produced and consumed **simultaneously**, whereas production and consumption of products can be separated. For example, a car can be produced first, sold a few months later, and then be consumed over a period of several years. For services, production and consumption has to take place in parallel. The production of the service creates the set of benefits, whose consumption cannot be postponed. For example, a restaurant service – preparing a meal and serving the customer – by and large has to be produced while the customer is receiving the service. As a consequence, customers participate in and affect the transaction, customers may affect each other, employees affect the service outcome, and centralization and mass production are difficult.

- Services are **perishable**, products are not. Services cannot be saved or stored. They cannot be returned or resold, and it is difficult to synchronize supply and demand.

The difference between products and services is not clear-cut. Often, services are augmented with physical products to make them more tangible. For example, luggage tags may be provided with a travel insurance policy. In the same way, products are augmented with add-on services, such as a guarantee, to improve the quality perception of the buyer. In the service marketing literature, a product–service continuum is used to indicate that there is no clear boundary between products and services. This product–service continuum has pure products at one end, pure services at the other, and product–service mixtures in between. Figure 14.10 shows some example products and services along this continuum.

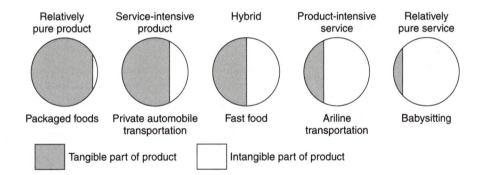

Figure 14.10 The product–service continuum (*Source*: L.L. Berry and A. Parasuraman, *Marketing Services: Competing Through Quality*, ©1991, The Free Press)

As this figure shows, products and services can be intertwined. In the case of fast food, both the product (the food) and the service (quick delivery) are essential to the customer. The quality of such a product–service mix is judged on both product and service aspects: does the food taste good and is it served quickly?

Let us return to the software engineering domain. A major difference between software development and software maintenance is the fact that software development results in a *product*, whereas software maintenance results in a *service* being delivered to the customer. Software maintenance has more service-like aspects than software development, because the value of software maintenance lies in activities that result in benefits for the customers, such as corrected faults and new features. Contrast this with software development, where the development activities themselves do not provide benefits to the customer. It is the resulting software system that provides those benefits.

As noted, the difference between products and services is not clear-cut. Consequently, this goes for software development and software maintenance as well. Figure 14.11 shows the product–service continuum with examples from the software engineering domain.

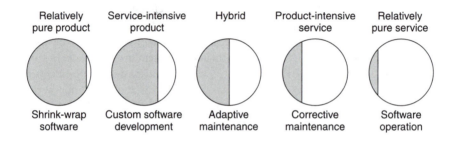

Figure 14.11 The product–service continuum for software development and maintenance

Service marketeers often use the gap model to illustrate how differences between perceived service delivery and expected service may come about. This gap model is depicted in Figure 14.12. Service quality is improved if those gaps are closed.

The difference between the perceived quality and the expected quality (gap 5 in Figure 14.12) is caused by four other gaps. These four gaps, and suggested solutions for bridging them, are:

Gap 1 The expected service as perceived by the service provider differs from the service expected by the customer

In the field of software maintenance, this difference is often caused by an insufficient relationship focus of the service provider. For example, a maintenance department may aim to satisfy certain availability constraints such as 99% availability, while the actual customer concern is with maximum downtime.

It is important for a maintenance organization to translate customer service expectations into clear service agreements. Preferably, the maintenance

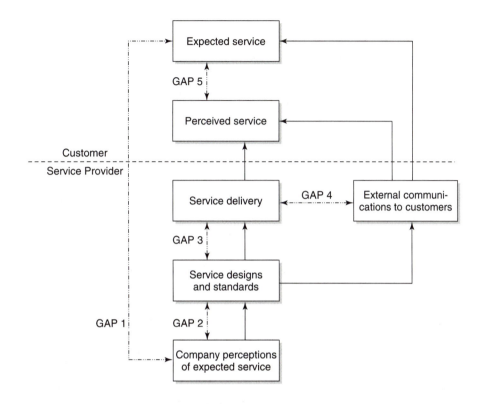

Figure 14.12 The gap model of service quality (*Reprinted with permission from*: A. Parasuraman, V.A. Zeithaml and L.L. Berry, A Conceptual Model of Service Quality and its Implication for Future Research, in *Journal of Marketing* **49**, Fall 1985, pp. 41–50. Published by the American Marketing Association.)

service commitments are specified in a contract – the **Service Level Agreement** – which specifies, amongst other things, the services themselves, the levels of service (i.e. how fast and reliably the service will be delivered), what happens if the service provider does not reach the agreed service levels, when and how the customer will receive reports regarding the services actually delivered, when and how the service level agreement will be reviewed, and so on.

Gap 2 The service specification differs from the expected service as perceived by the service provider

This may arise if the (internal) service designs and standards do not match the service requirements as perceived by the service provider. For example, the customer expects a quick restart of the system, while the standard procedure of the maintenance organization is focused on analyzing the reason for the crash.

The maintenance activities as specified in the service level agreement have to be planned. This includes the planning of the activities themselves, the transfer of the results to the customer, the planning of releases, the estimation of resources needed, the scheduling of maintenance activities, and the identification of possible risks. Explicitly basing the planning of maintenance activities on the commitments as agreed with the customer helps to close this gap.

Gap 3   The actual service delivery differs from the specified services

This is often caused by deficiencies in human resource policies, failures to match demand and supply, and customers not fulfilling their role. For example, customers may bypass the helpdesk by phoning the maintainer of their system directly, thereby hindering a proper incident management process.

The service level agreement states which maintenance activities are to be carried out, and how fast, reliably, etc. this should be done. In order to be able to report on the performance of the maintenance organization in this respect, information about the actual maintenance activities must be gathered. This information can be used to monitor maintenance activities and take corrective actions if necessary.

For example, when the customer reports a bug, information about the bug itself (originator, type, etc.) is recorded, as well as the reporting time, the time when corrective action was started and ended, and the time when the bug was reported as fixed. If this data indicates that the average downtime of a system exceeds the level specified in the service level agreement, the maintenance organization might assign more maintenance staff to this system, put maintenance staff on point-duty at the customer site, renegotiate the agreed upon service level, or take other action to realign agreement and reality.

By keeping a strict eye upon the performance of the maintenance organization and adjusting the maintenance planning or renegotiating the commitments with the customer when required, gap 3 is narrowed.

Gap 4   Communication about the service does not match the actual service delivery

This may be caused by ineffective management of customer expectations, promising too much, or ineffective horizontal communication. For example, a customer is not informed about the repair of a bug he reported.

An important instrument to help close this gap is event management. Event management concerns the management of events that cause or might cause the maintenance activities carried out to deviate from the levels promised in the service level agreement. An event is either a change request, such as a user request for a new feature, or an incident. Incidents are software bugs and other hazards that the maintenance organization has promised to deal with, such as, say, a server being down.

The main purpose of event management is to manage all those events. To do so, an event management library system is employed, often in the form of a 'helpdesk system'. The event management library system provides for the storage, update, and retrieval of event records, and the sharing and transfer of event records between the parties involved. This event management library system supports the communication with the customer about maintenance services delivered. It is also a highly valuable 'memory' for the maintainers: they may use the event library to search for similar incidents, to see why certain components were changed before, etc.[4]

Since the fifth gap is caused by the four other gaps, perceived service quality can be improved by closing those first four gaps, thus bringing the perceived quality in line with the expected quality. Since software maintenance organizations are essentially service providers, they need to consider the above issues. They need to manage their product – software maintenance – as a service in order to be able to deliver high quality.

14.5.3 Control of Maintenance Tasks

Careful control of the product is necessary during software development. The vast amount of information has to be kept under control. Documentation must be kept consistent and up to date. An appropriate scheme for doing so is provided by the set of procedures that make up configuration control; see Chapter 4. Configuration control pays particular attention to the handling of change requests. Since handling change requests is what maintenance is all about, configuration control is of vital importance during maintenance.

Effective maintenance depends on following a rigorous methodology, not only with respect to the implementation of agreed changes, but also with respect to the way change is controlled. Following IEEE Standard 1219, we suggest the following orderly, well-documented process for controlling changes during maintenance:

1. **Identify and classify change requests** Each change request (CR) is given a unique identification number and is classified into one of the maintenance categories (corrective, adaptive, perfective, preventive). The CR is analyzed to decide whether it will be accepted, rejected, or needs further evaluation. This analysis also results in a first cost estimate. The CR is finally prioritized and scheduled for implementation.

---

[4]Note that the focus of the event management library system differs somewhat from that of configuration management as discussed in the next section. Configuration management emphasizes the *internal* use of information about change requests and so on. Our description of event management focuses on the *external* use of essentially the same information. In practice, the two processes may well be combined.

2. **Analysis of change requests** This step starts with an analysis of the CR to determine its impact on the system, the organization, and possible interfacing systems. Several alternative solutions to implement the CR may be devised, including their cost and schedule. The results of the analysis are documented in a report. Based on this report, a decision is made whether or not the CR will be implemented. The authority for this decision is usually assigned to the configuration control board; see also Chapter 4.

3. **Implement the change** This involves the design, implementation, and testing of the change. The output of this step is a new version of the system, fully tested, and well documented.

The above steps indicate a maintenance model in which each change request is carefully analyzed and, if (and only if) the request is approved, its implementation is carried out in a disciplined, orderly way, including a proper update of the documentation. This control scheme fits in well with the **iterative-enhancement** model of software maintenance; see Figure 14.13. The essence of the iterative-enhancement model is that the set of documents is modified starting with the highest-level document affected by the changes, propagating the changes down through the full set of documents. For example, if a change request necessitates a design change, then the design is changed first. Only as a consequence of the design change is the code adapted.

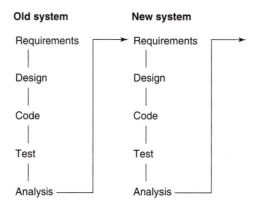

Figure 14.13 Iterative-enhancement model of software maintenance (*Source*: V.R. Basili, Viewing maintenance as reuse-oriented software development, *IEEE Software* **7**(1), pp. 19–25, ©1990, IEEE.)

Reality is often different. Figure 14.14 depicts the so-called **quick-fix** model of software maintenance. In the quick-fix model, you take the source code, make the necessary changes to the code and recompile the system to obtain a new version. The

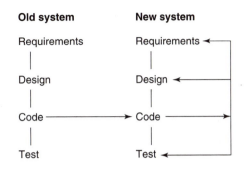

Figure 14.14 Quick-fix model of software maintenance (*Source: V.R. Basili, Viewing maintenance as reuse-oriented software development*, IEEE Software **7**, 1 (1990) 19–25, © 1990 IEEE.)

source-code documentation and other higher-level documents are updated after the code has been fixed and, usually, only if time permits.

In the latter scheme, patches are made upon patches and the structure of the system degrades rather quickly. Because of the resulting increase in system complexity and inconsistency of documents, future maintenance becomes much more difficult. To be realistic, the quick-fix model cannot be completely circumvented. In an emergency situation there is but one thing that matters: getting the system up and running again as fast as possible. Where possible though, the quick-fix model should be avoided. If it is used at all, preventive maintenance activities should be scheduled to repair the structural damage done.

In a normal, non-emergency situation, change requests are often bundled into **releases**. The user then does not get a new version after each and every change has been realized, but after a certain number of change requests has been handled, or after a certain time frame. Three common ways of deciding on the contents and timing of the next release are:

- fixed staff and variable schedule: In this scheme, there is a fixed number of people available for the maintenance work. The next release date is fixed in advance. Often, the release dates are scheduled at fixed time intervals, say every six months. The next release will contain all changes that have been handled within the agreed time frame. So the next release is always on time. There also is some flexibility as to the contents of the next release, since the maintainers and the customer do not fix the contents in advance.

- variable staff and fixed schedule: A release date is fixed in advance. The portfolio of change requests to be handled in this release is also negotiated and fixed in advance. Next, the number of people needed to implement the changes within the fixed time frame is decided. On the way, some renegotiation of both the contents and the schedule is possible. An advantage of this scheme is that change requests are assigned clear priorities and that communication with the customer about the contents of the next release is enforced.

- variable staff and variable schedule: As in the previous scheme, the portfolio of change requests to be handled in the next release is negotiated and fixed in advance. Then, the cost and schedule for this release are negotiated, and the number of maintainers required to achieve it is determined. This scheme requires more planning and oversight than the other two schemes. It is also likely to better accommodate the customer. As with ordinary development, schedule slippages and contents renegotiation are not uncommon in this scheme.

14.5.4 Quality Issues

Changing software impairs its structure. By a conscious application of software quality assurance procedures during maintenance, we may limit the negative effects. If we know the software quality factors that affect maintenance effort and cost, we may measure those factors and take preventive actions accordingly. In particular, such metrics can be used to guide decisions as to when to start a major overhaul of components or complete systems.

Quality control issues get quite some attention during software development. Software quality assurance however should broaden its scope to maintenance as well. The implementation of changes during maintenance requires the same level of quality assurance as development work. The ingredients of software quality assurance procedures, as discussed in Chapter 6, apply equally well to software maintenance.

Software quality assurance can be backed up by measurements that quantify quality aspects. With respect to maintenance, we may focus on measures which specifically relate to maintenance effort, such as counting defects reported, change requests issued, effort spent on incorporating changes, complexity metrics, etc.

Relationships between such measures can then be sought. Observed trends can be used to initiate actions, such as:

- If maintenance efforts correlate well with complexity metrics such as Henri and Kafura's information flow or McCabe's cyclomatic complexity (see Chapter 12), then these complexity metrics may be used to trigger preventive maintenance. Various studies have indeed found such correlations.

- If certain components require frequent changes or much effort to realize changes, then a redesign of such components should be given serious consideration.

- Metrics can be used to spot bad smells and initiate refactoring.

A particularly relevant issue during maintenance is to decide when to reengineer. At a certain point in time, evolving an old system becomes next to impossible and a major reengineering effort is required or the system enters the servicing stage. There are no hard figures on which to decide this, but certain characteristics certainly indicate system degradation:

- frequent system failures;

- overly complex program structure and logic flow;

- code written for previous generation hardware;

- running in emulation mode;

- very large components or subroutines;

- excessive resource requirements;

- hard-coded parameters that are subject to change;

- difficulty in keeping maintenance personnel;

- seriously deficient documentation;

- use of different coding patterns in different parts of the code;

- use of different technologies in a single system (especially proprietary technologies not supported any more);

- missing or incomplete design specifications.

The greater the number of such characteristics present, the greater the potential for redesign.

Improvements in software maintenance requires insight into factors that determine maintenance cost and effort. Software metrics provide such insight. To measure is to know. By carefully collecting and interpreting maintenance data, we may discover the major cost drivers of software maintenance and initiate actions to improve both quality and productivity.

14.6 SUMMARY

Software maintenance encompasses all modifications to a software product after delivery. The following breakdown of maintenance activities is usually made:

- **Corrective maintenance** concerns the correction of faults.

- **Adaptive maintenance** deals with adapting software to changes in the environment.

- **Perfective maintenance** mainly deals with accommodating new or changed user requirements.

- **Preventive maintenance** concerns activities aimed at increasing a system's maintainability.

'Real' maintenance, the correction of faults, consumes approximately 25% of maintenance effort. By far the larger part of software maintenance concerns the evolution of software. This evolution is inescapable. Software models part of reality. Reality changes and so does the software that models it.

Major causes of maintenance problems were discussed in Section 14.2: the existence of a vast amount of unstructured code, insufficient knowledge about the system or application domain on the part of maintenance programmers, insufficient documentation, and the bad image of the software maintenance department.

Some of these problems are accidental and can be remedied by proper actions. Through a better organization and management of software maintenance, substantial quality and productivity improvements can be realized. These issues were discussed in Section 14.5. Obviously, improved maintenance should start with improved development. Opportunities to improve the development process are a major topic in most chapters of this book.

A particularly relevant issue for software maintenance is that of reverse engineering, the process of reconstructing a lost blueprint. Before changes can be realized, the maintainer has to gain an understanding of the system. Since the majority of operational code is unstructured and undocumented, this is a major problem. Section 14.3 addresses reverse engineering, its limitations, and tools to support it.

The fundamental problem is that maintenance will remain a big issue. Because of the changes made to software, its structure degrades. Specific attention to preventive maintenance activities aimed at improving system structure are needed from time to time to fight system entropy.

Software maintenance used to be a rather neglected topic in the software engineering literature. Like programmers, researchers are more attracted to developing new, fancy methods and tools for software development. This situation has changed. Major journals regularly feature articles on software maintenance, there is an annual IEEE Conference on Software Maintenance (since 1985), and the journal *Software Maintenance and Evolution: Research and Practice* (launched 1989) is wholly devoted to it.

14.7 FURTHER READING

(Pigoski, 1996) is a textbook wholly devoted to software maintenance. (Lientz and Swanson, 1980) is a seminal booklet on software maintenance. It introduces the widely known categories of maintenance tasks and provides data on their distribution. More recent data on the distribution of maintenance tasks are given in (Nosek and Palvia, 1990), (Dekleva, 1992) and (Sousa and

Mozeira, 1998). (Chapin *et al.*, 2001) give a new classification of maintenance categories, including a separate category for user support. The maintenance life cycle stages are discussed in (Burch and Kung, 1997) and (Kung and Hsu, 1998). The distinction between an evolution stage and a servicing stage stems from (Bennett and Rajlich, 2000). The distribution of code-related maintenance activities is discussed in (Yu and Chen, 2006). The practice of software maintenance is discussed in (Singer, 1998) and (Tan and Gable, 1998).

The various types of reverse engineering are discussed in (Chikofsky and Cross II, 1990). The 100% functional equivalence issue in reverse engineering is discussed in (Bennett, 1998). Reverse engineering tools are discussed in (Biggerstaff *et al.*, 1994), (Jarzabek and Wang, 1998) and (Bellay and Gall, 1998). Fowler (1999) is the standard text for refactorinig. Mens and Tourwé (2004) provide a survey of software refactoring. Migration is discussed in (Rahgozar and Oroumchian, 2003) and (Bisbal *et al.*, 1999). Programming plans and beacons were originally proposed in (Soloway and Ehrlich, 1984) and (Brooks, 1983). Research addressing the role of these concepts in program comprehension processes is described in (Mayrhauser and Vans, 1995) and (Mayrhauser *et al.*, 1997). (LaToza *et al.*, 2006) discuss developer work habits, including code comprehension, during development and evolution. Example tools to help software maintenance include (Singer *et al.*, 2005) (support for browsing through software), (Rysselberghe and Demeyer, 2004) (visualization of change history), and (Ducasse *et al.*, 2006) (visualization of distribution of system properties).

Gîrba and Ducasse (2006) provide an overview of types of software evolution analysis. The distinction between version-centered and history-centered analysis is made in that article. (Gîrba *et al.*, 2004) discusses the 'yesterday's weather' approach to reverse engineering. Fischer and Gall (2004) and (Greevy *et al.*, 2006) discuss history-centered analysis.

Possible organizations of maintenance activities as well as their major advantages and disadvantages are discussed in (Swanson and Beath, 1990). Yeh and Jeng (2002) discuss the influence of departmentalization on software maintenance. The service perspective on software maintenance is discussed in (Niessink and van Vliet, 1999). The translation into a Capability Maturity Model aimed at maintenance processes is described in (Niessink and van Vliet, 1998a).

The IEEE Process Model for software maintenance is described in (IEEE1219, 1998). The iterative-enhancement and quick-fix models of software maintenance are discussed in (Basili, 1990). Approaches to scheduling releases are the topic of (Stark and Oman, 1997).

The cost of software maintenance, and empirical relations between quality aspects and cost are the topic of (Banker *et al.*, 1993), (Kemerer and Slaughter, 1997), (Henry and Cain, 1997), (Niessink and van Vliet, 1997), and (Koru and Tian, 2005). Indicators of system degradation are given in (Martin and Osborne, 1983).

Exercises

1. Define the following terms: corrective maintenance, adaptive maintenance, perfective maintenance, and preventive maintenance.

2. Discuss the major causes of software maintenance problems.

3. What is reverse engineering?

4. What is refactoring?

5. Characterize the evolution and servicing stage of software maintenance.

6. What is the difference between design recovery and redocumentation?

7. Characterize the version-oriented and history-centered analyses of software evolution data.

8. Why does corrective maintenance have more service-like aspects than product-like aspects?

9. Discuss the iterative-enhancement and quick-fix models of software maintenance.

10. Discuss the major impediments to fully-automated design recovery.

11. Discuss advantages of software configuration control support during software maintenance.

12. Discuss the possible structure and role of an acceptance test by the maintenance organization prior to the release of a system.

13. ♡ An alternative classification of maintenance and development activities is as follows:

    • Functional maintenance = corrective maintenance + adaptive maintenance + non-functional perfective maintenance (i.e. improving quality) + replacement of a system by a functional equivalent.

    • Functional development = functional perfective maintenance (i.e. adding new features) + development of new systems.

    Could this classification provide us with a better picture of the *real* maintenance effort? See also (Krogstie, 1994).

14. ♡ Assess opportunities of knowledge-based support for software maintenance (see (Devanbu *et al.*, 1991) for a very interesting application of such ideas).

15. ♡ Give a primary classification of your maintenance organization as W-, A-, or L-Type (see Table 14.3). What are the major strengths and weaknesses of your particular organization?

16. ♡ Does your organization collect quantitative data on maintenance activities? If so, what type of data and how is it used to guide and improve the maintenance process? If not, how is maintenance planned and controlled?

17. ♠ Study the technical documentation of a system whose development you have been involved in. Does the documentation capture the design rationale? In what ways does it support comprehension of the system? In hindsight, can you suggest ways to improve the documentation for the purpose of maintenance?

18. ♡ Discuss the impact of component reuse on maintainability.

19. ♡ Discuss the possible contribution of object-oriented software development to software maintenance.

20. ♡ Can you think of reasons why 10% change in a program of 200 LOC would take more effort than 20% change in a program of 100 LOC?

15

Software Tools

LEARNING OBJECTIVES

- To be able to distinguish various dimensions along which tools can be classified

- To be aware of the major trends in (collections of) software tools

- To appreciate the role of tools in the software development process

> Software development is generally supported by tools, ranging from those that support a single activity to integrated environments supporting a complete development process. In this chapter, we discuss the main classes of software development tools and their role in the development process.

The demand for software grows faster than the increase in software development productivity and available manpower. The result is an ever-increasing shortage of personnel; we are less and less able to satisfy the quest for software. To turn the tide, we must look for techniques that result in significant productivity gains.

One of the most obvious routes to pursue is automation itself. We may use the computer as a tool in the production of software. In the past, all sorts of things were automated, save software development itself. Programmers knew better than that.

We have long been accustomed to employ the computer as a tool for the implementation of software. To this end, programmers have a vast array of tools at their disposal, such as compilers, linkers, and loaders. Also during testing, tools such as test drivers and test harnesses have been used for a long time. The development of tools to support earlier phases of the software life cycle is more recent. One example of the latter is software to aid the drawing and validation of UML diagrams.

The use of software tools may have a positive effect on both the productivity of the people involved and the quality of the product being developed. Tools may support checking conformance to standards. Tools may help to quantify the degree of testing. Tools may support progress tracking. And so on.

The application of tools in the software development process is referred to as **Computer Aided Software Engineering** (**CASE**). Apart from the traditional implementation and test tools, CASE has a relatively short history. The first tools to support design activities appeared in the early 1980s. Today, the number of CASE products is overwhelming.

As the number of available CASE products proliferates, it becomes expedient to classify them. One way of doing so is according to the breadth of support they offer. Table 15.1 gives a classification of CASE products along this dimension. Some products support a specific task in the software development process. Others support the entire software process. The former are called **tools**, the latter **environments**. In between these two extremes it is useful to identify CASE products that support a limited set of activities, such as those which comprise the analysis and design stages. Such a coherent set of tools with a limited scope is referred to as a **workbench**.

Environments can be further classified according to the mechanism that ties together the individual tools that make up the environment. In a **toolkit**, tools are generally not well integrated. The support offered is independent of a specific programming language or development paradigm. A toolkit merely offers a set of useful building blocks. A **language-centered environment** contains tools specifically suited for the support of software development in a specific programming language. Such

Table 15.1 Classification of CASE products

CASE product	Supports
Tool	One task
Workbench	Limited set of activities
Environment	Entire software process
Toolkit	
Language-centered environment	
Integrated environment	
Process-centered environment	

an environment may be hand-crafted or generated from a grammatical description of the language. In the latter case, the environment tends to focus on the manipulation of program structures.

The essence of **integrated** and **process-centered environments** is the sharing of information between the tools that make up the environment. Integrated environments focus on the resulting product. The heart of an integrated environment is a data repository, containing a wealth of information on the product to be developed, from requirements up to running code. Process-centered environments focus on sharing a description of the software development process.

Obviously, classifying actual CASE products according to this framework is not always easy. For example, many environments that span the complete life cycle evolved from workbenches that supported either front-end activities (analysis and global design) or back-end activities (implementation and test). These environments tend to contain tools specifically geared at supporting tasks from the corresponding part of the life cycle, augmented by a more general support for the other phases (such as for editing, text processing, or database access).

Table 15.2 lists a number of dimensions along which CASE products can be classified. Using all of these dimensions to classify a CASE product yields a faceted classification scheme, which provides more information and is more flexible than the one-dimensional framework of Table 15.1.

No development method is suited for all classes of problems. Likewise, there is no CASE product for all problem classes. Specific properties of a given class of problems will impact the tools for that class. An important property of embedded systems is that the software is often developed on some host machine which is different from the ultimate target machine. Specific tools are required for the development of such systems, for instance tools that allow us to test the software on the host machine.

For many business applications, the human–computer interaction plays a prominent role, while the requirements analysis of such systems tends to be problematic. A development environment for such systems had better contain tools that support those aspects (analyst workbench, prototyping facilities, and facilities to generate screen layouts). As a final example, when developing real-time software, it would be preferable to have tools that allow us to analyze system performance at an early stage.

Table 15.2 Faceted classification structure for CASE products

Dimension	Typical values
Breadth of support	Tool, workbench, or environment
Class of problem	Embedded, business, real-time, . . .
Size of system	Small, medium, or large
User scale	Individual, family, city, or state
Number of sites	1, >1
Process scale	Product, people, or product-and-people
Process support	None, fixed, or variable
Execution paradigm	State machine, Petri net, production rules, procedures, . . .

A second dimension relates the set of tools to the size of the system to be developed. In practice, it shows that tool usage increases with problem size. For a small project, we may confine ourselves to a simple configuration control system, simple test tools, and a shared database system to store documents. In a medium-sized project, more advanced support could be used, for example, a structured database with objects such as design documentation, test plans, or code components. Certain traceability relations between objects, such as A uses B, or A implements B, could be maintained. For a medium-sized project, the toolset would also include tools to support management tasks, for example to create CPM or PERT charts. For a large project, we may require that the tools be mutually compatible. The toolset for a large project will generally also impose more constraints on their users.

The user scale refers to the number of users the product supports. Not surprisingly, the user-scale dimension is closely related to the system size dimension. Larger systems require larger development teams, don't they? Using a sociological paradigm, possible values along the user-scale dimension are called individual, family, city and state. Some products support the individual developer. These products are dominated by issues of software construction and the emphasis is on tools that support software construction: editors, debuggers, compilers, etc. CASE products that offer configuration management and system build facilities can be classified as belonging to the family model of software development environments. In the family model, a great deal of freedom is left to the individual developer, while a number of rules are agreed upon to regulate critical interactions between developers.

This model is not appropriate if projects get really big. Larger populations require more complicated rules and restrictions on individual freedom. Within my family, a few simple rules suffice (Jasper and Marieke take turns in washing dishes) and adjustments and local deviations are easily established (Jasper has a party today and asks Marieke to take over). Within a large company, policies have to be more strictly obeyed and cooperation between individuals is enforced (as in a city). Likewise, toolsets to support the development of large systems should enforce proper cooperation between individual developers.

A state may be viewed as a collection of cities. A company may be viewed as a collection of projects. In the state model, the main concern is with commonality and standardization, to allow developers to switch between projects, to be able to reuse code, designs, test plans, etc.

If development is done at more than one site, we need tools to facilitate collaboration and coordination. On one hand, tools such as those for configuration management and requirements management need to provide support to coordinate development work at multiple sites. On the other hand, tools from the realm of Computer-Supported Cooperative Work (CSCW) could be part of the tool suite. This dimension is also closely related to the user-scale and system-size dimensions, since larger projects tend to be distributed over multiple sites; see also Chapter 20.

The process scale specifies whether the CASE product supports code production activities, people activities, or both. CASE products focusing on code production concentrate on support for the evolution of software. They contain tools to write, compile, test, debug, and configure code. These are all activities done by a computer. Other CASE products concentrate on personnel interactions, such as the scheduling of review meetings. Still others do both. Values along this axis may be termed product, people, and product-and-people.

CASE products may or may not support the development *process*. If the development process is supported, some tools do so on the basis of a predefined model of the process. Others allow the user to define his own process model. If the CASE product supports the development process, it may employ various internal means of guiding the execution (or enactment) of the development process, such as state machines, Petri nets, production rules, or procedures.

The various approaches to collections of software tools are addressed using the simple classification scheme of Table 15.1. Toolkits are discussed in Section 15.1. UNIX is a prime example from this category. Section 15.2 discusses language-centered environments. This encompasses both environments created manually around some given programming language, and environments generated from a grammatical description of the program structures being manipulated. In both cases, the support offered mostly concerns the individual programmer. Sections 15.3 and 15.4 discuss integrated and process-centered environments, respectively. Since most workbenches may be viewed as trimmed-down integrated environments, workbenches are also discussed in Section 15.3.

The discussion below is fairly global in nature. We will skim over details of individual tools. Our aim is to sketch discernible trends in this area and to have a critical look at the possible role of tools in the software development process.

15.1 TOOLKITS

With a toolkit, developers are supported by a rather loosely-coupled collection of tools, each of which serves a specific, well-defined, task. The analogy with a carpenter is obvious. His toolkit contains hammers, screwdrivers, a saw, and so on. These tools each serve a specific task. However, they are not 'integrated' in the way a drill and its attachments are.

The prime example of a toolkit environment is UNIX. UNIX may be viewed as a general support environment, not aimed at one specific programming language, development method, or process model. UNIX offers a number of very convenient, yet very simple, building blocks with which more complicated things can be realized (Kernighan and Mashey, 1981):

- The file system is a tree. The leaves of this tree are the files, while inner nodes correspond to directories. A specific file can be addressed absolutely or relative to the current directory. The addressing is through a pathname, analogous to the selection of method names in Java. Directories are files too, though the user cannot change their contents.

- Files have a very simple structure. A file is but a sequence of characters (bytes). So there are no physical or logical records, there is no distinction between random access files and sequential access files, and there are no file types.

  An I/O device is a file too; if it is opened, it automatically activates a program which handles the traffic with that device. In this way, a user may write programs without knowing (and, indeed, without having to know) where the input comes from or where the output goes to.

- All system programs (and most user programs) assume that input comes from the user's terminal and output is written to that terminal. The user can easily redirect both input and output. Through a call of the form

  ```
  prog < in > out
  ```

  input is read from file `in`, while output is written to file `out`. The program itself need not be changed.

- UNIX offers its users a very large set of small, useful, programs. To name but a few: `wc` counts the number of lines, words, and characters in files; `lpr` prints files; and `grep` does pattern matching.

- Programs can easily be combined to form larger programs. If the output of one program is to serve as input to another program, they can be connected by a *pipe*, denoted by '|'. The following command makes a list of all file names and prints that list:

  ```
  ls | pr
  ```

There is no need for an auxiliary file to store intermediate results.

In this way, users are led to try to reach their goals by gluing existing components together, rather than writing a program from scratch. A disadvantage of UNIX is that there is little consistency in interfaces and the choice of command names. For different programs, the '-k' option, say, may well mean something rather different. To stop a dialog, you may try kill, stop, quit, end, leave, and a few others. If you get tired, CTRL-C is likely to work too.

The average UNIX user knows only a fairly limited subset of the available commands and tools (Fischer, 1986). It is quite likely that, after a while, a workable set of commands will be known and used, and then the learning process stops. Inevitably, the facilities offered under UNIX are far from optimally used.

In UNIX, the different tools have minimal knowledge of the objects they manipulate. Various integrated and process-centered environments have been built on top of UNIX. They make use of the attractive features of UNIX, but try to overcome its disadvantages by imposing more structure.

Besides tools that support the individual programmer, UNIX also offers support for programming-in-the-large, through configuration management and system build facilities such as SCCS and Make. These are discussed in Section 15.3.2.

15.2 LANGUAGE-CENTERED ENVIRONMENTS

Nowadays, most software is developed interactively, changes are made interactively, and programs are tested and executed interactively. Much research in the area of language-centered environments is aimed at developing a collection of useful, user-friendly, effective tools for this type of activity. Since most of these environments focus on supporting programming tasks, this type of environment is often called a **programming environment**. To emphasize their graphic capabilities to manipulate program constructs, they are sometimes called **visual programming environments**.

Environments that are built around a specific programming language exploit the fact that a program entails more than a mere sequence of characters. Programs have a clear structure. This structure can be used to make the editing process more effective, to handle debugging in a structured way, and so on. Knowledge of properties of the objects to be manipulated can be built into the tools and subsequently used by these tools. Well-known early examples of language-centered environments are Interlisp and the Smalltalk-80 environment.

Present-day language-centered environments generally come with a host of components that considerably ease software development. Examples of such environments include Microsoft Studio .NET and Eclipse. The support offered ranges from a set of APIs for generating user interfaces (such as Swing), to facilities for handling persistence (EJB) or creating Web applications (Ajax). The richness of features comes with a price: a rather long learning curve.

15.3 INTEGRATED ENVIRONMENTS AND WORKBENCHES

This section is devoted to CASE products that support (parts of) the software development process. Depending on the scope of the set of tools available, such an environment is called an Analyst WorkBench (AWB), a Programmer WorkBench (PWB), a Management WorkBench (MWB), or an Integrated Project Support Environment (IPSE); see also Figure 15.1. The acronym CASE (Computer-Aided Software Engineering) is often used to indicate any type of tool support in the software development process. The qualified terms Upper CASE and Lower CASE refer to tool support during the analysis–design and implementation–test phases, respectively.

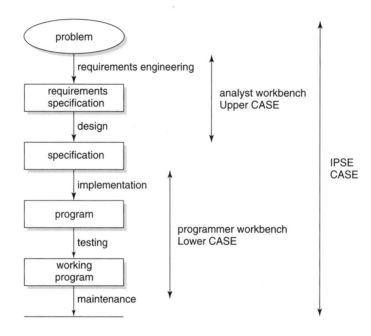

Figure 15.1 Scope of tool sets

In the ideal case, the choice of a specific set of tools will be made as follows. First, a certain approach to the software development process is selected. Next, techniques are selected that support the various phases in that development process. As a last step, tools are selected that support those techniques. Some steps in the development process may not be supported by well-defined techniques. Some techniques may not be supported by tools. Thus, a typical development environment will have a pyramid shape as in Figure 15.2.

In practice, we often find the reverse conical form: a barely developed model of the development process, few well-defined techniques, and a lot of tools. In this

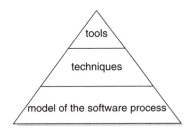

Figure 15.2 Support in a typical development environment

situation, the benefits of the tools are limited at best. To paraphrase the situation: for many a CASE, there is a lot of computer-aided and precious little software engineering.

15.3.1 Analyst WorkBenches

Analyst workbenches serve to support the activities in the early phases of software development: requirements engineering and (global) design. In these phases, analysis and design data is gathered. Often, a graphical image of the system is made, for instance in the form of a set of UML diagrams. From a practical point of view, important problems concern the drawing and redrawing of those diagrams and guarding the consistency and completeness of the data gathered. AWB tools specifically address these points.

The kernel of an AWB is a database in which the information gathered is stored. The structure of the database can be free or it can be derived from the techniques supported. The AWB also contains tools to support the following types of activity:

- Drawing, changing and manipulation of pictures: This may vary from simple drawing programs that have no knowledge of the pictures' semantics, to programs that have an elaborate knowledge of the semantics of the drawing technique in question. As far as the latter is concerned, we may think of automatic generation of pointers to subpictures, the automatic reconfiguration of pictures to circumvent intersecting lines, and so on. If the drawing technique has been sufficiently formalized, the user support can be comparable to that offered by a syntax-directed editor for programming languages.

- Analysis of data produced, as regards consistency and completeness: The possibilities of doing this are strongly dependent upon the degree to which the drawing technique itself imposes strict rules. There is a choice as to when this checking takes place. If the user is immediately notified when an error is made, there is little chance for errors to cascade. On the other hand, the freedom to 'play' during the exploratory development stages is also limited. If checking is done at a later stage, the user may continue on the wrong track for quite a while before detection, and it then becomes more difficult to identify the proper error messages.

- Managing information: A prime example is managing requirements. A simple way is to store them in a plain text document. More advanced tools allow for maintaining relations between requirements, tracing requirements to design documents, detecting and handling conflicts, and so on.

- Generating reports and documentation: It is important to be able to adapt the precise form of reports and documentation to the requirements of the user. For instance, internal standards of some organization may enforce certain report formats. It should be possible to configure the tools to adhere to these standards.

Further tools of an AWB may support, amongst others, prototyping, the generation of user interfaces, or the generation of executable code. (Post *et al.*, 1998) found that users perceive two types of (Upper-CASE) tool: those that are good at supporting analysis and design tasks and those that are good at code generation and prototyping. Apparently, the tools tend to emphasize one of these uses.

15.3.2 Programmer WorkBenches

A programmer workbench consists of a set of tools to support the implementation and test phases of software development. The term originated in the UNIX world (Dolotta *et al.*, 1978). The support offered by UNIX mainly concerns these types of activity. Many programming environments constructed around a certain programming language also support these phases in particular. In a PWB, we find tools to support, among others:

- editing and analysis of programs;

- debugging;

- generation of test data;

- simulation;

- test coverage determination.

The tools that support teamwork on large projects deserve our special attention. In a typical environment, a group of programmers will be working on the same system. The system will have many components, developed, tested, and changed by different people. During the evolution of the system, different versions of components will result. Automatic support for the control of such a set of components, both technically and organizationally, is a sheer necessity.

    One of the early systems for configuration control is the source code control system (SCCS), originally developed for IBM OS and best known from UNIX. SCCS enables the user to keep track of modifications in files (which may contain such diverse things as program code, documentation, or test sets). The system enables the user to generate any version of the system. New versions can be generated without old versions being lost. Important aspects of SCCS are:

- no separate copies of versions are kept: only the modifications (so-called deltas) to previous versions are stored;

- access to files is protected: only authorized users can make changes;

- each file is identified by author, version number, and date and time of modification;

- the system asks the user for information on the reason for a change, which change was made, where, and by whom.

Figure 15.3 illustrates the main operations provided by SCCS. Within SCCS, all information is kept in **s-files**. The operation `create` creates the s-file for the first time. If the original file is named `prog`, then the SCCS file is named `s.prog`. The operation `get` yields a read-only copy of the file requested. This read-only copy can be used for compiling, printing, and so on. It is *not* intended to be edited. The operation `edit` retrieves a copy to be edited. SCCS takes care of protection in the sense that only one person can be editing a file at one time. Finally, the `delta` operation stores the revised version of the file edited.

Versions of SCCS files are numbered, 1.1, 1.2, 1.3, 2.1, etc. The number to the left of the period is the major version number (release number). The number to the

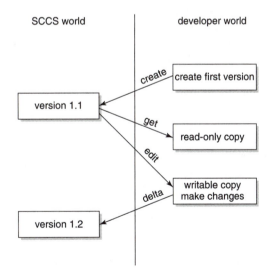

Figure 15.3 Main operations of SCCS

right of the period is the minor version number. The first version is numbered 1.1. By default, `get` and `edit` retrieve the latest version of a file, while `delta` results in an increase of the minor version number. If an older version is required or the major version number is to be increased, this must be specified explicitly.

The above scheme results in a linear sequence of versions. SCCS also provides the possibility of creating branches (**forks**), as illustrated in Figure 15.4. For example, starting from version 1.2 we may create versions 1.3, 1.4, etc to represent normal development of a system component, and versions 1.2.1.1, 1.2.1.2, etc to represent bug fixes in version 1.2. In SCCS, the merging of development paths must be done manually.

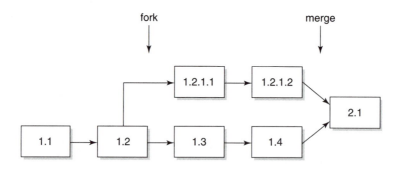

Figure 15.4 Forking and merging of development paths

When different versions of the same system are maintained in this way, the need to automate the construction of new executable versions arises. Make is a tool that does this (Feldman, 1978). Make uses a description of the various components of a system and their mutual dependencies. When generating a new executable system, Make inspects the date and time of the latest changes to components and only recompiles components when needed (i.e. components that have been changed since the last compilation). A tool such as Make not only saves machine time, but also ensures that the most recent version of each component is used.

The basic functionality of configuration control systems has not fundamentally changed since the development of SCCS in the early 1970s. Rather than keeping a copy of each version, SCCS and similar systems only keep track of what has changed from the previous version (the deltas). Nowadays, disk storage is not an issue and many software configuration systems use simple zip-like compression instead of deltas. Additional features offered in present-day systems are mainly directed at increasing the flexibility and usability of such systems:

- The ability to symbolically tag file versions: If the repair of some bug requires changes in a number of modules, each of these revised modules may be given the same tag, say `bug27`. In a subsequent build of the system, this tag `bug27` may then be used to reference file versions in which this bug has been taken care of. This frees the user from the need to remember that the bug concerns version 1.12 of module A, version 1.3.1.7 of module B, etc.

- The ability to automatically merge branches: This is by no means a foolproof operation and should be used with care. The possibility of merging branches hinges on the availability of appropriate merge tools. If changes are made in disjoint parts of a file, merge tools can generally merge these changes fully automatically.

- Flexible support for multiple developers working on the same system: In SCCS, only one person can be editing a file at a time. This rather restrictive scheme is known as **reserved checkout**. It may unnecessarily restrict the work in a team. For example, one developer may check out a file he is not going to work on until next week. However, the fact that he did so prevents other developers from working on that file during this week. In another model, known as **unreserved checkout**, each developer has a working copy of a file. After a while, one developer writes back his updated copy of that file, and other developers will be notified if they want to do the same. These other developers will then, one by one, have to merge their changes with the already updated copy.

- Management of **workspaces**: Checked-out files are put in a workspace. This may be as simple as the home directory of a developer, or more complex and supported by additional tools. For instance, as well as the files a developer is about to change, files that are needed to compile and test changes may be automatically downloaded.

- Support for communication within a development team: For example, if one developer checks out a file someone else is already working on, he may be given a notification of this, so that the developers can start a dialog and coordinate their activities. The latter type of support connects the pure archival function of configuration control systems with the communication and coordination functions of workflow management systems.

Language-centered environments, as discussed in Section 15.2, support the individual developer. These environments are dominated by issues of software construction. The emphasis is on tools that support software construction: editors, debuggers, compilers, etc. Toolsets that offer configuration management and system build facilities such as those offered by SCCS and Make can be classified as belonging to the family model of software development environments: a great deal of freedom is left to individual developers, while a number of rules are agreed upon to regulate critical interactions between developers.

Most programmer workbenches offer this family type of support. For example, Make assumes that files whose names end in .c are C source files. Members of the development family follow this rule and may even have agreed upon further naming conventions. The development environment however has no way of enforcing those rules. It is up to management to make sure that the rules are followed.

15.3.3 Management WorkBenches

A management workbench contains tools that assist the manager during planning and control of a software development project. Example tools in an MWB include:

- **Configuration control** Besides the control of software components as discussed in the previous section, we may also think of the control of other project-specific information, such as design and analysis data, or documentation. An essential aspect of this type of configuration control concerns the control of change requests. Changes are proposed, assessed, approved or rejected, given a priority and cost estimate, planned, and executed. The corresponding procedures are described in a configuration control plan. The administration and workflow of those change requests may well be supported through a tool. See also Chapter 4.

- **Work assignment** Given a number of components, their mutual dependencies, and resources needed (both people and hardware), tools can be used to determine critical paths in the network of tasks, and work packages may be assigned accordingly. This is a central feature of process-centered environments; see Section 15.4.

- **Cost estimation** Various quantitative cost-estimation models have been developed. These models yield cost estimates, based on project characteristics. Tools have been developed that assist in gathering quantitative project data, calibrating cost estimation models based on this data, and making cost estimates for new projects.

15.3.4 Integrated Project Support Environments

An integrated project support environment (IPSE) is meant to support all phases of the software life cycle. Thus, such an environment has to contain the various tools discussed in the previous sections. Environments that span the complete life cycle usually emphasize the support of either front-end activities (analysis and global design – Upper CASE) or back-end activities (implementation and testing – Lower CASE). They then contain tools specifically geared at supporting tasks from the corresponding part of the life cycle, augmented by more general support for the other phases (such as for editing, text processing, or database access).

When developing an IPSE, we may strive for either a strong or a weak integration of its tools. A strong integration, as realized in the language-centered environments discussed in Section 15.2, has both advantages (such as better control capabilities) and disadvantages. One disadvantage is that such an IPSE tends to be less flexible. If the tools are not integrated, as in UNIX, there is more flexibility. On the other hand, more stringent management control is then needed.

We may also look for intermediate forms. For example, all objects may be stored in the UNIX file system, controlled by SCCS, and the relationships between objects may be represented using a relational database system.

The heart of an integrated environment is the data repository, containing the information shared between the tools that make up the environment. The constraints imposed on the structure of this repository mirror the degree to which the tools are integrated. A stricter integration of tools allows for a stricter definition of the structure of the data they share, and vice versa.

15.4 PROCESS-CENTERED ENVIRONMENTS

In a process-centered software engineering environment (PSEE), a description of the software development process is shared by the tools that make up the environment. Not surprisingly, developments in process-centered environments are closely tied to developments in process modeling, and vice versa. For example, the kinds of description used in process modeling (state transition diagrams, Petri nets, and so on) are also the formalisms used in PSEEs. Process modeling is discussed in Section 3.7.

As with an integrated environment, a process-centered environment may cover the complete life cycle. As with an IPSE, a PSEE tends to be geared towards supporting tasks from a specific part of the software development life cycle. Since back-end activities (implementation and testing) are somewhat easier to structure and formalize, work on process modeling and PSEEs has concentrated on modeling and supporting back-end activities.

Figure 15.5 gives a model of the process of conducting a code review. The notation is that of Petri nets. In Section 3.7, this same figure was used to explain the role of different formalisms in process modeling. Here, we discuss its role in a process-centered software engineering environment.

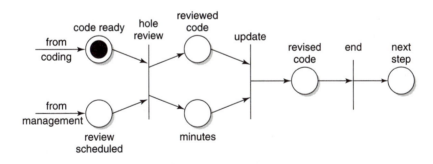

Figure 15.5 Petri net view of the review process

If the developer indicates that some piece of code is ready for review, the environment is notified and comes into a state as indicated in Figure 15.5. Parallel to the coding activity, management schedules a review meeting. Once this is done, the place[1] labeled `review scheduled` is marked. The support environment then 'knows' that the review can be held and may offer support for

---

[1]See Section 3.7 for the terminology of Petri nets.

doing so. In this way, the environment guides the developers and other participants through the steps of the review process, alerts them when certain actions
are required, maintains status information of code products and other pieces of
information, etc. Thus, PSEEs provide support for software development by automating routine tasks, invoking appropriate development tools, and enforcing rules and
practices.

Formal models of a software process are rigid. In practice, this rigidity is a
hindrance, since there will always be exceptions. For example, the minutes of a
review meeting might get lost, management may decide to skip a certain review
meeting, a review meeting may have to be rescheduled because some participant
was ill, etc. The Petri model of Figure 15.5 cannot cope with these situations.
A number of them can be accommodated by making the model more complex.
But the model will never cover all situations. There is thus a need to be able to
intervene. Some PSEEs, for example, offer a way of updating process models on
the fly. A fully satisfactory solution is difficult to find and the rigidity of formal
models is likely to continue to conflict with the requirements of flexibility in process
support.

This holds even more where it supports the early stages of software development. A designer or requirements engineer is not helped by an environment that
dictates the detailed order of process steps to be taken. Broadly speaking, we may
distinguish two types of activity: the unstructured, creative, and cooperative activities
that characterize the early stages of software development; and the repetitive and
structured activities that characterize the later stages. A similar dichotomy may be
observed in PSEEs. Those that focus on the early stages have much in common
with groupware and computer-supported cooperative work (CSCW) systems. These
PSEEs support coordination of activities, such as access to and sharing of information,
and cooperation activities, such as communication between people and scheduling
meetings. This type of support is becoming increasingly important in present-day
multisite development; see also Chapter 20. PSEEs focusing on the later stages have
much in common with workflow management and configuration control systems.
Present-day configuration control systems not only offer the basic versioning and
access capabilities known from systems such as SCCS (see Section 15.3.2) but they
also offer ways to define and enact software configuration tasks and policies. Some
even claim that configuration management tools are the 'real' PSEEs (Conradi *et al.*,
1998).

15.5 SUMMARY

Developments in the area of (integrated) collections of tools move very fast. For
many a facet of the software development process, good tools are available. In
this chapter, we have discussed the major developments as regards computer-aided
software engineering (CASE). We have done so using a simple, one-dimensional

classification of CASE products, which expresses the parts of the life cycle they support:

- a **tool** supports one specific task;

- a **workbench** supports a limited set of activities, such as those which comprise the implementation and testing stages;

- an **environment** supports the entire process.

We have further classified environments according to the mechanism that ties together the tools that make up the environment:

- In a **toolkit**, the tools are generally not so well integrated. A toolkit merely offers a set of useful building blocks. UNIX is a prime example of this.

- A **language-centered environment** contains tools specifically aimed at supporting software development in a specific programming language.

- An **integrated environment** contains tools that share information about the resulting product. This information is stored in a data repository, and the tools read and write this repository.

- A **process-centered environment** contains tools that share a description of the software-development process.

Though environments are supposed to cover the entire life cycle, they tend to emphasize certain parts of the process. They then contain tools specifically geared at supporting tasks from that part of the process, augmented by a more general, and often limited, support for the other parts. For example, language-centered environments tend to focus on the implementation and testing stages.

One of the major impediments to the widespread use of tools is their rigidity. Software tools are driven by formal models of what can and cannot be done. A tool for requirements engineering is likely to enforce certain rules of well-formedness on the diagrams it handles. A tool to support the testing process is likely to prescribe a certain order of process steps. The requirements engineer, though, may well want to play with ill-formed diagrams for a while. Likewise, the tester may want to deviate from the pre-established order of steps if circumstances require this. The tension between the demands for flexibility of tool users and those for formality of tool builders is one of the major challenging research themes in this area.

In a retrospective of PSEE research, Cugola and Ghezzi (1998) refer to this tension as the minimalist versus maximalist approaches. In a maximalist approach, the goal is to model all possible situations. A minimalist approach is more lightweight and acknowledges that humans play a decisive role in the decision process. A further corollary is that tools should support cooperation rather than automation.

An interesting open question is whether tools really help. Studies of tool adoption and usage show mixed results. Some conclude that tools offer real improvements, while others conclude that users have not found tools to be helpful. There are definitely certain impediments to tool adoption. Tools cost money, sometimes a lot of money. There is also a learning curve for tool users. Finally, there is quite a gulf between the state of the art as reported in this chapter and actual practice.

For many an organizational problem, automation seems to be the panacea. Likewise, the use of tools is often seen as panacea for our problems in software engineering: CASE as prosthesis. Tools, though, remain mere tools. Within the software development process, other factors play a role as well. If the tools do not fit the procedures used within your organization, they are likely to have a far from optimal effect. Also, tools cannot make up for an ineffective development method or badly qualified personnel. Good people deliver good products and mediocre people deliver mediocre products, irrespective of the tools they use.

15.6 FURTHER READING

An early taxonomy of CASE products is given in (Dart *et al.*, 1987). Fuggetta (1993) extended this framework with a category of 'process-centered environments'. The latter classification is used in this chapter. Additional dimensions for classifying CASE products are given in (Lott, 1993). Lundell and Lings (2004) discuss how perceptions of CASE have changed over the years. The sociological paradigm (individual, family, etc.) for the user scale stems from (Perry and Kaiser, 1991).

(Barstow *et al.*, 1984) is a collection of seminal articles on programming environments, including the UNIX toolkit approach and early language-centered environments such as Interlisp. The Source Code Control System (SCCS) is described in (Rochkind, 1975). The state of the art in configuration management is reflected in (Estublier *et al.*, 2005). Building tools have not changed much since Make (Feldman, 1978). A recent development in this area in the Java world is Ant (Serrano and Ciordia, 2004).

In the 1980s, tool research focused on creating integrated environments. (Tahvanainen and Smolander, 1990) is an annotated bibliography of articles on software engineering environments from that period. Subsequent research in the area of tools focused on PSEEs. The state of the art in this area is reflected in (Fuggetta and Wolf, 1996) and (Ambriola *et al.*, 1997). The case for more flexibility in software engineering environments is made in (Jankowski, 1994), (Cugola *et al.*, 1996), (Jarzabek and Huang, 1998), and (Cugola and Ghezzi, 1998).

Tool integration issues are addressed in (Sharon and Bell, 1995). Tools assessment is the topic of (Software, 1996b). Studies of tool adoption and usage can be found in (Iivari, 1996) and (Post *et al.*, 1998).

Exercises

1. What does the acronym CASE stand for?

2. Define the following terms:

   - tool,
   - workbench,
   - environment.

3. What are the main distinguishing features of:

   - a toolkit,
   - a language-centered environment,
   - an integrated environment, and
   - a process-centered environment.

4. What is the difference between Upper CASE and Lower CASE?

5. What is the basic functionality of a tool for configuration management?

6. Discuss the fundamental tension between formality and informality in tools.

7. Why is the user scale an important issue when considering the adoption of tools?

8. ♡ Defend the statement that configuration management tools are the only 'real' process-centered environments (see (Conradi *et al.*, 1998)).

9. ♠ For the development environment you are currently working in, prepare a list of:

   - utilities you use on a regular basis;
   - utilities you use infrequently or vaguely know about.

Next compare these lists with the manuals describing the environment. What percentage of the environment's functionality do you really need?

10. ♠ Select and evaluate some commercial UML modeling tool using the criteria given in (Zucconi, 1989) or (Baram and Steinberg, 1989).

11. ♡ Discuss the possible role of automatic support for configuration control in the management of artifacts other than source code modules.

12. ♡ One of the claims of CASE-tool providers is that CASE dramatically improves productivity. At the same time though, customers seem to be disappointed with CASE and take a cautionary stand. Can you think of reasons for this discrepancy?

13. ♡ Why is tool integration such an important issue?

Part III
Advanced Topics

CONTENTS

In this third part, we discuss a number of additional important issues concerning large-scale software development.

Chapter 16 addresses issues that have to do with human factors that are relevant for the development of interactive systems. The approach taken in this chapter can be summarized as 'The user interface *is* the system'.

The next three chapters deal with software reuse. Chapter 17 gives a broad overview of the topic and the other two chapters zoom in on specific forms of software reuse. Chapter 18 deals with component-based software engineering (CBSE). In CBSE, we try to compose systems out of ready-made building blocks, much like a car is composed out of ready-made building blocks. Chapter 19 deals with service orientation. A service can be seen as a component that is searched for and discovered dynamically.

Finally, Chapter 20 deals with global software development. Nowadays, software development often is not done by a collocated team. Rather, members of a team are scattered around the globe. This has repercussions for the way development projects are managed and executed.

16

User Interface Design

With Gerrit C. van der Veer, Open University, Heerlen, The Netherlands

LEARNING OBJECTIVES

- To be aware of different architectural styles for interactive systems

- To appreciate the role of different types of expertise in user interface design

- To be aware of the role of various models in user interface design

- To understand that a user interface entails considerably more than what is represented on the screen

- To recognize the differences between a user-centered approach to the design of interactive systems and other requirements engineering approaches

Software systems are used by humans. Cognitive issues are a major determinant of the effectiveness with which users go about their work. Why is one system more understandable than another? Why is system X more 'user-friendly' than system Y? In the past, the user interface was often only addressed after the system had been fully designed. However, the user interface concerns more than the size and placement of buttons and pull-down menus. This chapter addresses issues about the human factors that are relevant to the development of interactive systems.

Today, user needs are recognized to be important in designing interactive computer systems, but as recently as 1980, they received little emphasis.
Grudin (1991)

We can't worry about these user interface issues now. We haven't even gotten this thing to work yet!
(Mulligan *et al.*, 1991)

A system in which the interaction occurs at a level which is understandable to the user will be accepted faster than a system where it is not. A system which is available at irregular intervals or gives incomprehensible error messages, is likely to meet resistance. A 1992 survey found that 48% of the code of applications was devoted to the user interface, and about 50% of the development time was devoted to implementing that part of the application (Myers and Rosson, 1992). Often, the user interface is one of the most critical factors as regards the success or failure of a computerized system. Yet, most software engineers know fairly little about this aspect of our trade.

Users judge the quality of a software system by the degree in which it helps them to accomplish their tasks and by the sheer joy they have in using it. This judgment is to a large extent determined by the quality of the user interface. Good user interfaces contribute to a system's quality in the following ways (Bias and Mayhew, 1994):

- Increased efficiency: If the system fits the way its users work and if it has a good ergonomic design, users can perform their tasks efficiently. They do not lose time struggling with the functionality and its appearance on the screen.

- Improved productivity: A good interface does not distract the user, but rather allows him to concentrate on the task to be done.

- Reduced errors: Many so-called 'human errors' can be attributed to poor user interface quality. Avoiding inconsistencies, ambiguities, and so on, reduces user errors.

- Reduced training: A poor user interface hampers learning. A well-designed user interface encourages its users to create proper models and reinforces learning, thus reducing training time.

- Improved acceptance: Users prefer systems whose interface is well-designed. Such systems make information easy to find and provide the information in a form which is easy to use.

In a technical sense, the user interface often comprises one or more layers in the architecture of a system. Section 16.1 discusses two well-known architectural styles that highlight the place and role of the user interface in interactive systems. A common denominator of these and other schemes is that they separate the functionality of the system from the interaction with the user. In a similar vein, many software engineering methods also separate the design of the functionality from the design of the user interface. The design of the user interface then reduces to a mere design of the screen layout, menu structure, size and color of buttons, format of help and error messages, etc. User interface design then becomes an activity that is only started *after* the requirements engineering phase has finished. It is often done by software engineers who have little specialized knowledge of user interface design.

Software engineers are inclined to model the user interface after the structure of the implementation mechanism, rather than the structure of the task domain. For instance, a structure-based editor may force you to input $\uparrow 10\ 2$ in order to obtain 10^2, simply because the former is easier for the system to recognize. This resembles the interface to early pocket calculators, where the stack mechanism used internally shows itself in the user interface. Similarly, user documentation often follows implementation patterns and error messages are phrased in terms that reflect the implementation rather than the user tasks.

In this chapter we advocate a rather different approach. This approach may be summarized as 'The user interface *is* the system'. This broader view of the concept user interface and the disciplines that are relevant while developing user interfaces are discussed in Section 16.2. Within the approach discussed, the design of the user interface replaces what we used to call requirements engineering. The approach is inspired by the observation that the usability of a system is not only determined by its perceptual appearance in the form of menus, buttons, etc. The user of an interactive system has to accomplish certain tasks. Within the task domain, e.g. sending electronic mail or preparing documents, these tasks have a certain structure. The human–computer interaction (HCI) then should have the same structure, as far as this can be accomplished. Discovering an adequate structuring of the task domain is considered part of user interface design. This discovery process and its translation into user interface representations requires specific expertise, expertise that most software engineers do not possess. Section 16.5 discusses this eclectic approach to user interface design. Its main activities – task analysis, interface specification, and evaluation – are discussed in Sections 16.6 to 16.8.

In order to develop a better understanding of what is involved in designing user interfaces, it is necessary to take a closer look at the role of the user in operating a complex device such as a computer. Two types of model bear upon the interplay between a human and the computer: the user's mental model and the conceptual model.

Users create a model of the system they use. Based on education, knowledge of the system or application domain, knowledge of other systems, general world knowledge, and so on, the user constructs a model, a knowledge structure, of that system. This is called the mental model. During interaction with the system, this mental model is used to plan actions and predict and interpret system reactions. The mental model reflects the user's understanding of what the system contains, how it works, and why it works the way it does. The mental model is initially determined through metacommunication, such as training and documentation. It evolves over time as the user acquires a better understanding of the system. The user's mental model need not be, and often is not, accurate in technical terms. It may contain misunderstandings and omissions.

The conceptual model is the technically accurate model of the computer system created by designers and teachers for their purposes. It is a consistent and complete representation of the system as far as user-relevant characteristics are involved. The conceptual model reflects itself in the system's reaction to user actions.

The central question in human–computer interaction is how to attune the user's mental model and the conceptual model as well as possible. When this is achieved to a higher degree, an interactive system becomes easier to learn and easier to use. Where the models conflict, the user gets confused, makes errors, and gets frustrated. A good design starts with a conceptual model derived from an analysis of the intended users and their tasks. The conceptual model should result in a system and training materials which are consistent with the conceptual model. This, in turn, should be designed such that it induces adequate mental models in the users.

Section 16.4 discusses various models that play a role in HCI. As well as the aforementioned mental and conceptual models, attention is given to a model of human information processing. When interacting with a system, be it a car or a library information system, the user processes information. Limitations and properties of human information processing have their effect on the interaction. Knowledge of how humans process information may help us to develop systems that users can better cope with.

There are many factors that impact human–computer interaction. In this chapter, we just scratch the surface. Important topics not discussed include the socio-economic context of human–computer interaction, input and output media and their ergonomics, and workplace ergonomics. Section 16.10 contains some pointers to relevant literature.

16.1 WHERE IS THE USER INTERFACE?

A computerized library system includes a component to search the library's database for certain titles. This component includes code to implement its function as well as code to handle the interaction with the user. In the old days, these pieces of code tended to be entangled, resulting in one large, monolithic piece of software.

In 1983, a workshop on user interface management systems took place at Seeheim in West Germany (Pfaff, 1985). At this workshop, a model was proposed which separates the application proper from the user interface. This model has become known as the **Seeheim model**.

The Seeheim model (see Figure 16.1) describes the user interface as the outer layer of the system. This outer layer is an agent responsible for the actual interaction between the user and the application. It, in turn, consists of two layers:

- the presentation, i.e. the perceptible aspects including screen design and keyboard layout;

- the dialog, i.e. the syntax of the interaction including metacommunication (help functions, error messages, and state information). If the machine is said to apply a model of its human partner in the dialog, e.g. by choosing the user's native language for command names, this model is also located in the dialog layer.

This conceptualization of the user interface does not include the application semantics, or 'functionality'. In the Seeheim model, the tasks the user can ask the machine to perform are located in another layer, the application interface. Figure 16.1 shows the separation of concerns into three parts. For efficiency reasons, an extra connection is drawn between the application and the display. In this way, large volumes of output data may skip the dialog layer.

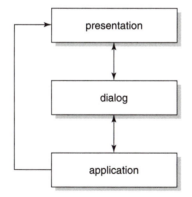

Figure 16.1 The Seeheim model

The Seeheim model provides some very relevant advantages. For example, we may provide the same outer layer to different applications. We may apply the same look and feel to a text editor, a spreadsheet, and so on, as in Microsoft products.

In this way, the user does not have to learn different dialog languages for different applications. Conversely, we may provide a single application to be implemented behind several different outer layers, so as to allow different companies to adopt the same application with their own corporate interface style.

In both these cases, it is assumed that the changes are likely to occur in the interface part of the system, while the application part remains largely unaffected. Alternatively, we may assume that the functionality of the system will change. We then look for an architecture in which parts of the system can be modified independently of each other. A first decomposition of an interactive system along these lines is depicted in Figure 16.2. Each component in this decomposition handles part of the application, together with its presentation and dialog. In a next step, we may refine this architecture such that the input or output device of each component may be replaced. The result of this is shown in Figure 16.3. This result is in fact the Model–View–Controller (MVC) paradigm used in Smalltalk. It is also the archetypal example of a design pattern; see Section 12.5. The dialog and application together constitute the model part of a component. In MVC, the output and input are called view and controller, respectively.

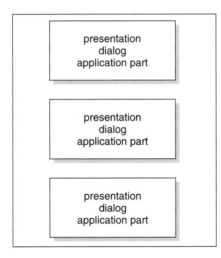

Figure 16.2 A part–whole decomposition of interactive systems

Both the Seeheim model and MVC decompose an interactive system according to quality arguments pertaining to flexibility. The primary concern in the Seeheim model is with changes in the user interface, while the primary concern of MVC is with changes in the functionality. This difference in emphasis is not surprising if we consider the environments in which these models were developed: the

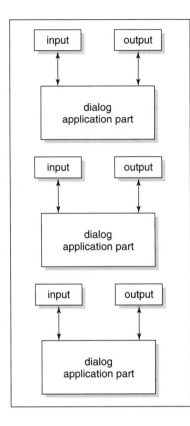

Figure 16.3 The Model – View – Controller paradigm for interactive systems

Seeheim model by a group of specialists in computer graphics and MVC in an exploratory Smalltalk software development environment. Both models have their advantages and disadvantages. The project at hand and its quality requirements should guide the design team in selecting an appropriate separation of concerns between the functionality proper and the part which handles communication with the user.

In many applications, the user interface part is running on one machine, the client, while the application proper is running on another, the server. This of course also holds for Web applications, where the user interface is in the browser. On one hand, there has been a tendency towards 'thin' clients, where *only* the user interface is located at the client side, while all processing takes place at the server side. However, in circumstances where one is not always connected to the Internet, e.g. with mobile devices, one would still like to continue work, and restore data once the connection is re-established. This gives rise to more data manipulation at the client side and, thus, 'fatter' clients (Jazayeri, 2007). The separation between user interface and application, then, is not the same as that between browser and server application.

16.2 WHAT IS THE USER INTERFACE?

The concept 'user interface' has several meanings. It may denote the layout of the screen, 'windows', or a shell or layer in the architecture of a system or the application. Each of these meanings denotes a *designer's* point of view. Alternatively, the user interface can be defined from the point of view of the intended *user* of a system. In most cases, users do not make a distinction between layers in an architecture and they often do not even have a clear view of the difference between hardware and software. For most users an information system as a whole is a tool to perform certain tasks. To them, the user interface *is* the system.

In this chapter, we use the term **user interface** to denote all aspects of an information system that are relevant to a user. This includes not only everything that a user can perceive or experience (as far as it has a meaning), but also aspects of internal structure and processes *as far as the user should be aware of them*. For example, car salesmen sometimes try to impress their customers and mention the horse-power of each and every car in their shop. Most customers probably do not know how to interpret those figures. They are not really interested in them either. A Rolls-Royce dealer knows this. His answer to a question about the horse-power of one of his cars would simply be: 'Enough'. The same holds for many aspects of the internal structure of an information system. On the other hand, the user of a suite of programs including a text editor, a spreadsheet, and a graphics editor should know that a clipboard is a memory structure whose contents remain unchanged until overwritten.

We define the user interface in this broad sense as the **user virtual machine** (UVM). The UVM includes both hardware and software. It includes the workstation or device (gadget) with which the user is in physical contact as well as everything that is 'behind' it, such as a network and remote data collections. In this chapter, we take the whole UVM, including the application semantics, as the subject of (user interface) design.

In many cases, several groups of users have to be distinguished with respect to their tasks. As an example, consider an ATM. One type of user consists of people, bank clients, who put a card into the machine to perform some financial transaction. Other users are specially trained people who maintain the machine and supply it with a stock of cash. Their role is in ATM maintenance. Lawyers constitute a third category of users of ATM machines. They have to argue in favor of (or against) a bank to show that a transaction has been fraudulent, using a log or another type of transaction trace that is maintained by the system. Each of these three user categories represents a different role in relation to the use of the ATM. For each of these roles, the system has a different meaning; each role has to be aware of different processes and internal structures. Consequently, each has a different interface. If we are going to design these interfaces, however, we have to design all of them, and, moreover, we have to design the relation between them. In other words, within the task domain of the ATM, we have to design a *set* of related UVMs, with respect to the tasks that are part of the various roles.

Not only will several groups of users have different interfaces to the same application, but sometimes a single user will have different interfaces to one and the same application as well. This is the case in particular when a user is accessing a system through different devices, such as a mobile phone and a laptop. Not only do these devices have different characteristics, such as the size of the screen and the number of buttons available, but the user is likely to be in a different mood as well: in a hurry and with a lot of distracting noise around him when working via the mobile phone, while in a more quiet environment when working on his laptop. Conceptually, this is not different from the multi-role situation sketched above. Technically, the multi-device user situation poses its own set of challenges (Seffah *et al.*, 2004).

We may look at the user interface from different viewpoints:

- how to design all that is relevant to the user (the design aspect)

- what does the user need to understand (the human side)

In principle these aspects have to be combined, otherwise the user will not understand the system's features. The next section is concerned with the human side. Later sections focus on the design aspects of the user interface.

16.3 HUMAN FACTORS IN HUMAN–COMPUTER INTERACTION

Attention to the user interface is often located in the later phases of the software life cycle. The design approach we elaborate in this chapter, however, requires attention to the human user (or to the different user roles) from the very start of the design process. The various design activities are carried out in parallel and in interaction with each other, even though a large design team may allocate to specialists the tasks of analyzing, specifying, and evaluating user interface aspects. The design of the user interface consists of a complex of activities, all of which are intended to focus on the human side of the system.

The human side cannot be covered by a single discipline or a single technique. There are at least three relevant disciplines: the humanities, artistic design, and ergonomics.

16.3.1 Humanities

In this view we pay attention to people based on psychological approaches (how do humans perceive, learn, remember, think, and feel), and to organization and culture (how do people work together and how does the work situation affect the people's work). Relevant disciplines are cognitive psychology, anthropology, and ethnography. These disciplines provide a theoretical base and associated techniques for collecting information on people's work as well as techniques for assessing newly designed tools and procedures. Designers of the virtual machine or user interface need some insight into the theories and experience with techniques from these disciplines. For example, in specifying what should be represented at a control panel, one may have to consider that less information makes it easier for the user to identify indications of process irregularity (the psychological phenomenon of attention and distraction). On the other hand, if less of the relevant information is displayed, the user may have to remember more, and psychology teaches us that human working memory has a very limited capacity.

16.3.2 Artistic Design

Creative and performing artists in very different fields have developed knowledge on how to convey meaning to their public. Graphical artists know how shapes, colors, and spatial arrangements affect the viewer. Consequently, their expertise teaches interface designers how to draw the attention of users to important elements of the interface. For example, colors should be used sparingly in order not to devalue their possible meaning. Well-chosen use of colors helps to show important relations between elements on the screen and supports users searching for relevant structures in information. Design companies nowadays employ graphical artists to participate in the design of representational aspects of user interfaces.

Complex systems often need a representation of complex processes, where several flows of activity influence each other. Examples of this type of work situation are the team monitoring a complex chemical process and the cockpit crew flying an intercontinental passenger airplane. In such situations, users need to understand complex relations over time. The representation of the relevant processes and their relations over time is far from trivial. Representing in an understandable way what is going on and how the relations change over time is only part of the question. Frequently, such complex processes are safety critical, which means that the human supervisor needs to make the right decision very soon after some abnormal phenomenon occurs, so immediate detection of an event as well as immediate understanding of the total complex of states and process details is needed. Experts in theater direction turn out to have knowledge of just this type of situation. This type of interface may be compared with a theater show, where an optimal direction of the action helps to make the audience aware of the complex of intentions of the author and the cast (Laurel, 1990, 1993). Consequently, theater sciences are another source for designing interfaces to complex processes.

Another type of artistic expertise that turns out to be very relevant for interface design is cinematography. Film design has resulted in systematic knowledge of the representation of dynamics and processes over time (May and Barnard, 1995). For example, there are special mechanisms to represent the suggestion of causality between processes and events. If it is possible to graphically represent the causing process with a directional movement, the resulting event or state should be shown in a location that is in the same direction. For example, in an electronic commerce system, buying an object may be represented by dragging that object to a shopping cart. If the direction of this movement is to the right of the screen, the resulting change in the balance should also be shown to the right.

In the same way there are 'laws' for representing continuity in time. In a movie, the representation of a continuing meeting between two partners can best be achieved by ensuring that the camera viewpoints do not cross the line that connects the location points of the two partners. As soon as this line is crossed, the audience will interpret this as a jump in time. This type of expertise helps the design of animated representations of processes and so on.

In general, artists are able to design attractive solutions, to develop a distinctive style for a line of products or for a company, and to relate the design to the professional status of the user. There are, however, tradeoffs to be made. For example, artistic design sometimes conflicts with ergonomics. When strolling through a consumer electronics shop you will find artistic variants of mobile phones, coffee machines, and audio systems where the designer seems to have paid a tribute to artistic shape and color, while making the device less intuitive and less easy to use, from the point of view of fitting the relevant buttons to the size of the human hand. A similar fate may befall a user interface of an information system.

16.3.3 Ergonomics

Ergonomics is concerned with the relation between human characteristics and artifacts. Ergonomics develops methods and techniques to allow adaptation between humans and artifacts (whether physical tools, complex systems, organizations, or procedures). In classical ergonomics, the main concern is anthropometrics (statistics of human measures, including muscle power and attributes of human perception). During the past 25 years, **cognitive ergonomics** developed as a field that focuses mainly on characteristics of human information processing in interaction with information systems. Cognitive ergonomics is increasingly considered to be the core view for managing user interface design. A cognitive ergonomist is frequently found to be the leader of the design team as far as the virtual machine is concerned.

For beginning users, the human–computer conversation is often very embarrassing. The real beginner is a novice in using a specific computer program. He might even be a novice in computer use in general. Sometimes he is also relatively new to the domain of the primary task (the office work for which he will use the PC or the monitoring of the chemical process for which the computer console is the front end). In such a situation, problems quickly reach a level at which an expert is asked for help and the user tends to blame the program or the system for his failure to use the new facility.

There seems to be a straightforward remedy for this dilemma: start by educating the user in the task domain, next teach him everything about the facility, and only thereafter allow him access to the computer. This, however, is only a theoretical possibility. Users will insist on using the computer from the outset, if they intend ever to use it, and introducing a task domain without giving actual experience with the system that is designed for the task is bad education. So the cure must be found in another direction. The designer of the system must start from a detailed 'model of the user' and a 'model of the task'. If he knows that the user is a novice both on the task domain and on the system, he will have to include options for learning both these areas at the same time.

In general, the system designer will try to apply cognitive ergonomic knowledge and adapt the interface to the intended task rather than vice versa. The system should be made transparent (unobtrusive) as far as anything but the intended task is concerned. This should facilitate the user's double task: to delegate tasks to the system and to learn how to interact with the system. However, in many cases this cannot be accomplished completely in one direction and a solution has to be found by adapting the human user to the artifact, i.e. by teaching and training the user or by selecting users that are able to work with the artifacts. Adapting the user to the artifacts requires a strong motive, though. Constraints of available technology, economic aspects, and safety arguments may contribute to a decision in this direction. A mobile phone has only a few keys and a fairly small screen. Instead of designing an 'intuitive' airplane cockpit that would allow an average adult to fly without more than a brief series of lessons, analogous to driving a car, most airlines prefer to thoroughly select and train their pilots.

Cognitive ergonomics developed when information technology started to be applied by people whose expertise was not in the domains of computer science or computer programming. The first ideas in this field were elaborated more or less simultaneously in different parts of the world, and in communities that used different languages, which resulted in several schools with rather specific characteristics. Much of the early work in the US and Canada, for instance, is based on applying cognitive ergonomics to actual design problems. Also, success stories (such as the development of the Xerox Star) were, after the fact, interpreted in terms of ergonomic design concepts (Smith *et al.*, 1982). Carroll (1990) describes this as 'the theory is in the artifact'. Conversely, European work in the field of cognitive ergonomics has concentrated on the development of models: models of computer users, models of human–computer interaction, models of task structures, and so on. By now, these differences are fading away, but a lot of important sources still require some understanding of their cultural background.

16.4 THE ROLE OF MODELS IN HUMAN–COMPUTER INTERACTION

The concept of a *model* has an important place in the literature on human–computer interaction and cognitive ergonomics. Models represent relevant characteristics of a part of reality that we need to understand. At the same time, models are abstract: they represent only what is needed, thus helping us to find our way in complex situations. We need to be aware of differences between types of model, though, and of the inconsistent use of names for the various types of model. First, we discuss the difference between internal and external models in human–computer interaction.

Internal models are models 'for execution'. Internal models use an agent (a human or a machine) who makes a decision based on the behavior of the model. If the agent is human, this model is termed a **mental model** in psychology. Humans apply these models whenever they have to interact with complex systems. We discuss mental models in Section 16.4.2.

If the agent is a machine, the internal model is a program or a knowledge system. For example, a user interface may retain a model of the user. In that case the literature mostly speaks of a **user model**: a model of the user that is used by the interface. The model could help the interface to react differently to different users or, alternatively, to adjust to the current user depending on the machine's understanding of that user's current goals or level of understanding. User models of this type may be designed to learn from user behavior and are commonly used in so-called intelligent user interfaces. A third type of internal model in machines is a model of the task domain, which enables the user and the system to collaborate in solving problems about the task. The latter type of internal model leads to systems that can reason, critique user solutions, provide diagnosis, or suggest user actions. User models are not discussed further in this book.

External models are used for communication and, hence, are first of all represented in some type of formalism (which could also be a graphical representation such as a Petri net or flow diagram). The formalism should be chosen in relation to what is being modeled, as well as to the goal of the communication. In designing user interfaces, there are several domains where external models are needed. Designers need to understand some relevant aspects of the user, especially human information processing. Cognitive psychology provides such types of knowledge, hence in Section 16.4.1 we briefly discuss a recent variant of the model of human information processing, only mentioning those aspects that are relevant when designing for users of computers. Another type of model is used in the various types of design activity. These external models help designers to document their decisions, to backtrack when one design decision overrules another, and to communicate the result of one design phase to people responsible for another phase (e.g. to communicate a view of the task to a colleague responsible for usability evaluation). In Section 16.4.3, we give some examples of external models used in various design activities. These models are the HCI-oriented counterparts of the requirements representation formats discussed in Chapter 9.

Some types of model, such as task knowledge models, refer to aspects that are both internal and external. Task knowledge is originally to be found in the memory of human beings, in documents about the work domain, and in the actual situation of the work environment. These are internal models, applied while doing the work. Designers need to understand this knowledge and apply it as the base of their design, hence they need to perform task analysis and model the task knowledge. This is an external model for use in design. Task models and task modeling are treated in Section 16.6.

16.4.1 A Model of Human Information Processing

The model of human information processing is an example of an external model. We only briefly mention some notions that need to be understood in analyzing human–computer interaction. We focus on human perception, memory, and the processing of information in relation to the input and output of the human in interaction with an outside system. Figure 16.4 depicts this model. In textbooks on psychology, a figure such as this is often adorned with formulae that allow calculation of the speed of processing, the effect of learning, etc.

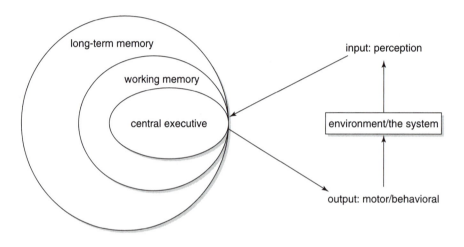

Figure 16.4 A model of human information processing

In modern cognitive psychology, perception (the input of human information processing) is considered to proceed through a number of phases:

1. Edge detection: the large amount of unstructured information that bombards our senses is automatically and quickly structured, e.g. into phonemes (hearing) or a '2.5-D sketch' based on movement, color, and location (vision).

2. Gestalt formation: a small number of understandable structures (such as a triangle, a word, and a tactile shape) known as 'gestalts' are formed, based on similarities detected in the sketch, on spatial relations and on simplicity.

3. Combination: the gestalts are combined into groups of segments that seem to belong together: an object consisting of triangles, cubes and cylinders; a spoken utterance consisting of a series of words.

4. Recognition: the group of segments is recognized as, for example, a picture of a horse or a spoken sentence.

The processing in the later phases is done less and less automatically. People are aware of gestalt formation and combination when any problem arises, for example because of irregularity or exceptional situations such as 'impossible' figures. Recognition leads to conscious perception.

The whole series of phases takes a fraction of a second. It takes more time when a problem occurs because of an unexpected or distorted stimulus. It takes less time when the type of stimulus is familiar. So we may train our computer users to perceive important signals quickly and we may design our signals for easy and quick detection and discrimination. Psychologists and ergonomists know when a signal is easy to detect, what color combinations are slow to be detected, and what sounds are easy to discriminate.

The output of human beings is movement. People make gestures, manipulate tools, speak, or use a combination of these. For computer use, manipulation of keys, mouse or touch-screen, and speaking into microphones are common examples of output. According to modern psychology, all those types of output are monitored by a central processing mechanism in the human. This central executive decides on the meaning of the output (say yes, move the mouse to a certain location, press the return key) but leaves the actual execution to motor processes that, in normal cases, are running 'unattended', i.e. the actual execution is not consciously controlled. Only in case of problems is attention needed. For example, if the location to be pointed to on the screen is in an awkward position, if a key is not functioning properly, or if the room is so noisy that the person cannot properly hear his own spoken command. So we should design for human movements and human measures. It pays to ask an ergonomist about the most ergonomic design of buttons and dials.

The central executive unit of human information processing is modeled as an instance that performs productions of the form `if condition then action`, where the `condition` in most cases relates to some perceived input or to some knowledge available from memory. The `action` is a command to the motor system, with attributes derived from working memory. The central executive unit has a very limited capacity. First of all, only a very small number of processes can be performed simultaneously. Secondly, the knowledge that is needed in testing the condition as well as the knowledge that is processed on behalf of the motor output has to be available in working memory. Most of the time, we may consider the limitations to result in the execution of one process at a time and, consequently, in causing competing processes to be scheduled for sequential execution based on perceived priority. For example, when a driver approaches a crossroads, the talk with his passenger will be temporarily interrupted and only resumed when the driving decisions have been made. The amount of available resources has to be taken into account when designing systems. For example, humans cannot cope with several error messages each of which requires an immediate decision, especially if each requires complex error diagnosis to be performed before reaction is feasible.

Working memory is another relevant concept in the model. Modern psychology presumes there is only one memory structure, **long-term memory**, that contains knowledge that is permanently stored. Any stimulus that reaches the central executive unit leads to the activation of an element in long-term memory. The activated elements together form the current working memory. The capacity of the set of activated elements is very limited. The average capacity of the human information processor is 5–9 elements. If new elements are activated, other elements lose their activation status and, hence, are no longer immediately available to the central executive. In other words, they are not in working memory any more.

Long-term memory is highly structured. One important type of relation concerns semantic relations between concepts, such as part-of, member-of, and specialization–generalization. In fact, each piece of knowledge can be considered a concept defined by its relation to other elements. Such a piece of knowledge is often called a **chunk**. It is assumed that working memory has a capacity of 5–9 chunks. An expert in some task domain is someone who has available well-chosen chunks in that domain, so that he is able to expand any chunk into relevant relations, but only when needed for making decisions and deriving an answer to a problem. If not needed, an expert will not expand the chunk that has been triggered by the recognition phase of perception or by the production based on a stimulus. For example, the sequence of digits '85884' could occupy five entries in working memory. However, if it is your mother's telephone number, it is encoded as such and occupies only one entry. When the number has to be dialed, this single entry is expanded to a series of digits again. Entries in working memory can thus be viewed as labels denoting some unit of information, such as a digit, your mother's telephone number, or the routine quicksort. In this way an expert can cope with a situation even with the restrictions on the capacity of working memory.

The structures in long-term memory are the basis for solving problems in a domain and for expertise. When working with a system, people develop a suitable knowledge structure for performing their tasks. If they are able to understand the system as much as they need (we defined this as the **virtual machine** in Section 16.2), they may develop a coherent and useful structure in long-term memory. As far as this structure can be considered a model of the system, we consider it to be the **mental model** of the system.

16.4.2 Mental Models of Information Systems

Mental models are structures in long-term memory. They consist of elements and relations between those elements. They represent relevant knowledge structures analogous to physical, organizational, and procedural structures in the world. These mental models become 'instantiated' when activated by an actual need, e.g. when one needs to make a decision related to an element of this knowledge. The activated mental model is, to a certain extent, run or executed in order to predict how the structure in the world that is represented by the mental model would behave in relation to the current situation and in reaction to the possible actions of the person. In the terminology introduced before, mental models are internal models.

When working with complex systems, where part of the relevant structure and processes of the system cannot be perceived by a human being or cannot be completely monitored, a mental model is needed to behave optimally in relation to the system. Hence, people develop mental models of such situations and systems. If the system is a computer system, there are four functions of using the system that require the activation of a mental model:

- When planning the use of the technology, users will apply their knowledge (i.e. their mental model) to find out for what part of their task the system could be used and the conditions for its use. Users will determine what they need to do beforehand, when they would like to perform actions and take decisions during the use of the system, and when they would abort execution or reconsider use.

Suppose I want to use our library information system to search for literature on mental models of computer systems. I may decide to search by author name. First, I must find one or a few candidate authors.

- During execution of a task with a system, there is a continuous need for fine-tuning of user actions towards system events. The mental model is applied to monitoring the collaboration and reconsidering decisions taken during the planning stage.

If the result of my search action is not satisfactory, I may decide to look up alternative author names or switch to a keyword search. If the keywords used by the system are keywords listed in the titles of publications, there is quite a chance that relevant literature is not found by a search using the keywords `mental model`. I may then consider other keywords as well, such as `human-computer interaction`.

- If the system has performed some tasks for the user and produced output, there is the need to evaluate the results, to understand when to stop, and to understand the value of the results in relation to the intended task. The mental model of the system is needed to evaluate the system's actions and output, and to translate these to the goals and needs of the user.

Some of the literature sources found may have titles that indicate a relation between mental models and learning, while others relate mental models to personality factors. I may decide to keep only those titles that relate mental models to HCI, since the others are probably not relevant.

- Modern computer systems are frequently not working in isolation and more processes may be going on than those initiated by current use. The user has to cope with unexpected system events, and needs to interpret the system's behavior in relation to the intended task as well as to the state of the system and the network of related systems. For this interpretation, users need an adequate mental model of the system and its relation to the current task.

I may accept a slow response to my query knowing that the answer is quite long and network traffic during office hours is heavy.

Mental models as developed by users of a system are always just models. They abstract from aspects the user considers not relevant and they have to be usable for a human information processor with his restricted resources and capacities. Consequently, we observe some general restrictions in the qualities of human mental models of computer systems. Norman (1983) has shown that mental models of systems of the complexity of a computer application have the following general characteristics:

- They are incomplete and users are generally aware of the fact that they do not really know all details of the system, even if relevant. They will know, if they are experts, where details can be found.

- They can only partly be 'run', because of the nature of human knowledge representation. I may know how to express a global replacement in my text editor (i.e., I know the start and end situation) without knowing how the intended effect is obtained.

- They are unstable. They change over time, both because of users using different systems and spoiling the knowledge of the previously applied system and because of new experiences, even if the user has been considered a guru on this system for the past ten years.

- They have vague boundaries. People tend to mix characteristics of their word processor with aspects of the operating system and, hence, are prone to occasionally make fatal errors based on well-prepared decisions.

- They are parsimonious. People like to maintain models that are not too complex and try to stick to enough basic knowledge to be able to apply the model for the majority of their tasks. If something uncommon has to be done they accept having to do some extra operations, even if they know there should be a simpler solution for those exceptions.

- They have characteristics of superstitions that help people feel comfortable in situations which they know they do not really understand. An example is the experienced user who changes back to his root directory before switching off his machine or before logging out. He knows perfectly well there is no real need for this, but he prefers to behave in a nice and systematic way and hopes the machine will behave nicely and systematically in return.

Designers of user interfaces should understand the types of mental structures users tend to develop. There are techniques for acquiring information about an individual user's mental models, as well as about the generic mental structures of groups of users. Psychological techniques can be applied and, in the design of new types of system, it is worthwhile to apply some expert help in assessing the knowledge structures that may be needed for the system, as well as those that may be expected to be developed by users. If the knowledge needed differs from the mental models developed in actual use, there is a problem and designers should ask for expert help before the design results in an implementation that does not accord with the users' models.

16.4.3 Conceptual Models in User Interface Design

A central part of user interface design is the stepwise-refined specification of the system as far as it is relevant for the user. This includes the knowledge the user needs in order to operate the system, the definition of the dialog between user and system, and the functionality that the system provides to the user. All that is specified in the design process is obviously also explicitly modeled, in order to make sure implementation does not result in a system that differs from the one intended. In cognitive ergonomics, all that is modeled about the system as far as relevant to its different sets of users is called the **conceptual model** of the system (Norman, 1983).

Formal design modeling techniques have been developed in order to communicate in design teams, to document design decisions, to be able to backtrack on specifications, and to calculate the effects of design specifications. Some techniques model the user's knowledge (so-called competence models), others focus on the interaction process (so-called process models), and others do both. Reisner's Psychological BNF (Reisner, 1981) is an example of a competence model. In this model, the set of valid user dialogs is defined using a context-free grammar. Process models may model time aspects of interaction, as in the Keystroke model (Card *et al.*, 1983) which gives performance predictions of low-level user actions. Task Action Grammar (TAG) (Payne and Green, 1989) is an example of a combined model. It allows the calculation of indexes for learning (the time needed to acquire knowledge) and for ease of use (mental load, or the time needed for the user's part of executing a command).

Moran (1981) was one of the first to structure the conceptual model into components, somewhat akin to the Seeheim model. Even though, at that time, command dialogs were the only type of interactive user interface available to the general public, his **Command Language Grammar** (CLG) still provides a remarkably complete view of the types of design decision to be made during user interface design. Additionally, Moran was the first to state that a conceptual model can be looked upon from three different viewpoints:

- The psychological view considers the specification as the definition of all that a user should understand and know about the new system.

- The linguistic view describes the interaction between human and system in all aspects that are relevant for both participants in the dialog.

- The design view specifies all that needs to be decided about the system from the point of view of the user interface design.

Moran distinguishes six levels in the conceptual model, structured in three components. Each level details concepts from a higher level, from the specific point of view of the current level. The formalism that Moran proposes (the actual grammar) would nowadays be replaced by more sophisticated notations, but the architectural concepts show the relevance of analyzing design decisions from different viewpoints and at the same time investigating the relationships between these viewpoints:

a. Conceptual component. This component concerns design decisions at the level of functionality: what will the system do for the users.

a.1 Task level. At this level we describe the task domain in relation to the system: which tasks can be delegated to the machine, which tasks have to be done by the user in relation to this (preparation, decisions in between one machine task and the next, etc.). A representation at this level concerns tasks and task-related objects as seen from the eyes of the user, not detailing anything about the system, such as 'print a letter on office stationery' or 'store a copy'.

a.2 Semantic level. Semantics in the sense of CLG concern the system's functionality in relation to the tasks that can be delegated. At this level, task delegation is specified in relation to the system. The system objects are described with their attributes and relevant states, and the operations on these objects as a result of task delegation are specified. For example, there may be an object `letter` with an attribute `print date` and an operation to store a copy in another object called `printed letters` with attributes `list of printed letters` and `date of last storage operation`.

In terms of the Seeheim model, this level describes the application interface.

b. Communication component. This component describes the dialog of the Seeheim model.

b.1 Syntax level. This level describes the dialog style, such as menus, form-filling, commands, or answering questions, by specifying the lexicographical structure of the user and system actions. For example, to store a letter, the user has to indicate the letter to be stored, then the storage location, then the storage command, and, finally, an end-of-command indication.

b.2 Keystroke level. The physical actions of the user and the system are specified at this level, such as clicking the mouse buttons, pointing, typing, dragging, blinking the cursor, and issuing beeping signals.

c. Material component. At this level, Moran refers to the domain of classical ergonomics, including perceptual aspects of the interface, as well as relevant aspects of the hardware. The presentation aspect of the Seeheim model is located at the spatial layout level.

c.1 Spatial layout level. The screen design, for example, the shape, color, and size of icons and characters on the screen, and the size of buttons, is specified at this level. This level is also intended to cover sound and tactile aspects of the interface (such as tactile mouse feedback) not covered by the hardware.

c.2 Apparatus level. At this level, Moran suggests we specify the shape of buttons and the power needed to press them, as well as other relevant hardware aspects.

Moran's CLG provides a fairly complete specification model for the user interface or UVM. The actual grammar representation is no longer relevant, but the layers and their relations are important, and the design models discussed in the next section cover most of them: task models relate to Moran's task level and the UVM specifications include the semantic level, the communication component, and parts of the spatial layout level.

16.5 THE DESIGN OF INTERACTIVE SYSTEMS

The concept *user interface* in this chapter denotes the complete UVM, the user's virtual machine. Traditional user interface design mainly concerns the situation of a single user and a monolithic system. In current applications, computers are mostly part of a network, and users are collaborating, or at least communicating, with others through networks. Consequently, the UVM should include all aspects of communication between users as far as this communication is routed through the system. It should also include aspects of distributed computing and networking as far as this is relevant for the user, such as access, structural, and time aspects of remote sources of data and computing. For example, when using a Web browser, it is relevant to understand mechanisms of caching and of refreshing or reloading a page, both in terms of the content that may have changed since the previous loading operation and in terms of the time needed for operations to complete.

These newer types of application bring another dimension of complexity into view. People are collaborating in various ways mediated by information technology. Collaboration via systems requires special aspects of functionality. It requires facilities for the integration of actions originating from different users on shared objects and environments, facilities to manage and coordinate the collaboration, and communication functionality. Such systems are often denoted as **groupware**. Modern user interface design techniques cater for both the situation of the classical single user system and groupware. We expect this distinction to disappear in the near future.

There are several classes of stakeholder in system development (see also Chapter 9). These include, at least, the clients, i.e. the people or organizations that pay for the design or acquisition of systems, and the users, i.e. the people or groups that apply the systems as part of their daily work, often referred to as the **end**

users. Throughout the process of design, these two classes of stakeholders have to be distinguished, since they may well have different goals for the system, different (and possibly even contradictory) knowledge about the task domain, and different views on what is an optimal or acceptable system. This does not mean that in certain situations these classes will not overlap. But even if this is the case, individual people may well turn out to have contradictory views on the system they need. In many situations there will be additional classes of stakeholders to cater for, such as people who are involved in maintaining the system, and people who need traces or logs of the system to monitor cases of failure or abuse, such as lawyers.

In relation to these different classes of stakeholders, designers are in a situation of potential political stress. Clients and users may have contradictory inputs into the specification of the system. Moreover, the financial and temporal constraints on the amount of effort to be invested in designing the different aspects of the system (such as specifying functionality and user interface, implementation, and testing) tend to counteract the designers' ambitions to sufficiently take care of the users' needs.

Making a distinction between classes of stakeholders does not solve the problem of user diversity. In complex systems design, we are confronted with different end users playing different roles, as well as end-user groups that have knowledge or a view on the task domain that need not be equivalent to the (average or aggregated) knowledge and views of the individuals.

16.5.1 Design as an Activity Structure

Viewing design as a structure of interrelated activities, we need a process model. The model we use will be familiar to readers of this book: it is a cyclical process with phases devoted to analysis, specification, and evaluation. Figure 16.5 depicts this process model.

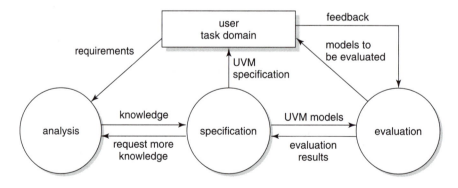

Figure 16.5 A process model for user interface design

Analysis: Since the system to be developed will feature in a task situation, we start with task analysis. We further structure this activity into the development of two models: task model 1, which models the current task situation, and task model 2, which models the task domain of the future situation, where the system to be developed will be used, including changes in the organization of people and work procedures. The relationship between task models 1 and 2 reflects the change in the structure and organization of the task world as caused by the implementation of the system to be developed. As such, the difference is relevant both for the client and the user.

The development of task model 2 from task model 1 uses knowledge of current inadequacies and problems concerning the existing task situation, needs for change as articulated by the clients, and insight into current technological developments. Section 16.6 discusses task analysis.

Specification: The specification of the system to be designed is based on task model 2. It has to be modeled in all details that are relevant to the users, including cooperation technology and user-relevant system structure and network characteristics. Differences between the specification of the new system (the user's virtual machine or UVM) and task model 2 must be considered explicitly and lead to design iteration. Specifying the UVM is elaborated in Section 16.7.

Evaluation: The specification of the new system incurs many design decisions that have to be considered in relation to the system's prospective use. For some design decisions, guidelines and standards might be used as checklists. In other situations, formal evaluation may be applied, using formal modeling tools that provide an indication of the complexity of use or learning effort required. For many design decisions, however, evaluation requires confronting the future user with relevant aspects of the intended system. Some kind of prototyping is a good way to confront the user with the solution proposed. A prototype allows experimentation with selected elements or aspects of the UVM. It enables imitation of (aspects of) the presentation interface, it enables the user to express himself in (fragments of) the interaction language, and it can be used to simulate aspects of the functionality, including organizational and structural characteristics of the intended task structure. We discuss some evaluation techniques in Section 16.8.

Figure 16.5 is similar to Figure 9.1. This is not surprising. The design of an interactive system as discussed in this chapter is very akin to the requirements engineering activity discussed in Chapter 9. The terminology is slightly different and reflects the user-centered stance taken in this chapter. For example, 'elicitation' sounds more passive than 'analysis'. 'Evaluation' entails more than 'validation'; it includes usability testing as well. Finally, we treat the user and the task domain as one entity from which requirements are elicited. In the approach advocated here, the user is observed *within* the task domain.

16.5.2 Design as Multi-Disciplinary Collaboration

The main problem with the design activities discussed in the previous section is that different methods may provide conflicting viewpoints and goals. A psychological focus on individual users and their capacities tends to lead to Taylorism, neglecting the reality of a multitude of goals and methods in any task domain. On the other hand, sociological and ethnographical approaches towards groupware design tend to omit analysis of individual knowledge and needs. Still, both extremes provide unique contributions.

In order to design for people, we have to take into account both sides of the coin: the individual users and clients of the system, and the structure and organization of the group for which the system is intended. We need to know the individuals' knowledge and views on the task, on applying the technology, and the relation between using technology and task-relevant user characteristics (expertise, knowledge, and skills). With respect to the group, we need to know its structure and dynamics, the phenomenon of 'group knowledge' and work practice and culture. These aspects are needed in order to acquire insight into both existing and projected task situations where (new) cooperation technology is introduced. Both types of insight are also needed in relation to design decisions, for functionality and for the user interface. Consequently, in prototyping and field-testing, we need insight into the acceptance and use by individuals and the effect of the new design on group processes and complex task dynamics.

For example, in a traditional bank setting, the client and the bank employee are on different sides of a counter. The bank employee is probably using a computer, but the client cannot see the screen, and does not know what the clerk is doing. In a service-oriented bank setting, the clerk and client may be looking at the screen *together*. They are together searching for a solution to the client's question. This overturns the existing culture of the bank and an ethnographer may be asked to observe what this new setup brings about.

The general framework for our approach to user interface design is depicted in Figure 16.6. It is a refinement of Figure 16.5, emphasizing the specialties involved in carrying out different activities. Task model 1 is based on knowledge of single users (psychological variables, task-related variables, knowledge, and skills) and on complex phenomena in the task situation (roles, official and actual procedures, variation in strategies, and variation in the application of procedures). The integration of this insight in a model often does not provide a single (or a single best) decomposition of tasks and a unique structure of relationships between people, activities, and environments. The model often shows alternative ways to perform a certain task, role-specific and situation-specific methods and procedures, and a variety of alternative assignments of subtasks to people. For example, the joint problem-solving approach to the bank counter, sketched out above, cannot be applied to the drive-in counter of the bank. The drive-in counter requires a different approach and a different user interface.

From this, and because of client requirements, compromises often have to be made in defining task model 2, the new task situation for which the technology

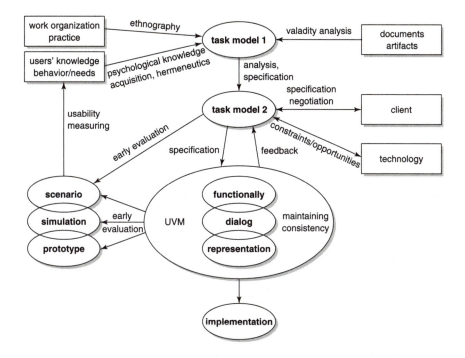

Figure 16.6 Structure of design team activities

has to be designed. This process includes the interpretation of problems in the current task situation, negotiation with the client regarding his conditions, and the resources available for design (including both financial impacts and time constraints). Ultimately, decisions have to be made about complex aspects, such as re-arranging the balance of power and the possibilities for users in various roles to exercise control.

Again, when detailed design decisions are being considered, early evaluation needs to include analytical methods (formal evaluation and cognitive walkthrough techniques) in combination with usability testing where users in different roles are studied both in the sense of traditional individual measures and in the sense of ethnographic interaction analysis.

16.6 TASK ANALYSIS

Analyzing a complex system means analyzing the world in which the system functions, the *context of use*, which comprises (according to standards such as (ISO 9241, 1996)):

- the users;

- the tasks;

- the equipment (hardware, software, and materials);

- the social environment;

- the physical environment.

If we design systems for the context of use, we must take these different aspects of the task world into consideration. In traditional literature on task analysis from the HCI mainstream, the focus is mostly on users, tasks, and software. Design approaches for groupware and computer-supported collaborative work (CSCW), on the other hand, often focus on analyzing the world first of all from the point of view of the (physical and social) environment. Recent approaches to task modeling include some aspects that belong to both categories, but it still looks as if one has to, by and large, opt for one view or the other. Section 16.6.1 presents task analysis approaches from the classical HCI tradition and distinguishes different phases in task analysis. Section 16.6.2 presents an ethnographic point of view, as frequently applied to the design of CSCW systems, where phases in the analysis process are hardly considered.

Jordan (1996), though originally working from an ethnographic approach and focusing on groupware applications, provides a view on analyzing knowledge of the task world that is broad enough to cover most of the context of use as now defined by ISO 9241 (1996). We illustrate Jordan's view in Section 16.6.3. The groupware task analysis (GTA) framework of modeling task knowledge combines approaches from both HCI and CSCW design. GTA is described in Section 16.6.4.

16.6.1 Task Analysis in HCI Design

Classical HCI features a variety of notions regarding task analysis. Task analysis can mean different activities:

- analyzing a current task situation,

- envisioning a task situation for which information technology is to be designed, or

- specifying the semantics of the information technology to be designed.

Many HCI task analysis methods combine more than one of these activities and relate them to actual design stages. Others do not bother about the distinction. For example, goals, operators, methods, and selection rules (GOMS, see (Card *et al.*, 1983)) can be applied for any or a combination of the above activities.

In many cases. the design of a new system is triggered by an existing task situation. Either the current way of performing tasks is not considered optimal, or the availability of new technology is expected to allow an improvement over current methods. A systematic analysis of the current situation may help formulate requirements and allow later evaluation of the design. In all cases where a current version of the task situation exists, it pays to model this. Task models of this type pretend to describe the situation as it can be found in real life, by asking or observing people who know the situation (see (Johnson, 1989)). Task model 1 is often considered to be generic, indicating the belief that different expert users have at their disposal basically the same task knowledge.

Many design methods in HCI that start with task modeling are structured in a number of phases. After describing a current situation (in task model 1), the method requires a re-design of the task structure in order to include technological solutions for problems and technological answers to requirements. Task model 2 is in general formulated and structured in the same way as task model 1. However, it is not considered a *descriptive* model of users' knowledge, though in some cases it may be applied as a *prescriptive* model of the knowledge an expert user of the new technology should possess.

A third type of modeling activity focuses on the technology to be designed. This may be considered part of task model 2. However, some HCI approaches distinguish specific design activities which focus on the technology (e.g. see (Tauber, 1990)). This part of the design activity is focused on a detailed description of the system as far as it is of direct relevance to the end user, i.e. the UVM. We separate the design of the UVM from the design of the new task situation as a whole, mainly because the UVM models the detailed solution in terms of technology, whereas task model 2 focuses on the task structure and work organization. In actual design, iteration is needed between the specification of these two models. This should be an explicit activity, making the implications of each obvious in its consequences for the other. Specifying the UVM is treated in more detail in Section 16.7.

HCI task models represent a restricted point of view. All HCI task modeling is rather narrowly focused, mainly considering individual people's tasks. Most HCI approaches are based on cognitive psychology. Johnson (1989) refers to knowledge structures in long-term memory. Tauber (1990) refers to 'knowledge of competent users'. HCI approaches focus on the knowledge of individuals who are knowledgeable or expert in the task domain, whether this domain already exists (task model 1) or still has to be re-structured by introducing new technology (task model 2 and the UVM).

As a consequence of their origin, HCI task models seldom provide an insight into complex organizational aspects, situational conditions for task performance, or complex relationships between tasks of individuals with different roles. Business processes and business goals (such as the service focus of a modern bank counter, which may be found in a business reengineering project) are seldom part of the knowledge of individual workers and, consequently, are seldom related to the goals and processes found in HCI task modeling.

Task analysis assumes there are tasks to analyze. Many current Web applications, though, are information-centric. The value of such systems is in the information they provide (Wikipedia, Amazon.com, and so on), and to a much lesser extent in the tasks they offer to the user. The key operation is searching. The developers seek to make searching simpler by organizing the information in a logical way, by providing navigation schemes, and so on (Nerurkar, 2001). The challenge for such applications is to induce the users to provide ever more information. This is another example of crowdsourcing, as already mentioned in Chapter 1.

16.6.2 Analysis Approaches for Collaborative Work

CSCW work stresses the importance of situational aspects, group phenomena and organizational structure and procedures. Shapiro (1996) even goes so far as to state that HCI has failed in the case of task analysis for cooperative work situations, since generic individual knowledge of the total complex task domain does not exist. The CSCW literature strongly advocates ethnographic methods.

Ethnographers study a task domain (or community of practice) by becoming a participant observer, if possible with the status of an apprentice. The ethnographer observes the world 'through the eyes of the aboriginal' and at the same time is aware of his status as an outside observer whose final goal is to understand and describe for a certain purpose and a certain audience (in the case of CSCW, a design project). Ethnographers start their observation purposely without a conceptual framework regarding characteristics of task knowledge, but, instead, may choose to focus on activities, environments, people, or objects. The choice of focus is itself based on prior ethnographic observations, which illustrates the bootstrapping character of knowledge elicitation in ethno-methodology. Methods of data collection nowadays start with video recordings of relevant phenomena (the relevance of which, again, can only be inferred from prior observation) followed by systematic transaction analysis, where inter-observer agreement serves to improve the reliability of interpretation. Knowledge of individual workers in the task domain may be collected as far as it seems to be relevant, but it is in no sense a priori considered the main source and is never considered indicative of generic task knowledge.

The ethnographic approach is unique in its attention to all relevant phenomena in the task domain that cannot be verbalized explicitly by (all) experts (see (Nardi, 1995)). The approach attends to knowledge and intentions that are specific for some actors only, to conflicting goals, to cultural aspects that are not perceived by the actors in the culture, to temporal changes in beliefs, to situational factors that are triggers or conditions for strategies, and to non-physical objects such as messages, stories, signatures and symbols, of which the actors may not be aware while interacting.

Ethno-methodology covers the methods of collecting information that might serve as a basis for developing task model 1 (and no more than this since ethno-methodology only covers information on the current state of a task domain). However, the methodology for the collection of data and its structuring into a complete task domain description is often rather special and difficult to follow in detail. The general impression is that CSCW design methods skip the explicit construction of task models 1 and 2 and, after collecting sufficient information on the community of practice, immediately embark on specifying the UVM, based on deep knowledge of the current task situation that is not formalized. This may cause two types of problem.

Firstly, the relationship between specifications for design and analysis of the current task world might depend more on intuition than on systematic design decisions. Secondly, skipping the development of task model 2 may lead to conservatism with respect to organizational and structural aspects of the work for which a system is to be (re)designed.

16.6.3 Sources of Knowledge and Collection Methods

Collecting task knowledge to analyze the current situation of a complex system has to start by identifying the relevant knowledge sources. In this respect, we refer to a framework derived from (Jordan, 1996), see Figure 16.7. The two dimensions of this framework denote where the knowledge resides and how it can be communicated. For example, A stands for the explicit knowledge of an individual, while D stands for the implicit knowledge of a group.

Sources of knowledge

Levels of communicability		individual	group
	explicit	A	C
	implicit	B	D

Figure 16.7 Dimensions of knowledge for complex task domains

Jordan's framework has been applied in actual design processes for large industrial and government interactive systems. We may expand the two factors distinguished from dichotomies to continuous dimensions to obtain a two-dimensional framework for analyzing the relevant sources of knowledge in the context of use. This framework provides a map of knowledge sources that helps us to identify the different techniques that we might need in order to collect information and structure this information into a model of the task world.

To gather task knowledge in cell A, psychological methods may be used: interviews, questionnaires, think-aloud protocols, and (single-person-oriented) observations. For knowledge in cell B, observations of task behavior must be complemented by hermeneutic methods to interpret mental representations (see (Veer, 1990)). For the knowledge referred to in cell C, the obvious methods concern the study of artifacts such as documents and archives. In fact all these methods are to be found in classical HCI task analysis approaches and, for that matter, the requirements elicitation techniques discussed in Chapter 9.

The knowledge indicated in cell D is unique in that it requires ethnographic methods such as interaction analysis. Moreover, this knowledge may be in conflict with what can be learned from the other sources. First of all, explicit individual knowledge often turns out to be abstract with respect to observable behavior and to ignore the situation in which task behavior is exhibited. Secondly, explicit group knowledge such as expressed in official rules and time schedules is often in conflict with actual group behavior, and for good reasons. Official procedures do not always work in practice and the literal application of them is sometimes used as a political weapon in labor conflicts, or as a legal alternative to a strike. In all cases of discrepancy between sources of task knowledge, ethnographic methods will reveal unique and relevant additional information that has to be explicitly represented in task model 1.

The allocation of methods to knowledge sources should not be taken too strictly. The knowledge sources often cannot be located completely in single cells of Jordan's conceptual map. The main conclusion is that we need different methods in a complementary sense, as we need information from different knowledge sources.

16.6.4 An Integrated Approach to Task Analysis: GTA

Groupware Task Analysis (GTA) is an attempt to integrate the merits from the most important classical HCI approaches with the ethnographic methods applied for CSCW (see (Veer and van Welie, 2003)). GTA contains a collection of concepts and their relations (a conceptual framework) that allows analysis and representation of all relevant notions regarding human work and task situations as dealt with in the different theories.

The framework is intended to structure task models 1 and 2, and, hence, to guide the choice of techniques for information collection in the case of task model 1. For task model 2, design decisions have to be made, based on problems and conflicts that are present in task model 1 and the requirement specification.

Task models for complex situations are composed of different aspects. Each describes the task world from a different viewpoint and each relates to the others. The three viewpoints are:

- **Agents**, often people, either individually or in groups. Agents are considered in relation to the task world. Hence, we make a distinction between agents as actors and the roles they play. Moreover, we need the concept of organization of agents. Actors have to be described with relevant characteristics (e.g. for human actors, the language they speak, their amount of typing skill, or their experience with Microsoft Windows). Roles indicate classes of actors to whom certain subsets of tasks are allocated. By definition, roles are generic for the task world. More than one actor may perform the same role and a single actor may have several roles at the same time. Organization refers to the relation between actors and roles in respect to task allocation. Delegating and mandating responsibilities from one role to another is part of the organization.

For example, an office may have agents such as 'a secretary', 'the typing pool', and 'the answering machine'. A possible role is 'answer a telephone call'. Sometimes it is not relevant to know which agent performs a certain role: it is not important who answers a telephone call, as long as it is answered.

- **Work**, in both its structural and dynamic aspects. We take task as the basic concept. A task has a goal as an attribute. We make a distinction between tasks and actions. Tasks can be identified at various levels of complexity. The unit level of tasks needs special attention. We need to make a distinction between

  - the **unit task**: the lowest task level that people want to consider in referring to their work
  - the **basic task** (after (Tauber, 1990)): the unit level of task delegation that is defined by the tool that is used, for example a single command in a command-driven computer application.

  Unit tasks are often role-related. Unit tasks and basic tasks may be decomposed further into (user) actions and (system) events, but these cannot really be understood without a frame of reference created by the corresponding task, i.e. actions derive their meaning from the task. For instance, hitting a return key has a different meaning depending on whether it ends a command or confirms the specification of a numerical input value.

  The task structure is often at least partially hierarchical. On the other hand, performance on certain tasks may influence the procedures for other tasks (possibly with other roles involved). For example, the secretary has to deliver the mail on time and may have to interrupt other tasks to be able to do so. Therefore we also need to understand task flow and data flow over time as well as the relationship between several concurrent flows.

- **Situation**. Analyzing a task world from the viewpoint of the situation means detecting and describing the environment (physical, conceptual, and social) and the objects in the environment. Each thing that is relevant to the work in a certain situation is an object in the sense of task analysis. Objects may be physical things, or conceptual (non-material) things such as messages, gestures, passwords, stories, or signatures. The task environment is the current situation for the performance of a certain task. It includes actors with roles as well as conditions for task performance The history of past relevant events in the task situation is part of the actual environment if this features in conditions for task execution.

16.7 SPECIFICATION OF THE USER INTERFACE DETAILS

Specifying details of the user interface means elaborating all aspects of the machine that are relevant for the user, hence the concept of a user virtual machine (UVM). When there are several types of user for the system, we need to specify several separate UVMs, since each user role is defined by another subset of tasks. As suggested by the Seeheim model, we need to consider the representation, the dialog, and the application, each in relation to the type of user (the role) on which we are focusing. The application proper, i.e. the functionality of the system, is the first aspect. It defines what the user can do with the system (cf. Moran's semantic level). Techniques for specifying the functionality are dealt with in Chapter 9.

The other activities in relation to the specification of the UVM concern the interaction between the user and the system, with its two aspects:

- the dialog (corresponding to the dialog layer in the Seeheim model, and the syntax and keystroke level in Moran's CLG), and

- the presentation interface (corresponding to the presentation layer in the Seeheim model, and Moran's spatial layout level).

The three components of the UVM lead to three specifications that are strongly related. The dialog and the presentation are two sides of the coin of user–system interaction, and both express, each in its own way, the semantics and functionality of the system.

16.7.1 Dialog

The dialog in modern user interfaces is frequently a combination of several dialog styles, such as command language, menu choice, answering of questions generated by the interface, fill-in-the-blanks forms, and direct manipulation of interface objects. For an overview of the various styles, and options for using them in different situations depending on task and user characteristic, see (Mayhew, 1992) and (Shneiderman and Plaisant, 2004). Dialog styles may often be seen as implementations of different dialog metaphors:

- In a command language or natural language, the user and the interface 'speak' to each other. Legal dialogs obey a certain grammar. The user feels in control as long as he understands what is possible and remembers the right terminology. The user does not perform a task directly but is rather obliged to persuade the system to perform it.

- When the user has to choose from a menu, click on an icon, fill in labeled slots in a form on the screen, or answer questions from the interface, the interface provides a structure where the user is prompted to react by selecting an option. The user does not have to remember too many options. On the other hand, he may not feel totally in control of the dialog.

- In a direct-manipulation-type interface, the user moves in a 'space' and, by acting in the space, shows the computer what he needs, whether the space is a two-dimensional screen where he may drag and drop icons, a 3-D virtual reality environment, or something in between ('augmented-reality interfaces'). The direct manipulation style provides the user with a sense of direct engagement. It feels as if the user is in direct contact with the objects from the task domain.

It makes sense to relate the metaphor to the actual task domain. For example, a space can be specified as a desktop, or a virtual library, depending on whether the task domain concerns the management of documents or a search for objects.

In specifying the dialog further, the syntax of the interaction has to be specified in detail, including the sequence of user actions. For example, in both Windows and the Macintosh interface, the user has to indicate the object first and then the operation. The reverse is true in the UNIX command language. Also, the lexicon has to be specified. This includes deciding on the verbal labels for objects and operations, the iconic representations, the gestures (such as a cross or a series of connected up and down strokes to indicate rubbing out on a drawing pad), and sounds. The lexicon includes both the symbols that the user can use in communicating with the machine and the symbols the machine will output to the user.

There are various modeling techniques for specifying the dialog. An example dialog specification technique is User Action Notation (UAN, see (Hix and Hartson, 1993)) which combines the specification of functionality with dialog details. UAN is relatively easy to use, especially since the actual formalism may to a large extent be tailored to the designer's needs without losing the benefits of a formal model. UAN provides a representation of the specification of the UVM with separate columns to specify user actions, interface actions, interface states, and connections to underlying system events. Each of these columns is filled in with the amount of detail the designer needs at a certain moment. Later on, any item may be refined. For example, the designer may specify a user action `enter pincode` and later on specify a detailed interaction `enter pincode` where he elaborates details of inputting each digit, erasing a wrong keystroke, and what the interface should show on the screen at each point in time.

16.7.2 Representation

This aspect of the UVM contains the details of the interface that determine the perceptible aspects. The lexicon indicated in the previous section includes all interface elements. Their representation concerns their shape, color, contrast, pitch, loudness, size, etc. Representation also concerns all aspects of screen design, such as the size of windows, the speed of movement displayed, and the timbre of generated sounds. The representation aspect may need the assistance of artists or at least specialists who understand the laws of graphical representation, sound representation, and animation.

This part of design is the one for which no general formal representation models have been developed. Sketches, video clips, and verbal descriptions of what one intends to have represented are commonly used, and frequent communication between the designer and the implementor is needed. Artists may have very useful ideas but may propose very convincing solutions that change the essence of the intended specification.

16.8 EVALUATION

Evaluation is needed whenever decisions are made in the course of the design process. This will be the case during both analysis and specification. Evaluating analysis decisions is mostly related to the phase where the future task world is envisioned. During the process of developing detail specifications of the UVM, many decisions have to be made that relate technical details to aspects of usability.

Evaluation does not solve problems, it merely points to them. A valid diagnosis often requires several complementary techniques as well as expertise. Evaluation is done by presenting design decisions such that questions can be answered. Sometimes the questions may be answered in an unbiased way by the designer himself (e.g. if indexes can be calculated in a straightforward way), but in many cases there is a need to include others in the evaluation process, either specialists in design or humanities, or stakeholders in the design.

16.8.1 Evaluation of Analysis Decisions

During the early development of task model 2 there is not enough detail to develop a prototype. However, scenarios can be developed regarding the future task world, and it can be modeled with the help of formalisms. Both scenarios and formalisms offer opportunities to apply evaluation techniques.

In **scenario-based evaluation**, scenarios will be developed concerning those parts of task model 2 that concern a change in comparison to the current situation. In this phase of the design, it is worthwhile to represent not only the new use of technology, but also the situational aspects of this use and the organizational consequences. Developing a scenario means describing a process of using the intended system in an actual situation and organizational setting. The scenario may be described verbally, but a video representation is often used because that may show more relevant situational details, even though the technology may be represented in a way that reveals no details (for example, a laptop may be represented by a sheet of paper if the details of the screens have not yet been decided).

In order to evaluate a scenario, a 'claims analysis' can be performed. Apart from the designer and the constructor of the scenario, (future) users, representatives of the client, and other relevant stakeholders may participate in the claims analysis. It often makes sense not to choose only representatives who have a positive attitude towards the intended change but also to include people who are afraid of the future developments or who have a pronounced opinion on the possible negative effects of future implementation. For each aspect of the task delegation to the new system that is an explicit change from the current system, the participants of the claims analysis try to identify:

- to what extent the change is providing a solution in the intended direction, and

- what the positive and negative side effects of the change are.

Another way to evaluate a scenario is to ask a group of stakeholders to act out the written scenario and videotape the performance, possibly collecting several takes where people change roles and where the non-believers, in particular, get a chance to show where things may go wrong. Analyses of this type will show not only the possible success of the envisioned changes but also the potential problems. The latter, in particular, are the basis for reconsidering decisions and for developing measures to counteract unwanted side-effects. The scenarios that are acted by stakeholders, in particular, often reveal possible changes in the design that may provide a breakthrough.

Formal evaluation techniques allows specific questions to be answered. For example, hierarchical task analysis (HTA) (Kirwan and Ainsworth, 1992) describes the task domain as a hierarchical structure of tasks and subtasks with a complete representation of the procedural structures of the decomposition. HTA formal evaluation may consider the length of a sequence of subtasks, given the relevant conditions. The same type of formalism allows an evaluation of possible modular procedures (similar subtrees that occur in different places and the aspects of consistency between their execution), which is indicative of the amount of learning involved for understanding the new task domain.

16.8.2 Evaluation of UVM Specifications

As soon as details of the UVM have been specified, other representations may be used for evaluation, even though it may still be worthwhile to analyze scenarios. At this stage in the design, scenarios are often elaborated and executed with the help of mock-up representations or simulations of the intended system, especially if hardware aspects in relation to the physical work conditions are expected to matter. The simulations concern the size, weight, and perceptible aspects of the intended UVM, even if the interactive aspects have not yet been specified. Many evaluation techniques from classical ergonomics may be applied as well (Corlett and Clark, 1995).

Formal evaluation will certainly play an important role for the UVM. Many formalisms have been developed with certain usability aspects explicitly in mind. For example, TAG allows us to measure ease of learning and use by indexing the complexity of rules and the number of features to be considered during each command to the machine; UAN representations allow systematic reasoning about dialog specification details.

Detailed specification of the UVM permits other evaluation techniques as well, in particular **heuristic evaluation** and **cognitive walkthrough**. In both cases, it is useful to employ experts in user interface design who have not been part of the team that developed the specification. Experienced designers know the criteria applied in these techniques and will have considered them during their decisions. Only somebody for whom the design is new can have an unbiased view concerning these criteria. A last type of evaluation technique, **user testing and observation**, requires future users to be involved and a working prototype. Obviously, a prototype may also be the basis for heuristic evaluation and a cognitive walkthrough.

Heuristic evaluation is based on some definition of usability. Usability is a complex of aspects such as ease of use, ease of learning, ease of recall after a period of not using a system (known as re-learnability), affection, help, likeability, etc. Approaches toward heuristic evaluation provide checklists of characteristics of the user interface or UVM that describe the different usability aspects. Such a checklist may also be applied as a guideline for making design decisions. Checklists exist in different forms, and often include a technique for calculating usability indexes. Each item may be checked when applicable and, additionally, each item that is diagnosed as non-optimal may give rise to design changes. Example items from such a checklist are (Shneiderman and Plaisant, 2004; Nielsen, 1993):

- **Use a simple and natural dialog** Humans can only pay attention to a few things at a time. Therefore, dialogs should not contain information that is irrelevant or rarely needed. Information should appear in a logical and natural order to ease comprehension.

- **Speak the user's language** A dialog is easier to understand if it uses concepts and phrases that are familiar to the user. The dialog should not be expressed in computer-oriented terms, but in terms from the task domain.

- **Minimize memory load** The user should not have to remember information from one part of the dialog to another. Long command sequences, menus with a large number of entries, and uncertainty about 'where we are' hamper interaction. There must be easy ways to find out what to do next, how to retrace steps, and get instructions for use.

- **Be consistent** Users should not have to wonder whether different words or actions mean the same thing. Metaphors should be chosen carefully, so as not to confuse the user.

- **Provide feedback** The system should keep the user informed of what is going on. If certain processes take a while, the user should not be left in the dark. A moving widget informs the user that the system is doing something; a percentage-done indicator informs him about the progress towards the goal.

- **Provide clearly marked exits** Users make mistakes, activate the wrong function, follow the wrong thread. There must be an easy way to leave such an unwanted state.

- **Provide shortcuts** Novice users may be presented with an extensive question–answer dialog. It gives them a safe feeling and helps them to learn the system. Experts are hindered by a tedious step-by-step dialog and the system should provide shortcuts to accommodate them.

- **Give good error messages** Error messages should be explained in plain language. They should not refer to the internals of the system. Error messages should precisely state the problem and, if possible, suggest a solution.

Items from such a checklist should be used with care, though. Design involves tradeoffs between conflicting goals. Consider for example the two function-key layouts in Figure 16.8. Interface designers might prefer the star as the best design. It is a symmetric design, consistent with directional indicators on a compass. Yet, studies have shown that the inverted 'T' is the most useful configuration. With the index finger on the cursor-left key and the ring finger on the cursor-right key, the middle finger can efficiently cover the cursor-up and cursor-down keys. Designers of computer games seem to have known this for quite a while.

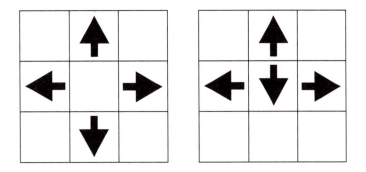

Figure 16.8 Two possible cursor key arrangements

Cognitive walkthroughs focus solely on the cognitive aspects of the dialog. The technique can be applied early in the specification phase and it helps to detect failures that would otherwise make the system incomprehensible for users. Like heuristic evaluation, it requires only a small number of expert colleagues who are confronted with the specification of the dialog and the content of the representation. Screen design need not have finished yet, but the information representation (wording, icons) of the screen must be known. The technique requires a specification of scenarios of normal, faultless dialog examples. A scenario might for example read as follows: 'when checking in you have to put your credit card in the slot; the machine will ask you to enter your pin code; you type . . . '. Based on a specification of this type, the start state is described to the evaluator, along with all information on the task as the user would know it, and the background of the user (education and systems experience). The evaluator is asked to answer a small set of questions about the next move. After these have been answered, the intended move is described with the resulting state of the interface, after which the evaluator is again asked the same set of questions.

An example of such a set of questions is:

- What should the user do now?

- Based on what knowledge or information would the user do this?

- What would the user expect to be the next step of the system?

Techniques such as this quickly expose any invalid expectations of user knowledge and understanding and any lack of relevant information at the interface. Additionally, they show inconsistencies in the interface information as well as inconsistencies in dialog conventions.

16.8.3 Evaluation of Prototypes

The proof of the pudding is in the eating. An evaluation should, at some point, be carried out with real users. As soon as a mock-up or simulation is available, users can be asked to perform tasks. We are then asking users to 'play a scenario' even if we do not mention this explicitly. As soon as details of the dialog have been established, a more interactive type of testing is possible.

Evaluation by the user is often based on a prototype implementation of the system. In early phases of detail design, the prototype will often not represent the total UVM. A single aspect of the task to be delegated, one instance of the dialog and representation with hardly any real functionality available, may be enough to detect problems early on. Several types of user testing may be done. Users may be provided with tasks or allowed to explore. Observations during the interaction, complemented with subsequent discussions with the user, may reveal problems and misunderstandings. In addition, user performance may be measured, for example, the time to complete a task or the frequency of errors. Users may be asked for their subjective understanding of the system; standardized measurement techniques are commercially available, focusing on subjective learnability, ease of use, and mental load.

ISO 9241 (1996) defines usability in terms of efficiency, effectiveness, and satisfaction. Usability evaluation of prototypes (and systems) is usually based on more specific definitions of usability characteristics, such as those defined in (Shneiderman and Plaisant, 2004; Nielsen, 1993). Figure 16.9 gives an overview of these usability characteristics. They have an almost one-to-one correspondence with the user interface quality factors as listed in the introduction to this chapter. For each of the usability characteristics, a number of (indirect) metrics exist. These metrics are gathered by observing users at work and by asking subjective questions.

ISO 9241	Shneiderman	Nielsen
Efficiency	Speed of performance	Efficiency
	Time to learn	Learnability
Effectiveness	Retention over time	Memorability
	Rate of errors by users	Errors/Safety
Satisfaction	Subjective satisfaction	Satisfaction

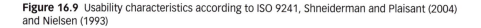

Figure 16.9 Usability characteristics according to ISO 9241, Shneiderman and Plaisant (2004) and Nielsen (1993)

16.9 SUMMARY

The user interface of a system is important. About half of the code of an interactive system is devoted to the user interface. Consequently, about half of the time and effort is spent on that interface as well. The quality of the user interface is a critical success factor. Good user interfaces increase the efficiency and productivity of their users, reduce errors and training time, and improve user acceptance.

In a technical sense, the user interface of a system often consists of two components or layers:

- a presentation component that handles the perceptible aspects of the interface, including screen design and keyboard layout;

- a dialog component that handles the syntax of the interaction, including metacommunication such as help functions and error messages.

As a result of this limited view of what a user interface is, it is often designed rather independently of the system's functionality. The design of the user interface is then seen as a separate activity, not in the mainstream requirements-engineering–design–implementation–testing phases. Chances are then that it does not get the attention it deserves.

In this chapter, we take a different stance. In the approach we sketch, the design of the interface and the design of the functionality go hand in hand. A provocative heading could have been 'The user interface *is* the system'. There are two main reasons for taking this broader view of what a user interface is:

- The system, and hence its interface, should help the user perform certain tasks. The user interface should therefore reflect the structure of the task domain. The design of tasks and the design of the corresponding user interface influence each other and should be part of the same cyclical process. Like quality, the user interface is not a supplement.

- The dialog and representation alone do not provide sufficient information to the user. In order to be able to work with a system, the user sometimes needs to know 'what is going on behind the screen'.

When thinking about user interface design, it is important to make a distinction between the user's mental model, the user virtual machine, and the conceptual model.

The mental model is a model in human memory. It is the user's model of the system he uses. It is based on education, knowledge of other systems, knowledge of the application domain, general knowledge about the world, etc. The mental model is used during interaction with the system, to plan actions and interpret system reactions. The mental model is often incomplete and inconsistent.

The user virtual machine (UVM) includes everything the user should know about the system in order to use it. It includes aspects ranging from the physical outlook of the computer and connected devices to the style of interaction and the form and content of the information exchange.

The conceptual model is the explicit model of the system created by designers and teachers. It is a consistent and complete representation of the system as far as relevant for the users. The conceptual model shows itself in the interface. If there is only one class of users, the user virtual machine and the conceptual model are the same. If there is more than one class of users (such as ATM clients, ATM maintainers, and lawyers), or the user uses more than one device, there is one UVM for each class, and the conceptual model is the union of those UVMs.

The central issue in human–computer interaction is to attune the user's mental model and the conceptual model as closely as possible. When this is achieved, the system becomes easier to learn and easier to use. When the models conflict, the user gets confused and starts making errors. Good design starts with the derivation of a conceptual model from an analysis of users and their tasks. This conceptual model is then built into the system (the UVM) in such a way that it induces adequate mental models in the users.

The design of a user interface involves different disciplines. Psychologists know how humans perceive, learn, remember, think, and feel, how people work together, and how the work situation affects work. Cognitive psychology, anthropology and ethnography provide techniques for collecting information on how people work. Artists know how to design attractive things that function effectively. Cognitive ergonomics is concerned with the characteristics of human information processing in interaction with information systems. Design teams for interactive systems may thus contain quite a variety of expertise alongside software engineering.

16.10 FURTHER READING

There is a growing collection of books on user interface design. Well-known textbooks are (Shneiderman and Plaisant, 2004) and (Sharp *et al.*, 2007). Newman and Lamming (1995) and (Dix *et al.*, 1998) cover most aspects of design, and are, at the same time introductory, i.e. they do not require too much background on the subject. Moran and Carroll (1996) consider the design process from the point of view of management and provide techniques to monitor the design space and design decisions.

The classical HCI approaches to task analysis are best exemplified in (Johnson and Johnson, 1991). Additional insight into methods of task knowledge elicitation may be found in (Sebillotte, 1988). General task analysis representation techniques are discussed in detail in (Kirwan and Ainsworth, 1992). Jordan and Henderson (1995) give a detailed account of ethnographic methods and techniques from the background of CSCW and groupware design.

For an overview of modeling techniques and examples see (Haan *et al.*, 1991). Task Action Grammar (TAG) is discussed in (Payne and Green, 1989), User Action Notation (UAN) in (Hix and Hartson, 1993), and Groupware Task Analysis (GTA) in (Veer and van Welie, 2003).

A classical collection of user interface guidelines can be found in (Smith and Mosier, 1986). Two volumes that consider dialog styles in detail are (Shneiderman and Plaisant, 2004) and (Mayhew, 1992). A view on details of representation and dialog design from an artistic point of view is presented in (Laurel, 1993). Representation aspects, as well as hardware aspects, are discussed in detail in (Corlett and Clark, 1995).

Nielsen and Mack (1994), (Jordan *et al.*, 1996), and Lindgaard (1994) provide collections of evaluation techniques for various stages in design. Carroll (1995) discusses scenario evaluation techniques, as well as the application of scenarios to other design phases.

Exercises

1. Define the following terms: mental model, conceptual model, and user virtual machine.

2. Discuss the differences between the Seeheim model and MVC.

3. Describe the role of cognitive ergonomics in user interface design.

4. Sketch a model of human information processing.

5. What is the difference between working memory and long-term memory?

6. In which ways is the user's mental model activated while using a computer system?

7. Describe the constituents of Command Language Grammar (CLG).

8. Discuss the differences between single-user systems and groupware with respect to task analysis.

9. Discuss the following user interface evaluation methods:

- scenario-based evaluation;
- heuristic evaluation;
- cognitive walkthrough.

10. ♡ Study the desktop metaphor as it is commonly used in user interfaces for PCs and workstations. Can you spot places where the metaphor breaks down or may even lead you astray?

11. ♡ Try to answer the following questions from the manual of your favorite word processor:

- How do I swap two paragraphs?
- How do I include the text of some other document at a given position?
- How do I let the page numbering start at 0 rather than 1?
- How do I align a picture at the top or bottom of the page?

Assess whether the user documentation is organized by the functionality offered or whether it addresses typical tasks faced by its users.

12. ♠ Discuss the requirements for online help facilities for a word processor.

13. ♡ Augment the waterfall model such that user interface issues are dealt with at appropriate phases.

14. ♠ Discuss the pros and cons of the following approaches to user interface development:

- discussing manually constructed usage scenarios with prospective users;
- prototyping screen displays and iteratively enhancing them;
- developing the user interface after the functional parts of the system are complete and accepted by the users;
- formally describing and analyzing the user interface prior to or concurrent with system design.

17

Software Reusability

LEARNING OBJECTIVES

- To appreciate various dimensions along which approaches to reuse may be classified

- To be aware of a number of composition-based and generation-based reuse techniques

- To see how reuse can be incorporated into the software life cycle

- To recognize the relation between reuse and various other software engineering concepts and techniques

- To understand the major factors that impede successful reuse

If we estimate the programmer population at three million people, and furthermore assume that each programmer writes 2 000 lines of code per year, 6 000 million lines of code are produced each year. There is bound to be a lot of redundancy in them. Reuse of software or other artifacts that are produced in the course of a software development project, may lead to considerable productivity improvements and, consequently, cost savings. This chapter gives an overview of reuse issues. Chapters 18 and 19 discuss two reuse technologies in more details: components and services.

Meanwhile Daedalus, tired of Crete and of his long absence from home, was filled with longing for his own country, but he was shut in by the sea. Then he said: 'The king may block my way by land or across the ocean, but the sky, surely, is open, and that is how we shall go. Minos may possess all the rest, but he does not possess the air.' With these words, he set his mind to sciences never explored before, and altered the laws of nature. He laid down a row of feathers, beginning with tiny ones, and gradually increasing their length, so that the edge seemed to slope upwards. In the same way, the pipe which shepherds used to play is built up from reeds, each slightly longer than the last. Then he fastened the feathers together in the middle with thread, and at the bottom with wax; when he had arranged them in this way, he bent them round into a gentle curve, to look like real birds' wings.
Ovid: Metamorphoses, VIII, 183–194.

Daedalus deserves a place in the mythology of software engineering. In King Minos' days, software did not exist; and yet the problems and notions which we still find in today's software engineering existed. One example is the construction of complex systems. Daedalus certainly has a track record in that field. He successfully managed a project that can stand a comparison with today's software development projects: the construction of the Labyrinth at Knossos.

After a while, Daedalus wanted to leave Crete, as narrated above in Ovid's words. King Minos, however, did not want to let him go. We know how the story continues: Daedalus flies with his son Icarus from Crete. Despite his father's warnings, Icarus flies higher and higher. He gets too close to the sun and the wax on his wings melts. Icarus falls into the sea and drowns. Daedalus safely reaches the mainland of Italy.

Daedalus' construction is interesting from the point of view of reuse. The fact that it concerns hardware rather than software is not important here. What concerns us in the present framework is the application of certain principles in the construction:

• **reuse of components**: Daedalus used real feathers;

• **reuse of design**: he imitated real wings;

- **glue to connect the various components**: at that time, people used wax to glue things together. The quality of the glue has a great impact on the reliability of the end product.

Through a justified and determined application of these principles, a successful and ambitious project (Daedalus' flight to Italy) was realized. An effort to storm heaven with insufficient technology turned into a disaster (Icarus' fall into the sea).

We make a small jump in history, to the end of the 1970s. The software crisis has been rampant for many years. The demand for new applications far surpasses the ability of the collective workforce in our field. This gap between demand and supply is still growing. Software reuse is one of the paths being explored in order to achieve a significant increase in software productivity.

Why code well-known computations over and over again? Cannot reliability and productivity be drastically increased by using existing high-quality software components?

It sounds too good to be true. But it isn't that simple. The use of existing software components requires standardization of naming and interfaces. The idea of gluing components together is not directly transferable to software.

Is software reuse a myth or can it really be achieved? In the following sections, we give an overview of the developments, opportunities, and expectations of software reusability. A tentative conclusion is that we should not expect miracles. By patiently developing a sound reuse technology, a lot of progress is possible. There is no philosopher's stone. There are, however, a great number of different developments that may reinforce and supplement one another.

The modern view does not restrict the notion of software reuse to component reuse. Design information can be reused also, as can other forms of knowledge gathered during software construction.

Software reuse is closely related to software architecture. A software architecture provides a context for the development of reusable building blocks. Conversely, a software architecture provides a skeleton into which building blocks can be incorporated. Attention to architectural issues is a prime software reuse success factor. A new style of software development, emphasizing component reuse within an architectural framework, is emerging. It is known as **Component-Based Software Engineering** (CBSE). Developments in interface technology such as provided by middleware interface description languages provide additional leverage for CBSE. Components that are dynamically discovered and deployed are called **services**. These two specific reuse technologies are discussed more extensively in Chapters 18 and 19.

Closely coupled to software reuse is software flexibility. Software is continuously adapting to changed circumstances. In developing the next release of a system, we would like to reuse as much as possible from the present release. This is sometimes considered to be software reuse. Flexibility aspects have been extensively discussed in previous chapters, notably Chapters 6 and 11, albeit not explicitly in the context of reusability.

Various aspects of software reuse are discussed in Sections 17.1 to 17.4. Section 17.1 discusses the main dimensions along which reuse approaches can be distinguished. Section 17.2 elaborates upon one of these dimensions, the type of product to be reused. Section 17.3 discusses another of these dimensions, namely the various process models incorporating reuse. Specific tools and techniques to support reuse are the topic of Section 17.4. Section 17.5 addresses the perspectives of software reuse. In particular, a domain-oriented, evolutionary approach is advocated. Finally, non-technical aspects of software reuse are addressed in Section 17.6.

17.1 REUSE DIMENSIONS

Software reuse has many dimensions or facets. The main dimensions along which approaches to software reuse can be distinguished are listed in Table 17.1. We discuss each of these dimensions in turn, by highlighting essential characteristics of extreme positions along the axes. Most reuse systems, however, exhibit a mixture of these characteristics. For example, a typical reuse system may use a combination of a compositional and a generative approach.

Table 17.1 Reuse dimensions

Dimension	Description
substance	components, concepts, procedures
scope	horizontal or vertical
approach	planned, systematic or ad hoc, opportunistic
technique	compositional or generative
usage	black-box, as-is or white-box, modified
product	code, object, design (architecture), text, . . .

The first dimension along which approaches to reuse may differ concerns the substance, the essence of the things that are reused. Most often, the things being reused are components. A component can be any piece of program text: a procedure, a module, an object-oriented class, etc. Components can be generic (data structures, such as binary trees or lists, widgets for graphical user interfaces, or sorting routines) or domain-specific. A point of recurring concern when reusing components is their quality, in particular their reliability. Instead of encapsulating a chunk of knowledge as a component in some programming language, we may also describe it at a more abstract level, for example as a generic algorithm, or a concept. Finally, rather than reusing product elements, we may also reuse process elements, such as procedures on how to carry out an inspection or how to prototype. To be able to do so, these process elements have to be formally captured, for example in a process model.

The scope of software reuse can be horizontal or vertical. In horizontal reuse, components are generic. They can be used across a variety of domains. A library of mathematical subroutines or GUI widgets is a typical example of horizontal reuse. In vertical reuse, components within a particular application domain are sought for. This often involves a thorough domain analysis to make sure that the components do reflect the essential concepts of the domain. The choice of a particular domain incurs a challenging tradeoff: if the domain is narrow, components can be made to fit precisely and the pay-off is high when these components are reused. On the other hand, the chance that these components can be reused outside this narrow domain is fairly small. The reverse holds for large domains.

Software reuse may be undertaken in a planned, systematic way or it may be done in an ad hoc, opportunistic fashion. Planned reuse involves substantial changes in the way software is developed. Extra effort is needed to develop, test, and document reusable software. Specific process steps must be introduced to investigate opportunities to reuse existing components. The economics of software development change, since costs and benefits relate to more than just the present project. Planned reuse requires a considerable investment up front. For a while, extra effort is needed to develop reusable components. Only at a later stage can the benefits be reaped. With the opportunistic approach, individuals reuse components when and if they happen to know of their existence, and when and if these components happen to fit. In this approach, components are not developed with reuse in mind. Populating a library with a large enough number of reusable components is often a problem when using the opportunistic approach. In the process-model perspective, the planned and opportunistic approaches to reuse are known as software development *for* reuse and software development *with* reuse, respectively.

In a composition-based technology, reuse is achieved by (partly) composing a new system from existing components. The building blocks used are passive fragments that are copied from an existing base. Retrieval of suitable components is a major issue here. In a generation-based technology, it is much more difficult to identify the components that are being reused. Rather, the knowledge reused (usually domain-specific) is to be found in a program that generates some other program. In a generation-based technology, reusable patterns are an active element used to generate the target system. Prime examples of these two technologies are subroutine libraries and application generators, respectively.

In a black-box reuse approach, elements are reused as-is: they are not modified to fit the application in which they are going to be incorporated. Often, the person reusing the component does not know the internals of the element. Commercial off-the-shelf (COTS) components are a prime example of this approach. Quality and the legal aspects of such components are critical issues. In a white-box approach, elements can be modified before they are incorporated. White-box reuse is most often done in combination with an opportunistic approach. Black-box reuse is 'safer' in that components reused as-is usually have fewer faults than components that are changed before being reused.

Finally, we may categorize reuse approaches according to the type of product that is reused: source code, design, architecture, object, text, and so on. Most often, some form of source code is the reuse product. There is a strong trend to capture reusable design knowledge in the form of design patterns and software architectures; see Chapter 11. Text is a quite different kind of reusable product, for instance in the form of pieces of documentation. The 'user manual' of a modern airplane, for example, easily runs to thousands of pages. Quite likely, each airplane is unique in some aspects and so is its documentation. By developing reusable pieces of documentation, the user manual can be constructed by assembling it from a huge number of documentation fragments.

17.2 REUSE OF INTERMEDIATE PRODUCTS

Libraries with ready-to-use pieces of code, such as those for numerical or statistical computations, have been with us for a long time and their use is widespread. This form of software reuse is not necessarily suited for other domains. In other domains we may be better off reusing 'skeleton' components, i.e. components in which some details have not been filled in yet. In an environment in which the same type of software is developed over and over again, these skeletons may be molded in a reusable design. A similar technique is to reuse the architecture of a software system, as is found in the construction of compilers, for example. These are all examples of composition-based reuse techniques.

By incorporating domain knowledge in *supporting* software, we arrive at the area of application generators and fourth-generation languages. These are examples of generation-based reuse techniques.

17.2.1 Libraries of Software Components

No one in his right mind will think of writing a routine to compute a cosine. If it is not built into the language already, there is bound to be a library routine cos. By investigating the question of why the reuse of mathematical functions is so easy, we come across a number of stumbling blocks that hamper the reuse of software components in other domains:

- **a well-developed field, with a standardized terminology**: 'cosine' means the same to all of us;

- **a small interface**: we need exactly one number to compute a cosine;

- **a standardized data format**: a real number may be represented in fixed point, floating point, or double precision, and that's about all.

Reuse of subroutines works best in an application domain that is well disclosed, one whose notions are clear and where the data to be used is in some standardized format.

The modern history of software reuse starts with McIlroy (1968), who envisaged a bright future for a software component technology at the NATO software engineering conference. In his view, it should be possible to assemble larger components and systems from a vast number of ready-to-use building blocks, much like hardware systems are assembled using standard components. We haven't got there yet. In order for large-scale reuse of software components to become feasible, we first have to solve the following problems:

- **Searching**: We have to search for the right component in a database of available components, which is only possible if we have proper methods available to describe components. If you do not know how to specify what you are looking for, there is little chance you will find it.

- **Understanding**: To decide whether some component is usable, we need a precise and sufficiently complete understanding of what the component does.

- **Adaptation**: The component selected may not exactly fit the problem at hand. Tinkering with the code is not satisfactory and is, in any case, only justified if it is thoroughly understood.

- **Composition**: A system is wired from many components. How do we glue the components together? We return to this topic in Section 17.4.1 and, more extensively, in Chapter 18.

To ease the searching process, hardware components are usually classified in a multi-level hierarchy. Since the naming conventions in that field have been standardized, people are able to traverse the hierarchy. At the lowest level, alternative descriptions of components are given, such as a natural language description, logic schema, and timing information, which describe different aspects of the components. These alternative descriptions further improve the user's understanding of these components.

Several efforts have been made to classify software components in a hierarchical fashion as well. One such effort is described in (Booch, 1987). In his taxonomy (see Figure 17.1), a component is first described by the abstraction it embodies. Secondly, components are described by their time and space behavior, for instance, whether or not objects are static in size or handle their own memory management.

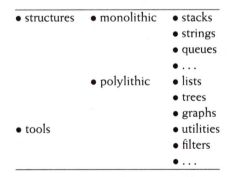

Figure 17.1 Part of a taxonomy of reusable software components

The retrieval problem for software components is very similar to that for textual sources in an ordinary library. Quite a number of classification, or indexing, techniques have been developed for the latter type of problem. Figure 17.2 identifies the main indexing techniques.

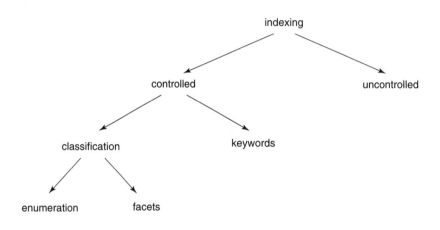

Figure 17.2 Main indexing techniques

An indexing scheme is either controlled or uncontrolled. In a controlled indexing scheme, classifiers are chosen from a finite set of terms. This set of terms may be predefined and immutable. It may also change over time, though only in a controlled way. With controlled indexing, a list of synonyms is often provided to make both searching and indexing more flexible. In an uncontrolled indexing scheme, there is no restriction on the number of terms. Uncontrolled indexing is mostly done by extracting terms from the entity to be indexed. For example, the terms that occur most frequently can be taken as index terms. An advantage of uncontrolled indexing is that it can be done automatically. A disadvantage is that semantic knowledge is lost.

In controlled indexing, one option is simply to use a list of keywords. This list is not ordered and there are no relations between the keywords. An advantage of this scheme is that it is easy to extend the set of index terms. In a classification scheme, on the other hand, the set of index terms is structured in some way. One way of doing so is through some enumerated hierarchical structure, as in Figures 17.1 and 17.2. The power of a hierarchical scheme is its structure. This same structure, however, is also a weakness.

An enumerated scheme offers one specific view on the structure of a domain. Figure 17.1 offers one such view on the domain of generic data structures. Figure 17.3 offers an alternative view on that same domain. In the latter scheme, the structural relationships between elements of a compound data structure have been used to set

structures	0–0	sets
	1–1	stacks
		queues
		lists
		. . .
	1–n	trees
	n–m	graphs

Figure 17.3 An alternative component hierarchy

up the taxonomy. For example, there is a 1–1 relationship between elements of a linear structure such as a list or queue. The taxonomies in Figures 17.1 and 17.3 both seem to be reasonable. Each of them can be used effectively, provided the user knows *how* the hierarchy is organized.

This phenomenon holds for component hierarchies in general. If you do not know how the hierarchy is organized, there is little chance that you will be able to find the component you were looking for.

Strictly enumerative schemes use a predefined hierarchy and force you to search for a node that best fits the component to be classified. Though cross-references to other nodes can be included, the resulting network soon becomes fairly complicated. Facetted classification has certain advantages over the enumerative classification used in the examples of Figures 17.1 and 17.3. A faceted classification scheme uses a number of different characteristics, or *facets*, to describe each component. For example, components in a UNIX environment could be classified according to the action they embody, the object they manipulate, the data structure used, and the system they are part of. Classifying a component is then a matter of choosing an n-tuple which best fits that component.

The essence of an indexing technique is to capture the relevant information of the entities to be classified. This requires knowledge of the kind of questions users will pose, as well as knowledge of the users' search behavior. This is difficult, which makes the development of an indexing language a far from trivial undertaking. Librarians know this. Software engineers responsible for a library of reusable components should know this too. Any user of the Internet will have experienced that finding something that exactly fits your needs is a very difficult task.

The examples contained in Figures 17.1 and 17.3 are somewhat misleading, in that the components found at the leaf nodes of the hierarchy embody abstractions that are all too well known. In other domains, there will be less mutual understanding as regards primitive concepts and their naming. Therefore, setting up a usable taxonomy, i.e. defining an indexing language, is likely to be much more difficult in other domains.

Once a set of candidate components has been found, we need to evaluate these components for their suitability in the current reuse situation. The main types of information useful for such an evaluation are:

- Quality information, for example, a rating for each ISO 9126 quality characteristic (see Chapter 6)

- Administrative information, such as the name and address of the developer, the component's modification history, and information on the price of reuse

- Documentation about what the component does and details about the internals of the component (if it may be adapted)

- Interface information (most often about the types of parameters)

- Test information, to help with testing the component in the reuse situation, such as a set of test cases with the associated expected results.

Valuable quality information is also provided by comments about the reuse history of the component: successful experiences,[1] critical notes about circumstances in which reuse was found to be less successful, and so on.

One further observation that can be made about the reuse of components regards their granularity. The larger a component is, the larger the pay-off will be once it is reused. On the other hand, the reusability of a component decreases as its size grows, because larger components tend to put larger constraints on their environment. This is analogous to Fisher's fundamental theorem of biology: the more an organism is adapted to some given environment, the less suited it is for some other environment.

Some actual experiences suggest that practical, useful component libraries will not contain a huge number of components. For example, Prieto-Diaz (1991a) reports that the asset collection of GTE went from 190 in 1988 to 128 in 1990. Poulin (1999) asserts that the best libraries range from 30 components to, in rare cases, as many as 250 components. For that reason, the classification and retrieval of components is often not the main impediment to a successful reuse program. Rather, filling the library with the *right* components is the real issue. This aspect will be taken up again in Section 17.5.

More detailed technical characteristics of components, their forms, their development and composition, are discussed in Chapter 18.

17.2.2 Templates

In the preceding section, we silently assumed library components to be ready-to-use pieces of code. The applicability of a component can be increased by leaving certain details unspecified. **Templates** or **skeletons** are 'unfinished' components. By *instantiating* them, i.e. by filling in the holes, a (re)usable component results.

---

[1] Be careful though. The software that caused the Ariane 5 disaster was reused from the Ariane 4 and *never* caused any problems there (Lions, 1996); see also Section 1.4.1. This phenomenon may be termed the antidecomposition property of software reuse: if a component has been successfully used in some environment, this does not imply that it can be successfully reused in some other environment.

An example of a possible template is a procedure that implements the quicksort algorithm. Details such as the bounds of the array to be sorted, the type of the array elements, and the relational operator used to compare array elements, are not important for the essence of the algorithm.

As more and more details are left open, a template can be applied more generally. However, there is a price to be paid. The cost of obtaining a complete application is likely to increase in proportion to the number of holes to be filled in.

Templates need not be constrained to just subroutines. It is realistic to think of a template that can be instantiated into a full program for a very specific application domain. Such templates are called application generators and are discussed in Section 17.2.4.

17.2.3 Reuse of Architecture

For each problem, we must look for an architecture which best fits that problem. An inappropriate architecture can never be the basis for a good system. The situation becomes rather different if a problem recurs over and over again in different variants. If a useful standard architecture exists for a particular type of problem, it can be applied in all future variants.

A prime area within computer science where a software architecture is routinely reused is in building compilers. Most compilers are built out of the same components: a lexical analyzer, a parser, a symbol table, a code generator, and a few others. There exist certain well-defined types of parser, such as LL(1) or LALR(1) parsers. There is a large body of theory about how compilers function and this theory is known to the people building compilers. In this way, a generally accepted standard architecture for compilers has evolved. Obviously, it has never been proved that this is the only, or best, way to build a compiler. But it constitutes a sound and well-known method of attacking problems in a notoriously difficult domain.

Large-scale reuse of architecture is still seldom found in other areas. The main reason is that a similar body of shared, crystallized knowledge just does not yet exist for most domains. We may, however, observe that this situation is changing rapidly. In many fields, people are explicitly building such a body of knowledge and molding it into the form of a software architecture. It may be called a domain-specific software architecture (DSSA), a product-line architecture (in which case the architecture provides the basis for a family of similar systems), or an application framework (if the emphasis is on the rapid generation of an application from existing building blocks); see also Chapter 11.

17.2.4 Application Generators and Fourth-Generation Languages

Application generators write programs. An application generator has a fair amount of application-domain knowledge. Usually, the application domain is quite narrow. In order to obtain a program, one obviously needs a specification of that program. Once the specification is available, the program is generated automatically.

The principle being used is the same as that behind a generic package or template: the actual program to be generated is already built into the application generator. Instantiation of an actual program is done by filling in a number of details. The difference is that the size of the code delivered is much bigger with an application generator than with a template. Also, the details are generally provided at a higher level of abstraction, in terms of concepts and notions drawn from the application domain.

An application generator can be employed in each domain with a structure such that complicated operations within that domain can be largely automated. One example is the production of graphical summaries from a database. So-called compiler compilers are another typical example of application generators: given a grammar (i.e. the details) of some programming language, a parser for that language is produced.

Fourth-generation languages or **very-high-level languages** (VHLLs) are often mentioned in the same breath with application generators. Fourth-generation languages offer programming constructs at a much higher level than third-generation programming languages. Model-driven development/architecture (MDD/MDA) may be seen as the ultimate form of this; see also Section 3.4.

Expressions from a given application domain can be directly phrased in the corresponding fourth-generation language. Consequently, the fourth-generation language must have knowledge of that application domain. This generally means that fourth-generation languages are only suited for one specific, limited, domain.

There is no fundamental difference between fourth-generation languages and application generators. When one wants to stress the generative capabilities of a system, the term application generator is mostly applied. The term fourth-generation language highlights the high-level programming constructs being offered. For many such systems, the terms are used interchangeably.

Application generators and fourth-generation languages potentially offer a number of cost savings, since implementation details need not be bothered with: less code is written, the software is more comprehensible, there are fewer errors, and the software is easier to maintain. In practice, this theory often does not come up to expectations. For one thing, the user may want something which is not offered by the system. In that case, a piece of handwritten code must be added to the software being generated automatically. By doing this, one of the main advantages of using fourth-generation languages, easily comprehensible programs at a high level of abstraction, is lost.

17.3 REUSE AND THE SOFTWARE LIFE CYCLE

Reuse affects the way we develop software. We may distinguish two main process models incorporating reuse:

- software development **with** reuse, and

- software development **for** reuse.

Both these approaches to reuse may be combined with any of the software life cycle models discussed earlier. Also, combinations of the 'with' and 'for' reuse models are possible.

The software-development-with-reuse model may be termed a *passive* approach to reuse. It presupposes a repository with a number of reusable assets. At some point during the development process, this repository is searched for reusable assets. If they are found, they are evaluated for their suitability in the situation at hand and, if the evaluation yields a positive answer, the reusable assets are incorporated. The process does not actively seek to extend the repository. As a side effect of the present project, we may add elements to the repository, but no extra effort is spent in doing so. For instance, we do not put in extra effort to test the component more thoroughly, to document it more elaborately, or to develop a more general interface to it. From a reuse perspective, the software-development-with-reuse approach is an opportunistic approach.

A pure software-development-with-reuse model is routinely applied in, e.g. circumstances where we need some mathematical routine. If our project requires some numerical interpolation routine, we search a mathematical library. We may find some routine which uses Gaussian interpolation, fits our needs, and decide to incorporate it. Most likely, the project will not result in a new interpolation routine to be included in the library.

Development with reuse is most often applied at the component level. It has its main impact, therefore, during the architectural design stage when the global decomposition into components is decided upon. We search the repository for suitable candidates, evaluate them, and possibly include them in our architecture. This is a cyclical process, since we may decide to adjust the architecture because of characteristics of the components found. The resulting process model is depicted in Figure 17.4. The model includes some further communication links between later phases of the software development life cycle and the repository. These reflect less far-reaching adaptations to the process model. For example, the repository may contain test cases that can be retrieved and used when testing the system, or we may be able to add our own test results to the repository.

The software-development-for-reuse process model constitutes an *active* approach to reuse. Rather than merely searching an existing base, we *develop* reusable assets. The software-development-for-reuse approach is thus a planned approach to reuse. Again, this approach most often involves reusable components, and we illustrate the approach by considering that situation. During architectural design, extra effort is now spent to make components more general, more reusable. These components are then incorporated into the repository, together with any information that might be of help at a later stage, when searching for or retrieving components. Software-development-for-reuse thus incurs extra costs to the present project. These extra costs are only paid back when a subsequent project reuses the components.

Software-development-for-reuse process models (see Figure 17.5) may differ with respect to the point in time at which components are made reusable and

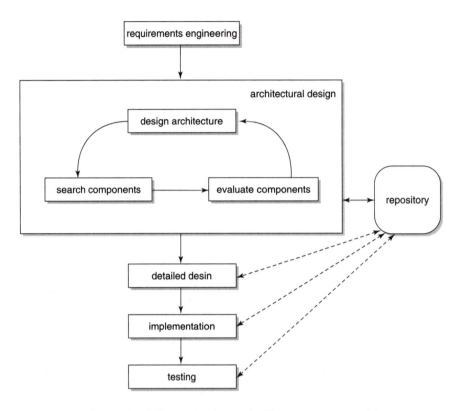

Figure 17.4 Software-development-with-reuse process model

incorporated in the repository. In one extreme form, reusable components are extracted from the system after it has been developed. This may be termed the a posteriori approach. In an a priori software-development-for-reuse approach, reusable components are developed *before* the system in which they are to be used. The latter approach has become known as the **software factory** approach.

If the architecture is developed for one specific problem, chances are that peculiarities of that situation creep into the architecture. As a result, components identified might fit the present situation very well, but they might not fit a similar future situation. The extra effort spent to make these components reusable then might not pay off. To prevent this, development for reuse generally involves a different requirements engineering process as well. Rather than only considering the present situation, the requirements for a family of similar systems are taken into account. So, instead of devising an architecture for the library of our own department, we may decide to develop an architecture which fits the other departments of our university as well. We may even decide to develop an architecture for scientific libraries in general. This more general requirements engineering process is known as domain engineering. The resulting architecture is also termed a product-line architecture; see also Section 18.4.

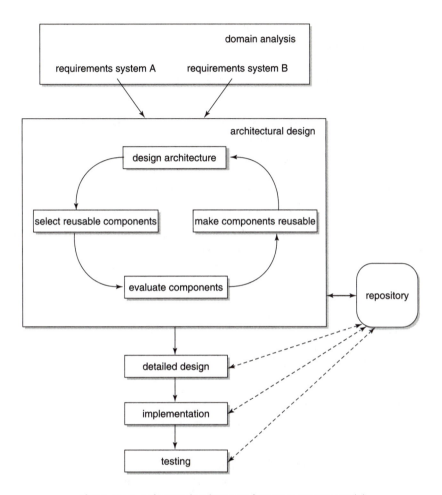

Figure 17.5 Software-development-for-reuse process model

A disadvantage of the model depicted in Figure 17.5 is that the development of components and the development of applications are intertwined. This may lead to tensions. For example, a manager responsible for the delivery of an application may be reluctant to spend resources on developing reusable components. An alternative form of the software-development-for-reuse model therefore is to have separate life cycle processes for the development of reusable components and the development of applications. This latter form is discussed in Section 18.3.

17.4 REUSE TOOLS AND TECHNIQUES

In this section, we consider a few concepts, methods and techniques that have a positive impact on software reuse. In doing so, we reconsider the approaches discussed in the previous section, thus establishing a relation between the reusable software assets discussed in the previous section and the notions discussed here.

17.4.1 From Module Interconnection Language to Architecture Description Language

The relation between different modules of a system can be formally expressed in a **module interconnection language** (MIL). A MIL is an important tool when designing and maintaining large systems consisting of many different modules. A MIL description is a formal description of the global structure of a software system. It can be used to verify the integrity of the system automatically. It can also be used to check whether the various modules conform to the agreed interfaces.

Figure 17.6 contains a small fragment of (hypothetical) MIL code to illustrate the general flavor. The example concerns the structure of a Key Word In Context (KWIC) index program using abstract data types (see (Parnas, 1972) for the description of this problem and its solutions). For each component, it specifies what the component provides to its environment and what it requires from its environment. The overall result is a complete 'uses' structure of the system. For each component, one or more implementations are also indicated. The composition given at the end of the description selects a number of building blocks defined previously.

MILs originated as a consequence of the separation between programming-in-the-small and programming-in-the-large. The essential ideas behind the development of MILs are:

- **A separate language for system design**: A MIL is not a programming language. Rather, it describes desirable properties of modules that are to become part of the system being considered.

- **Static type-checking between different modules**: This automatically guarantees that different modules obey the interface. An interface can only be changed after the corresponding change has been realized in the design.

- **Design and binding of modules in one description**: In the early days of programming-in-the-large the various modules of a system were assembled by hand. Using a MIL, it is done automatically.

- **Version control**: Keeping track of the different versions of (parts of) a system during development and maintenance requires a disciplined approach.

A number of different MILs have been developed. The basic concepts, however, are the same:

- **resources**: everything that can have a name in a programming language (constants, types, variables, and procedures) and can be made available by a module for use in another module;

```
system kwic
    provide kwic_system

    module control_mod
        provide procedure control
        require input_procs, output_procs
        implementation CONTROL
    end control_mod

    module input_mod
        provide package input_procs is
            ...
        end input_procs
        require store_procs
        implementation INPUT1 .. Java
        implementation INPUT2 .. Pascal
    end input_mod

    module store_mod
        provide package store_procs is
            procedure InitStore
            procedure PutCharacter(r, w, c, d)
            procedure CloseStore
            procedure Lines
            procedure Words(r)
            procedure Characters(r, w)
            procedure Character(r, w, c)
        end store_procs
        implementation STORE1 .. Java
        implementation STORE2 .. Pascal
    end store_mod

    ...

    COMPOSITION
    KWIC_SYSTEM_1 = [CONTROL, INPUT2, STORE2, SHIFT2, SORT2,
OUTPUT2]
end kwic
```

Figure 17.6 Partial MIL description of a KWIC-index system

- **modules**: make resources available or use them;

- **systems**: groups of modules which together perform a well-defined task. To the outside world, a system can be viewed as a single module.

The coupling between modules can be modeled as a graph: the nodes of the graph denote modules while the (directed) edges denote the 'uses' relation. Depending on the sophistication of the MIL, this graph can be a tree, an acyclic directed graph, or a directed graph without any restrictions.

To describe the architecture of a system, we need more than is generally provided by a MIL. MILs emphasize components and uses relations between components. In particular, MILs neither treat connectors as first-class citizens nor describe the architectural configuration (topology) of the system. MILs have evolved into architecture description languages (ADLs) that express the latter aspects also.

Figure 17.7 contains part of a (hypothetical) ADL-description of the same KWIC-index program using abstract data types. It defines `Store` as a component with an abstract data type interface. It also lists the various methods, with their signatures, that make up this interface. The main program, `kwic`, is a component too. Its interface is defined to be of type `filter`; both its input and output are streams of characters. The implementation part of `kwic` lists all components and connectors as instances of certain types of component or connector. Furthermore, all connections are made explicit, so that the topology of the system is completely specified. For example, a procedure call connector has two ends: a defining end and a calling end. The defining end of `P` in Figure 17.7 is connected to the routine `Putchar` of module `Store`, while its calling end is connected to the output routine of module `Input`.

MILs and ADLs generally have the same limitations: they only engage themselves in the *syntax* of interfaces. Whether the resources passed on are meaningful or not cannot be assessed.

With respect to the previous section we may note that MILs and ADLs fit in well with forms of reuse where design plays an essential role.

17.4.2 Middleware

In the object-oriented paradigm, it is often stated that two objects, a client and a server, have agreed upon some contract, whereby the client object is allowed to request certain services from the server object. A natural next step is to isolate the contents of this contract, or interface, from both client and server. This is essentially what happens in the Common Object Request Broker Architecture, CORBA.[2] CORBA has been developed by the Object Management Group (OMG), a multivendor effort to standardize object-oriented distributed computing. JavaBeans and Microsoft's COM and .NET are similar solutions to the problem of connecting components with a very long wire.

---

[2]CORBA, ORB, Object Request Broker, OMG-IDL, CORBAservices and CORBAfacilities are trademarks of the Object Management Group.

```
system kwic
    interface is type filter
        player input is StreamIn
        player output is StreamIn
    end interface
    implementation is
        uses Inp instance component Input
        uses Sto instance component Store
        uses Shi instance component Shift
        uses Sor instance component Sort
        uses Out instance component Output
        uses P instance connector ProcedureCall
        uses Q instance connector ProcedureCall

        connect input to Inp.in
        connect output to Out.out
        connect Inp.out to P.caller
        connect Store.Putchar to P.definer
        connect Out.in to Q.caller
        connect Sor.Ith to Q.definer
        ...
    end implementation
end kwic


component Store
    interface is type ADT
        player InitStore is RoutineDef signature ( → void)
        player PutCharacter is RoutineDef signature
            (int × int × int × char → void)
        player CloseStore is RoutineDef signature ( → void)
        player Lines is RoutineDef signature ( → int)
        player Words is RoutineDef signature (int → int)
        player Characters is RoutineDef signature (int × int → int)
        player Character is RoutineDef signature
            (int × int × int → char)
    end interface
    implementation is
        variant STORE2
end Store
```

Figure 17.7 Partial ADL description of a KWIC-index system

```
module KWIC{
    interface Store
        {void InitStore;
        void PutCharacter (in int l, in int w, in int c, in char d);
        void CloseStore;
        int Lines;
        int Words (in int l);
        int Characters (in int l, in int w);
        char Character (in int l, in int w, in int c);
        }
    interface Input ...
    interface Shift ...
    interface Sort ...

    ...
}
```

Figure 17.8 Partial IDL description of a KWIC-index system

CORBA interfaces are expressed in the Interface Definition Language (IDL). Figure 17.8[3] contains part of such an interface definition for the KWIC index program using abstract data types. IDL is a strongly typed language; it is not case-sensitive; and its syntax resembles that of C++. The interface construct collects operations that form a natural group. Typically, the operations of one abstract data type constitute such a group. For each operation, the result type is given, followed by the operation names, and finally the parameters. A result type of **void** indicates that no value is returned. Parameters are prefixed by either **in**, **out**, or **inout**, denoting an input, output, or input–output parameter.

Note the similarity between the texts of Figures 17.6, 17.7 and 17.8. Each of these figures expresses interfaces of components, though with a slightly different syntax and for slightly different purposes.

Middleware primarily shields underlying technology such as hardware, the operating system, and the network. It is a bridging technology. A key driver of middleware is to realize interoperability between independently developed pieces of a software system. It is often used as an integration technology in enterprise information systems. Component models on the other hand emphasize achieving certain quality properties for a collection of components that together make up a system. Component models generally focus on the conventions that components running on top of the middleware must satisfy. Some types of middleware can thus be part of a component model. The Corba Component Model (CCM) is a very relaxed component model. It imposes few constraints on top of its request–response type of

---

[3]Reserved words are printed in bold for legibility.

interaction. Other component models offer a lot more, though. Component models are discussed in Section 18.2.

17.5 PERSPECTIVES OF SOFTWARE REUSE

> Useful abstractions are discovered, not invented.
> Johnson and Foote (1988)

In any reuse technology, the building blocks being reused, whether in the form of subroutines, templates, transformations, or problem solutions known to the designers, correspond to crystallized pieces of knowledge, which can be used in circumstances other than the ones for which they were envisaged originally.

A central question in all the reuse technologies discussed above is how to exploit some given set of reusable building blocks. This is most paramount in various projects in the area of component libraries, where the main goal is to provide ways of retrieving a useable component for the task at hand.

Alternatively, we may look at software reusability from an entirely different angle: what building blocks do we need in order to be able to use them in different applications?

Reuse is not the same as reusability. Reuse of software is only profitable if the software is indeed reusable. The second approach addresses the question of how to identify a useful, i.e. reusable, collection of components in an organized way. Such a collection of reusable components is tied to a certain application domain.

When trying to identify a reusable set of components, the main question is to decide *which* components are needed. A reusable component is to be valued, not for the trivial reason that it offers relief from implementing the functionality yourself, but for offering a piece of the *right* domain knowledge, the very functionality you need, gained through much experience and an obsessive desire to find the right abstractions.

Components should reflect the primitive notions of the application domain. In order to be able to identify a proper set of primitives for a given domain, considerable experience with software development for that domain is needed. While this experience is being built up, the proper set of primitives will slowly evolve.

Actual implementation of those primitives is of secondary importance. A collection of primitives for a given domain defines an *interface* that can be used when developing different programs in that domain. The ideas, concepts, and structures that play an important role in the application domain have to be present in the interface. Reuse of that interface is more important than reuse of its implementation. The interface structures the software. It offers a focal point in designing software for that application area.

In (Sikkel and van Vliet, 1988), such a collection of primitives is called a domain-oriented virtual machine (DOVM). A domain is a 'sphere or field of activity or influence'. A domain is defined by consensus and its essence is the shared understanding of some community. It is characterized by a collection of common notions that show a certain coherence, while the same notions do not exist or do not show that coherence outside the domain. Domains can be taken more or less broadly. Example domains are, for instance:

- accounting software,

- accounting software for multinationals,

- accounting software for multinationals, developed by Soft Ltd.

All accounting software will incorporate such notions as 'ledger' and 'balance'. Accounting software for multinationals will have some notions in common that do not exist in accounting systems for the grocery store or the milkman, such as provisions for cross-border cash flow. Representation of notions in software developed by Soft Ltd. will differ from those of other firms because of the use of different methodologies or conventions.

The essential point is that certain notions play an important role in the domain in question. Those notions also play a role in the software for that domain. If we want to attain reuse within a given domain, these domain-specific notions are important. These notions have certain *semantics* which are fixed within the domain, and are known to people working in that domain. These semantically primitive notions should be our main focus in trying to achieve reusability.

For most domains, it is not immediately clear which primitives are the right ones. It is very much a matter of trial and error. By and by, the proper set of primitives show themselves. As a domain develops, we may distinguish various stages:

- At the start, there is no clear set of notions and all software is written from scratch. Experience slowly builds up, while we learn from previous mistakes.

- At the second stage, similar problems are being recognized and solved in a similar way. The first semantic primitives are recognized. By trial and error, we find out which primitives are useful and which are not.

- At the third stage, the domain is ripe for reuse. A reasonable amount of software has been developed, the set of concepts has stabilized, there are standard solutions for standard problems.

- Finally, the domain has been fully explored. Software development for the domain can largely be automated. We do not program in the domain any more. Instead, we use a standard interface formed by the semantic primitives of the domain.

Most reuse occurs at the last stage, by which time it is not recognized as such. A long time ago, computers were programmed in assembly language. In high-level languages, we 'just write down what we want' and the compiler makes this into a 'real' program. This is generally not seen as reuse any more. A similar phenomenon occurs in the transition from a third-generation language to a fourth-generation language.

From the reusability point of view, the above classification is one of a normal, natural, evolution of a domain. The various stages are categorized by reuse at qualitatively different levels:

- at the first stage, there is no reuse;

- at the second stage, reuse is ad hoc;

- at the third stage, reuse is structured. Existing components are reused in an organized way when new software is being developed;

- at the fourth stage, reuse is institutionalized and automated. Human effort is restricted to the upper levels of abstraction.

Within a given domain, an informal language is used. In this informal domain language, the same thing can be phrased in quite different ways, using concepts that are not sharply defined. Yet, informal language is understandable, because the concepts refer to a universe of discourse that both speaker and listener share.

Concepts in a formal language do not refer to experience or everyday knowledge. They merely have a meaning in some formal system. A virtual machine is such a formal system and its language is a formal language.

To formalize a domain is to construct a formal (domain) language that mimics an existing informal language. We then have to choose from the different semantic primitives that exist informally. Sometimes also, it is convenient to add new primitives that fit neatly within the formalized domain.

As an example of the latter, consider the domain of computerized typesetting. Part of formatting a document concerns assembling words into lines and lines into paragraphs. The sequence of words making up a paragraph must be broken into lines such that the result is typographically pleasing. Knuth and Plass (1981) describe this problem in terms of 'boxes', 'glue', and 'penalties'. Words are contained in boxes, which have a certain width. White space between words is phrased in terms of glue, which may shrink or stretch. A nominal amount of white space between adjacent words is preferred and a penalty of 0 is associated with this nominal spacing. Putting words closer together (shrinking the glue), or wider apart (stretching the glue), incurs a non-negative penalty. The more this glue is stretched or shrunk, the higher the penalty. The penalty associated with formatting a complete paragraph in some given way then is the sum of the penalties associated with the inter-word spacing within that formatted paragraph. The problem may now be rephrased as: break the paragraph into lines such that the total penalty is minimal. (Note that penalties may also be associated with other typographically less-desirable properties, such as hyphenation.) The notions 'box', 'glue', and 'penalty' give a neat formalization to certain aspects of typography. They also lead to an efficient solution for the above problem, using a dynamic programming technique.

In practice, formalizing is not a one-shot activity. Rather, it is an iterative process. The formalized version does not exactly describe the informal language. It fixes one possible interpretation. If we study its semantics, it may have some undesirable aspects. In due course, an acceptable compromise is reached between those who use the language (in higher domains) and those who implement it (in lower domains). Once the formal domain language is fixed, it also affects the informal domain language. People working within the domain start to use the primitives of the formal language.

It is now clear that it is, in general, not wise to go directly from stage one (no reuse) to stage three (structured reuse). Formalization has much in common with standardization. It has a solidifying effect on the semantic primitives of the domain. Our notion of these primitives changes, because we do not any longer consider them as coming from the intuitive universe of discourse, but as being based on the underlying formalism. A crucial question, namely whether we formalized the *right* semantic primitives, then becomes harder to answer.

Stage two (ad hoc reuse) is crucial. In this stage, we get insight into the application domain and discover *useful* semantic primitives. This experience, both in working with the primitives and in implementing them, is of vital importance for the formalization of the domain in the right way.

The above discussion suggests an evolutionary approach to reuse. To start with, potentially reusable building blocks can be extracted from existing software products. While gaining experience with the reuse of these building blocks, better insight is obtained and better abstractions of concepts and mechanisms from the application domain are discovered. The library of reusable building blocks thus evolves and stabilizes over time.

This evolutionary process can be structured and guided through **domain analysis**, a process in which information used in developing software for a particular domain is identified, captured, structured, and organized for further reuse. Domain analysts and domain experts may use a variety of sources when modeling a domain, including expert knowledge, existing implementations and documentation. They extract and abstract the relevant information and encapsulate them in reusable building blocks.

Domain analysis often results not only in a collection of reusable building blocks. It also yields a reusable architecture for that domain: the domain-specific software architecture, product-line architecture, or application framework mentioned in Section 17.2.3. To increase the reusability of these building blocks across different operating systems, networks, and so on, they are put on top of some middleware platform.

17.6 NON-TECHNICAL ASPECTS OF SOFTWARE REUSE

The problem is not lack of technology but unwillingness to address the most important issues influencing software reuse: managerial, economic, legal, cultural, and social.
Prieto-Diaz (1991b)

Myth #1: Software reuse is a technical problem.
Tracz (1988)

Until now, we have discussed only the technical aspects of software reuse. Software engineering is not only concerned with technical aspects but with people and other environmental aspects as well.

By being embedded within a society, the field of software engineering will also be influenced by that society. Software reuse in the US is likely to be different from software reuse in Japan or Europe. Because of cultural differences and different economic structures, it is not a priori clear that, say, the Toshiba approach to reuse can be copied by Europeans, with the same results.

Though our discussion so far has concerned the technical aspects of software reuse, it is not complete without a few words on non-technical issues. These non-technical issues are intimately intertwined with the more technical ones. Various practitioners in the field of software reuse have argued that the technology needed for software reuse is available, but that the main problems inhibiting a prosperous reuse industry are non-technical in nature.

Successful reuse programs share the following characteristics:

- Unconditional and extensive management support. A reuse program requires changes in the way software is developed. Management commitment is essential for making such changes work. In particular, building a base of reusable assets requires an initial investment which may not pay off for some time.

- Establishment of an organizational support structure. The organization must provide the initiative for the reuse program, funding, and policies. A separate body is needed to assess potential candidates for inclusion in the reuse library. A librarian is needed to maintain the library.

- Incremental program implementation. A first catalog with potential reusable assets can be built at a relatively low cost. Positive experiences with such an initial library will raise awareness and provide the necessary incentives (and funding) to expand the library, devise a classification scheme, etc.

- Significant success, both financial and organizational. Raytheon for example reports a 50% increase in productivity over a period of several years.

- Compulsory or highly incentivized. Programmers suffer from the 'not invented here' syndrome. By creating an environment that values both the creation of reusable software and the reuse of software, an atmosphere is established in which reuse may become a success.

- Domain analysis was conducted either consciously or unconsciously. Domain analysis identifies the concepts and mechanisms underlying some well-understood domain. This way, the *really* useful concepts are captured in reusable resources.

- Explicit attention to architectural issues, such as a common architecture across a product line.

Some of the non-technical aspects are discussed in the subsections below.

17.6.1 Economics

> Reuse is a long term investment.
> Tracz (1990)

Reuse does not come for free. In a traditional development environment, products are tailored to the situation at hand. Similar situations are likely to require slightly different products or product components. For a software component to become reusable, it has to be generalized from the situation at hand, thoroughly documented and tested, incorporated in a library and classification scheme, and maintained as a separate entity. This requires an initial investment, which only starts to pay off after a certain period of time. One of the real dangers for a software reuse program is that it gets trapped in a devil's loop of the kind depicted in Figure 17.9.

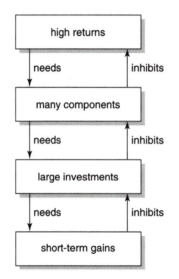

Figure 17.9 Software reuse devil's loop

The major factors that determine the cost of a reusable building block are:

- the initial development cost of that component,

- the direct and indirect costs of including the component in a library, and

- the cost of (possibly) adapting the component and incorporating it into the system under development.

It is obvious that the development of a reusable component is more costly than the development of a nonreusable component with the same functionality. Estimates of this extra cost vary from 50% to 100% (see also Section 7.1.5 on the COCOMO 2 cost estimation model). It depends on the usage frequency of the component whether its development eventually pays off.

More immediate returns on investment can be obtained if the reuse program starts small, with an initial library whose members are extracted from existing products. Expansion of the program can then be justified on the basis of positive early experiences. But even then, non-project-specific funds must be allocated to the reuse program.

The economic consequences of software reuse go beyond cost savings in production and maintenance. The nature of the software development process itself changes. Software becomes a *capital* good. High initial costs are coupled with returns over a longer time period. The production of software thus becomes a *capital-intensive* process (Wegner, 1984). The production of non-reusable software, on the other hand, is a *labor-intensive* process. Many man-months are spent, but the profits are reaped as soon as the project is finished.

Whereas labor-intensive software production tends to concentrate on finishing the project at hand on time and within budget, capital-intensive software production takes into account long-term business concerns such as the collective workers' knowledge and the collection of reusable assets. The software factory paradigm discussed earlier in this chapter as well as the various approaches emphasizing the architecture of a software system fit this view of the software development organization.

17.6.2 Management

> Myth #9: Software reuse will just happen.
> Tracz (1988)

Getting software reuse off the ground cannot depend on spontaneity. Rather, software production ought to be organized so that reuse is promoted. In Chapter 3, we noted that the traditional waterfall model tends to impede software reuse. In the waterfall model, emphasis is placed on measuring and controlling project progress. The product quality with respect to reusability is hard to measure. There is no real incentive to pursue reusability, since the primary (and often the only) goal is to finish the current project within time and budget. There is no motivation to make the next project look good. Consequently, software reusability tends to have a low priority.

If reuse is not a clear objective of our software development process, it is bound to remain accidental. Programmers tinker with code they have written before if and when they happen to notice similarities between successive problems. This unplanned approach to reuse is also known as **code scavenging** or **code salvaging**. This is distinct from the process of reusing software that was *designed* to be reused. In the life cycle perspective, this shows up as the difference between software-development-with-reuse and software-development-for-reuse.

In software-development-for-reuse, software reuse has been incorporated in the software development process. In this process model, reusable assets are actively sought. The concepts and mechanisms underlying some domain are identified and captured in reusable resources. The focus of software management then shifts from the delivery of individual products to maintaining and nurturing a rich collection of reusable artifacts. Some of the successful reuse programs, such as those reported in (Prieto-Diaz, 1991b), have followed this approach.

The library of reusable assets itself needs to be managed. An organizational infrastructure must be created which makes the library accessible (through documentation and classification schemes), assesses candidates for inclusion in the library, maintains and updates the library, etc. A separate organizational role, the librarian, may be created for this purpose. Its tasks resemble that of a database administrator.

One type of reuse only mentioned in passing is *reuse of good people*. Expert designers are worth their weight in gold. Every average programmer is capable of writing a complicated, large program. In order to obtain a better, smaller, more elegant, radically new solution for that same problem, we need a person who has bright ideas from time to time.

A major problem in our field is that managers are rated higher than programmers or designers. If you are really good, you will sooner or later, but usually sooner, rise in the hierarchy and become part of the management. According to (Brooks, 1987), there is only one way to counteract this phenomenon. To ensure that bright people remain system designers, we need a dual ranking scheme, one in which good designers have the same job prospects as good managers. Once again: the software process must be reconsidered as one of growing both people and the base of reusable assets (Curtis, 1989).

17.6.3 Psychology of Programmers

> Reusing other people's code would prove that I don't care about my work.
> I would no more reuse code than Hemingway would reuse other authors'
> paragraphs.
> Cox (1990)

Software reuse means that programmers have to adapt, incorporate, or rejuvenate software written by other programmers. There are two important psychological aspects to this process:

- Are programmers willing to do so?

- Are they capable of doing so?

The first aspect is often mentioned as a major stumbling-block to establishing a positive attitude towards software reuse. Barnes and Bollinger (1991) phrase this problem of image as follows: 'Anyone who has ever gone to an auto salvage yard to pick up a spare part for his old car "knows" what reuse is.'

Many authors suggest a solution to this problem that is both simple and effective: change the programming culture. The experiences at Raytheon and other places suggest that it is indeed possible, given the right incentives and, more importantly, a management attitude that pays attention to longer-term goals and developers' expectations about the nature of their work.

Research into the comprehensibility of software, such as reported in (Soloway and Ehrlich, 1984), shows that programmers use certain standard schemes in standard situations. Experienced programmers tend to get confused when a known problem has been tackled using (to them) non-standard solutions. As a consequence, the reusability of components is likely to be increased if the components embody abstractions the programmers are familiar with. Domain analysis addresses the same issues by trying to identify the notions that are shared by experts in a particular domain.

One side-effect of the use of standard designs and standard components is the increased comprehensibility of the resulting software. Once all programmers get used to the same house style, all programs read as if they were written by one team. Any team can understand and adapt a program written by another team. This effect is stronger if we are able to explicitly name these larger constructs, as is done with design patterns and architectural styles.

17.7 SUMMARY

Reuse projects vary considerably in a number of dimensions:

- The thing to be reused may be a concrete component such as a piece of code or a software architecture, a more abstract concept, or even a process element such as a procedure to handle change requests.

- The scope of reuse may be horizontal or vertical. In horizontal reuse, components are generic. In vertical reuse, they are domain-specific.

- The approach to reuse may be planned or opportunistic. In planned reuse, software is *designed* to be reused. In opportunistic reuse, software is reused haphazardly, if and when we happen to know of its existence, if and when it happens to fit the current situation. Planned reuse is software development *for* reuse, opportunistic reuse is software development *with* reuse.

- Reuse may be compositional or generative. A composition-based technology aims at incorporating existing components into software to be newly developed. In a generation-based technology, the knowledge reused is to be found in some program that generates some other program.

- Reuse may be black-box or white-box. In black-box reuse, elements are reused as-is. In white-box reuse, they may be adapted to fit the situation at hand.

Classification schemes for reusable elements resemble those for textual sources in an ordinary library. They vary from a simple Key Word In Context approach to fully automated keyword retrieval from existing documentation, and may even involve elaborate knowledge of the application domain. With respect to retrieval, systems may employ an extensive thesaurus to relate similar terms or offer browsing facilities to inspect 'similar' components.

Software reusability is an objective, rather than a field. It emerged as an issue within software engineering, not because of its appeal as a scientific issue per se, but driven by the expected gain in software development productivity.

The history of software reuse starts in 1968. At the first software engineering conference, McIlroy already envisaged a bright future for a software component technology, somewhat similar to that for hardware components. The first conference specifically devoted to software reuse was held in 1983 (ITT, 1983). Since then, the topic has received increased attention. Over the years, a shift in research focus can be observed from domain-independent technical issues, such as classification techniques and component libraries, to domain-specific content issues, such as architectural frameworks and domain analysis.

A central question in all reuse technologies discussed is how to exploit some set of reusable building blocks. As argued in Section 17.5, an equally important question is which building blocks are needed to start with. Answering the latter question requires a much deeper understanding of the software design process than we currently have.

Successful reuse programs share a number of characteristics:

- unconditional and extensive management support,

- an organizational support structure,

- incremental program implementation,

- significant success, both financial and organizational,

- compulsory or highly incentivized,

- domain analysis conducted either consciously or unconsciously,

- explicit attention to architectural issues.

Reuse is not a magic word with which the productivity of the software development process can be substantially increased at a stroke. But we do have a sufficient number of departure-points for further improvements to get a remunerative reuse technology off the ground. Foremost amongst these are the attention to non-technical issues involved in software reuse and an evolutionary approach in conjunction with a conscientious effort to model limited application domains.

17.8 FURTHER READING

The modern history of software reuse starts at the first NATO software engineering conference (McIlroy, 1968). The first conference specifically devoted to software reuse was held in 1983 (ITT, 1983). (Biggerstaff and Perlis, 1989) and (Freeman, 1987) are well-known collections of articles on software reuse. (Karlsson, 1995) is a good textbook on the subject. It is the result of an Esprit project called REBOOT. Amongst other things, it describes the software-development-with-reuse and software-development-for-reuse process models. (Reifer, 1997) and (Mili *et al.*, 2002) are other textbooks on software reuse. Frakes and Kang (2005) discuss the status of software reuse research.

The various reuse dimensions are discussed in (Prieto-Diaz, 1993). A survey of methods for classifying reusable software components is given in (Frakes and Gandel, 1990). Advice on when to choose black-box reuse or white-box reuse is given in (Ravichandran and Rothenberger, 2003). Selby (2005) discusses fault characteristics of black-box versus white-box reuse. The application of faceted classification to software reuse is described in (Prieto-Diaz, 1991a).

(Prieto-Diaz and Neighbors, 1986) gives an overview of Module Interconnection Languages. (Medvidovic and Taylor, 1997) gives an overview of major types of Architecture Description Languages. CORBA is described in (Siegel, 1995). (Emmerich *et al.*, 2007) give an excellent overview of research on middleware. References for component-based software engineering are given at the end of Chapter 18.

The non-technical nature of software reuse is discussed in (Tracz, 1988) and (Fafchamps, 1994). Software reuse success factors are discussed in (Prieto-Diaz, 1991b), (Rine and Sonnemann, 1998), (Fichman and Kemerer, 2001), (Morisio *et al.*, 2002a), and (Rothenberger *et al.*, 2003). Models to quantify reuse levels, maturity, costs and benefits are discussed in (Frakes and Terry, 1996). The Raytheon approach to software reuse is described in (Lanergan and Grasso, 1984). Experiences with successful reuse programs are collected in (Schaeffer *et al.*, 1993), (Software, 1994b), and (JSS, 1995b).

Exercises

1. What is the difference between composition-based reuse and generation-based reuse?

2. What is a faceted classification scheme?

3. What is the difference between horizontal and vertical reuse?

4. Describe the software-development-with-reuse process model. Where does it differ from the software-development-for-reuse process model?

5. Discuss the main differences between module interconnection languages (MILs) and architecture description languages (ADLs). How do these differences relate to software reuse?

6. How does CORBA promote reuse?

7. To what extent do you consider a domain-independent library of reusable software components a realistic option?

8. ♠ For a domain with which you are familiar, identify a set of potentially reusable software components and devise a classification scheme for them. Consider both a hierarchical and a faceted classification scheme and assess their merits with respect to ease of classification and search, and extensibility.

9. ♠ For the same domain, assess its maturity level and that of the components identified. Can you relate the maturity level of components to their perceived reusability?

10. ♡ Devise a managerial setting and a software development process model for a component-based software factory.

11. ♠ Assess one or more of the following domains and determine the extent and kind of reuse that has been achieved:

   • window management systems;
   • (2D) computer graphics;
   • user-interface development systems;
   • office automation;
   • salary administration;
   • hypertext systems.

12. ♡ For the domains studied in Exercise 11, is there any relation between the reuse level achieved and (de facto or de jure) standardization within the domain? Can you discern any influence of standardization on reuse, or vice versa?

13. ♠ Discuss possible merits of knowledge-based approaches to software reusability.

14. ♡ From your own past in software development, make an inventory of:

    • components developed by yourself which you reused more than once, and

    • components developed by others and reused by you.

    To what extent does the 'not-invented-here' syndrome apply to your situation? Is reuse in your situation accidental or deliberate? Were the components designed for reuse or was it, rather, a form of code scavenging?

15. ♡ Suppose you developed a routine to determine the inverse of a matrix. The routine is to be incorporated in a library of reusable components. Which aspects of this routine should be documented in order that others may determine the suitability of the routine for their application?

16. ♡ In developing abstract data types (ADTs), we try to strictly separate (and hide) implementation concerns from the users of those ADTs. To what extent could these implementation concerns be relevant to the person reusing them?

18

Component-Based Software Engineering

With Michel Chaudron, Technische Universiteit Eindhoven, The Netherlands, and Ivica Crnkovic, Mälardalen University, Sweden

LEARNING OBJECTIVES

- To understand the essentials of component-based software engineering

- To know the main characteristics of components and component models

- To be aware of software development processes for component-based systems

- To be aware of the mutual relations between software architecture and component models

> In component-based software engineering (CBSE), systems are assembled from existing components. In CBSE, there are independent development processes for components and for systems built out of components. Composing a system out of components is only possible if those components conform to the same set of standards, also known as their component model. Component models differ in the way they handle quality properties. Component models influence software architecture, and vice versa.

Chapter 17 gave a general discussion of software reuse. In this chapter, we focus on a specific type of reuse, that of components. A **component** is a building block for software, much like an LCD screen is a building block for a mobile phone and a rubber tire is a building block for a car. The idea behind **component-based software engineering** (CBSE) is to assemble systems out of existing, independently developed, components. CBSE entails more than the mere reuse of components, though. It also aims to increase the flexibility of systems through improved modularization.

The idea of separating the manufacturing of parts and the assemblage of those parts into a product was pioneered around 1800 in the production of rifles. This idea has fundamentally changed the hardware-manufacturing business. In this chapter, we discuss how to apply the same idea to the production of software. The production of software parts – the components – is separated from the assemblage of those parts into applications. As a consequence, there will be two separate development processes, one for components and one for applications. These processes are not independent. Applications need certain components and components had better be used in applications. So there are dependencies between the two development processes. These development processes and their dependencies are discussed in Section 18.3.

LEGO is often taken as an example of a component-based approach. LEGO is a set of building blocks in a large variety of shapes and colors. LEGO is sold in boxes that contain a number of blocks that can be composed to make up toys such as cars, trains or airplanes. In order to enable their composition, all LEGO blocks provide small cylindrical stubs on the top and complementary holes on the bottom of the shape. The conformance of the blocks to this convention ensures that blocks, possibly from different LEGO boxes, can be combined. Moreover, they can be combined into constructions other than the construction suggested by the manufacturer. Hence, LEGO blocks have the characteristic that they are easily composable and are generic. These are characteristics that we also look for in software components.

There are however, many more toys that consist of building blocks that can be assembled. Take, for example, Meccano and traditional jigsaw puzzles. While each of these can be combined with blocks of the same type (Meccano–Meccano, LEGO–LEGO, etc.), they cannot be combined with blocks of another type (e.g. Meccano–LEGO). This illustrates that composability of building blocks is related to the conformance to a set of conventions. This set of conventions is called a **component model**. Component models and components are discussed in Section 18.2.

Components are to become parts of bigger systems. As such, they have to fit the architecture of those systems. One possibility is to first design the architecture and then search for components that fit the architecture. A second possibility is to design an architecture of a family of (similar) systems and develop components that fit a variety of products within that family. A third possibility is to use a bottom-up approach in which the architecture is made to fit the available components. These different architectural approaches are discussed in Section 18.4.

A warning about terminology is warranted. In CBSE, the word 'component' has a more specific meaning than its meaning in Standard English. Whereas 'component' in general means 'part', in CBSE a 'component' is 'a piece of software that conforms to the rules of a particular software component model'. The component model used in one system may be very different from that used in another system. As a result, the notion of component differs between different types of domain. In the literature, the component model assumed is often implicit. Furthermore, in earlier chapters of this book we used the term 'component' in its general sense of 'part' or 'constituent'.

CBSE is not a goal in itself, but a means to an end. CBSE is aimed at contributing to the realization of the business goals of an organization. The main motivations for applying CBSE are the topic of Section 18.1.

18.1 WHY COMPONENT-BASED SOFTWARE ENGINEERING?

> It is not the strongest of the species that survive, nor the most intelligent,
> but the ones most responsive to change.
> Charles Darwin

CBSE contributes to the following business goals:

- CBSE increases the quality of software, especially its evolvability and maintainability. This holds for both the quality of individual components and for the quality of the architecture of systems built in a component-based way.

- CBSE increases the productivity of software development (more software per dollar).

- CBSE shortens the development time, and thus time to market, of software.

We explain these benefits in a bit more detail.

CBSE leads to a higher quality of individual software components in the following ways:

- CBSE requires us to make the dependencies of components explicit. This reduces programming errors that occur as a result of unknown or undocumented dependencies. Also, testing can be performed more effectively if dependencies are explicit.

- The more often a component is (re)used, the more likely it is that errors are found and removed. Errors may be uncovered during execution of a component or through the testing that is done before a component is integrated into a system.

- Before components are offered to other parties on a commercial basis, they must be tested thoroughly. Otherwise, the company that offers this component will lose its credibility and go out of business quickly.

- Components must be well-documented, otherwise parties other than the creator of the component have great difficulty in using the component.

Developing software in a component-based way requires a discipline of strict modularization. The strict modularization limits the domino effect of changes in the system. Hence, the effort needed to change a component-based system is likely to be less than the effort needed when the same changes are made to a system that is not modularized according to a component-based design discipline. This property improves maintainability. When subsystems are strictly modularized, it becomes easier to change parts to support new features. This improves the ability of the system to evolve.

CBSE increases productivity through the reuse of building blocks that have been developed in earlier efforts or by other parties. In order for this to enhance productivity, the acquisition and integration of a component should of course be cheaper than developing that component from scratch. This general characteristic of software reuse has been discussed in Chapter 17.

The size of professional software systems is in the order of millions of lines of code. The time needed to realize such software systems may span several years. CBSE contributes to reducing the development time of software by using existing components rather than developing components from scratch. Another way in which CBSE may reduce development time is by enabling concurrent development of components. Concurrent development of components is easier if components have minimal mutual dependencies, i.e. when components are loosely coupled. Any dependencies that do exist between components must be specified explicitly. Hence, in CBSE, components are designed and specified in such a way that they can be constructed independently of, and concurrently with, other components.

18.2 COMPONENT MODELS AND COMPONENTS

In the introduction to this chapter, we made an analogy with LEGO and Meccano and noticed that composing building blocks is feasible only if they conform to the same set of conventions.

In the world of engineering, the conventions for components are chosen such that they can be used for constructing systems with certain properties. For example, a racing car requires parts that are lightweight and aerodynamic in order to obtain an overall system that is fast. An army tank requires parts that are tough in order to make a robust system.

Software components encapsulate functionality in a form that conforms to a set of conventions. These conventions ensure composability and determine the properties of systems that can be built using a particular type of components. Rather than physical properties, such as weight and shape, software components are required to have properties such as computational efficiency, resource efficiency, and reliability. These characteristics are captured in the following definition.

A **component model** defines standards for:

- properties that individual components must satisfy, and

- methods, and possibly mechanisms, for composing components.

Informally, a component model defines the types of building block and the recipe for putting these building blocks together. This definition stresses a generic constraint: components are composable.

A **component** is a building block that conforms to a component model

The key aspect of this definition is composability. For software, composability may be achieved by using explicit interfaces for defining what is offered as well as what is required by a piece of software and by defining the manner in which a component can communicate with other pieces of software. Whereas composability is a necessary technical requirement, genericity is a desirable requirement from a business perspective. A generic component can be used more often and hence has greater potential for generating revenue. The genericity characteristic implies certain technical characteristics. For instance, components with lower coupling generally have fewer dependencies on their environment and, hence, can be applied in a wider context. The following definition of a component is more specific to software.

A **software component**:

- implements some functionality,

- has explicit dependencies through provided and required interfaces,

- communicates through its interfaces only, and

- has a structure and behavior which conform to an encompassing software component model; notably, this applies to the interfaces and patterns of communication of the component.

Whereas a component model defines a standard, a component technology is the collection of implementation artifacts that realize this standard.

A software **component technology** is the implementation of a component model by means of:

- standards and guidelines for the implementation and execution of software components, and

- executable software that supports the implementation, assembly, deployment, and execution of components.

There are many examples of software component technologies. A large number of component models is oriented towards business information systems. These include Enterprise JavaBeans (EJB) (Burke and Monson-Haefel, 2006), COM+ (Box, 1997), .NET (Chappell, 2006), and the CORBA-Component Model (CCM). Other component models are oriented towards embedded systems: the Robocop component model (Muskens *et al.*, 2005) for consumer electronics and the SaveCCM (Åkerholm *et al.*, 2007) for automotive systems. Each of these technologies embodies some underlying component model. Let's look at the .NET component technology as an example. Implementation support for .NET is provided by the Visual Studio .NET toolset which includes dedicated editors and compilers. Run-time support is provided by a run-time execution platform (called the common language run-time, CLR) that runs on top of the regular operating system.

The composability requirement for components entails the standardization of interfaces and interaction. These conditions may be sufficient to ensure composability at the implementation level of the component. However, much more can be said about properties that are generally desired from software components, such as component granularity, encapsulation, cohesion, or testability. These additional properties are related to general aspects of the design and development of components and are discussed in Chapter 12.

Although the definition of a component model allows a lot of freedom, in practice there is a lot of commonality amongst component models. Comparing component technologies shows that they standardize conventions that cover multiple stages of the development of components. In the next subsection we discuss how the standards defined by component models are related to different development stages of a component.

18.2.1 Component Forms in Component Models

When we look at the life cycle of a component, it passes through the following global stages, depicted in Figure 18.1: development, packaging, distribution, deployment, and execution. In the development stage, the design, specification, implementation, and meta data of components is constructed. In the packaging stage, all information that is needed for trading and deployment of the component implementation is grouped into a single package. The distribution stage deals with searching, retrieval, and transportation of components. The deployment stage addresses issues related to

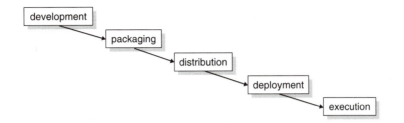

Figure 18.1 Stages of a component life cycle

the integration of component implementations in an executable system on some target platform. Finally, the execution stage deals with executing and possibly upgrading components.

Across these different stages of their life cycle, components are represented in different forms. In the development stage, components may be represented by means of a design or specification language, such as a set of UML diagrams, and as a set of source-code and configuration files, such as a directory with .c and .h files for C or a set of class files in case of Java, that together can be turned into executable code. In the packaging stage, the files that together form a component are bundled into a single unit, for example in a compressed file. In the distribution stage, packaged components are represented in a format that can be transmitted across a network or stored on some physical carrier such as a disk or memory stick. This may be standardized by a component model but, in general, distribution formats are from the area of distributed systems – nowadays, mostly Internet standards. At the deployment stage, components are unpackaged in a form that can be installed onto a target machine. In the execution stage, components take the form of blocks of code and data in the memory of a processor and cause a set of actions on this processor. All these forms are different views on, or manifestations of, what is logically a single building block.

Cheesman and Daniels (2000) introduce convenient terminology for denoting the different forms of components. Figure 18.2 shows the distinction between different forms of components that they introduced and the relations between them. Figure 18.3 shows how these different forms relate to different stages of development.

The **component specification** describes properties that are, or should be, realized by the corresponding component implementation. Many different properties may be included in a specification. A component specification typically includes the following important properties:

• functionality (what a component does),

• behavior (the order of actions a component performs),

• interaction potential (the ways according to which a component can interact with other software),

• quality properties such as performance and reliability.

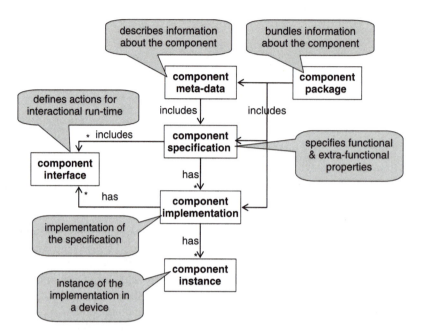

Figure 18.2 Characterization of component forms

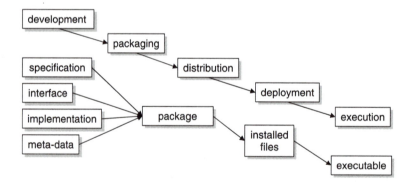

Figure 18.3 Forms of a component at different stages of the life cycle

Of course, these properties should be specified in a complete, precise, and verifiable way.

The interface of a component is defined in the design stage and continues to play an important role in execution time. A component interface defines the actions through which components may communicate with each other. Interfaces are offered by one component in order to be used by other components. The component that offers an interface is responsible for realizing the actions of the interface. The component that uses the actions of an interface only needs to know what the action achieves, not how it is achieved. In this sense, users of an interface are shielded from the machinery that is used to implement it. This shielding is a means of abstraction – details about the realization are omitted. As a result of this abstraction, different implementations of an interface may be used to realize some action without users of the interface being aware of it. This is, of course, the basic idea of information hiding, as discussed in Chapter 12.

A typical use of this property of interfaces is to replace a component by a newer version (see Figure 18.4). This figure shows that component P can be replaced by component P' if P' realizes the same interface Ix. Component R that uses interface Ix need not be changed. The component that offers an interface is called the provider of that interface; the component that uses the interface is called the requirer of the interface.

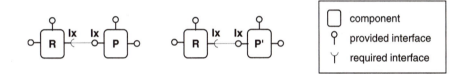

Figure 18.4 Component P can be replaced by component P' if P' realizes the same interface Ix

The purpose and scope of a component specification differ from the purpose and scope of a component interface. The most important difference is that specifications define a *realization contract*, while interfaces describe *usage contracts*. During development of a component, the specification is a prescription of what the implementation should realize. As such, the specification may include the definition of interfaces. Once the implementation of a component is finished, a specification describes what architects and developers who wish to use a component may want to know about it. Here, the specification is used to understand the component.

A component specification and an interface also differ in scope: if a component has multiple interfaces, these are all listed as part of the specification. The scope of a specification is the component as a whole. As such it needs to specify the way in which the interfaces of a component relate to each other.

A **component implementation** is a realization of a component specification. There has been some discussion on how strict the hiding of internals of components should be. The black-box requirement for components has been criticized as being too strong a constraint. For the purpose of tailorability or testability, components should disclose more of their internals. Several variants of black box have been proposed; they differ in the degree to which the internals of components can be inspected and changed by parties other than its developer:

- **Black-box component**: only the specification and the contract of the component are available to the user or integrator of a component.

- **Glass-box component**: the internals of the component may be inspected but not modified. The implementation can thus add information to the specification of the component.

- **Grey-box component**: part of the internals of a component may be inspected and limited extension or modification is possible; e.g. only certain methods may be defined or redefined by the user or integrator.

- **White-box**: the component is open to both inspection and modification by its user or integrator.

A **component package** is a unit of distribution. A package contains the implementation of a component, relevant data files, meta-data about the component, and meta data about the package. The **meta-data** of a package contains a table of contents of the files in the package. It may be compressed to improve download time, and encrypted and certified to improve security. It can be compared to the way a ZIP file can be used to package a collection of files into a single unit.

Finally, the **component instance** consists of the executable code and associated data in the target machine. The relation between a component implementation and a component instance is like the relation between a class and an object. The component instance will form part of the execution architecture of the running system. The execution architecture determines the performance of a system by defining the mapping of functionality onto run-time entities (such as processes and resources) in a system. The component instance has to conform to conventions that are dictated for this purpose by the software architecture.

18.2.2 Architecture and Component Models

Since the mid 1990s, software architecture has been recognized as an important inter- mediate artifact of software engineering projects. The goal of a software architecture is to define the key principles and guidelines for developing a software system such that the resulting system and process meets its functional and quality requirements (see Chapter 11).

The functional requirements can be achieved by defining a functional decom- position of a system. Functionality behaves relatively nicely in an additive manner: to increase the functionality of a system, we just add a new subsystem. Achieving the quality properties of a system is often more difficult. One complicating factor is that quality properties do not have the additive property, but are the collective result of interaction by all parts of a system. The performance of a system is not 'handled' by one component; it is 'everywhere'. In order to achieve some set of quality properties, all parts of a system must adhere to certain principles. Since quality is to a large extent determined by the software architecture (see Chapter 11), component-based software engineering requires that attention be paid to the software architecture.

To successfully develop systems in a component-based manner, an architectural plan needs to be in place that organizes how components fit together and how, once assembled, a system meets its quality requirements. In an ideal case, the development of a system is driven by an architecture that is developed up front. Based on this architecture, a component model is selected or a dedicated component model is developed such that the rules of the component model match those of the architecture. Examples of dedicated component models are the Koala model (Ommering *et al.*, 2000) developed for meeting resource constraints in consumer devices, and the SaveCCM (Åkerholm *et al.*, 2007) model developed for meeting dependability requirements in the automotive domain. As these examples illustrate, dedicated component models are developed in domains that have rather specific quality requirements.

Developing a proprietary component model takes a lot of effort. Therefore, a practical alternative is to select the architecture and component model in concert. To this end, a set of candidate architectures and a set of candidate component models are selected. The choice of a particular component model limits the possible architectures that can be realized. If a component model is not an ideal match with the target architecture, then some additional work is needed to provide extra features or eliminate (or hide) superfluous features. So, an architecture constrains the possible component models and a component model constrains the possible architectures. Typical issues that are the subject of architectural decisions which may influence the choice between a custom architecture and custom component model versus a commercial component model are: security mechanisms, transaction mechanisms, and scheduling policies. Typically, policies for such issues are hard-wired into commercial component models, but can be tailored when designing a custom component model.

There are different approaches to dividing the responsibility for managing quality properties between components and the execution platform. The different types of approach are characterized by the reference architectures shown in Figure 18.5. The grey areas in this figure denote the locations where logic resides that handles quality properties of the system. These reference architectures talk about quality properties in general. An instance of the architecture could be concerned with performance, security, reliability. There are two main dimensions in which these approaches differ in managing quality properties:

- The party that manages the property: Either the property is endogenous (that is, it is handled by the component) or it is exogenous (that is, it is handled by the system).

- The scope of management of the property: A property is managed on a per-collaboration basis or on a system-wide scale.

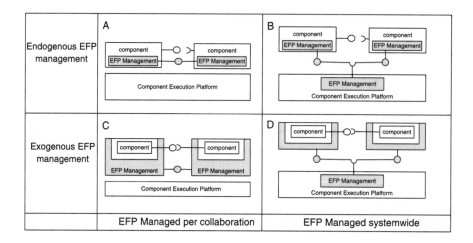

Figure 18.5 Management of quality, or extra-functional properties (EFP)

Many component models provide no specific facilities for managing quality properties. The way a property is handled is, in that case, left to the designers of the system; as a result, a property may not be managed at all (approach A, in Figure 18.5). This approach makes it possible to include policies for managing quality properties that are optimized towards a specific system and can also cater for adopting multiple policies in one system. This heterogeneity may be particularly useful when commercial off-the-shelf (COTS) components need to be integrated. On the other hand, the fact that such policies are not standardized may be a source of architectural mismatch between components.

The compatibility of components can be improved if the component model provides standardized facilities for managing quality properties (approach B in Figure 18.5). In this approach, there is a mechanism in the component execution platform that contains policies for managing quality properties for individual components as well as for quality properties involving multiple components. The ability to negotiate the manner in which quality properties are handled requires that the components themselves have some knowledge about how the quality properties affect their functioning. This is a form of reflection.

A third approach is that the components should be designed such that they address only functional aspects and no quality properties. Consequently, in the execution environment these components are surrounded by a container. This container contains the knowledge on how to manage quality properties. Containers can either be connected to containers of other components (approach C in Figure 18.5) or they can interact with a mechanism in the component execution platform that manages quality properties on a system-wide scale (approach D in Figure 18.5). Approach C manages interaction between two components. In approach D, the scope of the management can be global across the system.

The container approach is a way of realizing separation of concerns in which components concentrate on functional aspects and containers concentrate on quality aspects. In this way, components become more generic because no modification is required to integrate them into systems that may employ different policies for managing quality properties. Since in this approach components do not address quality properties, they are simpler and smaller, and hence cheaper to implement or integrate.

As well as the differences discussed above, component models also have a number of features in common. An overview of these common features is given in Table 18.1. The features common to component models are:

Table 18.1 Common features of component models

Infrastructure
Instantiation
Binding
Communication
Discovery
Announcement of capabilities
Component and application development support
Language independence
Platform independence
Analysis support
Support for upgrading and extension
Support for quality properties

- **Infrastructure** All component models provide an infrastructure: mechanisms for component instantiation, binding, communication, distribution of components over hardware, announcing capabilities of components and discovery of desired components. These mechanisms are needed to create a composition of components that can cooperate in performing a certain task.

- **Instantiation** A component instance is the instantiation of an executable component at a specific location in the memory of a device. The relation between a component instance and a component implementation is the same as that between an object and a class. Once in operation, each component instance may create and manage its own data structures. There are a number of different ways in which the instantiation can be achieved. The distinguishing factor is the element in the architecture that controls the instantiation. In existing component models, instantiation is typically controlled by the component infrastructure, a component container, or a component factory.

- **Binding** In the context of component-based systems, binding is the creation of a link between two or more component instances. Binding can be done at design-time, compile-time or run-time. At design time and compile time, the binding is done by the developer. These types of binding are called early binding. Run-time binding is also called late binding, or dynamic binding, since each invocation may, in principle, be to another instance of the component. The link between component instances may be used for communication and navigation. The distinguishing aspect of the different ways in which binding can be organized in a component model is the party that initiates the binding.

We distinguish first-party binding and third-party binding. In first-party binding, a component instance binds itself to another component. In third-party binding, a binding between component instances is created by a party other than those being bound. Consider the scenario where a binding is constructed between component A and component B. In first-party binding, component A asks a registry where to find component B and the registry provides A with a reference to B; A knows about the component which it wishes to collaborate. In third-party binding, another party, say C, manages the binding between A and B. C can connect A to B and acts as a controller; components A and B act as slaves to the controller.

- **Communication** To facilitate communication between components, a component infrastructure must provide some interaction mechanisms. The interaction styles supported are partially defined by the architectural styles that the component model supports. The communication styles that a component infrastructure supports determine a number of the quality properties that systems built using these components can obtain. For instance, some communication styles favor efficiency over flexibility. The most common style is request–response as implemented by method-calling. This style is the basis of all imperative programming languages and does not require any special facilities from the component infrastructure. The next most common style is events. The event style is often used in combination with request–response. It is typically used for notification, e.g. of exceptions. The publish–subscribe style of communication can be seen as a generalization of the event style to distributed systems. Streaming is often used in systems that are aimed at multimedia processing.

- **Discovery** A component model needs to define a mechanism by which components in the system can be discovered. A discovery mechanism is needed to support dynamic binding. Discovery mechanisms are most prominent in component models with run-time binding. In systems with design-time or compile-time binding, the discovery is typically guided by the designer or developer. In systems with run-time binding, a registry is commonly used for the discovery of components. Dynamic binding is a main characteristic of service-oriented architectures; see also Chapter 19.

- **Announcement of capabilities** Usually the capabilities of a component are expressed by the interfaces that it implements. The way in which interfaces

are specified differs between component models. Some component models introduce a special language for expressing interfaces; others use programming languages
to specify the interfaces.

- **Component and application development support** Component models have a
  variety development features. For example, COM and .NET support development
  of components independent of programming language, whereas Enterprise Java-
  Beans (EJB) supports platform independence.

- **Language independence** Some component models support development of components in different programming languages. In order to achieve interoperability
  between the components developed in different programming languages, the interfaces must be specified independent of the programming language. Usually an
  interface description language (IDL) is used for this purpose.

- **Platform independence** Some component models offer platform independence;
  this means that executable components can be executed on different platforms.
  This is usually achieved using an intermediate language. This intermediate language
  can be interpreted at run-time or compiled by a just-in-time (JIT) compiler.

- **Analysis support** During development of individual components and applications,
  it may be desirable to have analysis techniques. These techniques can be used to
  prove the correctness of the software or to predict quality properties of assemblies
  of components.

- **Support for upgrading and extension** Software evolves. The value and the
  economic lifetime of a device and the software on it can be increased by supporting
  the upgrading and extension of the software. Component models can support
  upgrading and extension at different stages of the software life cycle (design,
  compile time, run time, etc.). The current trend is that upgrading and extension is
  shifting more and more to the run-time phase of the software life cycle.

- **Support for quality properties** When developing software, the functionality of the
  software is not the only concern. We also have to deal with quality properties such
  as performance, security, and reliability. Which quality properties are important
  very much depends on the problem domain. The quality properties that are
  important may introduce all kinds of restrictions on a component model.

18.3 COMPONENT-BASED DEVELOPMENT PROCESS AND COMPONENT LIFE CYCLE

The process of component-based system development differs from the 'classical'
development processes of software systems as discussed in Chapter 3. The main
difference is in the separation of the development process of components from the
development process of systems. Since the component-based approach is a relatively

young approach in software engineering, the main emphasis in the area has been on the development of technologies, while process modeling for CBSE is still a relatively unexplored area. This section analyzes the basic characteristics of the component-based approach and its impact on the development process and life cycle models. The generic life cycle of component-based systems and the life cycle of components are discussed, and the different types of development processes are discussed in detail: architecture-driven component development, product-line development, and COTS-based development.

The main idea of the component-based approach is the building of systems from already existing components. This assumption has several consequences for the system life cycle:

- The development processes of component-based systems are kept separate from those of the components. The components should already have been developed, and possibly used in other products, when the system development process starts.

- Component assessment is a new, possibly separate, process for finding and evaluating components. Component assessment can be part of the main process but many advantages are gained if the process is performed separately. The result of the process is a repository of components that include specifications, descriptions, documented tests, and the executable components themselves.

- The activities in the component-based development processes are different from those in a non-component-based approach. For the system-level process, the emphasis is on finding the proper components and verifying and integrating them. For the component-level process, design for reuse is the main concern.

18.3.1 Component-Based System Development Process

To illustrate the specifics of the component-based development process we use the simple waterfall model as a reference. However, the illustration can relatively simply also be applied to other development processes. Figure 18.6 shows the main activities of a typical component-based waterfall life cycle model: requirements engineering, analysis and design, implementation, test, release, and maintenance.

The primary idea of the component-based approach is to (re)use the existing components instead of implementing them whenever possible. For this reason, the availability of existing components must be considered even in the requirements and design phases.

- **Requirements engineering**: In a non-component-based approach, the requirements specification is one of the inputs to the development of the system. In a component-based approach, it is somewhat different: the requirements specification also considers the availability of existing components. The requirements specification is not only input to the later stages, but is also a *result* of the design and

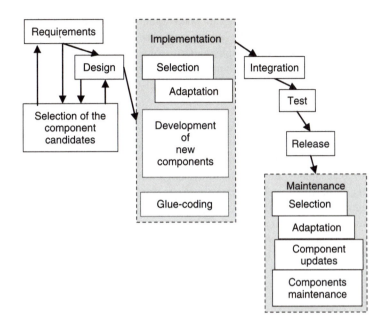

Figure 18.6 Component-based waterfall life cycle model

implementation decisions. This was touched upon when we discussed COTS selection in Section 9.1.5.

- **Analysis and design**: The design phase of component-based systems follows the same pattern as the design phase of customary development models. It consists of an architectural design phase followed by the detailed design phase. From the software architecture, the architectural components are identified. These components are not necessarily the same as the implementation components, but they should be identified and specified in the detailed design as assemblies of existing components. As in the requirements process, a tradeoff between the desired design and a possible design using existing components must be analyzed. In addition to this, there are many assumptions that must be taken into consideration during design. For example, it must be decided which component models will be used. This decision has an impact on the architectural model as well as on certain system quality properties.

- **Implementation**: The implementation phase includes less coding than in a more traditional development process for implementing functions and focuses more on the selection of available components. In an ideal case, there is no coding at all. In practice, components often have to be adapted to fit the requirements and design specification. Required functionality that is not provided by any existing component must be implemented and the relevant stakeholders have to decide whether these new functions are implemented in the form of new components that can be reused later. An inevitable part of the implementation of a component-based system is the 'glue' code which connects components, enables their intercommunication and, if necessary, solves possible mismatches. In the ideal case, glue code can be generated automatically.

- **Integration**: The integration phase includes activities that build the system from the incoming parts. The integration phase does not include 'creative' activities in the sense of creating new functions by producing new code. For this reason, it is desirable to automate and rationalize the integration process as much as possible. The integration phase is however very important, as it is the 'moment of truth'. Problems arise which are due to architectural mismatches of incoming components or unwanted behavior of different quality properties at the system level. That is why the integration phase is tightly connected to the system test phase in which the system functions and quality properties are verified.

- **Test**: In CBSE, the need for component verification is apparent since the system developers typically have no control over component quality, component functions, etc., as the components could have been developed in another project with other purposes. The tests performed in isolated components are usually not enough since their behavior can be different in the assemblies and in other environments. The Ariane example from Section 1.4.1 is a case in point.

- **Release**: The release phase includes packaging of the software in forms suitable for delivery and installation. The CBSE release phase is not significantly different from a 'classical' release phase.

- **Maintenance**: The maintenance approach of CBSE is to replace old components by alternative components or by adding new components to the system. The paradigm of the maintenance process is similar to that for development: find a proper component, test it, adopt it if necessary, and integrate it into the system.

Figure 18.6 shows a simplified and idealized process. Its assumption is that the components selected and used are sufficiently close to the units identified in the design process that the selection and adaptation processes require (significantly) less effort than the components' implementation. Further, the figure shows only the process related to system development and not the supporting processes that have to do with the assessment of components and the development of components.

18.3.2 Component Assessment

While development of component-based systems significantly decreases the detailed design and implementation effort during system development, it requires additional effort in other activities. For example, instead of implementing the required functions, developers have to search for components that provide such functionality. Developers must also verify that the selected components provide (or approximate) the desired functionality, and that they can successfully be integrated with other components. A consequence might be that the best components are not selected but rather the components that best fit together.

To make the system development process efficient, many assessment activities can be performed independently, separate from system development. A generic assessment process includes the following activities:

- **Find** From an unlimited component space, find the components that might provide the required functionality.

- **Select** The candidate components found are compared and ranked. A component that is most suitable for the given requirements and constraints is selected. The ranked list of components should be maintained throughout system development so that alternatives for a function can quickly be found.

- **Verify** Verification is part of the component selection process. The first level of verification includes testing functional and certain quality properties of a component in isolation. A second level of verification involves testing the component in combination with other components integrated in an assembly.

- **Store** When a component is assumed to be a good candidate for the current or future applications, it is stored in a component repository. The repository should not only include the component itself, but also additional information (meta-data) that can be useful in further exploitation of the component. Examples of such meta-data are measured results of component performance, known problems, response time, tests passed, and test results.

18.3.3 Component Development Process

The component development process is in many respects similar to the system development process: requirements must be captured, analyzed, and defined; the component must be designed, implemented, verified, validated, and delivered. When building a new component, developers will reuse other components and will use similar procedures of component evaluation as for system development. There is, however, a significant difference: components are intended for reuse in (many) different products, many of them yet to be designed. The consequences of this difference are the following:

- There is greater difficulty in managing requirements.

- Greater efforts are needed to develop reusable units.

- Greater efforts are needed to provide component specifications and additional material that help developers and consumers of the components.

Below, we highlight the specific characteristics of activities of a component development and maintenance process.

Requirements Engineering. Requirements specification and analysis is a combination of a top-down and a bottom-up process. The requirements elicitation should be the result of the requirements specification at the system level. However, since the components are also built for future systems, not even yet planned, these system requirements have not necessarily been identified. For this reason the process of capturing and identifying requirements is more complex. It must address ranges of requirements and possible reusability. Reusability is related to generality, thus the generality of the components should be addressed explicitly.

Analysis and Design. The input to the design phase in the component development process comes from system design, system constraints, and system concerns. Since such systems do not necessarily exist yet, the component designer must make many assumptions about the system. Many assumptions and constraints are determined by selecting a component technology. The component technology determines, for example, possible component interactions, certain solutions built into the technology (such as transactions or security mechanisms), and assumptions of system resources (such as scheduling policies). For this reason, it is most likely that a component model and a component technology that implements that model must be chosen at design time.

For a component to be reusable, it must be designed in a more general way than a component tailored for a unique situation. Components intended to be reused require adaptability. This increases the size and complexity of the components. At the same time, they must be concrete and simple enough to serve particular requirements in an efficient way. This requires more design and development effort. Developing a reusable component may require three to four times more resources than developing a component which serves a specific purpose (Mili *et al.*, 2002).

Implementation. Implementation of components is, to a large extent, determined by the component technology selected. The component technology provides support in programming languages and automation of component compositions. It may include many services and provide many solutions that are important for the application domain. Good examples of such support are transactions management, database management, security, and interoperability support for distributed systems provided by component technologies such as .NET, J2EE, or COM+.

Integration. Components are built to be easily integrated into systems. For this reason, integration considerations must be continuously in focus. Usually, component technology provides good support for components integration and integration is being performed on a daily basis.

Test. Test activities are of particular importance for two reasons. First, the component should be very carefully tested since its usage and environment context is not obvious. No specific conditions should be taken for granted, but extensive tests and different techniques of verification should be performed. Second, it is highly desirable that the tests and test results are documented and delivered with the component to system developers.

Release. Release and delivery of the components is the phase where (assemblies of) components are packaged into sets that are suitable for distribution and installation. Such a package not only includes the executable components, but also additional information and assets (meta-data that specifies different properties, additional documentation, test procedures, test results, etc.).

Maintenance. A specific aspect of maintenance in component-based systems is the relation between a component and the systems it is used in. If a bug in a component is fixed, the question is to which systems a new version of the component should be delivered. Who will be responsible for the update: the component producer or each of its consumers? There is also the question of who is responsible for component maintenance: is this a responsibility of the component producer or the producer of the system this component is part of? Do component producers have the obligation to fix bugs and support updates in the systems that make use of their components? Can they provide support in return for additional payment?

Even more difficult problems are related to 'blame analysis'. The issue is related to a manifestation of a fault and the origin of the fault itself. A fault might be detected in one component, but the cause of that fault might be in another component. For example, due to a high frequency of input in component A, component A requires more CPU time. As a consequence, component B does not complete its execution during the interval assumed by component C. Component C then issues a time-out error and a user of component C gets the impression that an answer from component C was not delivered. A first analysis shows that the problem is in component C, then B, then A, and finally in the input to A. The question is: who performs this analysis if the producers of components A, B, and C are different? Such situations can be regulated by contracts between the producers and consumers of the components, but this requires additional effort and, in many cases, it is not possible at all.

The above example shows that maintenance activities can be much more extensive than expected. For this reason, it is important that component producers build a strategy for performing maintenance and take corresponding actions to ensure the realization of this strategy. For example, component producers might decide to provide maintenance support; it is then important that they can reproduce the context in which the error manifested.

18.4 ARCHITECTURAL APPROACHES IN COMPONENT-BASED DEVELOPMENT

Industrial practice has established several approaches to using component-based development. These approaches, while similar in using component technology, have quite different processes and different solutions at the architectural level. In this section, we look at three approaches, all component-based, but with quite different assumptions, goals and, consequently, processes.

18.4.1 Architecture-Driven Component Development

This is a top-down approach. Here, components are identified as part of an architectural design. The componentization of the architecture serves as a way of achieving a high level of modularity. Components are not primarily developed for reuse, but rather as pieces to fit into the specified architectures (in the same way as pieces in a jigsaw puzzle). In the implementation, component-technologies (such as .Net) are used, but this is mainly because of the extensive support of component technology for modeling and specification, because of easier implementation, and the possibility of using standard services of a component technology. The genericity of these components is limited: they only have to fit the architecture they were designed for. Reusability and time-to-market issues are of less concern.

An example of this approach would be the software that controls flying an aircraft. It requires a dedicated architecture where each of the components has highly domain-specific functionality. However, a component-based approach would allow replacing of individual components by newer versions.

18.4.2 Product-Line Development

This approach has a strong top-down direction, but also some bottom-up elements. In contrast to the previous approach, this approach aims to enable efficient development of many variants of products – sometimes called a family of products or a product-line. Such families are common in consumer products such as mobile telephones, televisions, and home audio equipment. Product-line development tries to cater for easily making and maintaining many variants of a products with minimal technical diversity at minimal costs. The solution for this is sought in component-based architectures. This architecture defines the common parts of the system and the parts that are variable.

As an example of this approach, consider a product family of consumer electronics products which includes CD players, DVD players, and mobile phones. In this case, careful design of the architecture would allow an MP3 decoding component to be integrated into the architecture of the CD player, DVD player, and mobile phone.

The component-based character of the architecture plays a crucial role: it enables reuse of components and efficient integration. Composability, reusability, and time-to-market are equally important.

It is characteristic of product lines that the architectural solution has a direct impact on the component model. The component model must comply with the pre-defined reference architecture. In practice, many companies have developed their own component model that suits their proprietary architecture. A second characteristic of product-line architectures is a high degree of concurrency between the component development process and product development process and a combination of top-down and bottom-up procedures.

18.4.3 COTS-Based Development

This is mostly a bottom-up approach: it tries to assemble a system from existing components. The architecture of the system is secondary to the combinations of components that are available.

From the perspective of the system developer, the strongest driver for this approach is time to market: what components exist that we can quickly assemble into a system? For this approach to work, there must be component developers that aim at developing highly reusable functionality. Overall, this approach assumes that the system development process is completely separate from the development processes of components.

While the COTS approach gives instant value in new functionality, there are a number of problems in this approach that complicate its realization: because components were not designed to comply to a component model or to fit together, this approach may run into problems of composability. This may occur if the semantics are not clear or if architectural properties of the components are not properly and adequately documented. For COTS-based development, component assessment plays a much more important role than in the previous two approaches.

As an example of this approach consider a Web store. Web stores now have a fairly crystallized architecture that has a fair amount of commonality with the architecture of many business information systems. A Web-store system can be assembled by buying components that are sold as building blocks on the software market. Typical components include: database, Web server, search engine, payment handler, and stock-control system. In this case, a selection is made of which (combination of) components is most appealing and then an architecture is designed which integrates these components.

18.4.4 Selecting an Approach

Which of these approaches is best or most CBSE-specific? There is no definitive answer. After a surge of enthusiasm in both industry and research, the COTS components market has decreased and does not show revolutionary improvement. One of the reasons for that is that it is difficult to achieve reusability by being very general, effective, and simple and, at the same time, provide attractive functionality. Furthermore, there are problems of trustworthiness (who can guarantee that the component is correct?), component verification, and certification.

The product-line approach has been successful in many domains and its combination with CBSE is a promising approach. Possible threats are the increasing costs of development and maintenance of the component technologies developed internally, and the pace of technological innovations in compilers, debuggers, and integrated development environments. In some cases, the internally developed component technologies are replaced by widely used general-purpose component technologies, while keeping the overall product-line approach.

18.5 SUMMARY

The vision of assembling systems using independently developed components was first published by McIlroy (1968). In his paper, McIlroy identifies important concepts, such as component, binding, and variability. Following his paper on components, McIlroy worked on the pipes-and-filters mechanism in the Unix operating system. The composition mechanism of pipes and filters is still unique in its genericity and simplicity.

The goals of component-based software engineering are to

- reduce development time,

- improve productivity, and

- improve the evolvability and maintainability of software systems.

In order to enable composition of components the components need to be compatible. This compatibility is achieved by component models that define a set of conventions to which individual components must adhere. Component models are developed to satisfy the quality requirements of particular application domains. In this chapter, we have discussed the common features of component models.

To successfully develop systems in a component-based manner, an architectural plan needs to be in place that organizes how components fit together and how, once assembled, a system meets its quality requirements. An architectural plan is essential when reuse of components is needed across a family of related products, a so-called software product line.

The process of CBSE is characterized by a separation of the development processes of the individual components and the development process of the system that uses components.

18.6 FURTHER READING

(Szyperski, 1998) is a seminal book about component software; it contains chapters on CORBA, COM and JavaBeans. Wang and Qian (2005) discuss many different component models and give extensive code examples. (Heineman and Councill, 2001) is a comprehensive book on component-based software engineering that covers development processes, design methods, component technologies, and legal issues. Szyperski (2003) discusses the state of the art in component technology. Cheesman and Daniels (2000) discuss the design of component-based systems.

Architecture-driven component development is discussed in (Crnkovic and Larsson, 2002a). Software product lines are discussed in (Clements and Northrop, 2002) and (Weiss *et al.*, 1999). (Morisio *et al.*, 2002b) discuss COTS-based software development. Crnkovic and Larsson (2002b) discuss the challenges of component-based software development and illustrate them with a case study.

Research on CBSE has largely focused on mechanisms for modularization. Only recently, has the notion of composition become recognized as a subject of study in its own right. For example, mixins (Bracha and Cook, 1990) generalize the type of composition provided by the inheritance mechanism of object-oriented languages. (Achermann *et al.*, 2000) discuss language support that enables us to construct more complex composition recipes from simpler ones. Another direction of research is looking to identify the units of software that best match the needs of software engineers when assembling systems. Examples of other types of unit of composition are features (Turner *et al.*, 1999) and aspects (Suvee *et al.*, 2006).

Exercises

1. What is a component?

2. What are the benefits of CBSE?

3. How are components and component models related?

4. Discuss the stages of a component life cycle.

5. How does a component specification differ from a component interface?

6. Describe four ways in which quality can be managed in a component model.

7. What is the difference between early binding and late binding?

8. What is the difference between first-party binding and third-party binding?

9. How does the component-based software development process differ from the more traditional software development process discussed in Parts I and II of this book?

10. Why is a component assessment process needed in CBSE?

11. Why is software architecture important for CBSE?

12. Discuss the main differences between:

    - architecture-driven component development,
    - product-line development, and
    - COTS-based development.

13. What are differences between CBSE and reuse?

14. Recommend which aspects of a component should be covered by its specification.

15. ♡ Putting two stone bricks or blocks of LEGO together does not yield a stone brick or a LEGO block, but the result of such a composition is again composable. What is happening here? What is kept invariant by composition? What are the similarities and differences between composing with LEGO blocks and composing with software components?

16. ♠ Which mechanisms in different programming paradigms (imperative, functional, logical) can be considered as composition mechanisms? See, for example, (Assman, 2003).

17. ♡ Provide a list of issues that may cause incompatibility (and hence incomposability) between components.

18. ♡ Mechanisms in the execution platform play an important role in enabling run-time composition of software components. Are such infrastuctural mechanisms also needed for composing electronics components? Give reasons.

19

Service Orientation

LEARNING OBJECTIVES

- To understand the essentials of service orientation
- To know the characteristics of a service-oriented architecture (SOA)
- To know how Web services implement services
- To know the essentials of service-oriented software engineering (SOSE)

> In service orientation, a system is made up of services that are discovered dynamically. The use of services gives rise to a typical overall architecture: the service-oriented architecture (SOA). The usual implementation of a service-oriented system is via Web services that make heavy use of open standards. Service orientation is more than just a technology. It marks a shift from *producing* software to *using* software.

My wife and I like to visit the local Italian restaurant. It provides an excellent service. There is an elaborate menu to choose from. You can either pick individual dishes or select one of the suggested menus. The waiters are vintage Italian, but understand the orders if articulated carefully. The orders are communicated with the kitchen by yelling the number on the menu (I guess, because my Italian is quite bad). It seems to work, since invariably the dish asked for arrives at our table.

The Italian restaurant provides a service. The above story uses the three basic ingredients of services:

- **services**, which may consist of other services (the restaurant service consists of a choice of menus and drinks)

- **service descriptions** (the details listed on the menu)

- **service communication** (the yelling of orders).

Service orientation is a popular development model these days. It grew out of component-based software engineering (CBSE), and heavily uses the Web. A service resembles a component in CBSE; a service description resembles a CORBA or .NET description of a component; and service communication resembles a remote procedure call. Though services, service descriptions, and service communication resemble well-known concepts, they differ slightly from these concepts. Taken together, these differences make service-orientation really different from component-based approaches.

If one component in a component-based system makes use of another component, the selection of that component is made at design time. The caller knows all the details of the callee that it needs to know: name, parameters, quality. The composition can be tested before it is put into operation. There often are a lot of tacit dependencies between the two components: they most likely run, and have to run, on the same platform, for example.

This is not true if services are used. In a service-oriented system, one service (component) may ask for another service (component), but the selection is made dynamically. In a voice-recognition application, for example, we may need a service to remove noise from a taped message. There may be several candidate services that deliver the functionality asked for. They may differ in price, quality of the noise removal, speed, and so on. They may be written in different languages and run on different platforms. The selection of a specific noise-reduction service is done dynamically and, potentially, a different one may be chosen each time it is needed. This latter aspect is what makes a service-oriented approach truly different from CBSE.[1] The major characteristics of services are further discussed in Section 19.1.

The use of services gives rise to a service-oriented architecture (SOA) in which services interact through a messaging engine, the service bus. The coordination of services is taken care of in a dedicated coordination layer. The service-oriented architecture is discussed in Section 19.2.

The usual implementation of a service-oriented system is via Web services. Often, Web services and service orientation are viewed as synonyms. However, Web services are an *implementation* means to realize service-oriented systems. Web services make heavy use of a number of open standards, such as XML, SOAP, and others. Section 19.3 introduces the main open standards used to realize Web services. These standards describe only the syntax level. For example, SOAP is used to describe how services exchange messages. But it only describes the syntax of the messages, not their semantics. (Berners-Lee *et al.*, 2001) describe an extension of the current Web in which information has a meaning. This second-generation Web is called the 'semantic web'. In the semantic web, services also carry semantics. These semantics can be used in service discovery, composition, and so on. Second-generation Web services languages will exploit these semantics. These second-generation languages are beyond the scope of this chapter.

Service orientation has its impact on the various phases of the software development life cycle. This has resulted in the notion of service-oriented software engineering (SOSE), discussed in Section 19.4.

Service orientation is more than just a technology. Traditional software engineering approaches are geared towards the production of software. Organizations using these traditional approaches build complete software solutions or individual components. Their customers buy these solutions and then, usually, own them. They have to install the software on their machines, and receive regular patches or have to buy the next version or release.

This is not true in a service-oriented approach. Service orientation marks a shift from *producing* software to *using* software. In service orientation, an organization need not host the software, need not keep track of versions and releases, need not ensure that the software evolves with the wishes and requests of its users, and so on. The software is 'somewhere' and is deployed on an as-needed basis. To emphasize this shift in perspective, service-orientation is sometimes referred to as *software as a service* (SaaS).

---

[1] Actually, the difference is not as sharp as suggested here. We may argue that the use of such patterns as the factory pattern also allows for the dynamic selection of components.

19.1 SERVICES, SERVICE DESCRIPTIONS, AND SERVICE COMMUNICATION

The notion of service-oriented design goes back to the early 1990s. Service orientation has driven the 'intelligent network services' of the telecommunications domain. Telecommunications services such as free-phone (e.g., 800 services) and credit-card billing are built on top of complex distributed systems and require the cooperation of large numbers of computers, databases, peripherals, and networks (Margaria and Steffen, 2006).

In some sense, services are just like components: a system is made up of a collection of communicating services. Most of the important characteristics of services as listed in Table 19.1 resemble well-known characteristics of 'ordinary' components. If well-designed, ordinary components are also loosely coupled (this is one of the design criteria discussed in Chapter 12), adhere to a contract (often phrased in terms of pre- and post-conditions), hide their logic (information hiding), and so on. Yet, the characteristics of services differ subtly from those of software components, as discussed below.

Services can be discovered Services are discovered dynamically. This characteristic has repercussions for many of the other characteristics and makes services distinctly different from the components in a component-based system.

Service discovery means that, given a description of what the service is supposed to do (the contract), a dynamic search is done for candidate services that are capable of fulfilling that contract. This process is depicted in Figure 19.1. One service, the service requestor, sends a lookup request for another service to a service registry. If a suitable candidate service is found, its details are returned to the service requestor, which can then be bound to that candidate service, the service provider. Of course, the candidate service first has to register itself by publishing information in the registry. The registry thus acts like a phone directory.

Table 19.1 Main characteristics of services

Services can be discovered
Services can be composed to form larger services
Services adhere to a service contract
Services are loosely coupled
Services are stateless
Services are autonomous
Services hide their logic
Services are reusable
Services use open standards
Services facilitate interoperability

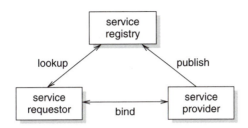

Figure 19.1 Service discovery and communication

Consider for example our library system. At the highest level, we might distinguish services that deal with membership administration, catalog administration, and a news service. The latter is intended to provide a window on the surrounding world to the community of library users. It may link to relevant government regulations, healthcare institutes, and so on. The news service may consist of a number of smaller, more specialized services, the invocation of which depends on the user query. It may invoke a service provided by the local hospital if the query concerns healthcare, a service provided by local government if the query concerns government regulations, or a Google-like service.

The suitability of a service for a given service consumer request depends on the contract it offers. The service consumer may also take other considerations into account when choosing a particular service. For instance, depending on demand load, complexity of the question, and other parameters, a service at a particular location may be selected. The dynamism of service orientation thus offers a way of optimizing use of computer resources.

Dynamic discovery can also be used to increase the robustness and fault tolerance of applications. In our news service example, the quality of answers to news requests may not be known in advance. So a query to one news service provider may yield an answer which is not considered adequate by the service requestor. The latter may then dynamically try another provider. The same can be done if a given news service provider fails to return an answer within a certain time frame. The result is a more robust, more fault-tolerant, service assembly.

Services can be composed to form larger services In our library system, services invoke other services to deal with part of their service offering. Viewed the other way round, these smaller services are composed to form larger services. Conceptually, this is not different from the way small components are building blocks for larger components in CBSE.

Services adhere to a contract If the query concerns healthcare, we may have other options besides the local hospital, such as health insurance companies and local drugstores. The services of insurance companies may require membership. The healthcare service may be slow and the information returned very reliable. The drugstore service may be fast but the information returned somewhat less

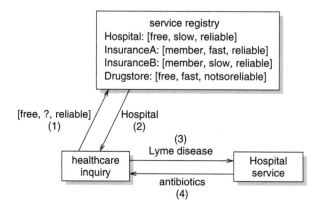

Figure 19.2 Example service discovery and communication

reliable. Figure 19.2 shows schematically how a healthcare query might be handled. Four candidate services have registered themselves in the registry: Hospital, InsuranceA, InsuranceB and Drugstore, together with their characteristics with respect to cost, speed, and reliability of information. If the healthcare inquiry service asks for a service which is both free and reliable, Hospital is selected, the link is made, and the query is executed.[2]

The input of the request to the registry should contain everything that is needed to do the search and return a satisfactory answer. In an ordinary component-based system, the invocation of a component contains all the information the called component needs to do its job but there is often a lot of tacit information shared between components. This tacit information is known to the designer, but is not explicitly encoded. It is shared knowledge between the components, but nowhere stated explicitly. Typically, this involves things such as:

• platform characteristics, such as the version of the database management system, the operating system, and the network and message protocols

• quality information, such as performance, reliability, availability, and so on

• design decisions that go beyond an individual component; for example, different components from an insurance portfolio may all tacitly assume that the renewal date is 1 April.

This information is not tacitly shared in a service-oriented system. Platform characteristics need not be the same for all components in a service-oriented setting. Web services (see Section 19.3) and the associated open standards allow for a smooth bridging of platform differences. Other types of information have to be made explicit,

---

[2]In Figure 19.2, the numbers in brackets indicate the order in which messages are exchanged.

though. Both components and services work according to a contract. In the case of components, this contract lists functional obligations. For services, the contract lists both functional and quality obligations.

If it is required that a service has certain performance characteristics, this has to be specified in the service request. And, conversely, candidate services have to publish their performance characteristics. During the search, performance requirements can then be compared against the performance offerings of candidate services and a suitable candidate can be chosen.

Not all quality information, however, is easy to specify. How for instance should the information reliability of the news services in our library example be specified? Is a choice between two options (`reliable` and `notsoreliable`) sufficient? And what do these qualifications mean?

For all types of quality information, the question remains how the service requestor should assure itself of the promised characteristics. A health insurance company may desire to present itself as a reliable source of information. But how can the news service know or ascertain that the promised information reliability level will indeed be reached? We may want to have stronger evidence than the mere promise of the service provider.

One possible way to handle this is to have an independent, trusted intermediary that collects evidence of the quality characteristics of a service. For example, if some party has been using the service and experienced certain quality levels, these can be reported to the trusted intermediary and can be used to update the available quality information of that service. This process is not that different from similar processes that have been proposed for collecting and disseminating quality information for commercial off-the-shelf (COTS) components. In the case of services, we need to explicitly model this information in such a way that it can be dynamically used by other services.

Collectively, the set of quality characteristics promised or required by a service is termed **Quality of Service** (QoS). This term is used in contexts such as telephony, networking, and streaming media to denote performance requirements one party asks for and another party has to comply with. A related term is **Service Level Agreement** (SLA). This notion also has been around for many years, most notably in deployment contexts, where the SLA describes certain levels of availability, throughput, and so on, that parties agree on. Both terms are used in the context of services to denote the quality part of a service contract.

A service may offer more than one QoS **level**. For instance, a voice-recognition service may offer a fast but somewhat noisy result, or a much better result at a slower speed. It is then up to the service consumer to choose between these QoS levels.

Services are loosely coupled Because of the dynamic discoverability, we cannot tacitly assume anything from a service found. Everything two interacting services need to know from each other has to be passed explicitly. A natural consequence then is that we aim for a situation in which they need as little information as possible. So we want services to be loosely coupled. This is a well-known decomposition criterion in every software design method. But in the realm of services, loose coupling also means loose coupling at the business level. A healthcare inquiry from the news service of the library system may be answered by a service provider hitherto completely unknown.

Services are stateless Since the selection of a service is done dynamically, potentially at least a different candidate may be selected each time a certain service is needed. At some point in time, service `InsuranceA` from health insurance company CompA might be selected, while next time service `Hospital` from the City Hospital might be the preferred option. The coupling between the library on one side and CompA and City Hospital on the other side is thus very loose. A consequence of this type of loose coupling is that services have to be stateless.

Services are autonomous; services hide their logic A service cannot retain information that is saved for a future invocation. The next invocation may well be to another service with the same functionality, but from a different provider.

In our library example, the news service has its own rules which determine how its process is structured. Its logic does not depend on other services of the library, such as those that have to do with membership administration or the catalog administration. This works two ways: the news service is autonomous and its internal logic is hidden.

Services are reusable A service models a business process. As such, a service is usually not very fine-grained. In our library example, one business process may have to do with the handling of fines, while another has to do with the complete administration of library items. Borrowing a book is not a business process and is not modeled as such in a separate service. Deciding on the proper granularity of services often raises much debate in service-oriented development. An important criterion is that services should be reusable.

Services use open standards In order that different companies can produce and use a variety of services, they communicate through open standards. When two applications cooperate through a proprietary standard, it may not be all that easy to change to another provider for either of them. If the provider of those applications does not disclose the way these applications interface, one is forced to change both. If the provider does disclose the interface, there might well not be a ready solution available, and a solution has to be developed that matches the particular interface. So the user organization in many cases is confronted with a package deal. This is known as *vendor lock-in*. Vendor lock-in does not occur if open standards are used. Any provider can decide to abide by those open standards, and thus enter the market. There are open standards for how services are described, how they communicate, how data is transferred between services, and so on. Some of the main open standards in use for service-oriented systems are discussed in Section 19.3.

Services facilitate interoperability A consequence of the use of open standards and the loose coupling between services is that interoperability is eased. In more classical approaches, the integration of, say, the news services provided by insurance companies and hospitals on the one hand, and a library information system on the other, poses challenges because of proprietary and incompatible data formats, platform differences, and so on. With services, these incompatibilities are partly hidden inside individual services, and partly subsumed by the open standards. Interoperability, within and across organizational boundaries, is thus made a lot easier.

The characteristics of services do not come about automatically. They have to be designed in. The service-oriented architecture (SOA), discussed in Section 19.2, promotes realization of those characteristics. Section 19.4 gives further guidelines for the design of services.

19.2 SERVICE-ORIENTED ARCHITECTURE (SOA)

A system that is composed of a collection of services that send and receive messages has an architecture, like any other system. If no structure is imposed on the way the services are connected through message sending, a bowl of spaghetti results: a spaghetti-oriented architecture. But this is not what we usually mean by the acronym SOA.

In the world of services, the term SOA is often used to denote any system built out of services or one utilizing Web services. We, however, confine the term to standing for a specific architectural style that has become widely used (see Figure 19.3). It has two layers of services, called the **business service layer** and **infrastructure service layer**. The services in these layers communicate through a **service bus**. Finally, the coordination of services is done in the **coordination layer**.

In this architectural style, services do not send each other messages directly, which would result in the spaghetti style mentioned above. Rather, they do so via a **service bus**, an event-based messaging engine. This bus acts as an intermediary

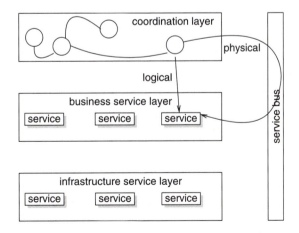

Figure 19.3 SOA architectural style

between services. Services send their messages to the bus, which in turn redirects them to the appropriate receiver of the message.

The service bus solves major complexity problems that often face application integration projects. This is also the area from which the service bus concept comes. A rather straightforward application integration effort consists of just putting a wrapper around existing legacy applications. These wrappers hide data formats and internal details and provide an XML-based Web interface instead. This is not a viable solution in the long run, though, because of platform differences between applications. To solve this type of integration problem, the notion of an enterprise service bus (ESB) was developed.

A similar type of bus is used in a service-oriented architecture . As well as routing messages, the service bus usually also takes care of a number of other issues that services have to deal with, such as:

- Mediation: protocol translation, data transformations, dealing with platform differences and other adaptations needed for services that use different protocols, data formats, and so on, to cooperate

- Quality of Service: issues that have to do with security, the reliable delivery of messages, and so on

- Management: monitoring or logging service usage and gathering audit information.

Conceptually, we have depicted the service bus as a centralized entity. It may be implemented as such, in a broker or hub style. It may also be implemented in a decentralized way, in smart endpoints of message exchanges.

The business service layer contains services that represent distinct pieces of business logic. The infrastructure service layer contains services that represent supporting activities, such as the storing and shipping of data.

Finally, the interaction between services has to be coordinated. For example, a sequence of services may have to be invoked in a certain order. Or, if a sequence of services is to be invoked to form one coherent transaction, we may want to ensure that the whole chain of services has been executed. If a failure is discovered somewhere in the chain, services that have already been executed have to be undone. To model service interaction, special languages have been developed that express these types of coordination issues. These coordination languages generally grew out of languages for workflow management.

Coordination languages for services come in two flavors: **orchestration** and **choreography**. In orchestration, there is a central place where coordination takes place. In choreography, there is no such central place: coordination is distributed. This resembles an orchestra with its conductor and a ballet performance, respectively. In practice, orchestration languages are used more often than choreography languages.

Logically, the coordination layer addresses services in the business and infrastructure service layer. Physically, this linkage is via the services bus, since all message exchanges go via this mediation component.

19.3 WEB SERVICES

Web services are an implementation way of realizing services. Web services use a standardized way to integrate services across the Internet. The main open standards used to realize Web services are:

- **Extensible Markup Language (XML)**, which has the primary goal of sharing data between applications

- **Simple Object Access Protocol (SOAP)**, used to transfer messages between services

- **Web Services Description Language (WSDL)**, used to describe available services

- **Universal Description, Discovery, and Integration (UDDI)**, used to list the available services.

In the context of Web services, XML is used to structure messages. In particular, SOAP messages, WSDL documents, and UDDI descriptions are all encoded as XML documents.

These open standards achieve interoperability between two services. What they do not achieve is integration of a *collection* of services. If a collection of services is to be integrated into a service-oriented system, there are certain global rules or constraints that such a conglomerate has to obey. For instance, if a complex insurance service consists of several smaller services, we may require that a transaction is completed entirely. If this cannot be achieved, parts that have been realized have to be undone. Also, we may wish to be able to roll back to earlier points in the process. This requires a language to express the flow of process steps. One such language is the **Business Process Execution Language for Web Services (BPEL4WS)**. This type of language is used at the coordination layer of the SOA (Figure 19.3).

Figure 19.4 gives an example of how we may combine WSDL and BPEL4WS in a typical application. WSDL is used to describe individual services. These services are implemented in some language, say Java. The flow of process steps is 'programmed' in BPEL4WS. Each individual process step refers to a service in WSDL. This can be applied recursively. So the complete composition as given in Figure 19.4 may be referred to as a service in some other WSDL description, and used as a single entity in another composition.

When two components (services, applications, and so on) communicate over a network, they do so via a protocol, such as FTP for file transfer and SMTP for mail transfer. These protocols provide containers of information, such as 'file' and 'mailbox', as well as operations to put information into those containers and get information out of them. In a similar way, Web services realize connectivity between network nodes. A SOAP message definition also provides for a container, and ways for the message sender to put the message into the container and for the message receiver to get the message out of the container. However, the SOAP user defines his own

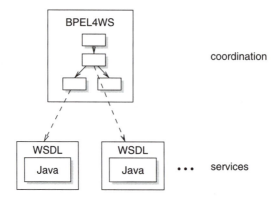

coordination

services

Figure 19.4 Coordination of Web services

message format in each SOAP definition. In that sense, SOAP is not a protocol, but a language to define new protocols. The same holds for WSDL and other Web services standards.

The Web services open standards form a stack, known as the Web services stack; see Figure 19.5. At the lowest level of this stack, we encounter the familiar network protocols. At the next level, SOAP deals with the interaction between services. WSDL and UDDI reside at the next higher level. They concern the description and discovery of services. At the highest level, BPEL4WS is concerned with the composition of services. At all levels above the network layer, XML is used as the document-representation language.

There are many other, more specialized open standards related to Web services. WS-Security for example deals with the integrity and confidentiality of messages. It describes how to make SOAP messages secure. WS-ReliableMessaging deals with the reliable delivery of messages. WS-Policy allows for the description of policies of service providers and consumers, with respect to QoS, for example. Further information on these open standards can be found at the websites of OASIS and W3C, the two main consortia in the area of Web services.

Figure 19.5 The Web services stack

The most popular underlying technology platforms to realize Web services are J2EE and .NET. J2EE provides different types of component, such as Enterprise JavaBeans (EJBs) and servlets, to realize Web services. The main API for processing messages is JAX-RPC (Java API for XML-based RPC). In the .NET environment, Web services are represented by units of programming logic called Assemblies. An Assembly consists of one or more classes. The .NET class library provides classes for processing SOAP messages, WSDL definitions, and so on.

19.3.1 Extensible Markup Language (XML)

XML grew out of HTML, the language used to describe the format and layout of Web pages. HTML has a fixed set of elements that are used to describe Web pages. In XML, elements are not predefined. The user of XML can define his own vocabulary in an XML schema. The vocabulary defines the language used in a specific set of documents. Documents can be encoded in XML conforming to the schema.

For instance, in our library system, we may have a schema called `library` that defines the syntax of documents that describe library items. All items in the library can be encoded using this schema. A small example is given in Figure 19.6.

```
<?xml version="1.0"?>
<!DOCTYPE library SYSTEM "library.dtd">

<libitem category="Novel">
    <title>What is the What< \title>
    <author>Dave Eggers< \author>
    <year>2007< \year>
< \libitem>
```

Figure 19.6 XML example

The first lines in the example tell us that XML version 1.0 is used, and the XML schema used is called `library`. The next lines have the familiar syntax of HTML, but the keywords used are different. These keywords are defined in the schema, in this case a Document Type Definition called `library.dtd`. The example describes one library item in the category `Novel`, and lists the title, author, and year of publication of that novel.

An XML schema defines one or more trees, nested categorizations of constructs. In the example of Figure 19.6, it is a very simple tree in which a `libitem` has three child nodes. XML provides a way to structure this type of hierarchical information. It is only about *syntax*. An XML document carries no semantics, though. Any XML document having a structure that conforms to the `libitem` schema will be accepted as a valid library item.

XML has evolved into more powerful languages that do allow for the inclusion of semantic information in documents. The main exponent of this is the Ontology Web Language (OWL). The semantic information included can be used in service discovery and mapping processes. Where XML is the basis for first-generation, syntax-based Web services, OWL is the basis for second-generation, semantics-based Web services.

XML is used to represent all kinds of data in Web services. Web services communicate by sending each other data formatted as XML documents. SOAP messages are XML documents, the entries in a UDDI are XML documents, and the service descriptions of WSDL are XML documents. XML documents are omnipresent in Web services. The flexibility of XML and its wide support in industry are a major factor in the success of Web services.

Often, items from different XML schema have to be combined in one document. Since names in a single XML document have to be unique, each vocabulary is given its own namespace, and names are then prefixed with a reference to the namespace where that name is defined. For example, `soap:binding` refers to `binding` as defined in the WSDL namespace for SOAP bindings (see Figure 19.7). It is customary to use the prefix `ths:` to refer to the current document ('this namespace').

19.3.2 Simple Object Access Protocol (SOAP)

The Simple Object Access Protocol is the format for exchanging messages between Web services. A SOAP message is sent from a SOAP sender of one service to the SOAP receiver of another service, possibly via SOAP intermediaries at intermediate services. The message is contained in a SOAP envelope. This envelope in turn has an optional header and a mandatory body. The header is like the address on an envelope or the header of an email message. It contains information that identifies intermediaries and meta information about the SOAP message. The body is the container for the actual data being transferred.

A SOAP message is unidirectional. It defines a message from one service to another, not a *conversation* between services. If we have to cope with conversation issues and state information that has to be kept between two messages, this has to be done at higher levels such as WSDL or BPEL4WS.

19.3.3 Web Services Description Language (WSDL)

WSDL is used to define individual Web services. A short example of a WSDL definition is given in Figure 19.7. This example shows the four main parts of a Web service definition:

- Web service interfaces, labeled `portType`. This is similar to a component interface as used in component-based software engineering. A service interface has a name and a series of operations.

```
<definitions name="HealthcareInformation"
    targetNamespace="http://example.org/HealthcareInformation
        .wsdl" >

    <message name="GetHealthcareInformationInput">
        <part name="body" element="xsd:
            HealthcareInformationRequest"\ >
    <message name="GetHealthcareInformationOutput">
        <part name="body" element="xsd:
            HealthcareInformationResult"\ >

    <portType name="HealthcareInformationPortType">
        <operation name="GetHealthcareInformation">
            <input message="ths:GetHealthcareInformationInput"\ >
            <output message="ths:
                GetHealthcareInformationOutput"\ >
        < \operation>
    < \portType>

    <binding name="HealthcareInformationSoapBinding"
        type ="ths:HealthcareInformationPortType">
        <soap:binding style = "document"
            transport = "someURI"\ >
        <operation name="GetHealthcareInformation">
            <input>
                <soap:body use = "literal"\ >
            < \input>
            <output>
                <soap:body use = "literal"\ >
            < \output>
        < \operation>
    < \binding>

    <service name="HealthcareInformationService">
        <port name="HealthcareInformationPort"
            binding="ths:HealthcareInformationSoapBinding">
            <soap:address location="http://example.org/
                HealthcareInformtion"\ >
        < \port>
    < \service>
< \definitions>
```

Figure 19.7 WSDL example

- Messages, labeled `message`. When an operation is executed, messages may be exchanged.

- Bindings, which define transport and format details for the operations and messages of an interface. An interface (portType) can have multiple bindings.

- Services, which describe the collection of endpoints for accessing a service. An endpoint, or port, is a combination of a binding and a network address. A service can have several ports of the same portType, but with different bindings. The behavior of these ports then is semantically equivalent, but one may, for instance, be faster than the other.

The portTypes and Messages describe the abstract interface description, while Bindongs and Services describe the concrete, implementation part of the service description.

The example in Figure 19.7 concerns the news component service of our library system. One of the operations of interface `HealthcareInformationPort-Type` is `GetHealthcareInformation`, which retrieves healthcare information. This operation is a request–response type of operation. It has an input message `GetHealthcareInformationInput` and an output operation `GetHealthcareInformationOutput`. Other possibilities are: one-way (only input), notification (only output) and solicit–response (output message followed by an acknowledgement).

Next a binding, `HealthcareInformationSoapBinding`, is defined and tied to an actual service found at `http://example.org/Healthcare Information`. It uses the WSDL 1.1 binding for SOAP 1.1 endpoints. The request–response combination used in `GetHealthcareInformation` need not be similarly combined in the actual binding. For example, the two messages may be exchanged in two actual communications.

This example only scratches the surface of WSDL. There are many other features that WSDL has, such as the ability to decompose large service descriptions into smaller ones, and the ability to describe faults, i.e. events that disrupt the normal flow of messages. Also, WSDL builds on and uses other open standards, such as those for building namespaces.

19.3.4 Universal Description, Discovery, and Integration (UDDI)

The UDDI is a registry of service descriptions. A UDDI allows one to publish and search for services. A UDDI registry is either public or private. The original vision behind UDDI was to have a huge public registry, very much like a phone directory, in which every organization would publish its services. Reality is different. Many organizations do not want their services to be made available outside the organization. Others only want to make services available to partner organizations. The current version offers different levels of visibility for service descriptions.

Entries in a UDDI registry have three main parts:

- `businessEntity`: information about the organization that publishes the services: name, description, a unique identifier, and so on

- `businessServices`: descriptive information about the actual services provided by the organization, such as a unique identifier for each service

- `bindingTemplates`: technical information to link services to implementation information; a binding template may point to a website or it may point to the actual service description.

Entries are stored in XML format. These entries are quite complex and are not really meant for humans. The keys used to identify an organization or service, for instance, can be readable names such as a domain name, but they often look like a rather complex bar code. Interaction with the registry is done by SOAP messages.

Having different registries rather than one global registry poses additional challenges very similar to the challenges of distributed databases. For instance, keys and other information may have to be mapped between registries. The interaction between a collection of registries has to obey the policies of the organizations that make use of those registries. The interface to such a set of UDDI registries is often through publishing and inquiry systems in which these policies are embedded. There is however no standard for how to encode the information to be published in a UDDI registry. If our news service looks for a service `HealthcareInquiry` and the hospital has published its service as `HealthcareInformation`, it will never be selected.

19.3.5 Business Process Execution Language for Web Services (BPEL4WS)

BPEL4WS is a language for programming-in-the-large. It has variables, `if-then-else` statements, `while` statements, and so on. But the elementary objects are not numbers and strings, but process steps. A BPEL4WS 'program' describes the workflow of a business process.

The three main parts of a BPEL4WS process definition are (see also Figure 19.8):

- partnerLinks, which define dependencies between services

- variables, which store information to be kept between service invocations

- a workflow model, which expresses the sequence of process steps to be executed.

A process has a number of partner services that participate in the process. For the news services, possible partner services are `HealthcareInformationService` (see Figure 19.7) and `HospitalInformationService`. For each such partner service, the BPEL4WS process definition provides a `partnerLinkType` element that identifies the corresponding `portType` elements from the WSDL definition.

```
<process name="NewsServiceProcess">
    <partnerLinks>
        ...
    < \partnerLinks>

    <variables>
        ...
    < \variables>

    <sequence>
        ...
    < \sequence>

< \process>
```

Figure 19.8 BPEL4WS skeleton process definition

```
<partnerLinks>
    <partnerLink name = "RequestLT"
        partnerlinkType="HealthcareInformationServicePortType"
        myRole="HealthcareInformtionServiceProvider"\ >
    <partnerLink name="HospitalRequestLT"
        partnerlinktype="HospitalInformationServicePortType"
        partnerRole="HospitalInformationServiceProvider"\ >
< \partnerLinks>
```

Figure 19.9 BPEL4WS partnerLinks

Figure 19.9 gives an example that defines two partnerlinkTypes: RequestLT and HospitalRequestLT. Two roles are distinguished for these links: myRole and partnerRole. myRole is used when the service is invoked by a client service, i.e. the service acts as a provider. partnerRole is used when the service invokes another service. The partnerRole then identifies the partner service that is invoked. A service can both be invoked and invoke other services in the same partnerLink. In that case, both roles occur in the same partnerLink.

Information on partner links is also embedded in the WSDL definition of services. It resembles the information given in Figure 19.9.

The variables part of a BPEL4WS process definition is used to store state information related to the workflow. For example, the news service may store the healthcare information received from, say, the drugstore service, examine its contents and invoke the hospital service if the information received is of low quality. Each variable has a type, which has to be given upon definition of that variable.

In a real news service interaction, there will be many requests for information, and many receipts, that co-exist, i.e. there will be many instances of the news service. Within a specific interaction, there thus has to be a way of connecting the right reply to a given request. This is similar to ordinary business transactions, where many orders may be 'alive' concurrently. It is customary to identify particular orders by a specific token, say a purchase order number, which is used during the whole workflow. It is used when the order is shipped, when it is being paid, when enquiries are made, and so on. In service interactions, similar tokens are used as part of the messages being exchanged. Messages are *correlated* to relate operations within a service instance, for example to connect a news reply to the corresponding request.

Finally, the `sequence` part of a BPEL4WS process definition gives the sequential order in which process steps are to be executed. BPEL4WS offers a number of constructs to express workflow logic in the process definition. Figure 19.10 gives a short example. The workflow starts with a `receive` construct, which means that the process waits for a matching message to arrive. Then, the `DrugstoreHealthcareInformation` service is invoked. This delivers an `OutputRequest` which is inspected in a BPEL4WS if statement. If the `Quality` element of the result is large enough, we're done. Otherwise, the `HospitalHealthcareInformation` service is invoked. Finally, the `reply` construct sends a result message as an answer to the `receive` construct. This pair constitutes the request–response operation that was mentioned in the WSDL `portType` of the healthcare information service.

BPEL4WS is an orchestration language. There is central control (just as the conductor of an orchestra is in control). In a choreography language, such as the Web Services Choreography Description Language (WS-CDL), no such central control exists. In a WS-CDL, each participant remains autonomous. A WS-CDL description

```
<sequence>
    <receive name = "InfoRequest"
        ...\>
    <invoke name="DrugstoreHealthcareInformation"
        ...\>
    <switch>
        <case condition="GetVariableProperty('OutputRequest',
            'Quality') '>' "threshold"" >
        < \case>
        <otherwise>
            <invoke name="HospitalHealthcareInformation"\>
        < \otherwise>
    <reply ...
    variable="InfoResult"\>
< \sequence>
```

Figure 19.10 Outline BPEL4WS workflow

defines a number of interactions (message exchanges) together with their ordering constraints. In particular, WS-CDL has no notion of global variables. Variables may be shared between participants in an interaction, so that state information can still be retained. Many other aspects of BPEL4WS show up in WS-CDL too, though sometimes under a different name. WS-CDL is not executable, while BPEL4WS is.

19.4 SERVICE-ORIENTED SOFTWARE ENGINEERING

Services, and compositions of services, need to be engineered too. This process is known as service-oriented engineering (SOE) or service-oriented software engineering (SOSE). At a global level, the SOSE life cycle is not different from the ordinary software life cycle, and consists of phases such as analysis, architecture, design, testing, construction. Each of the SOSE phases however is subtly different from its non-service-oriented counterpart. Below, we discuss the analysis, architecture, and design phases, since this is where the service-specific elements are most visible. An overview of these SOSE phases is given in Table 19.2. The process, of course, is not linear but iterative, both across and within phases.

Sometimes, a distinction is made between organizations that develop individual services and organizations that develop applications built out of a collection of available services. This is similar to software product-line development organizations, where a distinction is made between the component development organization and the application development organization. The latter develops the overall architecture and builds products using components developed by the component organization.

A service, be it simple or composite, models a business process. The first step in the analysis phase scopes the service: which business process will be handled by the service, what is its start and end, who are the participants, what is the input and output of the process? This first step determines the boundaries for the steps to follow.

Especially for larger business processes, there will be existing applications that automate part of the process. These may be (legacy) applications from within the organization, or components and services that may be acquired from elsewhere. The gap analysis step determines which existing elements can be reused in the realization of this service. The gap analysis is similar to a COTS selection process as discussed in Section 9.1.5.

Table 19.2   Main SOSE phases

SOSE phase	Detailed steps
Analysis	Determine scope
	Gap analysis
Architecture	Decompose process
	Compose specific SOA
Design	Design services and their interfaces
	Design business process

The architecture phase starts with a decomposition of the process into its constituent process steps and their interactions. Workflow modeling notations and languages can be used for this purpose. These resemble the process modeling notations discussed in Section 3.7. Usage scenarios are devised and used to manually test the process flow developed and identify any missing steps. These usage scenarios are also used to group services into composite ones.

Next, a particular instance of the SOA, as discussed in Section 19.2, is chosen. The service layers are determined, the Web services standards to be used are determined, as well as rules for how they are applied (such as which namespaces are used and where they are positioned).

Finally, the design phase concerns the design of individual services and their interfaces, as well as the detailed design of the service-oriented business process. In terms of the SOA architectural style, this concerns the detailed design of the service layers and the coordination layer, respectively. At the level of Web services, the former concerns the SOAP/WSDL level, while the latter concerns the BPEL4WS level.

Though SOSE and the more familiar software engineering approaches look similar, there are important differences for which no adequate SOSE solution has been found yet (see (Papazoglou *et al.*, 2006) and (Tsai *et al.*, 2007)):

- Existing software process modeling techniques and their notations (RUP, UML) are not very well suited for modeling business aspects. There exist numerous techniques and notations specifically aimed at the business level, such as the Business Process Modeling Notation (BPMN, see `www.bpmn.org`). BPMN is a graphical, flowchart-like notation for depicting workflows. It is still an open question as to how to combine existing software engineering techniques and notations with their business-oriented counterparts.

- For services, design principles such as coupling and cohesion apply as well. The precise definition of design principles for services and their associated measures are still open to debate.

- For services too, different versions exist in parallel. Version management for services has to be integrated with service discovery schemes, so that users can decide to keep using older versions even in the presence of newer ones.

- The engineering of services is collaborative and crosses organizational boundaries. The issues are similar to those found in global software engineering. For services, particular attention needs to be paid at integration issues at each phase of the life cycle. Different partners will use different techniques and notations for expressing requirements, designs, and so on.

- Certain engineering tasks have to be done at run time. If a new version of a service comes along, it has to be analyzed and tested while the complete service assembly of which it is part is up and running.

19.5 SUMMARY

Services have a long history in the world of telephony. Many of the achievements made there are currently being reinvented and translated to the general world of software engineering.

The most important characteristic that distinguishes services from ordinary software components is that services can be dynamically discovered, based on a description of what the service is supposed to accomplish. This description contains both functional and quality information. Service providers publish their service descriptions in a registry, after which service requestors can search the registry for candidate services.

The efforts to realize service orientation so far have been largely directed at the syntax level: how to program services, how to hook them together, and so on. The semantic level of domain-specific libraries of services has hardly been touched yet. This is similar to what happened in the area of reuse and components. Efforts to add a level of semantics are underway. (Berners-Lee *et al.*, 2001) describe an extension of the current Web in which information has a meaning. In this semantic Web, services also carry semantics. These semantics can be used in service discovery, composition, and so on. New standards are being developed in which this semantic information is embedded. XML is the basis for the first generation of Web services open standards. The Ontology Web Language (OWL) is the basis for the second, semantics-oriented, generation of standards.

The widely used service-oriented architecture (SOA) consists of a number of business and infrastructure services that communicate via a message engine, the service bus, and a coordination layer that handles the workflow of and interaction between the services.

The realization of services calls for specific software engineering techniques, service-oriented software engineering (SOSE). The main phases of the life cycle for developing services are the same as those for developing components. There are specific elements though, especially in the analysis and design phases, where the alignment between business aspects and technical solutions is stressed. There are also many open issues where it comes to the engineering of services.

19.6 FURTHER READING

(Erl, 2005) is a good textbook on service orientation. It makes a clear distinction between the conceptual issues and implementation issues incurred by Web services. (Papazoglou, 2008) is a very comprehensive textbook on Web services. (Turner *et al.*, 2003) describe the software-as-a-service (SaaS) concept. (CACM, 2003) and (CACM, 2006) are special journal issues that deal with service orientation. There is an annual International Conference on Service-Oriented Computing (ICSOC), in which research on service orientation is reported. One of the striking characteristics of the research reported there is that it seems disconnected from much of mainstream software engineering research.

Two important consortia in the area of open standards are the Organization for the Advancement of Structured Information Standards (OASIS) and the World Wide Web Consortium (W3C). Each has technical committees that endorse standards. W3C is known for its work on XML, SOAP, WSDL, and many other Web-related languages.

More information about XML can be found at www.w3.org/TR/XML. For OWL, see www.w3.org/2004/OWL. For SOAP 1.1, see www.w3.org/TR/soap. We used WSDL version 1.1 in the example in Section 19.3.3; see the W3C report at www.w3.org/TR/wsdl. More information about UDDI can be found at http://uddi.xml.org, hosted by OASIS. We used BPEL4WS version 1.1 in Section 19.3.5; see www-128.ibm.com/developerworks/library/specification/ws-bpel. BPEL4WS is developed by a consortium consisting of BEA Systems, IBM, and Microsoft, among others. It is being standardized as Web Services Business Process Execution Language (WSBPEL) by OASIS, see www.oasis-open.org. The Web Services Choreography Language (WS-CDL) is being developed by W3C; see www.w3.org/TR/ws-cdl-10. Peltz (2003) discusses the difference between orchestration and choreography. (Curbera *et al.*, 2002) provide an introduction to SOAP, WSDL, and UDDI. The research origins of middleware, including Web service middleware such as SOAP and WSDL, is discussed in (Emmerich *et al.*, 2007).

The platform technologies underlying Web services change quickly. Good starting points are http://java.sun.com/Webservices for Java developments and http://msdn2.microsoft.com/en-us/Webservices for .NET developments.

The SOSE life cycle discussed in Section 19.4 is loosely based on (Erl, 2005) and (Papazoglou and van den Heuvel, 2006). SOSE challenges are discussed in (Papazoglou *et al.*, 2006) and (Tsai *et al.*, 2007).

Exercises

1. What is a service?

2. Explain how service discovery works.

3. What are the main characteristics of services?

4. Explain the terms Quality of Service and Service Level Agreement in the context of service orientation.

5. Why is the use of open standards essential for realizing services?

6. What does the software-as-a-service (SaaS) perspective entail?

7. What is the Web services stack?

8. What are the main parts of a WSDL Web service definition?

9. Explain the role of BPEL4WS.

10. Describe the SOSE development life cycle.

11. Discuss the differences and commonalities between CBSE and SOA.

12. ♡ In terms of the categorization of viewpoints given in Chapter 11, how would you classify the view given in Figure 19.3? Can you think of other architecture viewpoints that might be relevant?

13. ♠ Write an essay on the prospective role of second-generation Web service languages in service orientation.

14. ♡ Write an essay on the role of version control in SOSE.

15. ♠ For a non-service-oriented system you have been involved in, identify the business functions supported and design a collection of services that could realize its functionality.

20

Global Software Development

LEARNING OBJECTIVES

- To understand the main issues that impact global software development

- To know different approaches for addressing the challenges of global software development

> In global software development projects, work is distributed over sites that operate in different time zones and geographical locations. People working at these different sites may differ widely in culture. The specific challenges imposed by this distance in time, place, and culture are discussed in this chapter. These challenges concern the way people communicate and collaborate, and the way work is coordinated and controlled.

A friend of mine runs a small Dutch software company that develops websites for organizations such as healthcare insurance agencies and municipal bodies. The requirements engineering and design is done in the Netherlands. Implementation and unit testing is outsourced to an Eastern European partner. Management and acceptance testing is again the responsibility of the Dutch company.

The reason for this division of labor is primarily cost – at the time of writing, salaries are still quite a bit lower in Eastern Europe than in the Netherlands. The technical competence of the Eastern European partner is very high. Consequently, the technical quality of their work is very high as well. But they have much less feeling for user interface issues. As long as all items appear on the website, they do not care so much about fonts, colors, and the like. The end result is that a lot of extra communication about these user interface issues is required, and the result often leaves much room for improvement.

Until fairly recently, software development was mostly a collocated activity. Today's software development often is a global activity. The challenges of the globalization of software development are discussed in Section 20.1 and Section 20.2 discusses ways to tackle these challenges.

Members of a collocated development team are usually housed within walking distance. Psychology tells us that if one has to walk more than 30 meters or climb the stairs, one is inclined to reinvent the wheel rather than ask a colleague. So, preferably, development teams share a project room or a 'war room'. Experimental studies such as (Teasley *et al.*, 2002) confirm that the frequent informal exchanges that result from being collocated foster collaboration, information sharing, mutual learning, and efficient communication. Communication between developers that are more than 30 meters apart is as infrequent as communication between developers at different sites. This is just one challenge of being global.

The tasks of the members of a software development team are interdependent. They coordinate their activities to reach a set of common goals and share the responsibility for reaching those goals. Traditional, collocated software development fits this picture. A global, or virtual, team has the same goals and objectives, but it has multiple sites. It operates across different time zones and geographical locations, and may involve different organizations. Members of a virtual team use a variety of media (telephone, email, teleconferencing, etc.) for communication.

Many organizations have outsourced or offshored[1] part of their work to lower the labor cost. Currently, mostly the 'low-end' tasks are offshored to low-wage countries, while 'high-end' activities such as requirements engineering and architecture remain in high-wage countries. It is by no means sure that situation will continue (Aspray *et al.*, 2006). But other factors also play a role when deciding on where to locate software development activities:

- faster delivery because of 'follow-the-sun' development: Software development is started by a team of developers at one development site and, when their work day ends, it is shifted to a team in a place where the work day is starting. In theory, work can continue around the clock.

- access to a larger pool of developers: In some countries there is a permanent shortage of skilled developers. To alleviate this problem, work can be moved to a country where there is an abundance of skilled developers.

- better modularization of work: By its nature, global development requires that work is split into modules that require as little communication between development teams as is possible. Global development thus encourages desirable design properties.

There is very little proof that these alleged advantages actually materialize (Conchúir *et al.*, 2006). For example, around-the-clock development often results in working shifts that overlap in time, so that developers at different sites can have direct contact. Work then shifts to these overlapping hours. It may also result in a lot of overtime at either side to make sure that direct contact is possible. Cost advantages are offset against higher travel costs, higher maintenance costs, and so on. Even if the wages at offshoring sites are about 10% of those in the Western hemisphere, actual cost savings are more likely to be in the 20–40% range (Matloff, 2005).

20.1 CHALLENGES OF GLOBAL SYSTEM DEVELOPMENT

The essence of a collocated team is that many things are shared. The team shares some set of tools and uses the same process. Team members have the same background and share an understanding of the job to be done. Team members share information at frequent informal meetings in the lobby or at the coffee machine. (Perry *et al.*, 1994) observed that developers in a particular organization spent up to 75 minutes per day in unplanned personal interaction. Sometimes, development teams share the same office area on purpose, to stimulate interaction and speed things up. A shared room is also one of the distinguishing practices of agile development.

These mechanisms all disappear when work is distributed. The challenges that face global software development all have to do with distance: temporal distance,

---

[1]Outsourcing means that work is done by a third party. Offshoring means that it is done in a different country from the contracting organization.

geographical distance, and sociocultural distance. Along a second dimension, the challenges of global software development can also be classified in three categories (Ågerfalk *et al.*, 2006):

- communication and collaboration between team members: Individual team members need to exchange information and work together.

- coordination between tasks: The work to be done at different sites needs to be coordinated.

- control of the work: Management must keep in control of the work done at different sites.

Table 20.1 lists the main challenges according to this two-dimensional classification. Below, we discuss each of the entries in this table. Note that many of the issues discussed are interrelated; the borders between entries are not that clear-cut.

Table 20.1   Challenges of global system development (based on (Ågerfalk *et al.*, 2006); (Clerc *et al.*, 2007))

	Distance		
	Temporal	Geographical	Sociocultural
Communication	Effective communication	Effective information exchange Build a team	Cultural misunderstandings
Coordination	Coordination costs	Task awareness Sense of urgency	Effective cooperation
Control	Delays	Accurate status information Uniform process	Quality and expertise

Effective communication When team members are at different locations, communication means are often asynchronous (email, for example). Asynchronous communication is less effective than synchronous communication. It is not possible to get an immediate clarification if a message is not understood. Problems may crop up at a later stage because people take the risk of *not* contacting a colleague at a remote site, but guess an answer and tacitly accept the risks.

Coordination costs For global software development projects, coordination costs are often larger than for collocated projects. In some cases, representatives from the client organization are located at a development site for the duration of the project.

Key people such as managers and architects frequently travel to the different teams to have onsite meetings. The infrastructure tends to be more expensive too, in terms of bandwidth, videoconferencing hardware and software, and so on.

Delays When an issue arises that requires information from another site, it often incurs a delay. One may have to wait for the next teleconference meeting, send an email and wait for the other side to react, and so on. Asynchronous communication easily leads to delays where the same issue in a collocated team would be dealt with immediately simply by walking down the corridor and engaging in a discussion with the person involved.

For example, suppose a change request only touches upon the code base owned by a local site. Any problems a developer may have in handling this request can be solved by consulting a nearby colleague. If on the other hand a change request is multi-site, a developer at one site may have to communicate with a colleague at another site. If he knows which person to contact, he can send him an email and wait for a reply. If not, he first has to find out which person to contact. Initiating contact in a global project is even more difficult if more than two people are involved. Either way, delays are incurred.

Effective information exchange When teams are at geographically different sites, there is less informal, unplanned contact. During unplanned meetings at the coffee machine, highly valuable and relevant information is exchanged. Small issues that are easily settled in an unplanned meeting in the hall by a collocated team may have to be 'saved' until the next formal teleconference meeting in a global setting. Chances are then that a number of these smaller issues remain unresolved for a long time or are forgotten altogether. Unplanned social meetings also help people build up an awareness of what is important and what is not, and what the future of the project will bring. These issues are often largest at the start of a project, simply because one doesn't yet know team members at the other sites.

Effective information exchange is especially important during the early stages of a project. Damian and Zowghi (2003) report difficulties in handling requirements in a global software development environment. An often-used medium for exchanging such information is email. But email is a poor medium in which to handle ambiguities and may lead to lengthy discussions without actually resolving the issue. Emails raising a difficult requirements issue may not be answered immediately and end up in a stack, ultimately to be forgotten.

In a global setting, partners in information exchange often speak a different native language. It then becomes more difficult to exchange requirements unambiguously. It may be difficult to find the proper terms for domain entities. Income tax laws in my country make use of very special regulations that are difficult to express at all, let alone unambiguously. Partners in another country will have difficulties in interpreting them properly; they may use their background knowledge of their own tax rules to infer a likely meaning. In such circumstances, it may take a long time before problems related to misunderstood requirements come to the surface.

Individual members of a global team often have difficulties identifying appropriate expertise at other sites. As a consequence, they do not know whom to contact with a specific information request. (Fussell *et al.*, 1998) identify four types of awareness problem in distributed teams:

- activity awareness: what are the others doing?

- availability awareness: when can I reach them?

- process awareness: what are they doing?

- perspective awareness: what are they thinking and why?

Ehrlich and Chang (2006) found that people communicate more frequently with someone else if they know what this person is working on, when they know this person from a previous project, or have some general idea about his knowledge and expertise. This suggests that improving awareness and familiarity of other team members in a global team helps. This and other studies also found that team boundaries are often permeable. People do not *only* rely on information from their immediate colleagues in the development team. They have a personal network that they rely upon, especially for technical matters.

In collocated teams, inadequate knowledge management is often compensated for by personal contact and knowing who knows what. Distributed teams need more thorough means of knowledge management. Local meetings may result in decisions that are not properly captured and disseminated to the other teams that need to know about them. The latter then have to guess things or rediscover them.

Build a team Building a team in a global development project is hampered because of the temporal and geographical distance. As a result, there is a higher chance of mismatches in terminology and definitions, resulting in communication overhead and delays.

Collocated teams tend to be more cohesive than global teams because of their daily interaction, physical proximity, similar background, and so on. In a global setting, team members from different sites may consider themselves as part of different teams rather than one global team. Such feelings may lead to a 'them and us' attitude between teams at different sites. This attitude is more likely to occur when the teams have different roles, such as a designer team at one site and a development team at another. This may result in negative attitudes and conflicts. Weak ties between team members impede the transfer of complex knowledge (Hansen, 1999). Usually, the knowledge that needs to be exchanged between sites of a distributed software development project is quite complex in nature. It would thus help to strengthen ties in a distributed software development project.

An issue closely related to team building is trust. Distance makes it difficult to build up relationships in which there is mutual trust. During the early phases, when requirements are being negotiated, trust is essential. Parties in this negotiating process may leave certain issues deliberately open or ambiguous. They may have a hidden agenda. Developers may keep things hidden from their manager to protect their position. Conversely, a manager may hide information from the developers so as not to alarm them at an early stage, and so on. In a collocated development team, many issues are resolved in open meetings. In a global setting, there is ample room for bilateral contact through emails, phone calls, and so on. Information then is spread to some people and not to others, possibly adding to the level of distrust. Distrust is further increased if emails are used as a weapon, for instance by copying management each time a problem is reported to a colleague.

If sites in a global project do not see themselves as partners, it may result in 'uncharitable' behavior (Herbsleb and Grinter, 1999). For instance, a person at one site might say that a certain change cannot be made. The recipient of this message at the other site may construe this as meaning that that person is not willing to make the effort.

People may feel that multi-site development is a first step towards reducing jobs. They will then not be inclined to communicate freely. If they do, their knowledge may be transferred to others, and they become easier to replace.

Task awareness In a global setting, work assignments may not be understood properly. This may easily lead to long discussions that add up to delays. For example, the precise distribution of responsibilities between a development team and the integration test team may not be understood properly and lead to long discussions between the two. Unlike single-site projects, in globally distributed projects, the amount of discussion generally does not decrease in the course of the project.

Team members do not only coordinate work through an input–process–output model. There is more to coordination of work than the formal exchange of messages. A team builds up a shared mental model of the work to be done. Team members have to *know* what is to be done, what the other team members know, and the goals of colleagues. By studying what designers do, (Curtis *et al.*, 1988) found that performance is improved when team members have a shared mental model. Building such a shared model is a lot easier when the team is collocated.

Sense of urgency Multi-site development may result in differences in the perceived sense of urgency of handling requests. For example, a developer at one site may ask for clarification of some requirement in an email to a colleague at another site. The person receiving the email may not read his email for a while, or postpone an immediate answer. The developer in turn may be sitting idle, waiting for a reply. Direct contact with colleagues at the same site makes it easier to convey the urgency of a help request. Asynchronous communication such as sending emails lowers the perceived sense of urgency. The lack of a sense of urgency induces delays.

Accurate status information In a global setting, it is difficult to exert effective control. For instance, if a team at one site exceeds its plan, that team can easily blame management at a remote site that 'has no idea of the complexity of our subsystem'.

Tracking status is essential in a global software development project. If code is developed at different sites and has to be integrated at a third site, management needs to have accurate status information. If the schedule slips at one development site, it will also slip at the integration site. If status information is inaccurate, it may easily give rise to feelings of frustration elsewhere.

Uniform process It is important to have a uniform process strategy. Having non-uniform processes introduces delays. For example, one site may have a dedicated team for integration testing, while integration testing may be the responsibility of each subsystem team at another site. The integration team needs assistance from developers when issues arise, and this is complicated when developers have to deal with different processes. At integration time, speed is paramount to quickly resolve bugs discovered.

Establishing a uniform process requires negotiation. It is part of establishing common ground between sites. It usually does not work to simply impose one site's process upon another. This creates 'them and us' feelings, as mentioned before, and inhibits mutual trust.

On the other hand, different sites are likely to use different tools and methods, because of history, culture, or other reasons. Management must be able to accommodate these differences. The manager has to become an orchestrator rather than a dictator.

Cultural misunderstandings There are different kinds of culture: corporate culture, technical culture, and national culture. Corporate culture has to do with the organization one works in. Some organizations for instance have an open communication culture, others communicate through formal channels only. Technical culture has to do with the development processes followed. Some organizations are much more concerned about the quality of products shipped than others. National culture has to do with differences between people from different parts of the world. In the words of Browning (1994):

> American managers have a hamburger style of management. They start with sweet talk – the top of the hamburger bun. Then the criticism is slipped in – the meat. Finally, some encouraging words – the bottom bun. With the Germans, all one gets is the meat. With the Japanese, all one gets is the buns; one has to smell the meat.

Culture is one of the most important challenges to be addressed in global software development. People from different parts of the world exhibit cultural differences. This ranges from simple dress codes, such as wearing a tie or not, to issues of hierarchy and structure, sense of time, and communication style. Cultural differences also impact the ease with which certain types of software can be developed. Middleware and embedded software are relatively culture-neutral. Application software, for example an end-user application to handle mortgages, is more culture-specific and thus requires more careful communication.

Hofstede (1997) deals with cultural differences at the national level. His book is based on research done between 1967 and 1973 at IBM, long before the era of global software development. Many years later, it was found to be very useful for designing user interfaces, in particular websites. And now it is found to be useful in grasping cultural issues in global software development. Hofstede distinguishes five dimensions along which cultural differences can be observed:

- **power distance** In a culture with high power distance, status, wealth, and similar factors determine one's hierarchical status. In a culture with low power distance, individuals are considered equal.

- **collectivism versus individualism** In a collectivistic culture, individuals are part of a group to which they are loyal. In an individualistic culture, everyone looks after himself, and personal interests take priority over those of the group one belongs to.

- **femininity versus masculinity** This dimension has to do with gender values, where the more masculine values are earnings, challenges, and recognition while the more feminine values are good working relationships, cooperation, and employment security.

- **uncertainty avoidance** This dimension reflects how tolerant people are when placed in an unfamiliar or new situation. A high value indicates that the culture is based on strict rules and procedures to mitigate uncertainty. A low value indicates the culture is more flexible in handling uncertainty.

- **long-term versus short-term orientation** Long-term orientation is characterized by values such as persistence in pursuing goals, observing order, thrift. Short-term orientation is characterized by protecting one's face, personal steadiness, respect for tradition.

Of these, power distance, collectivism versus individualism, and uncertainty avoidance have the strongest impact on global software development.

People from Asia value personal relationships within a team more than the task at hand. The North-American and European culture on the other hand is very task-oriented. In a cross-Pacific meeting, team members from Singapore and Thailand might first have some small talk and inform about family issues, while team members from North America skip the introductions and come to business right away. In other words, the Individualism Index (IDV) is higher for North-Americans and Europeans than it is for people from Asia.

People from different places also have a different power distance. This is relevant for hierarchical relations within teams. In Northern America and Europe, managers have to convince their team members and team members may argue with their manager's decisions. In Asia, people respect authority: the power distance is large. This might clash when people from different cultures get to work in the same team. An American manager may expect discussion and not get it; a manager from Asia may be surprised by the opposition he encounters from his American team members.

Finally, societies with a low value for uncertainty avoidance (UAI) have better mechanisms for coping with uncertainty. They can deal with agile approaches, ill-defined requirements documents, and so on. Cultures with a high value for UAI favor waterfall models, heavy processes, strict change control procedures. Latin America and Japan have a high UAI value, whereas North America and India have low UAI value. European scores are quite mixed.

Cultural differences thus impact global software development. It should be noted that most of the current insight is anecdotal and common sense. Hofstede's dimensions provide a way to categorize issues that play a role. The above statements about cultural differences between, say, Europe and Asia, are simplifications of reality. For instance, there are large regional differences within Europe. Though the power distance is low for most European countries, it is relatively high for Belgium and France (see (Hofstede, 1997)).

Effective cooperation Cooperation between team members from different cultures imposes problems: differences in vocabulary, a possible reluctance on either side to ask questions, differences in communication style, and so on. A team member one side, for instance, may prefer direct contact through a phone call or videoconference contact, while his colleague may prefer to send email.

In collocated projects, as well as multi-site projects, it is important to know 'who is who', to recognize individuals, and acknowledge their expertise. This is a lot easier when members are located at the same site. Once contact has been initiated, people are more willing to overcome cultural differences in order to communicate and cooperate effectively.

Quality and expertise It is difficult to assess the quality and expertise of remote partners. A CMM level 5 certificate in itself does not guarantee quality. What matters is the level of technical expertise, and this level is often difficult to assess from a distance.

20.2 HOW TO OVERCOME DISTANCE

Olson and Olson (2000) identified four concepts that are important for making distributed development succeed:

- common ground,

- coupling of work,

- collaboration readiness,

- technology readiness.

20.2.1 Common Ground

Common ground refers to the knowledge team members have in common, and that they are aware of. If you discuss part of a design with a close and knowledgeable colleague, mentioning the name of a particular design pattern might suffice, while a much longer explanation is used when explaining the same concept to a novice on the team. Non-verbal communication is taken into account as well, and may adjust our assumptions on the fly of what people know or understand. Common ground is established dynamically. This is much easier if the team is collocated.

Technology such as videoconferencing or other high bandwidth channels helps to establish common ground, but it remains a difficult issue. People prefer to contact a colleague from their own location, if there is one at the remote site. The more common ground people from different sites have, the easier communication is. For newly established teams, such common ground has to be developed, for instance through site visits.

It is better to do more frequent traveling at the beginning of the project, to build common ground. Travel can also be used to build liaisons. A person from site A who has traveled to site B is known to people at site B. Whenever they have questions regarding the work of site A, they are more likely to contact the person they know. One may even exploit this phenomenon and use it to *build* liaisons. For instance, that person may travel to site B regularly, to maintain and foster the mutual contacts.

Achieving common ground is also known as socialization. Socialization refers to the process by which one learns what behaviors are desirable, and which knowledge and skills are required to do one's job. The most obvious examples of socialization are the introduction of a new member to the team, and a kick-off meeting at the beginning of a global software development project. Socialization in global teams takes place both in face-to-face meetings, and through electronic media such as emails, teleconferencing, and so on. It is generally acknowledged that face-to-face meetings are essential. Since software development projects are usually quite long running, there may be a need to re-socialize (Oshri *et al.*, 2007): the ties established at the kick-off meeting simply fade away over time.

Since global software development projects tend to have regular face-to-face meetings, it is natural to incorporate the socialization aspects into those meetings. It is good practice to reserve some time specifically for socialization purposes. Otherwise the meeting will be completely filled with urgent project matters such as requirements conflicts, change requests, planning of the next release, and so on. The social element that 'comes for free' in a collocated project has to be planned for in a global project. Another way of implementing socialization is to have experts travel around or have the project manager visit sites outside the regular schedule of the face-to-face meetings.

Interaction in global software development often follows a rhythm: intense meetings are scheduled at regular intervals and in between those intervals interaction is less intense (Maznevski and Chudoba, 2000). The intense meetings are used to discuss important aspects, make far-reaching decisions such as the global partitioning of a system, and build relationships. The intervals between intense meetings tend to be shorter at the beginning of the project. They can be wider apart once the tasks are known. The reason for having periodic intense meetings rather than letting the situation at hand determine whether such a meeting is appropriate is logistical.

It is often not feasible to gather the project manager, lead architect, and end-user representative at short notice.

An extensive survey of outsourcing projects confirmed that intense interactions between sites is the most important success factor in such projects, more so than coordination tools, CMM level, and upfront investment in architectural modeling (Tiwana, 2004).

20.2.2 Coupling of Work

Coupling refers to the amount and extent of communication required in performing tasks. Collocated teams can communicate very effectively in informal ways. Ambiguities can easily be solved over a cup of coffee and are less likely to play a major role because of the common ground people share. Certain tasks, such as brainstorming over design issues, are very collaborative and difficult to handle in a distributed fashion. It is better to design the organization such that tasks that require much collaboration are done at the same spot. Tasks that require little interaction can be executed at different sites. So, programming or testing relatively independent subsystems can be done at different sites. Clear and unambiguous communication is of paramount importance in such circumstances, since there is likely to be less common ground between the sites.

20.2.3 Collaboration Readiness

If an organization has no culture of cooperation or sharing, it will have difficulty operating successfully in a global software development effort. The transition to a sharing and cooperating organization requires changing work habits, learning new tools, and so on. Incentives are needed to make employees change their habits and make them ready for collaboration. Collaboration readiness not only applies to individuals but also to the organization as a whole.

20.2.4 Technology Readiness

Finally, the technology has to be there. With the advent of the Web and the availability of advanced groupware tools, such as weblogs, wikis, and so on, this is less of an issue now than it was ten years ago. Global software development projects use these Internet technologies to support communication and collaboration in a variety of ways:

- Project management tools, usually workflow-oriented, allow people to synchronize their work.

- Web-enabled versions of familiar tools, such as those for requirements tracking, planning, budget, and so on help people to coordinate their work remotely. For example, (Lanubile *et al.*, 2003) discusses a Web-based support system for distributed software inspections.

- An infrastructure to automate builds and tests provides the ability to control them remotely (Spanjers *et al.*, 2006).

- Web-based project repositories, such as workspaces, store and share files intelligently between sites.

- Real-time collaboration tools bridge the soft skills gap in distributed work.

- Knowledge management technology finds information and people.

A lot of knowledge of a software development organization is kept in unstructured forms: FAQs, mailing lists, email repositories, bug reports, lists of open issues, and so on. Lightweight tools such as wikis, weblogs, and yellow pages are other examples of relatively unstructured repositories to share information in global projects. In the knowledge management literature, this strategy is known as the *personalization strategy*. Each person has his own way to structure the knowledge. The threshold for contribution is usually low, but the effort expended in finding useful information is higher. Another strategy is *codification*, where the knowledge is codified in a structured way that can be used while querying. An advantage of the codification strategy is that the information has the same form and structure. A disadvantage is the extra effort it takes to cast the information in the form required. A hybrid strategy may be used to have the best of both worlds (Desouza *et al.*, 2006).

(Gao *et al.*, 2002) describe PIMS, a Web-based problem information management system. PIMS not only provides Web-based access to support the various problem-reporting tasks, such as problem reporting, status tracking, and information search, but it also allows for customization. Different users of the system may configure their own workflow for handling problem reports, define their own report formats, and use their own data formats. Teams in a global software development project may thus employ their own local processes, yet communicate and coordinate their work through a shared system.

The mere availability of tools that support global development is not sufficient, though. Efficient use of these technologies also depends on properties of the organization (policies, rewards, incentives) and the degree to which people understand the technology (Orlikowski, 1992).

We may distinguish two types of communication media in global software development projects: simple media such as email messages and phone calls, and rich media such as teleconference meetings and site visits. In effective teams, form follows function (Maznevski and Chudoba, 2000): simple messages are handled by simple media, while complex messages are handled by rich media. In ineffective global teams, one may find lengthy discussions on somewhat irrelevant issues in a teleconference call, while essential decisions are communicated in a short email message.

It is important for an organization to capture the lessons learned to prevent future development projects making the same mistakes over and over again. Capturing the lessons learned is especially difficult in global software development projects because the knowledge is spread. The root cause of a certain performance problem may be a combination of decisions of a functional nature at one site and decisions about data storage at another.

One way to capture such lessons learned is through Communities of Practice (CoPs). A community of practice is a, usually informal, group of people who share certain knowledge. For instance, all software architects of an organization may form a community of practice. Such a community creates knowledge, shares it, may have regular meetings to discuss their field of expertise, and makes their knowledge accessible to others, for instance through a website. Many software development organizations have such communities of practice. They capture and foster the collective knowledge of the organization. Communities of practice often span boundaries: experts from different projects and different branches of the organization can be members of the same community.

20.2.5 Organizing Work in Global Software Development

There are two ways in which one may address the lack of informal communication in global software development projects:

- reduce the need for informal communication, and

- provide technologies that ease informal communication.

Usually, a combination of both is used.

Reducing the need or communication, be it formal or informal, is usually achieved through organizational means. Typically, people that have to interact a lot are located at the same site. This not only reduces the need for communication, but also makes the coordination of work a lot easier. For instance, experts in a certain area, such as user interfaces, are put together at the same site. User interfaces for all the systems of an enterprise are then developed at that site. Alternatively, the gross structure of the system, the architecture, can be used to divide work amongst sites. This can be seen as a variation of Conway's Law (Conway, 1968), which states that the structure of a product mirrors the organizational structure of the people who designed it. If three groups are involved in the development of a system, that system will have three major subsystems. This way of decomposing work is the programming-in-the-large equivalent of Parnas' advice to consider a module as a 'responsibility assignment rather than a subprogram' (Parnas, 1972). A third way is to split up tasks according to life cycle phases: design is done at one site, development at a second, testing at a third.

Each of these organizational means has advantages and disadvantages. Each may work well, but problems may arise if a lot of coordination is required that crosses the boundaries of the division. Many projects require more than one functional area. A system needs a user interface, a database, security protection, and so on. If each site has a specific expertise, many projects will require a lot of cross-site coordination. If different sites are responsible for different subsystems, problems may arise with tasks that involve more than one subsystem, such as integration testing. If different sites are responsible for different life cycle phases, this may incur delays. For instance, the development site may decide not to ship code to the testing site until all the components have been developed, and the site responsible for testing will have to wait for the code to be shipped.

Division of work amongst sites is not only guided by objective arguments. For instance, if different sites develop different components, a political battle may ensue as to who is going to develop which component. A component whose requirements are volatile, or one that critically depends on hardware that has not been acquired yet, may easily lead to problems and had thus better be the responsibility of someone else. On the other hand, a high-visibility component may be attractive to develop. This way, politics enters the picture when it comes to division of labor.

The three main ways of coordinating work in global software development are architecture, plans, and processes (Herbsleb and Grinter, 1999). The architecture of a system establishes a division of responsibilities into independent building blocks. The design and implementation of the building blocks may be assigned to different sites. Plans describe when milestones are reached and who does what. Processes describe *how* the software is going to be developed. All three are needed.

Global software development at first sight seems to better fit the more traditional development paradigms in which a lot of effort is spent at the beginning on delineating and documenting tasks. These tasks can then be assigned to different teams. Agile methods seem less fit for global software development, because of the need for very frequent communication and the onsite presence of a customer. Paasivara and Lassenius (2006) argue that many of the agile practices not only pose challenges for global system development, but can also be seen as benefits. Provided suitable tools for communication are in place, the frequent communication that is typical for agile projects may actually help communication in the project, foster team building, increase mutual awareness of people, and so on. Continuous integration and testing gives fast feedback, so that issues come to the front very quickly. Misunderstandings between teams thus have a better chance to surface quickly, before they become a big problem.

Global software development is orthogonal to outsourcing. Distributed teams may or may not be part of the same company. Most of the challenges are in essence independent of this distinction, but are likely to be larger in the case of outsourcing. In an outsourcing context, cultural differences tend to be larger, company policies might differ, and there is less background between the parties involved. This poses greater challenges for communication, coordination, and control. Partial answers to these greater challenges are dependencies (for example, all development is outsourced) and strict contractual agreements for controlling purposes.

20.3 SUMMARY

Global software development poses a number of challenges that have to do with distance in time, place, and culture. These challenges concern the way people communicate and collaborate, and the way work is coordinated and controlled. The most striking challenges concern:

- finding ways to deal with the lack of informal communication between team members, and

- handling cultural differences.

Software developers in a collocated team exchange a lot of valuable information in informal and unplanned meetings. The information exchanged is tacit and becomes part of the shared knowledge of that group of developers. Such informal exchange is not possible in a global development project and this needs to be catered for in a different way: through regular site visits, teleconferencing, Web-based tools to share knowledge, and so on. Intense interaction between sites is the most important success factor in global software development projects (Tiwana, 2004).

Cultural differences also impact global software development. The main dimensions along which cultural differences affect global software development are:

- power distance: Is a person's hierarchical status important or are individuals considered equal?

- collectivism versus individualism: Are individuals part of a group or do personal interests take priority?

- uncertainty avoidance: Is the culture flexible about uncertainty?

A number of techniques and tools are emerging to overcome the challenges of global software development. The International Conference on Global Software Engineering (ICGSE) is fully devoted to the topic. To paraphrase Brooks (1987): each of the many solutions proposed will contribute its mite. But we should not expect miracles. Distance still matters (Olson and Olson, 2000).

20.4 FURTHER READING

Case studies of global software development and the issues encountered are discussed by Damian and Zowghi (2003). (Herbsleb and Mockus, 2003) is an empirical study into delays induced by multi-site development. Further case studies are reported in (Herbsleb and Grinter, 1999), (Herbsleb *et al.*, 2005), (Casey and Richardson, 2006), (Damian, 2007), and (DeLone *et al.*, 2005). (Software, 2001) and (Software, 2006a) are special journal issues devoted to global software development. (Carmel, 1999) is a well-known textbook on global software development.

The 30 meter threshold for information exchange stems from (Allen, 1977). Different coordination mechanisms for distributed development are discussed in (Grinter *et al.*, 1999). Herbsleb (2007) provides a concise overview of the state of the art. (Desouza *et al.*, 2006) discuss knowledge management in global software development.

Critical success factors of multi-site development are discussed in (Olson and Olson, 2000). (Ramasubbu *et al.*, 2005) translate these success factors into a process maturity framework to deal with distributed development. (Hofstede, 1997) is the seminal text on cultural differences amongst organizations. Cultural issues in software development are given special attention in (Krishna *et al.*, 2004) and (Borchers, 2003).

Exercises

1. What is global software development?

2. In what ways does global software development incur delays?

3. What makes team building more difficult in global software development?

4. Discuss Hofstede's cultural dimensions and how they apply to distributed software development.

5. Why is common ground important in software development?

6. Explain how Conway's Law relates to global software development.

7. ♡ Write an essay on the role of informal communication in software development.

8. ♡ Suppose you have to manage a project with teams in Boston and Bangalore. The project has to develop a Web-based system that helps

people select their healthcare insurance. Discuss how you would split up tasks between those teams.

9. ♡ Discuss the advantages and disadvantages of using a personalization and codification approach to share knowledge between development sites.

Bibliography

Abdel-Hamid, T., Sengupta, K., and Ronan, D. (1993). Software Project Control: An Experimental Investigation of Judgment with Fallible Information. *IEEE Transactions on Software Engineering*, 19(6):603–612.

Aberdour, M. (2007). Achieving Quality in Open Source Software. *IEEE Software*, 24(1):58–64.

Abrahamsson, P., Salo, O., Ronkainen, J., and Warsta, J. (2002). Agile Software Development Methods. Technical report, VTT Publications 478, VTT, Finland.

Abran, A. and Robillard, P. (1992). Function Points: A Study of Their Measurement Processes and Scale Transformations. *Journal of Systems and Software*, 25(2):171–184.

Abran, A. and Robillard, P. (1996). Function Points Analysis: An Empirical Study of Its Measurement Processes. *IEEE Transactions on Software Engineering*, 22(12):895–910.

Achermann, F., Kneubuehl, S., and Nierstrasz, O. (2000). Scripting coordination styles. In Porto, A. and Roman, G.-C., editors, *COORDINATION 2000: Fourth International Conference on Coordination Languages and Models*, pages 19–35. Springer Verlag, LNCS 1906.

Adams, E. (1984). Optimizing Preventive Service of Software Products. *IBM Journal of Research and Development*, 28(1):2–14.

Ågerfalk, P., Fitzgerald, B., Holmström, H., Lings, B., Lundel, B., and Conchúir, E. (2006). A Framework for Considering Opportunities and Threats in Distributed Software Development. In *Proceedings International Workshop on Distributed Software Engineering*, pages 47–61. Austrian Computer Society.

Agrawal, M. and Chari, K. (2007). Software Effort, Quality, and Cycle Time: A Study of CMM Level 5 Projects. *IEEE Transactions on Software Engineering*, 33(3):145–156.

Åkerholm, M., Carlson, J., Fredrikson, J., Hansson, H., Håkansson, J., Möller, A., Pettersson, P., and Tivoli, M. (2007). The SAVE approach to component-based development of vehicular systems. *Journal of Systems and Software*, 80(5):655–667.

Albrecht, A. (1979). Measuring Applications Development Productivity. In *Proceedings Application Development Symposium*, pages 83–92. SHARE/GUIDE.

Albrecht, A. and Gaffney, J. (1983). Software Function, Source Lines of Code, and Development Effort Prediction: A Software Science Validation. *IEEE Transactions on Software Engineering*, 9(6):639–648.

Alexander, C. (1979). *The Timeless Way of Building*. Oxford University Press.

Alexander, C. (1999). The Origins of Pattern Theory. *IEEE Software*, 16(5):71–82.

Alexander, C., Ishikawa, S., and Silverstein, M. (1977). *A Pattern Language*. Oxford University Press.

Allen, T. (1977). *Managing the Flow of Technology: Technology Transfer and the Dissemination of Technological Information within the R&D Organization*. MIT Press.

Ambriola, V., Conradi, R., and Fuggetta, A. (1997). Assessing Process-Centered Software Engineering Environments. *ACM Transactions on Software Engineering and Methodology*, 6(3):283–328.

Arisholm, A. and Sjøberg, D. (2004). Evaluating the Effect of a Delegated versus Centralized Control Style on the Maintainability of Object-Oriented Software. *IEEE Transactions on Software Engineering*, 30(8):521–534.

Armour, P. (2001). Zeppelins and Jet Planes: A Metaphor for Modern Software Projects. *Communications of the ACM*, 44(10):13–15.

Armour, P. (2002). The Organism and the Mechanism of Projects. *Communications of the ACM*, 45(5):17–20.

Aspray, W., Mayadas, F., and Vardi, M., editors (2006). *Globalization and Offshoring of Software*. ACM.

Assman, U. (2003). *Invasive Software Composition*. Springer Verlag.

Atkinson, C. (2000). Socio-Technical and Soft Approaches to Information Requirements Elicitation in the Post-Methodology Era. *Requirements Engineering Journal*, 5(2):67–73.

Austin, R. and Devin, L. (2003). Beyond Requirements: Software Making as Art. *IEEE Software*, 20(1):93–95.

Avison, D., Gregor, S., and Wilson, D. (2006). Managerial IT Unconsciousness. *Communications of the ACM*, 49(7):89–93.

Baber, R. (1982). *Software Reflected*. North-Holland Publishing Company.

Babich, W. (1986). *Software Configuration Management*. Addison-Wesley.

Baddoo, N. and Hall, T. (2003). De-motivators for software process improvement: an analysis of practitioners' views. *Journal of Systems and Software*, 66(1):23–34.

Baker, F. (1972). Chief Programmer Team Management of Production Programming. *IBM Systems Journal*, 11(1):56–73.

Banker, R., Datar, S., Kemerer, C., and Zweig, D. (1993). Software Complexity and Maintenance Costs. *Communications of the ACM*, 36(11):81–94.

Banker, R., Kauffman, R., and Kumar, R. (1991). An Empirical Test of Object-Based Output Measurement Metrics in a Computer Aided Software Engineering (CASE) Environment. *Journal of Management Information Systems*, 8(3):127–150.

Baram, G. and Steinberg, G. (1989). Selection Criteria for Analysis and Design CASE Tools. *ACM Software Engineering Notes*, 14(6):73–80.

Barnard, H., Metz, R., and Price, A. (1986). A Recommended Practice for Describing Software Designs: IEEE Standards Project 1016. *IEEE Transactions on Software Engineering*, 12(2):258–263.

Barnes, B. and Bollinger, T. (1991). Making Reuse Cost-Effective. *IEEE Software*, 8(1):13–24.

Barstow, D., Shrobe, H., and Sandewall, E., editors (1984). *Interactive Programming Environments*. McGraw-Hill.

Basili, V. (1990). Viewing Maintenance as Reuse-Oriented Software Development. *IEEE Software*, 7(1):19–25.

Basili, V., Briand, L., Condon, S., Kim, Y.-M., Melo, W., and Valen, J. (1996). Understanding and Predicting the Process of Software Maintenance Releases. In *Proceedings International Conference on Software Maintenance (ICSM'96)*, pages 464–474. IEEE.

Basili, V., McGarry, F., Pajersky, R., and Zelkowitz, M. (2002). Lessons Learned from 25 Years of Process Improvement. In *Proceedings 24th International Conference on Software Engineering (ICSE24)*, pages 69–79. IEEE.

Basili, V. and Selby, R. (1987). Comparing the Effectiveness of Software Testing Strategies. *IEEE Transactions on Software Engineering*, 13(12):1278–1296.

Bass, L., Clements, P., and Kazman, R. (2003). *Software Architecture in Practice*. Addison-Wesley, second edition.

Batini, C., Ceri, S., and Navathe, S. (1992). *Conceptual Database Design: An Entity–Relationship Approach*. Benjamin Cummings.

Beck, K. (2000). *Extreme Programming Explained*. Addison-Wesley.

Beck, K. (2003). *Test-Driven Development*. Addison-Wesley.

Beck, K. and Cunningham, W. (1989). A Laboratory For Teaching Object-Oriented Thinking. In *OOPSLA '89 Proceedings, ACM SIGPLAN Notices 24(10)*, pages 1–6.

Beck, K. *et al.* (2001). Manifesto for Agile Software Development. http://agilemanifesto.org.

Beizer, B. (1995). *Black Box Testing*. John Wiley & Sons.

Bellay, B. and Gall, H. (1998). An Evaluation of Reverse Engineering Tool Capabilities. *Journal of Software Maintenance: Research and Practice*, 10:305–331.

Benington, H. (1983). Production of Large Computer Programs. In *Proceedings ONR Symposium (1956), reprinted in Annals of the History of Computing 5(4)*, pages 350–361.

Bennett, K. (1998). Do Program Transformations Help Reverse Engineering? In *Proceedings International Conference on Software Maintenance (ICSM'98)*, pages 247–254. IEEE.

Bennett, K. and Rajlich, V. (2000). Software Maintenance and Evolution: a Roadmap. In Finkelstein, A., editor, *The Future of Software Engineering*, pages 73–87. ACM Press.

Bergland, G. and Gordon, R. (1981). *Tutorial: Software Design Strategies*. IEEE, EZ389.

Berners-Lee, T., Hendler, J., and Lassila, O. (2001). The Semantic Web. *Scientific American*, 284(5):34–43.

Bersoff, E. and Davis, A. (1991). Impacts of Life Cycle Models on Software Configuration Management. *Communications of the ACM*, 34(8):104–118.

Beyer, H. and Holtzblatt, K. (1995). Apprenticing with the Customer. *Communications of the ACM*, 38(5):45–52.

Bias, G. and Mayhew, D., editors (1994). *Cost-Justifying Usability*. Academic Press.

Bieman, J., Jain, D., and Yang, H. (2001). OO Design Patterns, Design Structure, and Program Changes: An Industrial Case Study. In *Proceedings International Conference on Software Maintenance (ICSM'01)*, pages 580–589. IEEE.

Biffl, S. and Halling, M. (2002). Investigating the Influence of Inspector Capability Factors with Four Inspection Techniques on Inspection Performance. In *Proceedings 8th IEEE International Software Metrics Symposium*, pages 107–17. IEEE.

Biggerstaff, J., Mitbander, B., and Webster, D. (1994). Program Understanding and the Concept Assignment Problem. *Communications of the ACM*, 37(5):72–83.

Biggerstaff, T. (1989). Design Recovery for Maintenance and Reuse. *IEEE Computer*, 22(7):36–50.

Biggerstaff, T. and Perlis, A., editors (1989). *Software Reusability, Volume I: Concepts and Models, Volume II: Applications and Experience*. Addison-Wesley.

Binder, R. (2000). *Testing Object-Oriented Systems*. Addison-Wesley.

Bisbal, J., Lawless, D., Wu, B., and Grimson, J. (1999). Legacy Information Systems: Issues and Directions. *IEEE Software*, 16(5):103–111.

Blum, B. (1994). A Taxonomy of Software Development Methods. *Communications of the ACM*, 37(11):82–94.

Boehm, B. (1975). Some Experience with Automated Aids to the Design of Large-Scale Reliable Software. In *Proceedings International Conference on Reliable Software, ACM SIGPLAN Notices 10(6)*, pages 105–113. ACM.

Boehm, B. (1976). Software Engineering. *IEEE Transactions on Computers*, C-25(12):1226–1241.

Boehm, B. (1981). *Software Engineering Economics*. Prentice Hall.

Boehm, B. (1983). The Economics of Software Maintenance. In *Proceedings Software Maintenance Workshop*, pages 9–37. IEEE, 83CH1982-8.

Boehm, B. (1984a). Software Life Cycle Factors. In Vick, C. and Ramamoorthy, C., editors, *Handbook of Software Engineering*, pages 494–518. Van Nostrand Reinhold.

Boehm, B. (1984b). Verifying and Validating Software Requirements and Design Specifications. *IEEE Software*, 1(1):75–88.

Boehm, B. (1987a). Improving Software Productivity. *IEEE Computer*, 20(9):43–57.

Boehm, B. (1987b). Industrial Software Metrics Top 10 List. *IEEE Software*, 4(5):84–85.

Boehm, B. (1988). A Spiral Model of Software Development and Enhancement. *IEEE Computer*, 21(5):61–72.

Boehm, B. (1989). *Software Risk Management*. IEEE.

Boehm, B., Abts, C., Brown, A., Chulani, S., Clark, B., Horowitz, E., Madachy, R., Reifer, D., and Steece, B. (2000). *Software Cost Estimation with COCOMO II*. Prentice Hall.

Boehm, B. and Basili, V. (2001). Software Defect Reduction Top 10 List. *IEEE Computer*, 34(1):135–137.

Boehm, B., Brown, J., Kaspar, H., Lipow, M., MacLeod, G., and Merrit, M. (1978). *Characteristics of Software Quality*. Number 1 in TRW Series of Software Technology. North-Holland.

Boehm, B. et al. (1997). COCOMO II Model Definition Manual. Technical report, University of Southern California.

Boehm, B. and Sullivan, K. (1999). Software economics: status and prospects. *Information and Software Technology*, 41(14):937–946.

Boehm, B. and Turner, R. (2003). *Balancing Agility and Discipline*. Addison-Wesley.

Boehm, B. and Turner, R. (2005). Management Challenges in Implementing Agile Processes in Traditional Development Organizations. *IEEE Software*, 22(5):30–39.

Böhm, C. and Jacopini, G. (1966). Flow Diagrams, Turing Machines, and Languages With Only Two Formation Rules. *Communications of the ACM*, 9(5):366–371.

Bohrer, K., Johnson, V., Nilsson, A., and Rudin, B. (1998). Business Process Components for Distributed Object Applications. *Communications of the ACM*, 41(6):43–48.

Booch, G. (1987). *Software Components with Ada: Structures, Tools, and Subsystems*. Benjamin Cummings.

Booch, G. (1994). *Object-Oriented Analysis and Design with Applications*. Benjamin Cummings, second edition.

Booch, G., Rumbaugh, J., and Jacobson, I. (1999). *UML User Guide*. Addison-Wesley.

Borchers, G. (2003). The Software Engineering Impacts of Cultural Factors on Multi-cultural Software Development Teams. In *Proceedings 25th International Conference on Software Engineering (ICSE25)*, pages 540–545. IEEE.

Bounds, G., Yorks, L., Adams, M., and Ranney, G. (1994). *Beyond Total Quality Management*. McGraw-Hill.

Box, D. (1997). *Essential COM*. Addison-Wesley, Object Technology Series.

Bracha, G. and Cook, W. (1990). Mixin-Based Inheritance. In Meyrowitz, N., editor, *Proceedings of the Conference on Object-Oriented Programming: Systems, Languages, and Applications / Proceedings of the European Conference on Object-Oriented Programming*, pages 303–311. ACM Press.

Brooks, Jr., F. (1987). No Silver Bullet: Essence and Accidents of Software Engineering. *IEEE Computer*, 20(4):10–20.

Brooks, Jr., F. (1995). *The Mythical Man-Month*. Addison-Wesley, second edition.

Brooks, R. (1983). Towards a Theory of the Comprehension of Computer Programs. *International Journal of Man-Machine Studies*, 18:543–554.

Brown, W., Malveau, R., III, H. M., and Mowbray, T. (1998). *AntiPatterns: Refactoring Software, Architectures, and Projects in Crisis*. John Wiley & Sons.

Browning, E. (1994). Side by side: Computer chip project brings rivals together, but the cultures clash; Foreign work habits get in the way of creative leaps, hobbling joint research. Softball is not the answer. *Wall Street Journal*, May 3:page A1.

Budgen, D. (2003). *Software Design*. Addison-Wesley, second edition.

Burch, E. and Kung, H.-J. (1997). Modeling Software Maintenance Requests: A Case Study. In *Proceedings International Conference on Software Maintenance (ICSM'97)*, pages 40–47.

Burke, B. and Monson-Haefel, R. (2006). *Enterprise JavaBeans 3.0*. O'Reilly, fifth edition.

Buschmann, F., Meunier, R., Rohnert, H., Sommerlad, P., and Stal, M. (1996). *A System of Patterns*. John Wiley & Sons.

Bush, E. (1985). The Automatic Restructuring of COBOL. In *Proceedings Conference on Software Maintenance*, pages 35–41. IEEE.

Buxton, J. and Randell, B., editors (1969). *Software Engineering Techniques, Report on a Conference*. NATO Scientific Affairs Division, Rome.

CACM (1993a). Special Issue on Participatory Design. *Communications of the ACM*, 36(6).

CACM (1993b). Special Issue on Project Organization and Management. *Communications of the ACM*, 36(10).

CACM (1997). Special Issue: The Quality Approach: Is It Delivering. *Communications of the ACM*, 40(6).

CACM (2003). Special Issue: Service-Oriented Computing. *Communications of the ACM*, 46(10).

CACM (2006). Special Issue: Services Science. *Communications of the ACM*, 49(7).

Cameron, J. (1989). *JSP & JSD, The Jackson Approach to Software Development*. IEEE.

Campbell-Kelly, M. (2003). *From Airline Reservations to Sonic the Hedgehog*. MIT Press.

Card, S., Moran, T., and Newell, A. (1983). *The Psychology of Human–Computer Interaction*. Erlbaum.

Carmel, E. (1999). *Global Software Teams*. Prentice Hall.

Carmel, E., Whitaker, R., and George, J. (1993). PD and Joint Application Design: A Transatlantic Comparison. *Communications of the ACM*, 36(6):40–48.

Carroll, E. (2005). Estimating Software Based on Use Case Points. In *Conference on Object Oriented Programming, Systems, Languages and Applications (OOPSLA)*, pages 257–265. ACM.

Carroll, J. (1990). *The Nurnberg Funnell: Designing Minimalist Instruction for Practical Computer Skill*. MIT Press.

Carroll, J. (1995). *Scenario-Based Design*. John Wiley & Sons.

Casey, V. and Richardson, I. (2006). Uncovering the Reality Within Virtual Software Teams. In *Proceedings International Conference on Global Software Engineering (ICGSE'06)*. IEEE.

Cha, S., Leveson, N., and Shimeall, T. (1988). Safety Verification in MURPHY using Fault-Tree Analysis. In *Proceedings 10th International Conference on Software Engineering (ICSE10)*, pages 377–386. IEEE.

Chapin, N. (1987). The Job of Software Maintenance. In *Proceedings Conference on Software Maintenance*, pages 4–12. IEEE.

Chapin, N., Hale, J., Khan, K., Ramil, J., and Tan, W.-G. (2001). Types of software evolution and software maintenance. *Journal of Software Maintenance and Evolution: Research and Practice*, 13:3–30.

Chappell, D. (2006). *Understanding .NET*. Addison-Wesley.

Cheesman, J. and Daniels, J. (2000). *UML Components*. Addison-Wesley.

Chen, P. (1976). The Entity–Relationship Model: Toward a Unifying View of Data. *ACM Transactions on Data Base Systems*, 1(1):9–36.

Chidamber, S. and Kemerer, C. (1994). A Metrics Suite for Object Oriented Design. *IEEE Transactions on Software Engineering*, 20(6):476–493.

Chikofsky, E. (1990). CASE & Reengineering: From Archeology to Software Perestroika. In *Proceedings 12th International Conference on Software Engineering (ICSE12)*, page 122. IEEE.

Chikofsky, E. and Cross II, J. (1990). Reverse Engineering and Design Recovery: A Taxonomy. *IEEE Software*, 7(1):13–18.

Churcher, N. and Shepperd, M. (1995). Comments on 'A Metrics Suite for Object Oriented Design'. *IEEE Transactions on Software Engineering*, 21(3):263–265.

Ciolkowski, M., Laitenberger, O., and Biffl, S. (2003). Software Reviews: The State of the Practice. *IEEE Software*, 20(6):46–51.

Clarke, L., Podgurski, A., Richardson, D., and Zeil, S. (1989). A Formal Evaluation of Data Flow Path Selection Criteria. *IEEE Transactions on Software Engineering*, 15(11):1318–1332.

Clements, P., Bachman, F., Bass, L., Garlan, D., Ivers, J., Little, R., Nord, R., and Stafford, J. (2003). *Documenting Software Architectures: Views and Beyond*. Addison-Wesley.

Clements, P., Kazman, R., and Klein, M. (2002). *Evaluating Software Architectures: Methods and Case Studies*. Addison-Wesley.

Clements, P. and Northrop, L. (2002). *Software Product Lines: Practices and Patterns*. Addison-Wesley.

Clemmons, R. (2006). Project Estimation With Use Case Point. *Crosstalk*, 14(3).

Clerc, V., Lago, P., and Vliet, H. v. (2007). Global Software Development: Are Architectural Rules the Answer? In *Proceedings International Conference on Global Software Engineering (ICGSE'07)*. IEEE.

CMMI Product Team (2006). CMMI for Development. Technical report, CMU/SEI-2006-TR-008, Software Engineering Institute.

Coad, P. and Yourdon, E. (1991). *Object-Oriented Analysis*. Yourdon Press, second edition.

Coakes, J. and Coakes, E. (2000). Specifications in Context: Stakeholders, Systems and Modelling of Conflict. *Requirements Engineering Journal*, 5(2):103–113.

Cockburn, A. (1996). The Interaction of Social Issues and Software Architecture. *Communications of the ACM*, 39(10):40–46.

Cockburn, A. (2001). *Writing Effective Use Cases*. Addison-Wesley.

Cockburn, A. (2002). *Agile Software Development*. Addison-Wesley.

Cohn, M. (2006). *Agile Estimation and Planning*. Prentice Hall.

Coleman, D. (1996). Fusion with Use Cases: Extending Fusion for Requirements Modelling. Technical report, available through URL http://www.hpl.hp.com/fusion/index.html.

Coleman, D., Arnold, P., Bodoff, S., Dollin, C., Gilchrist, H., Hayes, F., and Jeremaes, P. (1994). *Object-Oriented Development: The FUSION Method*. Prentice Hall.

Collofello, J. and Woodfield, S. (1989). Evaluating the Effectiveness of Reliability-Assurance Techniques. *Journal of Systems and Software*, 9(3):191–195.

Colwell, B. (2002). Near Misses: Murphy's Law is Wrong. *IEEE Computer*, 35(4):9–12.

Conchúir, E., Holmström, H., Ågerfalk, P., and Fitzgerald, B. (2006). Exploring the Assumed Benefits of Global Software Development. In *Proceedings International Conference on Global Software Engineering (ICGSE'06)*. IEEE.

Conklin, J. (1987). Hypertext: An Introduction and Survey. *IEEE Computer*, 20(9):17–41.

Conklin, J. and Begeman, M. (1988). gIBIS: A Hypertext Tool for Exploratory Policy Discussion. *ACM Transactions on Office Information Systems*, 6(4):303–331.

Conradi, R. and Fuggetta, A. (2002). Improving Software Process Improvement. *IEEE Software*, 19(4):92–99.

Conradi, R., Fuggetta, A., and Jaccheri, M. (1998). Six Theses on Software Process Research. In Gruhn, V., editor, *Software Process Technology, 6th European workshop, EWSPT'98*. Springer Verlag, LNCS 1487.

Constantine, L. (1993). Work Organization: Paradigms for Project Management and Organization. *Communications of the ACM*, 36(10):34–43.

Conte, S., Dunsmore, H., and Shen, V. (1986). *Software Engineering Metrics and Models*. Benjamin Cummings.

Conway, M. (1968). How Do Committees Invent. *Datamation*, 14(4):28–31.

Cook, S., Harrison, R., Lehman, M., and Wernick, P. (2006). Evolution in software systems: foundations for the SPE classification scheme. *Journal of Software Maintenance and Evolution: Research and Practice*, 18(1):1–35.

Copeland, L. (2003). *A Practitioner's Guide to Software Test Design*. Artech House Publishers.

Corby, T. (1989). Program Understanding: Challenge for the 1990s. *IBM Systems Journal*, 28(2):294–306.

Corkill, D. (1997). Countdown to Success: Dynamic Objects, GBB, and RADARSET-1. *Communications of the ACM*, 40(5):48–58.

Corlett, E. and Clark, T. (1995). *The Ergonomics of Workspaces and Machines*. Taylor & Francis Ltd., London.

Costagliola, G., Ferrucci, F., Tortora, G., and Vitiello, G. (2005). Class Point: An Approach for the Size Estimation of Object-Oriented Systems. *IEEE Transactions on Software Engineering*, 31(1):52–74.

Côté, M.-A., Suryn, W., and Georgiadou, E. (2006). Software Quality Model Requirements for Software Quality Engineering. In *Proceedings 14th International Software Quality Management & INSPIRE Conference*.

Couger, J. and Zawacki, R. (1980). *Motivating and Managing Computer Personnel*. Wiley.

Cox, B. (1990). Planning the Software Industrial Revolution. *IEEE Software*, 7(6):25–33.

Crnkovic, I. and Larsson, M. (2002a). *Building Reliable Component-Based Software Systems*. Artech House.

Crnkovic, I. and Larsson, M. (2002b). Challenges of component-based development. *Journal of Systems and Software*, 61(3):201–212.

Crowston, K. and Howison, J. (2006). Assessing the Health of Open Source Communities. *IEEE Computer*, 39(5):89–91.

Cugola, G., di Nitto, E., Fuggetta, A., and Ghezzi, C. (1996). A Framework for Formalizing Inconsistencies and Deviations in Human-Centered Systems. *ACM Transactions on Software Engineering and Methodology*, 5(3):191–230.

Cugola, G. and Ghezzi, C. (1998). Software Processes: a Retrospective and a Path to the Future. *Software Process – Improvement and Practice*, 4(3):101–123.

Curbera, F., Duftler, M., Khalaf, R., Nagy, W., Mukhi, N., and Weerawarana, S. (2002). Unraveling the Web services Web: An introduction to SOAP, WSDL, and UDDI. *IEEE Internet Computing*, 6(2).

Currit, P., Dyer, M., and Mills, H. (1986). Certifying the Reliability of Software. *IEEE Transactions on Software Engineering*, 12(1):3–11.

Curtis, B. (1989). Three Problems Overcome with Behavioral Models of the Software Development Process. In *Proceedings 11th International Conference on Software Engineering (ICSE11)*, pages 398–399. IEEE.

Curtis, B., Krasner, H., and Iscoe, N. (1988). A Field Study of the Software Design Process for Large Systems. *Communications of the ACM*, 31(11):1268–1287.

Curtis, B., Krasner, H., Shen, V., and Iscoe, N. (1987). On Building Software Process Models Under the Lamppost. In *Proceedings 9th International Conference on Software Engineering (ICSE9)*, pages 96–103.

Curtis, B., Sheppard, S., and Milliman, P. (1979). Third Time Charm: Stronger Prediction of Programmer Performance by Software Complexity Metrics. In *Proceedings 4th International Conference on Software Engineering (ICSE4)*, pages 356–360. IEEE.

Cusumano, M. (1989). The Software Factory: A Historical Interpretation. *IEEE Software*, 6(2):23–30.

Cusumano, M. and Yoffe, D. (1999). Software Development on Internet Time. *Computer*, 32(10):60–69.

Damian, D. (2007). Stakeholders in Global Requirements Engineering: Lessons Learned from Practice. *IEEE Software*, 24(2):21–27.

Damian, D. and Zowghi, D. (2003). RE challenges in multi-site software development organizations. *Requirements Engineering*, 8:149–160.

Darcy, D. (2005). The Structural Complexity of Software: An Experimental Test. *IEEE Transactions on Software Engineering*, 31(11):982–995.

Darcy, D. and Kemerer, C. (2005). OO Metrics in Practice. *IEEE Software*, 22(6):17–19.

Darke, P. and Shanks, G. (1996). Stakeholder Viewpoints in Requirements Definition: A Framework for Understanding Viewpoint Development Approaches. *Requirements Engineering Journal*, 1:88–105.

Dart, S. (1990). Spectrum of Functionality in Configuration Management Systems. Technical report, CMU/SEI-90-TR-11, Software Engineering Institute.

Dart, S., Ellison, R., Feiller, P., and Habermann, A. (1987). Software Development Environments. *IEEE Computer*, 20(11):18–28.

Davenport, T. (1993). *Process Innovation: Reengineering Work through Information Technology*. Harvard Business School Press, Cambridge, MA.

Davis, A. (1993). *Software Requirements: Objects, Functions and State*. Prentice Hall, second edition.

Davis, A. (1995). Object-Oriented Requirements to Object-Oriented Design: An Easy Transition? *Journal of Systems and Software*, 30(1 & 2):151–159.

Davis, A. (2005). *Just Enough Requirements Management*. Dorset House.

Davis, G. (1982). Strategies for Information Requirements Determination. *IBM Systems Journal*, 21(1):4–30.

Dekleva, S. (1992). Delphi Study of Software Maintenance Problems. In *Proceedings International Conference on Software Maintenance (ICSM'92)*, pages 10–17. IEEE.

Delisle, N. and Garlan, D. (1990). Applying Formal Specification to Industrial Problems: A Specification of an Oscilloscope. *IEEE Software*, 7(5):29–37.

DeLone, W., Espinosa, J., Lee, G., and Carmel, E. (2005). Bridging Global Boundaries for IS Project Success. In *Proceedings 38th Hawaii International Conference on Information Sciences (HICSS)*, pages 1–10. IEEE.

DeMarco, T. (1979). *Structured Analysis and System Specification*. Prentice Hall.

DeMarco, T. (1982). *Controlling Software Projects*. Yourdon Press.

DeMarco, T. and Lister, T. (1989). Software Development: State of the Art vs. State of the Practice. In *Proceedings 11th International Conference on Software Engineering (ICSE11)*, pages 271–275. IEEE.

DeMarco, T. and Lister, T. (1999). *Peopleware: Productive Projects and Teams*. Dorset House, second edition.

DeMillo, R., Lipton, R., and Perlis, A. (1979). Social Processes and the Proofs of Theorems and Programs. *Communications of the ACM*, 22(5):271–280.

DeRemer, F. and Kron, H. (1976). Programming-in-the-large Versus Programming-in-the-small. *IEEE Transactions on Software Engineering*, 2(2):80–86.

Desouza, K., Awazu, Y., and Baloh, P. (2006). Managing Knowledge in Global Software Development Efforts: Issues and Practices. *IEEE Software*, 23(5):30–37.

Deursen, A. v., Hofmeister, C., Koschke, R., Moonen, L., and Riva, C. (2004). Symphony: View-Driven Software Architecture Reconstruction. In *Proceedings 4th Working IEEE/IFIP Conference on Software Architecture (WICSA4)*, pages 122–132. IEEE.

Devanbu, P., Brachman, R., Selfridge, P., and Ballard, B. (1991). LASSIE: A Knowledge-Based Software Information System. *Communications of the ACM*, 34(5):34–49.

Diaz, M. and Sligo, J. (1997). How Software Process Improvement Helped Motorola. *IEEE Software*, 14(5):75–81.

Dix, A., Finlay, J., Abowd, G., and Beale, R. (1998). *Human–Computer Interaction*. Prentice Hall.

Dobing, B. and Parsons, J. (2006). How UML is used. *Communications of the ACM*, 49(5):109–113.

Dobrica, L. and Niemelä, E. (2002). A Survey of Software Architecture Analysis Methods. *IEEE Transactions on Software Engineering*, 28(7):638–653.

Dolotta, T., Haight, R., and Mashey, J. (1978). UNIX Time-Sharing System: The Programmer's Workbench. *The Bell System Technical Journal*, 57(6):2177–2200.

Downs, E., Clare, P., and Coe, I. (1992). *SSADM: Structured Systems Analysis and Design Method*. Prentice Hall, second edition.

Ducasse, S., Gîrba, T., and Kuhn, A. (2006). Distribution Map. In *Proceedings International Conference on Software Maintenance (ICSM'06)*, pages 203–212. IEEE.

Dunsmore, A., Roper, M., and Wood, M. (2002). Further Investigations into the Development and Evaluation of Reading Techniques for Object-Oriented Code Inspection. In *Proceedings 24th International Conference on Software Engineering (ICSE24)*, pages 47–57. IEEE.

Dybå, T. (2005). An Instrument for Measuring the Key Factors of Success in Software Process Improvement. *Empirical Software Engineering*, 5(4):410–424.

Ehrlich, K. and Chang, K. (2006). Leveraging expertise in global software teams: Going outside boundaries. In *Proceedings International Conference on Global Software Engineering (ICGSE'06)*. IEEE.

Eischen, K. (2002). Software Development: An Outsider's View. *IEEE Computer*, 35(5):36–44.

El Emam, K., Benlarbi, S., Goel, N., and Rai, S. (2001). The Confounding Effect of Class Size on the Validity of Object-Oriented Metrics. *IEEE Transactions on Software Engineering*, 27(7):630–650.

El Emam, K., Drouin, J., and Melo, W. (1997). *SPICE: The Theory and Practice of Software Process Improvement and Capability Determination*. IEEE.

El Emam, K. and Madhavji, N. (1995). The Reliability of Measuring Organizational Maturity. *Software Process – Improvement and Practice*, 1(1):3–25.

Elshoff, J. (1976). Measuring Commercial PL-1 Programs Using Halstead's Criteria. *ACM SIGPLAN Notices*, 11(5):38–76.

Emmerich, W., Aoyama, M., and Sventek, J. (2007). The Impact of Research on Middleware Technology. *ACM SIGSOFT Software Engineering Notes*, 32(1):21–46.

Endres, A. and Rombach, D. (2003). *A Handbook of Software and Systems Engineering*. Pearson.

Epstein, R. (1997). *The Case of the Killer Robot*. John Wiley & Sons.

Erdogmus, H., Morisio, M., and Torchiano, M. (2005). On the Effectiveness of the Test-First Approach to Programming. *IEEE Transactions on Software Engineering*, 31(3):226–237.

Erl, T. (2005). *Service-Oriented Architecture: Concepts, Technology and Design*. Prentice Hall.

Estublier, J., Leblang, D., van der Hoek, A., Conradi, R., Clemm, G., Tichy, W., and Wiborg-Weber, D. (2005). Impact of Software Engineering Research on the Practice of Software Configuration Management. *ACM Transactions on Software Engineering and Methodology*, 14(4):383–430.

Fafchamps, D. (1994). Organizational Factors and Reuse. *IEEE Software*, 11(5):31–41.

Fagan, M. (1976). Design and Code Inspections to Reduce Errors in Program Development. *IBM Systems Journal*, 15(3):182–211.

Fagan, M. (1986). Advances in Inspections. *IEEE Transactions on Software Engineering*, 12(7):744–751.

Fairley, D. (2002). Making Accurate Estimates. *IEEE Software*, 19(6):61–63.

Fairley, R. and Wilshire, M. (2003). Why the Vasa Sank: 10 Problems and Some Antidotes for Software Projects. *IEEE Software*, 20(2):18–25.

Fang, Y. and Neufeld, D. (2006). Should I Stay or Should I Go? Worker Commitment to Virtual Organizations. In *Proceedings 39th Hawaii International Conference on Information Sciences (HICSS)*. IEEE.

Fayad, M. (1997). Software Development Process: A Necessary Evil. *Communications of the ACM*, 40(9):101–103.

Fayad, M. and Laitinen, M. (1997). Process Assessment Considered Wasteful. *Communications of the ACM*, 40(11):125–128.

Feldman, S. (1978). Make: A Program for Maintaining Computer Programs. Technical report, AT&T.

Fenton, N. and Pfleeger, S. L. (1996). *Software Metrics: A Rigorous & Practical Approach*. Thomson Computer Press, second edition.

Fetzer, J. H. (1988). Program Verification: The Very Idea. *Communications of the ACM*, 31(9):1048–1063. See also ref: *Communications of the ACM* 32(3):374–381 (1989) and 32(4):506–512 (1989).

Fichman, R. and Kemerer, C. (2001). Incentive Compatibility and Systematic Software Reuse. *Journal of Systems and Software*, 57(1):45–60.

Finkelstein, A., editor (2000). *The Future of Software Engineering*. ACM Press.

Fischer, G. (1986). From Interactive to Intelligent Systems. In Skwirzynski, J., editor, *Software System Design Methods*, volume 22 of *NATO ASI Series F: Computer and Systems Sciences*, pages 185–212. Springer Verlag.

Fischer, M. and Gall, H. (2004). Visualizing feature evolution of large-scale software based on problem and modification report data. *Journal of Software Maintenance and Evolution: Research and Practice*, pages 385–403.

Fitzgerald, B. and O'Kane, T. (1999). A Longitudinal Study of Software Process Improvement. *IEEE Software*, 16(3):37–51.

Fitzsimmons, A. and Love, T. (1978). A Review and Evaluation of Software Science. *ACM Computing Surveys*, 10(1):3–18.

Fjelstad, R. and Hamlen, W. (1979). Application Program Maintenance Study: Report to our Respondents. In *Proceedings of GUIDE 48*.

Flowers, S. (1996). *Software Failure: Management Failure*. John Wiley & Sons.

Floyd, C., Mehl, W.-M., Reisin, F.-M., Schmidt, G., and Wolf, G. (1989). Out of Scandinavia: Alternative Approaches to Software Design and System Development. *Human–Computer Interaction*, 4:253–350.

Folmer, E., van Gurp, J., and Bosch, J. (2003). A Framework for Capturing the Relationship between Usability and Software Architecture. *Software Process Improvement and Practice*, 8(2):67–87.

Fowler, M. (1999). *Refactoring: Improving the Design of Existing Code*. Addison-Wesley.

Fowler, M. (2003). Who Needs an Architect. *IEEE Software*, 20(5):11–13.

Fowler, M. (2004). *UML Distilled*. Addison-Wesley, third edition.

Frakes, W. and Gandel, P. (1990). Representing Reusable Software. *Information and Software Technology*, 32(10):653–664.

Frakes, W. and Kang, K. (2005). Software Reuse Research: Status and Future. *IEEE Transactions on Software Engineering*, 31(7):529–536.

Frakes, W. and Terry, C. (1996). Software Reuse: Metrics and Models. *ACM Computing Surveys*, 28(5):415–435.

Frankl, P. and Weiss, S. (1993). An Experimental Comparison of the Effectiveness of Branch Testing and Data Flow Testing. *IEEE Transactions on Software Engineering*, 19(8):774–787.

Frankl, P., Weiss, S., and Hu, C. (1997). All-Uses vs Mutation Testing: An Experimental Comparison of Effectiveness. *Journal of Systems and Software*, 38(3):235–253.

Frankl, P. and Weyuker, E. (1993a). A Formal Analysis of the Fault-Detection Ability of Testing Methods. *IEEE Transactions on Software Engineering*, 19(3):202–213.

Frankl, P. and Weyuker, E. (1993b). Provable Improvements on Branch Testing. *IEEE Transactions on Software Engineering*, 19(10):962–975.

Freeman, P., editor (1987). *Tutorial: Software Reusability*. IEEE, EZ750.

Freeman, P. and Wasserman, A., editors (1983). *Tutorial: Software Design Techniques*. IEEE EZ514.

Fuggetta, A. (1993). A Classification of CASE Technology. *IEEE Computer*, 26(12):25–38.

Fuggetta, A. and Wolf, A., editors (1996). *Software Process – Improvement and Practice*. John Wiley & Sons.

Fussell, S., Krut, R., Lerch, F., Scherlis, W., McNally, M., and Cadiz, J. (1998). Coordination, Overload and Team Performance: Effects of Team Communication Strategies. In *Proceedings ACM CSCW '98*, pages 275–284.

Gamma, E., Helm, R., Johnson, R., and Vlissides, J. (1995). *Design Patterns: Elements of Reusable Object-Oriented Software*. Addison-Wesley.

Gane, C. and Sarson, T. (1979). *Structured Analysis and Systems Analysis: Tools and Techniques*. Prentice Hall.

Gao, J., Itaru, F., and Toyoshima, Y. (2002). Managing Problems for Global Software Production – Experience and Lessons. *Information Technology and Management*, 3:85–112.

Garlan, D., Allen, R., and Ockerbloom, J. (1995). Architectural Mismatch: Why Reuse Is So Hard. *IEEE Software*, 12(6):17–26.

Garlan, D., Kaiser, G., and Notkin, D. (1992). Using Tool Abstraction to Compose Systems. *IEEE Computer*, 25(6):30–38.

Garmus, D. and Herron, D. (1996). *Measuring the Software Process: A Practical Guide to Functional Measurements*. Prentice Hall.

Gartner (2001). Describing the Capability Maturity Model. *Measure IT*. Gartner Inc, http:///www.gartner.com/measurements.

Garvin, D. (1984). What does 'Product Quality' really mean? *Sloan Management Review*.

Gelperin, D. and Hetzel, B. (1988). The Growth of Software Testing. *Communications of the ACM*, 31(6):687–695.

Genuchten, M. v. (1991). *Towards a Software Factory*. PhD thesis, Technical University of Eindhoven, The Netherlands.

Gibson, V. and Senn, J. (1989). System Structure and Software Maintenance Performance. *Communications of the ACM*, 32(3):347–358.

Gilb, T. (1988). *Principles of Software Engineering Management*. Addison-Wesley.

Gilb, T. and Graham, D. (1993). *Software Inspection*. Addison-Wesley.

Gîrba, T. and Ducasse, S. (2006). Modeling history to analyze software evolution. *Journal of Software Maintenance and Evolution: Research and Practice*, 18:207–236.

Gîrba, T., Ducasse, S., and Lanza, M. (2004). Yesterday's Weather: Guiding early reverse engineering efforts by summarizing the evolution of changes. In *Proceedings International Conference on Software Maintenance (ICSM'04)*, pages 40–49. IEEE.

Glass, R. (2003). *Facts and Fallacies of Software Engineering*. Addison-Wesley.

Godfrey, M. and Tu, Q. (2000). Evolution in Open Source Software: A Case Study. In *Proceedings 2000 International Conference on Software Maintenance (ICSM'00)*, pages 131–142. IEEE.

Goguen, J. (1986). An Introduction to OBJ: A Language for Writing and Testing Formal Algebraic Program Specifications. In Gehani, N. and McGettrick, A., editors, *Software Specification Techniques*, pages 391–419. Addison-Wesley.

Goguen, J. and Jirotka, M., editors (1994). *Requirements Engineering: Social and Technical Issues*. Academic Press, Boston.

Goguen, J. and Linde, C. (1993). Techniques for Requirements Elicitation. In *Proceedings 1st International Symposium on Requirements Engineering (RE93)*, pages 152–164, San Diego. IEEE.

Goodenough, J. and Gerhart, S. (1975). Toward a Theory of Test Data Selection. *IEEE Transactions on Software Engineering*, 1(2):156–173.

Gopal, A., Krishnan, M., Mukhopadhyay, T., and Goldenson, D. (2002). Measurement Programs in Software Development: Determinants of Success. *IEEE Transactions on Software Engineering*, 28(9):863–875.

Gordon, V. and Bieman, J. (1994). Rapid Prototyping: Lessons Learned. *IEEE Software*, 12(1):85–95.

Gotel, O. and Finkelstein, A. (1994). An Analysis of the Requirements Traceability Problem. In *Proceedings International Conference on Requirements Engineering*, pages 94–101. IEEE.

Gotterbarn, D. (1999). How the New Software Engineering Code of Ethics Affects You. *IEEE Software*, 16(6):58–64.

Gotterbarn, D., Miller, K., and Rogerson, S. (1999). Computer Society and ACM Approve Software Engineering Code of Ethics. *IEEE Computer*, 32(10):84–88.

Grady, R. and Caswell, D. (1987). *Software Metrics: Establishing a Company-Wide Program*. Prentice Hall.

Grady, R. and van Slack, T. (1994). Key Lessons in Achieving Widespread Inspection Use. *IEEE Software*, 11(4):46–57.

Greevy, O., Ducasse, S., and Gîrba, T. (2006). Analyzing software evolution through feature views. *Journal of Software Maintenance and Evolution: Research and Practice*, pages 425–456.

Grinter, R., Herbsleb, J., and Perry, D. (1999). The Geography of Coordination: Dealing with Distance in R&D Work. In *Proceedings GROUP'99*, pages 306–315. ACM.

Grossman, M., Aronson, J., and McCarthy, R. (2005). Does UML make the grade? Insights from the software development community. *Information and Software Technology*, 47(6):383–397.

Grudin, J. (1991). Interactive Systems: Bridging the Gaps Between Developers and Users. *IEEE Computer*, 24(4):59–69.

Guindon, R. and Curtis, B. (1988). Control of Cognitive Processes during Design: What Tools Would Support Software Designers? In *Proceedings CHI'88*, pages 263–268. ACM.

Gunning, R. (1968). *The Technique of Clear Writing*. McGraw-Hill.

Gyimóthy, T., Ferenc, R., and Siket, I. (2005). Empirical Validation of Object-Oriented Metrics on Open Source Software for Fault Prediction. *IEEE Transactions on Software Engineering*, 31(10):897–910.

Haan, G. d., van der Veer, G., and van Vliet, J. (1991). Formal Modelling Techniques in Human–Computer Interaction. *Acta Psychologica*, 78:27–67.

Hall, T. and Fenton, N. (1997). Implementing Effective Software Metrics Programs. *IEEE Software*, 14(2):55–65.

Halstead, M. (1977). *Elements of Software Science*. North-Holland Publishing Company.

Hamlet, D. and Taylor, R. (1990). Partition Testing Does Not Inspire Confidence. *IEEE Transactions on Software Engineering*, 16(12):1402–1411.

Hansen, M. (1999). The Search-Transfer Problem: The Role of Weak Ties in Sharing Knowledge across Organization Subunits. *Administrative Science Quarterly*, 44(1):82–111.

Harel, D. (1988). On Visual Formalisms. *Communications of the ACM*, 31(5):514–530.

Harrison, W. (2004). Clueless–and Oblivious. *IEEE Software*, 21(3):5–7.

Harrold, M. (1999). Testing Evolving Software. *Journal of Systems and Software*, 47(2/3):173–181.

Harrold, M., Offutt, A., and Tewary, K. (1997). An Approach to Fault Modeling and Fault Seeding Using the Program Dependence Graph. *Journal of Systems and Software*, 36(3):273–295.

Hatley, D. and Pirbhai, I. (1988). *Strategies for Real-Time System Specification*. Dorset House.

Hatton, L. (2007). How Accurately Do Engineers Predict Software Maintenance Tasks? *IEEE Computer*, 40(2):64–69.

Heemstra, F. (1989). *How Much Does Software Cost?* PhD thesis, Technical University of Eindhoven, The Netherlands. In Dutch.

Heineman, G. and Councill, W. (2001). *Component-Based Software Engineering: Putting the Pieces Together*. Addison-Wesley.

Henderson Sellers, B. (1992). Modularization and McCabe's Cyclomatic Complexity. *Communications of the ACM*, 35(12):17–19.

Henri, S. and Kafura, D. (1981). Software Structure Metrics Based on Information Flow. *IEEE Transactions on Software Engineering*, 7(5):510–518.

Henry, J. and Cain, J. (1997). Comparison of Perfective and Corrective Software Maintenance. *Journal of Software Maintenance: Research and Practice*, 9:281–297.

Herbsleb, J. (2007). Global Software Engineering: The Future of Socio-technical Coordination. In *Proceedings 29th International Conference on Software Engineering (ICSE29)*. ACM.

Herbsleb, J. and Grinter, R. (1999). Architectures, Coordination, and Distance: Conway's Law and Beyond. *IEEE Software*, 16(5):63–70.

Herbsleb, J. and Mockus, A. (2003). An Empirical Study of Speed and Communication in Globally-Distributed Software Development. *IEEE Transactions on Software Engineering*, 29(3):1–14.

Herbsleb, J., Paulish, D., and Bass, M. (2005). Global Software Development at Siemens: Experience from Nine Projects. In *Proceedings 27th International Conference on Software Engineering (ICSE27)*, pages 524–533. IEEE.

Herbsleb, J., Zubrow, D., Goldenson, D., Hayes, W., and Paulk, M. (1997). Software Quality and the Capability Maturity Model. *Communications of the ACM*, 40(6):30–40.

Highsmith, J. (2004). *Agile Project Management*. Addison-Wesley.

Hirschheim, R. and Klein, H. (1989). Four Paradigms of Information Systems Development. *Communications of the ACM*, 32(10):1199–1216.

Hitz, M. and Montazeri, B. (1996). Chidamber and Kemerer's Metrics Suite: A Measurement Theory Perspective. *IEEE Transactions on Software Engineering*, 22(4):267–271.

Hix, D. and Hartson, H. (1993). *Developing User Interfaces: Ensuring Usability Through Product and Process*. John Wiley & Sons.

Ho, W. and Olsson, R. (1996). A Layered Model for Building Debugging and Monitoring Tools. *Journal of Systems and Software*, 34(3):211–222.

Hødalsvik, G. and Sindre, G. (1993). On the purpose of Object-Oriented Analysis. In *OOPSLA'93 Proceedings, ACM SIGPLAN Notices 28 (10)*, pages 240–255.

Hofman, H. and Lehner, F. (2001). Requirements Engineering as a Success Factor in Software Projects. *IEEE Software*, 18(4):58–66.

Hofmeister, C., Kruchten, P., Nord, R., Obbink, H., Ran, A., and America, P. (2007). A General Model of Software Architecture Design Derived from Five Industrial Approaches. *Journal of Systems and Software*, 80(1):106–126.

Hofstede, G. (1997). *Culture and Organizations*. McGraw-Hill.

Hops, J. and Sherif, J. (1995). Development and Application of Composite Complexity Models and a Relative Complexity Metric in a Software Maintenance Environment. *Journal of Systems and Software*, 31(2):157–169.

Hosier, W. (1961). Pitfalls and Safeguards in Real-Time Digital Systems With Emphasis on Programming. *IRE Transactions on Engineering Management*, pages 99–115.

Howden, W. (1982). Validation of Scientific Programs. *ACM Computing Surveys*, 14(2):193–227.

Howden, W. (1985). The Theory and Practice of Functional Testing. *IEEE Software*, 2(5):6–17.

Humphrey, W. (1988). Characterizing the Software Process: A Maturity Framework. *IEEE Software*, 5(2):73–79.

Humphrey, W. (1989). *Managing the Software Process*. SEI Series in Software Engineering. Addison-Wesley.

Humphrey, W. (1996). Using a Defined and Measured Personal Software Process. *IEEE Software*, 13(3):77–88.

Humphrey, W. (1997a). *Introduction to the Personal Software Process*. Addison-Wesley.

Humphrey, W. (1997b). *Managing Technical People*. Addison-Wesley.

Humphrey, W., Kitson, D., and Kasse, T. (1989). The State of Software Engineering Practice: A Preliminary Report. In *Proceedings 11th International Conference on Software Engineering (ICSE11)*, pages 277–288. IEEE.

Hunt, A. and Thomas, D. (2003). *Pragmatic Unit Testing*. The Pragmatic Bookshelf.

IEEE610 (1990). *IEEE Standard Glossary of Software Engineering Terminology*. IEEE Std 610.12.

IEEE730 (1998). *IEEE Standard for Software Quality Assurance Plans*. IEEE Std 730.

IEEE828 (1998). *IEEE Standard for Software Configuration Management Plans*. IEEE Std 828.

IEEE829 (1998). *IEEE Standard for Software Test Documentation*. IEEE Std 829.

IEEE830 (1998). *IEEE Recommended Practice for Software Requirements Specifications*. IEEE Std 830.

IEEE983 (1986). *IEEE Standard on Software Quality Assurance Planning*. IEEE Std 983.

IEEE1012 (2004). *IEEE Standard for Software Verification and Validation Plans*. IEEE Std 1012.

IEEE1016 (1987). *IEEE Recommended Practice for Software Design Descriptions*. IEEE Std 1016.

IEEE1219 (1998). *IEEE Standard for Software Maintenance*. IEEE Std 1219.

IEEE1471 (2000). IEEE Recommended Practice for Architectural Description of Software-Intensive Systems. Technical report, IEEE.

Iivari, J. (1996). Why are CASE tools not used? *Communications of the ACM*, 39(10):94–103.

Inverardi, P. and Jazayeri, M., editors (2006). *Software Engineering Education in the Modern Age*. Springer Verlag, LNCS 4309.

Ishikawa, K. (1985). *What Is Total Quality Control? The Japanese Way*. Prentice Hall.

ISO 9126 (2001). *ISO/IEC 9126-1: Software Engineering – Product Quality – Part 1: Quality Model*. ISO.

ISO 9241 (1996). ISO DIS 9241-11, Ergonomic Requirements for Office Work with Visual Display Terminals (VDTs): – Part 11: Guidance on Usability. Technical report, ISO.

ITT (1983). *Proceedings Workshop on Reusability in Programming*. ITT.

Jackson, M. (1975). *Principles of Program Design*. Academic Press.

Jackson, M. (1983). *System Development*. Prentice Hall.

Jackson, M. (2001). *Problem Frames*. Addison-Wesley.

Jankowski, D. (1994). The Feasibility of CASE Structured Analysis Methodology Support. *ACM Software Engineering Notes*, 19(2):72–82.

Janzen, D. and Saiedian, H. (2005). Test-Driven Development: Concepts, Taxonomy, and Future Direction. *IEEE Computer*, 38(9):43–50.

Jarzabek, S. and Huang, R. (1998). The Case for User-Centered CASE Tools. *Communications of the ACM*, 41(8):93–98.

Jarzabek, S. and Wang, G. (1998). Model-based Design of Reverse Engineering Tools. *Journal of Software Maintenance: Research and Practice*, 10:353–380.

Jazayeri, M. (2007). Some Trends in Web Application Development. In *Proceedings 29th International Conference on Software Engineering (ICSE29)*. IEEE.

Jeffries, R., Anderson, A., and Hendrickson, C. (2001). *Extreme Programming Installed*. Addison-Wesley.

Jeske, D. and Zhang, X. (2005). Some successful approaches to software reliability modeling in industry. *Journal of Systems and Software*, 74(1):85–100.

Jézéquel, J.-M. and Meyer, M. (1997). Design by Contract: The Lessons of Ariane. *IEEE Computer*, 30(1):129–130.

Johnson, H. and Johnson, P. (1991). Task Knowledge Structures: Psychological Basis and Integration into System Design. *Acta Psychologica*, 78:3–26.

Johnson, L. (1998). A View From the 1960s: How the Software Industry Began. *IEEE Annals of the History of Computing*, 20(1):36–42.

Johnson, P. (1989). Supporting System Design by Analyzing Current Task Knowledge. In Diaper, D., editor, *Task Analysis for Human–Computer Interaction*. Ellis Horwood, Chichester.

Johnson, R. and Foote, B. (1988). Designing Reusable Classes. *Journal of Object Oriented Programming*, 1(1):22–35.

Jonassen Hass, A. (2002). *Configuration Management Principles and Practice*. Addison-Wesley.

Jones, C. (1986). *Programming Productivity*. McGraw-Hill.

Jones, C. (1989). Software Enhancement Modelling. *Journal of Software Maintenance: Research and Practice*, 1(2):91–100.

Jones, C. (1999). The Euro, Y2K, and the US Software Labor Shortage. *IEEE Software*, 16(3):55–61.

Jones, C. (2006). The Economics of Software Maintenance in the Twenty First Century, Version 3, February 14, 2006. Technical report, http://www.spr.com.

Jordan, B. (1996). Ethnographic Workplace Studies and CSCW. In Shapiro, D., Tauber, M., and Traunmueller, R., editors, *The Design of Computer Supported Cooperative Work and Groupware Systems*, pages 17–42. North-Holland, Amsterdam.

Jordan, B. and Henderson, A. (1995). Interaction Analysis: Foundations and Practice. *The Journal of the Learning Sciences*, 4(1):39–103.

Jordan, P., Thomas, B., Weerdmeester, B., and McClelland, I. (1996). *Usability Evaluation in Industry*. Taylor & Francis, London.

Jørgensen, M. (2004). A review of studies on expert estimation of software development effort. *Journal of Systems and Software*, 70(1-2):37–60.

Jørgensen, M. (2005). Practical Guidelines for Expert-Judgment-Based Software Effort Estimation. *IEEE Software*, 22(3):57–63.

Jørgensen, M. and Grimstad, S. (2004). Over-optimism in Software Development Projects: "The winner's curse". *Improve, Software Process Improvement Newsletter*, (4).

Jørgensen, M., Teigen, K., and Moløken, K. (2004). Better sure than safe? Over-confidence in judgement based software development effort prediction intervals. *Journal of Systems and Software*, 70(1-2):79–93.

JSS (1995a). Special Issue on Software Metrics. *Journal of Systems and Software*, 31(2).

JSS (1995b). Special Issue on Software Reuse. *Journal of Systems and Software*, 30(3).

Juristo, N., Moreno, A., and Silva, A. (2002). Is the European Industry Moving toward Solving Requirements Engineering Problems? *IEEE Software*, 19(6):70–77.

Juristo, N., Moreno, A., and Vegas, S. (2004). Reviewing 25 Years of Testing Technique Experiments. *Empirical Software Engineering*, 9:7–44.

Kamsties, E. and Lott, C. (1995). An Emperical Evaluation of Three Defect-Detection Techniques. In Schäfer, W. and Botella, P., editors, *Software Engineering ESEC '95, LNCS 989*, pages 362–383. Springer Verlag.

Kaner, C. and Bond, W. (2004). Software Engineering Metrics: What Do They Measure and How Do We Know. In *Proceedings 10th International Software Metrics Symposium (Metrics 2004)*, pages 1–12. IEEE.

Kano, N. (1993). Kano's Methods for Understanding Customer-defined Quality. *Center for Quality of Management Journal*, 2(4):3–36.

Karlsson, E.-A., editor (1995). *Software Reuse: A Holistic Approach*. John Wiley & Sons.

Karlström, D. and Runeson, P. (2005). Combining Agile Methods with State-Gate Project Management. *IEEE Software*, 22(3):43–49.

Karner, G. (1993). Metrics for Objectory. Technical report, Diploma Thesis, University of Linköping, LiTH-IDA-Ex-9344:21.

Kazman, R., Bass, L., and Klein, M. (2006). The essential components of software architecture design and analysis. *Journal of Systems and Software*, 79(8):1207–1216.

Keen, P. (1991). *Shaping the Future: Business Design through Information Technology*. Harvard Business School Press, Cambridge, MA.

Keil, M. and Carmel, E. (1995). Customer–Developer Links in Software Development. *Communications of the ACM*, 38(5):33–44.

Kemerer, C. (1993). Reliability of Function Points Measurement. *Communications of the ACM*, 36(2):85–97.

Kemerer, C. and Porter, B. (1992). Improving the Reliability of Function Point Measurement: An Empirical Study. *IEEE Transactions on Software Engineering*, 18(11):1011–1024.

Kemerer, C. and Slaughter, S. (1997). Determinants of Software Maintenance Profiles: An Empirical Investigation. *Journal of Software Maintenance: Research and Practice*, 9:235–251.

Kernighan, B. and Mashey, J. (1981). The UNIX Programming Environment. *IEEE Computer*, 14(4):12–24.

King, D. (1988). *Creating Effective Software: Computer Program Design Using the Jackson Methodology*. Yourdon Press.

Kirwan, B. and Ainsworth, L. (1992). *A Guide to Task Analysis*. Taylor & Francis, London.

Kitchenham, B., Jeffery, D., and Connaughton, C. (2007). Misleading Metrics and Unsound Analysis. *IEEE Software*, 24(2):73–78.

Kitchenham, B. and Pfleeger, S. (1996). Software Quality: The Elusive Target. *IEEE Software*, 13(1):12–21.

Kitchenham, B., Pfleeger, S., and Fenton, N. (1995). Towards a Framework for Software Measurement Validation. *IEEE Transactions on Software Engineering*, 21(12):929–943.

Klein, G., Jiang, J., and Tesch, D. (2002). Wanted: Project Teams with a Blend of IS Professional Orientations. *Communications of the ACM*, 45(6):81–87.

Knight, J. and Ammann, P. (1985). An Experimental Evaluation of Simple Methods for Seeding Program Errors. In *Proceedings 8th International Conference on Software Engineering (ICSE8)*, pages 337–342. IEEE.

Knight, J. and Myers, E. (1993). An Improved Inspection Technique. *Communications of the ACM*, 36(11):50–61.

Knuth, D. and Plass, M. (1981). Breaking Paragraphs Into Lines. *Software, Practice & Experience*, 11:1119–1184.

Kohno, T., Stubblefield, A., Rubin, A., and Wallach, D. (2004). Analysis of an Electronic Voting System. In *Proceedings IEEE Symposium on Security and Privacy*, pages 27–42.

Koontz, H. and O'Donnell, C. (1972). *Principles of Management: An Analysis of Managerial Functions*. McGraw-Hill.

Koru, A. and Tian, J. (2005). Comparing High-Change Modules and Modules with the Highest Measurement Values in Two Large-Scale Open-Source Products. *IEEE Transactions on Software Engineering*, 31(8):625–642.

Kotonya, G. and Sommerville, I. (1997). *Requirements Engineering, Processes and Techniques*. John Wiley & Sons.

Krasner, G. and Pope, S. (1988). A cookbook for using the Model–View–Controller user interface paradigm in Smalltalk-80. *Journal of Object Oriented Programming*, 1(3):26–49.

Kraut, R. and Streeter, L. (1995). Coordination in Software Development. *Communications of the ACM*, 38(3):69–81.

Krishna, S., Sahay, S., and Walsham, G. (2004). Managing Cross-Cultural Issues in Global Software Outsourcing. *Communications of the ACM*, 47(4):62–66.

Krogstie, J. (1994). On the Distinction between Functional Development and Functional Maintenance. *Journal of Software Maintenance: Research and Practice*, 7:383–403.

Kruchten, P. (1995). The 4 + 1 View Model of Architecture. *IEEE Software*, 12(6):42–50.

Kruchten, P. (1999). The Software Architect. In *Software Architecture (WICSA1)*, pages 563–583. Kluwer Academic Publishers.

Kruchten, P. (2003). *The Rational Unified Process: An Introduction*. Addison-Wesley, third edition.

Kruglinski, D. (1996). *Inside Visual C++*. Microsoft Press.

Kung, H.-J. and Hsu, C. (1998). Software Maintenance Life Cycle Model. In *Proceedings International Conference on Software Maintenance (ICSM'98)*, pages 113–121.

Kuvaja, P., Simila, J., Krzanik, L., Bicego, A., Koch, G., and Saukonen, S. (1994). *Software Process Assessment and Improvement: the BOOTSTRAP approach*. Blackwell Publishers, Oxford, UK.

Lamsweerde, A. v. (2001). Goal-Oriented Requirements Engineering: A Guided Tour. In *Proceedings 5th International Symposium on Requirements Engineering (RE'01)*, pages 1–13. IEEE.

Lanergan, R. and Grasso, C. (1984). Software Engineering with Reusable Designs and Code. *IEEE Transactions on Software Engineering*, 10(5):498–501.

Lange, C., Chaudron, M., and Muskens, J. (2006). UML Software Architecture and Design Description. *IEEE Software*, 23(2):40–46.

Lanubile, F., Mallardo, T., and Calefato, F. (2003). Tool Support for Geographically Dispersed Inspection Teams. *Software Process Improvement and Practice*, 8(4):217–231.

LaToza, T., Venolia, G., and DeLine, R. (2006). Maintaining Mental Models: A Study of Developer Work Habits. In *Proceedings 28th International Conference on Software Engineering (ICSE28)*, pages 492–501. ACM.

Laurel, B., editor (1990). *The Art of Human–Computer Interface Design*. Addison-Wesley.

Laurel, B. (1993). *Computers as Theatre*. Addison-Wesley.

Lawrence, M. (1981). Programming Methodology, Organizational Environment, and Programming Productivity. *Journal of Systems and Software*, 2:257–269.

Lea, D. (1994). Christopher Alexander: An Introduction for Object-Oriented Designers. *ACM Software Engineering Notes*, 19(1):39–46.

Lederer, A. and Prasad, J. (2000). Software management and cost estimating error. *Journal of Systems and Software*, 50(1):33–42.

Leffingwell, D. and Widrig, D. (2000). *Managing Software Requirements – A Unified Approach*. Addison-Wesley.

Lehman, M. (1974). *Programs, Cities and Students: Limits to Growth?* Number 9 in Inaugural Lecture Series. Imperial College, London.

Lehman, M. (1980). Programs, Life Cycles, and Laws of Software Evolution. *Proceedings of the IEEE*, 68(9):1060–1076.

Lehman, M. (1987). Process Models, Process Programs, Programming Support. In *Proceedings 9th International Conference on Software Engineering (ICSE9)*, pages 14–16. IEEE.

Lehman, M. and Belady, L., editors (1985). *Program Evolution*. Number 27 in APIC Studies in Data Processing. Academic Press.

Lehman, M., Ramil, J., Wernick, P., Perry, D., and Turski, W. (1997). Metrics and Laws of Software Evolution – The Nineties View. In *Proceedings 4th International Symposium On Software Metrics (Metrics 97)*, pages 20–32. IEEE.

Lethbridge, T., Singer, J., and Forward, A. (2003). How Software Engineers Use Documentation: The State of the Practice. *IEEE Software*, 20(6):35–39.

Leveson, N. (1986). Software Safety: What, Why, and How. *ACM Computing Surveys*, 18(2):125–164.

Leveson, N. (1991). Software Safety Issues in Embedded Computer Systems. *Communications of the ACM*, 34(2):34–46.

Leveson, N. (1992). High-Pressure Steam Engines and Computer Software. In *Proceedings 14th International Conference on Software Engineering (ICSE14)*, pages 2–14. IEEE.

Leveson, N. and Turner, C. (1993). An Invesigation of the Therac-25 Accidents. *IEEE Computer*, 26(7):18–41.

Li, W. and Henry, S. (1993). Object-Oriented Metrics that Predict Maintainability. *Journal of Systems and Software*, 23(2):111–122.

Lientz, B. and Swanson, E. (1980). *Software Maintenance Management*. Addison-Wesley.

Linden, F. v. d. and Müller, J. (1995). Creating Architectures with Building Blocks. *IEEE Software*, 12(6):51–60.

Lindgaard, G. (1994). *Usability Testing and System Evaluation*. Chapman & Hall, London.

Lindvall, M., Muthig, D., Dagnino, A., Wallin, C., Stupperich, M., Kiefer, D., May, J., and Kähkönen, T. (2004). Agile Software Development in Large Organizations. *IEEE Computer*, 37(12):26–34.

Linger, R., Mills, H., and Witt, B. (1979). *Structured Programming: Theory and Practice*. Addison-Wesley.

Lions, J. (1996). Ariane 5 Flight 501 Failure: Report by the Inquiry Board. Technical report, http://www.cs.vu.nl/ hans/ariane5report.html.

Lott, C. (1993). Process and Measurement Support in SEEs. *ACM Software Engineering Notes*, 18(4):83–93.

Loucopoulos, P. and Karakostas, V. (1995). *Systems Requirements Engineering*. McGraw-Hill.

Lubars, M., Meredith, G., Potts, C., and Richter, C. (1992). Object-Oriented Analysis for Evolving Systems. In *Proceedings 14th International Conference on Software Engineering (ICSE14)*, pages 173–185. IEEE.

Lundell, B. and Lings, B. (2004). Changing perceptions of CASE technology. *Journal of Systems and Software*, 72(2):271–280.

Lyons, M. (1981). Salvaging Your Software Asset (Tools Based Maintenance). In *AFIPS Conference Proceedings*, volume 50, pages 337–341.

Lyu, M., editor (1995). *Handbook of Software Reliability Engineering*. McGraw-Hill.

Macala, R., Stuckey, Jr., L., and Gross, D. (1996). Managing Domain-Specific, Product-Line Development. *IEEE Software*, 13(3):57–68.

MacLean, A., Young, R., Bellotti, V., and Moran, T. (1991). Questions, Options, and Criteria: Elements of Design Space Analysis. *Human–Computer Interaction*, 6:201–250.

Macro, A. and Buxton, J. (1987). *The Craft of Software Engineering*. Addison-Wesley.

Maiden, N., Gizikis, A., and Robertson, S. (2004). Provoking Creativity: Imagine What Your Requirements Could Be Like. *IEEE Software*, 21(5):68–75.

Maiden, N. and Ncube, C. (1998). Acquiring COTS Software Selection Requirements. *IEEE Software*, 15(2):46–56.

Mäntylä, M., Vanhanen, J., and Lassenius, C. (2003). A Taxonomy and an Initial Empirical Study of Bad Smells in Code. In *Proceedings International Conference on Software Maintenance (ICSM'03)*, pages 381–384.

Maranzano, J., Rozsypal, S., Zimmerman, G., Warnken, G., Wirth, P., and Weiss, D. (2005). Architecture Reviews: Practice and Experience. *IEEE Software*, 22(2):34–43.

Margaria, T. and Steffen, B. (2006). Service Engineering: Linking Business and IT. *IEEE Computer*, 39(10):45–55.

Martin, J. (1991). *Rapid Application Development*. MacMillan.

Martin, R. (2002). *Agile Software Development, Principles, Patterns and Practices*. Prentice Hall.

Martin, R. and Osborne, W. (1983). *Guidance on Software Maintenance*. National Bureau of Standards, Washington. NBS Special Publication 500-106.

Mata-Toledo, R. and Gustafson, D. (1992). A Factor Analysis of Software Complexity Measures. *Journal of Systems and Software*, 17(3):267–273.

Matloff, N. (2005). Offshoring: What Can Go Wrong? *IT Pro*, July/August:39–45.

Maximilien, E. and Williams, L. (2003). Assessing Test-Driven Development at BM. In *Proceedings 25th International Conference on Software Engineering (ICSE25)*, pages 564–569. IEEE.

May, J. and Barnard, P. (1995). Cinematography and Interface Design. In Nordby, K. *et al.*, editors, *Human–Computer Interaction: Proceedings Interact'95*, pages 26–31. Chapman and Hall.

Mayhew, D. (1992). *Principles and Guidelines in Software User Interface Design*. Prentice Hall.

Mayrhauser, A. v. and Vans, A. (1995). Program Comprehension During Software Maintenance and Evolution. *IEEE Computer*, 28(8):44–55.

Mayrhauser, A. v., Vans, A., and Howe, A. (1997). Program Understanding Behaviour during Enhancement of Large-scale Software. *Journal of Software Maintenance: Research and Practice*, 9:299–327.

Maznevski, M. and Chudoba, K. (2000). Bridging Space Over Time: Global Virtual Team Dynamics and Effectiveness. *Organization Science*, 11(5):473–492.

McCabe, T. (1976). A Complexity Measure. *IEEE Transactions on Software Engineering*, 2(4):308–320.

McCall, J., Richards, P., and Walters, G. (1977). Factors in Software Quality. Technical Report RADC-TR-77-369, US Department of Commerce.

McClure, R. (1968). Production-Management Aspects. In Naur and Randell (1968), page 72.

McConnell, S. (2006). *Software Estimation: Demystifying the Black Art*. Microsoft Press.

McCracken, D. and Jackson, M. (1981). A Minority Dissenting Position. In Cotterman, W. *et al.*, editors, *Systems Analysis and Design: A foundation for the 1980's*, pages 551–553. North Holland.

McDowell, C., Werner, L., Bullock, H., and Fernald, J. (2006). Pair Programming Improves Student Retention, Confidence, and Program Quality. *Communications of the ACM*, 49(8):90–95.

McIlroy, M. (1968). Mass-Produced Software Components. In Naur and Randell (1968), pages 88–98.

Medvidovic, N. and Taylor, R. (1997). A Framework for Classifying and Comparing Architecture Description Languages. In Jazayeri, M. and Schauer, H., editors, *Proceedings 6th European Software Engineering Conference, LNCS 1301*, pages 60–76. Springer Verlag.

Medvidovic, N. and Taylor, R. (2000). A Classification and Comparison Framework for Software Architecture Description Languages. *IEEE Transactions on Software Engineering*, 26(1):70–93.

Mens, T. and Tourwé, T. (2004). A Survey of Software Refactoring. *IEEE Transactions on Software Engineering*, 30(2):126–139.

Meservy, T. and Fenstermacher, K. (2005). Transforming Software Development: An MDA Road Map. *IEEE Computer*, 38(9):52–58.

Metzger, P. (1987). *Managing Programming People*. Prentice Hall.

Meyer, B. (1985). On Formalism in Specifications. *IEEE Software*, 2(1):6–26.

Meyer, B. (1992). Design by Contract. *IEEE Computer*, 25(10):40–51.

Meyer, B. (1996). Reality: A cousin twice removed. *IEEE Computer*, 29(7):96–97.

Mili, H., Mili, A., Yacoub, S., and Addy, E. (2002). *Reuse-Based Software Engineering*. Wiley.

Miller, B., Fredrikson, L., and So, B. (1990). An Experimental Study of the Reliability of UNIX Facilities. *Communications of the ACM*, 33(12):32–44.

Mills, H., Dyer, M., and Linger, R. (1987). Cleanroom Software Engineering. *IEEE Software*, 4(5):19–25.

Mintzberg, H. (1983). *Structures in Fives: Designing Effective Organizations*. Prentice Hall.

Mockus, A., Fielding, R., and Herbsleb, J. (2000). A Case Study of Open Source Software Development: The Apache Server. In *Proceedings 22nd International Conference on Software Engineering (ICSE22)*, pages 263–272. IEEE.

Mohagheghi, P., Anda, B., and Conradi, R. (2005). Effort Estimation of Use Cases for Incremental Large-Scale Software Development. In *Proceedings 27th International Conference on Software Engineering (ICSE27)*, pages 303–311. IEEE.

Moran, T. (1981). The Command Language Grammar: A Representation of the User Interface of Interactive Computer Systems. *International Journal of Man-Machine Studies*, 15(1):3–50.

Moran, T. and Carroll, J. (1994). *Design Rationale: Concepts, Techniques, and Use*. Lawrence Erlbaum Associates.

Moran, T. and Carroll, J. (1996). *Design Rationale: Concepts, Techniques and Use*. Lawrence Erlbaum Associates, New Jersey.

Morisio, M., Ezran, M., and Tully, C. (2002a). Success and Failure Factors in Software Reuse. *IEEE Transactions on Software Engineering*, 28(4):340–357.

Morisio, M., Seaman, C., Basili, V., Parra, A., Kraft, S., and Condon, S. (2002b). COTS-based software development: Processes and open issues. *Journal of Systems and Software*, 61(3):189–199.

Motschnig-Pitrik, R. (1996). Analyzing the Notions of Attribute, Aggregate, Part and Member in Data/Knowledge Modeling. *Journal of Systems and Software*, 33(2):113–122.

Moynihan, T. (1996). An Experimental Comparison of Object-Orientation and Functional-Decomposition as Paradigms for Communicating System Functionality to Users. *Journal of Systems and Software*, 33(2):163–170.

Moynihan, T. (2000). Coping with 'requirements-uncertainty': the theories-of-action of experienced IS/software project managers. *Journal of Systems and Software*, 53(2):99–109.

Mulligan, R., Altom, M., and Simkin, D. (1991). User Interface Design in the Trenches: Some Tips on Shooting from the Hip. In *Proceedings CHI'91*, pages 232–236. ACM.

Musa, J., Iannino, A., and Okumoto, K. (1987). *Software Reliability: Measurement, Prediction, Application*. McGraw-Hill.

Muskens, J., Chaudron, M., and Lukkien, J. (2005). A Component Framework for Consumer Electronics Middleware. In Atkinson, C., Bunse, C., Peper, C., and Gross, H.-G., editors, *Component-Based Software Development for Embedded Systems*. Springer, LNCS 3778.

Mustapic, G., Wall, A., Norström, C., Crnkovic, I., Sandström, K., Fröberg, J., and Andersson, J. (2004). Real World Influences on Software Architecture – Interviews with Industrial System Experts. In *Proceedings 4th Working IEEE/IFIP Conference on Software Architecture (WICSA4)*, pages 101–111. IEEE.

Myers, B. and Rosson, M. (1992). Survey on User Interface Programming. In *Human Factors in Computing Systems, Proceedings SIGCHI'92*, pages 195–202. ACM.

Myers, G. (1979). *The Art of Software Testing*. John Wiley & Sons.

Myers, G. (2004). *The Art of Software Testing*. Wiley, second edition.

Myers, W. (1986). Can Software for the SDI ever be Error-Free? *IEEE Computer*, 19(10):61–67.

Myers, W. (1988). Shuttle Code Achieves Very Low Error Rate. *IEEE Software*, 5(5):93–95.

Mylopoulos, J., Chung, L., Liao, S., Wang, H., and Yu, E. (2001). Exploring Alternatives during Requirements Analysis. *IEEE Software*, 18(1):92–96.

Nardi, B., editor (1995). *Context and Consciousness: Activity Theory and Human Computer Interaction*. MIT Press, Cambridge MA.

Naur, P. and Randell, B., editors (1968). *Software Engineering: Report on a Conference*. NATO Scientific Affairs Division, Garmisch.

Nelson, E. (1966). *Management Handbook for the Estimation of Computer Programming Costs*. Systems Development Corp. AD-A648750.

Nerurkar, U. (2001). Web User Interface Design: Forgotten Lessons. *IEEE Software*, 18(6):69–71.

Neumann, P. (1995). *Computer-Related Risks*. Addison-Wesley.

Neumann, P. (2004). The Problems and Potentials of Voting Systems. *Communications of the ACM*, 47(10):29–30.

Newman, W. M. and Lamming, M. G. (1995). *Interactive System Design*. Addison-Wesley.

Nielsen, J. (1993). *Usability Engineering*. Academic Press.

Nielsen, J. and Mack, R. (1994). *Usability Inspection Methods*. John Wiley & Sons.

Niessink, F. and van Vliet, H. (1997). Predicting Maintenance Effort with Function Points. In *Proceedings International Conference on Software Maintenance (ICSM'97)*, pages 32–39. IEEE.

Niessink, F. and van Vliet, H. (1998a). Towards Mature IT Services. *Software Process – Improvement and Practice*, 4(2):55–71.

Niessink, F. and van Vliet, H. (1998b). Towards Mature Measurement Programs. In Nesi, P. and Lehner, F., editors, *Proceedings 2nd Euromicro Conference on Software Maintenance and Reengineering*, pages 82–88. IEEE.

Niessink, F. and van Vliet, H. (1999). Software Maintenance from a Service Perspective. Technical report, Vrije Universiteit.

Norden, P. (1970). Useful Tools for Project Management. In Starr, M., editor, *Management of Production*, pages 71–101. Penguin Books.

Norman, D. (1983). Some Observations on Mental Models. In Gentner, D. and Stevens, A., editors, *Mental Models*, pages 7–14. Erlbaum.

Nosek, J. and Palvia, P. (1990). Software Maintenance Management: Changes in the Last Decade. *Journal of Software Maintenance: Research and Practice*, 2(3):157–174.

Offutt, A., Harrold, M., and Kolte, P. (1993). A Software Metric System for Module Coupling. *Journal of Systems and Software*, 20(3):295–308.

Offutt, A. and Lee, S. (1994). An Emperical Evaluation of Weak Mutation. *IEEE Transactions on Software Engineering*, 20(5):337–344.

Olson, G. and Olson, J. (2000). Distance Matters. *Human–Computer Interaction*, 15(2/3):139–178.

Ommering, R. v., van der Linden, F., Kramer, J., and Magee, J. (2000). The Koala Component Model for Consumer Electronics Software. *IEEE Computer*, 33(3):78–85.

Orlikowski, W. (1992). Learning from Notes: Organizational Issues in Groupware Implementation. In *Proceedings ACM Conference on Customer-Supported Cooperative Work (CSCW'92)*. ACM.

Oshri, I., Kotlarsky, J., and Willcocks, L. (2007). Global software development: Exploring socialization and face-to-face meetings in distributed strategic projects. *Journal of Strategic Information Systems*, 16:25–49.

Osterweil, L. (1987). Software Processes Are Software Too. In *Proceedings 9th International Conference on Software Engineering (ICSE9)*, pages 2–13. IEEE.

Oz, E. (1994). When Professional Standards are Lax: The CONFIRM Failure and its Lessons. *Communications of the ACM*, 37(10):29–36.

Paasivara, M. and Lassenius, C. (2006). Could Global Software Development Benefit from Agile Methods? In *Proceedings International Conference on Global Software Engineering (ICGSE'06)*. IEEE.

Page, D., Williams, P., and Boyd, D. (1993). *Report of the Inquiry into the London Ambulance Service*. South West Thames Regional Health Authority.

Papazoglou, M. (2008). *Web Services: Principles and Technology*. Pearson.

Papazoglou, M., Traverso, P., Dustdar, S., and Leymann, F. (2006). Service-Oriented Computing: Research Roadmap. In *Dagstuhl Seminar Proceedings 05462, Service Oriented Computing*, http://drops.dagstuhl.de/opus/volltexte/2006/524.

Papazoglou, M. and van den Heuvel, W.-J. (2006). Service-oriented design and development methodology. *International Journal of Web Engineering and Technology*, 2(4):412–442.

Parnas, D. (1972). On the Criteria to be Used in Decomposing Systems Into Modules. *Communications of the ACM*, 15(12):1053–1058.

Parnas, D. (1978). Designing Software for Ease of Extension and Contraction. In *Proceedings 3rd International Conference on Software Engineering (ICSE3)*, pages 264–277. IEEE.

Parnas, D. (1985). Software Aspects of Strategic Defense Systems. *ACM Software Engineering Notes*, 10(5):15–23.

Parnas, D. (1987). SDI 'Red Herrings' Miss the Boat. *IEEE Computer*, 20(2):6–7.

Parnas, D. and Clements, P. (1986). A Rational Design Process: How and Why to Fake it. *IEEE Transactions on Software Engineering*, 12(2):251–257.

Parnas, D. and Lawford, M. (2003a). Inspection's Role in Software Quality Insurance. *IEEE Software*, 20(4):16–20.

Parnas, D. and Lawford, M. (2003b). The Role of Inspection in Software Quality Assurance. *IEEE Transactions on Software Engineering*, 29(8):674–676.

Parnas, D. and Weiss, D. (1987). Active Design Reviews: Principles and Practices. *Journal of Systems and Software*, 7(4):259–265.

Parrish, A. and Zweben, S. (1995). On the Relationships Among the All-Uses, All-DU-Paths, and All-Edges Testing Criteria. *IEEE Transactions on Software Engineering*, 21(12):1006–1009.

Patel, S., Chu, W., and Baxter, R. (1992). A Measure for Composite Module Cohesion. In *Proceedings 14th International Conference on Software Engineering (ICSE14)*, pages 38–48. IEEE, Melbourne.

Payne, S. and Green, T. (1989). Task-Action Grammar: The model and its Developments. In Diaper, D., editor, *Task Analysis for Human–Computer Interaction*, pages 75–105. Ellis Horwood, Chichester.

Peltz, C. (2003). Web Services Orchestration and Choreography. *IEEE Computer*, 36(10):46–53.

Perry, D. and Kaiser, G. (1991). Models of Software Development Environments. *IEEE Transactions on Software Engineering*, 17(3):283–295.

Perry, D., Staudenmayer, N., and Votta, L. (1994). People, Organizations, and Process Improvement. *IEEE Software*, 11(4):36–45.

Perry, D. and Wolf, A. (1992). Foundations for the Study of Software Architecture. *ACM Software Engineering Notes*, 17(4):40–52.

Peter, L. and Hull, R. (1970). *The Peter Principle*. Pan Books.

Peterson, J. (1981). *Petri Net Theory and the Modelling of Systems*. Prentice Hall.

Petroski, H. (1994). *Design Paradigms: Case Histories of Error and Judgment in Engineering*. Cambridge University Press.

Pfaff, G., editor (1985). *User Interface Management Systems*. Springer Verlag.

Pfleeger, S. (1995). Maturity, Models and Goals: How to Build a Metrics Plan. *Journal of Systems and Software*, 31(2):143–155.

Pfleeger, S. (2000). Risky business: what we have yet to learn about risk management. *Journal of Systems and Software*, 53(3):265–273.

Pigoski, T. (1996). *Practical Software Maintenance*. John Wiley & Sons.

Pohl, K. (1993). The Three Dimensions of Requirements Engineering. In Rolland, C., Bodart, F., and Cauvet, C., editors, *Proceedings Fifth International Conference on Advanced Information Systems Engineering (CAISE'93)*, pages 275–292. Springer Verlag.

Pohl, K., Böckle, G., and van der Linden, F. (2005). *Software Product Line Engineering*. Springer Verlag.

Porter, A., Siy, H., Mockus, A., and Votta, L. (1998). Understanding the Sources of Variation in Software Inspections. *ACM Transactions on Software Engineering and Methodology*, 7(1):41–79.

Porter, A., Siy, H., Toman, C., and Votta, L. (1997). An Experiment to Assess the Cost-Benefits of Code Inspections in Large Scale Software Developments. *IEEE Transactions on Software Engineering*, 23(6):329–346.

Porter, A., Votta, Jr., L., and Basili, V. (1995). Comparing Detection Methods for Software Requirements Inspections: A Replicated Experiment. *IEEE Transactions on Software Engineering*, 21(6):563–575.

Post, G., Kagan, A., and Keim, R. (1998). A Comparative Evaluation of CASE Tools. *Journal of Systems and Software*, 44(2):87–96.

Poston, R. (1987). Preventing Most-Probable Errors in Requirements. *IEEE Software*, 4(5):81–83.

Potts, C. (1993). Software-Engineering Research Revisited. *IEEE Software*, 10(5):19–28.

Poulin, J. (1999). Reuse: Been There, Done That. *Communications of the ACM*, 42(5):98–100.

Power, L. and Weiss, Z., editors (1987). *Addendum to the Proceedings of OOPSLA87*. ACM.

Prieto-Diaz, R. (1991a). Implementing Faceted Classification for Software Reuse. *Communications of the ACM*, 34(5):88–97.

Prieto-Diaz, R. (1991b). Making Software Reuse Work: An Implementation Model. *ACM Software Engineering Notes*, 16(3):61–68.

Prieto-Diaz, R. (1993). Status Report: Software Reusability. *IEEE Software*, 10(3):61–66.

Prieto-Diaz, R. and Neighbors, J. (1986). Module Interconnection Languages. *Journal of Systems and Software*, 6:307–334.

Procaccino, J., Verner, J., and Lorenzet, S. (2006). Defining and Contributing to Software Development Success. *Communications of the ACM*, 49(8):79–83.

Putnam, L. (1978). A General Empirical Solution to the Macro Software Sizing and Estimating Problem. *IEEE Transactions on Software Engineering*, 4(4):345–361.

Raba (2004). Trusted Agent Report Diebold AccuVote-TS Voting System. RABA Technologies.

Rahgozar, M. and Oroumchian, F. (2003). An effective strategy for legacy systems evolution. *Journal of Software Maintenance and Evolution: Research and Practice*, 15:325–344.

Rainer, A. and Hall, T. (2003). A quantitative and qualitative analysis of factors affecting software processes. *Journal of Systems and Software*, 66(1):7–22.

Ramasubbu, N., Krishnan, M., and Kompalli, P. (2005). Leveraging Global Resources: A Process Maturity Framework for Managing Distributed Development. *IEEE Software*, 22(3):80–86.

Ramos, I., Berry, D., and Carvalho, J. (2005). Requirements engineering for organizational transformation. *Information and Software Technology*, 47(5):479–495.

Ravichandran, T. and Rothenberger, M. (2003). Software Reuse Strategies and Component Markets. *Communications of the ACM*, 46(8):109–114.

Raymond, E. (1999). *The Cathedral and The Bazaar*. O'Reilly.

Reddin, W. (1970). *Managerial Effectiveness*. McGraw-Hill.

Redmond, J. and Ah-Chuen, R. (1990). Software Metrics: A User's Perspective. *Journal of Systems and Software*, 13(2):97–110.

Redwine, S. and Riddle, W. (1985). Software Technology Maturation. In *Proceedings 8th International Conference on Software Engineering (ICSE8)*, pages 189–200. IEEE.

Reifer, D. (1997). *Practical Software Reuse: Strategies for Introducing Reuse Concepts in Your Organization*. John Wiley & Sons.

Reifer, D. (2000). Web Development: Estimating Quick-to-Market Software. *IEEE Software*, 17(6):57–64.

Reisner, P. (1981). Formal Grammar and Human Factors Design of an Interactive Graphics System. *IEEE Transactions on Software Engineering*, 7(2):229–240.

Reiss, S. (1990). Connecting Tools Using Message Passing in the Field Environment. *IEEE Software*, 7(4):57–66.

Rettig, M. (1991). Nobody Reads Documentation. *Communications of the ACM*, 34(7):19–24.

Riehle, D. (2007). The Economic Motivation of Open Source Software: Stakeholder Perspectives. *IEEE Computer*, 40(4):25–32.

Rifkin, S. (2001). What Makes Measuring Software So Hard? *IEEE Software*, 18(3):41–45.

Rine, D. and Sonnemann, R. (1998). Investments in Reusable Software. A Study of Software Reuse Investment Success Factors. *Journal of Systems and Software*, 41(1):17–32.

Robertson, J. (2002). Eureka! Why Analysts Should Invent Requirements. *IEEE Software*, 19(4):20–22.

Robillard, P. and Kruchten, P. (2003). *Software Engineering Process with the UPEDU*. Addison-Wesley.

Rochkind, M. (1975). The Source Code Control System. *IEEE Transactions on Software Engineering*, 1(4):364–370.

Rothenberger, M., Dooley, K., Kulkarni, U., and Nada, N. (2003). Strategies for Software Reuse: A Principal Component Analysis of Reuse Practices. *IEEE Transactions on Software Engineering*, 29(9):825–837.

Rothermel, G. and Harrold, M. (1996). Analyzing Regression Test Selection Techniques. *IEEE Transactions on Software Engineering*, 22(8):529–551.

Royce, W. (1970). Managing the Development of Large Software Systems: Concepts and Techniques. In *Proceedings IEEE WESCON*, pages 1–9. IEEE.

Royce, W. (1998). *Software Project Management: A Unified Framework*. Addison-Wesley.

Rozanski, N. and Woods, E. (2005). *Software Systems Architecture: Working with Stakeholders using Viewpoints and Perspectives*. Addison-Wesley.

Rumbaugh, J., Blaha, M., Premerlani, W., Eddy, F., and Lorensen, W. (1991). *Object-Oriented Modeling and Design*. Prentice Hall.

Rumbaugh, J., Jacobson, I., and Booch, G. (1999). *The Unified Modeling Language Reference Manual*. Addison-Wesley.

Rysselberghe, F. v. and Demeyer, S. (2004). Studying Software Evolution Information By Visualizing the Change History. In *Proceedings International Conference on Software Maintenance (ICSM'04)*, pages 328–337. IEEE.

Saaty, T. (1990). *Multicriteria Decision Making: The Analytic Hierarchy Process*. Volume I, AHP Series, McGraw-Hill.

Sawyer, S. (2001). A Market-Based Perspective on Information Systems Development. *Communications of the ACM*, 44(11):97–102.

Schach, S., Jin, B., Yu, L., Heler, G., and Offutt, J. (2003). Determining the Distribution of Maintenance Categories: Survey versus Measurement. *Empirical Software Engineering*, 8:351–365.

Schaeffer, W., Prieto-Diaz, R., and Matsumoto, R., editors (1993). *Software Reusability*. Ellis Horwood.

Schwaber, K. and Beedle, M. (2002). *Agile Software Development with Scrum*. Prentice Hall.

Sebillotte, S. (1988). Hierarchical Planning as a Method for Task-Analysis: The Example of Office Task Analysis. *Behaviour and Information Technology*, 7(3):275–293.

Seffah, A., Forbrich, P., and Javahery, H. (2004). Multi-devices "Multiple" user interfaces: development models and research opportunities. *Journal of Systems and Software*, 73(2):287–300.

Selby, R. (2005). Enabling Reuse-Based Software Development of Large-Scale Systems. *IEEE Transactions on Software Engineering*, 31(6):495–510.

Selby, R., Basili, V., and Baker, F. (1987). Cleanroom Software Development. *IEEE Transactions on Software Engineering*, 13(9):1027–1037.

Serrano, N. and Ciordia, I. (2004). Ant: Automating the Process of Building Applications. *IEEE Software*, 21(6):89–91.

Shapiro, D. (1996). Ferrets in a Sack? Ethnographic Studies and Task Analysis in CSCW. In Shapiro, D., Tauber, M., and Traunmueller, R., editors, *The Design of Computer Supported Cooperative Work and Groupware Systems*. North-Holland, Amsterdam.

Sharon, D. and Bell, R. (1995). Tools That Bind: Creating Integrated Environments. *IEEE Software*, 12(2):76–85.

Sharp, H., Rogers, Y., and Preece, J. (2007). *Interaction Design: Beyond Human–Computer Interaction*. Wiley, second edition.

Shaw, M. (1996). Some Patterns for Software Architectures. In *Proceedings Second Workshop on Pattern Languages for Programming*. Addison-Wesley.

Shaw, M. and Clements, P. (1996). A Field Guide to Boxology: Preliminary Classification of Architectural Styles for Software Systems. Technical report, Carnegie Mellon University/Software Engineering Institute.

Shaw, M., DeLine, R., Klein, D., Ross, T., Young, D., and Zelesnik, G. (1995). Abstractions for Software Architecture and Tools to Support Them. *IEEE Transactions on Software Engineering*, 21(4):314–335.

Shaw, M. and Garlan, D. (1996). *Software Architecture: Perspectives on an Emerging Discipline*. Prentice Hall.

Shepperd, M. (1990). Design Metrics: An Empirical Analysis. *Software Engineering Journal*, 5(1):3–10.

Shepperd, M. and Ince, D. (1993). A Critique of Three Metrics. *Journal of Systems and Software*, 26(3):197–210.

Shneiderman, B. and Plaisant, C. (2004). *Designing the User Interface: Strategies for Effective Human–Computer Interaction*. Addison-Wesley, fourth edition.

Siegel, J. (1995). *CORBA Fundamentals and Programming*. John Wiley & Sons.

Sikkel, K. and van Vliet, J. (1988). Growing Pains of Software Reuse. In *Proceedings Software Engineering in the Nineties*. SERC, Utrecht.

Simmons, P. (1996). Quality Outcomes: Determining Business Value. *IEEE Software*, 13(1): 25–32.

Singer, J. (1998). Practices of Software Maintenance. In *Proceedings International Conference on Software Maintenance (ICSM'98)*, pages 139–145. IEEE.

Singer, J., Eles, R., and Storey, M.-A. (2005). NavTracks: Supporting Navigation in Software Maintenance. In *Proceedings International Conference on Software Maintenance (ICSM'05)*, pages 325–334. IEEE.

Smith, D., Irby, C., Kimball, R., Verplank, W., and Harslem, E. (1982). Designing the Star User Interface. *Byte*, 7(4):242–282.

Smith, S. and Mosier, J. (1986). Design Guidelines for User–System Interface Software. Technical report, MITRE Corporation.

Software (1994a). Special Issue on Process Improvement. *IEEE Software*, 11(4).

Software (1994b). Special Issue on Systematic Reuse. *IEEE Software*, 11(5).

Software (1996a). Special Issue on Managing Large Software Projects. *IEEE Software*, 13(4).

Software (1996b). Special Issue on Software Tools Assessment. *IEEE Software*, 13(5).

Software (1997a). Special Issue on Managing Risk. *IEEE Software*, 14(3).

Software (1997b). Special Issue on Measurement. *IEEE Software*, 14(2).

Software (1999). Special Issue on Critical Success Factors. *IEEE Software*, 16(3).

Software (2000). Special Issue: Software Estimation. *IEEE Software*, 17(6):22–70.

Software (2001). Special Issue: Global Software Development. *IEEE Software*, 18(2).

Software (2003). Special Issue: State of the Practice in Software Engineering. *IEEE Software*, 20(6).

Software (2005). Special Issue: Adapting Agility. *IEEE Software*, 22(3):17–49.

Software (2006a). Special Issue: Global Software Development. *IEEE Software*, 23(5).

Software (2006b). Special Issue: Software Architecture. *IEEE Software*, 23(2):22–87.

Soloway, E. (1986). Learning to Program = Learning to Construct Mechanisms and Explanations. *Communications of the ACM*, 29(9):850–858.

Soloway, E. and Ehrlich, K. (1984). Empirical Studies of Programming Knowledge. *IEEE Transactions on Software Engineering*, 10(5):595–609.

Sommerville, I. (2005). Integrated Requirements Engineering: A Tutorial. *IEEE Software*, 22(1):16–23.

Sommerville, I., Bentley, R., Rodden, T., and Sawyer, P. (1994). Cooperative System Design. *The Computer Journal*, 37(5):357–366.

Sommerville, I. and Sawyer, P. (1997). Viewpoints: principles, problems and a practical approach to requirements engineering. *Annals of Software Engineering*, 3:101–130.

Soni, D., Nord, R., and Hofmeister, C. (1995). Software Architecture in Industial Applications. In *Proceedings 17th International Conference on Software Engineering (ICSE17)*, pages 196–207. IEEE.

Sousa, M. and Mozeira, H. (1998). A Survey on the Software Maintenance Process. In *Proceedings International Conference on Software Maintenance (ICSM'98)*, pages 265–274. IEEE.

Spanjers, H., ter Huurne, M., Graaf, B., Lormans, M., Bendas, D., and van Solingen, R. (2006). Tool Support for Distributed Software Engineering. In *Proceedings International Conference on Global Software Engineering (ICGSE 2006)*, pages 187–198. IEEE.

Spector, A. and Gifford, D. (1986). A Computer Science Perspective of Bridge Design. *Communications of the ACM*, 29(4):267–283.

SPIP (2006). Special Issues: Understanding Free/Open Source Software Development Processes. *Software Process: Improvement and Practice*, 11(2):93–211.

Stålhane, T., Borgersen, P., and Arnesen, K. (1997). In Search of the Customer's Quality View. *Journal of Systems and Software*, 38(1):85–94.

Stapleton, J., editor (2003). *DSDM: Business Focused Development*. Addison-Wesley, second edition.

Stark, G. and Oman, P. (1997). Software Maintenance Management Strategies: Observations from the Field. *Journal of Software Maintenance: Research and Practice*, 9:365–378.

Stevens, W., Myers, G., and Constantine, L. (1974). Structured Design. *IBM Systems Journal*, 13(2):115–139.

Stroud, J. (1967). The Fine Structure of Psychological Time. *Annals NY Academy of Sciences*, 138:623–631.

Succi, G., Pedrycz, W., Stefanovic, M., and Miller, J. (2003). Practical assessment of the models for identification of defect-prone classes in object-oriented commercial systems using design metrics. *Journal of Systems and Software*, 65(1):1–12.

Suryn, W., Hailey, V., and Coster, A. (2004). Huge potential user base for ISO/IEC 90003. *ISO Management Systems*, July/August 2004:34–39.

Sutcliffe, A. (1988). *Jackson System Development*. Prentice Hall.

Sutcliffe, A., Maiden, N., Minocha, S., and Manuel, D. (1998). Supporting Scenario-Based Requirements Engineering. *IEEE Transactions on Software Engineering*, 24(12):1072–1088.

Sutton, S., Heimbigner, D., and Osterweil, L. (1990). Language Constructs for Managing Change in Process-centered Environments. In *SIGSOFT'90, Proceedings of the Fourth Symposium on Software Development Environments*. ACM.

Suvee, D., Fraine, B. D., and Vanderperren, W. (2006). A Symmetric and Unified Approach Towards Combining Aspect-Oriented and Component-Based Software Development. In *Proceedings 9th International SIGSOFT Symposium on Component-Based Software Engineering (CBSE 2006)*, pages 114–122. Springer Verlag, LNCS 4063.

Swanson, E. and Beath, C. (1990). Departmentalization in Software Development and Maintenance. *Communications of the ACM*, 33(6):658–667.

Symons, C. (1988). Function Point Analysis: Difficulties and Improvements. *IEEE Transactions on Software Engineering*, 14(1):2–11.

Szyperski, C. (1998). *Component Software: Beyond Object-Oriented Programming*. Addison-Wesley.

Szyperski, C. (2003). Component Technology: What, Where, and How? In *Proceedings 25th International Conference on Software Engineering (ICSE25)*, pages 684–693. IEEE.

Tahvanainen, V.-P. and Smolander, K. (1990). An annotated CASE Bibliography. *ACM Software Engineering Notes*, 15(1):79–92.

Taivalsaari, A. (1993). On the Notion of Object. *Journal of Systems and Software*, 21(1):3–16.

Tan, W.-G. and Gable, G. (1998). Attitudes of Maintenance Personnel Towards Maintenance Work: A Comparative Analysis. *Journal of Software Maintenance: Research and Practice*, 10:59–74.

Tanenbaum, A., van Staveren, H., Keizer, E., and Stevenson, J. (1983). A Practical Toolkit for Making Portable Compilers. *Communications of the ACM*, 26(9):654–662.

Tapscott, D. and Caston, A. (1993). *Paradigm Shift: The New Promise of Information Technology*. McGraw-Hill.

Tauber, M. (1990). ETAG: Extended Task Action Grammar – a Language for the Description of the User's Task Language. In Diaper, D. *et al.*, editors, *Proceedings INTERACT '90*. Elsevier, Amsterdam.

Teasley, S., Covi, L., Krishnan, M., and Olson, J. (2002). Rapid Software Development through Team Collocation. *IEEE Transactions on Software Engineering*, 28(7):671–683.

Tiwana, A. (2004). Beyond the Black Box: Knowledge Overlaps in Software Outsourcing. *IEEE Software*, 21(5):51–58.

Tockey, S. (2004). *Return on Software: Maximizing the Return on Your Software Investment*. Addison-Wesley.

Tracz, W. (1988). Software Reuse Myths. *ACM Software Engineering Notes*, 13(1):17–21.

Tracz, W. (1990). Where Does Reuse Start? *ACM Software Engineering Notes*, 15(2):42–46.

Trammell, C., Binder, L., and Snyder, C. (1992). The Automated Production Control Documentation System: A Case Study in Cleanroom Software Engineering. *ACM Transactions on Software Engineering and Methodology*, 1(1):81–94.

Tripp, L. (1988). A Survey of Graphical Notations for Program Design – An Update. *ACM Software Engineering Notes*, 13(4):39–44.

TrSE (1998). Special Issue on Scenario Management. *IEEE Transactions on Software Engineering*, 24(12).

Tsai, W.-T., Wei, X., Paul, R., Chung, J.-Y., Huang, Q., and Chen, Y. (2007). Service-oriented system engineering (SOSE) and its applications to embedded system development. *Service-Oriented Computing and Applications*, 1(1):3–17.

Turner, C., Fuggetta, A., Lavazza, L., and Wolf, A. (1999). A conceptual basis for feature engineering. *Journal of Systems and Software*, 49(1):3–15.

Turner, M., Budgen, D., and Brereton, P. (2003). Turning Software into a Service. *IEEE Computer*, 36(10):38–45.

Tyree, J. and Akerman, A. (2005). Architecture Decisions: Demystifying Architecture. *IEEE Software*, 22(2):19–27.

Veer, G. v. d. (1990). *Human–Computer Interaction: Learning, Individual Differences, and Design Recommendations*. PhD Dissertation, Vrije Universiteit, Amsterdam.

Veer, G. v. d. and van Welie, M. (2003). Groupware Task Analysis. In Hollnagel, E., editor, *Handbook of Cognitive Task Design*, pages 447–476. Lawrence Erlbaum.

Verner, J. and Cerpa, N. (1997). Prototyping: Does Your View of its Advantages Depend on Your Job. *Journal of Systems and Software*, 36(1):3–16.

Vessey, I. and Conger, S. (1994). Requirements Specification: Learning Object, Process, and Data Methodologies. *Communications of the ACM*, 37(5):102–113.

Vliet, H. v. (2006). Reflections on Software Engineering Education. *IEEE Software*, 23(3):55–61.

Vlissides, J., Coplien, J., and Kerth, N., editors (1996). *Pattern Languages of Program Design, Vol. 2*. Addison-Wesley.

Wallace, L. and Keil, M. (2004). Software Project Risks and Their Effect on Project Outcomes. *Communications of the ACM*, 47(4):68–73.

Walston, C. and Felix, C. (1977). A Method of Programming Measurement and Estimation. *IBM Systems Journal*, 16(1):54–73.

Wang, A. and Qian, K. (2005). *Component-Oriented Programming*. Wiley.

Warnier, J.-D. (1974). *Logical Construction of Programs*. Stenfert Kroese.

Weber, D. (1996). Change Sets Versus Change Packages. In Sommerville, I., editor, *Proceedings Workshop on Software Configuration Management (SCM6)*, pages 25–35. Springer, LNCS1167.

Wegner, P. (1984). Capital-Intensive Software Technology. *IEEE Software*, 1(3):7–45.

Wegner, P. (1992). Dimensions of Object-Oriented Modeling. *IEEE Computer*, 25(10):12–21.

Weidenhaupt, K., Pohl, K., Jarke, M., and Haumer, P. (1998). Scenarios in System Development: Current Practice. *IEEE Software*, 15(2):34–45.

Weinberg, G. (1971). *The Psychology of Computer Programming*. Van Nostrand Reinhold.

Weiss, D., Tau, C., and Lai, R. (1999). *Software Product-Line Engineering*. Addison-Wesley.

Weller, E. (1993). Lessons from Three Years of Inspection Data. *IEEE Software*, 10(5):38–45.

Wendel, I. (1986). Software Tools of the Pleistocene. *Software Maintenance News*, 4(10):20.

Weyuker, E. (1988). The Evaluation of Program-Based Software Test Data Adequacy Criteria. *Communications of the ACM*, 31(6):668–675.

Weyuker, E. (1990). The Cost of Data Flow Testing: An Empirical Study. *IEEE Transactions on Software Engineering*, 16(2):121–128.

Weyuker, E. (1993). More Experience with Data Flow Testing. *IEEE Transactions on Software Engineering*, 19(9):912–919.

Whittaker, J. (2000). What Is Software Testing? And Why Is It So Hard. *IEEE Software*, 17(1):70–79.

Whittaker, J. and Voas, J. (2000). Toward a More Reliable Theory of Software Reliability. *IEEE Computer*, 33(12):36–42.

Wiborg-Weber, D. (1997). Change Sets versus Change Packages: Comparing Implementations of Change-Based SCM. In *Proceedings 7th International Workshop on Software Configuration Management (SCM7)*, pages 25–35. Springer LNCS 1235.

Wiegers, K. (2002). *Peer Reviews in Software – A Practical Guide*. Addison-Wesley.

Wieringa, R. (1996). *Requirements Engineering: Frameworks for Understanding*. John Wiley & Sons.

Wieringa, R. (1998). A Survey of Structured and Object-Oriented Software Specification Methods and Techniques. *ACM Computing Surveys*, 30(4):459–527.

Wing, J. (1988). A Study of 12 Specifications of the Library Problem. *IEEE Software*, 5(4):66–76.

Wohlwend, H. and Rosenbaum, S. (1994). Schlumberger's Software Improvement Program. *IEEE Transactions on Software Engineering*, 20(11):833–839.

Wolverton, R. (1974). The Cost of Developing Large-Scale Software. *IEEE Transactions on Computers*, pages 615–636.

Wood, M., Roper, M., Brooks, A., and Miller, J. (1997). Comparing and Combining Software Defect Detection Techniques. In Jazayeri, M. and Schauer, H., editors, *Proceedings 6th European Software Engineering Conference, LNCS 1301*, pages 262–277. Springer Verlag.

Xia, F. (2000). On the Concept of Coupling, its Modeling and Measurement. *Journal of Systems and Software*, 50(1):75–84.

Yeh, D. and Jeng, J.-H. (2002). An empirical study of the influence of departmentalization and organizational position on software maintenance. *Journal of Software Maintenance and Evolution: Research and Practice*, 14:65–82.

Yourdon, E. and Constantine, L. (1975). *Structured Design*. Yourdon Press.

Yu, L. and Chen, K. (2006). An Empirical Study of the Maintenance Effort. In *Proceedings 8th International Conference on Software Engineering and Knowledge Engineering (SEKE)*, pages 242–245.

Zelkowitz, M. (1988). Resource Utilization During Software Development. *Journal of Systems and Software*, 8(4):331–336.

Zhu, H. (1996). A Formal Analysis of the Subsume Relation Between Software Test Adequacy Criteria. *IEEE Transactions on Software Engineering*, 22(4):248–255.

Zhu, H., Hall, P., and May, J. (1997). Software Unit Test Coverage and Adequacy. *ACM Computing Surveys*, 29(4):366–427.

Zucconi, L. (1989). Selecting a CASE Tool. *ACM Software Engineering Notes*, 14(2):42–44.

Index